THE TOP TEN

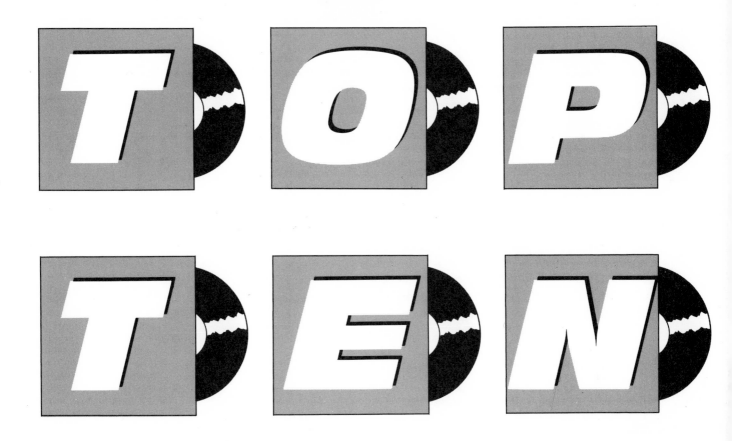

1956-Present

by Gary Theroux
and Bob Gilbert

A FIRESIDE BOOK
Published by Simon and Schuster
New York

Lest We Forget

Many thanks for photos and photo-finding assistance to the fine folks at the following labels: A&M, ABC, Ariola America, Atlantic, Avco, Bell, Buddah, Cadence, Cameo/Parkway, Canadian-American, Capitol/UA, Capricorn, Casablanca, Challenge, Chelsea, Chess/Checker, Colgems, Elektra, EMI America, Fantasy, Hi, Invictus, Juana, Laurie, Mala, MAM, MCA, Mercury/Phonogram, MGM, Monument, Motown, Neighborhood, Ode, Pacific, Philadelphia International, Phillies, Polydor, Private Stock, RCA, Reprise, Rocket, Roulette, RSO, Scepter, Shelby Singleton/Sun, Soul City, Sussex, Swan Song, Threshold, TK, T Neck, 20th Century, Valiant, Vanguard, Vee Jay, Warner Brothers, and White Whale. Also hat tips to ABC-TV, Bagdasarian Productions, Banner Talent Associates, CBS-TV, Columbia Pictures, Drake-Chenault Enterprises, Filmmation Associates, NBC-TV, and Paramount Pictures. Finally, these individuals: Pat Boone, Don Cornelius, Veronica Davis, Elliot Lurie, Penny Stallings, Dean Torrence, Lawrence Welk, Shawn Willcuts, Ken Williamson, and Tsuyoshi Yamaoka.

Pop Record Research is one of the world's largest archives of information on the hits and hitmakers—bios, photos, reviews, clippings, films, videotapes, and the records themselves. For more information, write: Pop Record Research, 19 Linden Avenue, Pelham, New York 10802.

Copyright © 1982 by Gary Theroux and Bob Gilbert
All rights reserved
including the right of reproduction
in whole or in part in any form
A Fireside Book
Published by Simon and Schuster
A Division of Gulf & Western Corporation
Simon & Schuster Building
Rockefeller Center
1230 Avenue of the Americas
New York, New York 10020

FIRESIDE and colophon are registered trademarks of Simon & Schuster

Designed by H. Roberts Design

Manufactured in the United States of America
Printed and bound by the Murray Printing Co.
10 9 8 7 6 5 4 3 2 1
Library of Congress Cataloging in Publication Data
Theroux, Gary.
   The top ten.
   "A Fireside book."
   1. Music, Popular (Songs, etc.)—United States—
History and criticism.   2. Musicians—Biography.
I. Gilbert, Bob.   II. Title.
ML3477.T5   1982   784.5'00973   82-10478
ISBN: 0-671-43215-X

This book is dedicated to everyone
who ever gave of their time, money, and talents
in an effort to try and cut a hit record—
and never made it.

GARY (age 5): Mom, what is rock 'n' roll?
MOM (age 38): Sewage with a beat.

ACKNOWLEDGMENTS

I'll try to keep this list from looking like a lyric sheet from "Life Is a Rock (but the Radio Rolled Me)" but it won't be easy.

First off, let me salute all the people—in many capacities—who have made and delivered the music that has meant so much to millions. In particular, let me thank the musicians, singers, writers, producers, arrangers and industry personnel who have, over the years, allowed me to stick microphones in their faces and ask them about their work. I only wish I could have used even more of their remarks in this book.

Most of the photos reproduced here came from the files of Pop Record Research. In addition, the following people and organizations contributed pictures, comments, advice, connections, and good will: Steve Allen, Jan Azrak, Ross Bagdasarian, Jr., Banner Talent Associates, Mark Barkan, Jeff Barry, Perry Bodkin, Jr., Pat Boone, Jimmy Bowen, Boudleaux and Felice Bryant, Freddie Cannon, Jerry Capehart, Harry Casey, Lee Castle, George Cates, Gayle Cobb, Don Cornelius, Ron Dante, Joan Deary, Dusty DeRousse, Helen DeWitty, George Duning, Arthur Everett, Filmmation Associates, Peter Fletcher, Rebecca Fox, Rollie Flynn, Sandy Friedman, Jerry Fuller, Sandy Gaylen, Bob Gilbert, Deena Goldstein, Johnny Hayes, Sharon House, Gordon Jenkins, John Kay, Kenny Kerner, Frederick Knight, Harvey Kubernik, Art Laboe, Chris Lamson, Margo Lewis, Ronnie Lippin, Elliot Lurie, Beverly Magid, Ray Manzarek, George Martin, Tom McConnell, Sara McMullen, Angela Miller, the Million Dollar Quartet #2 (Bill Drake, Gene Chenault, Mark Ford, and Bill Watson), MTM Productions, Don Noble, Chris Peake, Peter Perkins, Dee Presley, Buck Ram, Jim Ramsey, the Record Depot, Rogers and Cowan, Carol Saro, Warren Seabury, John Sebastian, Ned Shankman, Dick Shehan, Kyo Shiree, Shelby Singleton, Major Bill Smith, Solters & Roskin, J. Randy Taraborrelli, Dean Torrance, Paul Vance, Betty Walton, Wayne Weinberg, and Norman Whitfield.

Listings were compiled through an analysis of national trade chart activity, major market radio air play, industry sales figures, and music licensing tally reports. Bob Gilbert and I both contributed to the statistical work.

And finally, a very special thanks to the three people who kept me fed, loved, and solvent during the long year that this book was in production: Marjorie Theroux, Paul Theroux, and Joan Holpuch. Without their support, encouragement, and constant inquiries ("Isn't it done *yet*?") this volume might still be only a pipedream.

—Gary Theroux

CONTENTS

1 9 5 6   2

1 9 5 7   14

1 9 5 8   26

THE
TOP TEN

NINETEEN FIFTY-SIX was the first solid year in rock 'n' roll history. There had been hits before, but the music didn't really take off until it developed an explosive catalyst—a charismatic messiah—in the person of Elvis Presley.

The pop scene he invaded was one of mellow conformity. Radio stations played what we now call "easy listening" music, or MOR (middle of the road). That was the rule—but there certainly were exceptions. Rough, rumbling "Honky Tonk," born informally at a late-night jam session, became an instrumental classic. Doo-wop made strong inroads, thanks to the Platters, the Five Satins, and the Teenagers (featuring Frankie Lymon). Early "girl groups" were heard, such as the Teen Queens, Patience and Prudence, and the Chordettes. Buchanan and Goodman introduced the "break-in record," a zany collection of excerpts from other people's hits (for

their trouble, they nearly lost everything in lawsuits).

Show tunes dominated the LP charts, thanks to such powerful productions as *Oklahoma, Carousel, Picnic, The King and I, High Society* and *The Eddy Duchin Story*. The original cast album of *My Fair Lady* began an incredible nine-and-a-half-year run, including *four years* in the national top ten.

The generation gap had just begun. It had been a hairline crack for over a decade, but was now starting to widen. Records like Kay Starr's "Rock and Roll Waltz" captured the moment—awkwardly, to be sure, but then again, it was an awkward time. "Whatever will be, will be," sang Doris Day. "The future's not ours to see."

For the old guard, brought up on big bands and sentimental crooners, perhaps that was just as well.

The cultural phenomenon known as **Elvis Presley** exploded in January 1956—the month he recorded and unleashed "Heartbreak Hotel." Before the year was out, he would make two top-grossing movies *(Love Me Tender* and *Loving You),* cut two number-one albums *(Elvis Presley* and *Elvis),* and place an unbelievable seventeen songs on the national charts ("Heartbreak Hotel," "I Was the One," "Blue Suede Shoes," "Money Honey," "I Want You, I Need You, I Love You," "My Baby Left Me," "Don't Be Cruel," "Hound Dog," "Blue Moon," "I Don't Care if the Sun Don't Shine," "Love Me Tender," "Any Way You Want Me," "Love Me," "When My Blue Moon Turns to Gold Again," "Paralyzed," "Old Shep," and "Poor Boy"). The King of Rock 'n' Roll had arrived, and no one was ever to forget him.

The supper club sensation of 1956 was the "exotic" beat of calypso, as popularized by native New Yorker **Harry Belafonte**. A frustrated actor, he'd appeared in Otto Preminger's *Carmen Jones* (1954), with his singing voice, in grand Hollywood tradition, dubbed in by somebody else. Harry's *Calypso* LP included the classic "Banana Boat (Day-O)," as well as his first big hit, "Jamaican Farewell" (whose lyrics mention "Kingston Town" and inspired the name of the Kingston Trio). Belafonte was a favorite of folk fans well into the sixties, thanks to top-selling albums like *Belafonte, An Evening with Harry Belafonte, Harry Belafonte at Carnegie Hall, Jump Up Calypso,* and *The Midnight Special.* One cut of the last LP features guitar work by one of Harry's lesser-known but most fervent admirers. Yes, it was Belafonte, not Woody Guthrie, who was the idol of young Bob Dylan.

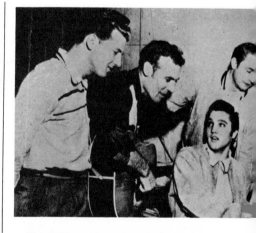

The Million-Dollar Quartet: Carl Perkins recalled the events of December 9, 1956, at the Sun Record Studio in Memphis: "You see, it was my recording session, and Jerry Lee Lewis was recording with me. Johnny Cash was in the studio, and then Elvis walked in. My session just kind of flew apart because we were glad to see him. We hadn't seen him for a good little while, any of us, and it turned into a big jam session. We all got singing, and just let the tapes roll. Elvis says in one place, 'Carl, let's rock this thing and see if it rocks.' And I'm on guitar, you know, and Elvis is playing piano, and he says, 'Yeah, man, that's the way to rock, never played it at this speed.' You can really hear rock 'n' roll being born, right there on that tape."

The unforgettable **Nat King Cole** came to television in 1956, with his own fifteen-minute program. It was one of the first network variety series hosted by a black performer. Nat began his career as a barroom piano player. One night he was asked to sing by a boisterous, tipsy patron. "We don't sing," Nat replied softly, but the club's manager ordered him to comply. With great reluctance, Nat stepped up to the microphone, and his remarkable tenure as a classic crooner was under way. Cole became known as "the merry balladeer," and over the next twenty-two years he put nearly eighty songs on the charts. His TV series, sadly, went mostly unsponsored and failed after barely a year. Advertisers claimed fear of racial boycotts, and several NBC affiliates refused to carry the program at all. Nat died in 1965, without ever knowing how successful his daughter, Natalie, would turn out to be.

Back in '56, no one could guess the extent of rock's life span. Hollywood, though, was willing to gamble that the craze might last a few weeks—long enough to crank out a handful of low-budget movies. Two of those films starred the original King of Rock 'n' Roll—the first artist to put a rock song on the pop charts ("Crazy Man Crazy" in '53). **Bill Haley,** who fused R&B with western swing, was one of the creators of rock 'n' roll in the early fifties. His biggest hit, "Rock Around the Clock," first thundered from the soundtrack of *The Blackboard Jungle* (1955), resulting in that film's being banned in Britain for eleven years. In America, though, the song was such a smash that two more movies were built around it: *Rock Around the Clock,* and *Don't Knock the Rock.* The original single went on to sell more than twenty-five million copies, making it the best-selling rock record in history. Later it was heard in *American Graffiti* (1973), *Superman* (1978), and the TV series "Happy Days." Haley became a legend and toured the world for twenty-seven years, until his death in 1981.

THE TOP 40

1. Don't Be Cruel/Hound Dog, *Elvis Presley*
2. Heartbreak Hotel, *Elvis Presley*
3. My Prayer, *Platters*
4. The Wayward Wind, *Gogi Grant*
5. Lisbon Antigua, *Nelson Riddle*
6. Whatever Will Be, Will Be, *Doris Day*
7. The Great Pretender, *Platters*
8. The Poor People of Paris, *Les Baxter*
9. Moonglow and Theme from "Picnic," *Morris Stoloff*
10. Memories Are Made of This, *Dean Martin*
11. The Rock and Roll Waltz, *Kay Starr*
12. Canadian Sunset, *Hugo Winterhalter*
13. I Want You, I Need You, I Love You, *Elvis Presley*
14. Hot Diggity, *Perry Como*
15. Honky Tonk, *Bill Doggett*
16. Blue Suede Shoes, *Carl Perkins*
17. I Almost Lost My Mind, *Pat Boone*
18. No Not Much, *Four Lads*
19. Love Me Tender, *Elvis Presley*
20. Green Door, *Jim Lowe*
21. Why Do Fools Fall in Love?, *Teenagers*
22. I'm in Love Again, *Fats Domino*
23. Just Walkin' in the Rain, *Johnny Ray*
24. Allegheny Moon, *Patti Page*
25. Tonight You Belong to Me, *Patience and Prudence*
26. Ivory Tower, *Cathy Carr*
27. Standing on the Corner, *Four Lads*
28. See You Later, Alligator, *Bill Haley and His Comets*
29. Sixteen Tons, *Tennessee Ernie Ford*
30. Flying Saucer, *Buchanan and Goodman*
31. I'll Be Home, *Pat Boone*
32. Band of Gold, *Don Cherry*
33. Magic Touch, *Platters*
34. Be-Bop-a-Lula, *Gene Vincent*
35. On the Street Where You Live, *Vic Damone*
36. Moonglow and Theme from "Picnic," *George Cates*
37. True Love, *Bing Crosby and Grace Kelly*
38. A Tear Fell, *Teresa Brewer*
39. Born to Be with You, *Chordettes*
40. The Fool, *Sanford Clark*

THE TOP 10 LPs

1. Calypso, *Harry Belafonte*
2. My Fair Lady, *Original Cast*
3. The King and I, *Original Soundtrack*
4. The Eddy Duchin Story, *Original Soundtrack*
5. Elvis Presley, *Elvis Presley*
6. High Society, *Original Soundtrack*
7. Songs for Swingin' Lovers, *Frank Sinatra*
8. Belafonte, *Harry Belafonte*
9. The Platters, *Platters*
10. Oklahoma, *Original Soundtrack*

Fats Domino was at his peak in 1956, with seven songs on the charts. Among them: "I'm in Love Again," "My Blue Heaven," and his all-time biggest, "Blueberry Hill." He sang another of his 1956 hits, "Blue Monday," on camera in the first wide-screen color rock movie, *The Girl Can't Help It,* which also starred Little Richard, Gene Vincent, Eddie Cochran, and the Platters. Fats came from New Orleans, where his distinctive brand of blues, boogie-woogie, and simple rhythm had captivated fans since the late forties. Antoine Domino's nickname came as the result of his first single, "The Fat Man." Pop audiences discovered him in 1955 via "Ain't That a Shame," and after that it was hit after hit—nearly seventy chart songs in all over the next fourteen years.

10

Memories Are Made of This
DEAN MARTIN

Dino Crocetti was one of six children, born in Steubenville, Ohio, to a $30-a-week immigrant barber. Although he recalled being a "fairly cocky kid" with no lack of self-confidence, he was a poor student, and dropped out of school in the ninth grade. He then embarked on a number of odd jobs: mill hand, drugstore clerk, coal miner, wire bundler, and gas station attendant. He delivered bootleg hootch and dealt blackjack in the backroom of a hometown smoke shop. His father gave him $5 to enroll in barber school, but instead he went into boxing as Kid Crochet, at $25 a bout. After thirty bouts someone bashed his nose, and young Dino gave up the fight game.

He'd always liked music; as a Boy Scout, he was the Troop 10 drummer. When he got a wind-up phonograph, he used to sing along to Bing Crosby and Russ Columbo records. He was twenty-seven years old when—having tried everything else he could think of—Dino decided to try making it as a professional singer.

His first job was with bandleader Sammy Watkins in Cleveland. After that, Dino went solo, anglicized his name, and got a nose job. He played clubs around the east, and then, in 1946, was booked into the prestigious Five Hundred in Atlantic City. Also on the bill was a nineteen-year-old comedian named Jerry Lewis, whose act consisted of simply pantomiming to records. The owner was looking for a comedy *team,* and on impulse, just threw the two together. For their first show they followed a script. "We laid the biggest bomb in nightclub history," Dino recalled. There was no opportunity to find more material, so the next time they went on, they ad-libbed ("we had courage"). The audience loved it and them, and their rate went from $350 to $25,000 a week. Within a matter of months, Dean Martin and Jerry Lewis were major stars.

Their film career took off three years later with *My Friend Irma,* and continued through sixteen pictures: *My Friend Irma Goes West* (1950), *At War with the Army* (1950), *That's My Boy* (1951), *Sailor Beware* (1951), *Jumping Jacks* (1951), *The Stooge* (1953), *Scared Stiff* (1953), *The Caddy* (1953), *Money from Home* (1953), *Living It Up* (1954), *Three Ring Circus* (1954), *You're Never Too Young* (1955), *Artists and Models* (1955), *Pardners* (1956), and *Hollywood or Bust* (1956).

In 1950, Dean signed with Capitol, and began cranking out hit records as well. In 1955, he decided to try one offered to him by Terry Gilkyson, a former member of the folksinging Weavers. Terry, who had also written "The Cry of the Wild Goose," composed "Memories Are Made of This" with his musical partners, Richard Dehr and Frank Miller. Fourteen months later, as the Easy Riders, they were to have their own million-selling hit, "Marianne."

Dean's version of the song broke late in November 1955, and was the first number-one single of the new year. It stayed at the top for more than a month, and remained a best-seller well into the summer. It became a staple of his act, and even today people associate its sound with the events and happenings of early 1956.

Memories are made of this.

Moonglow and Theme from Picnic

MORRIS STOLOFF

Philadelphia-born Morris Stoloff took up the violin at the age of sixteen, and later joined the L.A. Philharmonic. When movies began to talk in 1928, he got a job at Paramount, leading the studio band. A short time later he took over the Columbia Pictures Orchestra, and became that company's general music director. For nearly thirty years, he oversaw the scoring of every Columbia feature, and along the way, won three Oscars and eighteen other Academy Award nominations. Among his screen credits are *The Jolson Story* (1946), *The Eddy Duchin Story* (1956), and the original *Gidget* (1959).

Morris helped put together a lot of soundtrack albums; however, his name only appeared on the pop singles chart once—for conducting "Moonglow and Theme from *Picnic*." It was a deceptively clever track, conceived and orchestrated by one of his staff arrangers, George Duning.

Duning, who also wrote the *Picnic* theme, spent eighteen years in the big bands before joining Columbia as a composer in 1946. Once with the studio, he began turning out about a score a month—music for nearly three hundred pictures in all during his tenure.

"I never professed to be a songwriter," Duning admitted. "I'm a background writer, a score writer. But I'd seen the stage version of *Picnic* in New York, and when I heard that Josh Logan was going to turn it into a film, I became very interested. I felt very close to the story because my people are all from the Midwest, and the characters in the script—some of them, anyway—could have been my relatives.

"So, about two or three months before shooting began, I wrote a *Picnic* theme, and Josh just loved it. He agreed to use it in the picture, but then said that there was an old Mills Brothers tune, "Moonglow," that he also wanted to use. We approached

the publisher of that song, but what they wanted for sync rights was fairly high at the time. So, we tried to talk Josh into using something from the Columbia Pictures library, for which we didn't have to pay any sync rights. He said he had used "Moonglow" on the stage, and wanted to use it in the film. He was a volatile person, and superstitious about the song. We agreed and negotiated for the sync rights.

"I got the record that Josh had used in New York and re-recorded it for the movie. I was lucky to get three of the four boys who played on the original disc. They took that track and used it while filming the boat dock dance scene.

"When they finally finished the picture, Josh viewed the rough cut with Morris and me to decide on the cueing, the spotting. When we got to that scene where William Holden and Kim Novak move in toward each other, it was like an explosion from Josh. He cried, 'Stop, stop right here.' We stopped the film, and he said, 'Right here is where I want to hear George's theme.' I don't know why he picked this number, but 'twenty-seven violins,' he said, 'I want to hear it played by twenty-seven violins.' Morris said, 'Well, look Josh, you can't do that. They've already shown a little band playing onstage. To suddenly have all those violins come in wouldn't be realistic.' But Josh was adamant. Then he left and went back to New York.

"Morris asked me to come up with something—to possibly play the *Picnic* theme over the 'Moonglow' track. I said, 'Not if you want to match the thirty-two bars to thirty-two bars. It's impossible.' Morris said, 'Take your time. Forget everything else you're doing and see what you can come up with.'

"So, I spent four or five days in my office, and it actually turned out to be one of the times when my conservatory training finally came to good use.

Naturally, I had to retain the original rhythm. What I wound up doing was starting my theme—not at the beginning, where the chorus of 'Moonglow' would start—but somewhere within the 'Moonglow' song. Then, by extending my bridge, I was able to make the two songs match over that original track.

"From then on was history. That thing was on the hit parade for twenty-seven weeks, and made it to number one. It's one of the most fortunate and exciting things that happened to me in all the years I've been in this business."

George Duning went on to score many other productions, including such TV series as "Star Trek." Later, he was named to the Board of Directors of ASCAP. Morris Stoloff retired in the mid-sixties and died in 1980.

8

Poor People of Paris
LES BAXTER

I started in music when I was five years old," said Les Baxter. "I was a child prodigy pianist and student at the Detroit Conservatory of Music. I started composing at a very young age, and continued when I went to high school. I played several instruments: woodwinds, concert piano. I was always studying and always ahead of my class in whatever I was doing, musically.

"I left high school a year early because I felt I was ready to go to college. I got a scholarship and enrolled without my parents even knowing about it. I proceeded through college rather quickly, and have an LL.D. degree from Pepperdine.

"I signed with Capitol in 1950, and introduced a style known as 'exotic music' with my album, *Music Out of the Moon.* Then, in 1951, they gave me a piece called 'Because of You.' I did an arrangement on it with a vocal group, and it hit. They gave me another single to do—'Blue Tango'— and it hit in 1952. After that were 'April in Portugal' and 'Ruby' (1953), 'The High and the Mighty' (1954), 'Unchained Melody' and 'Wake the Town and Tell the People' (1955).

"Most of these were European melodies, the start of a whole trend called 'continental music.' Following 'April in Portugal,' there was every type of European title you can think of. One of them was 'Poor People of Paris.'

"I thought this kind of music was simplistic. But it was good for the pop field, because every song was a little concert piece, a little musical picture of its own. 'Poor People of Paris' was more than just a pop hit. It was a Paris bistro of the 20s in feel. It sounds like it was made today because it has a basic, contemporary rhythm.

"There isn't much of a story behind 'Poor People of Paris.' It came from Europe, was semi-hot there, so we jumped on it. I had a flair for European music, thought of Paris in the 20s when I heard it, and just arranged

those colors into it. There are no interesting or bizarre stories connected with my work. It's just like sitting down to type. You just press the keys and go. I was an arranger, and that was just a professional job of arranging."

"Poor People of Paris" was first sung as "La goulant du pauvre (The Ballad of Poor John)" in France by Edith Piaf. It told the story of a young man who wound up with "the wrong sort of girls." After Piaf's version began to take off, Capitol's European rep excitedly telegraphed the home office in Hollywood—garbling the title in the process. As a result, we in America

have come to know the tune, incorrectly, as "Poor People of Paris."

Les' single broke in early February 1956, and topped the charts for six weeks, beginning in March. In all, it spent nearly six months on the best-seller lists.

Les Baxter never did have another big 45, but didn't really need one. His albums of exotic music sold well, and in 1959 he wrote another million-seller, "Quiet Village," which became a hit for Martin Denny. In later years he became a concert conductor and scored more than 150 TV shows and motion pictures.

The Great Pretender

THE PLATTERS

The Platters were formed in 1953 by bass singer and comedian Herbert Reed. The first person he hired was a tenor, Tony Williams, who was then working as a form block maker at Douglass Aircraft. Next he brought in David Lynch, a cab driver, as second tenor. To round out the group, he found Paul Robi, a New Orleans piano player who could also sing baritone.

This quartet auditioned for songwriter-producer Buck Ram, who got them a recording contract with Federal Records. The deal was blown, however, when the boys showed up two hours late for their first and only Federal session. On that date, though, they cut one take of a tune called "Only You."

At that time, Buck was also managing the Penguins, who were then hot with the single "Earth Angel." Mercury wanted to sign the Penguins, and Buck agreed, but only if they'd also take his new act, the Platters. Mercury balked, but later, grudgingly, gave in. As things turned out, the Penguins never had another hit, but the Platters went on to bring millions to the label.

In 1955, the Platters re-recorded "Only You" for Mercury, and it became one of the biggest hits of the year. Shortly afterward, they added a fifth member to the group, Zola Taylor, formerly of the Queens. These five sang on every other Platters hit of the fifties.

Their next record was "The Great Pretender," written by Alanzio Taylor. Buck Ram liked the song and purchased all rights to it for $25. He worked out an arrangement for the song between Platters' performances in Las Vegas. "We were at the Flamingo Hotel," Buck recalls, "and things were so noisy with the slot machines and everything that I actually finished the tune in the men's washroom. I took it to Tony, and he

rejected it. He said it was a hillbilly song. I said, 'Tony, I don't care if it's a Chinese song, I want you to try it.' So he did, and it was wonderful. The song sold 500,000 copies the first week it was out."

"The Great Pretender" entered the pop charts in November 1955 and quickly climbed into the national top ten. By February 1956, it was the number-one record in the country, and it remained a strong seller for nearly six months.

The Platters, of course, went on to score many more hits in 1956, including "(You've Got the) Magic Touch," "My Prayer," "You'll Never Never

Know," and "On My Word of Honor." They also appeared in their first of four motion pictures, *Rock Around the Clock,* and turned up numerous times on television. They became the most successful singing group of the fifties and in fact outsold every other recording act around, with the exception of Elvis Presley.

"The Great Pretender" marked a high point in the evolution of pop R&B. It kicked off a new trend of vocal class and musicianship in group arrangements. Its full orchestral background and vocal smoothness were both innovations at the time and stylistic trailblazers for years to come.

Whatever Will Be, Will Be (Que Sera, Sera)

DORIS DAY

Doris von Kappelhoff was born in Cincinnati, Ohio, the daughter of a choirmaster and music teacher. As a child, she had hopes of becoming a professional tap dancer, but after an auto accident injured her right leg, she turned to singing. Bandleader Barney Rapp was the one who renamed her, taking his cue from the song "Day by Day."

In 1945, Doris recorded her first number-one record, "My Dreams Are Getting Better All the Time," with the Les Brown orchestra. A few months later, she teamed with Les again to cut "Sentimental Journey," one of the best-selling singles of the decade.

Doris's movie career began in 1948 in *Romance on the High Seas* but didn't hit its peak until 1956 in Alfred Hitchcock's *The Man Who Knew Too Much.* It was the most challenging role of her career, and also provided Doris with the tune that was to become her theme song. Co-composer Jay Livingston recalled how the tune came about.

"In a picture called *The Barefoot Contessa* (1954), Rosanno Brazzi marries Ava Gardner and takes her to his family castle in Italy. Cut into a stone of the castle is the motto, 'Che sera, sera.' It means 'what will be, will be.' I copied this down in the dark, because songwriters are always on the alert for good song titles. 'Vaya Con Dios' had recently been a hit, and this sounded like a similar good idea. Ray Evans and I were working at Paramount, but we had time between assignments so we wrote it as a pop tune.

"About two weeks later, we were called to the office of the head of the music department to meet with Alfred Hitchcock. He told us that Paramount was insisting that Doris Day have a new song to sing in *The Man Who Knew Too Much.* He said, 'I don't want a song,' which didn't make us feel too welcome. But he said that he had worked out a good story point, so that the song would fit well into the story of the picture. He said that he wanted a song that Doris could sing to her little boy, and that foreign words in the title wouldn't hurt because her co-star, Jimmy Stewart, was in the diplomatic service and worked in a lot of European capitals. In other words, he described 'Que Sera, Sera.' His parting words were, 'I don't know what kind of a song I want.' We said we would get to work and write something for him.

"As we left, I said to Ray, 'We've *got* that song.' He said, 'I know.' So we waited for two weeks so that Hitchcock would think we were working hard, and then made an appointment to play it for him. As I was playing and singing it for him, I had no idea what he was thinking. When I finished, he said, 'Gentlemen, I told you I didn't know what kind of a song I want.' Then he thrust his finger at me and said, '*That's* the kind of a song I want,' and walked out. It was a typical Hitchcock dramatic exit.

"We changed 'Che,' the Italian spelling, to 'Que,' the Spanish spelling, because we figured there were more Spanish people in the world. However, the legal department wouldn't let us use that title. So we had to call it 'Whatever Will be, Will Be,' with 'Que Sera, Sera' in parentheses. Doris didn't want to record the song, but studio pressure made her do it. A friend of mine was at the recording session and told me that she sang it through once—one take only—and said, 'That's the last time you'll ever hear that song.' That was no reflection on her—we've all been wrong in picking hits."

"Whatever Will be, Will Be" went on to win an Oscar as the best song from a motion picture in 1956. It also turned up in two later Doris Day films, *Please Don't Eat the Daisies* (1960) and *The Glass-Bottomed Boat* (1966). She also used it as the theme song for her television series, which ran on CBS from 1968 to 1973.

Doris Day's relaxed vocal style helped make her one of the top moneymakers at Columbia Records during the fifties. She was a star in her first film and remained a star until she retired in 1975. Eleven of her thirty-nine pictures are among the largest-grossing films of all time. She was—quite clearly—one of the most successful female stars to emerge during the immediate postwar years.

Lisbon Antigua
NELSON RIDDLE

Nelson Riddle grew up in the wilds of northern New Jersey, surrounded by lots of trees and plenty of popular music. "We lived in the middle of a forest," he explained. "It was very overgrown, and my family was kind of isolated." For fun, the Riddles turned to simple pastimes, like the joys of homemade song. "My father was an amateur musician, and had a little band, maybe four or five men. They would use our living room as a rehearsal area in the evenings. If I was permitted to stay up—I was only five or six years old at the time—I would listen to the music, and got a feel of the sound of the mid-twenties. Many years later, I was to recall those experiences while writing the score of *The Great Gatsby* (1974), for which I was lucky enough to win an Academy Award.

"I started to study the piano at the age of eight. At about fourteen, I picked up the trombone and became a member of the school band. After graduation, I worked in several traveling orchestras—first small ones, then more important ones. Among the people I worked for were Charlie Spivak, Bob Crosby, and Alvino Rey. I finally spent a year [1944] with Tommy Dorsey, for whom I played trombone. I was in his band when they recorded 'On the Sunny Side of the Street' and 'Opus One.' I idolized Tommy—the quality he insisted on, and the music I got to play."

After leaving the army in 1946, Nelson spent six months in New York, honing his skills as a freelance arranger for Les Elgart, Elliot Lawrence, and other bandleaders. That December, he moved to Los Angeles and got a job in the NBC music department. He stayed there until the spring of 1950, when the network decided to "let him go."

"Les Baxter was doing some dates with Nat King Cole at the time," Nelson recalled, "and he asked me to come up with a couple of the arrangements. One was for a song called 'Mona Lisa,' which eventually climbed to number one. Capitol Records liked that, so they hired me on as a house arranger and conductor."

Nelson worked with nearly every act on the Capitol roster, most notably in support of Frank Sinatra. Beginning in 1953 with "Young at Heart," he was behind almost every important Sinatra single of the fifties, including "Love and Marriage," "Learnin' the Blues," "All the Way," "Chicago," and "Witchcraft." His innovative arrangements helped the songs transcend their own time.

In those days, it was accepted practice for the big record companies to pirate songs from the small labels. And that's exactly how Nelson came by the song that got him his first gold record. It had originally been recorded by a Mexican group, Los Churambalis.

"Soon afterward," says Nelson, "a picture was made at Republic with Ray Milland. It featured some pretty photography of Lisbon, and I was hired to do the musical score. As the film was called *Lisbon,* I worked variations of the song throughout a great deal of it."

The song "Lisbon Antigua" (the title means "In Old Lisbon") was first published in Lisbon, Portugal, in 1937, as "Lisboa Antigua." It was written by Raul Portela, with Portuguese words by Jose Galhardo and Amadeu do Vale (Nelson's version, of course, was only an instrumental). Later, English lyrics were written by Harry Dupree.

"Lisbon Antigua," recorded late in 1955, entered the pop charts in November of that year. It spent twenty-

nine weeks on the best-seller lists, peaking at number one for four weeks in February 1956. Two follow-up singles also made the top forty in 1956: "Port au Prince" and the "Theme from *The Proud Ones.*" Nelson later had one other hit single, "The *Route 66* Theme," which reached the top thirty in the summer of 1962.

"Lisbon Antigua" sparked a long and successful career for Nelson Riddle. It called attention to his arranging and conducting skills and opened the door to many jobs, scoring and writing music for dozens of TV shows, movies, and record albums. He became one of the most respected artists in his field—and has remained so for more than a quarter of a century.

The Wayward Wind
GOGI GRANT

Audrey Brown had been out of high school for only a short time when she decided that working as a clerk-typist in Los Angeles was not the most exciting thing she could do. So Audrey auditioned for a series of TV talent shows, and did well enough on them for her to consider making singing a full-time career.

She worked with a vocal coach for about three months and then went to Gold Star Studios in Hollywood to record some samples of her voice. The owner of the studio, Stan Ross, was impressed. He got in touch with an agent friend at MCA, and before long, Audrey Brown had her first recording contract.

"I became Gogi Grant when I signed with them," she explained. "It was Dave Kapp who insisted on changing my name. He said that 'Gogi' had come to him in a dream, although I later found out that he had lunch every day in a little restaurant called Gogi's La Rue."

The earliest records by Gogi Grant were poor sellers, and after two failed, she was "released" from her contract. However, in 1955, Gogi was picked up by another label, Era, which was then itself struggling to get off the ground. Her first single for them, "Suddenly There's a Valley," put both Gogi and the new company on the map. Its success, in the fall of 1955, was due in no small part to an aggressive twenty-eight-day promotion tour across the country.

When Gogi got back, arrangements were made for the recording of a follow-up song, entitled "Who Are We?"

"I was in the Era offices," she recalled, "and was preparing for the session with Buddy Bregman, my arranger and conductor. As we were going over the material, Herb Newman, one of the owners of Era, called me into one of the other rooms. He pulled out of a desk this brown, time-worn manuscript, and explained

to me that it was a song he had written with a friend of his while they were at UCLA. It had obviously been written for a robust male singer, and the lyric was in the first person, with lines like '*I* was born in a lonely town,' rather than 'he was.' Well, Herb sang that song for me, and I said, 'You know, I feel that music is moving toward songs of this nature—western-type songs. Give it to me, and let me change a few of the words,' which I did.

"We recorded 'The Wayward Wind' in the last fifteen minutes of a three-hour session. 'Who Are We?' was the crux of that session, and so was the first one released. However, it hardly sold at all. And then we released 'The Wayward Wind,' and it took off—I mean, it really took off.

"In the years since then I've realized how many kinds of people that song touched. I guess, for the male population, it touched their wanderlust—their dreams of freedom to just go off and have adventures. As I sang it, from the female point of view, it's a sad song, you know, to have fallen in love with a man who just can't settle down. It's a crazy record. It appealed to every kind of group: bankers, cowboys, housewives, teenagers."

A year after "The Wayward Wind," Gogi Grant was heard on film as the singing voice of Ann Blyth in *The Helen Morgan Story*. She was also heard, and seen, in *The Big Beat,* a landmark music movie in which she starred. Others in the cast included Harry James, the Mills Brothers, the Diamonds, the Del-Vikings, Charlie Barnet, Freddy Martin, Fats Domino, the Four Aces, Russ Morgan, George Shearing, and Cal Tjader.

Gogi Grant continued recording for RCA and Liberty in the late fifties and early sixties, but never managed to come up with another "Wayward Wind." "I got married in 1959 and continued to appear live, but when my son was born in 1965, I just had

the desire to stay home." She made her last recordings in 1970 and then retired.

She still has a room full of awards, citations, and the gold record plaque she received—to her surprise—on "The Steve Allen Show." "The fact was, Elvis Presley was the hot number, and we had to knock off his number one, 'Heartbreak Hotel,' with 'The Wayward Wind.' And indeed we did, for six weeks, until July 28, 1956. That's when 'The Wayward Wind' was knocked off itself, by "I Want You, I Need You, I Love You'—by Elvis Presley."

My Prayer
THE PLATTERS

The Platters were really spinning in 1956. No less than eleven of their songs appeared on the national pop charts, including "Only You," "The Great Pretender," "(You've Got the) Magic Touch," and "My Prayer." Each one captured the essence of the Platters' popularity—the four key ingredients that made their music magic.

First of all, there was Tony Williams, their brilliant, soaring lead singer. He set the pace with his smooth, flowing style. His forte was sweet ballads, and that's probably why the Platters never really got into rock 'n' roll. Instead, they offered an update on the tender Ink Spots sound.

The Platters also went in for timeless tunes, the kind of music that could transcend its own era. Their manager, Buck Ram, had the group revive many standards, or sing songs that he thought would not date easily. "All our lyrics and melodies spoke of romance," Buck said, "and that's not going out of style."

The group also relied on showmanship—timed choreography, tight harmonies, and impeccable performances. Over the years, they toured the world, performing in more than thirty countries. They played everything from Foreign Legion outposts to ancient Roman arenas. They were the guests of kings and presidents and sang in nearly every major auditorium in America.

Their fourth strong point was the relationship between Buck Ram and Tony Williams. "We were inseparable," Buck recalled. "It was almost like being wed. I would toss out song ideas and suggest ways to work them into the act. Tony and I would fight constantly, and often in the studio he would insist on his own way. Sometimes he was right, and sometimes not. But the important thing was that the song would survive, and the best version was the one that got released.

"Now, 'My Prayer' was the very first

song that Tony sang for me. It was the one that he and the group auditioned with, way back at the very beginning. I thought it was great, and I wanted to do it, but Mercury said no—I don't know why. We had to fight for every song we ever recorded. Anyway, we did the song one night, and Mercury buried it in an album. So I told my friend Alan Freed, the disc jockey, about it, and he heard it, and he liked it. But even he couldn't get Mercury to release it as a single. Finally, Alan told them he'd heard that the Four Aces were going to cut the song. Well, that record was out in two weeks, and you know the rest."

"My Prayer" was actually an updated version of a song known as "Avant de Mourir." The original composer was a man named George Boulanger. In 1939, English songwriter Jimmy Kennedy revised the tune and retitled it "My Prayer."

The Platters' single was released in June 1956 and reached number one two months later. In all, it spent twenty-three weeks on the pop charts.

The success of "My Prayer" and other Platters hits led the group to a TV contract with NBC. From October 1956 through June 1957, they were regulars on the Jonathan Winters show. After it was canceled, they returned to Hollywood and appeared in *Rock All Night* (1957), *The Girl Can't Help It* (1957), and *Girls' Town* (1959). The hits kept on rolling, as well: "I'm Sorry," "Twilight Time," "Smoke Gets in Your Eyes," "Enchanted," "Harbor Lights," and many more.

On June 6, 1960, Tony Williams left the group to embark on an ill-fated solo career. He introduced his replacement, Sonny Turner, on the very same day. Over the next few years, David, Paul, and Zola also left, leaving only Herb Reed and new personnel. In 1966, Herb and his set of Platters made a brief comeback, thanks to a tune called "With This Ring."

Heartbreak Hotel
ELVIS PRESLEY

The story of the Presley era is filled with the fireworks of sudden, startling success, the shock of an ever-increasing and almost incredible amount of money, and the noise and tumult of public controversy that surrounded Presley, at least for a while, like a hurricane. Almost everything about him was out of the ordinary, including the fact that at birth he was the surviving member of a set of twins named Jesse Garon and Elvis Aron. As a young boy in Tupelo, Mississippi, Presley often sang in church, and later he became known as the third member of a trio (along with his mother and father) that sang at camp meetings, revivals, and church conventions. When the boy won a music contest at a local fair by singing "Old Shep," his parents bought him his first guitar for $12.98.

In 1953, a recent high school graduate and a $35-a-week truck driver for the Crown Electric Company in Memphis, Presley wandered into the Sun Record Company to make a solo recording for his mother. One year later, he was asked to make a record for Sun as a professional. On the basis of that record, called "That's All Right Mama," he was taken under the direction of Col. Tom Parker, who remained his manager throughout his career.

Elvis toured the south in 1955 and, on one swing through Florida, "discovered" the song with which he would revolutionize the music business. It was conceived by Tommy Durden, who got the idea after reading a suicide note printed in the local paper. Entitled "I Walk a Lonely Street," the note was rewritten into "Heartbreak Hotel" by Tommy and his friend Mae Boren Axton. They presented the song to Elvis in his hotel room and he liked it right away, but then the Colonel stepped in, and "something happened that I never cared for," according to Mae's son, songwriter Hoyt Axton. "Parker said Elvis wanted

a third of the writers' credit, which I think is kind of cheap, you know. But at the time no one knew how big a star Elvis could turn out to be."

Steve Sholes, A&R manager at RCA in Nashville, had an inkling, though. At his insistence, RCA bid for the young performer's contract, and got it for $35,000—a then unheard-of price for a virtually untried artist.

On January 5, three days before his twenty-first birthday, Elvis entered the RCA Recording Studios at 1525 McGavock Street in Nashville. It was a crude facility, so primitive that a stairwell at the back of the building had to serve as the echo chamber.

With Elvis that day were his regular side men: guitarist Scotty Moore, bass player Bill Black, drummer D. J. Fontana, pianist Floyd Cramer, and producer-guitarist Chet Atkins. Elvis himself showed up in very tight pink slacks, which, during the recording of "Heartbreak Hotel," split right down the back. He had to make a quick wardrobe change right there in the studio. When Chet tossed the ripped pair out into the hall, a secretary asked

whom they belonged to. "Elvis," Chet replied. "Pick 'em up and keep 'em. They'll be worth a fortune someday."

Elvis first sang his song publicly on January 28, when he made his television debut on Tommy and Jimmy Dorsey's CBS series "Stage Show." The network was swamped with phone calls, telegrams, and letters, and Dorothy Kilgallen wrote in her column, "The kid had no right behaving like a sex maniac on a national show." Elvis was back the next week, though, and the next week, and the next. By February 22, "Heartbreak Hotel" was on the charts, and within a short time it was the number-one record in the country. It was to remain America's best-selling single for nearly two months.

In April 1956, Elvis flew to Hollywood for a Paramount screen test. He appeared in color on the "Milton Berle Show." He played Vegas, and his very first million-seller was exploding from radios and jukeboxes everywhere. He was then just twenty-one years old. No one could have known that at that point, his life was already half over.

Hound Dog and Don't Be Cruel

ELVIS PRESLEY

Elvis and his clothes designer, Mr. Nudy.

At the same session that yielded "Heartbreak Hotel" and "I Was the One," Elvis Presley recorded his second single, "I Want You, I Need You, I Love You." Released in May 1956, it too became a million-seller, with the flip side, "My Baby Left Me," also getting a lot of play. But it was Elvis's next record that became his all-time classic—the biggest hit of the biggest star the world has ever known.

The story of the A side began in 1952, with a white drummer and vibes player named Johnny Otis. He was an R&B deejay and the leader of a hot black blues band in L.A. Johnny asked Jerry Lieber and Mike Stoller to write some material for his band, including a 300-pound songbird named Big Mama Thornton. Jerry and Mike watched her rehearse one day and came away awed. For Mama, they wrote "Hound Dog" as a kind of country blues, with a loping rhythm patterned after "Louisiana music." It became her first and only hit—a number-one R&B record in the spring of 1953.

Elvis didn't hear the song until three years later, during his disastrous one-week run in April 1956 at the Frontier Hotel in Las Vegas (somehow, Elvis did not appeal to middle-aged gamblers). It seems that while walking through the hotel lounge, Elvis caught the act of Freddie Bell and his Bellboys, which included a comic takeoff on Big Mama's record. The Bellboys, fun lovers that they were, had tampered with the lyrics, adding "you ain't never caught a rabbit" and other lines that were not part of the original verse. Elvis thought that their parody was hilarious and added the song to his repertoire of live material. It got a great response in concert, but he didn't want to record it. Steve Sholes at RCA, after much argument, persuaded Presley to cut a version of it.

On July 1, Elvis sang "Hound Dog" on Steve Allen's NBC-TV comedy series. Steve Allen recalled: "I made the decision to have him wear tails, rather than raunchy Levi's, or whatever he might have worn otherwise; and we got a funny-looking basset hound and sat it on a low Greek column; and he sang the song to the dog, which made it a comedy spot."

The day after that appearance, Elvis entered RCA's New York studios and, after several rehearsal takes, recorded "Hound Dog." Afterward, during a coffee break, Steve Sholes told Elvis that he had another song he wanted him to hear. With that, Steve pulled out a demonstration record of "Don't Be Cruel," written by Otis Blackwell, an R&B singer whom Elvis had long admired. Elvis loved it. He changed the words and music slightly, adapting it to fit his style, and in short order another great master had been captured on tape.

"Hound Dog" and "Don't Be Cruel" were issued back to back in July 1956. At the end of the month, as "I Want You, I Need You, I Love You" reached number one, "Hound Dog" made its first appearance on the national charts. The next week, "Don't Be Cruel" debuted, and by mid-August both songs were sharing the number-one spot. They remained there clear through till November, when they were bounced out by—you guessed it—another Elvis record, "Love Me Tender." Elvis dominated the number-one spot like no other artist in 1956, occupying the top of the charts for twenty-five of the fifty-two weeks.

On September 9, Elvis made his first of three appearances on the "Ed Sullivan Show." He sang "Don't Be Cruel," "Hound Dog," "Ready Teddy," and "Love Me Tender" (the last was the theme song of his first motion picture). It was estimated that fifty-four million people—82.6% of the TV audience—were tuned in that night, a record not broken until 1964, by the Beatles.

Today, of course, it is fun to recall the controversy that engulfed Elvis in that first year as an international star. It was generated mostly by his uninhibited physical gyrations during each song, and partly by the equally uninhibited response of his audience. Girls wept at the sight of him. His home in Memphis was watched day and night by little bands of adolescent girls eager for a glimpse of their idol. It was a phenomenon that had happened before in America (and would happen again), but it had never before reached precisely the Presley point of sheer mania.

AS ROCK 'N' ROLL BEGINS to catch on across the country, record sales jump, topping $400 million in 1957. Everywhere you turn, new groups seem to be popping up—the Miracles, the Kingston Trio, and others. Lead singers, such as Jackie Wilson of the Dominoes and Frankie Lymon of the Teenagers, launch spectacular solo careers. Elvis Presley buys his dream home, Graceland, for $100,000, while Chuck Berry, on tour in Denver, meets the eleven-year-old autograph hound who inspires "Sweet Little Sixteen." Jerry Lee Lewis and his father sell thirty-three dozen eggs to finance a trip to Memphis, where Jerry Lee camps on the doorstep of Sun Records until he wins an audition. And in England, musicians are swept up in a craze known as skiffle,

popularized by a twenty-five-year-old folksinger named Lonnie Donnegan. John Lennon and Paul McCartney have a skiffle group, the Quarrymen, and in their spare time write songs—in their own, very different style. One of them, "Love Me Do," is destined to be their first hit as the Beatles, five years in the future. And back in the States, Tod Storz and Gordon McLendon can be found sitting in a bar next to the jukebox. They're observing people punch up the same songs over and over, and it occurs to them: Why not have a radio format that concentrates on only the biggest hits? They decide to call it "Top Forty," and a whole new era of broadcasting is under way.

Dick Clark sits atop some of the more than 700,000 mail ballots that poured into his office when he asked home viewers to vote for their favorite dancing couple on "American Bandstand." Produced in Philadelphia and premiering coast to coast on August 5, 1957, it was the first network series ever devoted to rock 'n' roll music. The format was simple—every weekday, on camera, teens would dance to America's top-ten singles. Guest stars would drop by to sing their latest hits, and new records would be rated by a panel of rock fans. Dozens of dress and dance crazes began and ended on the show, which did much to popularize Philadelphia as a major music center in the late fifties and early sixties. "American Bandstand" became a TV institution and, eventually, ABC's longest-running series ever.

"The Adventures of Ozzie and Harriet" was television's longest-running situation comedy—fourteen years, from 1952 to 1966. Ozzie and Harriet Nelson played themselves, as did their two sons, David and Ricky. One night (in real life), **Ricky Nelson** was out on a date when suddenly an Elvis song came over the car radio. The girl swooned and, to save face, Ricky blurted that he, too, was going to cut a record, even though he had no such intention. His date laughed in his face—giving Ricky all the motivation he needed to carry out his boast. Nelson's favorite tune at the time was Fats Domino's "I'm Walkin'," and he sang it on TV on April 10 in an episode called "Rick the Drummer." Within a week, his version was a radio hit, and it eventually sold over a million copies. That was the first of more than fifty songs he'd put on the charts during the next sixteen years—in one of the most successful music careers ever.

Rock Rock Rock marked the motion picture debut of **Chuck Berry,** a master craftsman and one of the first singer-songwriters to capture the essence of rock 'n' roll. Chuck was as clever as he was comical, and he understood teens: their rapture, rebellion, fears, and fantasies. With amazing empathy, he said out loud what young Americans felt in their hearts: "It's gotta be rock 'n' roll music," and that's all there was to that. "Johnny B. Goode," "Sweet Little Sixteen," "Maybellene," "Roll Over Beethoven," "School Day"—these songs and more, coupled with Chuck's remarkable writing, singing, and performing style, made him one of the most arresting and influential recording stars of all time. Appearing with Chuck in *Rock Rock Rock* were the Moonglows, the Flamingoes, and the Johnny Burnette Trio. Other music movies of 1957 included *April Love* with Pat Boone and Shirley Jones; *Jailhouse Rock* with Elvis; *Untamed Youth* with Eddie Cochran; *Jamboree* with Fats Domino, Buddy Knox, Carl Perkins, and Charlie Gracie; and *Mr. Rock 'n' Roll* with Alan Freed, Little Richard, Clyde McPhatter, and Brook Benton.

Little Richard was a churning, burning, raving wildman, one of the most exciting performers in rock 'n' roll history. His trademark was a scream, and in the mid-fifties, he injected a lot of raucous fun and maniacal energy into a relatively dull music scene. Little Richard wrote nearly all his own hits—mostly nonsense lyrics set to a wild, driving beat. The frenzy began with "Tutti Frutti" in 1956 and barreled on through "Long Tall Sally," "Slippin' and Slidin'," "Rip It Up," "Jenny Jenny," "Keep A Knockin'," and "Good Golly, Miss Molly." Then, in 1957, while flying to Australia, Richard looked out his window and saw one of the engines burst into flame. He swore that if the plane landed safely, he'd give up "the Devil's music" and enter the ministry. It did, and he did, abruptly ending a whirlwind career. In the late sixties, Richard made a remarkable comeback as a top concert attraction, but he gave it up again after a few years and is now a full-time evangelist.

After a brief but meteoric rise to stardom, **Buddy Holly** was at the top of the rock world in 1957. Three of his songs were major hits, including "Oh Boy," "Peggy Sue," and "That'll Be the Day." A shy young man from Lubbock, Texas, Buddy developed a vocal catch—the "Holly Hiccup"—that was unique and lastingly influential. Dozens of stars have admitted a great debt to Buddy, from Tommy Roe and Bobby Vee to Bob Dylan and the Beatles. Holly had a nervous, excited style, plus a vulnerability that set him apart from other rockabilly types. His backup band, the Crickets, had a clear, clean sound and opened up new possibilities for guitar-based rock 'n' roll groups. Buddy's sudden death at the age of twenty-one turned him into a legendary figure, revered and honored by many around the world. Linda Ronstadt, the Rolling Stones, and others continue to cut Holly songs, and his musical legacy includes some of the finest rock 'n' roll records ever produced.

When **Elvis'** first film, *Love Me Tender,* was released, the demand for prints was so great that Paramount had to have more copies made and shipped than for any other picture in the studio's history. That demand did not subside for his second movie, *Loving You.* Filmed in color, it caught Presley's early stage act better than any of his other motion pictures. Also in 1957, Elvis' third movie was released—*Jailhouse Rock.* Its theme of lawlessness brought new charges that Presley was leading a wave of "juvenile delinquency."

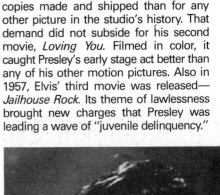

THE TOP 40

1. Love Letters in the Sand, *Pat Boone*
2. Young Love, *Tab Hunter*
3. All Shook Up, *Elvis Presley*
4. Little Darlin', *Diamonds*
5. Young Love, *Sonny James*
6. Tammy, *Debbie Reynolds*
7. So Rare, *Jimmy Dorsey*
8. Bye Bye Love, *Everly Brothers*
9. Round and Round, *Perry Como*
10. Don't Forbid Me, *Pat Boone*
11. Jailhouse Rock, *Elvis Presley*
12. Teddy Bear, *Elvis Presley*
13. Wake Up Little Susie, *Everly Brothers*
14. Party Doll, *Buddy Knox*
15. Come Go with Me, *Del-Vikings*
16. Diana, *Paul Anka*
17. Too Much, *Elvis Presley*
18. It's Not for Me to Say, *Johnny Mathis*
19. Banana Boat (Day-O), *Harry Belafonte*
20. Honeycomb, *Jimmie Rodgers*
21. You Send Me, *Sam Cooke*
22. A White Sport Coat, *Marty Robbins*
23. Send for Me, *Nat King Cole*
24. Singing the Blues, *Guy Mitchell*
25. Banana Boat, *Tarriers*
26. Butterfly, *Andy Williams*
27. Silhouettes, *Rays*
28. That'll Be the Day, *Crickets*
29. School Day, *Chuck Berry*
30. Searchin', *Coasters*
31. Gone, *Ferlin Husky*
32. Butterfly, *Charlie Gracie*
33. I'm Gonna Sit Right Down and Write Myself a Letter, *Billy Williams*
34. Dark Moon, *Gale Storm*
35. Whole Lotta Shakin' Goin' On, *Jerry Lee Lewis*
36. Fascination, *Jane Morgan*
37. A Teenager's Romance, *Ricky Nelson*
38. Marianne, *Terry Gilkyson and the Easy Riders*
39. I'm Walkin', *Fats Domino*
40. Teenage Crush, *Tommy Sands*

THE TOP 10 LPs

1. My Fair Lady, *Original Cast*
2. Around the World in 80 Days, *Original Soundtrack*
3. Oklahoma, *Original Soundtrack*
4. Hymns, *Tennessee Ernie Ford*
5. Calypso, *Harry Belafonte*
6. Love Is the Thing, *Nat King Cole*
7. The King and I, *Original Soundtrack*
8. Songs of the Fabulous Fifties, *Roger Williams*
9. Film Encores, *Mantovani*
10. The Eddy Duchin Story, *Original Soundtrack*

10

Don't Forbid Me
PAT BOONE

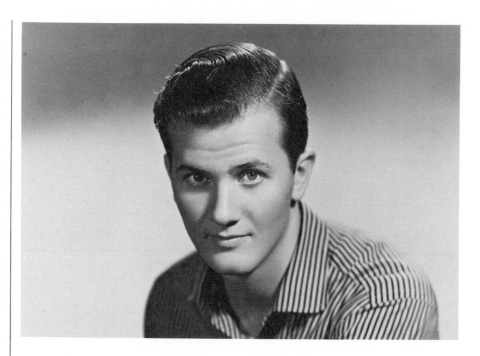

"To me, what makes my emergence and my career such a miracle or phenomenon is that nobody in my family had any contact with show business," said Pat Boone. "I played a little ukulele, sang at a lot of weddings and funerals, but that was all at first. Later I emceed a local radio show called 'Youth on Parade' and eventually won a Nashville talent contest. I then appeared on Ted Mack's 'Original Amateur Hour' four times and on 'Arthur Godfrey Time.' Randy Wood of Dot Records saw me on TV, called my folks, and suggested that we get together. I met with Randy and he said, 'You ought to be recording for us. When I find a song I think could be a hit, I'll ring you up.' I thought he'd forgotten about it, but eight months later he called and the song was 'Two Hearts.' We went to Chicago, recorded it, and that became my first hit."

"Two Hearts," in the spring of 1955, kicked off one of the most prodigious and durable careers in pop music history. A direct descendant of frontiersman Daniel Boone, Charles Eugene "Pat" Boone blazed his own trail in the fifties and sixties, opening doors for many kinds of music and emerging as the third most successful recording artist of his time, behind Elvis and the Beatles. He placed no less than sixty songs on America's hit parade, fifteen of which were top-ten singles. He remained on the charts for more than two hundred consecutive weeks, having at least one song in contention every week—an all-time record.

Pat became best known as a clean-cut alternative to Elvis Presley, and a popularizer of rock, country and R&B material ignored by much of the general public. Such songs were often considered crude and unlistenable in their original versions, but acceptable when "cleaned up" and sung more smoothly by Pat. His early hits included "Ain't That a Shame" and

"At My Front Door" (both 1955). Later there were "I'll Be Home," "Tutti Frutti," "Long Tall Sally," "I Almost Lost My Mind," "Friendly Persuasion" and "Chains of Love" (all 1956). In the fall of that year, Pat recorded his second of five number-one songs: "Don't Forbid Me."

"That was such a fluke," he remembered. "Somebody had sent it in, and it was one of the tunes that Randy had picked for me to record. Billy Vaughn came up with a pretty good arrangement, but in the studio we skipped it and worked on other stuff.

"Now today you spend $100,000 and fifty hours to get one song down. In those days, you went in and recorded for three hours—maybe a half hour over if you were really working on something—and you just had to get things right in that time. In this case, we managed to get down a couple of things that Randy really liked, and he was relaxed. He said, 'Look, there's no point in starting another song. We've got what we came for, and there's only twenty

minutes left. Let's just call it quits, and let the musicians go home early.'

"I went over to Billy Vaughn and said, 'What about this song, Billy? We didn't get to it.' And he said, 'Yeah, it's too bad. This is a nice song. I think it could be a hit.' He started playing it for me, and when he got to that low note—'Hold me in your lovin' arms'—'arms' dropped down almost below the range of normal hearing.

"Now I'm a frustrated bass. I always listen to low notes, and love to sing low. As soon as I heard that—he didn't even have to play it all the way through—I sort of had goose bumps, and thought this could be a real big hit. I ran into the control room and said, 'Randy, hold the musicians. Let's run this one over.' He said, 'We've only got about fifteen minutes left.' I said, 'Well, I think this thing could pay for the whole session.' So he said, 'O.K., let's run over this song for Pat.' We did, and got the whole song down in fifteen minutes. Six weeks later it was number one. It was just a runaway smash."

Round and Round
PERRY COMO

Pierino Roland Como was born the seventh son of a seventh son, in the mining town of Canonsburg, Pennsylvania. At the age of fifteen he opened his own barber shop, and he often sang pop songs of the day while going about his work. Among his customers were traveling musicians, more than a few of which were impressed by the lad's voice and personality. In 1933, Perry was offered a job singing with a dance band, for the overwhelming salary of $28 a week. This meant giving up the $125 a week he was already making, a real risk in the worst slump of the Depression. But finally he decided to give music a try.

Perry developed his early style by studying his idol, Bing Crosby. "He set the pattern for all of us," said Como. "He was an easygoing, relaxed crooner. He didn't have a great voice; none of us do. But he communicated naturally, selling a song by making it believable."

By 1936, Perry was the featured vocalist with the big band of Ted Weems. Every Sunday they would broadcast coast to coast, and Como quickly built up a national following. Things looked bright until 1942, when Weems broke up his orchestra and went into military service. Discouraged, Perry almost went back to cutting hair, but his wife insisted, "You can't quit now. Something's bound to happen."

And of course, something did. Perry was booked into New York's Copacabana nightclub, and the engagement was "a smash." Como got his own radio show and a contract with Victor Records. In 1944, the hits began with a top-ten song, "Long Ago (and Far Away)." The next year, there were "Temptation," "If I Loved You," "Dig You Later (A Hubba-Hubba-Hubba)," and "'Til the End of Time"—all million-

sellers. Some of these tunes were introduced in musical films that he made, such as *Something for the Boys* (1944), *If I'm Lucky* (1946), and *Words and Music* (1948).

"I like things like 'Dreamer's Holiday,' or anything by Rodgers and Hart or Rodgers and Hammerstein," said Perry. "Or Jimmy Van Heusen. He wrote most of the stuff for Bing's pictures. 'Give Me Your Hand,' 'Some Enchanted Evening'—these are great songs, and I love to sing them. People come to my concerts to see what I do—whatever that might be—and to hear things like 'When You Were Sweet Sixteen,' 'Prisoner of Love,' 'Surrender.' You can go right down the line. 'Catch a Falling Star'. . . . And I enjoy doing them, because if I didn't, I wouldn't walk out there."

In the dozen years between 1944 and 1956, Perry Como placed nearly seventy songs on the charts. There were all kinds, from neo-operatic ballads to novelties, from Christmas carols to rock. In fact, he recorded the very first rock record ever released by RCA, "Ko Ko Mo."

"If I had chosen all of my music, I would probably still be cutting hair or something," Perry said with a grin. "My commercial sense was just not that great. There was a song in 1952 that I didn't want to do at first. It was off meter, as far as I was concerned. But it went to number one—'Don't Let the Stars Get in Your Eyes.' "

Early in 1957, Perry was persuaded to record a kind of song that he had rarely tried before. It was a round, and in fact was called "Round and Round." It had been written a few weeks before by Joe Shapiro and Lou Stallman. Perry introduced the song on his NBC-TV variety series. It got a tremendous response, not only from his television audience, but from record buyers and critics as well. It became his fifteenth

million-seller and stayed on the charts for nearly seven months.

In an interview conducted around that time, Perry was asked about the rock 'n' roll invasion. "I think what they're selling the kids today is that beat," he said. "You can play 'Stardust' or 'Deep Purple' for them, and if it doesn't have that 'thing' going on in the back, they say, 'Well, that's square. That's for old people.' But it's still beautiful music to us.

"Twenty years from now, or ten years from now, I can imagine somebody singing 'you ain't nothin' but a hound dog.' A lot of thirty- to fifty-year-olds may get a little sick about that. But this is *their* music, and someday it'll probably become the standard music."

Bye Bye Love
THE EVERLY BROTHERS

Don and Phil Everly were born in Brownie, Kentucky, and raised on the road, all over the South and Midwest. Their parents, Ike and Margaret, were stars of their own country radio show, broadcast weekly by KMA in Shenandoah, Iowa. When Don was six and Phil was eight, they made their professional debut on that program, telling jokes, singing, and playing guitar. After that, they accompanied their parents everywhere on tours.

The Everly family act broke up once the brothers had graduated from high school. Don and Phil moved to Memphis with dreams of carving out their own musical career. While still in their teens, they were already show biz veterans, able to handle the ups—and the downs.

"We were getting some money from our parents," Phil recalled, "but not enough to really live on. They were doing the best they could, but nobody actually had any money. In fact, in 1956, we only worked about three gigs, and those were way below scale. We'd drive three hundred miles, and earn maybe $10 apiece. And we were expected to kick back $5 to the promoter."

Columbia Records beckoned later that year, releasing the very first Everly Brothers single: "Keep a-Lovin' Me." "It laid a complete ostrich egg," said Phil. "We cut some other things, but they were never even issued. I think they burned the tapes."

The Everly parents, though, never gave up on their sons; Ike, in fact, raved about the boys to anyone who would listen. "He opened a little barber shop, and I was one of his customers," recalled songwriter Boudleaux Bryant. "Every time I came in, he'd tell me about Phil and Don. Eventually my publisher, Wesley Rose, sent a demo of the brothers to Archie Bleyer, who was then setting up a country division of Cadence Records. Archie thought it was great and immediately said he'd take them on."

Along with other songwriters, Boudleaux was invited to submit material for the Everlys' consideration. "I had this song which had been turned down by twenty-nine other performers. My wife and I had written it for a country duet, Johnny and Jack—Johnny being Johnny Wright, the husband of Kitty Wells. Johnny said it was all right, but they wouldn't do it because they already had enough material for their next session. So I sent it to Elvis, Porter Wagoner, anybody we could think of, but nobody got excited about it until the Everlys came along."

"When we cut 'Bye Bye Love,'" said Phil, "we were starving to death, and I'd imagine we would have done anything. The main reason we cut the record was for the session money—the fee you get for recording. I think at the time we were getting about forty dollars a side. Donald put an intro on it that he had made up for another song, and we cut the thing in about three hours. I don't think anybody figured it to be a number one."

"Bye Bye Love" broke onto both the pop and country charts in mid-May of 1957 and within a few weeks was also outselling nearly everything in the R&B field. By the end of the month, the boys had been admitted to the Grand Ole Opry, and soon after, they were startling country fans with their use of drums onstage. Such percussion instruments had rarely been seen at the Opry, and some considered their use a sacrilege. But this was the dawn of a new age—the rockabilly rebels had arrived.

"Rock 'n' roll is just an extension of country music," stated Phil. "Buddy Holly, Jimmy Bowen, Buddy Knox, Roy Orbison, Elvis Presley, Don and I—we were part of the country-rock contingent. Rock 'n' roll is just a northern term, anyway. If that phrase hadn't caught on, we would have been called 'new wave country.'

"You know, in that first year, 1957, we had two million-sellers in a row—'Bye Bye Love' and 'Wake Up Little Susie.' Yet the two of us were still only making about $500 a night. That's almost laughable today, since that's what we pay sidemen now. But somehow it didn't seem to matter to us. We could feel new ground being broken, and I'm glad that Don and I got into it when we did. Being at the beginning of anything can be the greatest joy in your life, because it can never be taken away."

So Rare

JIMMY DORSEY

The career of Jimmy Dorsey began in a family quartet led by his father, a music teacher. Rounding out the group was his sister, Mary, and younger brother, Tommy. From there, Jimmy and Tommy put together their first orchestra, Dorsey's Novelty Six, which they called "the jazz band of them all." Two years later, they became Dorsey's Wild Canaries, one of the first jazz bands to appear on radio.

After that act broke up, the brothers made their recording debut with Billy Lustig's Scranton Sirens. In 1924, they joined Eddie Elkins and his California Ramblers. They continued to free lance and work as session musicians until 1934, when they launched the Dorsey Brothers Orchestra.

Jimmy and Tommy had opposite personalities, and sometimes their rivalry would flare into out and out combat. One night, at the Glen Island Casino, they broke into a fist fight onstage. A short time later, Jimmy criticized the tempo of a song. Tommy glared at him icily, grabbed his horn, and stormed off. They were not to share a bandstand again for nearly twenty years.

The brothers formed rival groups, and both became leading figures in the Big Band Era. Jimmy's greatest success came in the early forties, with twenty-three top-ten hits. In 1941, he had four top-ten singles in a row—"Amapola," "My Sister and I," "Green Eyes," and "Maria Elena." Other big Jimmy Dorsey records included "Tangerine," "Besame Mucho," "Blue Champagne," and his theme song, "Contrasts."

In 1953, Jimmy broke up his big band, and the brothers were reunited in a new Dorsey Brothers Orchestra. They entered television, and hosted their own series, "Stage Show," which ran on CBS between July 1954 and September 1956. Two months later, at the age of fifty-one, Tommy choked to death in his sleep. Jimmy then carried on alone—to the final triumph of his life.

"I was their TV musical director," said Lee Castle, who also doubled as lead trumpet player. "What happened was, Lee Carlton of Fraternity Records really liked this old song, 'So Rare,' from 1937. I can tell you now, I'd never have picked it, and I don't know anyone else who would have either. Jimmy Dorsey wouldn't have picked it. But Harry had a lot of faith in it, and put a lot of money behind it. He got a good arranger, Lou Douglas, and set a deal up for Jimmy to record it.

" 'So Rare' had a good backbeat to it, a simple backbeat, and that's what made it work. That's why rock 'n' roll came through—because it simplified the dance rhythm. Jazz bands were playing so damn 'modern' that they got out of hand. People couldn't whistle or tap their feet to what they were doing. So, the folks went elsewhere, back to the real beat. After all, what makes people dance is the rhythm. If all you're going to give them is be-bop and modern jazz stuff, they're not going to be able to move. And people have to dance if they want to stay young.

"Jimmy took a lot of takes. He was never easily satisfied with anything. He was trying to get a certain sound, and finally, after a long time, he got it. That was the take they released, and it was a hit."

"So Rare" broke onto the pop charts in mid-February 1957, and hung on for an incredible thirty-eight weeks. It peaked in June, the month Jimmy Dorsey was given his gold record. Then, on June 12, he died of cancer, at the age of fifty-three.

"Jimmy was the best saxophone player in the world," said Lee in 1981. "The most generous man, the most sensitive guy I ever met—a real human being. And 'So Rare' is still going big, even today. I now lead the Jimmy Dorsey Orchestra, and we play all over the world, forty-four weeks a year. I have to do that song twice a night. Everybody wants 'So Rare.' I tell you—it's enough to drive you nuts."

Tammy
DEBBIE REYNOLDS

Mary Francis "Debbie" Reynolds was born in El Paso, Texas, but grew up in Southern California. In high school, she played French horn with the Burbank Youth Symphony. Then, in 1948, she won the "Miss Burbank" beauty contest, and was given a screen contract with MGM. Over the next seventeen years, she was to make more than forty movies, including *Singin' in the Rain* (1952), *The Tender Trap* (1955), *Goodbye Charlie* (1964), *The Unsinkable Molly Brown* (1964), and *Divorce American Style* (1967). She also cut two of the biggest pop records of the fifties.

The first came from her fourth picture, *Two Weeks with Love,* which featured actor Carlton Carpenter. The song was a high-speed gibberish duet of jungle romance—"Abba Daba Honeymoon." In the spring of 1951, it sold more than a million copies on the MGM label.

More films followed, and in 1957, Debbie was loaned out to Universal to co-star in *Tammy and the Bachelor.* It was the story of a country girl

who fell for a pilot she nursed back to health after a plane crash. Music for the movie was provided by the songwriting team of Jay Livingston and Ray Evans.

"According to the original script," recalled Ray, "Tammy had to sing a song in her attic room while gazing wistfully out the window. Someone overheard her, and asked what the song was. She said it was a song her great-grandmother used to sing, and had been handed down through the family. That dictated the style of song: it had to have an old 'folk-type' flavor. The problem was to have the character sing a song about herself. We solved that by making the title a quote—that is, 'I hear the cottonwoods whisp'ring above, "Tammy, Tammy, Tammy's in love."'"

"The song was played for me," said Debbie, "and I thought it was lovely. It's a very pretty song, very sweet, very plaintive, the kind of song I like. I cut it with just a piano player, and then we shot the scene as I lip-synched. Afterwards they added more instruments to the track and I went

down to listen to it. That's when I discovered who had 'ghosted' the arrangement—Henry Mancini! I knew it had to have been a pretty good somebody."

Ray continued. "Universal owned a record company called Coral, and they were obligated to release the song. The head of the label, Bob Thiele, didn't think it would sell anything, so instead of recutting it as a record, he decided to just lift the soundtrack. It ran three-and-a-half minutes, which at that time was usually the death knell for records, because deejays were clamoring for two-minute stuff."

"The picture was released," said Debbie, "and was not terribly successful. Then the song came out, took off, and hit number one on the charts. I was in Europe when they called me, and I laughed; I said, 'You have to be kidding.' I had just married Eddie Fisher—he had had thirty-one straight hits—and for me to have one was startling."

"Tammy" broke onto American radio in mid-July 1957, and by August was the best-selling record in the country. It remained a big hit for more than thirty weeks, selling well over two million copies. It also sparked the re-release of *Tammy and the Bachelor,* which became a box-office smash.

"The role and the record were good for my career then," said Debbie, "but in later years, very bad. People wouldn't let me grow up—they still thought of me as Tammy."

Debbie, of course, did transcend the role, and went on to make many more feature films, two TV series, and a permanent place for herself on the Las Vegas nightclub circuit. She also opened a health spa—"Debbie's Place"—where she still works out.

And Tammy? Debbie never repeated the part, but the character turned up in several movie sequels and, in 1965, a short-lived television show.

Young Love
SONNY JAMES

Sonny James won his first musical honor in 1934, when he was four years old. He and his mother, father, and sister Thelma took first place in a folk music contest. Singer Kate Smith gave Sonny her own prize of a silver dollar and predicted a future of "great artistic achievement" for the young singer. She was certainly right about that.

Born and raised in Hackleburg, Alabama, "Sonny" James Louden spent most of his early years on stage or on the radio. At the age of five, he defeated fifty-two other hopefuls for a full-time radio contract with a station in Birmingham. By the time he was ten, he had mastered the violin and had won three tri-state and two mid-South championships. By 1947, he had learned nearly every instrument in the orchestra and was the featured vocalist on a Dallas radio show.

Sonny spent fifteen months in Korea in the early fifties, entertaining the troops with his fiddle, guitar, and unique delivery. He was uncertain, though, about his future, when he returned to the States in 1952. A Nashville friend, Chet Atkins, introduced him to record producer Ken Nelson. Upon hearing some of the material Sonny had written overseas, Nelson asked him to record, and thus began a long and productive musical relationship.

The very first Sonny James record to make any noise was "For Rent," which became a country hit in the spring of 1956. Elvis Presley, though, had just exploded nationwide, and in comparison, the success of Sonny's little single seemed minimized. As a result, Sonny decided to try next for the kind of song that could go over in any field, be it country, pop, or rhythm and blues. The search ended in November when another old friend, music publisher Bill Lowery, came up with "Young Love."

The song had been written a few months earlier by two young Atlantans, Carole Joyner and Ric Cartey, who happened to be dating at the time. Cartey had recorded the song for RCA Victor, but his single had flopped. Lowery played a tape of "Young Love" for Sonny, who said that he "immediately liked it" and wanted to give it a try.

Sonny worked out a new arrangement for the song and began recording it in the studio. During the session, debate arose over the balance between the drum work and Sonny's acoustic guitar. Finally, it was decided to place the guitar out front, thus establishing what became known as the "Sonny James sound."

The single was released early in December and broke onto the pop and country charts shortly before Christmas 1956. One week afterward, two other renditions had joined it—one by actor Tab Hunter and another by a Canadian vocal group, the Crew Cuts. All three versions managed to become major hits, landing in the national top twenty by February.

Sonny himself always regarded "Young Love" with particular fondness, remembering it as the turning point in his career. He knew he'd found a good song, but never dreamed that it would go on to sell more than three million copies. He also couldn't have guessed that "Young Love" was to define his whole recording style—one of the most durable, and successful, in country music history.

Little Darlin'
THE DIAMONDS

The Diamonds got together in Canada, at the University of Toronto, and, in their earliest days, were Ted Kowalski (tenor), Bill Reed (bass), Phil Letitt (baritone), and Stan Fisher (lead). In the fall of 1954, they went to audition for a TV program. They never got a chance to be on the show, but while waiting in the hallway, they met a CBC technician—and aspiring singer—named David Somerville. They went with him into an empty studio and, after a little harmonizing, accepted him as a fifth member of the group. A short while later, the boys were booked to appear at St. Thomas Aquinas Church for a hometown music show. At the last minute, Stan Fisher backed out, saying that music had taken him away from his studies. Dave Somerville replaced him as lead singer, a role he would remain in for the next eight years.

At this point, the boys finalized their group name, which had been suggested by Ted Kowalski. The word *diamond* had class, he felt, and it would be easy to make diamond emblems to wear on their suit coats. Not only that, but they could take cardboard squares and tilt them into diamond-shaped posters, with each guy's photo in one of the corners. The others thought these were terrific ideas, and before long, the Diamonds were in hot demand in Canada and upstate New York. Audiences were amazed by their quick-study skills— their ability to master flawless impressions of nearly any other act, regardless of style.

By January 1956, the boys were recording for Mercury, and their first assignment was to remake a Teenagers record, "Why Do Fools Fall in Love?" Although they didn't outsell the original group, the Diamonds did do well enough to get locked in a bag, as far as their label was concerned. The boys begged for original material, but Mercury almost always gave them "proven songs," those which had

already become hits for other artists. "We did so many cover versions back then," said John Felten, who replaced Ted Kowalski. "Mercury used to really push us because we could come in and do them in a hurry. They had very good distribution in those days. A lot of times a smaller label would release a record, and Mercury could cut a cover on it as much as two or three weeks later and still beat that first single to almost every city." That was the case with "Little Darlin'," a song originally recorded by the Gladiolas. The Diamonds' version hit the charts nearly a month before the Gladiolas' record even got off the ground.

"They were a bunch of young guys who showed up in Nashville one day at this little record shop," recalled John. "The owner had a little studio in the back, and he'd record just about anybody who'd walk in the door. His equipment was awful. It just couldn't compete with what studios in the big cities had. That's why the Gladiolas' record never made it. It just sounded bad. It wasn't the group's fault."

The leader of the Gladiolas, Maurice Williams, was the composer of "Little Darlin'." He'd written the song two years before, at the age of fifteen. At the time, he'd been trying to date two girls simultaneously and had been caught in the arms of one by the other. After finally making his choice, he sat down at the piano and wrote to his "little darlin'" that he'd been "wrong to love two."

"Little Darlin'" was recorded at Universal Studios in Chicago in February 1957. Less than one month later, it was on the charts, where it remained for a very impressive twenty-six weeks. It was the biggest record the Diamonds ever had, out of more than a dozen hits.

The Diamonds went on to record several more "novelty tunes," such as "High Sign," "Walking Along," and "She Say (Oom Dooby Doom)." They

also cut one other million-seller, "The Stroll," which, happily for them, was the "original" song that they had hoped for for so many years.

"The Diamonds were different from most of the fifties groups," John explained. "Most of the groups in that era were made up of guys who got together to make records. The Diamonds, on the other hand, started out to be live entertainers. We did, between 1956 and 1968, over ten thousand shows—thirty-three dates on "American Bandstand" alone. We were really a performing group that got lucky with records."

All Shook Up

ELVIS PRESLEY

By 1957, Elvis Presley was more than just the hottest name in music. He was also a marketing marvel, capable of moving a mountain of merchandise through mere name association. Hundreds of firms eagerly bid for the right to use the Presley endorsement, and before long, 188 products had been so licensed. Among them were lipsticks (in Hound Dog Orange, Tutti Frutti Red, and Heartbreak Hotel Pink), T-shirts, pencils, purses, mittens, socks, games, guitars, shoes, binders, bubble gum, scarves, skirts, mirrors, trading cards, pins, stuffed hound dogs, phonographs, statues, soft drinks, dancing dolls, greeting cards, knit pajamas, wallets, necklaces, ties, hats, cologne, scrapbooks, teddy bears, sweaters, rings, charm bracelets, bookends, key chains, photo albums, plastic busts, handkerchiefs, buttons, wrist watches, diaries, combs, molded plastic painted figures, hairbrushes, and 8 × 10 luminous pictures. It was estimated that, in 1957 alone, the sale of these items grossed over $55 million.

This, of course, was aside from Elvis's main product, which was phonograph records. In 1956, he achieved the greatest sales ever in one year—over ten million records sold. In 1957, he continued the pace, with two new albums—his first Christmas effort, and the soundtrack of *Loving You.* Both reached number one on the LP charts.

Elvis began the year, not in a recording studio, but in a hospital. The date was January 4, and the occasion was his pre-induction army physical. As expected, he easily made the grade. Two days later, he was in New York, performing live on the "Ed Sullivan Show." He sang seven songs and, for the first and only time, was televised from the waist up only (the wiggle of "Elvis the Pelvis" was considered too much for home viewing). It would be his last TV appearance for more than three years.

And speaking of "Too Much," that was the title of Elvis' first single of 1957. It spent most of February as the number-one record in the country. The next month, Elvis bought himself a house—Graceland, a sprawling estate on the edge of Memphis.

In April, his tenth million-seller topped America's hit parade. It was "All Shook Up," a record destined to spend more consecutive weeks on the pop charts than any other Elvis Presley song. It had been written by Otis Blackwell, the composer of Elvis' favorite song, "Don't Be Cruel." Presley was eager to record another Blackwell tune. But he wasn't completely satisfied with the song in its original form. With Blackwell's consent, he rewrote some of the words and recorded it early in 1957. Lyrically, "All Shook Up" was built around a well-used fifties expression. When the words were combined with the rolling rhythm of a boogie-woogie piano, the effect was incredible. "All Shook Up" spent thirty weeks on the best-seller lists, including eight weeks at number one.

In July, Elvis's second movie, *Loving You,* was finally released. The title song became a good-sized hit, but it was the other side of the record, another tune from the movie, that became a number-one smash: "(Let Me Be Your) Teddy Bear." A few months later, "Jailhouse Rock" became both a box-office bonanza and Presley's sixth single to top the charts. By the end of 1957, Elvis had sold over twenty-eight million records.

Perhaps the Presleymania that gripped the United States in 1957 was best summed up by a report in the

St. Petersburg (Florida) *Evening Independent.* This is how it read, in part: "The Pied Piper of rock 'n' roll, a swivel-hipped, leg-lashing entertainment bomb, blasted the downtown area into chaos all day yesterday. Screaming, fainting teenagers lined the streets early to catch a glimpse of Elvis Presley, a rockabilly gyrating singer who's shattered show business with his sultry style. He hit St. Petersburg with the effect of a small H-bomb, sending fans into mass hysteria and receiving an ovation rarely seen on the Suncoast." And that's the way it went, in city after city.

Young Love
TAB HUNTER

Arthur Andrew Kelm never knew his father. He was raised by his mom, a New York physiotherapist, who later let him adopt her maiden name of Gelien. At fifteen, he ran away from home and, lying about his age, signed up for a two-year hitch in the Coast Guard. After getting out, he developed championship ability as an ice skater and a fervent love of horses. His dream was to someday show hunters and jumpers professionally. However, there was little call for his combination of skills, and within a few months, Arthur was forced to get by on whatever odd jobs he could find.

By 1948 he was working in a sheet metal plant, where, by chance, he was discovered by Dick Clayton, a veteran talent scout. Clayton was impressed by the young man's good looks and introduced him to agent Harry Wilson. Harry told Arthur that he had a future in show business if only he'd change his name. "You could take 'Hunter' from the horses," Harry said, "but then we have to tab you with something first." Out of that came one of the most famous stage names in history.

Tab Hunter made a quick screen test in the summer of 1948 and then was cast in *Island of Desire,* his first starring film. After that came a long list of pictures, including *Saturday Island* (1952), *Gun Belt* (1953), *Damn Yankees* (1958), *The Pleasure of His Company* (1960), *The Golden Arrow* (1962), *Birds Do It* (1966), *Hostile Guns* (1967), *Judge Roy Bean* (1972), and *The Temper Tramp* (1973). He also tackled TV, appearing on a number of dramatic anthology shows, such as "Climax"; "The Hallmark Hall of Fame" and "Playhouse 90," for which he earned an Emmy nomination.

Tab's looks and talent made him a natural teen idol—the epitome of all that was "right" for a young man in the fifties. It was inevitable that he would branch out into making of records.

"That all came about through Randy Wood," said Tab. "Randy had a really good tune called 'Young Love.' He played the Sonny James version for me and said, 'I'd like you to record this song,' and I said, 'O.K., fine.' And then I sat down with Billy Vaughn and we started to work on it, Christmas week of '56, for the Dot label.

"After we cut the record, Dot sent it to a lot of distributors, and in no time at all, bang, it just shot right up the charts. I was really surprised how quickly it got up there. The first time I heard it on the air I was driving along and pulled my car over to the side to listen to it. It sounded like a weak, scared me, but it also had a nice, personal tone. Randy always used to say you can tell if a tune is going to make it by how it sounds on a car radio.

"A few months later, I had another big hit, 'Ninety-nine Ways.' But I was unable to continue recording because Warner Brothers refused to let me. I was actually under contract to Warner Brothers for everything, including records. Then they started their own label—I guess they wanted a piece of the action—and they picked tunes for me. I had one small hit with them in 1959—'Apple Blossom Time.' I wasn't terribly happy there, because I wanted my freedom. I finally bought back my contract—it cost me $100,000—and I did a TV series, "The Tab Hunter Show," in 1960 and 1961. We had a dreadful time slot, opposite the last half of the "Ed Sullivan Show." How can you compete against jugglers, dancing bears, and the Vienna Boys' Choir?

"After that I wanted to work, but couldn't get a job in Hollywood. People kind of turned their backs on me, so I went to Europe and starting making films over there. When I got back, I became a pioneer in American dinner theater, and I've been working in those ever since."

In 1977, Tab appeared in nineteen episodes of the TV series "Forever Fernwood." In 1981, he starred in the film *Polyester* and sang the title tune. Chris Stein from Blondie scored the whole movie, and Deborah Harry did the lyrics. She also did backup vocals for Tab. In 1982, he portrayed a teacher in the motion picture *Grease II.*

Love Letters in the Sand

PAT BOONE

In 1956, Pat Boone was the second most successful hitmaker of the year, following Elvis Presley. In 1957, those positions reversed, as Pat surged ahead with five distinctive singles. Both sides of each release made the charts, with three songs going all the way to number one.

The five were "Don't Forbid Me"/ "Anastasia," "Why Baby Why"/"I'm Waitin' Just for You," "Love Letters in the Sand"/"Bernardine," "Remember You're Mine"/"There's a Gold Mine in the Sky" and "April Love"/"When the Swallows Come Back to Capistrano." Of those, one became Pat's all-time biggest hit—a four-and-a-half-million seller. It was a tune written in 1931 by Nick Kenny, a sports columnist for the New York *Daily Mirror;* his brother, Charles; and J. Fred Coots.

" 'Love Letters in the Sand,' " recalled Pat, "now that was a song Randy Wood of Dot Records liked ever since Bing Crosby recorded it many years before. Frankly, I didn't share his enthusiasm for the song, because by that time I was much more in tune with rock 'n' roll. It just didn't sound commercial to me—it didn't seem like the kind of thing that was happening then.

"Anyway, we recorded it once and Randy liked it, but something else got put out instead. Later, we tried it again, but it still just seemed to lie there. Randy loved it, but the song never moved me. Finally, we had three different versions in the can, all cut at different sessions.

"It was then that I made my first movie, *Bernardine,* and Johnny Mercer wrote the title theme. It was a sophisticated, tongue-in-cheek sort of slick lyric with a lot of inner rhymes, for which he was noted. I was thrilled that Johnny Mercer would write a song for my movie, but I thought they were kidding themselves about it becoming a hit. It wasn't rock, and what was happening then was rock 'n' roll.

"Well, we needed something to put on the B side of 'Bernardine,' and the studio wanted another song in the movie. It didn't have to be tied in with the plot—just a song that I'd sing to myself in a back room. Randy convinced the people at 20th that 'Love Letters in the Sand' would work perfectly, and they agreed. They didn't care what it was. So we did 'Love Letters in the Sand,' and I lip-synched it in the movie.

"Then the single came out, and 'Bernardine' took off. It was getting all the promotion as the title theme, and even today when I travel around the world—especially the Orient—it's still a big request item.

"But at the same time, deejays flipped the record over and played the other side—'Love Letters in the Sand.' I don't know what that song had, and I still don't. Even now when I hear it I'm amazed that it was such a runaway smash. Once on the "Merv Griffin Show," Dick Clark conducted a little quiz. He asked which of these singles was on the charts the longest: 'Hey Jude' by the Beatles, 'Don't Be Cruel' by Elvis Presley, or 'Love Letters in the Sand.' Merv guessed 'Don't be Cruel.' I thought it was 'Hey Jude,' but it turned out to be 'Love Letters in the Sand.' It was around for thirty-one weeks—a record."

Pat's single broke in early May 1957, and in June began its seven-week run as America's most popular song. Later in the year, "April Love" also reached number one, and lasted six months on the charts.

Pat Boone went on to have many more hit records, including "A Wonderful Time Up There" (1958), "Twixt Twelve and Twenty" (1959), "Welcome New Lovers" (1960), "Moody River" (1961), and "Speedy Gonzales" (1962). He also hosted three TV shows, starred in more than a dozen films, and became a best-selling author.

"I was not a watershed performer," said Pat. "However, I did act as a sort of catalyst—making rock more acceptable, and allaying fears that parents and ministers had about this revolutionary new music. Elvis and I were compared because we were successful at the same time; in fact, a media feud was even created between us. But actually we had many of the same fans; he appealed to one set of their instincts, I appealed to another. He was the rebel, breaking rules and winning, while I was the conformist, playing by the rules and still winning. I think most people identified with that."

1958

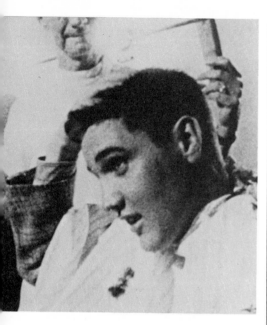

NINETEEN FIFTY-EIGHT was another milestone year in pop history. Over a billion dollar's worth of music had been sold since "Heartbreak Hotel," and now many of the best recordings were gaining new recognition. The RIAA began auditing record company books, and when they came across a million-seller, they certified it "gold." NARAS was formed and began offering its Grammy Awards. The first stereo LPs appeared, and for the first time, U.S. record sales topped $500 million a year.

Parents, teachers, and civic groups stopped laughing at rock 'n' roll in 1958. The silly fad once joked about now loomed as a very real threat to their music, morals, and lifestyles. "Why Don't They Understand?" asked George Hamilton IV in his biggest hit of the year. "Don't Ask Me Why," replied Elvis. "Rave On," said Buddy Holly, and Danny and the Juniors responded: "Rock and Roll Is Here to Stay."

Joachim Krauledat remembers 1958 as the year he escaped East Germany under Communist gunfire. A decade later, he'd return the thunder as John Kay, leader of Steppenwolf. Sam and Dave, the Brothers Four, the O'Jays, and Dion and the Belmonts all got together in 1958. And it was that summer that America got its first taste of heavy metal music. A single called "Rumble," performed on a $4 guitar, introduced Link Wray and His Ray Men. Incredibly, they had actually cut the song four years before!

March 24 was a cold, rainy, depressing day in Memphis—the day **Elvis Aron Presley** was drafted into the army. It cost the United States $400,000 in taxes alone, with Presley's own income dropping from over $100,000 to $78 a month. At Fort Chaffee, Oklahoma, Elvis was given the standard GI haircut, for which he paid the going army rate of sixty-five cents. He caught some of the hair in one hand and blew it toward the photographers. "Hair today, gone tomorrow," he said with a grin, but to millions of fans, his two-year stay in Germany was no joke. More than 10,000 letters arrived each week, many addressed simply "Elvis, U.S. Army." While overseas, Presley was to meet his future wife, Priscilla Beaulieu, who was then fourteen years old.

Dick Clark became a nearly ubiquitous personality on ABC when he took on a prime-time rock 'n' roll half-hour on February 15—"The Saturday Night Beechnut Show." Already the host of "American Bandstand" weekdays, Dick had to commute to New York from Philadelphia every weekend just to host this live, landmark program. Guests on the premier telecast included Johnnie Ray, Pat Boone, Chuck Willis, Connie Francis, Jerry Lee Lewis, and the Royal Teens.

The career of **Jerry Lee Lewis** was in full frenzy in 1958, when he starred in his second motion picture, *High School Confidential.* The film began with Jerry Lee in the back of a truck, whipping through the frantic title theme. He was an outrageous performer—self-confident, swaggering—but his arrogance was compensated for by a supreme talent. He was a master interpreter, capable of taking nearly any song and making it sound custom-written just for him. That, and the relentless rhythm of his pumpin' piano, helped make Jerry Lee one of the great originals of rock. Other music films of 1958 included *Hot Rod Gang* with Gene Vincent, *Sing Boy Sing* with Tommy Sands, *King Creole* with Elvis, and *Keep It Cool* with Paul Anka, Danny and the Juniors, Julius LaRosa, Wink Martindale, Della Reese, Roy Hamilton, and the Royal Teens.

The **Coasters** had an entirely different black sound: a raw, unpolished, urban brand of hard R&B. The group featured a wide range of comical singers who all seemed to have an offbeat, vaudevillian sense of humor. Coasters records were a kind of social satire set to a okay beat. "Young Blood," "Searchin'," "Poison Ivy," "Charlie Brown," "Along Came Jones"—each one of these songs was a comic cameo, a parody of teen or ghetto life. Most of their music was written by their producers, Jerry Lieber and Mike Stoller, who gave the group their name because they had developed on the West Coast. In 1958, the Coasters topped the charts for the first and only time with "Yakety Yak," a single highlighted by the nifty sax of King Curtis.

Antirock hysteria, which had been building for several years, reached a zenith in 1958 as civic groups, government agencies, and moralists rallied to stamp out the music that was "ruining our youth." The New York *Daily News* called it a "barrage of primitive jungle beat rhythm" and suggested making rock dancing illegal without written parental consent. In Asbury Park, New Jersey, one newspaper claimed that twenty-five "vibrating teens" had to be hospitalized after a rock 'n' roll record hop. In San Antonio, city council members banned rock from jukeboxes near public pools because it "attracted undesirable elements given to practicing their spastic gyrations in abbreviated bathing suits." In Nashville, Elvis was hung in effigy, and a deejay burned six hundred of his records in the city park. Some radio programmers banned rock music as "not up to station standards," while others said they couldn't "morally justify" playing it over the air. Another disc jockey tried to start a campaign to "eliminate certain 'wreck and ruin' artists." But the beat went on.

Johnny Mathis was one of the big stars of 1958. At one time he thought about becoming an English teacher or athletic coach. However, in 1955, he signed with Columbia Records and began his remarkable career as a consummate ballad singer. His voice was bell-like, fluid, caressing—the essence of romantic imagery. "Chances Are," "A Certain Smile," "It's Not for Me to Say," "Wonderful! Wonderful!"—these songs became middle-of-the-road classics in the late fifties. Johnny became known as the "king of necking music," and, with the lights down low, millions cooed and snuggled to his romantic LPs. Mathis was a prodigious record seller, with more than fifty gold and platinum albums. One of them, *Johnny's Greatest Hits,* stayed on the charts for nearly ten years—an incredible achievement by any standards.

THE TOP 40

1. Nel Blu Dipinto Di Blu, *Domenico Modugno*
2. All I Have to Do Is Dream, *Everly Brothers*
3. Patricia, *Perez Prado*
4. Witch Doctor, *David Seville*
5. It's All in the Game, *Tommy Edwards*
6. Tequila, *Champs*
7. Bird Dog, *Everly Brothers*
8. Catch a Falling Star, *Perry Como*
9. Little Star, *Elegants*
10. Return to Me, *Dean Martin*
11. Sail Along Silvery Moon, *Billy Vaughn*
12. Twilight Time, *Platters*
13. Purple People Eater, *Sheb Wooley*
14. At the Hop, *Danny and the Juniors*
15. Get a Job, *Silhouettes*
16. Don't, *Elvis Presley*
17. He's Got the Whole World in His Hands, *Laurie London*
18. It's Only Make Believe, *Conway Twitty*
19. Yakety Yak, *Coasters*
20. Poor Little Fool, *Ricky Nelson*
21. Secretly, *Jimmie Rodgers*
22. Rockin' Robin, *Bobby Day*
23. Tea for Two Cha Cha, *Warren Covington and the Tommy Dorsey Orchestra*
24. Tom Dooley, *Kingston Trio*
25. Sweet Little Sixteen, *Chuck Berry*
26. Wear My Ring Around Your Neck, *Elvis Presley*
27. Topsy Part 2, *Cozy Cole*
28. Stood Up, *Ricky Nelson*
29. Just a Dream, *Jimmy Clanton*
30. Who's Sorry Now?, *Connie Francis*
31. Splish Splash, *Bobby Darin*
32. A Wonderful Time Up There / It's Too Soon to Know, *Pat Boone*
33. Tears on My Pillow, *Little Anthony and the Imperials*
34. Sugartime, *McGuire Sisters*
35. Chantilly Lace, *Big Bopper*
36. The Stroll, *Diamonds*
37. Lollipop, *Chordettes*
38. When, *Kalin Twins*
39. Looking Back, *Nat King Cole*
40. Book of Love, *Monotones*

THE TOP 10 LPs

1. The Music Man, *Original Cast*
2. Johnny's Greatest Hits, *Johnny Mathis*
3. South Pacific, *Original Soundtrack*
4. My Fair Lady, *Original Cast*
5. Come Fly with Me, *Frank Sinatra*
6. Warm, *Johnny Mathis*
7. Sing Along with Mitch, *Mitch Miller*
8. Around the World in 80 Days, *Original Soundtrack*
9. Ricky, *Ricky Nelson*
10. Tchaikovsky: Piano Concerto No. 1, *Van Cliburn*

Return to Me

DEAN MARTIN

Dean Martin and Jerry Lewis. In the early fifties, one would have been hard-pressed to come up with a more popular comedy team. They were a top box-office draw for six years in a row, and in 1955 their annual net income ran into the millions. "I knew that ninety percent of the audience was watching Jerry," said Dean, "and he was a very funny guy. But let me tell you something else. I knew in my *guts* that I was funnier than he was."

Martin and Lewis split up in 1956 for the same reason that made them work: an absolute contradiction in style. Easygoing Dean contrasted sharply with madcap Jerry, who seemed to think of himself as a second Charlie Chaplin. Martin got tired of playing "stooge" to such "genius," and finally walked out. "Even the best of associations," he said, "can wear thin."

Jerry went on to make a long string of profitable films and incredibly, even scored a top-ten hit, "Rock-a-Bye Your Baby with a Dixie Melody," in 1956.

Dean, though, had less luck. He wanted to make "serious pictures," but was cast instead in a box-office bomb, *Ten Thousand Bedrooms* (1957).

Dean's record career also sagged. In the glory days, he'd had eight top-forty hits: "I'll Always Love You" (1950), "If" (1951), "If You Belong to Me" (1952), "That's Amore" (his first million-seller, 1953), "Sway" (1954), "Memories Are Made of This" (his second million-seller and first number one, 1955), "Innamorata" (1956), and "Standing on the Corner" (1956). Since splitting with Lewis, however, nothing he recorded seemed to click with America's deejays.

Rock bottom came in 1957, in a Pittsburgh nightclub. It was his final booking, with no other dates on the agenda. If Dean Martin had a message for his fans at that time, it was very clear—Return to Me.

And the call came from the Coast. Would Dean accept less than one-tenth of his former salary to appear in a film with Marlon Brando?

That picture, *The Young Lions,* helped revitalize Martin's career in 1958. And the same year, he cut the song that turned out to be his third million-selling single.

Danny diMinno wrote the words of "Return to Me (Ritorna a me)" in 1957, setting them to the music of Carmen Lombardo. Carmen was the singing, sax-playing brother of Guy, the big band leader. Besides composing such classics as "Boo Hoo," "Coquette," and "Sweethearts on Parade," Carmen also served as his brother's musical director.

Dean's version of "Return to Me" took off late in March 1958, and reached the peak of its popularity in mid-May. In total, it spent almost five months as one of America's best-selling singles.

The career of Dean Martin contin-ued to flourish in the fifties; there were more hits ("Angel Baby," "Volare"), more films (*Rio Bravo*), concert dates and several television specials. In the sixties, there was even greater success, sparked off by the million-seller "Everybody Loves Somebody." In the face of the Beatles, Cream, and the Rolling Stones, low-keyed Dean managed to rack up another ten top-forty hits. In 1965, he launched "The Dean Martin Show," a TV variety hour that lasted for nine seasons. In 1967, commenting, "God! I am not worth it," he signed a three-year, $34 million NBC contract. A year later, he was making more money annually than any other single person in the history of show business.

Through it all, Dean kept up his image as a cool, laid-back entertainer. "I'm no singer," he explained. "I can carry a tune, and I have an easy style, but we crooners get by because we're fairly painless."

Little Star
THE ELEGANTS

Vito Picone and Carmon Romano grew up in Staten Island, New York, intrigued by streetcorner harmony. In 1956, they joined the Crescents, which cut one record and then fell apart. In 1957, Vito and Carmon decided to form their own doo-wop group, and hit the streets looking for talent.

The first person they found was a mutual friend, Artie Venosa, who became their first tenor. Second tenor was a schoolmate of Vito's, Frankie Fardogno. Artie then brought in a bass man, Jimmy Moschella. Carmon sang baritone, Vito took the leads, and their quintet was complete. Now all they needed was a name.

For that, the boys looked no further than a nearby billboard. It advertised "Schenley, the liquor of elegance." With a minor spelling change, the group had a name that they felt was classy and unique.

The Elegants then began searching for material. They found it in "Twinkle, Twinkle, Little Star," a nursery rhyme written by Wolfgang Amadeus Mozart in 1761, at the age of five. Vito and Artie switched it around a little bit, and shortened the title to "Little Star."

Next, the group descended on Hull Records, the label home of their musical idols, the Heartbeats. They were signed to Hull's publishing company, Keel Music, and a recording session was set up. On that date, ten sides were cut, including "Getting Dizzy" and "Little Star."

Hull then sold the masters to ABC Paramount, which placed them on their own subsidiary label, Apt. In mid-July 1958, "Little Star" took off, peaking at number one in August. In all, it spent nearly five months on the charts.

Over the next four years, the Elegants released another seven singles, on Apt, Hull, United Artists, Photo, and ABC Paramount. All of them were absolute flops, completely missing the charts. In 1962, the group gave up, and went their separate ways. Today, Carmon is a hairdresser, Jimmy a bus driver, Artie a construction worker, and Frankie is employed by the New York Sanitation Department. Vito sells used cars.

And the Elegants? Well, they joined the Singing Nun, the Hollywood Argyles, Zager and Evans, and the Silhouettes as the five acts of the fifties and sixties who reached number one their first time out and were never heard from again.

AN
APT
RECORD

Keel Music Pub. Co.,
Inc. (BMI)
Time 2:37

25005
(45-15013)

LITTLE STAR
(Venosa - Picone)
THE ELEGANTS

Catch a Falling Star
PERRY COMO

Perry Como was perhaps the only former barber in history who had the street his shop was on renamed in his honor. He was also one of the most prolific hitmakers of all time, with more than one hundred charted sides to his credit. Over a thirty-year span, he found success in films, on stage, on radio, on records—and on TV.

Perry was starring on the "Chesterfield Supper Club" when it made the big move from NBC radio in 1948. Two years later, he started a program under his own name for CBS-TV. On September 17, 1955, Perry returned to NBC, where he remained a network fixture until 1963.

"The Perry Como Show" was as easygoing and relaxed as its star. (Bob Hope called Como "the Sleeping Prince"; others referred to him as "Perry Coma.") Every week, Mr. C would come out on an empty stage, chat for a few moments, sit on a stool, and croon the pop hits of the day. More often than not, they were his: "Hot Diggity," "More," "Glendora," "Kewpie Doll," "Delaware," "Just Born," "Juke Box Baby"—the list went on and on. Oddly enough, his theme song, "Dream Along with Me," was a flop when released as a single in 1956. Often Perry would appear in a cardigan sweater, which started a fad and grew into a kind of unofficial trademark. "I hated those things," he recalled. "They were made of alpaca and itched like hell." The show was broadcast from a studio known simply as "54." Later, that room was converted into a disco and became the focal point of Chic's 1979 record, "Le Freak."

Early in 1958, Perry introduced a song on the show that was to win him his only Grammy Award. "It was

the first thing I ever wrote," said co-composer Paul Vance. "I got an idea for some lyrics for this funny little tune I had made up. So I wrote them down and took them to my friend, Wally Schuster, a music publisher. I said, 'Do you want to listen to something I wrote?' He said, 'You can't even speak English. You got a Brooklyn accent, and you're gonna write songs?' And I said, 'Well, do you wanna listen?' And he said, 'Well, I don't have time, but I'll send you to somebody else.' So he sent me to the office of another publisher, Fred Fisher. I sang him the song a cappella, and he said, 'The lyric is sensational. But why don't you get somebody to do something about the tune?' Some guy in the office suggested Lee Pockriss, so I met him and went over to his place, and we finished the song in about half an hour.

"We took it back to Fred Fisher, and then he called and told us that Perry Como was going to do our song. Then he said there was this new team, Burt Bacharach and Hal David, and they'd written the song that was going to be on the other side, 'Magic Moments.' He said, 'Famous Music is gonna put a lot of money behind 'em, and we're only a small company, and I don't think we can buck them.' And so the record came out, and there was no A or B side marked. But we were very lucky. On the TV show, Perry introduced our song first—and all hell broke loose."

"Catch a Falling Star" and "Magic Moments" both debuted on the charts in mid-January 1958. Although both sides became hits, "Magic Moments" got no higher than the low twenties. "Catch a Falling Star" went on to become the A side all the way, spending more than five months on America's best-seller lists. It was Perry's sixteenth million-seller and the first

record ever to be certified gold by the RIAA. Later, it earned a Grammy as the Best Male Solo Vocal Performance.

After his series went off in 1963, Perry continued to make occasional TV specials, tour, and record whenever he could. He became the only performer in history to put major hits on the charts in the forties, fifties, sixties, and seventies. His last top-ten single, 'It's Impossible," was a Grammy nominee in 1970.

"I was fifty-eight when I made that record. But age, you know, means very little. Half the time, I feel like I'm still sixteen years old. I just hope that I'm remembered as someone who sang a song, enjoyed himself, and made a lot of people happy. It's made me happy, certainly."

Bird Dog
THE EVERLY BROTHERS

There were people, sad to say, who lumped Don and Phil Everly in with the flukes of '57. "Those harmonic hicks," wrote one critic, "are like all the other rock 'n' roll stars. A flash or two, and then they'll crawl back to the farms where they belong." But the brothers, like rock 'n' roll itself, returned like storm troopers in 1958, coming back stronger and even better than ever. Out of four singles, they pulled seven hits, including four that made the national top ten! The first, "This Little Girl of Mine," was followed by "All I Have to Do Is Dream," backed with "Claudette." "Bird Dog" and "Devoted to You" came next, and then "Problems," backed by "Love of My Life."

" 'Bird Dog' was clearly a novelty tune," recalled Phil, "and the other side was a ballad. The title 'Bird Dog' gave you no hint of what the song was about—you really had to listen to it. Again, both sides were written by our friends Boudleaux and Felice Bryant. They were very good writers for us. Just about anything they came up with had something to it that was different, a little bit unusual. The lyrics were about the cleverest piece of words I'd ever heard."

Boudleaux Bryant had based the song on a phrase he'd heard in childhood. "My father used to describe someone who was just a little of a reprobate—not really disreputable, but just sort of a character—as a bird. And then the phrase 'He's a dog' came to my mind as a kind of put-down of a person. It was a kind of stream-of-consciousness thing. When the words came together, 'bird dog,' that was it. The rest of the song just fell in place."

"Bird Dog" fit in with the Everlys' recording philosophy at that time. "When we were recording," explained Phil, "we tried to have a similar thread running through all our music. But we couldn't repeat. If you repeat, you're being dishonest, so we always tried to mix things up as much as possible. 'Devoted to You,' for example—that was a new style of harmony we were trying, new for us at least. But we had the same band, the same guys we used on 'Bye Bye Love' and 'Wake Up Little Susie.' Don played guitar, and so did Chet Atkins. I think he's about the greatest there is. And we had Hank Harlan—he wrote 'Sugarfoot Rag'—on the session. Floyd Cramer played piano. In those days, we had no written arrangements at all. It was more of a spontaneous thing, from the musicians, Don and I, Archie Bleyer, and anybody else who wanted to suggest something."

"Bird Dog" and "Devoted to You" both broke on U.S. radio stations in August 1958. Within a month they were top sellers in all three categories of music—pop, country, and rhythm and blues. Although both songs became major hits, it was "Bird Dog" that emerged as the most requested and most frequently played side.

Also in 1958, the Everlys went to England on their first international tour. Over there, they were mobbed by crowds as thick as those they'd experienced stateside—maybe even thicker. Among those deeply affected by the brothers' combination of heartfelt singing, country picking, and solid rocking beat were four young men who were later to call themselves, in tribute, "the Four-everlys." After a while, the quartet was to change its name again, to the Beatles.

Tequila
THE CHAMPS

The story of the Champs began in late 1957 with songwriter-guitarist Dave Burgess. One of his tunes, "I'm Available," was then a top-ten hit for Margie Rayburn on Liberty Records.

Dave worked as an A&R man for Challenge Records, a label owned and operated by former cowboy star Gene Autry. "He was like a second father to me," recalled Dave. "I had been writing for him ever since I was a teenager."

Dave came up with an instrumental called "Train to Nowhere." "Everybody thought it had a hit sound, so we decided to form our own little group to record it." For the session, he recruited three guys from a quartet that had been playing club dates around Southern California. They were Dale Norris (lead guitar), Danny Flores (sax), and Gene Alden (drums). He also hired studio musician Cliff Hils to play bass.

"The day prior to recording," said Dave, "we met in our rehearsal room on Sunset Boulevard and went over 'Train to Nowhere.' Then we tried to come up with an idea for the B side."

Danny Flores suggested a tune that he had thought up while visiting Tijuana. He and the others had played it in clubs as a kind of extended jam in which everybody soloed. Burgess listened to the song and then made one suggestion. "Danny, who was the sax player, had a real low voice. I thought it would be kind of an idea, since he drank tequila a lot, to have him stop and shout 'tequila' on the record." Danny agreed.

"The next day we went into the studio and had a normal three-hour session," Dave explained. "Then we said, 'Let's go ahead and do the B side.' We did one take on 'Tequila,' and not even after we finished did we realize what we had." The assembled musicians thought so little of the track that they didn't even stick around to listen to the playback.

When the record was about to be released, a meeting was held to choose a name for the impromptu group. "Gene's horse, as most people know, was named Champion," said Dave. "So we decided to call ourselves the Champs in honor of that horse."

The single was released early in 1958, and to Dave's surprise, was flipped over by radio programers. "Those were the days when deejays used to listen to both sides of a record," he said. " 'Tequila' took off and became a multi-million seller."

The tune broke in mid-February and was immediately covered by bandleader Eddie Platt on ABC Paramount Records. While his version climbed into the top twenty, the original surged to number one in March. Their single spent five weeks as America's favorite 45; nineteen weeks, in total, on the hit parade. It was also a top-five record in England, and number one on the U.S. R&B charts.

"That was the first year of the Grammy Awards, and the category in which we were placed was peculiar," said Dave. "Nat King Cole, George Shearing, Perez Prado, and the Champs were all nominated for 'Best Rhythm and Blues Recording,' but I don't think any of us could have been classified as genuine rhythm and blues. I certainly didn't think we'd win

over all those people, but we did, and I'm very grateful for that."

The Champs immediately hit the road to capitalize on their good fortune, but as they hadn't really worked out a stage act, they weren't too successful. One promoter even paid them off early, just so he could book someone else in their place. They had better luck in the studio, and had several small follow-up hits: "El Rancho Rock" (1958), "Too Much Tequila" (1960), and "Limbo Rock" (1962). The latter song, with added lyrics, became a vocal hit for Chubby Checker.

The Champs' other big problem had to do with perpetually changing personnel. Cliff Hils didn't want to go on the road at all; Gene Alden and Danny Flores quit in three months. Jimmy Seals and Dash Crofts were among the many musicians who replaced them. Eventually, Glen Campbell took over rhythm guitar. Six months after that the Champs officially broke up.

"I keep my Grammy Award right here in a display case in my office," said Dave, who is now the owner of Republic Records. "And I still think about those days sometimes. We felt that we really started something with a kind of Latin rock long before the Tijuana Brass came along."

It's All in the Game

TOMMY EDWARDS

In the 1940s, Tommy Edwards was a hometown radio star, singing and playing piano on his own program in Richmond, Virginia. He often took his show on the road, appearing in nightclubs and cocktail lounges all over the East and Midwest. In his spare time, he tried writing songs, and in 1946, he sold his first one to a publisher. It was "That Chick's Too Young to Fry," which later became a hit for Louis Jordan.

In 1950, Tommy moved to New York and started making the rounds of music publishers and record companies, trying to place his songs. To save money, he'd sung all his demonstration records himself. At MGM, he found himself caught up in a round of excitement among the company's officials. It took him a few minutes to realize that the excitement was more for his wistful voice than for the song itself. The very next week Tommy stood before a microphone in MGM's New York recording studios, waxing his first four sides under an exclusive recording pact. Included in the quartet of tunes was "All Over Again," the song that had given him his first lucky break.

In 1951, Tommy scored with two hits for the label, "Morning Side of the Mountain" and "It's All in the Game." The latter tune had been composed in 1912 by Charles Gates Dawes, a Chicago banker who eventually wound up as vice president of the United States (1925–1929) under Calvin Coolidge. Lyricist Carl Sigman added words to the song (which

Dawes called "Melody in A Major") some thirty-nine years later.

Tommy's later records for MGM were all bombs, and by 1958 the label was ready to drop him from their roster. However, stereo was just coming in, so at the last session in his contract, Tommy was asked to re-record his hits in stereo. Tommy rearranged "It's All in the Game" to give it a more contemporary, rock 'n' roll feel, and the label was so impressed that they released it as a demonstration of MGM stereo. To their amazement, the new version became an overnight smash hit—in fact, one of the biggest hit records of 1958.

"It's All in the Game" broke onto the charts in late August and by October was the number-one song in the country. It spent twenty-two weeks on the best-seller lists and sold more than three and a half million copies.

His career revitalized, Tommy went on to place thirteen more songs on the pop charts over the next two years. They included "Love Is All We Need" (1958); "Please Mr. Sun" backed with a new version of "Morning Side of the Mountain" (1959); "My Melancholy Baby" (1959), and "I Really Don't Want to Know" (1960). Ironically, his last charted song was titled "It's Not the End of Everything" (1960). But it was.

In the sixties, Tommy's career went into a steady decline, even as the popularity of "It's All in the Game" continued. In 1964, the song became a hit again for British rock star Cliff Richard. Early in 1968, Tommy drifted

back to his hometown, broke and almost forgotten. The owner of a local club cleaned him up, bought him a suit, and signed him to appear that very night. He opened to a packed house of friends, well-wishers, and curiosity seekers.

On October 22, 1969, Tommy died at the age of forty-seven. Had he lived only a few months more, he would have seen the song that made him a star become a hit for the fourth time—in still another version, by the Four Tops.

Witch Doctor

DAVID SEVILLE

I was born in Fresno, California," said Ross Bagdasarian, better known as David Seville. "Fresno is the largest grape- and raisin-growing center in the world. There are some people there, too. Some of these people are my family.

"My father was a grape grower, so it seemed logical (to my father) that I become a grape grower. At the age of nineteen I decided that farming was a wonderful life—for my father. I had been going to the local college trying to find out how not to be a grape grower, but I couldn't find any answers, so I went to New York and became an actor.

"After a fling at legit theater, I spent the following four years in the Air Force and spent one year in England and one in France. After the war I went back to Fresno and found a beautiful girl whose name is Armen and married her. I had decided by then that maybe my father had been right, so I went into the business of grape farming. Armen stuck it out with me, and after a full year of frustration, I harvested the grapes, only to find the bottom had fallen out of the market. Armen and I ate a lot of grapes that year.

"Later, we moved to Los Angeles. We had $200, two children, and an unpublished song called "Come On-a My House." I kept singing the song to anyone who would stand still long enough for the first chorus, and pretty soon Columbia Records heard about it and Rosemary Clooney recorded it. I started getting acting parts in pictures, and while I was acting I was writing songs.

"In October of 1956, I decided to try my hand at recording some of my stuff, so I concocted the name David Seville after hearing my version of "Armen's Theme." The name seemed to fit the mood of the song. Anyway, it all worked very nicely and I kept the name.

"How did I come to write 'Witch Doctor'? Well, as usual I was looking for an idea. I wanted to write an unusual novelty song. The month was January 1958; my mind was a little madder than its normal semi-orderly state of confusion. I looked up from my desk and saw a book, *Duel with the Witch Doctor.* All the teenage records that were selling seemed to have one thing in common—you couldn't understand any of the lyrics—so I decided to have the Witch Doctor give advice to the lovelorn in his own language—a kind of qualified gibberish.

"After recording the orchestra track, I spent two months trying to think of a voice for the Witch Doctor. I had recorded instruments at half speed, playing them back at normal speed. Why not do the same with a voice—the Witch Doctor's voice?

"At home, I sang the words at half speed into my tape machine and played them back normally. Before the first walla-walla-bing-bang had ended, Armen and our three children burst into the room asking what was happening. That was all I needed to drive me forward—an understanding, bright family.

"I finished the record and played it for Si Waronker of Liberty Records. He flipped, stopped all other business, and in a matter of twenty-four hours, the record had been released. It sold over a million and a half."

Ross Bagdasarian went on to develop his concept into an even greater achievement—the Chipmunks—the most successful novelty creation in history (over twenty-five million

records sold). The multitrack, multispeed recording techniques he pioneered are now taken for granted and used for both voice and music effects.

"I must say that all the insanity had paid off handsomely. The Chipmunks and I own, among other things, our own vineyard—two hundred and twenty acres of Thompson seedless grapes. The name 'The Chipmunk Ranch' appears on a huge sign over the entrance to the ranch, and on any given day, tourists can be seen photographing the ranch and asking the field workers if Alvin is around.

"All I can say is I don't mind if you go deer hunting, trout fishing, or fox trapping—but don't dare touch the hair on a chipmunk."

3

Patricia
PEREZ PRADO
and HIS ORCHESTRA

Damaso Perez Prado, who gained fame in the late forties and early fifties as "El Rey del Mambo" ("The King of the Mambo") was born in Cuba, in the city of Matanzas. There he received his musical training, and played piano and organ in the Orquesta Casino de la Playa, Cuba's leading big band. In 1942, while experimenting with syncopation, he developed a concept that came to be known as "the Mambo." He wrote his rhythm into arrangements for local groups, but no one seemed interested in using them then.

After several frustrating years, Perez left Cuba in 1948, taking his mambo beat with him. He formed a new band, and started recording a series of dance instrumentals in RCA's Mexico City studios. The mambo then began to catch on in Mexico, and soon after, was widely imitated throughout Latin America.

A few copies of Perez's singles happened to make their way north, and were heard by U.S. bandleader Stan Kenton. He put the word out that "Prado from Mexico" had something progressive jazz fans had to hear. RCA obliged by switching Perez over to their regular pop label, making his records available in the United States for the first time.

Then, in 1951, Prado visited the American west coast with a big band heavy on the brass. On his opening night in September, dancing was impossible at the Zenda Ballroom in L.A.; thousands of curious patrons jammed every inch of the hall. His tour—the first of many—was a smashing success, inspiring "Metronome" to call Prado's "the swingingest jazz band in this country." Many bookings followed, in theaters, nightclubs, TV, and motion pictures.

By 1954, the mambo had become one of the most popular rhythms in America. Everybody seemed to be using it, from Perry Como ("Papa Loves Mambo") to Rosemary Clooney ("Mambo Italiano"). Then, in 1955, RKO decided to use mambo music in their new Jane Russell movie, *Underwater.* They asked Perez to recut, for the soundtrack, a song he had first recorded in 1951: "Cherry Pink and Apple Blossom White." His startling new version, featuring a wild trumpet solo by Billy Regis, not only wound up as number one, but also as the biggest hit single of 1955 (and is still RCA's best-selling instrumental ever).

Perez managed to live quite nicely off that trumpet bit for several years, but eventually the mambo was superseded by another Latin sound, the cha-cha-cha. In scrambling to find a second gimmick, Prado remembered the organ—an instrument all but abandoned by pop musicians at that time. He wrote another instrumental, dubbed it "Patricia," and cut the song for RCA.

"Patricia" took off early in June 1958, and by July was clearly the hottest 45 in America. It was number one on the pop and R&B charts, and a top-twenty country record. It remained on the hit parade for a full six months, sparking a boom in organ sales. In 1961, it was heard again on the soundtrack of *La Dolce Vita.*

Perez Prado never had another big hit, although he tried for several more years (in 1961, he caused a few ripples with "The Patricia Twist"). Eventually, he retired, and now lives in Mexico City.

All I Have to Do Is Dream
THE EVERLY BROTHERS

By the spring of 1958, Don and Phil Everly had been stars for less than one year. In that time, though, they had scored two immense, classic hits—"Bye Bye Love" and "Wake Up Little Susie"—as well as placed another song, "This Little Girl of Mine," in the national top thirty. The boys had appeared on nearly every major American TV variety series, from the "Ed Sullivan Show" to Dick Clark's "American Bandstand." They had won the hearts of millions of fans—not just rock and country, but mainline pop and even rhythm and blues. It had been revealed that, in a time of strict musical categories, they'd become a "crossover act" completely by accident. They'd been hired to head up the country wing of Cadence Records, but their singles, by mistake, had been mailed to pop radio stations without being marked "country." Since they were on a pop label, deejays had assumed they were pop and played them accordingly. Mainstream listeners were at first shocked, then thrilled, by the Everlys' unusual sound.

"At that time," recalled Don, "we were following the tradition of the standard country duet, something that had been around in the country field for a long, long time. It goes on back to the Bailes Brothers, the Louvin Brothers, the Blue Sky Boys, and many, many more. It's really a traditional form of country music for two brothers to sing together. Our national acceptance, and wordwide acceptance, just came when they started to call it rock 'n' roll. Our style was a mixture of country and other sounds. The arrangements, I think, were affected a lot by R&B. I know I was a great fan of Bo Diddley, and I tried to incorporate some of his rhythm things into our music.

"In the spring of 1958, we thought the time was right for a ballad from the Everly Brothers. We turned again to Boudleaux and Felice Bryant, and

they came up with a great one—'All I Have to Do Is Dream.' "

It was a romantic ballad of unrequited love, as Boudleaux Bryant explained. "It was just one of those quickies that came out of the blue," he said. "I think we wrote it in about fifteen minutes. We were just writing scads and scads of songs, knowing that the Everlys were coming up for a session. Once they were hot, we wanted to have more records by them. We wrote many songs for them that they did not do. For a while, we wrote loads of songs that were directly aimed at their style of singing—with their harmonics built into the songs."

"All I Have to Do Is Dream" broke onto American radio in April 1958 and within a month was the number-one

record across the board—on the pop, country, and rhythm and blues charts. (The flip side, "Claudette," also became a hit. It had been written by Roy Orbison about his wife, who later died in a motorcycle crash.)

"If you ever have a universal hit, it can become a universal hit all over again," said Boudleaux. "Human nature doesn't change very rapidly. The song will always have whatever quality appealed to human nature in the first place." For that reason, "All I Have to Do Is Dream" has passed into our folklore as a perennial standard—a hit of the fifties, sixties, and seventies. Richard Chamberlain revived it in 1963, and in 1970, it became a duet all over again, for Glen Campbell and Bobbie Gentry.

Nel Blu, Dipinto Di Blu (Volare)

DOMENICO MODUGNO

Domenico Modugno (pronounced mo-*doon*-yo) was born in Polignano a Mare, Italy. His father, a poor policeman, taught him a few simple songs, and at the age of fourteen, Domenico composed his first tune, a lullaby called "Ninna Nanna." He saved his money, bought an accordion, and began his career by serenading the girlfriends of other boys.

After finishing school, Domenico moved to Rome, hoping to strike it rich as a singing movie star. However, the only work he could find was as a waiter or part-time factory worker. Eventually he was drafted and wound up spending several years in the Italian military. Once freed of that, he enrolled at Rome's Experimental Movie Center, where he studied alongside the then-unknown Sophia Loren.

Domenico slowly got small film parts and then landed his dream role—as a balladeer in *Il Mantello Rosso* (The Red Cloak). The exposure won him fame and a radio job, performing on the variety show of Italian comic Walter Chiari. In 1955, Domenico toured the United States and Canada, playing clubs like the Blue Angel in New York. The next year, he landed the part of Athos on "The Three Musketeers," a thirteen-week TV series produced in Europe. In 1957, he returned to music and wrote "Lazzarella," which took second place at the Neapolitan Song Festival.

In 1958, a friend, Franco Migliacci, came to Domenico with a song idea he said was inspired by the back of a cigarette pack. Domenico composed some music, and the two of them wrote the words. The result sounded romantic, although the song never actually mentioned love. Instead, it took the listener on a fantasy flight through "Nel Blu, Dipinto di Blu," or "the blue, painted blue."

Domenico entered his song in the San Remo Festival of Music and walked away with top honors. Released in Italy, his single sold nearly a million copies when first issued on the Fonit label. Decca picked up the American rights and released it stateside in July 1958. On August 4, the record broke onto the U.S. charts, and in two weeks it had displaced Rick Nelson's "Poor Little Fool" as number one.

Deejays were blitzed with requests for "that new foreign song." Listeners identified its ethnic origin as everything from French, Dutch, Spanish, and German to Greek, Polish, Hebrew, and even Latin. They also didn't know what to call it, with some asking for "Nelly Blue," "Domingo," or "Blue Nell Rides a Blue Pinto." English lyrics were written by Mitchel Parish, who retitled the song "Volare" ("to fly" in Italian). Adding to the confusion were more than a dozen quickly recorded cover versions by everyone from the McGuire Sisters to Dean Martin. (Dean's record was the only serious competition at the time; it reached number fifteen on the charts and sold over a million copies. In 1960, Bobby Rydell revived the song, taking it into the top five.)

Meanwhile, Decca was also blitzed. Their pressing plants, used to runs of 30,000 copies a day for run-of-the-mill best-sellers, were shipping out more than 60,000 copies of "Nel Blu" daily. Eventually, Domenico's record sold over three million singles in the U.S. Adding all the cover versions, the song sold over eight million.

In August 1958, Domenico flew to New York for appearances on the *"Ed Sullivan Show,"* and in nightclubs, at $5,000 a week. Later that year, at the very first Grammy Awards, his record was voted Best Male Vocal Performance, Song of the Year, and Record of the Year.

Domenico never had another U.S. hit but did win the San Remo Festival three more times, in 1959 (with "Piove," better known as "Ciao Ciao Bambina"), 1962 ("Addio, Addio"), and 1966 ("Dio Come Ti Amo"). Worldwide, his record sales now exceed 20 million.

In his native country, Domenico Modugno remained a star for many years. No one dared compete with him as a composer, actor, and singer all rolled into one. To this day, he still proudly bears the nickname given to him a long time ago: "The Music Genius of Italy."

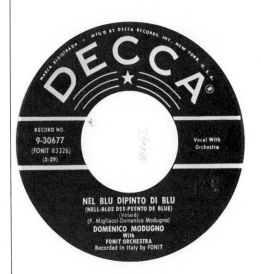

They called it **"The Biggest Show of Stars for 1959,"** and that it was—a package tour featuring Bill Haley and His Comets, the Big Bopper, Dion and the Belmonts, Ritchie Valens, the Platters, Frankie Avalon, and Buddy Holly. One night, after playing to a thousand screaming fans in Clear Lake, Iowa, Buddy, Ritchie, and the Bopper chartered a plane to take them ahead of the troupe to Fargo, North Dakota. There, at an all-night laundry, they hoped to get their clothes washed. There was a light snow blowing up shortly after 2 A.M. when the single-engine Beechcraft Bonanza, piloted by Roger Peterson of Dwyer's Flying Service, took off in a northwesterly direction toward Fargo. The plane managed to cover fifteen miles without incident, and then suddenly nosedived into the lonely farmyard of Albert Juhl. No one survived the crash. Years later, Don McLean was to call February 3, 1959, "the day the music died," in "American Pie."

NINETEEN FIFTY-NINE was more than just the end of a decade. It was the end of an age—the first great era of rock 'n' roll history. Out of country, pop, and R&B had come the early pioneers: Bill Haley, Chuck Berry, Fats Domino, Little Richard, Elvis Presley, Buddy Holly, and Jerry Lee Lewis (just to name a few). In a few short years, each had made an indelible mark on the music, and for many, their time had come and already gone. They were innovators, but there'll always be innovators, as long as people are restless for change, development, and excitement.

The pop scene in 1959 was a musical grab bag of fading styles and rising stars. Vocal groups like the Ames Brothers called it quits, while in Detroit, Mary Wilson, Flo Ballard, and Diana Ross were getting their act together as the Primettes. We wanted the extraordinary, and in our search, many of us turned to novelty records: "Alvin's Harmonica," "Deck of Cards," "The Little Space Girl," "Say Man," "I Got a Wife," "The Class," "Uh Oh Part 2," "Ragtime Cowboy Joe," "The Happy Reindeer," "Three Stars," and "The Battle of Kookamonga." The record market topped $600 million for the first time, with LP sales especially strong. One hot album, released by RCA Victor, failed to even mention the artist's name—anywhere—on either side of the jacket. There was only a title: "For LP Fans Only." However, the smiling face of Elvis Presley on the cover was all the public needed to know.

"Your Hit Parade" began on radio in 1935 and moved over to television fifteen years later. The format was simple: As the top tunes of the week were counted down, a regular cast, including crooner **Johnny Desmond,** sang them. This was fine, as long as you liked the song and didn't care who performed it. But in the mid-fifties, this program ran into trouble, mainly with rock 'n' roll records they couldn't avoid, or handle either. It was no longer the *song* that became a hit—it was a *specific recorded performance.* Cover versions just didn't make it with an increasingly sophisticated audience. On April 24, 1959, the curtain rang down for the last time on "Your Hit Parade."

His style was called "ecstasy pop," and his fans knew him as "Mr. Excitement." **Jackie Wilson** was a fiery, sexy, soulful singer whose passionate live shows were unequaled by any other performer. After such hits as "That's Why," "Lonely Teardrops," "To Be Loved," and "I'll Be Satisfied," Jackie began his movie career in *Go Johnny Go.* Also in the cast were Alan Freed, Eddie Cochran, the Cadillacs, Jimmy Clanton, the Flamingoes, Ritchie Valens, and Chuck Berry. Other music films of the year included *College Confidential* with Conway Twitty, *Gidget* with the Four Preps, *Hound Dog Man* with Fabian and Dodie Stevens, and *Jukebox Rhythm* with Johnny Otis, Jack Jones, Earl Grant, and the Nitwits (soon to be known as the Playmates).

In November 1959, investigations began in Washington, D.C., of alleged bribery of disc jockeys. It was charged that deejays accepted "payola"—money and other gifts in exchange for giving certain records preferential air play. (Many lawmakers were convinced that this was the only way that "rock 'n' roll and other trash" ever got on the radio.) A parade of broadcasters testified before Congress, including one of rock's most vocal champions, legendary deejay **Alan Freed**. The legislators decided to make an example of such an outspoken figure, the man tabbed with giving the music its name in the early fifties. They threw the book at him, and within days Freed lost both his "Big Beat" radio program and his local TV series. After years of delays, he was finally convicted of "commercial bribery" and given a six-month suspended sentence and a $500 fine. Later the amount was reduced to $300 because by then Alan Freed was broke. Two years later, he died.

The **Drifters** were formed in 1953 as a vocal backdrop for their first lead singer, Clyde McPhatter. However, they didn't achieve any real success until their manager, George Treadwell, fired the entire personnel in 1959. Another group, the Crowns, became the "new" Drifters and scored a million-seller with their very first release, "There Goes My Baby." More than a dozen other hits followed in the early sixties, including "On Broadway," "Up on the Roof," "Under the Boardwalk," and "Save the Last Dance for Me." The Drifters' pioneering use of strings, horns, and orchestral effects changed the face of R&B and set the stage for slick Motown music to come.

THE TOP 40

1. Mack the Knife, *Bobby Darin*
2. Battle of New Orleans, *Johnny Horton*
3. Venus, *Frankie Avalon*
4. Lonely Boy, *Paul Anka*
5. Personality, *Lloyd Price*
6. The Three Bells, *Browns*
7. Dream Lover, *Bobby Darin*
8. Come Softly to Me, *Fleetwoods*
9. Put Your Head on My Shoulder, *Paul Anka*
10. Sleepwalk, *Santo and Johnny*
11. Kansas City, *Wilbert Harrison*
12. Stagger Lee, *Lloyd Price*
13. Mr. Blue, *Fleetwoods*
14. Smoke Gets in Your Eyes, *Platters*
15. Charlie Brown, *Coasters*
16. There Goes My Baby, *Drifters*
17. Pink Shoelaces, *Dodie Stevens*
18. Quiet Village, *Martin Denny*
19. Sea of Love, *Phil Phillips*
20. 'Til I Kissed You, *Everly Brothers*
21. A Big Hunk of Love, *Elvis Presley*
22. I'm Gonna Get Married, *Lloyd Price*
23. A Teenager in Love, *Dion and the Belmonts*
24. It's Just a Matter of Time, *Brook Benton*
25. A Fool Such as I, *Elvis Presley*
26. Sorry, *Impalas*
27. Donna, *Ritchie Valens*
28. The Happy Organ, *Dave "Baby" Cortez*
29. My Heart Is an Open Book, *Carl Dobkins, Jr.*
30. Don't You Know, *Della Reese*
31. Lipstick on Your Collar, *Connie Francis*
32. What a Difference a Day Makes, *Dinah Washington*
33. Sixteen Candles, *Crests*
34. Lavender Blue, *Sammy Turner*
35. Kookie, Kookie, Lend Me Your Comb, *Edd "Kookie" Byrnes and Connie Stevens*
36. Waterloo, *Claude King*
37. Red River Rock, *Johnny and the Hurricanes*
38. Primrose Lane, *Jerry Wallace*
39. Deck of Cards, *Wink Martindale*
40. Seven Little Girls Sitting in the Back Seat, *Paul Evans*

The **Kingston Trio** did not invent folk music; they just made it immensely popular in the late fifties and early sixties. Dave Guard, Bob Shane, and Nick Reynolds first sang for free beer in college hangouts. Then, one night, they heard another performer sing a ninety-year-old ballad called "Tom Dula." They cleaned up the lyrics and included it as "Tom Dooley" on their first Capitol LP. In January 1959, it became both a million-selling single and album, igniting not only the Trio's career, but the whole folk boom of the early sixties.

THE TOP 10 LPs

1. Peter Gunn, *Original Soundtrack*
2. Gigi, *Original Soundtrack*
3. South Pacific, *Original Soundtrack*
4. From the Hungry i, *Kingston Trio*
5. At Large, *Kingston Trio*
6. Sing Along with Mitch, *Mitch Miller*
7. Inside, *Shelley Berman*
8. Exotica Vol. 1, *Martin Denny*
9. My Fair Lady, *Original Cast*
10. Flower Drum Song, *Original Cast*

Sleepwalk
SANTO and JOHNNY

*I*nstrumentals have always held a special place next to the consoles of disc jockeys. In the fifties and early sixties, they were considered a flexible kind of sound: something to talk over, use as a theme or background effect, and fade out of at will (in order to hit the regularly scheduled news on time). Such practices didn't reflect a lot of respect for instrumentals as recorded works, but at least it got them on the air. And, every once in a while, one moved beyond "filler" status and became a genuine hit. Instrumentals had a particularly good year in 1959, with twenty-eight moving into the national top forty. Of those, an even dozen managed to enter the top ten. They were, in order of release, "Manhattan Spiritual" by Reg Owen and His Orchestra, "Petite Fleur" by Chris Barber's Jazz Band, "Peter Gunn" by Ray Anthony, "The Happy Organ" by Dave (Baby) Cortez, "Guitar Boogie Shuffle" by the Virtues, "Quiet Village" by Martin Denny, "Only You" by Franck Pourcel's French Fiddles, "Forty Miles of Bad Road" by Duane Eddy, "Red River Rock" by Johnny and The Hurricanes, "Sleepwalk" by Santo and Johnny, "Teen Beat" by Sandy Nelson, and "In the Mood" by Ernie Fields and His Orchestra.

Of those, the biggest was "Sleepwalk," composed and performed by Santo Anthony and Johnny Steven—the Farina brothers.

Santo and Johnny were born in Brooklyn, New York. Santo started to play the steel guitar when he was nine years old, and later mastered Spanish guitar. He passed along what he knew to Johnny, who took up rhythm guitar at the age of twelve. They played together regularly while in high school, and by 1955 were well-established local favorites. Their lives became an endless round of parties, teen dances, variety shows, and club work.

The two brothers, aged twenty-one

and eighteen, wrote "Sleepwalk" in 1959 with their sister, Ann Farina. They recorded it at Trinity Music in New York, backed by the orchestra of Bob Davie. The disc was then leased to Canadian-American Records for release.

The appeal of "Sleepwalk," according to one critic, was "the pulsating, slow background beat of Johnny's rhythm guitar" set against the "melancholy, somewhat exotic melody of Santo's steel guitar."

The record broke in early August 1959, quickly rising to the top of the charts in September. It stayed number one for two weeks, and a best-seller for eighteen. After their hit came a major personal tour of the U.S., "their distinctive brand of Hawaiian-flavored R&B delighting audiences everywhere," according to one source. In three years, the brothers traveled over 100,000 miles.

Unlike many instrumental hitmakers, Santo and Johnny were actually able to place follow-up records on the

charts. In December 1959, "Teardrop" climbed to number twenty-three. In later years they had mild success with "Caravan" (1960), "Twistin' Bells" (1961), and "I'll Remember in the Still of the Night" (1964).

They also did well as LP sellers. Their first album, titled *Santo and Johnny,* went top-twenty in 1960, and remained on the hit parade for almost six months. The next LP, *Encore,* did even better, rising to number eleven and charting almost nine months. A third album, *Hawaii,* lasted thirteen weeks, peaking at eighty.

While his first love was playing the guitar, Johnny's other great passion was record collecting, and a good portion of his royalties went toward expanding that hobby. The two brothers, though, did stick together for many years, earning a comfortable income from live performances and a long string of instrumental "mood" LPs.

Put Your Head on My Shoulder

PAUL ANKA

As a young child, Canadian-born Paul Anka dreamed of becoming an actor or a writer. That all changed after he was thrown out of a shorthand class, and into a music class. Before long, Paul discovered how easy it was for him to pick out melodies on the piano.

Paul began to skip school and hang out in clubs, studying the stage technique of various singers. He took up guitar and started to write songs, playing them for anyone who would listen. He even organized a trio, the Bobbysoxers, which performed at the 1955 Central Canada Exposition (before breaking up). He won a number of amateur talent contests, and as his confidence grew, he felt sure that he was ready for the big time.

In August 1956, Paul traveled alone to Los Angeles, seeking out arranger Ernie Freeman, who had produced the Cadets' hit, "Stranded in the Jungle." Although only fifteen years old, he convinced Ernie to let him cut a single with the Cadets as his backup group. The result, "Blauwildesbestfontein," was a flop, and Anka had to work a month as a movie usher to earn his fare home.

Undaunted, Paul tried again in April 1957. Borrowing $100 from his father, he flew to New York, where friends let him sleep in a bathtub during his visit. On his first day in town, Paul hustled his way into the offices of ABC Paramount Records and cornered staff producer Don Costa. Don was amazed by the young man's brashness and agreed to listen to his four-song repertoire. One tune had been inspired by Paul's brazen crush on his brother's baby-sitter (Diana Ayoub), who was five years older than Paul. Costa was so impressed that he immediately arranged to have Anka's father flown to New York to sign a recording contract for his underage son.

That night, at his friends' kitchen table, Paul worked on his song until the wee small hours. The following afternoon, he awoke and breezed into the ABC recording studio. Without rehearsal, he cut "Diana" in one take, backed by a five-piece band and three session singers ("For padding," he explained). The single went on to become the biggest hit in ABC Paramount history, selling more than eight million copies.

And Paul Anka was just getting started.

In 1958, he put seven more songs on the charts, including "You Are My Destiny," "Crazy Love," "Let the Bells Keep Ringing," and "(All of a Sudden) My Heart Sings." He also teamed with Johnny Nash and George Hamilton IV for an obsequious novelty single, "The Teen Commandments." Paul made his first movie, *Let's Rock,* in 1958, and later in the year wrote a hit for Buddy Holly—"It Doesn't Matter Anymore."

In 1959, Paul scored his first number-one record with "Lonely Boy." Like nearly all his own hits, Paul had written it from his own experience. His next single came about the same way.

"It was kind of an interesting record," Paul recalled. "At that time I was traveling around the country to many major cities, doing hops for deejays and various high schools. It was one of the only means of promotion back then. While I was singing, I noticed that everybody's head was on somebody else's shoulder. I had never heard a song that expressed that feeling. So, one night after a hop, I went back to my hotel room and wrote 'Put Your Head on My Shoulder.' It just seemed like a natural idea for a song."

And it was, especially in context with Paul's budding romance with Annette Funicello, who was then a Mouseketeer on the "Mickey Mouse Club" television show. Paul dedicated the song to her, as he did a later hit, "Puppy Love."

"I think 'Put Your Head on My Shoulder' was the turning point in my career," Paul was to say years afterward. "Prior to that time, I was writing teen songs for a teen audience and, of course, I was a teenager myself. But this was my first solid copyright song, and did a lot to help ease my transition into an older crowd."

8

Come Softly to Me
THE FLEETWOODS

The Fleetwoods began as a vocal duet, formed in 1958 by two seniors at Olympia High School in Olympia, Washington. Barbara Ellis and Gretchen Christopher felt there was something missing, though, so they invited a friend, Gary Troxel, to accompany them on trumpet. After a short time, it became obvious that Gary was not much of a trumpet player, so instead, he hummed his part. They all liked the effect so much that he was added as a third "vocalist." The new trio decided to call themselves Two Girls and a Guy.

Barbara and Gretchen told Gary about a song they'd been working on, "Come Softly to Me." From its original concept, it had grown into a ten-minute epic with dozens of verses. Gary helped them cut the song down and, in lieu of his trumpet, suggested a gentle background chant. The group tried to arrange the song several different ways and finally felt that it worked best with Gary taking over the lead.

"We sang the song for the first time at a school talent show," Gary recalled, "and it went over real big with the kids. Gretchen sent a tape recording of us to Bob Reisdorff, who was a record distributor in Seattle. As it happened, a new label was being formed at the time, Dolphin Records, and we were the first act signed by the company. Everything seemed to fall in place for us in just over two months."

It was about this time that the group's name was changed—entirely by accident. While talking on the phone with Barbara one day, Bob remarked that the group should call themselves something simple, like his telephone exchange, which was "Fleetwood." The others thought that was a fine idea, and they made the change in time for the release of their first record.

As expected, "Come Softly to Me"

broke in the Northwest, causing so much excitement that Liberty Records stepped in and bought the master for national distribution. In less than a month, it was the number-one song in the country, which it remained for four full weeks. In all, "Come Softly to Me" spent more than a third of the year on America's best-seller list.

The Fleetwoods went on in 1959 to top the charts again, with a second million-seller, "Mr. Blue." They appeared on "American Bandstand" and the "Ed Sullivan Show," and then the naval reserve stepped in and took Gary away. While on leave in 1961, he rejoined the group for what turned out to be their final top-ten hit—ironically titled "Tragedy."

In 1962, Gary got out of the navy, but by then, internal friction was beginning to pull the trio apart. There were a few more hits, but when their record contract ran out in 1965, the three decided to go their separate ways.

The Fleetwoods had given the world some of the most quietly stunning harmonies ever recorded. But the time had come to move on.

Dream Lover

BOBBY DARIN

Robert Walden Cassotto was born in poverty, in perhaps the worst, most run-down section of the Bronx in New York City. His father, a small-time gangster, had died before Robert was born, leaving the young boy to be brought up by his mother, a former entertainer, and his older sister, Nina. Many observers, including Robert himself, pointed to his dismal beginnings as the source of his relentless drive and ambition—a compulsion that helped make him one of the hottest stars of the late fifties and early sixties.

A skinny, sickly kid, Robert suffered recurring attacks of rheumatic fever from the age of eight, and had to receive his primary education at home

from his mother. She also taught him music, and he mastered the piano, bass, vibraphone, guitar, and drums. As a teenager, he used those skills while performing in hotels in the Catskill Mountains, singing, playing his instruments, and emceeing shows for $15 a week.

After a year of drama study at Hunter College in New York, Robert joined forces with a high school friend—an up and coming music publisher named Don Kirshner. Together they managed to make ends meet by creating radio commercials for local merchants. Robert wrote and sang the jingles, while Kirshner sold them. In March 1956, Robert decided to stop working anonymously and plucked a new last name for himself out of the phone book. As Bobby Darin, he made his first television appearance on the Dorsey Brothers' "Stage Show," just two months after Elvis made his TV debut on the same program. The video exposure, on which he was billed as "the nineteen-year-old singing sensation," led to a one-year contract with Decca Records. Unfortunately, he was unable to come up with a hit during his run with that company. A "failure," he was forced to seek out a new deal and finally signed with the Atco label.

Again a year went by. Several more records came out, all flops. Depressed, Bobby dropped in at the house of a friend, New York disc jockey Murray the K. Murray's mother, as a joke, suggested the song title "Splish Splash, Takin' a Bath." To carry the gag further, Bobby sat down at the piano and set the title to music. Twelve minutes later, "Splish Splash," which eventually sold over a million copies, had been written. It was one of the first rock 'n' roll songs recorded on an eight-track tape machine, which

allowed voices and other effects to be added after the framework of the song had been laid down.

The success of "Splish Splash" kicked Bobby's career into high gear. He was a guest on nearly every important variety series and caused a sensation with his cocky, self-assured nightclub act. With his brash demeanor, bouncy songs, and snapping fingers, he was hailed as "the next Sinatra," "the best since Jolson," and in the words of Ed Sullivan, "the greatest rhythm singer in the world." Oddly, Darin had not been that confident about "Splish Splash." As insurance, he had recorded another song, "Early in the Morning," and had it released under the name of the "Rinky Dinks." In August 1958, both singles were riding high on the charts.

As a follow-up to "Splish Splash," Atco put out a second hard-rock dance record, "Queen of the Hop." It, too, made the national top ten, and it helped set the stage for 1959—the most exciting period ever in the life of Bobby Darin.

In April 1959, along came the single that demonstrated the versatility of pop's saucy new singer. Bobby Darin wrote and produced both "Dream Lover" and "Bullmoose," which featured the piano talents of Neil Sedaka. The single climbed the charts rapidly and remained a best-seller for nearly a quarter of the year.

Shortly after the release of "Dream Lover," Bobby was interviewed by *Life* magazine. To the interviewer's amusement, he said that he wanted to be a legend by the time he was twenty-five. Almost mockingly, the *Life* editors used that line as the banner headline over their story about him. Little did they, or anyone, know that immortality was only a few weeks away for the amazing Mr. Darin.

The Three Bells

THE BROWNS

Jim Ed Brown, a music major in college, began his career as the result of a family dare. His older sister, Maxine, teased him into entering a local talent show, in which he won first prize. He then called her up from the audience, and made her join him in a duet. The pair was so successful that evening that they were immediately signed by station KLRA for their program, "Barnyard Frolics."

From there, they went to Shreveport, and spent a year and a half as featured performers on the "Louisiana Hayride." Kid sister Bonnie came into the act in 1955, and that same year, the Browns entered television as regulars on ABC's "Ozark Jubilee."

In 1956, they began recording for RCA, and had a top-ten country hit with "I Take the Chance." Then, Jim Ed was called for army service, and younger sister Norma Brown had to fill in on live dates. For recording, Jim hoarded passes, and got out whenever he could. There were more hits, but more hassles, and by 1959, the Browns were ready to throw in the towel.

"We came into Nashville with the sole intent of telling RCA we were going to quit the business," said Jim Ed. "And 'The Three Bells' was going to be our swan song."

"The Three Bells" was written in 1945, as "Les Trois Cloches," by the French composer Jean Villard. English lyrics were written in 1948 by Bert Reisfield. The song didn't become a hit in America, though, until 1952, when Columbia released a version by Les Compagnons de la Chanson.

"I saw them perform it on the 'Ed Sullivan Show,' " said Jim Ed. "I really loved it. I was in my senior year then, and we started singing it in the high school choir.

"Maxine, Bonnie and I wanted to do the song for a long time, and we remembered it. The problem was, it was too lengthy for a commercial record—over six minutes. So Chet Atkins, Anita Kerr, and the three of us sat down one day, and shortened it. We reduced it by about half."

"The Three Bells" was released late in July 1959, and entered the country, pop, and R&B charts almost immediately. It rose through August, selling as many as 100,000 copies a week. In September, it reached number one, with sales ultimately topping three million.

The Browns, wisely, changed their minds about breaking up. TV appearances and world tours came next.

"Our sound was unusual for that time," explained Jim Ed. "We didn't sound like the rest of the country singers, and we weren't suited for the pop field either. So we just kept traveling about, trying to get another good record."

Ultimately, they found two which became both pop and country hits: "Scarlet Ribbons" (1959) and "The Old Lamplighter" (1960).

The Browns continued to place songs on the country charts until 1967. Then, on October 10, they sang together for the last time as part of the forty-second anniversary show of the Grand Ole Opry. With the retirement of his sisters, Jim Ed forged on, carving out a successful career as a solo performer.

"I still get requests for 'The Three Bells,' " he said. "You know, a lot of people think the Jimmy Brown in the song is me. Actually, it was just a coincidence. Until I came along, there were no Jim Browns or Jimmy Browns in my family. That is, as far as I know."

Personality
LLOYD PRICE

Lloyd Price was born in Crescent City, Louisiana, near New Orleans. As a child, he started singing in the church choir, encouraged by his mother, a gospel singer, and his family, jazz and blues musicians.

In high school, he took up the trumpet and organized his own five-piece band to play at dances and social events. While he was still only a sophomore, his group became the "house band" at WBOK radio and was heard behind station announcements and I.D. breaks.

Lloyd scored a lot of commercials during this time, and one of his jingles drew listener requests for a recorded version. He lengthened it into a complete song and went to Art Rupe, the owner of Specialty Records, for an audition. Art was just about ready to leave for the airport but agreed to stay long enough to listen to the one tune. Lloyd was so uptight that he literally began to cry as he sang "Lawdy Miss Clawdy."

Art canceled his plane reservation and remained to record the seventeen-year-old singer. In a dream come true, Lloyd's long-time idol, Fats Domino, provided his band and played piano on the session. "Lawdy Miss Clawdy" became one of the biggest R&B hits of 1952. It has been covered over the years by everyone from Elvis Presley to the Buckinghams. It sold over a million copies—without ever entering the pop chart.

Lloyd had three other R&B hits: "Oooh Oooh Oooh" backed with "Restless Heart" in 1952 and "Ain't It a Shame" in 1953. Then, in 1954, he was suddenly drafted into the army. Lloyd got himself assigned to Special Services, where he put together a military band. This outfit toured Japan, Korea, and Okinawa, providing backup for visiting stars.

Sgt. Lloyd Price was discharged in 1957 and immediately looked up an old friend, Harold Logan, who became his business manager. In a very unusual move at the time, they set up their own production company and leased masters to ABC. The first one, "Just Because," became a top-thirty pop hit that April.

Late in 1958, Lloyd released "Stagger Lee," which became his first number-one single in February 1959. After that came "Where Were You (on Our Wedding Day)." These records gave a first taste of the Price hit formula. A capable blues balladeer, he was most at home with peppy, up-tempo songs. Lloyd surrounded himself with a hard-charging brass and reed section, which matched his husky, handsome vocals. Despite this barrage of sound and rhythm, he made his presence felt.

Lloyd's next 45, "Personality," was one he composed with Harold Logan (Price wrote or co-wrote nearly everything he recorded). It combined bump-and-grind percussion, a catchy chorus, and his own pop adaptation of the "New Orleans sound." Released in May 1959, "Personality" peaked in June and became a massive hit. It spent more than four months on the U.S. charts and went top ten in England.

The single also gave Lloyd a well-deserved nickname—"Mr. Personality." For years he'd been known as "the friendly, good-natured singer with the biggest smile in town." He was a charismatic performer, drawing large crowds on a hectic schedule of one-night stands, nightclub dates, and TV appearances.

Over the next couple of years, Lloyd continued to chart records for ABC: "I'm Gonna Get Married" and "Come into My Heart" in 1959 and "Lady Luck" and "Question" in 1960. After that, he formed his own label, Double L, and had one final hit, "Misty," in 1963.

Of all the artists who emerged from the New Orleans scene, Lloyd Price and Fats Domino were the most

successful—and among the only ones to profit from their music. With his earnings, Lloyd set up a grant for poor blacks to go to college. In the late sixties, he made many cross-country tours, fronting a nine-piece band. Finally, after nearly twenty years in the music business, Lloyd opened a nightclub in New York's Times Square—and called it Lloyd Price's Turntable.

Lonely Boy
PAUL ANKA

*I*n 1959, at the age of seventeen, Paul Anka became the youngest self-made millionaire in history. He had the voice, the looks, the talent, and the drive to really sell himself and the many hit songs he wrote. In the late fifties and early sixties, he redefined just what a teen idol could be.

But amid all the glory—the triumphs and the accolades—Paul Anka also knew personal heartache. In early February 1959, while touring the Midwest, three members of his troupe—Buddy Holly, Ritchie Valens, and the Big Bopper—were killed in a plane crash. Paul had just written a song for Buddy, who was one of his best friends. The tune—Holly's last hit—was ironically titled "It Doesn't Matter Anymore."

A few weeks later, tragedy struck again, and this time much closer to home. Paul learned that his mother, then only in her late thirties, was dying of a liver ailment. "I gave her things she had never had, like her own home," he recalled. "And every one of my hits, I played for her first, down in the basement. I sent her to every doctor I could find." But in the end, Paul's mother died.

"At the time, I was really into the music scene, traveling around the world. But in moving so much, I never had time to spend with the people really close to me, or even a lot of people my age. I guess I realized that there had to be a little more to life than this, because I had needs that were not fulfilled. I wanted to experience more than just the success syndrome. I was reaching out, saying, 'Hey, I want somebody to share this with me.' 'Lonely Boy' came out of that."

In the summer of 1959, "Lonely Boy" became Paul Anka's first number-one record. He sang it in his second movie, *Girls' Town* (1959), in which he co-starred with Mel Tormé

and Mamie Van Doren. Four years later, Paul made a documentary film about himself and used it as a title theme. That picture won Paul eight international awards, including Canadian Film of the Year.

Paul Anka continued to place hit songs on the charts well into the sixties. Among the biggest were "It's Time to Cry" (1959), "Puppy Love," "My Home Town" and "Summer's Gone" (1960), "The Story of My Love," "Tonight My Love Tonight" and "Dance On Little Girl" (1961), and "Love Me Warm and Tender," "A Steel Guitar and a Glass of Wine," and "Eso Beso" (1962). In 1963, he released a sequel to his first big hit and called it "Remember Diana." That single was to be his last top-forty record for several years.

In the late sixties, Paul concentrated on nightclub appearances and songwriting. During this period, he wrote such hits as "She's a Lady" for Tom Jones and "My Way" for Frank Sinatra. But still, Paul longed for the spotlight.

In 1974, he finally made his comeback with "You're Having My Baby," a duet with Odia Coates. It became his first number-one record in fifteen years—since "Lonely Boy" in 1959. After that, there were several more hits: "One-Man Woman/One-Woman Man" in 1974, and "I Don't Like to Sleep Alone," "There's Nothing Stronger Than Our Love," and "Times of Your Life" in 1975.

"His voice," wrote *Time* magazine in 1961, "sounds as if his shirt collar is too tight." The same article went on to describe Anka fans as "teenage nuts." Yet, those "nuts" could identify with the many moods and emotions of Paul Anka records. His talent—and their bucks—helped make the young man from Canada one of the most successful artists of the twentieth century.

Venus

FRANKIE AVALON

Frank Avallone grew up in the same south Philadelphia neighborhood as another future teen idol, James Darren. As a child, he first wanted to be a boxer but changed his mind at the age of ten after seeing Kirk Douglas in *Young Man with a Horn* (1950). Kirk's performance inspired Frank to talk his father into buying him a trumpet. Before long, Frank was being called a prodigy, and he was signed to RCA's subsidiary label, X. His first two records, "Trumpet Sorrento" and "Trumpet Tarantella," were both instrumentals, credited to "11-Year-Old Frankie Avalon." However, neither one was a hit.

Determined not to be a has-been at twelve, Frankie joined a pop group called Rocco and the Saints and toured with them to Atlantic City. His trumpet skills there led to a series of TV appearances on the shows of Paul Whiteman, Ray Anthony, and Jackie Gleason. Occasionally on these programs, Frankie would put his trumpet down and sing.

Rocco and the Saints were signed by Bob Marcucci and Peter De Angelis, owners of Chancellor Records. After one unsuccessful release, "Cupid," Avalon went solo with "Teacher's Pet," the tune he sang in his debut motion picture, *Disk Jockey Jamboree* (1957).

His next recording session did not start off well. After blowing a number of takes, Avalon, as a gag, held his nose as he sang "Dede Dinah." Marcucci and De Angelis, who had written the song, thought the effect was so hysterical that they issued that take as a single. In the spring of 1958, it became Frankie's first gold record. A few months later, Frankie also held his nose on "Gingerbread"—and it, too, made the national top ten. A third hit, "I'll Wait for You," came out at the end of the year.

Early in 1959, a songwriter named Ed Marshall told Frankie he had a tune he wanted him to hear. Sitting at the piano, he sang and played "Venus." Frankie became very excited and asked if anyone else had heard the song. Ed explained that Al Martino had and was planning to record it on an album. Frankie called his producers, and brought the song to them. Within three days, a session was set up. It took nine takes to perfect "Venus," but afterward everyone agreed that it was something special. The record was released about three days later, and in little more than a week it had sold over a million copies.

Frankie Avalon had more big hits in 1959: "A Boy Without a Girl," backed with "Bobby Sox to Stockings," "Just Ask Your Heart," and a second number-one song, "Why." He became one of the hottest teen idols of the late fifties and early sixties and appeared frequently on "American Bandstand."

In 1960, Frankie turned most of his attention to movies. He appeared in *Guns of the Timberland* with Alan Ladd and *The Alamo* with John Wayne. After that came *Voyage to the Bottom of the Sea* (1961), *The Carpetbaggers* (1962), and *Beach Party* (1963), his first of nine films with Annette Funicello. Later pictures included *Beach Blanket Bingo* (1964), *Ski Party* (1965), *How to Stuff a Wild Bikini* (1967), *The Million Eyes of Su Muru* (1968), and *Skiddoo* (1969).

In the seventies, Frankie divided his time between personal appearances, occasional movies (*The Take; Grease*), and a summer TV series ("Easy Does It" in 1976). "It was about that time that a lot of my contemporaries were getting back in the recording studio again," Frankie said. "There was Anka, Sedaka, Vinton, and I thought, well, let me give it a try. Fourteen different labels passed on me, and then Billy Terrell of DeLite Records came up with the idea of remaking 'Venus' disco style. I wasn't too thrilled about it. I really didn't want to touch that song. It was such a big record, and such a good record. How do you top a song like that?"

The new version of "Venus" didn't top the original, but it did become a major disco hit in 1976. "It was all right, but I still prefer the original," Frankie said. "I'm still proud of that record, and in my opinion, it's the *only* record I've ever recorded."

Battle of
New Orleans

JOHNNY HORTON

Johnny Horton was raised on a farm in Tyler, Texas, where his mother taught him how to play guitar at the age of eleven. He went to college on a basketball scholarship, but rather than study assignments, Johnny would spend hours writing songs and eventually lost all interest in going to school. One day he just dropped out, grabbed his guitar, and headed north—to Alaska—where the rush was on in the fishing industry.

In 1950, Johnny moved to Los Angeles and found another job, again in fishing. In his free time, he played songs for his friends, who urged him to enter a country music contest at the Harmony Park Corral. Johnny did enter, won first place, and wound up with his own radio show over KXLA. Billed as "The Singing Fisherman,"

Johnny also appeared on local TV.

In 1955, Johnny became a regular on the "Louisiana Hayride," which was broadcast every Saturday night out of Shreveport. During the week he toured nightclubs, dances, and county fairs and became known as one of the hardest-working entertainers on the honky-tonk circuit. He brought his brand of music to the Grand Ole Opry and, for a while, even hosted a television series in his home town.

Johnny recorded occasionally for Mercury and Dot during this period. However, it wasn't until he signed with Columbia Records that he started to place songs on the country charts. His first hits were "Honky Tonk Man" (1956), "I'm a One-Woman Man" (1956), "I'm Coming Home" (1957), and "All Grown Up" (1958). Then, in 1959, he released "When It's Springtime in Alaska," a number-one country smash that remained a top seller for a full six months. After that, Johnny needed something equally strong. He selected "The Battle of New Orleans."

It was a remarkable song about a remarkable fight—one of the most pointless military exercises in history. The Battle of New Orleans was part of the War of 1812, which had *ended* two weeks before the legendary battle took place. However, this news had not yet filtered down to the troops. So, on January 8, 1815, Andrew Jackson and his band of American sharpshooters decimated the ranks of British forces, led by Commander Pakenham. In celebration, a tune called "The Eighth of January" was written. It became a nineteenth-century "hit" and was played all over the country, especially at square dances. Then, 140

years later, a schoolteacher from Snowball, Arkansas—Jimmy Driftwood—added words to the song. It was his version that was condensed, polished, and finally published in 1959 and recorded by Johnny Horton.

"The Battle of New Orleans" was a number-one single that summer, on both the pop and country charts (as an R&B record, it reached number three). It sold a million copies in less than seven weeks and wound up winning two Grammy Awards, as both Song of the Year and Best Country and Western Recording. Oddly enough, it was banned in Canada by radio programers who feared that Queen Elizabeth, then visiting their country, might hear it and be offended. Homer and Jethro cut their own satiric version, "The Battle of Kookamonga." To everyone's surprise, their comic cover also became a top-ten pop hit.

In the spring of 1960, Johnny had another big pop and country smash, "Sink the Bismarck," which he had helped write. Then, on November 5, he finished a show in Austin, Texas, and prepared to drive back to Nashville. On Route 70, near the tiny town of Milano, there was a grinding collision, and Johnny Horton was killed instantly.

Two weeks after the crash, deejays across America paid tribute by giving massive air play to what they thought would be the very last Johnny Horton release. It was the title theme from a new film starring John Wayne, Ernie Kovacs, and Fabian. Country, pop, and R&B stations joined together, to help make "North to Alaska" his second—and final—million-selling single.

Mack the Knife

BOBBY DARIN

"Sometime between 'Queen of the Hop' and 'Dream Lover,' I went in to record my first album," recalled Bobby Darin. "It was titled *That's All,* and one of the things in that album was a song that changed my entire life. Now, it may sound funny today, but at first I didn't want that song released as a single record. You see, I had established a pattern with 'Splish Splash,' 'Dream Lover,' and songs like that. This one was so unusual that I was afraid that it would break things up. I mean, it was fine for the album—it helped sell the album for about three or four months. But then Atco pulled the song as a single anyway, and as we all know, it went on to become a phenomenal hit record. It would be really wonderful if something like that came along every day, but, of course, if it did, it wouldn't be a phenomenon."

Bobby Darin was speaking of "Mack the Knife," a grisly, show-stopping number first heard more than thirty years before in Berlin. At that time, it was titled "Moritat" and was a scathing attack on German society and pop culture. Bertolt Brecht and Kurt Weill composed it as the main theme for their *Threepenny Opera,* a musical satire set in 1837 in Soho, the seediest, most crime-ridden district of London. In the play, a master thief and cutthroat is betrayed by a woman.

The Threepenny Opera was translated into English by Marc Blitzstein, who cleaned up the plot and also rewrote most of the song lyrics. In the process, "Moritat" was transformed into "Mack the Knife." Over two dozen artists tried recording the theme in 1956, when the show opened as a revival off Broadway. Five versions became major hits, including those of Louis Armstrong, Lawrence Welk, Richard Hayman and Jan August, Billy Vaughn, and the Dick Hyman Trio. Bobby's single, three years later,

outsold not only all these, but also every other record—of any kind— released in 1959.

Darin's rendition seemed to appeal to adults as well as rock 'n' rollers, and that's perhaps why it captured the Grammy Award as Record of the Year. Bobby was named Best New Artist of 1959, even though he'd been recording for quite a few years by then. His single broke onto the charts in the last week of August and hung in there for a solid six months. For more than two months, it reigned supreme.

Bobby Darin's "Mack the Knife" opened many important doors, including the golden gate to Hollywood. In 1959, Darin was signed by both Paramount Pictures and Universal-International. His first movie, *Come September* (1960), was shot in Italy, where he met, and later eloped with, his leading lady, Sandra Dee (their marriage ended in 1967). In 1962, Bobby had five films running at the same time. Then came *Captain Newman, M.D.,* for which he won an Academy Award nomination in 1963, and four other films.

The hits, of course, kept on coming as well: "Beyond the Sea" (1960), "You Must Have Been a Beautiful Baby" (1961), "Things" (1962), "You're the Reason I'm Living" (1963), "If I Were a Carpenter" (1966), and well over a dozen more.

As the sixties rolled on, Bobby became politically preoccupied. After the death of his hero, Robert Kennedy, he threw away his hairpiece, started calling himself "Bob Darin," and recorded albums full of folk rock that no one wanted to hear. His heart rate began to rise dangerously. In February 1971, two plastic valves were implanted in his chest during nine hours of open heart surgery.

One of Bobby's long-time dreams was to have his own TV series, which finally happened in the summer of

1972. "The Bobby Darin Amusement Company" was "a comedy show with music," according to producer Saul Ilson. The program was canceled in April 1973.

Late in 1973 Darin checked into Cedars of Lebanon Hospital in L.A. with heart trouble. "For thirty years," he bravely joked to the press, "I've expected to die." On December 20, that prediction came true. Bobby Darin was thirty-seven years old.

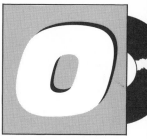

STEREO WAS THE BUZZWORD in 1960, the year the Osmonds and the Band were both formed, and Janis Joplin graduated from high school. In New York, *Bye Bye Birdie,* a musical based loosely on Elvis' army induction, opened on Broadway. At the same time, Presley got out of the service and joined Frank Sinatra on a TV special that also introduced Frank's young daughter, Nancy. Later in the year she wed Tommy Sands, and Bobby Darin married Sandra Dee. Two Cowsills, Susan and John, were born, and we lost two performers, Jesse Belvin and Johnny Horton, in separate car crashes. Lead singers went solo in droves; Dion left the Belmonts, Johnny Maestro the Crests, Tony Williams the Platters, and Ben E. King said goodbye to the Drifters. Dick Clark testified in Senate payola hearings, and it was the first year of "The Twist."

When US 53310761 was released from the army on March 5, 1960, in the midst of one of the worst blizzards Fort Dix, New Jersey, had ever seen, he was greeted by an avalanche of newspaper, radio, and TV reporters as well as wistful and loyal teenage fans who had stood for hours in deep snow and bitter cold to catch the merest sight of **Sergeant Elvis Presley** in uniform. By this time, there was a feeling that members of the press had subtly swung to Presley's side and, if not quite ardent fans of the singer, were impressed by the dignified and quite natural way in which he handled his army stretch. His totally relaxed and cordial stance at the Fort Dix press conference added to the picture of a maturing personality, and it is no exaggeration to say that Presley won a mighty victory both at Fort Dix and at his press conference on the way home to Memphis by remaining—of all peculiar things in show business—himself.

"The Ed Sullivan Show"—television's longest-running variety series—was carried over CBS every Sunday night for twenty-three years. Its host, a former newspaper columnist, couldn't sing or dance but knew who could, and booked them on the program. His first guests, on June 20, 1948, were Dean Martin and Jerry Lewis; over the years, virtually every important act of the fifties and sixties stopped by, from Elvis Presley to the Beatles. Ray Bloch led the house orchestra; genial Art Hannes was Ed's announcer. The series went off the air on June 6, 1971, and three years later Sullivan died.

Duane Eddy, whose bass guitar prowess earned him the nickname "Mr. Twang," scored his biggest of more than two dozen hits with the title theme from *Because They're Young* (also in the cast: Dick Clark and James Darren). Darren also turned up in *All the Young Men,* Frankie Avalon in *The Alamo,* Paul Anka in *Girls' Town,* and Conway Twitty in *Platinum High School.* In an odd switch, Louis Armstrong starred in *The Beat Generation,* while Chuck Berry appeared in *Jazz on a Summer's Day.* As usual, there were a couple of Elvis movies: *G.I. Blues* and *Flaming Star.*

For some reason, 1960 was a good year for comedy and novelty records, both albums and singles. Top forty 45s included "Mr. Custer" (Larry Verne), "Yogi" (the Ivy Three), "Got a Girl" (the Four Preps), and "Bad Man Blunder" (the Kingston Trio). "Hot Rod Lincoln" was recorded by both Johnny Bond and Charlie Ryan, "Alley Oop" by the Hollywood Argyles and Dante and the Evergreens. The Chipmunks offered "Rudolph the Red-Nosed Reindeer," "Alvin's Orchestra," and even "Alvin for President" (although most folks seemed to pass on that one). On the LP side, *Let's All Sing with the Chipmunks* was big, as was *Rejoice Dear Hearts* by Brother Dave Gardner, *Woody Woodbury Looks at Love and Life,* and *The Button-Down Mind of Bob Newhart.* But the champion comic of 1960 was a fast-talking, stream-of-consciousness comedian by the name of **Shelley Berman.** Not only was his LP *Edge* a big hit, but two other Berman releases, *Inside* and *Outside,* were among the top-selling ten albums of the year.

From his first wailing "We-e-e-l-l" to the last crunching guitar chord, **Eddie Cochran** was rock 'n' roll incarnate. His music spoke the language of the life-loving young—frustrated people who wanted to enjoy their youth without being hassled. A soulful singer and brilliant guitarist, Eddie Cochran knew how to write and deliver the feeling. His 1958 classic, "Summertime Blues," is often pointed to as an example of the essence of rock 'n' roll:

direct, powerful communication through simple musical means. The same can be said of "Skinny Jim," "Nervous Breakdown," "C'mon Everybody," "Somethin' Else," and more. In 1960, he went on tour with Gene Vincent, electrifying crowds in England and Europe. On the way to the airport and home, his taxi went into a skid and slammed into a lightpost. Eddie never regained consciousness and died hours later. He was twenty-two.

THE TOP 40

1. Theme from *A Summer Place,* *Percy Faith*
2. It's Now or Never, *Elvis Presley*
3. He'll Have to Go, *Jim Reeves*
4. Cathy's Clown, *Everly Brothers*
5. The Twist, *Chubby Checker*
6. I'm Sorry, *Brenda Lee*
7. Running Bear, *Johnny Preston*
8. Stuck on You, *Elvis Presley*
9. Handy Man, *Jimmy Jones*
10. Teen Angel, *Mark Dinning*
11. Everybody's Somebody's Fool, *Connie Francis*
12. Itsy Bitsy Teenie Weenie Yellow Polka Dot Bikini, *Brian Hyland*
13. Save the Last Dance for Me, *Drifters*
14. My Heart Has a Mind of Its Own, *Connie Francis*
15. El Paso, *Marty Robbins*
16. Greenfields, *Brothers Four*
17. Only the Lonely, *Roy Orbison*
18. Walk Don't Run, *Ventures*
19. Wild One, *Bobby Rydell*
20. Sweet Nothin's, *Brenda Lee*
21. Chain Gang, *Sam Cooke*
22. Alley Oop, *Hollywood Argyles*
23. Baby (You've Got What It Takes), *Brook Benton and Dinah Washington*
24. Puppy Love, *Paul Anka*
25. Good Timin', *Jimmy Jones*
26. What in the World's Come Over You, *Jack Scott*
27. Sink the Bismarck, *Johnny Horton*
28. Night, *Jackie Wilson*
29. Where or When, *Dion and the Belmonts*
30. Why, *Frankie Avalon*
31. Kiddio, *Brook Benton*
32. Please Help Me, I'm Falling, *Hank Locklin*
33. Sixteen Reasons, *Connie Stevens*
34. Mr. Custer, *Larry Verne*
35. Because They're Young, *Duane Eddy*
36. Let It Be Me, *Everly Brothers*
37. I Want to Be Wanted, *Brenda Lee*
38. Burning Bridges, *Jack Scott*
39. Paper Roses, *Anita Bryant*
40. Beyond the Sea, *Bobby Darin*

THE TOP 10 LPs

1. The Sound of Music, *Original Cast*
2. Button Down Mind, *Bob Newhart*
3. Sold Out, *Kingston Trio*
4. Sixty Years of Music America Loves Best, *Various Artists*
5. Heavenly, *Johnny Mathis*
6. Here We Go Again, *Kingston Trio*
7. Inside, *Shelley Berman*
8. Faithfully, *Johnny Mathis*
9. Elvis Is Back, *Elvis Presley*
10. Encore of Golden Hits, *Platters*

The **Ventures'** story started in 1958, when a Seattle construction worker, Don Wilson, spotted a guitar in the car of his new boss, Bob Bogle. The two men began to talk music, and before long were moonlighting in local clubs with two other musicians. "Although he doesn't know it, Chet Atkins was responsible for our first big single," said Bob. "He'd recorded 'Walk Don't Run' on one of his albums, and I dug the way he played. I couldn't match his style, so we decided to cut our own version." With the aid of a home tape recorder, they did just that. "Walk Don't Run" became a million-seller in 1960, and the prototype for many "surf" instrumentals to come.

Teen Angel

MARK DINNING

ark Dinning was born in Grant County, Oklahoma, the youngest son in a farm family of five girls and four boys. His father and uncles were evangelist singers, exposing Mark to gospel music at an early age. When not at church, Mark sometimes stayed home with his eleven-year-old baby-sitter, Clara Ann Fowler. Later she was to change her name to Patti Page.

In the early forties, Mark's older brother Wade took three of his sisters, Ginger, Jean, and Lou, up to Chicago to try out for the "Barn Dance Show" on KFH. They were accepted and soon were playing alongside such notables as Les Paul and Mary Ford, Pat Buttram, and the Hoosier Hot Shots. After a while, people began asking when Mark was going to join the family act. Ken White, A&R director for the Dinning Sisters, even came down to the farm and tried to audition the young man. However, at thirteen, Mark was far too shy for show biz.

A few years later, the family moved to Tennessee and bought another farm just outside of Nashville. The Dinning Sisters became regulars on the Grand Ole Opry and even cut a million-selling single, "Buttons and Bows." Mark was impressed with his sisters' popularity but still insisted that show business was not for him. He had already made plans for the future: He was going to become a turkey farmer.

Then, when Mark was seventeen years old, his father gave him an electric guitar. He toyed around with it at first, but then discovered the fun of simple folk music. Before long, Mark was appearing in local clubs, often in duets with his brother Ace.

Shortly after graduating from high school, Mark was drafted into the army and wound up at an isolated outpost in the Mojave Desert. He brought his guitar along to pass the time and spent many lonely nights picking and singing to the prairie dogs. One day he made a vow that as soon as he got out, he'd waste no time in landing a recording contract.

His discharge came through in 1957, and Mark headed directly for Nashville. He was auditioned by music publisher Wesley Rose, who immediately placed a call to Mitch Miller at Columbia Records in New York. Mitch, however, had just signed an unknown of his own, Johnny Mathis, on the very same day and was not looking for any more new talent. So Mark continued to hammer on doors and, six weeks later, closed a deal with MGM Records.

His first few releases were not too successful—"Shameful Ways," "A Million Tears," and other songs that went nowhere. Then, in early 1959, Jean Dinning came across a magazine article about a frustrated deejay. He was upset by parents who had "given up" on their children, writing

them off as "little devils." In his experience, he'd met hundreds of young people whom he described as "teen angels." Jean Dinning was fascinated by the phrase and, along with Red Surrey, turned it into a tear-stained ballad for her little brother.

"Teen Angel" was recorded late in 1959 and arrived at most radio stations right around Christmas. It quickly climbed the charts all through January, and by February it was the number-one record in the country. Some program directors refused to play it, saying that the story line was "too bloody." In England, it was banned completely. But it did open the door to TV, concerts, and fame for Mark Dinning. He toured America and Australia and turned up on "American Bandstand" more than fifteen times.

After "Teen Angel," Mark recorded several more singles, including "A Star Is Born," "The Lovin' Touch," and "Top Forty News, Weather, and Sports." None of them made much of an impact, and by the mid-sixties his recording career was over.

Mark continued, though, as a live performer, and still travels about six months of the year. Backed by an automatic rhythm and percussion machine, he's a one-man show—singing, playing his guitar, and remembering his one bright moment in the spotlight.

Handy Man

JIMMY JONES

Jimmy Jones was born in Birmingham, Alabama, but grew up in New York. "I started with a group called the Sparks of Rhythm; that was about 1955," he recalled. "I stayed with them for about two or three months and then formed my own group." He also formed his own label, which he cheerfully named "Good Records." "That was my thing—happy songs. I produced a tune on my label by the El-Chords. It sold a quarter of a million copies in New York alone."

Jimmy also wrote and recorded a number of singles for other companies, including Apollo, Savoy, Rama, and Epic. "I did a thing for Arrow Records with the Jones Boys called 'Whistlin' Man.' I wrote that, too. It was a lot similar to 'Handy Man.'"

Most of Jimmy's income, though, came from making demonstration records for various New York song publishers. "The first big song that Fabian had, I did the demo on that. Also, 'Hey Little Girl.'

"And then I got married. One night, I was in bed worried, because I had to pay my rent the next day, and I didn't have any money. Now, I had been thinking about 'Handy Man,' but couldn't get that song to hang together right. Then, about one or two o'clock in the morning, the punch hit—the 'come-a, come-a' rhythm idea. My wife was pregnant at the time, but I woke her up in the middle of the night and said, 'Hey, how do you like this: Come-a, come-a, come-a?' And she said, 'Aw, all right, whatever,' 'cause to her it didn't sound like anything at all. But I knew that it did.

"So I finished the song up and took it downtown the next day to the music publishers in the Brill Building. The first guy I talked to wouldn't accept it—he said it was crap, really. But he was nice. He said, 'I'll give you $25, but you just bring me in a better song than this.' So, instead of 'Handy Man,' I wrote him a thing called 'I Got a Girl to Live Next Door.' And we all know what happened with that song—nothing.

"So I went back on the street, and ran into Otis Blackwell. He was with Shalimar Music, which was one of the largest publishers down in that area at the time. I had done some demonstration records for him before, and he could go in and get three or four hundred dollars advance money for each record. So now he wanted a couple of dollars; he said that if I would let him be twenty-five percent writer on the song, he could get some money on it.

"We made a demonstration record—just a piano, a drum, and me singing—and took it back in to Shalimar. They liked it so much that, instead of sending it around to other artists, they decided to record me on it.

"I cut 'Handy Man' in April of 1959, at Regent Sound Studios. I did one take. Shalimar made a deal with Cub Records, and they released the song in June. And then nothing happened. It was a really tough time for me. Demo work was slowing up so I had to get a job on the side in a snack bar. Then in October, a deejay in Pittsburgh named Porky Chadwick broke the record. I didn't find out about it till December. After New Year's, the whole country went on it. It sold two and a half million copies in two and a half months.

"After that, I cut another song, 'Good Timin',' and it went like wildfire. 'Good Timin' ' just went straight up in May of '60. I sold close to two million records or more off of that. I did a lot of tours; I was on the 'Stars of '60' with Lloyd Price, Laverne Baker, the Coasters, the Isley Brothers. I went to Europe and was very happy to find 'Handy Man' and 'Good Timin' ' in the British top ten."

Jimmy Jones continued to record for several more years but never was able to recapture the magic of his first two hits. He later became a record producer, and he raised two daughters and a son. Today they perform as the Jones Family, and Jimmy sings in the New York area.

Stuck on You

ELVIS PRESLEY

During his two years in the army, Elvis Presley continued to storm the charts, and, as usual, both sides of his singles became top-selling hits. In 1958, there were "Don't" / "I Beg of You"; "Wear My Ring Around Your Neck" / "Doncha Think It's Time"; "Hard Headed Woman" / "Don't Ask Me Why"; and "One Night" / "I Got Stung." In 1959, the million-sellers rolled on with "A Fool Such as I" / "I Need Your Love Tonight" and "A Big Hunk of Love" / "My Wish Came True."

Presley began 1960 by releasing his second "greatest hits" album—*50,000,000 Elvis Fans Can't Be Wrong: Elvis' Gold Records Volume 2.* On March 20, fifteen days after he got out of the army, Elvis drove to Nashville for his first recording session of the decade. Present that day were three men who were to make up the backbone of his studio band for the next several years: guitarist Hank Garland, drummer Buddy Harmon, and pianist Floyd Cramer. Also on hand were old cronies Scotty Moore (lead guitar) and D. J. Fontana (percussion). The only man missing was bass player Bill Black, who had dropped out to form his own combo for Hi Records (in 1960, Bill was to rack up five hits, including an instrumental remake of a Presley hit he'd played on; "Don't Be Cruel").

The boys embarked on an all-night session, and among the songs laid down were "Stuck on You" and "Fame and Fortune," the A and B sides of Elvis' first post-army single. Predictably, both songs became big hits, "Stuck on You" rising to the number-one spot in April. Weeks before, RCA anticipated the demand by arranging for an initial run of one million pressings. By the time the single was released, though, advance orders topped that figure by more than 275,000 copies—an unprecedented amount at that time.

Elvis sang the two songs publicly for the first time on March 26. The occasion was the taping of a Frank Sinatra television special called "Welcome Back Elvis." Forty minutes into the show, Presley went into "Fame and Fortune." Afterward, he cued his backup singers, the Jordanaires, and introduced "Stuck on You." He shimmied, shook, and danced about the stage. There was no question—Elvis was back, this time to stay.

It was ironic that Elvis made his TV return on the same bill with Frank Sinatra. Only three years before, Frank had called rock 'n' roll "phony and false, written and played for the most part by cretinous goons." He admitted, though, that Elvis had "a natural, animalistic talent." In 1977, on the death of Presley, Sinatra told the press that there had been "many accolades uttered about his talent and performances through the years, all of which I agree with wholeheartedly. I shall miss him dearly as a friend. He was a warm, considerate, generous man."

Elvis was paid $125,000 for six minutes' work on the Sinatra special—the highest fee ever paid for a single guest appearance on television to that time. After the show aired May 12, his manager, Col. Parker, announced that Presley's TV fee from then on would be $150,000. "I don't want Elvis competing with his own movies," Parker said. Presley was not to appear on television again for nearly nine years.

Hollywood had indeed beckoned, though. The Colonel arranged for Elvis to star in three pictures a year, at a minimum of $1 million apiece. Presley only made two films, though, in '60—the inevitable army movie, *G.I.*

Blues, and one of his best motion pictures ever, a western called *Flaming Star.*

When Presley entered the army, one critic wrote: "The Elvis virus has at long last been isolated. Before Presley learns how to salute properly, his public will have forgotten him." As is common among critics of all varieties, it was simply wishful thinking. Six months into 1960, one fact had become crystal-clear: The Presley career was bigger than ever. The hits were coming thick and fast, and his films were breaking all his own box-office records. A Gallup poll revealed the staggering truth—that Presley's first name had become better known than any two names in the world.

Running Bear
JOHNNY PRESTON

John Preston Courville was born in Port Arthur, Texas, and began singing in his high school choir. While still a student, he formed his own band, the Shades, and began performing at dances around the area. Before long, they were one of the hottest groups in southern Texas and had caught the eye of the local media.

One night, while playing in a honkytonk in Beaumont, Johnny was approached by two men—Bill Hall, a record producer, and J. P. Richardson, a songwriter and deejay, better known as the Big Bopper of KTRM. Between sets, they asked him if he'd like to record a few singles. Johnny's answer was a big smile and a happy yes. The session did not go well, though—Johnny was nervous—and the resulting tapes were scrapped.

A short time later, J.P. contacted Johnny again and said that he had written a sure-fire hit record for him. Johnny asked what the song was, but the Bopper wouldn't tell him. "I just want to know," the Bopper barked, "if you're willing to give it another try." Johnny said that he was.

"Well, we just drove over to Houston one Sunday morning," Johnny recalled. "There was the Bopper and me, and Bill Hall, who was also our personal manager. And George Jones,

the country singer, he came along for the ride. So we got to the studio, and that's the first I ever heard of the song. J.P. played me the song, and said, 'John, if you record this, I guarantee that it'll be a smash.' Now, he'd already written two or three hits, so you'd think I'd agree with him, but actually I was kind of skeptical. I said, 'Well, I do blues; this isn't like anything we do in the clubs. I just don't know if this song is what everybody's looking for.' But he persisted, and fortunately, I was wrong.

"When we actually cut the record, we needed some war whoops in the background. So if you listen carefully, you can hear J.P., Bill Hall, George Jones, and Pappy Daily doing those oonka-chunkas behind me.

"It was a very good record for me, and J.P. had faith in it from the time we cut it until the day Mercury released it."

Unfortunately, J. P. Richardson did not live long enough to see his predictions come true. On February 3, 1959, he was killed in a plane crash, along with Buddy Holly and Ritchie Valens.

"Mercury didn't think it would be a good idea to put out the record, so soon after J.P.'s death, so they held on to it for eight months," Johnny

said. "It finally came out in October 1959. I remember saying to him, 'What do I do if this song hits? Where do I go from here?' He said, 'Well, son, relax and just follow the bouncing ball.' So that's what we did, and probably, to some extent, that's what led to my downfall. Instead of sticking to a certain style and making the most of it, we looked around and tried to ride with whatever was selling. All my records sounded different, 'cause I tried so many different styles. The public didn't know what Johnny Preston was, and, well, a recording career is never very long. I just slowly kind of slipped by the wayside."

Before he did, though, Johnny had two other big hits in 1960: "Cradle of Love," and "Feel So Fine."

"I recorded quite a bit more for Mercury, and then went on to Kapp, Imperial, Capitol, ABC Paramount, and 20th Century-Fox. It was a pleasure while it lasted. I did quite a bit of touring and got to see Europe, Australia, the Philippines, Japan, and all over the United States. I'll say this: I thank everybody from the bottom of my heart for the opportunity to entertain. I wouldn't trade my memories for anything in the world."

I'm Sorry
BRENDA LEE

Five-foot, one-inch Brenda Lee once gave a command performance for Queen Elizabeth of England. Her Majesty said, "You've certainly come a long way to sing for us." Brenda looked up and said, "I've come a long way, period." And indeed she had.

Brenda Mae Tarpley was born in the charity ward of Emory University Hospital in Atlanta, Georgia. Her family was very, very poor, and things went from bad to worse in 1952, when her father, a carpenter, was killed on the job. Her interest in music started early; according to her mother, when Brenda was three years old, she could hear a song twice and then sing it word for word.

As early as age four, it was evident that Brenda had a strong voice and the confidence to share it in front of an audience. She sang "Take Me out to the Ball Game" at the annual spring festival in town and won a first-place trophy. The community rallied behind Brenda, and following an audition for "Starmaker's Revue," she became a regular performer on the Atlanta-based radio program.

"Too Young" was the first song that Brenda sang on the air, but even at seven, she was not too young for a TV appearance. She performed "Hey Good Lookin' " for the producers of "TV Ranch" on Atlanta's WAGA. It was about this time that she dropped the "Tarp" from her name, and became simply Brenda Lee.

When she was nine years old, her family moved to Augusta, Georgia, where she met country star Red Foley. Foley got her a contract with Decca Records. She was to stay with the label for twenty-one years, longer than any other artist except Bill Monroe.

Brenda was eleven years old when her first recording session was held, on July 30, 1956. Supervising that day was Owen Bradley, who went on to produce all of her million-selling singles. "I remember when we started on that first take," he said. "All of a sudden she yelled, 'Stop, stop, he missed a note,' and pointed straight at the bass player. The bass player had missed a note and no one else had caught it."

One of Brenda's earliest recordings was "Dynamite," in 1957. It wasn't a big seller, but did inspire her lifelong nickname: "Little Miss Dynamite." Two years later, she finally cut the record that made her a star—"Sweet Nothin's."

"What I was singing about on that record, thirteen-year-old girls just weren't doing," she recalled later, "and neither was I. I was playing with paper dolls, and I didn't know what the lyrics meant. I just sang them the way I thought they should be sung."

But there was a lot of talk about how Brenda could sing, and make her songs believable, when she was only thirteen years old. "That's the problem we had in cutting 'I'm Sorry,' " she explained. "They said, 'Nobody's gonna believe a girl this age with unrequited love on her hands.' Ronnie Self, the same gentleman who wrote 'Sweet Nothin's,' brought me 'I'm Sorry,' and I loved the song, but the record company wouldn't let me do it. We held it—we said, 'Will you let us keep it?'—I think we must have held that song about three years before we ever cut it. We had just about given up hope, but then one night we had about ten minutes left over on a session. My manager, just for old times' sake, since we'd been bringing the song to every session, said, 'Well, why don't we try "I'm Sorry"?' Well, we didn't even have an arrangement, but everybody said, 'O.K.,' so we cut it in two takes. I think we rehearsed it once and then cut it, and we used three strings. That was one of the first times that strings were used on a pop session in Nashville. I just believed in that song—it was a good little ballad—and it sold six million records and has become a standard."

The other side of the single turned out to be a hit as well. "That's All You Gotta Do," composed by Jerry Reed, climbed the charts to number six.

The Twist
CHUBBY CHECKER

Ernest Evans was born in South Carolina, but grew up in Philadelphia, where he lived with his parents and two brothers, Spencer and Tracy. When he was a small boy, his mom took him to see Sugar Charles Robinson, a child piano prodigy. Ernest was so impressed that he vowed to someday enter show business. At age eight, he took the first step by organizing the Quantrells, his own streetcorner harmony group.

By the time he was in high school, Ernest had mastered the drums, piano, and a large number of vocal impressions. He made up little dances, and along with a friend, Fabian Forte, entertained classmates whenever he could. He also sang and cracked jokes at his after school job, delighting customers in the Ninth Street meat market.

The store owner, Henry Colt, was impressed, and began showing off his employee to anyone who would listen. Eventually, he arranged for Ernest to sing on a private recording for Dick Clark. The result was a Yuletide novelty, "The Class," on which Ernest did impressions of several top recording stars. Dick sent it out as a Christmas card in 1958, and it got such good response that Cameo-Parkway released it commercially, and signed Ernest early in 1959.

During "The Class" sessions, Dick's wife asked the young singer what his name was. "Well," he replied, "my friends call me Chubby." As he had just completed his imitation of Fats Domino, she smiled and said, "Like in Checker?" That little play-on-words got an instant laugh, and stuck—inspiring Ernest Evans' new professional name.

While all of this was going on in Philadelphia, more history was being made at the Peacock Club, a roadhouse in Atlanta, Georgia. Hank Ballard and the Midnighters were playing there, and had worked up a little dance routine to liven their act.

Hank wrote a tune to go along with it, and three weeks later, on November 11, 1958, he and the boys recorded the original version of "The Twist."

King Records slapped the song on the B side of "Teardrops on Your Letter," which made the R&B top ten in the spring of 1959. Then deejays turned the record over, and started playing the other side. Kids loved "The Twist," and Dick Clark noticed that right away. He booked Hank Ballard and the Midnighters on his show, "American Bandstand," but for some reason they failed to show up. Dick then suggested that someone else cut a twist record, and recommended Danny and the Juniors. When that group was unable to get it together in the studio, Henry Colt stepped in, and insisted that his protégé be given a shot at the song. Within a short time, Chubby had sung his parts over an already-recorded instrumental track.

His backup vocalists—doing the "boogly-boogly shoos'—were the Dreamlovers, a doo-wop quintet that later made the top ten with "When We Get Married" (1961).

Bernie Lowe, the president of Cameo-Parkway, was not impressed with Chubby's recording, and felt that, at best, it might be usable "someday" as a flip side. For that reason, it took nearly fourteen months—from June 1959 to August 1960—for the Checker record to reach the national charts.

Chubby worked hard promoting it, undertaking a nonstop round of interviews, TV dates, and live appearances. After three weeks of demonstrating the Twist, he had lost nearly thirty pounds and was still losing. But in September 1960, the loser became a heavyweight winner, as "The Twist" by Chubby Checker finally became America's number-one single.

Cathy's Clown
THE EVERLY BROTHERS

By 1960, the innovative Everlys had become a major part of the Nashville music scene. The sound of country had changed considerably since their early days, with Don and Phil playing no small role in its evolution. "People were really conservative in Nashville when we arrived," said Phil. "And there we were, still teenagers, wearing duck-tails, pink shirts, and pegged pants." In four years, the brothers had helped break down the barriers between country and other kinds of music and paved the way for the new, more pop-oriented "Nashville Sound."

"I think one of the things that helped was the fact that we never set out to become teen idols," said Phil. "Oh, we got a little taste of it, as did Buddy Holly, but we never got as much of it as, say, Elvis Presley. Guys didn't feel they had to back away from us because their girlfriends were getting silly. It took some fellows a long time to admit that they liked Presley, because he was so attractive to the ladies."

The Everly Brothers had racked up a dozen hits by the time the sixties rolled around—everything from "Bye Bye Love" and "Wake Up Little Susie" to their latest: "Poor Jenny," "Take a Message to Mary," and "'Til I Kissed You." The last-mentioned song, written by Don, showcased the Everlys' songwriting abilities—a talent they would draw upon more and more in the coming decade.

In January 1960, Don and Phil put out "Let It Be Me," their eighth and final top-ten single released on Cadence. For months, the brothers had argued with label owner Archie Bleyer over money, musical direction, and artistic control of their records. A few weeks later, they announced a split with Archie and a move to Los Angeles. They had signed a million-dollar deal with Warner Brothers, becoming that company's first venture into contemporary country.

Neil Diamond was one guest on Phil and Don Everly's TV series.

"We tried about eight things but weren't satisfied with them," recalled Phil, "and then Warner's called, asking for something to release. We told them to hold off, we'd get something, and then Donald came up with the idea of 'Cathy's Clown.' What spread the song, of course, was the name Cathy, plus the 'Grand Canyon Suite'—dum-ta-dum, which he adapted. It turned out to be one of our biggest ever."

"Cathy's Clown" became a number-one single in both the pop and R&B fields (oddly enough, country stations didn't play it). It peaked in June 1960, spending five weeks at the very top of the charts.

After the success of "Cathy's Clown," the boys felt confident enough to compose more and more of their own material. Phil came up with their next hit, "When Will I Be Loved," while Don wrote its follow-up, "So Sad." In 1961, their hits continued with "Walk Right Back," "Ebony Eyes," and "Don't Blame Me." The next year, there was "Crying in the Rain," and "That's Old Fashioned."

Also in 1962, the brothers, fearing the draft, enlisted in the Marine Corps Reserves and served six months of active duty. It was a costly time out, as the loss of momentum severely crippled the Everlys' career. Although they continued to cut records for more than a decade, the brothers never again scored a major hit single.

They rolled on, however, as a popular concert attraction. In 1970, ten years after "Cathy's Clown," Don and Phil got their own TV series, a summer replacement for the "Johnny Cash Show." In 1974, Phil hosted a "rap 'n' rock" television program called "In Session."

The Everly Brothers' partnership lasted for more than twenty years, until their breakup on a Friday the 13th, in July 1973. During a performance at the John Wayne Theater at Knotts' Berry Farm in Buena Park, California, Don suddenly walked off the stage and into history. "I'm tired of being booked as a relic of the past," he told reporters. "After more than two decades, I'm tired of being an Everly Brother."

He'll Have to Go

JIM REEVES

A remarkable musical story began on a day in 1928—that of James Travis Reeves, the Galloway, Texas, farm boy whose career was to last a lifetime—and many, many years beyond. On that day, an oil company worker fixed up a battered guitar for five-year-old Jim and taught him his first basic chords. At nine, Jim sang on the radio, and by high school, he was a regular performer at teenage dances and social events. He also drew people to the ballpark, where his skill as a pitcher attracted scouts from the St. Louis Cardinals. He signed with the team but soon after shattered both his ankles and all dreams of ever making it in professional sports.

Jim then turned to radio, becoming a newscaster and deejay for KGRI in Henderson, Texas (later on, he was to buy that station, along with WMTS in Murfreesboro, Tennessee). From there, Jim moved to KWKH, the home of the "Louisiana Hayride." He announced the Saturday night show and sometimes got to sing a few numbers. On one occasion, he was heard by Fabor Robinson, the owner of Abbott Records, who quickly put Jim under contract. It was on Abbott that Jim released his first country hit, "Mexican Joe," in 1952. It became a number-one C&W single.

In 1955, Jim joined the Grand Ole Opry and switched labels to RCA Victor. He wrote his first hit for the new company, "Yonder Comes a Sucker," and then began to turn out an impressive string of other country hits. In 1957, one of them managed to reach number twelve on the pop charts. It was called "Four Walls" and served to introduce the general public to the velvet voice of "Gentleman Jim."

Two years later, while out for a drive, Jim heard, for the first time, "He'll Have to Go"—on his car radio. The song had been written by Joe and Audrey Allison, a young couple who suffered from "telephone trouble." It seemed that Audrey had a very soft voice, and whenever Joe would phone her, she could barely be heard. He'd have to say, "If you can't talk louder, put your mouth closer to the phone." That gave Audrey the idea for the song, and one day the two of them sat down and completed it. Central Songs placed the tune with Billy Brown, a new artist on Columbia, and it was his record that Jim Reeves heard in the spring of 1959.

Jim wanted very much to record the song, but decided to wait six months and see if anything happened with Billy Brown's record. Nothing did, so on October 15, he entered the RCA studios in Nashville and laid down his own version. Chet Atkins was producer on that session, with Floyd Cramer playing piano, Bob Moore on bass, and Jim himself taking lead guitar. Everyone agreed that the finished track was a good recording, but nobody thought it was really anything special. So a decision was made to "throw the song away" by putting it on the back side of Jim's next single.

In November, that record, "In a Mansion Stands My Love," was released and RCA sat back, waiting for the expected hit. But it didn't come. Then, in December, country deejays flipped the single over and started playing "He'll Have to Go." In January, pop radio stations picked it up, and soon after, R&B stations were playing it as well. By early spring, it was one of the top-selling records in all three categories of music. Jim wound up with two Grammy nominations and the biggest hit single of his career—over three million copies sold.

Jim Reeves went on to place dozens of other songs on the pop and country charts. Often, both sides appeared, including "I Missed Me" and "Am I Losing You?" (1960); "Losing Your Love" and "What I Feel in My Heart"

(1961); and "Adios Amigo" backed with "I'm Gonna Change Everything" (1962). In 1963, he flew to Africa, where *Kimberly Jim,* his only motion picture, was filmed.

Jim Reeves was piloting his own plane on the night of August 31, 1964. He radioed the control tower that he was "running into heavy rain," and then suddenly all contact was lost. Twelve planes, two helicopters, and four hundred people on the ground searched for two days, before finding the wreckage in heavy brush.

Far from dimming his stature as a country music superstar, Jim Reeves's death actually enhanced his career, elevating him to legendary status and giving birth to "the Jim Reeves Effect." Amazingly, Jim's songs continued to appear on the country charts many years after his death.

It's Now or Never

ELVIS PRESLEY

One of America's best-selling albums in the summer of 1960 was *Elvis Is Back*—Presley's first post-army LP. Among the best-selling 45s was his biggest hit single of the year—one that spent five weeks at the top of the U.S. hit parade.

"It's Now or Never" was loosely based on another song, "O Sole Mio," which had been popularized by Elvis' favorite operatic tenor, Mario Lanza. The tune had been written in 1901 by two Italians, lyricist G. Capurro and composer Eduardo di Capua. Forty-eight years later, crooner Tony Martin had a major pop hit with it, under the title of "There's No Tomorrow." In 1960, two American writers, Aaron Schroeder and Wally Gold, adapted the song into "It's Now or Never."

Presley's version became an unbelievable worldwide smash, with more than five million copies sold in the United States alone. According to the *Guinness Book of World Records*, global sales topped twenty million. Elvis himself called it his "best recording ever," replacing his old favorite, "Don't Be Cruel." The B side of the single was "A Mess of Blues," which also got a good bit of air play.

"It's Now or Never" marked a significant change in Elvis' style. He had recorded ballads before, but this was the beginning of his drift away from rock 'n' roll rhythms—the sound that had made him a star. Some radio stations that had previously shunned Presley music programed "It's Now or Never" and his later hits in the same "easy listening" bag. RCA and the Colonel must have noticed this, because Elvis's next single was even further removed from his rockabilly roots. It was "Are You Lonesome Tonight?," a vaudeville recitation that had been written in the twenties. It sold a million copies its first week out and spawned a flurry of "answer records" ("Yes, I'm Lonesome Tonight," "Who's Lonesome Tonight?," "Oh How I Miss You Tonight," and others).

By October 1960, Elvis had recorded twenty-six singles and had earned thirty-three gold records (some of which, of course, were albums). All kinds of reasons, some of them fanciful, were advanced to explain the continuing Presley success. One theory had it that by disappearing into the army at the height of his career, Presley had left his fans drooling for more; absence had only made their hearts grow fonder. This was a fine theory except for one thing: Presley did not disappear into the army; he was drafted into it with about as much say as to the direction his army life would take as had any other GI.

Another theory stressed the goodwill he had gained by not taking the easy out in the army as an entertaining GI; this undoubtedly had an effect upon his public, although not enough to explain thoroughly the way his career took off at his discharge. A third theory came from the teenagers themselves, and it went something like this: Elvis simply outgrew all the things parents and other adults didn't like about him, and got better at all the things the teenagers already liked about him. In other words, he grew up.

Theme from A Summer Place

PERCY FAITH

*I*n 1915 when Percy was seven, he took up music—first the violin, and later piano. By eleven, he was earning three dollars a week, banging a battered upright as accompaniment to silent films at a hometown movie house. Every night as the lights dimmed he'd dream he was a concert pianist, and at fifteen, he gave his first recital at the Toronto Conservatory of Music.

Percy's future seemed bright until 1926, when his three-year-old sister's clothing caught fire. Having nothing else around, he beat out the flames with his bare hands, suffering such severe burns that doctors ordered him away from pianos for at least five years.

Percy was devasted, but instead of giving up, he decided to throw himself into new studies of composition and orchestration. Freed of classical confines, he discovered more satisfying ways of expressing his musical being. He started writing scores for local bands, and soon organized his own group to conduct on the radio. He developed a lush string sound that grew to become his trademark.

In 1933, the Canadian Broadcasting Company hired Percy as a staff arranger and conductor, and gave him his own radio show "Music by Faith." It became a top-rated program, and in 1938 Mutual picked it up for broadcast in America. Two years later, Percy was in the States, guest-hosting "The Carnation Contented Hour." His three-week on-air audition worked out so well that he stayed with the series for seven years, and became an American citizen. In 1947 he was named musical director of "The Coca-Cola Show," and then "The Woolworth Hour."

Percy was hired by Columbia Records as their Director of Popular Music in 1950. His boss, Mitch Miller, had just come in as the Director of Popular A&R. Faith's assignment was to help Miller in the search for new material, and to arrange for and accompany the growing list of singers Miller was hiring.

Percy had several hits in the early fifties: "I Cross My Fingers," "All My Love" (both 1950), and "On Top of Old Smokey" (1951), which featured a vocal by Burl Ives. In 1952, his Latin-flavored "Delicato," with Stan Freeman on harpsichord, was a number-one success. He didn't have a gold record, though, until 1953, and the "Theme from *Moulin Rouge*." It too was a chart-topper, and according to *Cashbox*, was the best-selling single of the year.

As leader of the Columbia house orchestra, Percy backed countless performers, and often took on outside projects. In 1955, his scoring of *Love Me or Leave Me* earned him an Academy Award nomination. The bulk of his career, though, was spent cutting instrumental versions of other people's hits—"mood music" it was called—and his album sales over the years were more than respectable. It was while cutting one such album that Percy found his greatest success.

The recording of the "Theme from *A Summer Place*" was just another routine assignment for Percy. The film, released in 1959, was a lushly photographed soaper of adultery and teenage love, set at a resort house on the Maine coast.

Percy Faith's version of the title theme broke in mid-January 1960, and by March was the number-one single in the country. It stayed at the top for nine weeks—longer than any other single in 1960—and quickly sold more than two million copies. When the Grammies were passed out, it was a shoo-in as Record of the Year. And when the film was reissued, it did considerably better.

Percy had another hit in 1960, "Theme for Young Lovers," and in 1969, earned a second Grammy for the "Love Theme from *Romeo and Juliet*." He continued to turn out profitable LPs, and in 1976, released a disco version of the "Theme from *A Summer Place*."

When Percy died on February 9 of that year, forty-five of his albums were still in the Columbia catalog. He was one of the people who helped build that label into a giant of the industry.

1961

NINETEEN SIXTY-ONE was the year that the FCC gave its O.K. to FM stereo, and a Marty Robbins record, "Don't Worry," introduced the sound of a fuzz guitar. It was also the time that we first heard embryonic hits by a lot of people who would become much bigger stars later: Glen Campbell ("Turn Around Look at Me"), Aretha Franklin ("Won't Be Long"), Paul Revere and the Raiders ("Like Long Hair"), Tony Orlando ("Halfway to Paradise"), the Spinners ("That's What Girls Are Made For"), and Gladys Knight and the Pips ("Every Beat of My Heart"). The Beach Boys and Lettermen formed their respective groups, John Stewart joined the Kingston Trio, and Frank Sinatra kicked off his Reprise label with "The Second Time Around." Elvis Presley got a plaque from RCA commending him for selling more than $76 million worth of records in five years. Leif Garrett was born, Ricky Nelson dropped the "y" from his name, and Bob Dylan played Carnegie Hall—to fifty-three people.

After several name and personnel changes, a new British band called the **Beatles** began to jell in 1960. The band members were John Lennon, rhythm guitar; George Harrison, lead guitar; Paul McCartney, bass; and Pete Best, drums. By 1961, the Beatles were appearing regularly at the Cavern Club in Hamburg, Germany, and in May they were considered good enough to back Tony Sheridan at a Polydor recording session. Five months later, Raymond Jones walked into NEMS record shop in Liverpool and asked owner Brian Epstein for a copy of "My Bonnie"—one of the tunes recorded during that session. Intrigued to find that a Liverpool group had actually cut a record, Brian visited the Cavern Club over a lunch hour and became fascinated with the Beatles' charisma (but not their approach). On December 3, he sat down with the boys and discussed becoming their manager. They thought it was a good idea, so he arranged an audition with Decca Records in London. George sang "The Sheik of Araby," and Brian predicted that someday they'd be "bigger than Elvis." Decca threw all five of them out of the building.

The **Chipmunks** came to prime-time television in 1961 on "The Alvin Show." They had first been heard in 1958, on a record created by Ross Bagdasarian. "I wanted to try for a Christmas novelty, so I recorded these little half-speed voices, like I'd done on 'The Witch Doctor.' I decided that I should, as David Seville, have a conversation with them, and perhaps even an argument. The idea for names came quickly—Simon, after Si Waronker of Liberty Records; Theodore, for my engineer, Ted Keep; and Alvin, after another label executive, Al Bennett." "The Chipmunk Song" went on to win three Grammies, inspire five hit sequels, and sell more than twelve million copies (it's revived every year). In 1979, the fuzzy three returned on a platinum album—*Chipmunk Punk.*

Connie Francis, the most successful female solo singer of the sixties, starred and performed the title song in her first motion picture, *Where the Boys Are.* (It was her twenty-first hit out of more than fifty chart entries.) Ray Charles appeared in *Swinging Along,* Pat Boone in *All Hands on Deck,* and Bobby Darin in *Come September.* It was a good year for twist movies: *Hey Let's Twist,* with Joey Dee; and *Twist Around the Clock,* with Chubby Checker, Dion, and the Marcels. Chubby and Dion also turned up in *Teenage Millionaire* with Jimmy Clanton and Jackie Wilson. Elvis went *Wild in the Country* and visited *Blue Hawaii.*

Sam Cooke was the son of a Chicago minister, and started singing with gospel groups in the early fifties. At the age of twenty-one, Sam went against his father's wishes and secretly began recording pop songs. One of the first was "You Send Me," a million-seller in the winter of 1957. After that came "Chain Gang" (1960), "Cupid" (1961), "Bring It on Home to Me" (1962), "Another Saturday Night" (1963), "Good Times" (1964), "Shake" (1965), and others. Sam Cooke wrote nearly all of his own hits, and many have become hits again for artists like Cat Stevens, Johnny Nash, Herman's Hermits, Doctor Hook, and the Animals. He died in 1965, the victim of a motel shooting in Los Angeles.

The Motown Record Corporation got off the ground in the early sixties, thanks in large part to a Detroit group known as the **Miracles.** The quintet auditioned before a fledgling songwriter/producer named Berry Gordy, Jr., who was then in the process of forming his own label. Gordy was impressed with the Miracles' material—most of it written by their leader, Smokey Robinson—and took them under his wing. Late in 1960 they released a Robinson original, "Shop Around," which became a number-one single early in 1961. It was the first million-seller for Motown, and the first of many gold records for one of the best-loved and most-imitated groups of the decade.

Although we were already more than a year into the new decade, fans of fifties R&B were not ready to give up the fight for their kind of music. Once again, doo-woppy records were all over the place, from "My True Story" by the Jive Five to "Angel Baby" by Rosie and the Originals. Barry Mann asked, "Who Put the Bomp (in the Bomp-Bomp-Bomp)," while Shep and the Limelites crooned, "Daddy's Home." Even a couple of fifties flops—the Edsels' "Rama Lama Ding Dong," and "There's a Moon Out Tonight" by the Capris—got reissued in 1961 and finally became hits. "In the Still of the Night" by the Five Satins returned to the charts for a *third* time. The whole nostalgic craze was encapsulated by Little Caesar and the Romans, in **"Those Oldies But Goodies (Remind Me of You)."**

THE TOP 40

1. Tossin' 'n' Turnin', *Bobby Lewis*
2. Michael, *Highwaymen*
3. Calcutta, *Lawrence Welk*
4. Runaway, *Del Shannon*
5. Exodus, *Ferrante and Teicher*
6. Pony Time, *Chubby Checker*
7. Will You Love Me Tomorrow?, *Shirelles*
8. Raindrops, *Dee Clark*
9. Travelin' Man, *Ricky Nelson*
10. Cryin', *Roy Orbison*
11. Wooden Heart, *Joe Dowell*
12. Running Scared, *Roy Orbison*
13. Take Good Care of Her, *Adam Wade*
14. Mother-in-Law, *Ernie K-Doe*
15. Boll Weevil, *Brook Benton*
16. Last Night, *Mar-Keys*
17. One Hundred Pounds of Clay, *Gene McDaniels*
18. I Fall to Pieces, *Patsy Cline*
19. Wonderland by Night, *Bert Kaempfert*
20. Are You Lonesome Tonight?, *Elvis Presley*
21. Where the Boys Are, *Connie Francis*
22. My True Story, *Jive Five*
23. Shop Around, *Miracles*
24. Wheels, *Stringalongs*
25. Quarter to Three, *Gary U.S. Bonds*
26. Blue Moon, *Marcels*
27. Last Date, *Floyd Cramer*
28. Dedicated to the One I Love, *Shirelles*
29. North to Alaska, *Johnny Horton*
30. He Will Break Your Heart, *Jerry Butler*
31. Don't Worry, *Marty Robbins*
32. Hit the Road Jack, *Ray Charles*
33. The Mountain's High, *Dick and Dee Dee*
34. Sad Movies, *Sue Thompson*
35. A Thousand Stars, *Kathy Young and the Innocents*
36. Bristol Stomp, *Dovells*
37. Apache, *Jorgen Ingmann*
38. Wheels, *Billy Vaughn*
39. Daddy's Home, *Shep and the Limelites*
40. On the Rebound, *Floyd Cramer*

THE TOP 10 LPs

1. Camelot, *Original Cast*
2. Exodus, *Original Soundtrack*
3. Great Motion Picture Themes, *Various Artists*
4. The Sound of Music, *Original Cast*
5. Calcutta, *Lawrence Welk*
6. G.I. Blues, *Original Soundtrack*
7. Never on Sunday, *Original Soundtrack*
8. Knockers Up, *Rusty Warren*
9. Sing Along with Mitch, *Mitch Miller*
10. At Carnegie Hall, *Harry Belafonte*

10

Cryin'
ROY ORBISON

Roy Orbison's career started in Wink, Texas, heart of the oil country, where he was born on April 23, 1936. His mother, Nadine, was a nurse; his father, "Orbie," a roughneck foreman in the oil fields. At age six, Roy began taking lessons on his father's guitar and by his early teens was writing songs and playing in local talent shows. With his first group, the Wink Westerners, he even had his own radio show, broadcast over KVWC in Vernon.

After summers working the oil rigs, Roy entered North Texas State College as a geology major. There he met Pat Boone, whose early rock 'n' roll success—as well as Elvis Presley's—inspired Roy to try entering the recording field himself.

"In 1956," Roy recalled, "I went back to West Texas, played and sang all summer with a group, and then got a couple of television shows on different local stations. Then I went to Norman Petty's studio in Clovis, New Mexico, and started recording."

In 1956, his first single, "Ooby Dooby," climbed to fifty-ninth place on the pop music charts, eventually selling more than 300,000 copies. Besides the first of many nicknames, "Oobie," the record earned Roy a contract with the legendary Sun label of Memphis. Two years later, his song "Claudette," written about his wife, was picked up by the Everly Brothers as the B side of "All I Have to Do Is Dream." When "Claudette" also became a hit, climbing into the top thirty, Wesley Rose signed Roy to Acuff-Rose, one of Nashville's top music publishers, and became his personal manager.

In 1960, Roy Orbison exploded with "Only the Lonely," his third release on the Monument label. It sold over two million copies and paved the way for "Blue Angel" (1960), "I'm Hurtin' " (1961), and Roy's first number-one record, "Running Scared" (1961).

Then, in the fall of 1961, Roy partic-ipated in the most fruitful recording session of his career.

"We recorded 'Cryin',' 'Blue Bayou,' 'Candy Man,' and 'Mean Woman Blues' all in the same evening," Roy said. "That's four hit sides in one session. After doing 'Cryin' ' and 'Blue Bayou,' we let the strings go home, and jammed on 'Candy Man' and 'Mean Woman Blues.'

"The song 'Cryin' ' was based on a true experience. It may not be completely apparent from the lyric, but I was dating this girl, and we broke up, and then I saw her again as I went to get a haircut. She waved, and I didn't; I just got in the car and then left and went on down the street, and then I felt real bad about it. I decided to put my feelings into the words of a song.

"One thing that was an undercurrent, I believe, in everything we did was the blues. It's a southern thing, you know, to sing about sorrow—to get it off your mind."

"Cryin'," backed with "Candy Man," was released in early August 1961. "Candy Man" appeared on the charts first, followed by "Cryin' " one week later. Both sides became big hits, but it was "Cryin' " that soared to the top—and remained a hot seller for more than three months.

Roy Orbison specialized in emotional, powerful songs that personified rock 'n' roll melodrama at its best. Among his admirers was another legendary performer, Elvis Presley.

"All I know for sure is we were very close friends," said Roy, "as close as you can be in this business. We both started out with the same company, the same manager, the same booking agent, the same everything. The first girl I ever dated on the road, my first tour, had dated Elvis the last time he was through.

"I know one of Elvis' all-time favorite records through the years was 'Cryin'.' I heard he sent someone ninety miles to get a copy when it first came out. He had a few of my records, I know, on his jukebox, and the last time I saw him he introduced me as 'one of the greatest singers in the world.' "

Travelin' Man

Ricky Nelson

It was the dawn of the big band era—1935—when maestro Oswald "Ozzie" Nelson married his comely girl singer, Peggy Lou Snyder (better known as Harriet Hilliard). They produced a couple of kids, David and Ricky, and in 1944, launched a radio series based on their family life. "The Adventures of Ozzie and Harriet" caught on, and in 1949, their real sons joined the cast.

In 1952, the family was heard, and seen, in a feature film: *Here Come the Nelsons.* It did well enough at the box office to inspire a television series—one which was to run an incredible fourteen years.

On one real-life night in 1957, sixteen-year-old Ricky was driving a date home after a less than spectacular evening. Suddenly, an Elvis song came over the radio, and the girl began to swoon. Hoping to save a little face, Ricky calmly said, "Well, you know I'm going to be making a record soon, too." The girl laughed in his face, giving Ricky all the motivation he needed.

With the help of his friends, the Four Preps, Ricky made his singing debut at a Hollywood High concert. Ozzie, meanwhile, worked up an episode in which his young son could showcase his new single. It aired on April 10, 1957, and three weeks later, "I'm Walkin' " was on the charts. It eventually went top ten, selling over a million copies on the Verve label.

The industry was impressed, especially Lou Chudd of Imperial Records. He said so to Ozzie the next time he saw him, adding, "I wish I had that kid under contract." Ozzie explained that Ricky *had never actually signed* with Verve. Amazed, Lou moved fast,

whipping up a record deal within hours.

Ricky's career on Imperial was nothing short of phenomenal—thirty-six charted songs in just over five years. Fifteen of them went top ten, including "Be Bop Baby" (1957), "Believe What You Say" (1958), "Poor Little Fool" (1958), "Lonesome Town" (1958), "It's Late" (1959), "Young World" (1962), "Teenage Idol" (1962), and "It's All Up to You" (1963). Usually both sides of his singles were hits, as in 1961, when Ricky recorded "Hello Mary Lou" and "Travelin' Man."

"I used to have to wait for my wife to get off from work," said composer Jerry Fuller, "and since there was this little park close by, I'd go there, sit with my guitar, and write songs.

"I'd been thinking about this idea of a guy traveling everywhere, so one

day I brought along a world atlas and started picking out all these different places and things. Then I tried to remember what they called girls in each of those countries. Had I been a little more learned at the time, I would have said 'wahini' instead of 'pretty Polynesian baby.' If you listen very carefully to the lyrics, they're somewhat immature, with very simple words. I think the whole thing took me about twenty minutes to complete. Then I made a demo of it, with Glen Campbell and Dave Burgess of the Champs behind me.

"I actually wrote the song for Sam Cooke—I was a big Sam Cooke fan. I took it up to his manager, J. W. Alexander, whose office was right next door to Lou Chudd's at Imperial. I had to leave the tape off.

"I didn't know Joe Osbourne then, but he was Ricky's bass player; he was at Imperial and heard J.W. play the demo. Joe went next door and said, 'Hey, can I hear that song again?' J.W., who had already dropped the tape in the garbage, pulled it out and said, 'Here, you can have it.' Joe played the song for Ricky, Ricky liked it, and so they cut it."

At the same session, Ricky also recorded "Hello Mary Lou." Issued back-to-back on the same single, both songs became top-ten hits for Ricky, and in June 1961, "Travelin' Man" reached the very top.

"The first time I heard that song broadcast was on 'Ozzie and Harriet,'" said Jerry, "and that was a big thrill for me. They played it at the end of the show, and it was the first time anything of mine had ever been played on TV. What a boost! And that was the biggest single he ever had."

Raindrops
DEE CLARK

Delecta "Dee" Clark was born in Blythsville, Arkansas, but grew up on the west side of Chicago. At thirteen, he formed a group called the Hambone Kids, and recorded a song called "Hambone" for the Okeh label. A kind of Bo Diddley beat rhythm record, it became a small regional hit in the Midwest. Later, Dee sang gospel with the Thompson Community Singers, and a high school quintet, the Goldentones.

Dee took to hanging around the studios of KGES radio, the home of disc jockey Herb Kent, who called himself the "Kool Gent" on the air. Kent got the Goldentones a contract with Vee Jay Records, and they thanked him by changing their name to the Kool Gents.

Dee wound up writing most of the Kool Gents pop material, all of which flopped in the mid-fifties. In 1957, he left the group and began his own solo career. At first, he tried imitating two major soul stars of the day—Clyde McPhatter and Little Richard—but didn't have any real success until he started to sound like himself. In 1958, he wrote what became his first hit, "Nobody But You."

After that came "Just Keep It Up" and "Hey Little Girl," both top-twenty singles in the summer of 1959. "How About That" made the national top forty in 1960, followed by "Your Friends" in the spring of 1961. Then it was time for Dee to release his biggest record of all time.

"Raindrops" was conceived on the road, during a driving rain. Dee was on the turnpike, coming back to Chicago from New York. At the wheel was his guitar player and friend, Phil Upchurch. As the thunderstorm continued, Dee concentrated on the windshield wipers and became swept up in their rhythm. "Oh rain, oh rain," he began to think, and the idea for a song started to germinate. He fumbled around in the glove compartment for his writing tablet and slowly began to sketch a rough idea for his tune. By the time they got to Chicago, Dee was sure he had something big. And, of course, he did.

Phil helped him finish the song, and soon after, it was recorded. A cloudburst effect was put at the beginning, and that, plus Dee's plaintive wail, helped put the tune over. "Raindrops" entered the pop charts in mid-May 1961, and by July had become one of the best-selling singles of the year. It stayed a top seller for nearly four months.

Dee continued to record for more than a decade—on Vee Jay, Constellation, Columbia, Wand, Liberty, United Artists, Rocky and Chelsea. At one point, he even put out a record called "Raindrops '73." However, he was never able to fully recapture the magic of his original hit. He entered the nightclub circuit, and played frequently around L.A., Atlanta, and Orlando, Florida. In 1978, he returned to Chicago, his base of operations.

Will You Love Me Tomorrow

THE SHIRELLES

Addie Harris, Beverly Lee, Doris Kenner, and Shirley Owens started singing together in junior high school, in Passaic, New Jersey. Then they called themselves the Poquellos, which is Spanish for "birds." Within a short time, they had their own band, and were appearing frequently at parties and school events.

A classmate, Mary Jane Greenberg, was impressed with their sound. She convinced her mother, Florence, that something had to be done to promote the girls' career. Mrs. Greenberg agreed, and formed her own production company, Tiara Records. Soon after, Tiara became Scepter Records, with the young quartet as its first act.

Florence didn't care much for the name "Poquellos," and suggested something else, like the "Honeytones." The girls thought that was much too corny. Instead, they chose "The Shirelles," because "it had a nice ring to it"—not as a play on their lead singer's name.

Their first major hit, "Will You Love Me Tomorrow," was also the first real success for the song's composers, Gerry Goffin and Carole King.

"Carole was just seventeen at the time," recalled Shirley. "She brought us the song, played it as a demo, and frankly, we couldn't stand it. It sounded like a hillbilly song to us—real country and western—certainly out of our league. We were still in high school and were afraid of what our friends might say if we sang anything that corny.

"Well, a few changes were made, and at the session it came out great, just completely different. Carole wound up playing kettle drums, because she couldn't get the drummer to give her what she wanted. She did a fantastic job. We still thank her for the song."

"Will You Love Me Tomorrow" broke in late November 1960. It climbed the charts steadily, reaching number one in February 1961. Few songs in release that year could match it for honesty and explicitness.

The Shirelles went on to place nearly two dozen other songs on the hit parade. Among them: "Dedicated to the One I Love" and "Mama Said" (1961), "Baby It's You" and "Soldier Boy" (1962), and "Everybody Loves a Lover" and "Foolish Little Girl" (1963). They were the most important female pop group of the early sixties—until 1964, when superseded by the Supremes.

And even today, if you ring Carole King's doorbell you'll hear those familiar chimes—"Will You Love Me Tomorrow."

Pony Time
CHUBBY CHECKER

Dateline: New York, 1961. The State Safety Council announces that of fifty-four cases of back trouble reported in a single week, forty-nine were due to "too much twisting." The dance craze has turned into a windfall for chiropractors, who are making money hand over fist from patients who develop what they have named the "twister back."

"The dance is actually a good way to build up muscle tone in the back," reports a spokesman. "Many twisters have lost inches around the waist." Osteopaths say that if people get more exercise, they'll be in better condition to do such a strenuous dance."

The Twist, of course, was *the* dance phenomenon of the early sixties. It had many variations, including the Bowler's Twist, the Oliver Twist, the Percolator Twist, the Peppermint Twist, the Pulley, the Organ Grinder's Twist, the Sharpie, the Jockey's Twist, the Seventh Inning Stretch, the Wind-up, the Lasso, and the Fly. At the same time, other dances were also gaining fleeting fame: the Hully Gully, the Madison, the Popeye, the Mashed Potato, the Jerk, the Dog, the Monkey, the Frug, the Waddle, the Block, the Bugaloo, the Philly Skate, the Locomotion, the Sanctification, the Beulah Wig, the Hucklebuck, the Alligator, and the Funky Broadway, to name a few.

Many of these movements were invented and/or popularized by the most important disco artist of all time—a young Philadelphian who used the name of Chubby Checker. Although best remembered for the Twist, Chubby also kicked off more than his share of other dance crazes. The most popular of these was one he launched in 1961—the Pony.

The song itself was hardly new—in fact, it was a rewrite of "Boogie Woogie," a tune written and first recorded by Clarence "Pinetop" Smith in 1928. Clarence, who was called "Pinetop" because of his conical head,

invented the term "boogie woogie" and was one of the pioneers in that style.

The adaptation known as "Pony Time" was written in 1960 by Don Covay and John Berry, who had previously worked together in a Washington doo-wop group, the Rainbows. When that outfit broke up, the two continued writing as a team, with Don still hoping to break in as a recording artist. Don cut the original version of "Pony Time" with the Goodtimers, an obscure act, on the tiny Arnold label. When the song began to take off locally, it was brought to the attention of Chubby, who covered it right away.

Both records entered the national charts at the same time, the last week in January 1961. The Goodtimers got to number sixty and faded in nine weeks. Chubby, though, went all the way to number one, and stayed there much of March. In all, his version spent sixteen weeks on the best-seller list.

Chubby continued in his role as the King of Dance Rock for several more

years, placing more than thirty dance and folk hits on the charts. "Dance the Mess Around," "The Fly," "The Twist," and "Let's Twist Again" were all big in 1961, with the latter tune winning a Grammy for Best Rock 'n' Roll Performance. In 1962, the beat went on with "Slow Twistin'," "Dancin' Party," "Popeye the Hitchhiker" and "Limbo Rock." "Let's Limbo Some More" came along in 1963, along with "20 Miles," "Birdland," and "Twist It Up."

After that, Chubby got into calypso-folk music, with "Loddy Lo," "Hooka Tooka," "Hey Bobba Needle" and "Lazy Elsie Molly." His last top-forty hit was "Do the Freddie" in 1965.

Chubby is married to a former Miss World, and continues to tour extensively. "My philosophy," he says, "is to sing as many happy songs as possible and to make people feel good."

And Don Covay? Well, he finally made the top thirty as a vocalist in 1973, with "I Was Checkin' Out, She Was Checkin' In."

Exodus
FERRANTE AND TEICHER

Even in their heyday, Ferrante and Teicher were something of a musical mystery. Hardly anybody could recall their first names, and few could tell them apart in photographs. Their black-rimmed spectacles, patent leather shoes, electric red jackets and matching pompadour toupees became as famous as their nickname, "The Movie Theme Team." They were the most popular piano duo ever, cutting over sixty LPs during the sixties, and selling more than twenty million records. To some, their music was "middlebrow muzak"; but to their label, they were the most consistent of all stars on the UA roster.

Arthur Ferrante and Louis Teicher were child prodigies who started picking out tunes on the piano when they were about two years old. The Ferrantes of New York City and the Teichers of Wilkes-Barre, Pennsylvania, decided to enroll their sons at Manhattan's Juilliard School of Music. The two boys worked together with the same teachers, studying theory, composition, orchestration, and conducting. Another part of the curriculum required playing ensemble music with another pianist, and the pair, matched so well in age and talent, began to play duets at one piano. A friendship grew, and while still teens, Arthur and Louis agreed to form a professional twin-piano act. After graduation they looked for work, but found little call for their particular kind of musical specialty.

Ferrante and Teicher then returned to Juilliard where they taught for three years and further developed their skills. They experimented with gadgetry, extending the range of their instruments with strips of sandpaper, cardboard wedges, and other devices. They reached into their instruments, plucking, strumming, and pounding on the strings. By 1947 they felt ready to go for broke, and bought an old delivery truck to cart their belongings. Over the next twelve years, they

toured America, playing in ballparks, gyms, cafeterias and boxing rings. Three vehicles and twelve engines later, their reputation was strong enough to warrant a major label contract with United Artists Records.

In July 1960, the duo hit with their first million-seller, "Theme from *The Apartment*," on which they were backed by a full symphony orchestra. Many so-called experts predicted failure for the record, but 750,000 copies were sold in the first three weeks. After that, Ferrante and Teicher changed their concerts from nearly all classical to nearly all popular numbers. They also began covering every movie theme they could get their hands on.

In November 1960, the team released "Exodus," the title tune from a sprawling history of Palestinian liberation. Otto Preminger, who directed the motion picture version, turned it into a real marathon, running nearly three-and-a-quarter hours. The stars were Paul Newman and Eva Marie Saint, along with Ralph Richardson, Peter Lawford, Lee J. Cobb and Sal Mineo.

Ferrante and Teicher equaled the grandeur of the movie, and in doing

so, typified their own twin-piano attack. While one man picked out the melody, the other was free to tack on frills—end-to-end keyboard ripples, tinsely effects and cascading strings. The result was a single that outsparkled competing 45s by Mantovani, Eddie Harris, and others. By January 1961, Ferrante and Teicher had clearly cut the most popular rendition, and within weeks it was certified as a million-seller. Later, composer Ernest Gold picked up both an Oscar and a Grammy award for writing what turned out to be the Song of the Year.

Ferrante and Teicher recorded prolifically for decades, cutting more than 150 albums over the next twenty years. In 1961, their version of "Tonight" from *West Side Story* became a third top-ten single. In 1969, their fourth gold 45 was the title theme from *Midnight Cowboy*.

They are still a popular concert attraction, and still practice from four to six hours a day, seven days a week, at home, on the road, or wherever they happen to be. As Louis explained, "Having talent is one thing, but you have to work at it constantly to keep your gift sharp."

Runaway

DEL SHANNON

Charles Westover was born in Coopersville, Michigan, where he bought his first guitar at age fifteen. He didn't know how to play the instrument, and no one cared to teach him, so he had to invent his own kind of "music lessons." Every Saturday night, he would sneak into roadside dance halls and stand quietly near the stage, watching the pickers' hands, studying their technique. Eventually, he absorbed not only a style but much of their rebel spirit and a strong liking for country and western music.

Charles made the football team in high school and often performed with his guitar at assemblies just before the game. He didn't actually like to play football; his idea of a good time was to stay in the shower room, experimenting with echo and practicing his falsetto. His father became quite upset at this, preferring that Charles participate out on the field. More than once, the elder Westover kicked his son out of the house along with "that blasted guitar."

After high school, Charles was drafted and spent some time as a GI in Germany. Upon his return, he began to accept club dates and became friends with WHRV deejay Ollie McLaughlin. In 1960, Ollie recorded one of those club dates and sent the tape to Embee Productions in Detroit. It was accepted, and Charles was flown to New York for a session with Big Top Records. Nothing came of it, though, and Charles returned home disappointed.

Back in Michigan, Charles got a part-time job selling carpets. He realized that changes had to be made in his life, and he decided to start with his name. His boss at the carpet store had just bought a Cadillac, and Charles knew that someday he'd have to get one of those. And a local prizefighter was about to turn pro under the name of Mark Shannon. By combining the middle syllable of "Cadillac" with

"Shannon," he came up with his new name.

A few weeks later, at the Hi-Lo Club in Battle Creek, Del Shannon was performing with Max Crook, a keyboard player who specialized on the "musitron," a kind of electronic organ. Max was playing an improvisational solo when suddenly he hit upon an unusual chord change, using minors—A minor and G. It was so catchy that Del immediately shouted out, "Hit those chords again!"

Over the next fifteen minutes, pop history was made by Del, Max, and the band. Del had already written some lyrics, but the music for his new song hadn't quite jelled yet. Then, in a twinkling, it all came together and "Runaway" was born.

Another session was quickly lined up. At the studio, they were given only ninety minutes to cut "Runaway," a B side, and several other tunes.

"Runaway" was released in late February 1961 and steadily climbed the charts all through March. By late April, it was the number-one record in the country, and went on to sell more than four million copies.

Later in 1961, Del Shannon had two

more big hits: "Hats Off to Larry" and "So Long Baby." In 1962, there was "Hey Little Girl" and in 1963, "Little Town Flirt." In 1964, he changed labels to Amy and cut "Handy Man" and "Keep Searchin'." His last big record was "Stranger in Town," in 1965. He wrote every one of his million-selling hits.

In the late sixties, Del found new fame in other ways: as a composer ("I Go to Pieces" for Peter and Gordon), arranger ("Baby It's You" by Smith), and producer ("Gypsy Woman" by Brian Hyland). In the seventies, he bought up all his old masters and the publishing rights to his songs. He also worked extensively with Jeff Lynne and with the Electric Light Orchestra. In 1980, Tom Petty produced some new Del Shannon records, using the Heartbreakers as his backup band.

Del Shannon now lives in Southern California and sometimes drives by a big retail carpet store. "Whenever I do that," he said, "I always think of 'Runaway' and how that one little record saved me from having to work in those places. That's got to be a fate worse than death."

Calcutta
LAWRENCE WELK

The son of an immigrant black-smith, Lawrence Welk was born in a sod farmhouse in Strasburg, North Dakota, a mostly German-speaking community. His schooling ended with fourth grade, and the young boy worked every day in the wheat fields. At night, the Welks entertained themselves by forming a family band. Lawrence performed on the accordion—an instrument he had been taught to play by his father.

Lawrence also appeared at weddings, barn dances, and church socials. He drifted in and out of several bands, usually getting fired after a short time for playing too loudly or off-key. Eventually he realized that he had his own musical ideas, and if he wanted anyone to follow his lead, he'd just have to organize his own ensemble.

That happened in 1927, when he put together Lawrence Welk's Hotsy Totsy Boys. They gained fame as local radio stars, broadcasting over WNAX in Yankton, South Dakota.

In 1938, while playing at Pittsburgh's William Penn Hotel, Welk read a fan letter that described his band as "sparkly and bubbly, like champagne." He decided to call his style "champagne music," and perfected a way of popping his cheek to sound like an exploding cork. Those trademarks, along with his famous backdrop—a cascade of bubbles—would remain mainstays of his stage act.

In 1944, Lawrence made his top-ten debut with "Don't Sweetheart Me" on Decca. It was the first of nineteen songs he'd put on the charts over the next twenty-one years. His next big hit, "Oh Happy Day," was in 1953. By then, Welk was already established as an L.A. TV star, with a weekly program on KTLA. Originally booked to run four weeks, it lasted four years—until picked up by the ABC network in 1955.

By 1956 Lawrence was selling a million assorted records a year for Coral. However, the gold didn't really start to flow until he changed labels. The first inkling of what was to come was "Last Date," a hit in December 1960. And then came "Calcutta."

"We were on Dot Records by then," recalled George Cates, Welk's musical director. "Randy Wood was the owner of the company and a good friend. He brought us the song, a version recorded in Germany by the Werner Muller Orchestra. We listened to the record because it had begun to make some noise in Europe."

"I liked it very much right from the start," Lawrence said. "I consider 'Calcutta' to be champagne music. Anything that has a sparkling feel, an effervescent feel, is music I call champagne music. It's supposed to give you a lift."

"We figured we couldn't compete with Werner's big string sound, so we decided to try the song another way," continued George. "Now Lawrence has always been flipped about harpsichords, and we had bought a great big one. I had just come back from Brazil, and thought because of Percy Faith's success with 'Delicato' we could give the song a South American feel, with maracas and the harpsichord. We decided to do it that way, with voices and a Latin rhythm section.

"What was hard in the studio was that all the rhythm leaked in every time the harpsichord was opened to get a sound. Finally, we put a microphone *inside* the harpsichord and wrapped the whole thing in a 'moth-ball' so that no sound could get in. Frank Scott, who played the harpsichord, had to have an earphone coming back from the booth so he could hear what he was playing. Out in the studio, the rest of the band couldn't hear the harpsichord at all; there was so much leakage. But it was an exciting sound, and by the time we got one take of it, we knew we didn't have to do another."

The original A side of the 45 was "My Grandfather's Clock." "That's what they were playing in Texas when the single first came out. Then, they turned it over and 'Calcutta' broke open all over. Maybe it was the unusual sound of the record. The harpsichord itself came off not unlike a baroque instrument."

"Calcutta" had been written in 1958 by German composer Heino Gaze as "Tivoli Melody." As "Calcutta" by Lawrence Welk it took off in mid-December 1960. It reached number one in February, spending seventeen weeks on the charts. Remarkably, it was also top ten R&B.

Michael
THE HIGHWAYMEN

The Highwaymen got together as college classmates at Wesleyan University in Middletown, Connecticut. They were all honor students and members of a local fraternity called EQV. As freshmen, the boys assembled their act for a campus party, and had such a good time singing together that they decided to form a more permanent association.

Dave Fisher, their organizer and lead tenor, took on the banjo, recorder, bongos, and arrangements for the group. Bob Burnett, Wesleyan's pole vault champion, also sang tenor, played bongos, and brought along his maracas. Steve Trott, president of the fraternity, became their third tenor, and also played guitar, which he had learned from a Mexican garbageman.

The fourth member, Steve Butts, was on crutches, as a result of childhood polio. A bass, he also served as sportscaster for the campus radio station. Rounding out the ensemble was Chan Daniels, a baritone. His specialty was the charango, a South American instrument made from an armadillo shell.

Collectively, they made up a kind of "Kingston Quintet," differing from other folk acts of the time by their use of both American and foreign material. They sang each song straight in its original language, recalling the ancestry of various members in Mexico, Brazil, Australia, and Europe.

The fellows polished their act in the frat house basement, performing unofficially before preoccupied pool shooters. After a number of successful local dates, one boy's father suggested that they contact talent agents in New York. In November 1960, they took that advice, and met Ken Greengrass, who became their manager. He arranged an audition with United Artists Records, and soon after the Highwaymen were on the road to fame.

Among the tunes chosen for their

first album was "Michael," a century-old traditional folk song. It had originated in the pre-war South, among slaves who commuted daily between the mainland and their quarters on offshore islands. The Highwaymen released their rendition in January 1961, and had to wait more than six months for the tune to take off. Finally, Dick Smith at WORC in Worcester broke the record in mid-July. By September it was the number-one record in the country, with sales eventually topping three million.

The Highwaymen appeared on the TV shows of Ed Sullivan and Johnny Carson, and had offers to perform for as much as $2,500 a night. However, they turned down most tours and personal appearances, preferring to concentrate on their studies. Their singing, in Chan Daniels' words, was just "a hobby in overdrive." They did manage to earn over $100,000 in 1961, and the next year, have a second top-twenty hit with "Cottonfields."

Bob and Steve graduated in 1962 and "left show business for good."

The Highwaymen became a quartet, with the addition of former Cumberland Three member Gil Robbins. In 1963, Bob returned, and stayed with the group until they finally broke up in 1964. The name "Highwaymen" was then sold to ABC Records, which applied it to a totally unrelated and unsuccessful folk-rock band.

Dave Fisher became a songwriter, Gil Robbins an actor, and Steve Butts a college administrator. Bob Burnett became a lawyer and Steve Trott became L.A.'s Chief Deputy District Attorney. Chan Daniels found work as a record company executive, and died of pneumonia in August 1975.

The Highwaymen regrouped in the late seventies for one final single. On one side was a re-make of their classic "Michael"; on the other side, though, was an original tune, which, sadly, did not become a hit. It was a tongue-in-cheek recap of what had happened to the "Highwaymen" in the ensuing years, "It's a Long Way Down from Number One."

Tossin' and Turnin'

BOBBY LEWIS

Bobby Lewis spent most of his early life in an orphanage in Indianapolis, Indiana. When he was five years old, the directors of the orphanage sponsored him for some piano lessons. He showed such a remarkable flair for music that, after that, he was often chosen for singing roles in grade school productions. He joined the glee club and sang with it in a series of radio concerts.

At the age of twelve, Bobby was adopted and taken to Detroit, where he began a long string of unusual odd jobs. One of the first was delivering ice in twenty-five- or fifty-pound chunks. He also mopped floors, sold shoes, and drove a coal delivery truck, until he overturned it one day. He worked at a neighborhood hotel as porter, bellhop, and desk clerk. After four weeks of lugging bags, dodging complaints, and tangling wires on the switchboard, Bobby quit in disgust. There had to be an easier way to earn a dollar. The year was 1948, and he was all of sixteen years old.

Bobby headed downtown and came across a theater advertising "The Bimbo Show." He went inside and watched the display of mild talent. He joined the troupe as a singer and stayed, without pay, for six months. After that, only show biz work would do. In rapid succession, he became a nightclub entertainer, a magician's helper, and a sand dancer. He joined a circus, and, when not carrying water, cleaning equipment, or setting up

rides, he provided musical accompaniment for the various acts. At the time, he was just learning guitar, and his picking left something to be desired. Ticket sales began to drop off, and when the finger of suspicion was pointed at him, Bobby strode behind the main tent and smashed his guitar over a rock.

Bobby returned to Indianapolis and began accepting small gigs in local nightclubs. In one, he met guitarist Wes Montgomery and his brother Monk, who was a bass player. They formed a combo, along with ballad singer Lucy Johnson. It was at this point that Bobby really came into his own as an interpreter of boogie blues.

In 1956, Bobby signed with Spotlight Records and recorded "Mumbles Blues." It was not a national hit but earned him a regular spot on the daytime TV show of Ed MacKenzie, then the number-one deejay in Detroit. He also turned up on the Soupy Sales show and appeared live with Soupy at the Coliseum.

In 1958, Bobby tried recording again, this time with a song called "Oh Mr. Somebody." It was a flop, but attracted the attention of Jackie Wilson, who invited Bobby to come to New York and sing. For the next two years, Bobby made the East Coast circuit—the Howard Theater in Washington, the Royal in Baltimore, and the Apollo in New York City. Bobby

became the master of ceremonies in these places, sharing the bill with Brook Benton, James Brown, Hank Ballard, Jackie Wilson, and Little Willie John.

Success still eluded him, however, so he returned to New York City. One day, while walking through Tin Pan Alley, he happened to stop in at the offices of a tiny new record label, Beltone. On impulse, he asked for an audition, and the company was more than happy to give him one. They handed him "Tossin' and Turnin'," which had been co-written by staff songwriter Joe Rene and Ritchie Adams, the former lead singer of the Fireflies. Bobby handled it so well that a date was immediately set for a recording session. Bobby never thought it would become a hit record—"not in my wildest dreams"—but it certainly was, for twenty-three weeks in 1961.

Later that same year, Bobby had another top-ten single, "One Track Mind." He continued to record for several more years but never managed to come up with the same magic again. In 1962, one of his attempts was "I'm Tossin' and Turnin' Again."

Today, Bobby lives in New York and continues to perform, both as a singer and as an actor. He's also a producer, reuniting old acts and introducing new ones. He still regards "Tossin' and Turnin' " as "a great experience, and the numero uno event of my life."

1962

IN 1962, the Alan Price Combo became the Animals; the Righteous Brothers, Standells, McCoys, and Rolling Stones each formed their respective groups. Robert Allen Zimmerman changed his name to Bob Dylan and wrote "Blowin' in the Wind." Pat Boone scored his last top-ten hit, "Speedy Gonzales," and Foster Sylvers was born. New names on the pop charts included Marvin Gaye ("Stubborn Kind of Fellow"), Dionne Warwick ("Don't Make Me Over"), and Carole King ("It Might As Well Rain Until September"). TV stars had hits: Walter Brennan ("Old Rivers"), Richard Chamberlain ("Theme from *Dr. Kildare*"), and Johnny Crawford ("Your Nose Is Gonna Grow"). A&M began with "The Lonely Bull" . . . "Telstar" took off . . . Chuck Berry landed in jail . . . and the Everlys wound up in the army. It was 1962—the year the Beatles added Ringo Starr and cut "Love Me Do."

Mitch Miller, a one-time oboe player with various symphony orchestras, found his greatest fame in the fifties and early sixties as an arranger, conductor, producer, label executive, and video host. In 1950, he became the Director of A&R for Columbia Records, responsible for the sound and style of countless performers (from Tony Bennett to Barbra Streisand). He also recorded, under his own name, eleven gold "singalong" albums, as well as "The Yellow Rose of Texas" (1955), one of the best-selling singles in history. By 1962, Miller had brought his LP concept to television, in an hour-long variety series. Home viewers were invited to "follow the bouncing ball" and "Sing Along with Mitch," as the lyrics to songs were superimposed on the screen. Rock was never featured, as Mitch was a long-time foe of that kind of music. In fact, he kept the Columbia roster nearly rock-free until 1965, when he was replaced by Clive Davis.

U.S. record sales jumped seven percent in 1962, thanks in no small way to the incredible popularity of the Twist and dance rock in general. If you faced a jukebox that year, hot little quarters in hand, you would most likely have had to choose from the following: "The Twist," "The Peppermint Twist," "Slow Twistin'," "Dear Lady Twist," "Twistin' the Night Away," "Twist Twist Senora," "The Percolator Twist," "Twist and Shout," "The Soul Twist," "Hey Let's Twist," "Twistin' Matilda," "Twist-Her," "Bristol Twistin' Annie," "Twistin' Postman," "The Alvin Twist," "Twistin' with Linda," "The Patricia Twist," "Twistin' U.S.A.," "The La Paloma Twist," "The Oliver Twist," "Twistin' White Silver Sands," "The Basie Twist," "The Guitar Boogie Shuffle Twist," "Twistin' All Night Long," "Everybody's Twistin'," and "Do You Know How to Twist." If you didn't, there were always "The Locomotion," "The Monster Mash," "Mashed Potato Time," "Gravy (On My Mashed Potatoes)," "The Wah Watusi," "Limbo Rock," "Let's Dance," "Dancin' Party," "Havin' a Party," "Party Lights," "The Cha Cha Cha," "Popeye (The Hitchhiker)," and "Hully Gully Baby." Or, you might have punched a Bobby Rydell favorite: "I'll Never Dance Again."

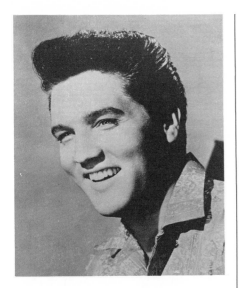

Follow That Dream was Elvis's best comedy ever, with excellent acting and a soundtrack to match. His other two films of the year were *Kid Gallahad* and *Girls Girls Girls.* Music movies of '62 also included *Don't Knock the Twist* with Chubby Checker, Gene Chandler, and the Dovells; *Follow the Boys* with Connie Francis; *State Fair* with Pat Boone, Bobby Darin, and Ann-Margret; *It's Trad Dad* with Gene Vincent, Del Shannon, and Gary U.S. Bonds; *Lonely Boy* with Paul Anka; and *Disneyland After Dark* with Bobby Rydell, Annette Funicello, and Louis Armstrong.

The last surviving heirs of the New York doo-wop sound were the **Four Seasons**, a group that titled themselves after a hometown bowling alley. Their style was built around the incredible falsetto of their lead singer, Frankie Valli, whose vocal range extended over three octaves. Their first hit, "Sherry," was cut in 1962, only fifteen minutes after being written. After that came more than three dozen other charted sides, including "Walk Like a Man" (1963), "Rag Doll" (1964), "Let's Hang On" (1965), and "Working My Way Back to You" (1966). The Four Seasons were as fiercely supported in the east as their chief rivals, the Beach Boys, were out west. Ironically, their biggest hit was also their last— "December 1963" (1976). Frankie Valli recorded it with other singers, after all the original members had left the group.

Phil Spector was one of the most respected and influential record producers of the sixties. His recording sessions were musical marathons, running all night if need be, until horns, guitars, drums, and voices blended perfectly. No one else lavished such care, time, and money on 45 rpm records—and no one else ever had so many hits. Of the first thirty singles that Spector produced for his own label, Philles Records, twenty-seven made the charts, nine were top ten, and three reached number one. His artist roster included the Crystals, Ronettes, Righteous Brothers, and Bob B. Soxx and the Blue Jeans; he also worked with the Drifters, Gene Pitney, Ike and Tina Turner, and the Beatles.

THE TOP 40

1. Stranger on the Shore, *Mr. Acker Bilk*
2. Mashed Potato Time, *Dee Dee Sharp*
3. I Can't Stop Loving You, *Ray Charles*
4. The Twist, *Chubby Checker*
5. The Stripper, *David Rose*
6. Johnny Angel, *Shelley Fabares*
7. The Wanderer, *Dion*
8. Roses Are Red, *Bobby Vinton*
9. The Locomotion, *Little Eva*
10. Hey! Baby, *Bruce Channel*
11. Peppermint Twist, *Joey Dee and the Starliters*
12. Duke of Earl, *Gene Chandler*
13. Soldier Boy, *Shirelles*
14. The One Who Really Loves You, *Mary Wells*
15. Let Me In, *Sensations*
16. Palisades Park, *Freddy Cannon*
17. It Keeps Right On a-Hurtin', *Johnny Tillotson*
18. Ramblin' Rose, *Nat King Cole*
19. Moon River, *Henry Mancini*
20. Midnight in Moscow, *Kenny Ball*
21. Breaking Up Is Hard to Do, *Neil Sedaka*
22. You'll Lose a Good Thing, *Barbara Lynn*
23. The Lion Sleeps Tonight, *Tokens*
24. Wolverton Mountain, *Claude King*
25. Twistin' the Night Away, *Sam Cooke*
26. Slow Twistin', *Chubby Checker*
27. Do You Love Me, *Contours*
28. Sherry, *Four Seasons*
29. Good Luck Charm, *Elvis Presley*
30. Walk On By, *Leroy Van Dyke*
31. I Know, *Barbara George*
32. The Wah-Watusi, *Orlons*
33. Monster Mash, *Bobby "Boris" Pickett*
34. Twist and Shout, *Isley Brothers*
35. Break It to Me Gently, *Brenda Lee*
36. Playboy, *Marvelettes*
37. Can't Help Falling in Love, *Elvis Presley*
38. Sealed with a Kiss, *Brian Hyland*
39. Love Letters, *Ketty Lester*
40. She Cried, *Jay and the Americans*

THE TOP 10 LPs

1. West Side Story, *Original Soundtrack*
2. Blue Hawaii, *Original Soundtrack*
3. Camelot, *Original Cast*
4. Breakfast at Tiffany's, *Original Soundtrack*
5. Time Out, *Dave Brubeck*
6. At Carnegie Hall, *Judy Garland*
7. The Sound of Music, *Original Cast*
8. West Side Story, *Original Cast*
9. Your Twist Party, *Chubby Checker*
10. Vol. 2, *Joan Baez*

West Side Story was basically an updated adaptation of Shakespeare's *Romeo and Juliet,* set in the street gang atmosphere of late fifties New York. All the chief components were meant to represent aspects of modern American youth, not least of which was the considerable impact of rock 'n' roll music. However, composer Leonard Bernstein and lyricist Stephen Sondheim had little actual contact with young people, and so their "rock 'n' roll" ballads came off more like Italianesque jazz. Nevertheless, *West Side Story* was an immense hit as a stage play, motion picture, and record album. The LP, released late in 1961, was a 1962 sensation—a chart-topper that remained on the best-seller list for 198 weeks.

Hey! Baby
BRUCE CHANNEL

Bruce Channel (pronounced sha-*nell*) was born in Jacksonville, Texas, to a family that he described as "musical." He taught himself guitar and was singing and playing by the time he was five. Bruce began writing songs at an early age and, in order to hear what they sounded like, formed his first band at fourteen. After that, he went through a succession of groups, experimenting with style and lyrics, looking for that right combination.

In the mid-fifties, the Channels moved to Dallas, and there Bruce found more avenues to develop his talent. Before long, he was in heavy demand to perform at youth centers, benefits, high school hops, parties, and local gatherings. His father made note of this popularity and, after some family discussions, agreed to accompany the young singer to Shreveport, where he could audition for the "Louisiana Hayride." The producer of the radio show, Tillman Franks, was impressed with Bruce and booked him for a single appearance. It went over so well that Bruce was signed on as a regular, and for the next six months he drove in every weekend to perform.

Meanwhile, Bruce was honing his writing skills. Among his favorite recording stars at the time were the Platters, and he was determined to come up with a song that they would want to record. After many attempts, he finally completed a ballad called "Dream Girl." However, he was unable to find anyone who could get his composition to the group. Rather than throw it away, he decided to record it himself, along with a number of other tunes he'd been working on. Among them was a song he had written with a girlfriend, Margaret Cobb.

"There's not a whole lot of story behind 'Hey! Baby,' " Bruce recalled. I sat down one day and just fooled around with my guitar. I tried to figure out some different chord progressions from what I'd been playing, and

suddenly up popped this little riff. It was a real simple thing—A, F sharp, B, E. Margaret was there, and we just wrote it. It didn't take long to write, maybe ten minutes, and there it was.

"After the session we decided to put 'Dream Girl' and 'Hey! Baby' back to back on the same single. The A side—the one we wanted to get air play on—was 'Dream Girl.' Well, after a few spins, deejays flipped the record over and started playing 'Hey! Baby.' It was a total surprise to me when it started moving."

"Hey! Baby" took off late in 1961, as a local release on the Le Cam label. After impressive sales around the East Texas area, Smash Records bought the master and reissued it nationally. "Hey! Baby" entered the pop charts in January 1962 and rose steadily, reaching number one two months later. It spent three weeks as America's favorite single, fifteen weeks in total on the record charts.

After "Hey! Baby," Smash had first-refusal rights on all later Bruce Channel masters recorded by Le Cam. They picked up several, including "Number One Man" and "Come On Baby," but none was able to duplicate the success of "Hey! Baby." In the meantime, though, Bruce made four tours of Europe, starring in his own show, which proved to be very popular. At one stop, in New Brighton, his band was booked to play the Castle, a nightclub right across from Liverpool. Their opening act was a little-known local group called the Beatles. John Lennon was intrigued by the instrumental break in "Hey! Baby" and asked to be taught how to perform it. Bruce's harmonica player was more than happy to oblige. Less than a year later, the Beatles released their first hit single, "Love Me Do," featuring a lengthy harmonica solo—by John Lennon.

In the early seventies, Bruce Channel returned home to stay and bought a house in Grapevine, Texas. He still

writes and records occasionally, but now works full time for the Parks Department. Someday he hopes to cut another record with the power of "Hey! Baby," but in the meantime he's content to have other artists, such as Mel Tillis and Conway Twitty, record his songs. As for his old harmonica player, he continued to struggle on for many years before finally resurfacing with his own hit single in 1981: "Giving It Up for Your Love," by Delbert McClinton.

The Locomotion

LITTLE EVA

E va Narcissus Boyd was born in Belhaven, North Carolina, one of a family of fourteen. At fifteen, she moved to New York, where relatives put her up while she finished high school. To help out with expenses, Eva took some babysitting jobs, one of which was with a young songwriting couple, Gerry Goffin and Carole King.

At that point, Eva was torn between becoming a nurse or a vocalist. "I'd lived around music all my life," she said, "singing in church, at school, whenever I was asked and sometimes when I wasn't asked." To pass time at the Goffin residence, Eva often sang to herself, imitating her favorite performers, such as Dee Dee Sharp.

One night, as Gerry and Carole were coming home, they overheard "Mashed Potato Time" wafting out from inside the house. They were impressed with Eva's pleasant voice and enthusiastic sound. "You should be cutting demos," they said, and in fact they had a melody right then that they'd been working on. Carole sat down at the piano, and as she played, Eva began inventing dance steps. They reminded Gerry of the movement of a train, and he excitedly sketched out some lyrics. Within a few minutes, "The Locomotion" was on paper.

The Goffins took Eva to their publisher, Aldon Music, where she demonstrated the song and dance for owners Al Nevins and Don Kirshner. Their intention was to place the tune with a pop singer who had requested material from the firm. However, when Eva finished, everyone agreed she should cut the song.

Carole worked up an arrangement, borrowing somewhat from the Marvelettes' "Please Mr. Postman." She then helped her husband produce the record. According to a studio musician on the session, Gerry "almost stood on his head to achieve the sound he wanted." The backup singers were the Cookies, later to have hits on their own ("Chains," "Don't Say Nothin' Bad About My Baby," etc.).

"The Locomotion" was the first release on the Goffin's own label, Dimension Records. It broke late in July 1962, and rocketed up the charts. By August, it was the number-one song in the country—and the start of a whole new dance craze.

Over the next year, Little Eva had two more big hits, both written and produced by Goffin and King: "Keep Your Hands Off My Baby" (1962) and "Let's Turkey Trot" (1963). She later recorded for the Amy and Spring labels, but never again with the same success. Today she lives in New York, and occasionally turns up at revival concerts.

Eva, who had a range of one octave and six, always regarded "The Locomotion" as "the most important event in my life. I was a little worried that I might disappoint people, but once I realized that the entire Nevins-Kirshner team was behind me, my fright disappeared."

In 1974, "The Locomotion" returned in a new version by Grand Funk. Like Little Eva's original, it, too, became a number-one record.

Roses Are Red

BOBBY VINTON

Bobby Vinton, the son of a locally popular big band leader, was born in Canonsburg, Pennsylvania, a suburb of Pittsburgh. As a child, his parents urged him to study music, but like most young boys, he preferred sports to practicing. Soon though, he began to enjoy what his father had made a career of, and at fifteen Bobby organized his own ensemble.

"I always wanted a big band with a young sound for young people," he said. "I was sure that kids of my generation wanted a full swinging group that would play rock 'n' roll with a solid beat." At that point, Bobby was only a musician, playing trumpet, sax, clarinet and oboe. He had no ambi-

tion to become a vocalist, but sometimes to break routine, he sang an occasional number.

Bobby paid his way through Duquesne University by leading his own group, playing proms, sock hops, and local nightclubs. After graduation, he wound up in the army—on trumpet—in a military band. While in the service he played a lot of football, and briefly toyed with the idea of becoming a professional athlete. Most of his time, though, was spent in solitude—later, the inspiration for one of his biggest hits, "Mr. Lonely."

Once out of the army, Bobby formed a new group, which appeared on NBC's "Saturday Prom" TV show. They backed Sam Cooke, Bobby Vee,

and other guests, and in 1960, were given their own label contract with Epic Records. Bobby's first album as a bandleader was "Dancing at the Hop"—a flop if ever there was one.

After a second LP also bombed, Epic decided to drop the new act from its roster. While sitting in an office, waiting to get his walking papers, Bobby happened to look his contract over one last time. To his surprise, he discovered that he had one more session—two sides—allotted to him. He began to listen to a stack of rejected demo records, hoping for a song that might turn his career around.

Bobby was interrupted by an Epic executive, who began talking about the band not making it, the amount of money they'd spent, and so forth. Vinton cut him off.

"Hey, wait a minute," he said. "Cut me as a singer."

The Epic man laughed. "You can't sing. You're a jazz musician."

"Well, I'll tell you," replied Bobby. "I just found a song on this reject pile that's so commercial I think anyone could sing it and have a hit." He placed the demo on the turntable and played it a second time. Afterward, he just grinned. "Well, it's either this," he said, "or the big band."

The man from Epic was not impressed. "All right Bobby, we'll try it," he sighed. "Let's cut it as a single and see what happens."

What did happen was mostly the result of Vinton's own promotion. He bought many of the early copies, and then hired a gorgeous girl to carry the record and roses around to disc jockeys. In June, the tune broke onto the pop charts, and by July it was the number-one song in the country. Ultimately, it sold more than three million copies.

"I don't have a voice like Sinatra or Como," admitted Vinton. "That's why I had to work to make my career happen."

The Wanderer

DION

"I was raised in the Bronx," Dion recalled. "Perhaps you could say I was forced up. I was ten when a friend of my father's visited our house one afternoon. His guitar and voice filled the room. The music stayed with me long after he left. When my parents bought me an $8 guitar in a pawn shop, I painted it with friends' names, then gave it to a cousin as I outgrew it. It was an antique Gibson, a collector's item that would be worth $500 now.

"At twelve, I heard 'Honky Tonk Blues' by Hank Williams, became an immediate fan, and started a record collection. Soon I had learned two hundred country songs by heart. In spite of my shyness, I began playing and singing in school plays, church dances, and talent shows.

"Nearly every person in my neighborhood belonged to a gang when I was a teenager. Friends of mine died from drugs and street wars. Like everyone else, I acted tough, hiding the real feeling inside. These were difficult times for me. My guitar got me through them.

"By this time I was into Chuck Berry, Elvis Presley, Fats Domino, and the Drifters. I taped a song for my mother and gave it to her for Valentine's Day. She was so proud of me she played it for anyone who would listen. Someone asked to borrow it, saying they knew people at a new record company. Next thing I knew I was called for an audition at Laurie Records.

"I rounded up the best of the street corner singers I knew in the Bronx. We rehearsed on the Sixth Avenue D train to Manhattan. That was the beginning of Dion and the Belmonts. We were hot stuff! We sang in the streets, subway stations, elevators, everywhere. Our two biggest records were 'A Teenager in Love' [1959] and 'Where or When' [1960]. Soon we were working the top concerts in the nation, touring with Bobby Darin, the Everly Brothers, Sam Cooke, Johnny Mathis, and many others. It was a baffling but beautiful feeling to suddenly find crowds waiting outside my dressing room window.

"In 1960 I began recording on my own, singing some original Bronx blues like 'Lonely Teenager,' 'Lovers Who Wander,' 'Little Diane,' and 'Love Came to Me.' The two biggest were 'Runaround Sue' and then 'The Wanderer.' That was about a kid in my neighborhood who had tattoos all over his body. He had 'Flo' tattooed on his left arm and 'Mary' on his right, and every time he went out with a different chick, he'd add her name to his collection. Sometimes, if things got bad, he'd have a name covered up with a panther or a rose or something. And then he got 'Rosie' on his chest. It's crazy, but we all kind of looked up to him, and my friend Ernie Maresca wrote a song about the guy.

"I'll never forget recording that song. We had Mickey Baker, of Mickey and Sylvia, on guitar. We brought our girlfriends down to the studio to sit around and watch us scream out some rock 'n' roll. It was a happening, and it was a lot of fun."

About a year after recording "The Wanderer," Dion moved over to the Columbia label. They tried to change his street-tough image and make him more "respectable"—a "suit and tie" singer with adult appeal, somewhat akin to a young Andy Williams. But the rock 'n' roll hits continued: "Ruby Baby," "Donna the Prima Donna," and "Drip Drop," all in 1963.

"But in 1964 the Beatles changed the pop musical scene. The new guitar sound was electric. During the mid-sixties I worked quietly on the acoustical guitar, improving as a songwriter. By 1968, I had come a long way musically from the street corner sounds of Dion and the Belmonts. 'Abraham, Martin and John' was different from anything I had ever done. It brought me to the coffeehouse circuit."

In 1972, Dion got back together with

his old group and recorded a classic live album, *Reunion: Dion and the Belmonts Live at Madison Square Garden*. Since that time, he has cut LPs in a variety of styles, including one entitled *Return of the Wanderer*. In the late seventies, Dion became a born-again Christian, and after that he pretty much restricted his music to gospel songs.

Johnny Angel
SHELLEY FABARES

I never did, nor to this day do I consider myself a singer," said Shelley Fabares. "While the whole experience of 'Johnny Angel' was wonderful, it was also quite frightening because I couldn't really sing. I remember my absolute panic going into the recording studio. There was Hal Blaine on drums, Glen Campbell on guitar, and they had just finished a session with Sinatra or Tony Bennett. I thought I'd just die.

"The way it all started was, I was doing 'The Donna Reed Show' and in between the second and third year our producer, Tony Owen, came to Paul Petersen and me and said he had a wonderful idea for the next season. 'We're going to have you two sing some songs,' he said, 'and we'll write some scripts around them.' Both Paul and I said, 'That's very interesting, but we can't sing.' Particularly *I* said that. Paul had more guts than I had then; he wasn't quite as frightened. I became absolutely paralyzed. The thought of standing up and singing something made my knees weak. I kept saying, 'No, I'm not going to do it, I can't do it.' Finally Mr. Owen said, 'Well, gee, do you want to be on the show next year?' And I said, 'Gee, yeah.' So he said, 'Well, then sing.'

"We went in and made records on the huge soundstage at Columbia. Paul and I each sang one song separately and one together. They were horrendous. My only thought was that that would be the end of it. They would see that we weren't just being obstinate—we really couldn't sing. We were told that they were going to send what we did to Columbia Pictures' record division, which was called Colpix. The next thing Paul and I knew, a producer from New York by the name of Stu Phillips was saying that he thought he could do something with us."

Stu Phillips picked up the story. "Actually, the song I wanted to do with Shelley was some other tune," he said. "However, Screen Gems [the TV arm of Columbia Pictures] decided that the lyrics were too risqué to put on television. I said, 'My God, I've got to find another song.' So I went through my briefcase and the only thing I could find that was reasonably a girl's song was this 'Johnny Angel,' which was actually a jazz piece. One of the writers was a jazz musician. It was not meant to be a rock 'n' roll song at all. But it was the only thing I had that they would accept, lyrically."

"I cut that song at United Recorders on Sunset Boulevard," recalled Shelley. "I found that if I sang very softly, I'd feel more courageous and even sound better. They double-tracked my voice and used an echo chamber effect. My backup singers were the Blossoms. I don't recall the session taking very long at all.

"They wrote a script around 'Johnny Angel' in which I sang it at a school show. The absolute next thing I remember was Tony Owen coming on the set, shaking his head back and forth, and saying, 'You won't believe how many records you sold today.' It got to be a joke."

"It was one of those things that surprised everyone," said Stu. "I wouldn't have bet anything in my pocket on it becoming a hit. I thought I blew it with Shelley. I just didn't know. It was a jazz song done by a singer who couldn't sing in a rock 'n' roll style. What else was against it? Everything, you know."

"I think it broke first in Boston,"

Shelley said, "and I remember when I first found out it had gone to number one. I was flat on my back in bed with mononucleosis."

"Johnny Angel" took off early in March 1962, and reached the top of the charts in April. In all, it spent more than three months as one of America's best-selling singles. Later in the summer, Shelley followed her gold record with another hit: "Johnny Loves Me." Concurrently, Paul Petersen did well with "She Can't Find Her Keys" (1962) and the million-selling "My Dad" (1963).

"The main thing that people say to me about 'Johnny Angel' is that it was something special and endearing," said Shelley. "It had a pleasant sound, and they identified with the character I played on TV. She was a very distinctive role model for the time, and the song itself—well, it was a very good song."

The Stripper
DAVID ROSE and HIS ORCHESTRA

David Rose was born in London and intended to become a railroad engineer. However, he got sidetracked into music, and wound up as a composer, arranger, and leader of his own orchestra. He conducted symphonies all over the world, earning renown for the brilliance and originality of his string arrangements. Yet his biggest hit—a total fluke—was a bawdy instrumental, recorded off-the-cuff with a brass section.

David moved to America when he was four and later attended the Chicago Musical College. After graduation, he served as an arranger/pianist in several midwestern bands, including that of Ted Fiorito. David also worked in local radio, and in 1936 formed his first orchestra.

Two years later, he moved to L.A. and became music director of the Mutual radio network. He had his own coast-to-coast series, and in 1942, introduced a tune he had written called "Holiday for Strings." Recorded for RCA early the next year, it became a million-seller and brought him international fame. In 1951, the song was revived by Red Skelton, who used it as his TV theme for the next twenty years (and employed Rose as his television musical director).

After the war, David kept busy conducting for radio and TV and recording for MGM. His specialty, mood albums of lush string music, sold in appreciable quantities. He was credited with being the first to use an echo chamber and other special effects on his LPs.

And then it happened in 1958.

"We had a string album to do—eleven numbers in one night," said David. "I knew my brass section would be left just sitting there, so for laughs I brought in a little tune I had written for a television show called 'Burlesque' with Dan Dailey. It was only eight bars, strip music, really. I thought it would be fun for the boys to clown around

with a bit. I elongated the thing and we recorded it in just one take, as a joke. I made private copies and gave one to each of the boys in the orchestra. The master tapes of the session were then sent back to New York and filed. MGM didn't think it was right to put out 'The Stripper' along with all of my string things."

David soon forgot about the track, and for good reason. By that time, he had become the most prolific composer of television music in the business. In 1959, no less than twenty-two series used his theme songs—every show from "Sea Hunt" to "Highway Patrol." He won two Emmys that year, including one for his work on "Bonanza." He also won a Grammy in 1959 for "Like Young," recorded with André Previn on piano.

"Accidents do happen," said David. "In 1962, MGM decided to make the picture *Sweet Bird of Youth,* with Paul Newman and Geraldine Page. As part of the score, they chose to use 'Ebb Tide,' which had already been a hit [for Frank Chacksfield in 1953]. They wanted a new version to help promote the movie, so they asked me to cut one quickly. I did—just that one track—and rushed it on to MGM. I didn't have anything for a flip side, so they went through my unreleased tapes looking for anything to slap on the back of the single. Someone found 'The Stripper' tape, and that became the B side of the 45.

"The next thing I knew, I got a phone call from somebody, saying, 'Turn on the radio. Your number is being played, and has been played for half an hour.' There was this deejay—Robert Q. Lewis—who was taking requests and playing my record. No matter what people asked for, he yelled 'Here it comes!' and put on 'The Stripper.' He did that for forty-five minutes in a row."

Other deejays heard about it, and added "The Stripper" to their playlists. It broke nationally in mid-May

1962 and by July was the number-one song in America. Despite being banned by some radio stations as "obscene," it remained a best-seller for nearly four months.

David Rose never had another hit record, but did very well in later years composing and arranging for movies and TV shows. He was in demand as a guest conductor for various orchestras, including the Chicago, Milwaukee, and San Francisco symphonies. He also led the Pasadena Pops and staged his own concerts at the Hollywood Bowl.

The Twist (1962)

CHUBBY CHECKER

It was the fall of 1960, and all across the country, radios rocked to the number one sound of "The Twist," by Chubby Checker. Young America loved and danced to that record, while their elders, by and large, looked the other way. According to convention, rock 'n' roll was strictly for adolescents—hardly of interest to mature, respectable adults. For that reason, many grown-ups simply ignored the growing rock scene, smug in the satisfaction that they were above such "musical nonsense." From attitudes like that arose the Generation Gap—a chasm that grew wider and deeper with each passing year.

But there were bridges, and one of the most remarkable began imperceptively, on October 13. It was then that a Passaic, New Jersey, twist band began three trial nights at a neighborhood bar in downtown Manhattan. They brought in such crowds that their engagement was extended—and extended again—to thirteen months. With the added revenue came alterations, and gradually, the look of the room began to improve. New York's elite trickled in, and with them, the relentless gossip press.

In the fall of 1961, Cholly Knickerbocker, a columnist for the *Journal-American,* happened to spot Prince Serge Obolensky out on the dance floor, happily twisting up a storm. Breathlessly, Cholly carried full details of this "scoop" in the next day's edition. Society's lemmings immediately rationalized that if a prince was doing something, it had to be *the thing to do.* Overnight, the Twist became acceptable for adults, and anybody who was anybody had to do it in that same tiny bar—the Peppermint Lounge.

The media, always alert for scenes of celebrities slumming, gave the craze

front page priority. Young and old, from Maine to California, were swept into Twistomania with astonishing speed. A nationwide survey, conducted in October 1961, revealed that ninety percent of those polled agreed that the Twist was America's most popular dance. Twist music turned up at everything, from high school hops to the most posh of upper crust parties. Even on the set of Liz Taylor's new movie, *Cleopatra,* the cast and crew were seen doing the Twist between takes.

Record shops and radio stations were bombarded with requests for "The Twist," and many deejays complied by giving the song extra spins as an oldie. However, as demand mounted, program directors were forced to add the single to their current playlists. By mid-November, it had re-entered the national charts, and in January it achieved a stunning, unprecedented feat—reaching number one a second time around. No other record before or since has matched that achievement. Combining its '61–'62 run with its eighteen weeks of popularity in 1960, "The Twist" spent an amazing nine months total on the U.S. best-seller lists.

"The Twist" revitalized American nightlife, touching off this country's first coast-to-coast disco craze. Many clubs, unable to afford live entertainment, were teetering on the brink of bankruptcy. Suddenly, all they needed was a record player, a couple of speakers, and a handful of rock 'n' roll singles. Chairs were pushed back, rugs rolled up, and a new kind of nitery was born—the "discotheque" (a French word, meaning "dancing to records"). Some clubs, such as the Peppermint Lounge, combined live and recorded music, and even had their own custom variations on

the dance. At the Peppermint Lounge, that house band—Joey Dee and the Starlighters—developed "The Peppermint Twist"—a number-one hit in 1962.

As for Chubby Checker, his star burned all that much brighter, as he became the hottest entertainer in show biz. He also became a merchandising marvel, selling millions of Twist shoes, T-shirts, ties, jeans, dolls, raincoats, chewing gum, and nighties. Most of all, though, Chubby was a catalyst, bringing together, for the first time, people of many age, race, social and economic groups. And he did it all with a single 45 rpm record.

"The Twist." According to the industry bible, *Billboard* magazine, it's the most successful single they've charted in more than forty-odd years.

I Can't Stop Loving You

RAY CHARLES

Ray Charles Robinson was not born blind; only poor, in Albany, Georgia.

"There was an old gentleman named Mr. Wiley Pittman," said Ray, "and he had a beat-up piano on his porch. I'd go over and stand there and listen, and pretty soon he'd move over and make room for me. I'd sit down and bang away up on the high keys. I wasn't playin' nuthin'. He knew it, but he'd smile and say, 'Thass good, thass so good, sonny. But you gotta practice.' "

By the time Ray was six, physical darkness—a kind of glaucoma—had begun to set in. "People should never be bitter about anything," he went on. "They should learn to keep fighting for themselves." The source of this philosophy was his mother's advice: "You're blind, not stupid, Ray. You lost your sight, not your mind."

At ten, his father died; five years later, his mother, too. At St. Augustine's School for the deaf and blind, he learned to read and write Braille, to play piano and clarinet, and how to memorize music—sometimes as much as 2,000 bars at a time. He also dropped his surname, to avoid being confused with boxer Sugar Ray Robinson.

After leaving school, Ray traveled with a hillbilly band, the Florida Playboys. "I always loved that kind of music," he said. "It's honest music, and I never missed hearing the Grand Ole Opry."

Ray began recording for a small label, Swingtime, and in 1954 his contract was bought by Atlantic Records. His first session for the new company was held in a radio station studio, and had to stop every fifteen minutes for local newscasts. Between interruptions, they cut what became his biggest hit single at that time, "I Got a Woman." It outraged the gospel world, which rightly charged that Ray had taken sacred music and secularized it. It was, in fact, Ray's rewrite of

an old hymn, "My Jesus Is All the World to Me." Despite the protests, Ray added more gospel flavor to his sound. The pinnacle was "What'd I Say," released in 1959 and banned by many U.S. radio stations. It was the turning point in Ray's career, and his first major pop single.

Ray's next top-forty record was "I'm Movin' On," and that's what he did. In November 1959 he signed a contract with ABC Paramount Records. It gave him a royalty estimated at three times the amount paid to the average performer and all rights to the original tapes of his records, which he then leased back to ABC Paramount.

Ray's first number-one record came along in 1960: "Georgia on My Mind," the winner of two Grammy Awards. He also picked up Grammies for the LP *Genius of Ray Charles* and the single "Let the Good Times Roll." In 1961, there were three more hits: "One Mint Julep," "Unchain My Heart," and "Hit the Road Jack."

Late in the year, Ray phoned Sid Feller, his A&R producer in New York, and requested that a tape be made of "all the great country and western songs." Sensing what his star had in mind, Feller immediately called the president of ABC Records, who became equally upset. A black man singing country and western songs? "It's not commercial," they cried. They

pleaded with Ray to forget the idea, but, of course, he wouldn't.

Among the tunes that Ray selected was one written in 1957 by Don Gibson. He was hoping to write a ballad of lost love, but after several lines were put down, he looked back and saw the words "I can't stop loving you." "That would be a good title," he thought, and then rewrote the song in its present form. On the same day, he also wrote "Oh Lonesome Me."

The latter tune became Don's first million-seller in 1958. Ray liked both Gibson numbers, but felt there was more potential in "I Can't Stop Loving You."

Ray's album, *Modern Sounds in Country and Western Music,* was released in January 1962. It rocked the music industry. On April 23, Ray's version of "I Can't Stop Loving You" was issued as a single. Distributors were confounded. They called ABC, asking, "What is this? A joke?" The so-called joke was number one for more than a month and won a Grammy Award as the Best R&B Record of the Year.

His hits did not stop there; nearly seventy Ray Charles sides made the charts in the fifties, sixties, and seventies. Among his more notable later releases: "You Don't Know Me" and "You Are My Sunshine" (1962), "Take These Chains from My Heart" and "Busted" (1963), and "Crying Time" (1966). The latter two were also Grammy winners, as was "Living for the City" (1975).

"The important thing is that you feel your music," said Ray. "Really feel it and believe it. That conviction carries over to the public.

"I try to bring out my soul so that people can understand what I am. I want people to feel my soul, and I've got to hear myself in a song. Soul is when you can take a song and make it a part of you—a part so real, so true, people think it must have happened to you."

Mashed Potato Time

DEE DEE SHARP

Dee Dee Sharp's career began with an ad in the newspaper, placed there by Cameo Parkway Records. They were looking for someone who could read music, play piano, and sing backup vocals. She could do all those things, and had been looking for a way to earn extra money. So, without telling her parents, she left school early one day, went down, and applied for the job.

Dee Dee was met at the door by songwriter Dave Appel, leader of the Applejacks. He asked the fourteen-year-old what she wanted, and when she said "to audition," he laughed. Just then Chubby Checker walked in, and was apprised of the situation. "Give the kid a break," he said, and they did, hiring her on the spot.

Dee Dee sang backups every day after school for the next two years, working with Freddie Cannon, Bobby Rydell, the Orlons and others. Then, in 1962, she ran into Chubby again. He had just cut a version of "Slow Twistin'," but it lacked the punch of earlier efforts. Label owner Bernie Lowe had suggested adding a female vocalist, to "round out the sound."

"I remember you," said Chubby. "You're the little girl that came in that day. How'd you make out?"

"O.K.," answered Dee Dee. "I'm still working."

"Well," he continued, "I've got some songs. How'd you like to sing with me?"

"I don't care," she replied. "I'll sing with anybody. It doesn't make any difference."

Chubby and Dee Dee then entered the studio; she ad-libbed a vocal part, and their record was complete. Bernie Lowe, sitting on the other side of the glass, was blown away by her talent. He decided to waste no time in recording her very first solo single. "I want to do it tonight," he said.

Dee Dee was a little frightened by that prospect. Her grandfather, a minister, ruled the family, and she was

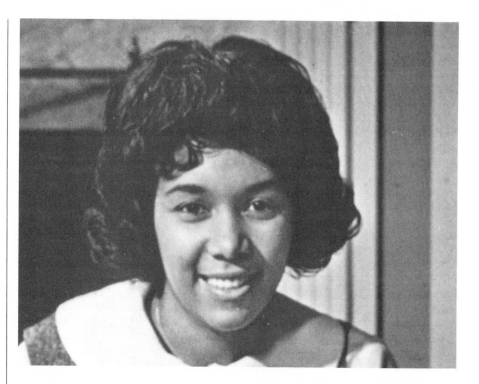

sure that he and the rest of the clan would not approve. But if she was going to "get killed," she figured she might as well go all the way. She recorded "Mashed Potato Time."

Two days later, Bernie Lowe told her that she had to change her name. At that time, Dion DiMucci was a big star, and Bernie felt that no one would believe her real name: Dione LaRue. Since she sang in the key of D sharp, he recommended "Dee Dee Sharp." She agreed, and that's what went on the records.

"Mashed Potato Time" and "Slow Twistin' " both broke early in March 1962. Dee Dee appeared on "American Bandstand," singing, dancing, and showing everybody how to mash potatoes with their feet. The silliness of the whole thing seemed to work in its favor; by May, "Mashed Potato Time" was one of the best-selling singles in America.

Overlooked through it all were two important facts: "I had two left feet," recalled Dee Dee. "I never could

dance, and had nothing to do with making up the dance. I just sang the song and hoped no one would ever ask me to demonstrate." Her cousins tried to teach her the step, but eventually gave up. "I did as much as needed to get by," she said. "I guess deep down I didn't want to learn it because I felt so awkward." Her other hidden secret: she didn't like the taste of mashed potatoes.

Dee Dee followed her record with—what else—another dance number called "Gravy." It made the top ten, as did "Ride" (1962) and "Do the Bird" (1963). Her last good seller was "Wild," a song inspired by her feelings for her fiancé, Kenny Gamble. They were married in 1967.

"The reason I stopped singing," she said, "was that I wanted to be a wife and mother. I like to cook, I like to clean, and I love Kenny (a part-owner of Philadelphia-International Records).

"I was in the right place at the right time—thanks to Chubby."

Stranger on the Shore

MR. ACKER BILK

Bernard Stanley Bilk grew up around music—mostly the religious kind, since his mother was a church organist and his father a Methodist lay preacher, in Bristol, England. Bernard himself, though, didn't get involved until 1947, when he was eighteen years old. At the time, he was in Egypt, serving three months in a military prison for falling asleep on guard duty. Having nothing better to do, he took up the clarinet to pass the time.

After getting out of the army, Bernard worked for a while as a blacksmith. It was tough, dirty work, and finally he decided that making music might be a more comfortable way to earn a living. He joined the Ken Colyer group and spent several years learning jazz and developing his style.

In 1958 he formed his own ensemble and called it the Paramount Jazz Band. They played clubs for a while around the Bristol area and then headed for Düsseldorf, where they found work as a jazz act in local beer cellars. Slowly, their reputation grew, and before long they were the most successful exponents of a sound known as "trad jazz," which was simply a reworking of the American New Orleans style.

In 1960, independent producer Denis Preston discovered the band and brought them to London to cut a few sides for his company, Record Production. One of the first things they did was "Summer Set," a tune written by their pianist, Dave Collett. It became a fairly big hit for them that year in England. Label credit was given to "Mr. Acker Bilk," *acker* being a slang term for "mate" or "buddy."

In 1961, the band released an album entitled *Sentimental Journey.* One of the tracks was "Jenny," a gentle instrumental written by Bilk and named after one of his children. About that same time, the BBC hired him to write a signature theme for its chil-

dren's TV series, "Stranger on the Shore." Pressed for time, Acker pulled out "Jenny," retitled it, and performed it on the show. The response was so strong that the track was issued as a single, to tie in with the program. It became an overnight hit and went on to spend nearly forty weeks on the British charts—longer than any other record in history up to that time.

Atco released the single in America early in 1962, and by May it was firmly entrenched in the number-one spot. In all, it spent twenty-one weeks on the U.S. best-seller list.

"Stranger on the Shore" sold its first million by April 1962, but for one

reason or another, it did not receive its RIAA Gold certification for another five years. By then, its worldwide sales were estimated at well over four million. The song was nominated for two Grammy Awards in 1962: Best Instrumental Theme and Best Performance by an Orchestra, or Instrumentalist with Orchestra, Not for Jazz or Dancing. However, it lost both.

Acker Bilk didn't seem to mind. His trad jazz fad lasted for another two years, and afterward, he was still regarded as Britain's top jazz clarinetist. With his bowler hat and colored waistcoat, he remained a popular U.K. personality for a long, long time.

IN 1963, THE BEATLES made their 294th and final appearance at the Cavern Club. The Stones cut their first record, "Come On," and the Kinks, Yardbirds, Mindbenders, Turtles, and Herman's Hermits all formed their respective groups. Paul Anka, Brenda Lee, and Chubby Checker each got married (no, not to each other). Les Paul and Mary Ford split up, as did the Springfields (allowing Dusty Springfield to start her solo career). Other lead singers on the move: Glenn Yarborough, who left the Limeliters; Len Barry, the Dovells; and Wilson Pickett, the Falcons. Jimmy Osmond was born, Dinah Washington died, and Patsy Cline was killed in a plane crash. The brother of Bobby Hebb was murdered, inspiring Bobby to write his only big hit, "Sunny." And the gross income of Elvis Presley—to this point—was estimated at $20 million.

Hootenanny—a word invented by Woody Guthrie in the forties—became the title of television's first folk music series on April 6. Every week, ABC cameras visited a different college campus, capturing guest artists in live performances before students. Jack Linkletter played host to a wide variety of collegiate favorites, including the Limeliters, the Chad Mitchell Trio, and the **Rooftop Singers.** The latter group, comprised of Erik Darling, Lynne Taylor, and Bill Svanoe, were then hot with the hits "Tom Cat" and "Walk Right In." "Hootenanny" went off the air on September 12, 1964.

Bobby Rydell, who ranked second only to Chubby Checker as a "Philadelphia Sound" superstar, appeared with Ann-Margret in *Bye Bye Birdie,* a musical farce that satirized Presley-type phenomena and teen culture in general. Other music movies included *Just for Fun,* with Bobby Vee, Johnny Tillotson, and Freddie Cannon; *Live It Up,* with Kenny Ball and Gene Vincent; and *What a Crazy World* with Freddie and the Dreamers. Johnny Cash, Sheb Wooley, the Brothers Four, and George Hamilton celebrated the folk craze in *Hootenanny Hoot;* Elvis starred in *Fun in Acapulco* and *It Happened at the World's Fair.*

Surf music was one of the trends of 1963, thanks to the Surfaris ("Wipe Out"), Beach Boys ("Surfin' U.S.A."), and especially **Jan and Dean.** The California duo got together in high school, and made their first recordings in Jan's garage on a couple of home tape recorders. "Jennie Lee" (1958) came out of that, as did "Baby Talk" (1959). Eventually, the boys signed with Liberty Records, and in 1963 released "Surf City," a chart-topping million-seller. Jan and Dean music celebrated the California lifestyle—sand, surf, hot rods, bikinis, skateboards, popsicles, and good times with golden girls. They had fun making their records, and the good cheer and good humor always shone through. Their later hits included "Honolulu Lulu," "Drag City," "The Little Old Lady (from Pasadena)," and "Ride the Wild Surf."

Another major folk act of the time was put together by promoter Albert Grossman, who hoped to duplicate the great success of the Kingston Trio. His creation, **Peter, Paul and Mary,** earned two Grammy Awards with their first top-ten hit, "If I Had a Hammer," in 1962. However, it was the following year that turned out to be their biggest ever, with "Puff the Magic Dragon," "Stewball," and a pair of songs written by another Grossman client,

Bob Dylan: "Don't Think Twice, It's All Right" and "Blowin' in the Wind." PP&M was a unique outfit for a number of reasons, not least of which was their overt political posing. They also did not sing harmonies; rather, were three solo voices in counterpoint. Later hits included "I Dig Rock 'n' Roll Music" (1967) and "Leavin' on a Jet Plane" (1969), after which they departed with the decade.

The fastest-selling disc of all time, according to the *Guinness Book of World Records,* is **"John Fitzgerald Kennedy: A Memorial Album,"** an LP recorded the day of Kennedy's assassination—November 22, 1963. At 99 cents, it sold four million copies in six days (December 7–12), ironically topping the previous speed record set by the comedy album *The First Family* (1962), which had also been about the Kennedys. In 1964, JFK made the LP charts with six more releases, two of which entered the top twenty (*The Presidential Years* and *Memorial Tribute Broadcast*).

THE TOP 40

1. End of the World, *Skeeter Davis*
2. Blue Velvet, *Bobby Vinton*
3. Rhythm of the Rain, *Cascades*
4. Fingertips—Pt. II, *Little Stevie Wonder*
5. Surfin' U.S.A., *Beach Boys*
6. He's So Fine, *Chiffons*
7. Can't Get Used to Losing You, *Andy Williams*
8. Hey Paula, *Paul and Paula*
9. She's a Fool, *Leslie Gore*
10. So Much in Love, *Tymes*
11. It's All Right, *Impressions*
12. I Will Follow Him, *Little Peggy March*
13. My Boyfriend's Back, *Angels*
14. Sugar Shack, *Jimmy Gilmer and the Fireballs*
15. Puff, *Peter, Paul, and Mary*
16. Washington Square, *Village Stompers*
17. Limbo Rock, *Chubby Checker*
18. Walk Like a Man, *Four Seasons*
19. Sukiyaki, *Kyu Sakamoto*
20. Go Away Little Girl, *Steve Lawrence*
21. I'm Leavin' It Up to You, *Dale and Grace*
22. Telstar, *Tornadoes*
23. Mockingbird, *Inez Foxx*
24. I Love You Because, *Al Martino*
25. Return to Sender, *Elvis Presley*
26. Walk Right In, *Rooftop Singers*
27. You're the Reason I'm Living, *Bobby Darin*
28. Up on the Roof, *Drifters*
29. Surf City, *Jan and Dean*
30. If You Wanna Be Happy, *Jimmy Soul*
31. Big Girls Don't Cry, *Four Seasons*
32. Blowin' in the Wind, *Peter, Paul, and Mary*
33. It's My Party, *Leslie Gore*
34. Easier Said Than Done, *Essex*
35. Deep Purple, *Nino Tempo and April Stevens*
36. Pipeline, *Chantays*
37. Wipeout, *Safaris*
38. Wild Weekend, *Rockin' Rebels*
39. Blame It on the Bossa Nova, *Eydie Gormé*
40. Our Day Will Come, *Ruby and the Romantics*

THE TOP 10 LPs

1. West Side Story, *Original Soundtrack*
2. Peter, Paul, and Mary, *Peter, Paul, and Mary*
3. Movin', *Peter, Paul and Mary*
4. In Concert, *Joan Baez*
5. I Left My Heart in San Francisco, *Tony Bennett*
6. Moon River, *Andy Williams*
7. Lawrence of Arabia, *Original Soundtrack*
8. The Days of Wine and Roses, *Andy Williams*
9. Pot Luck, *Elvis Presley*
10. The Barbra Streisand Album, *Barbra Streisand*

The **Ronettes** got together in 1959, making their professional debut at the Peppermint Lounge in New York City as part of Joey Dee's revue. Phil Spector discovered them there in 1963, and within a few months had co-written and produced their all-time biggest hit, "Be My Baby." Later Ronettes records included "Baby I Love You," "The Best Part of Breakin' Up," "Do I Love You," and "Walkin' in the Rain" (all 1964). Four years later, lead singer Ronnie Bennett became the baby of Phil Spector; they were married in Hollywood.

So Much in Love

THE TYMES

The story of the Tymes began in 1956, when George "The Great One" Hilliard met Norman "The Dressy One" Burnett at a summer camp. The two became friends and, that fall, got together with Albert "Caesar" Berry and Donald "The Chief" Banks. This quartet became the Latineers—a popular vocal group at record hops, talent shows, and supper clubs around Philadelphia.

Then in 1960, a fifth member was added—lead singer George Williams, who came to be known as "the black Bing Crosby." At this point, the group decided to change their name and selected "the Tymes," in honor of their favorite New York newspaper.

The sound they developed was clearly an anachronism—polished, precise—a throwback to the barbershop harmonies of the thirties and forties. Their idols were the Ink Spots, Platters, and Mills Brothers, and they emphasized the point by always wearing tuxedos and patent leather shoes. They were "smooth singing, finger-snapping daddies of love," according to one press release; "the love group," because of their cool, swooning style.

In April 1963, the Tymes turned up on a radio variety show broadcast by WDAS. A Cameo Records executive heard them and signed them to his label. The next step was finding a piece of material for their debut release.

"I came up with that," said George. "You see, that was a very romantic time for me. This lady and I were very tight, and we used to walk through this little park in North Philadelphia. I used to say a lot of things that were romantic, I guess, and one day I started to get these words together as we strolled along. She said, 'Say, you ought to try to do something with that.' So I wrote down the lyrics, and the other guys agreed to do the song."

The group cut a rough demo, which

captured the basic melody and first verse of the tune, which was then called "The Stroll."

"We gave it to Cameo, but didn't hear anything from anybody. We all figured, well, we blew our big shot. So we called our producer, Billy Jackson, and he said, 'Hey, we've been trying to find you guys. We think you've really got something here.'"

Billy and arranger Roy Straigis changed the song a little and renamed it "So Much in Love" (to avoid confusion with the Diamonds' record "The Stroll"). It was Billy's idea to add sound effects—the birds, the seashore, and so forth—to make the record more romantic.

"So Much in Love" turned into a dreamy, sentimental song, accented by popping fingers and a gentle, wistful mood. It broke onto the charts in June 1963 and one month later was America's best-selling 45. It remained a major hit all summer long.

Pop critics were quick to point out that George had a sound very similar

to that of Johnny Mathis. Most groups would deny such a fact, but the Tymes actually capitalized on it. As their next release, they remade "Wonderful! Wonderful!," a 1957 Mathis hit. In the fall of 1963, it went top ten, something the Mathis version never did.

The group's last Cameo hit was in the spring of 1964, "Somewhere," from the score of West Side Story. Over the next few years, they cut mostly show tunes and standards. In 1968, they surfaced briefly on Columbia with "People" from Funny Girl.

The Tymes' last major hit was a real surprise—a disco record, in the fall of 1974. RCA was so impressed with "You Little Trustmaker" that deejay copies were pressed in gold vinyl—a first in the company's history. Their confidence paid off, as the record sold 100,000 copies its first week and went on to sell a million.

And, oh, yes—George married the girl with whom he was "So Much in Love."

She's a Fool

LESLEY GORE

The daughter of a Tenafly, New Jersey, bathing suit manufacturer, Lesley Gore was never really interested in singing until her sixteenth birthday party. To enliven the festivities, she sang a few songs, and decided that it would be fun to become a recording star. After five weeks of voice lessons, she made a demo tape which was circulated among the record companies. Twelve different labels offered contracts, with the winning bid coming from Mercury Records. Producer Quincy Jones picked up the story:

"We were having an A&R meeting when Irving Green, the president of Mercury, brought a tape of this unknown singer, and asked if anyone of the staff felt they could do something with her. All hands froze but mine rose, for I felt something in her voice, a sound that hadn't been explored before. On a whim I decided to take on the project of recording Lesley, and after we started hitting I knew that my conscience had led me right."

Lesley's first singles, "It's My Party" and "Judy's Turn to Cry," began an impressive string of ten gold records. The flip side of "Judy," "Just Let Me Cry," was written by Ben Raleigh and Mark Barkan. After it became a million-seller, they were asked to come up with more material. As it happened, they already had a tune ready—one previously rejected.

"We used to go to E. B. Marks, a publisher who let songwriters use their pianos to write songs," said Mark. "I remember 'She's a Fool' came very quickly, in about forty-five minutes. We actually wrote it with the Chiffons in mind. I recall specifically playing it for the Tokens, who were managing the Chiffons at the time. There was a little odd structure in the chorus that went from an E flat chord (in the key of C) to the F, and that threw them off. In those days, everyone was used to just two or three chord songs, so this was a little unusual. It was a simple song, but they couldn't understand what could be done with it. I remember as we walked out the door, I said, 'We'll bring it over to Lesley Gore; she'll record it, and it'll be a big hit!'

"We went right over to Lesley—she liked it—and suggested doing a modulation on every verse.

"The record jumped on the charts on the heels of 'Judy's Turn to Cry,' and there was a problem. Somehow, Mercury had sent out 150,000 *unmixed* copies by mistake. It was slowing down on the charts, not taking those ten point jumps.

"I think it was her producer, Quincy Jones, who discovered the problem. He went and told everybody, 'Hey, this isn't mixed! Let's get the mix!' So when they got the mix out, all the disc jockeys got a hold of the right version and started playing it. In no time it went up into the top five.

"I think there are a number of reasons why 'She's a Fool' did so well. It was following on the heels of two huge hits, a number one and a number two. Another reason was, I think, that E flat chord in the key of C—that little difference for the ear to hear. Also, the story line was right on the money.

"Lesley's records were a continuing story of the same character in various different settings. That may be one of the reasons why she had such consistent success."

Lesley's later releases included "You Don't Own Me," "That's the Way Boys Are," "I Don't Wanna Be a Loser," and "Maybe I Know" (all 1964). In 1965, there were "Look of Love," "Sunshine, Lollipops and Rainbows," and "My Town, My Guy, and Me." Her last big single was "California Nights" in 1967.

"Initially it felt quite strange when the hit records stopped coming," said Leslie. "I had been accustomed to them for three years, so when things came to a halt it was a bit of a trauma. I quickly learned that there was more to life than hits; I sorted out my realities, so to speak, went back to school, and polished up the thing that I knew best: music. I never dealt with it as the death of a career; I looked at it as a hiatus period."

Hey Paula
PAUL and PAULA

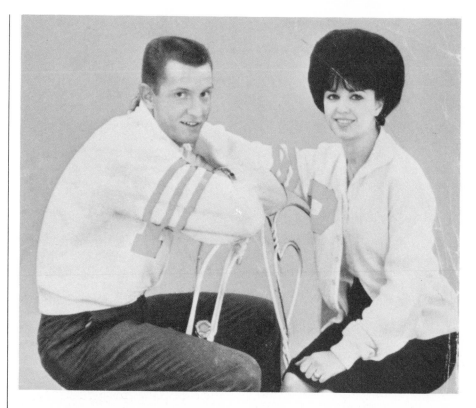

*I*n the fall of 1962, a radio station in Brownsville, Texas, announced a special broadcast to benefit the American Cancer Society. Volunteer performers were invited to come and donate their services before the mike. At nearby Howard Payne College, two students figured it would be fun to appear on the program. They were Ray Hildebrand, from Joshua, Texas, and Jill Jackson, from McCaney, Texas.

On the program, the team sang an original tune written a few days before by Ray. It went over so well that it was suggested that they make a professional recording of the song. So encouraged, Ray and Jill drove to Fort Worth in November 1962, hoping for an audition with Major Bill Smith, the owner of LeCam Records.

At the studio, the two were told that Major Bill was about to record some-one else, and could not see them that day. Determined to get a hearing, they decided to hang around just in case something happened. Something did.

"I was waiting for Amos Milburn, Jr., the son of the famous blues singer, and he didn't show up," recalled Smith. "That meant I had five musicians coolin' their heels at $5 apiece. So Marvin Montgomery said, 'Bill, there's a couple of kids out there that would like to see ya'. I said, 'O.K. What have they got?' He said, 'They've got a couple of little ol' songs and one of them's pretty good.' So I said, 'O.K. Let's record.'

"So in walks this little bitty, beautiful black-haired chick—that was Jill Jackson—and Ray Hildebrand. I said to Ray, 'Let's hear what you got, so he strummed the guitar, and sang, 'Hey-ay Paula. . . .' I said, 'O.K., boy, stop heyin', let's record.' I told Bob Sullivan—he's the engineer on all my hits—to turn the machine on. On the first take, Ray popped his 'P.' 'Let's do it again,' I said. It took two takes, and we cut 'Hey Paula.'

"I said, 'What do you call this song?' He said, 'I call it "Paul and Paula." ' I said, 'What do you call yourselves?' He said, 'Jill and Ray.' I said, 'Let's call it "Hey Paula" by Jill and Ray,' and that's the way it came out on the LeCam label.

"I then went to Nashville to pitch the thing to Ewart Abner, who was with Vee Jay Records. Ewart turned me down and took another instrumental I had called 'The Pink Character Song.' So I decided to release the record myself. I pressed it up on Election Day, 1962, and KSJZ Radio was the first station to play 'Hey Paula.'

"Then Shelby Singleton got wind of this thing. He was with Mercury, and he called me because it had sold sixteen thousand records in one day in Atlanta. He wanted the master, but said, 'Hey, this is stupid. "Hey Paula" by Jill and Ray? We're gonna change their name to Paul and Paula.' So I give Shelby Singleton credit for that idea. At first, Jill and Ray didn't like it, because everybody in Texas knew them as Jill and Ray. But they got used to it."

Singleton released the tune on Mecury's subsidiary label, Philips. It broke nationally right after Christmas 1962, and spent three weeks in February at number one. Incredibly, it also hit number one on the R&B charts as well. In all, it spent fifteen weeks on the best-seller list, moving more than two million copies worldwide.

Soon after "Hey Paula," Jill and Ray got married—but not to each other. This caused some problems on the road, and one night, while part of a Dick Clark Caravan of Stars, Ray got "tired and miserable" and flew home to Texas. Finally, in 1965, the team officially broke up.

Ray later found work as a songwriter and record producer, but eventually left the music business. Jill went on as an active performer, working as a solo act in Texas.

Can't Get Used to Losing You

ANDY WILLIAMS

Andy Williams began his singing career in his hometown of Wall Lake, Iowa, a farming community with a population of 749. His father, Jay Williams, a railway mail clerk, was the leader of the local Presbyterian church choir. To prove he was an active doer rather than a passive follower, the senior Williams, his wife, Florence, and their four sons—Bob, Don, Dick, and Andy—became the entire choir.

The group made a strong impression on the local citizenry and soon had their own radio show over WHO in Des Moines. They moved on to WLS in Chicago, and later to WLW in Cincinnati. Encouraged with this early success, the family then moved west to California, while Andy was still attending high school, and settled in Los Angeles.

For the next few years, the Williams Brothers continued to work on local radio stations in California. In 1946, the four boys joined with comedienne Kay Thompson. The troupe, known as Kay Thompson and the Williams Brothers, made its nightclub debut in 1947. For six years the act toured the United States and Europe.

Finally, in 1953, they broke up, and so did the Williams Brothers. Andy now faced an important decision—should he give up show biz, team with another group, or try to make it alone?

He opted for the solo route and wound up in New York with Steve Allen's "Tonight Show." A two-week commitment stretched into almost three years, and Andy was on his way.

While a "Tonight Show" regular, Andy was signed to Cadence Records by label owner Archie Bleyer. This contract led to ten albums and sixteen charted songs over a six-year period. Among the biggest hits were "Canadian Sunset" (1956), "Butterfly" and "I Like Your Kind of Love" (1957), "Are You Sincere?" and "Promise Me Love" (1958), "Hawaiian Wedding Song" and "Lonely Street" (1959), and "Village

of St. Bernadette" (1960). During this same time—the late fifties—Andy starred on three summer TV series, each on a different network.

Finally, on September 27, 1962, "The Andy Williams Show" began as a weekly prime-time NBC program. During its first season, it won an Emmy Award as the Best Musical-Variety Series. It was part comedy, part song, and the perfect vehicle for exposing hit records.

Andy changed labels to Columbia and began releasing LPs and singles. They sold moderately well, but below expectations. Andy then decided to tie in an album with a current motion picture. One of the biggest at the time was Blake Edwards's *Days of Wine and Roses,* starring Jack Lemmon and Lee Remick. So, with the aid of arranger-conductor Robert Mersey, Andy recorded an LP titled after the film.

Naturally, the song "Days of Wine and Roses," written by Johnny Mercer and Henry Mancini, was chosen as the first single. For the B side, Columbia threw on the least commercial filler track from that album. It, of course, turned out to be "Can't Get Used to Losing You."

The composers of that tune were "Doc" Jerome Pomus and Mort Shuman, one of the finest pop songwriting teams of the early sixties. Among their credits: "She's Not You," "Surrender," "This Magic Moment," "Teenager in Love," and "Save the Last Dance for Me." They were glad to have Andy record one of their songs, but certainly didn't think it would go on to become a hit.

Then Andy sang "Can't Get Used to Losing You" on his TV show. The single was released, but flipped by deejays. Early in March, the B side entered the pop charts, trailed—two weeks later—by the A side. By April, "Can't Get Used to Losing You" was a major smash—and the flip, an also-ran.

"Can't Get Used to Losing You"

became Andy Williams' all-time best-selling single, and the album it came from, his first gold LP. *Billboard* magazine called it the Best Vocal Album of 1963. Afterward, Andy had several more chart hits, including "Hopeless" (1963), "A Fool Never Learns" (1964), and "Love Story" (1971).

Andy continued on TV (with a two-year interruption) until July of 1971. Since then, he's devoted himself to live appearances, TV specials, and the Andy Williams San Diego Open Golf Tournament.

He's So Fine

THE CHIFFONS

The Chiffons did not go out of their way to become stars. They were close friends who attended the big R&B shows at the Apollo in New York. Afterward, they'd go back to their school lunchroom and imitate what they'd seen, just for the fun of it.

One day, the girls were overheard by a piano-playing friend, Ronnie Mack, who asked them to help him record a demo of some of his songs. He rounded up $25—the cost of an hour of studio time—and they cut as many tunes as they could. Nothing much came of it, and by the time graduation rolled around, the girls had pretty much forgotten about the session.

Meanwhile, Ronnie was playing the tape for anyone who would listen. Finally, it was heard by the Tokens, who were then hot from their hit, "The Lion Sleeps Tonight." They agreed to produce finished versions of several of the songs, including "He's So Fine." Ronnie found the girls again, and brought them to Manhattan's Mirror Sound Studios. There, in short order,

new recordings of the best tunes were made.

The completed masters were sold to Laurie Records, a local label made famous by Dion and the Belmonts. For six months, the girls heard nothing. Then, Ronnie called, and announced that "He's So Fine" was selling at the rate of five thousand copies a day. The girls were thrilled, and in late February their single broke onto the national charts. In April, it reached number one and stayed there for four weeks.

The Chiffons immediately began work on a follow-up. Under the Tokens' direction, over $20,000 was spent on backup musicians and endless studio time. Finally, Carole King stepped in and offered the girls a completed track, featuring the voice of Little Eva. Eva's voice was erased, the Chiffons' dropped in, and a single released. "One Fine Day" soared to number five in the summer of 1963.

By that time, the Chiffons were angry. Because of the $20,000 spent on musicians and studio time, each Chiffon had only made about $1,000

from "He's So Fine." They sued, and broke free of the Tokens. However, as the girls could neither write, produce, nor play instruments, they found themselves unable to make any more records.

Instead, they hit the road, saw America, and became the first U.S. girl group to tour with the Beatles. They made a film, *Discotheque Holiday,* and in 1966, scored a brief comeback with the top-ten single, "Sweet Talkin' Guy." Then, in 1969, lead singer Judy Craig retired from the grind. The others—Barbara Lee, Patricia Stelley, and Sylvia Peterson—went on, and still make appearances as the Chiffons in the New York area.

And as for "He's So Fine"? Well, eventually the copyright owners sued George Harrison, claiming that his "My Sweet Lord" was a direct steal of their melody. George put up a good fight, but wound up losing his court battle. Today all royalties from "My Sweet Lord" go to the heirs of Ronnie Mack, who died of Hodgkin's disease during the sixties.

Surfin' U.S.A.
THE BEACH BOYS

The Beach Boys began in a bedroom shared by three brothers in Hawthorne, California. It was there that Brian, Carl, and Dennis Wilson—all fans of the Everly Brothers, Hi-Los, and Four Freshmen—tried to imitate their idols' harmony styles. Eventually the boys' cousin, Mike Love, and a school friend, Al Jardine, joined in. The five worked up an intricate vocal style that sounded so exciting that they decided to form a group, and call it Carl and the Passions.

At about this time, surfing was catching on big around Southern California, and Dennis became an early proponent (his nickname at Hawthorne High actually was "Surfin'"). With great enthusiasm, he suggested that the new group put together a song based on the surfing craze. Mike came up with some words, Brian with some music, and before long they had written a tune called "Surfin'."

The boys then changed their name to the Pendletones (after a kind of windbreaker favored by surfers) and recorded their song for a local label, X Records, in 1961. However, the company folded right after that, and the master was passed on to another firm. Re-released on the Candix label in February 1962, "Surfin'" made the national charts, climbing to number seventy-five in March. The record, though, was not credited to the Pendletones. At the last minute—without telling the group—Candix publicist Russ Regan had changed their name to "the Beach Boys."

Candix folded in the spring of 1962, and so the brothers' father, Murry Wilson, took the Beach Boys' material to other labels. The masters were turned down everywhere, even though Murry's asking price was only $100. Finally Nick Venet, a house producer at Capitol Records, showed interest and put the group under contract. It was at this point that Al

Jardine left to begin studies at dental school. His replacement was David Marks, another friend who played rhythm guitar. David was to appear on all the Beach Boys recordings released through the end of 1963.

The single, "409," backed with "Surfin' Safari," was their first for Capitol, issued in May of 1962. The original A side was "409," but it faltered, and after a few months the record was flipped over. "Surfin' Safari" finally made it to number fourteen in November, becoming the Beach Boys' first real national hit.

The group began 1963 with one of their biggest singles ever, "Surfin' U.S.A.," a virtual checklist of all the best surfing spots in the country. The tune was adapted from "Sweet Little Sixteen," Chuck Berry's big hit of 1958, with new lyrics by Brian Wilson. However, when the single was released, only Brian's name was listed as a composer. Chuck Berry sued over this and eventually won his case: today, all pressings credit Chuck Berry, and only Chuck Berry, as writer of this song.

"Surfin' U.S.A." became a monster hit in the spring of 1963; even the flip

side, "Shut Down," got lots and lots of play. The next two Beach Boys singles were also double-sided hits: "Surfer Girl," backed with "Little Deuce Coupe," and "In My Room," backed with "Be True to Your School." Also in 1963, the Beach Boys played a concert with Jan and Dean and wound up performing on one of their albums. Brian and Jan Berry even wrote together; one of their songs, "Surf City," turned into Jan and Dean's biggest hit single ever. It was also the first surf single ever to make it to number one.

The Beach Boys always said that they never really sang about surfing; they simply used surfing "as a way to sing about freedom." Be that as it may, there were only two members of the group who even *tried* the sport—Dennis, an avid champion, and Alan, who nearly drowned while trying. Brian, their chief composer, used the slang of the surf better than any other songwriter of the sixties. Yet he himself rarely, if ever, went to the beach.

"I was scared of the water," he said, in all seriousness. "It *really* scared me."

Fingertips—Pt. II
STEVIE WONDER

Born in Saginaw, Michigan, Stephen Judkins Hardaway was the third of six children whose family later moved to Detroit. Blind since birth, Stevie never looked upon it as a handicap. "I did what all the kids my age were doing," he said. "I played games, rode bikes, and climbed trees." His introduction to music came when an uncle gave him a six-hole harmonica on a chain, which Stevie wore around his neck. After that, he sat by the hour in front of the radio, playing along with bluesmen Little Walter and Jimmy Reed.

In 1961, he was brought to Motown by a young friend's big brother, Ronnie White of the Miracles. "I didn't realize I was going through an audition," Stevie recalled. "I was just having fun singing." Berry Gordy, the president of Motown, was so impressed with the young man's natural style that he immediately signed him up. Gordy also gave him his stage name—"Little Stevie Wonder, the Ten-Year-Old Genius."

Motown was a special place for their "Little Wonder." "Everyone over eleven was my parent. Wanda of the Marvelettes would always tell me if she thought I was eating too much candy. All the musicians and artists watched over me. I used to get in a lot of trouble then. I loved to play jokes on people. I knew the com line numbers of everyone at Motown, and would change my voice and say, 'This is Berry. I want you to get Stevie that tape recorder right away. He's a great new artist, so it's O.K. He'll have it back in a few days.' After they fell for this about three times, and never got the tape recorder back, they gave me a recorder as a belated birthday present. I had turned eleven that May, and received the tape recorder that September."

Stevie was on the label for nearly two years before his career took off. Three early singles failed, as did his first LP, *The Jazz Soul of Little Stevie.*

In that album was the original studio version of "Fingertips."

Motown then decided to give Stevie exposure by taking him on one of their package tours, "the Motortown Revue." "As it became necessary to go on the road, I couldn't keep up with my school studies," he explained. "And no one came along who was qualified to tutor me. Because of this, my teachers told me that I should stop pursuing music, and continue my education. They informed me that they could legally keep me in school. I went into the bathroom and cried and prayed that God would allow me to remain in the industry. One of my teachers told me that I had three strikes against me—I was poor, black, and blind. I should buckle down and try to forget music."

One stop on the tour was the legendary Apollo Theater in New York. Motown crews were there, recording each show, and in one performance, Stevie roused the crowd so highly that a totally improvised reprise of "Fingertips" extended the song beyond its normal length. "On the *Jazz Soul* album we recorded 'Fingertips' in the key of G," Stevie explained. "On stage, we decided to change the key to C, and that's when the excitement started."

Stevie's live version was released on an album entitled *The 12-Year-Old Genius.* From there, the track was pulled as a single, and because of its length, was split over two sides. Initially, Part I was considered the A side, but deejays quickly flipped the record, and began playing the side with the improvisation. Issued on June 22, 1963, "Fingertips—Pt. II" was an instant-add on radio stations across the country. It reached number one in August, spending nearly four months on the charts.

Stevie went on to score three dozen top-forty hits in the sixties and seventies. He made several films and concert tours, and gained great

renown as a popular album artist. On August 5, 1975, he signed the biggest contract in the history of the recording industry. It called for guarantees to Stevie, over a seven-year period, of more than thirteen million dollars. That unprecedented sum was equal to the deals of Neil Diamond and Elton John combined.

"It was a learning experience," said Stevie, of "Fingertips." "That's what the journey of life is: to learn, experience, and remember. I like to think that my music means me, how I feel and what I want to say."

Rhythm of the Rain

THE CASCADES

According to one source, the Cascades were "a clean cut bunch of skindiving mountaineers" who "specialized in soft, pretty, summery sounds." The group consisted of John Gummoe, Eddie Snyder, Dave Stevens, Dave Wilson, and Dave Zabo—all from San Diego, California.

The quintet built its reputation at parties and school dances in the Southern California area. Eventually, they became kind of a house band at one of the most popular local clubs, the Peppermint Stick. There they were seen by an executive from Valiant Records, who auditioned them and signed them to his label.

Their very first recording session was held late in 1962 at Gold Star Studios in Hollywood. John Gummoe brought in three songs to record, all written recently. One of them was "Rhythm of the Rain."

"It was a relatively simple session—not complicated at all," recalled arranger Perry Bodkin, Jr. "They weren't terribly difficult to record. John Gummoe was a very good lead singer. He was very musical. He already had the song pretty much laid out the way he wanted to do it.

"I think my biggest contribution was a little sort of musical figure behind the tune. All the way through you hear a celeste piano thing that goes deet doo deet doo-deet doo, deet doo deet-doo. I remember sitting at the piano and finding that figure and everybody saying, 'Oh yeah, that's great!'

"The record starts off with a thunderclap and some rain. At Gold Star there were two sound effects records—birds and surf, and thunder and rain. Those same effects must have turned up on at least three or four major hit records. The Ronettes' 'Walkin' in the Rain' was one of them, absolutely, because Phil Spector produced all his stuff there."

The smooth sound of the Cascades brought them immediate success in 1963; "Rhythm of the Rain" broke in the U.S. during the second week of January. It peaked at number three in March, spending a total of sixteen weeks amid America's best-sellers. It was also a top-five hit in England, when released there on the Warner Brothers label.

The Cascades issued an album called *Rhythm of the Rain,* and then tried to follow the success of their single with another song, "Shy Girl," in April 1963. It failed to generate much interest, so deejays flipped the 45 over and started to play the other side, "The Last Leaf." It struggled to number sixty on the charts and then expired. After that, the group moved to RCA Victor, and cut "For Your Sweet Love"—another flop—in December 1963.

The Cascades toured extensively for the next decade and a half, playing mostly colleges, hotels, and nightclubs. They occasionally released singles on small regional labels, but none managed to click. In 1969, they were given one last chance by a major, Uni, which issued "Maybe the Rain Must Fall." It rose to number sixty-one and then vanished.

The Cascades continued to perform live until the mid-seventies, when they broke up back in their old home town.

Blue Velvet

BOBBY VINTON

After the success of "Roses Are Red," Bobby Vinton won a poll as "the most promising male vocalist of 1962." Over the next dozen years he more than kept that promise, selling in excess of thirty million records.

In 1963, Burt Bacharach wrote a major hit for Bobby, "Blue on Blue." As a follow-up, Vinton decided to do an "all-blue" album of "all-blue" material. Some of the early choices were easy: "Blue Hawaii," "My Blue Heaven," and "It's Been a Blue, Blue Day." Then a friend in Nashville suggested another "blue" number— "Blue Velvet."

Bobby had always liked the song, especially the way Tony Bennett introduced it in 1951. (Three years later, it was covered for the R&B market by the Clovers.) Bobby decided to add the tune to his album and was very pleased with the result.

He was startled, though, when his record company called, saying that they wanted to put it out as a single. Bobby agreed that it was "a pretty song," but felt it was inappropriate for the time. "This is an age of really hard music," he said. "I don't think record buyers today want soft sounds." Epic executives thought otherwise.

Over Vinton's protests, "Blue Velvet" was released on a 45 in early August 1963. It sped up the charts, spending three weeks at number one in September—fifteen weeks on the best-seller list over all. "It just goes to show," he said, "what I know about hit music." Within a matter of days, the tune had become his second gold record.

Vinton's career was at a peak in 1963; he was so popular, in fact, that eight orchestras bearing his name

were on the road, one of them led by his father. He had several other top-forty hits that year, including "Let's Kiss and Make Up," "Trouble Is My Middle Name," and "Over the Mountain."

Bobby closed out 1963 with his third number-one song, "There! I've Said It Again." Early the next year, it was bounced from the top spot by "I Want to Hold Your Hand," the first U.S. Beatles hit. The British invasion of 1964 washed many of Bobby's contemporaries off the charts, but somehow Vinton survived. Indeed, '64 was probably his best year ever: "My Heart Belongs to Only You," "Tell Me Why," "Clinging Vine," and his fourth number one, "Mr. Lonely."

Bobby went on to chart more than two dozen other songs, among them, "Long Lonely Nights" (1965), "Coming Home Soldier" (1966), "Please Love Me Forever" (1967), and "I Love How You Love Me" (1968). In 1974, he staged a dramatic comeback with his own composition, "My Melody of Love." After spending $50,000 of his own money producing the song, he took it to seven major record companies for distribution. They all turned him down. The eighth company, ABC Records, decided to take a chance, and within three months, "My Melody of Love" was the number-one song in the nation. It was embraced by Polish Americans around the country as their new national anthem, and Bobby, in turn, became their "Polish Prince."

Vinton hosted his own syndicated TV series in 1975–76, and continued as a popular nightclub performer. He was, in fact, the only known entertainer to hold three simultaneous contracts with major Las Vegas hotels: The MGM Grand, The Flamingo Hilton and the Riviera.

Summing up his career, Bobby looked back laughingly at an article in *Life* magazine entitled, "So Who Is This Bobby Vinton?" which appeared in 1965. The article described Bobby as the "most successful unknown in show business." Said Bobby, "That just goes to show you. I'm still here, and they're gone!!"

The End of the World

SKEETER DAVIS

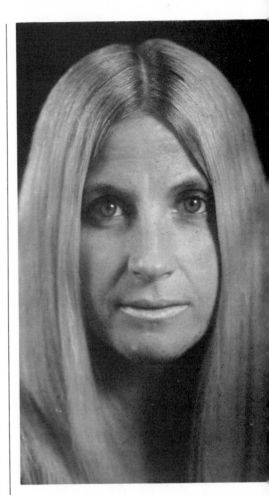

Mary Francis Penick, the eldest of seven children, was born in a rundown house just outside of Dry Ridge, Kentucky. While still in her teens, she worked up a vocal duet with her best friend, Betty Jack Davis. For billing purposes, they decided to call themselves the Davis Sisters—Bee Jay and Skeeter. The latter was a nickname given to Mary by her grandfather, who said that as a child she zipped around just like a mosquito.

The girls played a few local clubs in the area and then began broadcasting in 1949 over WLAX in Lexington. More radio dates and Grand Ole Opry appearances followed, culminating in a record contract with RCA Victor. On August 2, 1953, the duo performed over WWVA in Wheeling, West Virginia, and then set off by car for Cincinnati. Shortly after crossing the Ohio state border, their auto was struck head on by another motorist who swerved over the divider line. Betty Jack was killed instantly; her partner escaped virtually unscathed. Skeeter, though, was emotionally devastated and didn't sing again for another six months.

A week after the crash, the girls' first single, "I Forgot More Than You'll Ever Know," entered the country charts. It eventually climbed to number one, inspiring RCA to press Skeeter to continue the act with Bee Jay's sister, Georgia. The new combination failed to work out—there were no more hits, and the pair did not get along together. Eventually, their squabbles led to a split.

A couple of years went by, and then Steve Sholes signed up Skeeter again. She got quite a bit of deejay play but no big hits for some time.

Then in 1959, Skeeter made the country top five with a song called "Set Him Free." More successes

followed, including "Homebreaker," "Am I That Easy to Forget?," and "(I Can't Help You) I'm Falling Too." The last, an answer record to Hank Locklin's "Please Help Me I'm Falling," crossed over onto the pop charts and became Skeeter's first top-forty record. Her next single, "My Last Date (with You)," did the same (it was a vocal version of Floyd Cramer's "Last Date").

The country hits continued, and then in 1962, Summit Music sent a most unusual song to the attention of Chet Atkins at RCA. The composer was Sylvia Dee, the same woman who, in 1951, had provided Nat King Cole with his biggest-ever record, "Too Young." The new tune had been inspired by the death of Sylvia's father, an event she likened to "the end of the world." A trembling, part-spoken ballad, it was a lament of broken love and emotional loss. Chet Atkins felt it would make a perfect tribute to Bee Jay, and easily convinced Skeeter to record it. "One thing about Skeeter," Chet said, "was that she didn't sound all that well when singing by herself. But if you let her add her own harmony, she could sound really sensational. So I always had her sing along to tapes of herself. You could stack on as many voices as you wanted, and the result was terrific. Before she came along, we'd actually done very little multitrack recording."

"The End of the World" was released late in 1962 and peaked on both the pop and country charts early the next spring. It was also an international hit—a top-twenty record in England and abroad. Later in 1963, she entered the pop top ten for a second time with "I Can't Stay Mad at You." Over the next decade, she was to score more than a dozen additional hits, all on the country charts.

Today, Skeeter occasionally reflects on her days in the poplight, when she regularly appeared on the TV shows

of Dick Clark and Duke Ellington, and even sang on a Rolling Stones special. "I got a gold record from South Africa, and a silver record from Norway, and various other awards that I'm proud of, but because of 'The End of the World' and some other records that got on the pop charts as well as country, some folks thought I wasn't country anymore. But I've stayed with the Grand Ole Opry since joining in 1959, which proves that my heart's in the country. I'll probably never have another one like 'The End of the World,' and frankly, I don't think I'd want another one."

1964

THANKS TO AN INCREASED interest in LPs, U.S. record sales hit an all-time high in 1964, topping $700 million. Since the decade began, $3.3 billion worth had been sold—a figure greater than that for all of the fifties. *Hello, Dolly!* and *Funny Girl* both opened on Broadway, while on TV, a new show called "The Hollywood Palace" premiered. Among the first guests were the Rolling Stones. "Their hair is not long," remarked host Dean Martin. "It's just smaller foreheads and higher eyebrows." Later, the Stones' Mick Jagger met a new girlfriend—Marianne Faithful. Sonny and Cher were married; the Byrds and Styx got together (separately). Johnny Burnette drowned, Jim Reeves died in a plane crash, and Sam Cooke was shot to death. Little Stevie Wonder dropped the "little," Bing Crosby got his own TV show, and the Isley Brothers hired a $30-a-night backup guitarist—Jimi Hendrix. It was 1964—the year the Beatles held down the top five slots simultaneously on *Billboard*'s Hot 100 chart. (It was the week of April 4; they also occupied numbers 16, 44, 49, 69, 74, 84, and 89.)

On September 16, ABC introduced "Shindig," a prime-time rock 'n' roll variety series hosted by former deejay Jimmy O'Neill. Other regulars included Bobby Sherman, the Righteous Brothers, and a house band known as the Shindogs (featuring, at various times, Delaney Bramlett, Glen Campbell, David Gates, Billy Preston, and Leon Russell). The Beatles turned up on the October 7 show; later, the Stones, Kinks, **Byrds** (pictured), and Everly Brothers also made appearances. In 1965, the Who made their American TV debut on the program. "Shindig" was canceled on January 8, 1966 to make room for "Batman."

The Beatles starred in their first film in 1964: a "fictionalized documentary" called *A Hard Day's Night,* directed by Richard Lester. Ringo came up with the title, while United Artists came up with the bucks—a minuscule budget of only $500,000. The picture went on to earn more than $13.5 million and two Academy Award nominations. The title song also won a Grammy as the Best Performance by a Vocal Group. Other 1964 music movies included *Bikini Beach,* with Frankie Avalon, Annette Funicello, and Stevie Wonder (Frankie and Annette also turned up in *Beach Party* and *Muscle Beach Party*); *Get Yourself a College Girl* with the Animals, the Standells, and the Dave Clark Five; *Ferry Cross the Mersey* with Gerry and the Pacemakers; *Kissin' Cousins* with Elvis; *Ride the Wild Surf* with Fabian, Tab Hunter, and Shelley Fabares; *Just for You* with the Bachelors, Peter and Gordon, and Freddie and the Dreamers; *Looking for Love* with Connie Francis; *For Those Who Think Young* with James Darren and Nancy Sinatra; and the legendary *T.A.M.I. Show,* featuring live performances by Jan and Dean, the Rolling Stones, Chuck Berry, James Brown, Marvin Gaye, the Beach Boys, Leslie Gore, Billy J. Kramer, Gerry and the Pacemakers, Smokey Robinson and the Miracles, and the Supremes. Who could ask for anything more?

The British Invasion began in 1964 when TWA Flight 101 touched down at New York's Kennedy Airport. On board were the **Beatles,** bringing with them social, cultural, and musical revolution. Their success opened the door to America for countless English acts to follow: the Animals, Manfred Mann, the Dave Clark Five, Peter and Gordon, the Honeycombs, Dusty Springfield, the Kinks, Billy J. Kramer, the Rolling Stones, Chad and Jeremy, the Bachelors, Petula Clark, the Searchers, Freddie and the Dreamers, Tom Jones, the Seekers, Gerry and the Pacemakers, the Nashville Teens, Wayne Fontana and the Mindbenders, the Fortunes, Herman's Hermits, the Zombies, the Silkie, the Moody Blues, the Yardbirds, and many, many more.

Following the breakthrough of the Beatles, dozens of British stars stormed the American charts, many emulating the happy sound and well-scrubbed looks of those four adorable moptops. The **Rolling Stones,** however, took a different approach—coming on, in the words of one critic, like "dirty, unwashed enemies of the public decency." On their album covers they didn't even smile—they *scowled*—setting a whole trend for other bands who shared their "street-tough" stance. While the Fab Four seemed perfectly content to hold a girl's hand, the Stones were obviously reaching elsewhere. Their version of a Buddy Holly song, "Not Fade Away," marked their stateside debut (it made the top fifty in July). After that came "Tell Me" (in August) and "It's All Over Now" (in September). Then, in December, Mick Jagger, Keith Richard, Brian Jones, Charlie Watts, and Bill Wyman made the U.S. top ten for the first time with "Time Is on My Side." It was really that bluesy, prophetic record that established the Rolling Stones—a group that would still be rocking and rolling two decades later.

Another key British Invasion band was **Herman's Hermits,** easily one of the best-loved and best-remembered of the era (Elvis called them one of his favorite English acts). Originally the Heartbeats, they changed their name because of their lead singer, Peter Noone, who bore a strong resemblance to Sherman, a cartoon character on the "Bullwinkle" TV series. The Hermits specialized in good-time, easy-rocking songs, with catchy melodies, fine harmonies, and solid instrumental back-up. Churning out material for the group were some of the best pop tunesmiths of the day: Gerry Goffin and Carole King, Ray Davies, P. F. Sloan, Graham Gouldman, and others. The boys made their debut in October 1964 with "I'm into Something Good". After that came nine top-ten records in a row, including "Listen People," "I'm Henry VIII I Am," and "Mrs. Brown You've Got a Lovely Daughter." Herman's Hermits continued their unbroken string of hits well into 1968, earning several trade awards and setting box office records around the world (one summer, they were second only to the Beatles as a concert attraction). The band broke up in 1972; in 1980, Peter Noone returned in a New Wave-ish outfit, the Tremblers.

THE TOP 40

1. I Want to Hold Your Hand, *Beatles*
2. She Loves You, *Beatles*
3. Hello, Dolly!, *Louis Armstrong*
4. Oh, Pretty Woman, *Roy Orbison*
5. I Get Around, *Beach Boys*
6. My Guy, *Mary Wells*
7. Everybody Loves Somebody, *Dean Martin*
8. Where Did Our Love Go, *Supremes*
9. Love Me Do, *Beatles*
10. People, *Barbra Streisand*
11. Java, *Al Hirt*
12. A Hard Day's Night, *Beatles*
13. Glad All Over, *Dave Clark Five*
14. Under the Boardwalk, *Drifters*
15. Love Me with All Your Heart, *Ray Charles Singers*
16. Little Children, *Billy J. Kramer*
17. Chapel of Love, *Dixie Cups*
18. Louie Louie, *Kingsmen*
19. We'll Sing in the Sunshine, *Gale Garnett*
20. Last Kiss, *J. Frank Wilson*
21. Suspicion, *Terry Stafford*
22. Dominique, *Singing Nun*
23. Bread and Butter, *Newbeats*
24. Please Please Me, *Beatles*
25. Rag Doll, *Four Seasons*
26. Dawn, *Four Seasons*
27. There, I've Said It Again, *Bobby Vinton*
28. Doo Wah Diddy, *Manfred Mann*
29. Dancing in the Street, *Martha Reeves and the Vandellas*
30. Since I Fell for You, *Lenny Welch*
31. Forget Him, *Bobby Rydell*
32. World Without Love, *Peter and Gordon*
33. It Hurts to Be in Love, *Gene Pitney*
34. Dead Man's Curve, *Jan and Dean*
35. Come a Little Bit Closer, *Jay and the Americans*
36. Wishin' 'n' Hopin', *Dusty Springfield*
37. Popsicles and Icicles, *Mermaids*
38. Don't Let the Rain Come Down, *Serendipity Singers*
39. Baby Love, *Supremes*
40. Can I Get a Witness, *Marvin Gaye*

THE TOP 10 LPs

1. Honey in the Horn, *Al Hirt*
2. Blowin' in the Wind, *Peter, Paul and Mary*
3. Hello Dolly!, *Original Cast*
4. West Side Story, *Original Soundtrack*
5. Meet the Beatles, *Beatles*
6. The Barbra Streisand Album, *Barbra Streisand*
7. The Second Barbra Streisand Album, *Barbra Streisand*
8. Peter, Paul and Mary, *Peter, Paul and Mary*
9. Louie Louie, *Kingsmen*
10. Catch a Rising Star, *John Gary*

Most girl groups of this period fell into one of two categories: they were either sweet, cuddly, and lovable—or they were not. It was a golden age for "punk goddesses"—tough on the outside, yet warm and willing on the inside. One of the most successful of these was the **Shangri-las,** two sets of twin sisters from New York City. Their records were perfect three-minute melodramas: a blend of strings, sound effects, and intimate girl gossip. "Remember Walkin' in the Sand," "Leader of the Pack," and "Give Him a Great Big Kiss" were all big in 1964; in '65, "Give Us Your Blessings" and "I Can Never Go Home Anymore." Their last hits were in 1966: "Long Live Our Love," and the eerie "Past, Present and Future."

10

People
BARBRA STREISAND

When Barbra Streisand first listened to the inner voice that told her to "go west young girl" and seek her fortune, the trip meant only a forty-minute subway ride from her home in Flatbush to the show business world of Manhattan. The year was 1957, and she was only fifteen years old.

She quickly landed parts in such plays as *The Desk* and *Picnic,* and the next year, after graduating from high school, moved permanently to the theater district. She found a place to live, lined up a day job, and began taking evening drama classes.

Her first break came on April 5, 1961, when she made her network television debut on the old "Tonight Show" featuring Jack Paar. Jack happened to be off that night, so Barbra was met instead by guest host Orson Bean. Her attire that evening was a plain black dress adorned with an antique vest, which she had picked up in a Salvation Army store.

A few months later, Barbra appeared off-Broadway in *Another Evening with Harry Stoones,* a show that happened to close after one night. In the audience, though, was producer David Merrick, who gave her the part of Miss Marmelstein in his latest project, *I Can Get It for You Wholesale.* Shortly after it opened in March of 1962, Barbra fell in love with her leading man—a young unknown by the name of Elliot Gould. She invited him to share her junk-filled, rat-infested apartment, which was located over a fish market. At first, Elliot refused to even enter the building, but in due course he got used to the smell, and before long they were married.

In the meantime, *I Can Get It for You Wholesale* was released as an original cast LP, with Barbra's performance clearly the best part of the record. Columbia then stepped in with a lucrative solo contract, and in April 1963, issued *The Barbra Streisand Album.* It quickly became a top-ten

hit, and remained on the LP charts for more than one hundred weeks. Later, it won two Grammy Awards: Best Female Vocal Performance and, most notably, Album of the Year. In a veritably short period of time, Barbra had rocketed from total obscurity to international fame—and, of course, her ascent was only beginning.

More best-selling LPs followed: *The Second Barbra Streisand Album* and, inevitably, *The Third Barbra Streisand Album.* Then, on March 26, 1964, she opened on Broadway in the title role of *Funny Girl,* a play inspired by the life and loves of vaudeville comedienne Fanny Brice. For the first time, Barbra played "the Streisand character"—a plucky, wisecracking, Jewish cinderella, who, through sheer audacity, rose to heights unattainable by mere beauties. The emotional high point came when "Fanny" grew up, and shedding her youthful awkwardness, walked onstage to sing "People."

Her song brought down the house, and in early April a single's version entered the American pop charts. By

June it was one of the best-selling records in the country, and Barbra's very first hit 45. It earned her a Grammy Award as the Best Female Vocal Performance of 1964. A second Grammy was given to Peter Matz for his Best Accompaniment arrangement. The song also inspired an album called *People*—Barbra's first number one LP.

In 1968, Streisand made her motion picture debut in the film version of *Funny Girl.* For her efforts she won a Golden Globe Award, and was named Star of the Year by the National Association of Theater Owners. She also shared the Oscar for Best Actress with Katharine Hepburn.

Obviously, Barbra identified very closely with Fanny Brice; both were "Funny Girls" who, through their own actions had made it with very little compromise. "I arrived," said Streisand, "without having my nose fixed, my teeth capped, or my name changed. That was very gratifying to me."

Love Me Do
THE BEATLES

The Beatles story on record began in 1961 when they recorded "My Bonnie" as a backup band for Tony Sheridan. It was that single that inspired Brian Epstein to seek them out and eventually become their manager. On June 6, 1962, the Beatles auditioned for George Martin, the A&R director of EMI Parlophone Records. George Martin saw something in them and on sheer intuition signed them to his label.

Martin studied the band and decided that Pete Best, the Beatles' drummer, had to be replaced. The other three agreed to this, and so, shortly before their first EMI session on September 11, Pete was asked to leave. He later recorded briefly on his own and even released an LP entitled *Best of the Beatles.* At last word, he was operating a forklift truck at a warehouse in London.

The first song the Beatles chose to record for EMI was "Love Me Do," one of about fifty songs that John and Paul had put together in 1957, while trying to refine their writing style. During that period, the boys studied music trade papers and tried to write in whatever form was predicted as "the next big thing." But it was only when they started writing what worked for *them* that the two began to turn out bonafide hit songs.

When the Beatles showed up at EMI Studios to record "Love Me Do," they brought along their new drummer, Ringo Starr, to "break in." George Martin, though, was not about to risk having the date loused up by a musician he didn't know. Instead, he brought in his own man, Andy White. Ringo retreated to a corner, looking depressed for much of the session.

It took seventeen takes to perfect "Love Me Do," each one engineered by Norman "Hurricane" Smith. Ringo played drums on at least one take and tambourine on another. On every take, John Lennon threw in a harmonica solo, inspired by Delbert McClinton on Bruce Channel's "Hey! Baby" (one of his favorite records) and Frank Ifield's "I Remember You." The effect made "Love Me Do" a "pretty funky record," in John's words, and was repeated on "Please Please Me" and "From Me to You." After that, Lennon dropped it, fearing that the harmonica might become "a predictable gimmick."

At the same session, the boys managed to record another song, "P.S. I Love You," which had also been conceived by Paul. Ringo played maracas on this cut, with Andy White again on drums.

After the session was over, George Martin had trouble choosing one song over another as an A side for the single. Peggy Lee had a record called "P.S. I Love You." It might be confusing, he figured, if the Beatles also put one out. For that reason, Martin decided—with some reluctance—to mark "Love Me Do" as the A side. He also decided in a last-minute change of heart to release the version of "Love Me Do" with Ringo playing drums.

Issued October 5, 1962, "Love Me Do" climbed to number seventeen on the U.K. hit parade, thanks mainly to strong sales in Liverpool. Later, the single was offered to EMI's American affiliate, Capitol Records, for stateside release, along with "Please Please Me," "From Me to You," "Twist and Shout," "She Loves You," and other early material. Capitol rejected the songs outright as "noncommercial" and offered them gladly to any other U.S. label crazy enough to take them on. Vee Jay agreed to take twelve of the tunes and packaged them in an album called *Introducing the Beatles,* released in America on July 23, 1963 (oddly enough, they chose an alternate take of "Love Me Do" with Andy White on drums and Ringo on tambourine). It was the boys' first LP issued in America, and it was a flop—until the Beatles boom began with "I

Want to Hold Your Hand." On April 27, 1964, Vee Jay reissued "Love Me Do" backed with "P.S. I Love You" on their subsidiary label, Tollie Records. It took a month, but at the end of May, "Love Me Do" hit the top of the charts as the most popular song in the country ("P.S. I Love You" was in the top ten).

It was the spring of 1964, and America was bedazzled by the first bright blooms of Beatlemania. Little did we know that we had only turned the first page in the incredible story of the Fab Four.

Where Did Our Love Go

THE SUPREMES

The story of the Supremes began in 1959 in Detroit's Brewster Housing Projects. An all-male group, the Primes, went around the neighborhood looking for volunteers to form a female counterpart—to sing with them at dances, hops, and talent shows. Florence Ballard was interested; she called a schoolmate, Mary Wilson, who then contacted a neighbor, Diana Ross. The boys worked with the girls for hours until their protégés seemed good enough to be known as the Primettes.

The Primes and Primettes sang around town anywhere they could showcase their talent. The Primettes even added an accompanist, Marvin Tauplin.

Then Diana moved to Bellmont Street on the north side of Detroit. About four or five doors away lived Smokey Robinson, leader of a big local group, the Miracles. Diana was in awe of them; they had actually cut a record, "Got a Job," an answer to the Silhouettes' "Get a Job." She watched them rehearse on the basement steps, got to be good friends with the Robinson family, and ate, even slept there. She told Smokey that she had a group and would like to audition for him.

One day, Smokey announced a rehearsal at the home of his girlfriend, Claudette. "Bring your group," he said, "and we'll listen." The Primettes and Marvin showed up and went through several numbers. "Well, keep practicing," said Smokey, "and maybe I can get you an audition with Berry Gordy." He then invited Marvin to join *his* group. And Marvin did.

Smokey actually did get the girls into Motown, but the only reason Berry heard them was because he happened to be strolling through the studio. The Primettes sang "I Want a Guy" for him, and he told them to go back to school and return after graduation.

Berry finally signed the trio in 1961, and gave them one day to come up

with a better group name. After polling the employees at Motown, the best they could come up with was a name suggested by a secretary—"the Supremes." Berry Gordy gave it his stamp of approval and it immediately went on their first single release, "I Want a Guy"—a record that sold less than one hundred copies.

The group floundered for about two years, often working as background singers for Marvin Gaye, Marv Johnson, and others. Then Gordy hooked them up with the writing and production team of Brian Holland, Lamont Dozier, and Eddie Holland. After six flops in a row, the Supremes recorded "When the Lovelight Comes Shining Through His Eyes." That record—the first Supremes/Holland-Dozier-Holland collaboration—reached number twenty-three in January 1964.

The next single, "Run Run Run," was a bomb, but in June the girls were given "Where Did Our Love Go." Mary Wilson said, "Well, I don't think it's very good," and Diana agreed, but Berry told them to sing it anyway. H-

D-H recruited everyone they could find to stomp on a long piece of elevated plywood—the marching sound that opens "Where Did Our Love Go"—and the song was recorded.

The Supremes then left on a month-long road tour as part of the Dick Clark Caravan of Stars (which paid $50 a week). Midway through the tour, they began to get calls for "that very sexy sounding, very young sounding record." In their absence, Berry Gordy had pulled "Where Did Our Love Go" out of the can for release. "We had no idea what was going to come out," said Diana. "I don't know if it was my voice [as lead singer] or the nice clear master they had of it. But it was melodic, had a lot of oohs, and just kept repeating, 'Baby, baby.' "

Shortly after their return from the tour, in August 1964, "Where Did Our Love Go" became the third single in Motown history to reach number one. It sold more than two million copies, and was the first of five consecutive number ones the Supremes would rack up in less than twelve months.

Everybody Loves Somebody

DEAN MARTIN

"When I first came to Reprise Records, I looked over the artist roster, and saw the name of Dean Martin," said producer Jimmy Bowen. "I'd always been a big fan of his, and knew right away that he was the guy I wanted to produce.

"I did an album with him of country songs, and then told him that we had to do something contemporary, because we needed a hit single. He said, 'O.K., but before we do, I want to cut a mood album.' You see, when Dean would finish working at the Sands Hotel in Las Vegas, he'd go out to the little lounge they had and sing with a trio. They'd do a lot of old standards and people just loved it. So Dean wanted to do an album like that, and call it 'Dream with Me.'

"I found four or five musicians, set up a studio with mood lighting, and we began to record. On the last night we had booked, we were doing some song or another, and Dean said, 'Aw, I don't want to do this one.' I said, 'Well, we have to have one more tune to finish the LP.' Then Ken Lane, Dean's piano player and conductor—he'd been with him for years—said, 'Why don't you do my song?' Ken started playing 'Everybody Loves Somebody' on the piano. I said, 'God, I love that song,' so we did it in the mood of that LP.

"After the session was over, I told Dean: 'That's our record! We've got to recut that with the big orchestra—speed it up a little—make it pop!' He just looked at me like I was crazy. Here I'd been trying to get him

to go contemporary—you know, be modern—and do it with what he considered an old song.

"You see, I'd never heard it. I thought Ken Lane had just written the tune. They were all laughing at me, because Dinah Washington had cut it, Sinatra had cut it, a whole lot of people had already recorded the song. So, the following week, I went to Vegas, bought Dinah's record and a couple of other versions, and listened to them. I got our arranger, Ernie Freeman, on the phone, and we booked a session for the following Wednesday or Thursday. On that date, we went in and cut the single version of 'Everybody Loves Somebody.'

"Now that song—that arrangement—was not typical of the kind of music happening at that time. It was kind of against the marketplace. They

put it out, but after about four or five weeks, they dropped it. I mean, there was just no action on it. And then a station in Worcester, Massachusetts, went on it, and at the same time a top-forty station in New Orleans did, and the phones lit up. About ten days later we had one day where we had to order 60,000 singles. It just exploded. It was the start of his second career."

Sixteen years after being written, "Everybody Loves Somebody" took off in late June 1964. It swiftly became a gold record, and by August, was the top-selling single in the country.

"Dean really got a kick out of that," added Jimmy. When 'Everybody Loves Somebody' went number one, he had one of his people send a telegram to Elvis Presley. It said, 'Well, if you can't handle the Beatles, I will.' "

6

My Guy
MARY WELLS

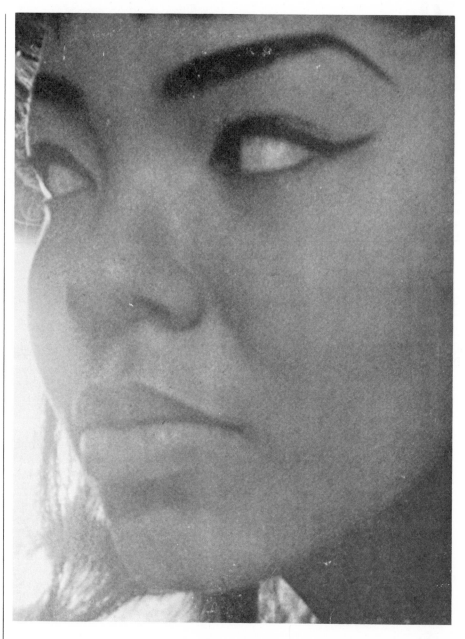

Mary Esther Wells began singing publicly at the age of ten, at church and school events. By her mid-teens, she was performing at parties and writing songs.

One day, Mary heard about "open-house auditions," held every Friday night by Motown's Berry Gordy. Mary didn't think she could ever become an artist, but did want to get into the music business. So, she wrote a song for one of her idols, Jackie Wilson, whose records were produced by Gordy. When Berry heard the tune, he suggested that she record it, and signed her to his label.

In 1961, "Bye Bye Baby," which took twenty-two takes to get right, became the third-ever release on Motown. A regional hit, it climbed to number forty-five in *Billboard.* It was a start.

After that, Mary Wells could do no wrong. Every one of her Motown singles made the national top forty—sometimes, both sides. In 1962, "The One Who Really Loves You" and "You Beat Me to the Punch" were both top ten. In 1963, there were more hits: "Two Lovers," "Laughing Boy," "Your Old Stand-By," "You Lost the Sweetest Boy," and "What's Easy for Two Is So Hard for One." The Beatles called her their favorite girl singer, and she toured with them in 1963 and 1964. Later, she returned the compliment by cutting an LP, *Love Songs to the Beatles.*

Although signed by Motown as a songwriter, most of Mary's music was written by other people—usually, Smokey Robinson. They'd sit down at the piano, he'd play, and she'd sing. They'd go over and over each song, and each time she'd add a little bit more of her own personality. Eventually, they'd work up a finished version, complete with Mary's ad libs.

In 1964, Smokey came up with "My Guy."

"Now that was a complete change for me," said Mary. "I think during that time Smokey and I were maturing, you know, we were becoming adults. Each tune gets better and better, the more you write. And 'My Guy'—well, that was a *great* tune. It's a standard, a standard song today."

"My Guy" was recorded in March 1964 and entered the pop charts one month later. It peaked in May, becoming Motown's very first single to reach number one.

I Get Around

THE BEACH BOYS

The Beach Boys began 1964 with a personnel change, as Al Jardine returned from dental school and rejoined the others. When he did, David Marks, who had been playing rhythm guitar in his absence, left to form his own ill-fated group, Dave Marks and the Marksmen.

The Beach Boys' first release of 1964 was "Fun Fun Fun," a classic teen dream documentary and one of their best car songs ever. Like "Surfin' U.S.A.," "Fun Fun Fun" owed a great debt to Chuck Berry. The opening riff, for example, was lifted directly from "Johnny B. Goode." The song reached number five in the spring on the American charts but bombed overseas.

The Beach Boys, at this point, were a cult band in England. They hadn't sold many records, yet were appreciated by a good number of influential British musicians. In the summer of 1964, on England's top rock TV show "Ready Steady Go," the Rolling Stones endorsed the Beach Boys and in particular their latest release, "I Get Around." That's all it took to send thousands of U.K. teens flocking to record shops; and before long, the Beach Boys had their first top-ten hit in England. In America, the record reached number one.

"I Get Around" marked a turning point in the content of Beach Boys songs. They still sang about fun and lighthearted romance, but the boys were outgrowing Southern California high school culture. In "I Get Around," they're "bugged drivin' up and down the same old strip" and are looking for "a new place where the kids are hip." Brian was then in his early twenties, and as the composer of "I Get Around"—and the Beach Boys' chief songwriter—his thoughts were drifting elsewhere. The uncertainties and responsibilities of early adulthood loomed larger than ever. This concern was echoed on the hit flip of "I Get Around"—"Don't Worry Baby"—as well as in the next Beach Boys' smash, "When I Grow Up (to Be a Man)."

In December 1964, "Dance Dance Dance" entered the top ten, and, quite unexpectedly, Brian married his long-time sweetheart, Marilyn Rovell (who had been one of the cheerleaders on "Be True to Your School"). Shortly after that, on December 23, Brian suffered a nervous breakdown. He dropped out of the group as an active performer and was replaced by a little-known session guitarist named Glen Campbell. On April 9, 1965, Glen in turn was replaced by Bruce Johnston.

The Beach Boys continued to be top hitmakers for the rest of the decade, and among their many chart songs were "Do You Wanna Dance," "Help Me Rhonda" (a second number one), "California Girls," and "The Little Girl I Once Knew" (all 1965); "Barbara Ann," "Sloop John B," "Good Vibrations" (a third number one), and "Wouldn't It Be Nice" (all 1966); "Heroes and Villains" and "Darlin'" (1967), "Do It Again" (1968), and "I Can Hear Music" (1969). Many of these songs were written by Brian in his living room, on an upright piano, seated in a giant sandbox. Brian used to like to squish sand through his toes while he wrote; he found the feeling "inspiring."

The Beach Boys were undisputed leaders in the sixties sound of California sun, surf, and good-time music (their only "rivals" were their friends and frequent performing partners, Jan and Dean). The timelessness of Beach Boys music was reaffirmed in 1974 when radio station KHJ in Los Angeles ran a promotion called the Firecracker 500. All weekend, listeners voted for their favorite records, and to everyone's surprise, the winner was a single cut before many of the voters were born—"Surfin' U.S.A." Capitol reissued the record, and to their shock it became a national top-forty hit all over again. That sparked a Beach Boys

repackage, *Endless Summer,* which climbed to the top of the LP charts. A few months later, the "fluke" was repeated when *Spirit of America,* another double compilation, also reached number one.

In 1976, many people named the Beach Boys as our unofficial Bicentennial band. There was also another top-ten single, "Rock 'n' Roll Music."

In 1981, after twenty years together, the Beach Boys still ruled as one of the country's hottest concert attractions.

Oh, Pretty Woman

ROY ORBISON

"As I write songs, I sing them," said Roy Orbison. "In other words, I have to sing them to write them, because it's all from my mind. So I write the lyrics and the melody all at the same time. They're welded together, more or less. And then, when the song is finished, I sometimes have to perform it, too, because not a lot of other people can. I prefer to sing the songs that I write, so I can make sure that they're performed the way I wrote them.

"By the time I started recording, I'd been playing the guitar for twelve years. So, starting at age six, playing the guitar and singing was a natural thing for me. Buddy Holly, of course, had played for a good while. Elvis had played and sung from, well, not as early as I did, but early in life. So it all sort of came together about 1955—late '55, when we were trying to express ourselves through playing and singing. Our influences were about the same—the Ink Spots, Bill Monroe—actually everyone from Lefty Frizzell to Perry Como. We listened to and played everything that we liked, and there was good in most everything we heard."

Roy Orbison drew from many sources in writing and singing the songs that made him a legend among performers. During the sixties, Roy established himself as a rock balladeer without peer, thanks to an absolutely majestic voice and his soulful songs. They included "Only the Lonely" (1960), "Running Scared" (1961), and a two-sided hit, "Cryin' " backed with "Candy Man" (1961). In 1962, there was "Dream Baby," "The Crowd," "Leah," and "Working for the Man." The next year, Roy was on the charts five times, with "In Dreams," "Falling," "Mean Woman Blues," "Blue Bayou," and his Christmas record, "Pretty Paper."

Roy spent a lot of time on the road and, on one tour in the early sixties, headlined in Europe on a bill that also featured the Beatles.

In 1964, Roy had one of his biggest years ever, starting with a top-ten single entitled "It's Over." After that, he topped the charts with an all-time classic inspired by an offhand quip.

"My wife was going to town, and I asked her, 'Do you need any money?' Well, Bill Dees, the same co-writer that worked with me on 'It's Over,' was there, and he said, 'A pretty woman never needs any money.' And then he said, 'Hey, how about that for a song title?' I said, 'No, that won't make it, but "Pretty Woman" will.' So, by the time my wife got back from the grocery store, we'd written 'Oh, Pretty Woman,' and I played it for her. The whole thing came that fast."

"Oh, Pretty Woman" was released in August 1964 and by October was the number-one single in the country. It earned a Grammy nomination as the Best Rock 'n' Roll Recording of the year, but lost out to "Downtown."

Shortly after "Oh, Pretty Woman," Roy was offered a million-dollar deal to switch from Monument to MGM Records, which offered "greater freedom" and the possibility of movie and TV roles. Roy accepted, but wound up making only one film—a Civil War comedy called *The Fastest Guitar Alive* (1967). Roy wrote the background score and most of the songs for the film, but his actual hits for MGM were few and far between.

In the late sixties, Orbison's life was marred by career setbacks and personal tragedies. His "pretty woman," Claudette, was killed in a motorcycle crash; and in 1968, two of his sons perished in a fire at his home near Nashville.

Roy's international popularity, though, lives on, as does his music. In 1976, Nazareth cut "Love Hurts," a song first recorded as an Orbison B side. Linda Ronstadt had a million-seller with his "Blue Bayou" in 1977, and Don McLean covered "Cryin' " in 1981. And at the same time, Roy finally won the Grammy Award that had eluded him for so many years. The Best Country Performance by a Duo or Group with Vocal was "That Lovin' You Feelin' Again" by Roy Orbison and Emmylou Harris.

Hello, Dolly!
LOUIS ARMSTRONG

Louis Armstrong was one of the masters of jazz. Born in New Orleans at the turn of the century, he spent his early years as a trumpet player in the bands of King Oliver and Fletcher Henderson. He later led his own groups, including the Hot Five, the Hot Seven, and the All-Stars.

Sometimes, Louis put down his trumpet, and vocalized. At first, he specialized in scat singing, but quickly branched into other styles. His cheerful, rhythmic sound was inimitable—as was his distinctive gravel voice.

Louis appeared in over thirty-five motion pictures, beside everyone from Frank Sinatra to Herman's Hermits. He also toured extensively, becoming a kind of goodwill ambassador for American jazz all over the world.

Occasionally, his name turned up on the pop charts. In the fifties, he had such hits as "I Get Ideas" and "A Kiss to Build a Dream On" (1951), "Takes Two to Tango" (1952), and "A Theme from *The Three Penny Opera*" and "Blueberry Hill" (both 1956).

Then, in 1964, Louis cut his all-time biggest record. To him it was just another track on an LP of show tunes. In fact, he had never even heard of the Broadway show it came from.

"Jack Lee, one of the men from my publishing company, brought it to him," recalled composer Jerry Herman. "It was an approach, and a very daring one, because no one realizes it now, but that song was written to be an 1890s production number, and had no relation to the kind of music that Louis had been associated with. It was just an odd idea that Jack had. He brought the song to him, and he did that arrangement, and you know the rest of the story. It helped the show, me, Louis, everybody. Because it was the title song, it could only help the show. It made those words famous: 'Hello, Dolly!' "

Louis' single broke onto the radio in mid-February 1964, amid the onslaught of the Beatles. In May it became the first record to knock the Beatles off the top of the pops. It clung to the charts for five months, ultimately selling more than two million copies. At the time, Louis Armstrong was sixty-three years old.

The success of "Hello, Dolly!" only intensified the warm affection shared between Louis and the American public. In 1969, the stage show was made into a film, and in the movie, Louis sang his song to "Dolly," portrayed by Barbra Streisand. To fans and critics alike, it was clearly the high point of the picture.

Louis died on July 6, 1971, just two days after his seventy-first birthday. Five years later, a statue was erected in his honor in New Orleans—in Louis Armstrong Park.

She Loves You

THE BEATLES

The Beatles' first hit in America was "I Want to Hold Your Hand," which debuted on the charts on January 18, 1964. One week later, a second record appeared—one that had been gathering dust at U.S. radio stations for more than four months. It was "She Loves You," a song that, over the next fifteen weeks, America was to come to love almost as well.

Paul and John started working on "She Loves You" while riding in a van on their way to a hotel in Newcastle. Paul's original arrangement was "a kind of gospel call-and-response thing" with two of the fellows singing "she loves you" and the other two coming back with "yeah, yeah, yeah." After kicking it around, they abandoned that concept as "crummy" but at least agreed on the basic premise of a song called "She Loves You." After arriving at their hotel, Paul and John went straight to their room, and a few hours later, they emerged with the tune in its final form.

George Martin first heard "She Loves You" in the studio, while seated, as was his custom, on a high stool. Paul and John stood before him, singing and playing acoustic guitars. George Harrison stood off to one side, joining in on the choruses. Martin thought the song was great, but there was one thing that struck him as a bit odd. That was the close, when they ended on a singing chord that was sort of a major sixth (Harrison doing the sixth and the others doing the third and fifth). "It's a great chord," said the boys. "Nobody's ever heard that before."

"Well, actually, it is a bit old-fashioned," replied Martin. "Glenn Miller used to do arrangements like that years ago."

"Well, none of our people know that, do they?"

George Martin had to agree—and, of course, that chord became a major part of the song.

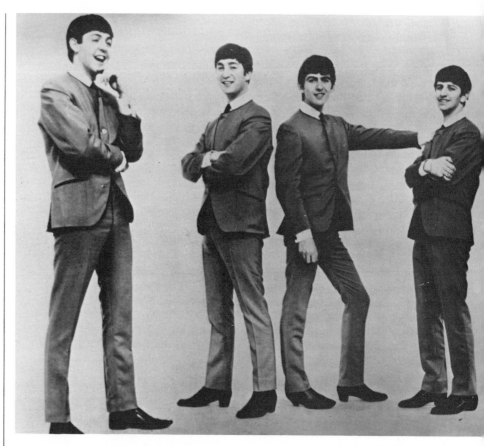

"She Loves You" contained all the classic elements of the early Beatles sound, from Ringo's buoyant drum fills to the boosted level of McCartney's bass. It also introduced the "yeah, yeah, yeah" hook, a phrase that instantly became synonymous with Beatlemania and rock 'n' roll (they were to reuse it in several songs, most notably in the closing seconds of "Hey Jude"). A decade later, some countries were still issuing decrees banning Beatles haircuts and "yeah, yeah, yeah music."

"She Loves You" was recorded on July 1, 1963, and first released in England on August 23. By September, it was the number-one record in Britain, and would remain so for a total of five weeks. On September 16, it was issued in the United States on the Swan label (after being rejected by EMI's American affiliate, Capitol Records). It didn't make the pop charts, though, until January 25, 1964. The Beatles were filmed performing the song, and on January 3, a clip from that movie was shown on NBC-TV's "Jack Paar Show." It was the first time the Beatles were shown on U.S. television, and six days before their historic appearance on the "Ed Sullivan Show."

On January 29, the Beatles were persuaded to record "She Loves You" and "I Want to Hold Your Hand" in German, for release in that country. Reluctantly, they obliged, and for that reason "Sie Liebt Dich" and "Komm, Gib Mir Deine Hand" exist. It's a tribute to the intensity of Beatlemania that, even as "She Loves You" was the number-one record in America, "Sie Liebt Dich" was also a U.S. chart item.

I Want to Hold Your Hand

THE BEATLES

February 1963: The fuse is lit in England, with the Beatles' first national tour, first national TV appearance, and first number-one record, "Please Please Me."

August 1963: "She Loves You" tops the British chart, with advance orders of a half million copies.

October 1963: Another U.K. TV date, this time on "Saturday Night at the London Palladium." The crowd outside is worked into a frenzy that, for the first time, is given a name: Beatlemania. Six days later, on the 19th, the boys record a song Paul and John had written on a bus in Yorkshire. "I like it," says John. "I think it has a beautiful melody." They call it "I Want to Hold Your Hand," and there are advance orders for one million copies—unheard of in England.

November 1963: On the 29th, "I Want to Hold Your Hand" is released in the U.K., one copy being sent airmail to New York. The record goes immediately to the top of the British charts.

December 1963: On the 29th, at 12:50 in the afternoon, New York's WMCA-AM becomes the first radio station in America to broadcast "I Want to Hold Your Hand."

January 1964: Amid a $50,000 Capitol advertising campaign, "I Want to Hold Your Hand" is released stateside on the 13th (on the 18th it enters the U.S. charts at number eighty-three). On the 20th, Capitol issues the LP *Meet the Beatles.* It's destined to be the largest-selling album in history, up to that time.

February 1964: While appearing at the Olympia Theatre in Paris, the Beatles receive word that "I Want to Hold Your Hand" has reached number one in the States. Six days later, on the 7th, 100 policemen, 200 reporters, and more than 10,000 teenagers greet them at New York's Kennedy Airport. They appear twice on the "Ed Sullivan Show," giving Sullivan the highest rating in TV history to that time. Statisticians claim that during this month, the Beatles account for sixty percent of all single records sold in America.

March 1964: "I Want to Hold Your Hand" is finally knocked out of the number-one slot—by "She Loves You." Capitol claims first-day sales of 940,225 on "Can't Buy Me Love." On the 31st, *Billboard*'s chart has "Can't Buy Me Love" at number one, "Twist and Shout" at two, "She Loves You" at three, "I Want to Hold Your Hand" at four, "Please Please Me" at five, and five other Beatles songs in various other positions. By the end of this month, Beatles singles sales in the U.S. will have grossed $17.5 million.

April 1964: The Beatles film *A Hard Day's Night.*

May 1964: "Love Me Do" reaches number one in America.

June 1964: So far, the Beatles have placed twenty songs on the U.S. charts in only six months. Besides those mentioned above, they include "I Saw Her Standing There," "P.S. I Love You," "From Me to You," "You Can't Do That," "All My Loving," and "Thank You Girl."

July 1964: Royalty attends the world premiere of *A Hard Day's Night* at the London Pavilion on the 6th. The title tune is released as a single, as are two other songs from the movie: "And I Love Her," and "I'll Cry Instead."

August 1964: The Beatles tour America and are paid $1,933 a minute to appear at the Hollywood Bowl.

September 1964: The Beatles boom in merchandising rolls on, with Beatles dolls, games, buttons, wigs, T-shirts, jewelry, hair spray, trading cards, wallpaper, Beatlenut ice cream, and more.

October 1964: Barclay's Bank in England rates the Beatles as "a national asset," noting that the export of their records has made "a major contribution" to Britain's balance of payments.

November 1964: Capitol issues a double-hit single: "She's a Woman" and "I Feel Fine." Also released is the *Beatles Story* LP.

December 1964: *Beatles '65* becomes the eleventh Beatles album to make the charts in one year. Others are *The Beatles vs. the Four Seasons, Jolly What! The Beatles and Frank Ifield, The Beatles with Tony Sheridan and Their Guests, The Beatles' Second Album, Something New, The American Tour with Ed Rudy, Songs, Pictures and Stories of the Fabulous Beatles,* and *A Hard Day's Night.*

And Beatlemania had only begun.

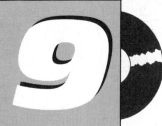

1965

BILL GRAHAM PROMOTED his first San Francisco show in 1965, the year record sales topped $800 million for the first time. A number of new groups got together: the Youngbloods, Canned Heat, the Association, Jefferson Airplane, the Nitty Gritty Dirt Band, Pink Floyd, and the Doors. Bill Black, Nat King Cole, and Alan Freed all passed away; Dean Martin and Steve Lawrence each got their own TV shows. Notable new names on the pop charts included Mitch Ryder ("Jenny Take a Ride"), Donovan ("Catch the Wind"), the Lovin' Spoonful ("Do You Believe in Magic"), and the Guess Who ("Shakin' All Over"). Many radio stations banned a record that made it to number one anyway—Barry McGuire's "Eve of Destruction." Elvis invited the Beatles to his home, but they were so in awe of him that they just sat, staring at him for a long time. Finally Elvis said, "Look, if you're just going to sit there and stare at me all night, I'm going to bed." That broke the ice—and the five of them jammed until dawn. It was 1965, the year Ray Charles was arrested for possession of some heroin—to be exact, a planeload.

Bob Dylan was just another raspy-voiced harmonica player until 1963, when he rewrote an old blues standard, "No More Auction Block for Me," into "Blowin' in the Wind." Peter, Paul and Mary covered the song, making pop protest big business. Dylan's label then promoted him as "a spokesman for his generation," and in the summer of 1965, Bob struck gold as a vocalist with "Like a Rolling Stone." After that, he took special delight in writing musical questions without answers— murky, paranoid nightmares—which fans searched fruitlessly for some kind of cosmic truth. "Positively Fourth Street" was a hit later in 1965; in 1966, there were "Rainy Day Women #12 and 35" and "I Want You." Dylan's last top-twenty singles were "Lay Lady Lay" (1969) and "Knockin' on Heaven's Door" (1973).

Beginning on June 27, Dick Clark produced and hosted "Where the Action Is," a daytime half-hour of rock 'n' roll on ABC. Regular performers included Linda Scott ("I've Told Every Little Star"), Steve Alaimo ("Every Day I Have to Cry"), and, most notably, **Paul Revere and the Raiders,** who became "overnight" stars thanks to the video exposure. Tommy Boyce and Bobby Hart wrote the series' theme song, which Freddie Cannon turned into a major hit (under the title "Action"). Among those making their earliest television appearances on the show were Sonny and Cher (on July 30). "Where the Action Is" went off the air on March 31, 1967.

The **Dave Clark Five,** the most intense of all the early British Invasion groups, sang and starred in *Catch Us If You Can,* their answer to the Beatles' *A Hard Day's Night* (the Beatles responded, in kind, with *Help*). Herman's Hermits appeared in *Hold On* (with Shelley Fabares), *Go Go Mania* (with the Animals), and *When the Boys Meet the Girls* (with Connie Francis, Sam the Sham, and Louis Armstrong). Frankie Avalon and James Brown were featured in *Ski Party,* Rick Nelson in *Love and Kisses,* Jim Reeves in *Kimberly Jim,* and Elvis in *Girl Happy, Tickle Me,* and *Harum Scarum.* It was also a good year for beach movies: *Beach Ball* (the Supremes, Four Seasons), *Swinging Summer* (Righteous Brothers, Rip Chords), *Girls on the Beach* (Beach Boys, Leslie Gore), *Wild on the Beach* (Sonny and Cher, Sandy Nelson), and *How to Stuff a Wild Bikini* (Annette Funicello, Buster Keaton).

The hard English sound took various forms during the mid-sixties; one group, the **Kinks,** sounded like they were using hammers on their guitars on such tunes as "You Really Got Me" and "All Day and All of the Night." Their biggest record, "Tired of Waiting for You," came out in 1965, as did "Set Me Free," "Who'll Be the Next in Line," and "A Well-Respected Man." The Kinks were one of Britain's premier garage bands, adapting their name from the slang word "kink," meaning "unusual," "far out," or "freaky." They got their distorted sound by sticking knitting needles in their amplifiers. Later hits included "Sunny Afternoon" (1966), "Lola" (1970), and "A Rock 'n' Roll Fantasy" (1978).

The **James Brown** story began in January 1956, when he cut "Please, Please, Please" in a radio station studio. It became an R&B million-seller, and the first of more than a hundred charted sides for the one they called "The Godfather of Soul." In 1965, James earned a Grammy Award for "Papa's Got a Brand New Bag," his first top-ten pop hit. After that came "I Got You" (1965), "It's a Man's Man's Man's World" (1966), "Cold Sweat" (1967), "I Got the Feelin'" (1968), and many more. One of the hardest-working men in show business, Brown played over three hundred live dates a year, carefully investing the proceeds in real estate, publishing companies, and the ownership of all of his own masters. Eventually, he built an empire that included his own castle (with moat and drawbridge), a huge fleet of cars, an armada of airplanes, and the Macon, Georgia, radio station he once shined shoes in front of.

THE TOP 40

1. Wooly Bully, *Sam the Sham and the Pharaohs*
2. I Can't Help Myself, *Four Tops*
3. Satisfaction, *Rolling Stones*
4. You've Lost That Lovin' Feelin', *Righteous Brothers*
5. Downtown, *Petula Clark*
6. You Were on My Mind, *We Five*
7. Help!, *Beatles*
8. Crying in the Chapel, *Elvis Presley*
9. My Girl, *Temptations*
10. The "In" Crowd, *Ramsey Lewis Trio*
11. King of the Road, *Roger Miller*
12. I Got You Babe, *Sonny and Cher*
13. Can't You Hear My Heart Beat, *Herman's Hermits*
14. This Diamond Ring, *Gary Lewis and the Playboys*
15. The Birds and the Bees, *Jewel Akens*
16. Back in My Arms Again, *Supremes*
17. Help Me Rhonda, *Beach Boys*
18. Mrs. Brown, You've Got a Lovely Daughter, *Herman's Hermits*
19. Shotgun, *Junior Walker and the All-Stars*
20. Stop in the Name of Love, *Supremes*
21. Mr. Lonely, *Bobby Vinton*
22. Hang on Sloopy, *McCoys*
23. Come See About Me, *Supremes*
24. Mr. Tambourine Man, *Byrds*
25. Unchained Melody, *Righteous Brothers*
26. Love Potion #9, *Searchers*
27. Eve of Destruction, *Barry McGuire*
28. Hold Me, Thrill Me, Kiss Me, *Mel Carter*
29. I Feel Fine, *Beatles*
30. Silhouettes, *Herman's Hermits*
31. The Jerk, *Larks*
32. I'll Never Find Another You, *Seekers*
33. Cara Mia, *Jay and the Americans*
34. Ticket to Ride, *Beatles*
35. Cast Your Fate to the Wind, *Sounds Orchestral*
36. What the World Needs Now Is Love, *Jackie DeShannon*
37. Yes, I'm Ready, *Barbara Mason*
38. What's New Pussycat, *Tom Jones*
39. She's Not There, *Zombies*
40. The Name Game, *Shirley Ellis*

THE TOP 10 LPs

1. Mary Poppins, *Original Soundtrack*
2. My Fair Lady, *Original Soundtrack*
3. Fiddler on the Roof, *Original Cast*
4. Beatles '65, *Beatles*
5. The Sound of Music, *Original Soundtrack*
6. Goldfinger, *Original Soundtrack*
7. Dear Heart, *Andy Williams*
8. Where Did Our Love Go, *Supremes*
9. Introducing, *Herman's Hermits*
10. People, *Barbra Streisand*

Also in 1965, *The Sound of Music* became an incredibly popular album and movie—the winner of six Academy Awards including Best Picture. The blockbuster Rodgers and Hammerstein musical was based on the actual adventures of the von Trapp Family Singers, a choral group that toured Europe for ten years before fleeing Nazi persecution in 1938. Julie Andrews played a former nun who organized the act around seven motherless kids—the offspring of Baron Georg von Trapp, a retired World War I naval hero. The real-life group, relocated in America, continued to perform together until 1958, when they gave their farewell concert.

The "In" Crowd
THE RAMSEY LEWIS TRIO

Chicago-born Ramsey Lewis began receiving classical instruction at the piano when he was six years old. "By the time I was twelve or thirteen, I wanted to pursue a career as a classical musician," he said. "I soon realized, however, that there was little room for black people in classical music."

At about this time, Ramsey was introduced to the piano stylings of Art Tatum and Errol Garner by his father. "I didn't try my hand at playing jazz until I was fifteen. Tatum, Garner, and Oscar Peterson were no doubt my early influences. But as I got older, I ceased to be impressed by any one musician. I would listen to one pianist for his technique, another for his harmonic treatment. I learned to imitate Tatum, Peterson, Kelly, Garland. But I began to find that if you are true to your art, you'll have

to search for your personal identity, and at some point it will begin to emerge and crystallize."

In 1950, Ramsey joined the Cleffs, a local band that included bassist Eldee Young and drummer Isaac "Red" Holt. When the Cleffs broke up six years later, the three men formed the Ramsey Lewis Trio. The new group played around DePaul University, where Ramsey was a student, and also in Chicago clubs and on the road. They eventually signed a contract with Argo Records, a subsidiary of Chess.

Nine years and several albums later, the trio was booked into the Bohemian Caverns, a popular night spot with the "in crowd" of Washington, D.C. A live LP was planned, and Ramsey had carefully worked out their repertoire, to be recorded over three nights (May 13–15, 1965). Shortly before the first night's taping, Ramsey dropped into a coffee shop across the street from the club. He happened to mention to the waitress that he was looking for one more song to complete the album. She asked if he had heard the new Dobie Gray record, "The In Crowd," which had been out for about six months. He hadn't, so she played it for him on the jukebox. Ramsey listened to the song several times and decided to include it in their opening night's performance. The song went over so well that it became the high point of their LP. Released as a single, it swiftly became a million-seller, and overnight the Ramsey Lewis Trio became the most popular jazz combo in America.

Success brought many long-sought rewards. Their booking fee shot from $2,500 to $6,500 for one-week club

dates, and the trio played Carnegie Hall to standing-room-only crowds. Their albums sold well, and there were follow-up hits: "Hang On Sloopy" (1965) and "A Hard Day's Night" (1966). Both were cut in the same vein as "The In Crowd"—jazzy instrumental remakes of other artists' vocal hits.

It all came crashing down in the spring of 1966, when Eldee and Isaac decided to form their own combo. Inner tension was the reason—too much attention paid to Ramsey and disagreements over musical direction. Ramsey wanted to stick to jazz, while the others favored the popular field ("soul swinging," they called it). Eldee and Isaac put together the Young-Holt Trio, later known as Young-Holt Unlimited, and scored a gold record, "Soulful Strut," in January 1969.

As for Ramsey Lewis, he just found other musicians and plowed ahead with "Wade in the Water," a top-twenty single in September 1966. Although later releases did not sell as well, Ramsey continued his award-winning ways ("The In Crowd" had copped a '65 Grammy for Best Instrumental Jazz Performance by a Small Group). In 1966, "Hold It Right There" earned him a Grammy for the Best R&B Group Performance, Vocal or Instrumental. He also picked up a third Grammy (Best R&B Instrumental) for a 1973 re-recording of "Hang On Sloopy."

In later years, Ramsey Lewis switched styles many times, bouncing from straight jazz to rhythm and blues, middle-of-the-road, and electronic funk. He also helped develop the sound of Earth, Wind and Fire and influenced many jazz-rock musicians.

9

My Girl
THE TEMPTATIONS

Eddie Kendricks used to live four doors down from Paul Williams in Birmingham, Alabama. The first time they met, Paul threw a bucketful of mop water on him. There was a brief scuffle, but they came out of it the best of friends.

The two moved to Detroit, where they formed the Primes in 1956. After several personnel changes, they became the Temptations in 1961. Other original members included Melvin Franklin, Elbridge Bryant, and Otis Williams (of Otis Williams and the Distants). A few years later, Bryant left; he was replaced by David Ruffin.

The group began recording in 1962 and had their first major hit in 1964, "The Way You Do the Things You Do." It was followed by two lesser chart records, "I'll Be in Trouble" and "Girl (Why You Wanna Make Me Blue)." That same year also marked their first album release, *Meet the Temptations.*

Then, in 1965, along came their very first number-one record. It grew out of a club date they played at the 20 Grand in Detroit. Smokey Robinson was in the audience and heard David sing a song made famous by the Drifters. Smokey was knocked out by the way David handled himself on the lead vocal. Afterward, he came up to David and said, "Hey, man, I'm gonna write a tune for you." Smokey then put together "My Girl" with another of the Miracles, Ronnie White.

By then, both groups were playing a week's engagement at the Apollo Theater in New York. Smokey brought a demo tape with him, and all week long, after every show, he'd go up to the Temptations' dressing room (they were on the top floor), and they'd rehearse the song over and over again. Otis Williams recalled saying at the time that "this might really be something. It wasn't until we got back home, though, and recorded it, and

Smokey put the strings on it, that I realized that it really did sound like a number one."

"My Girl" was released on January 9, 1965, and entered the pop charts one week later. Propelled by the slow, pulsating bass that opens the song and the harmony that builds in stair-steps, it gradually drifted to the top of the charts, peaking in March. It was the Tempts' first gold record, and the harbinger of many more to come.

Over the next few years, the Temptations were to grow into one of the classic soul groups of the sixties. They

cut seventeen hit albums and nearly two dozen top-forty singles during that time. Among their biggest songs were "Ain't Too Proud to Beg," "Beauty Is Only Skin Deep," and "I Know I'm Losing You" (1966); "All I Need," "You're My Everything," and "It's You That I Need" (1967); "I Wish It Would Rain," "I'm Gonna Make You Love Me" (with the Supremes), and "Cloud Nine" (1968); and "Runaway Child Running Wild," "Don't Let the Joneses Get You Down," and "I Can't Get Next to You" (1969). The last song was their second number one.

Crying in the Chapel

ELVIS PRESLEY

Elvis Presley put thirty-seven songs on the charts in the early sixties, including "Surrender," "I Feel So Bad," "His Latest Flame," "Little Sister," and "Can't Help Falling in Love" (1961); "Good Luck Charm," "She's Not You," "Return to Sender," and "Follow That Dream" (1962); "One Broken Heart for Sale," "Devil in Disguise," and "Bossa Nova Baby" (1963); and "Kissin' Cousins," "Such a Night," and "Ain't That Lovin' You Baby" (1964).

By 1965, Elvis was more than just a rock singer—he was the highest-paid entertainer in show biz. His royalties from record sales that year were $1,125,000, and his total take for the year, well over $5 million. As of April, the seventeen Elvis films by then in release had grossed between $125 million and $135 million worldwide. And Presley had sold 100 million records to date—with a cash value of $150 million.

Elvis' biggest single of 1965 was his version of "Crying in the Chapel," a country gospel song that had already been a big hit four times—by four different artists—in 1953. Knoxville composer Artie Glenn had written it for his son, Darrell, who introduced the song on Valley Records in July 1953. Two weeks later, June Valli had covered it, and before another week went by, Rex Allen was out with a third top-ten version. The fourth hit reading, by Sonny Til and the Orioles, reached the charts on August 15, 1953, and is sometimes—erroneously—called the very first rock 'n' roll record. It's not rock, of course, but a ballad, and hardly even the "original" version of the song. (On top of that, Bill Haley's "Crazy Man, Crazy" predated it by three months.)

Elvis Presley cut the tune in 1960, shortly after his discharge from the army. It was intended for his album *Elvis Is Back*, but because of legal problems, it was kept off the LP, and on the shelf, for a full five years. In April 1965, it was finally issued as, of all things, one side of a "Gold Standard" oldies single. It's hard to understand how an unheard, unreleased track could be passed off as a vintage million-seller, but that's exactly what RCA tried to do that spring. Instead, radio stations played it as a "new" Elvis record, and by June, it was among the hottest 45s.

"Crying in the Chapel" eventually found its way onto Presley's second religious album, *How Great Thou Art,* which came out in March 1967. That LP went on to earn a Grammy as the Best Sacred Performance. In 1972, Elvis won a second Grammy for "He Touched Me," that year's Best Inspirational Performance, Non-Classical. It seems incredible, but the King of Rock 'n' Roll never won a Grammy for the kind of music he made most famous. There were many more hits after "Crying in the Chapel"—sixty-eight, in fact, before Presley's death in 1977.

Because of Presley, pop music once and for all took its dominant characteristics—mainly the driving, regular beat—from country western repertoire and absorbed the whole colorful spectrum of gospel music and rhythm and blues into its mainstream. Because of Presley, too, young unknown artists, eager for the big break, took heart at his success and revolutionized pop singles recording in this country; they became within a few years the big stars in the field while displacing the old, familiar names whose presence on a recording was, at one time, the assurance of a hit. Those days quickly vanished as the singles record market became dominated, more and more, by younger and younger teenagers, most of whom were girls attracted to the Presley personality.

Despite the original predictions about him, Elvis Presley became one of the half-dozen chief members of the show business establishment, and to him can be given the headiest compliment of all: He changed the entire course of international pop music and set the path it would take for the rest of our lifetimes.

7

Help!
THE BEATLES

The Beatles released five singles in 1965, and, as expected, all of them became number-one records. The first, "Eight Days a Week," came out on February 15, just eight days before the group turned up in the Bahamas, ready to begin work on their second motion picture. Their first, *A Hard Day's Night,* had, of course, been a resounding success, and so this time Richard Lester was going to film the boys in color, on a budget that was more than twice the size (roughly $1.25 million).

Ringo had done a good job at coming up with a name for their first picture, and so the group turned to him again for another snappy suggestion. Ringo hesitated only briefly and then said, "Eight Arms to Hold You." That sounded all right to the other three, and so production began using that name. After a few weeks, though, the group became less enchanted with Ringo's phrase, especially when it came time to start writing a title song. Richard Lester then recommended something very simple, maybe even one word, that no one could say was either bad or good. Finally, the boys agreed on *Help!*—because, in their minds, it fit very well with the picture as released.

Most of the writing of the song "Help!" was done by John, who later referred to it as "the finest piece of music I ever wrote." "Help!" was more than just a catchy little movie theme to him; he saw it as a "very personal" record, "a cry from the heart." Like nearly all of John's songs, it was written in the first person and reflected his inner feelings. "Help!" worked because he meant it when he wrote it and when he sang it ("It's real," said John). He would hasten to add that it was the *song* that meant so much to him, and not the Beatles' *recorded performance.* John always felt that the Beatles' record had been performed too fast in their zeal to make the song commercial.

The Beatles cut "Help!" on April 13, 1965, and released it as a single on July 19. It was an instant number one in England, selling 500,000 copies in one week (800,000 in three weeks). In America, it sold a million copies in one week and spent most of September at the top of the singles chart.

The film *Help!* came out ten days after the single, with the world premiere in London on July 29 (it opened in New York on August 23). It shattered box office records set by *A Hard Day's Night,* eventually earning more than $13.5 million in worldwide rentals and TV sales. With their characteristic odd humor, the boys dedicated their movie to Elias Howe, the American who invented the sewing machine in 1846.

The Beatles' other activities during the year included stirring up a storm of controversy on June 12, when each received a Member of the Order of the British Empire award from the Queen. Many previous recipients were outraged and mailed back their medals

in protest. The Beatles, however, were very proud of their honor.

In late summer, they toured the United States again, making a very memorable appearance before 55,000 at New York's Shea Stadium on August 16. The $304,000 taken in that day was said to be the largest gross in show biz history up to that time.

And, of course, the hits just kept on coming: "Ticket to Ride" in the summer, "Yesterday" in the fall and three new album packages: *Beatles VI,* the *Help!* soundtrack, and *Rubber Soul.* (There was also a reissue of the Vee Jay material on *The Early Beatles.*)

How long could the Beatles' magic last? Well, by the end of 1965, the Fab Four had survived a year and eleven months longer than many pundits had predicted. Each new achievement seemed as if it had to be the crowning capper to their career. But the Beatles went on and on, dazzling and leading the music world, and the best was yet to come.

You Were on My Mind
WE FIVE

*I*n the early sixties, two of the overriding pop scenes in San Francisco were jazz and folk. Setting the pace for the latter was the Kingston Trio, a group that rose to prominence under the direction of Frank Werber. Later in the decade, flower power, hippie blues, and psychedelic rock took over. Out of somewhere in the middle came We Five—a quintet that billed itself as the first "electric band" to emerge from that city.

The roots of We Five can be traced back to 1962, and a local folk group called the Ridge Runners. Their bass singer, Michael Stewart, just happened to have a brother, John, who was one of the Kingston Trio. Through this connection, Michael was able to have some Ridge Runner material recorded by the more popular act. Eventually, John was able to arrange an audition for the Ridge Runners with Frank Werber, who was then the Trio's manager. Frank's advice to them was to abandon the folk idiom, and search for their own unique sound. For the next two years, they tried to do exactly that.

In 1964, Werber formed Trident Productions, and agreed to listen to Michael's group again. By that time, it had reorganized several times, finally coalescing on the campus of California's Mt. St. Antonio College. Besides Michael, the line-up featured baritone Robert Jones (guitar), tenor Jerry Bergen (guitar), tenor Peter Fullerton (drums), and soprano Beverly Bivens (lead vocals). They had also adopted a shorter collective name: We Five.

Werber liked what he heard, and figured he could do something with this quintet. For another eight months, he coached them — rehearsing, grooming, and polishing an act. Then, on April 20, 1965, he took them to the

Columbus Recording Studio in the Columbus Tower in San Francisco. There, We Five recorded "You Were on My Mind," a song written by singer Sylvia Fricker, of the Canadian folk team, Ian and Sylvia.

Werber sold the resulting master to A&M Records, which released it in mid-July. At the end of the month, it began to take off, and by September, was one of the best-selling singles of the year.

We Five went on to place only one other song on the charts—the ironically titled "Let's Get Together." By the time it became a hit in December 1967, internal dissension had reduced the group's number down to two. Pete and Jerry tried to struggle on by adding Jerry's wife Debbie, but somehow audiences never seemed to accept a three-member We Five.

Numerous reunion attempts have not been successful.

Downtown

PETULA CLARK

Petula (pronounced pe-*choo*-la) Sally Olwen Clark was born in Epson, England. She never really liked her first name, so at the age of seven she began insisting that everyone call her Sally, or at least "Pet." The latter stuck and became her lifelong nickname.

At the dawn of World War II, Pet's father took her to the Criterion Theatre, where the BBC was allowing children to send radio messages to loved ones overseas. During the broadcast an air raid began, and Pet started singing to calm the frightened children. The ploy worked, and the BBC was impressed enough to give her her own show, "Pet's Parlour."

When she turned twelve, Pet signed a film contract with J. Arthur Rank, the British movie magnate, who placed her in more than two dozen pictures. She became England's answer to Shirley Temple, and after a while she came to resent being known as "a sweet little girl." When audiences refused to let her grow up, she slipped away to France and began to take vocal lessons, hoping to inject a little sex in her voice and change her image.

Pet's recording career got under way in 1950, when she recorded a song called "Gondolier." Her record company, Vogue, asked her to cut it also in French, and the result was a bilingual hit. More chart singles followed, including three million-sellers: "Romeo," "Monsieur," and "Chariot." With the arrival of Le Twist in France, Pet became the darling of the pop music scene there, thanks to her record "Ya Ya Twist." For that tune she received the Grand Prix National de Disque Français. Pet was in her element. She learned the language, married a Frenchman (the promotion manager of Vogue), and settled in Paris.

One day, Pet met Tony Hatch, a Buckingham Palace musician who dabbled in A&R for Pye Records. He brought her an instrumental of his and asked for her opinion. She called it "marvelous" and suggested that he add words to it. The result was a composition so big that Pet was forever to divide her life into B.D. and A.D.—before and after "Downtown."

By the fall of 1964, Pet had already sold more than twenty million records in Europe and had pretty much written off any chance of cracking the U.S. market. In fact, only one European woman had ever scored a number-one single in America, and that was Vera Lynn, with "Auf Wiederseh'n Sweetheart," back in 1952. What chance did Pet have, after trying for fourteen years?

Enter Joe Smith, an enterprising young executive from Warner Brothers Records. While on a trip to Paris, Joe heard the French version of "Downtown" (it had been recorded in several languages). He quickly secured rights to release the song in English, in America. When it broke in mid-December, Pet could not believe the flood of telephone offers she received. Unfortunately, she could not accept any of them, as she was booked—at strictly "B.D." rates—for the next eight months. She did, though, manage to squeeze in one live "Ed Sullivan Show" appearance.

"Downtown" became a monster hit, not only in the U.S. (where it sold three million) but also in Canada, Britain, and most of Western Europe. It won the Grammy Award for Best Rock and Roll Recording of 1964, and led to three other nominations (Record of the Year, Best Vocal Performance, Female and Best New Artist of 1964). In a bizarre twist, the record was nominated *again* in 1965, for Best Vocal Performance, Female.

Pet Clark went on to rack up more than a dozen U.S. hits over the next four years. Among them were "I Know a Place" (a '65 Grammy winner), "My Love" (another number one, in 1966), "Don't Sleep in the Subway" (a triple

Grammy nominee in 1967), and "Kiss Me Goodbye" (her last big record, in 1968). She also made two more films: *Finian's Rainbow* (1968) and *Goodbye Mr. Chips* (1969).

"There are times when I'd just like to start all over again," said Pet. "What happens in this business is that you make a name for yourself, and then you find yourself being locked in by it. Sometimes I think there must be better things I can do than sing these silly songs—more useful things. But then I get the letters, scores of them. People tell me how much a song means to them, how it helped them through a problem. That's when I feel it's all worthwhile again."

You've Lost That Lovin' Feelin'

RIGHTEOUS BROTHERS

Bill Medley and Bob Hatfield grew up in Southern California, unrelated and unknown to each other. After high school, each began his own musical career, establishing a small combo and playing local clubs. Bill put together a group called the Paramours, while Bobby sang with the Variations. They started to attract a cult following and, before long, were in competition. One day, the first tenor of the Paramours quit, and Bill asked Bobby to replace him. Bobby agreed, and the two soon discovered a "magic" in singing together. Their R&B style, later known as "blue-eyed soul," attracted large crowds, as few whites were "singing black" in the early sixties.

The Paramours broke up, overshadowed by their two lead singers. Bobby and Bill needed a new name and got one from black friends who came to hear them in clubs. At that time, if you had a good-looking coat, it was called "righteous." And if you were well liked, you were known as a "brother." As Bobby and Bill were both good dressers and were admired by blacks, their fans came to call them "the righteous brothers." The name stuck.

By 1963, the team was selling out nightclubs all over Southern California. They signed with Moonglow Records and scored two big local hits, "Little Latin Lupe Lu" and "My Babe." In 1964, they joined the Beatles' first American tour and were thus exposed to the entire nation. As a result of that connection, they were invited to sing on the premiere telecast of "Shindig" on September 16. The Righteous Brothers went over so well that they were signed as regulars and remained with the show during its entire network run.

The boys' biggest break, though, came in a meeting with the legendary Phil Spector, who signed them to a recording contract. He produced their first record for Phillies, "You've Lost

That Lovin' Feelin'." The song is generally regarded as Phil Spector's greatest achievement as a record producer. He's also listed as a cowriter, although most of the credit should go to Barry Mann and Cynthia Weil. "Phil influences more than he writes," said Cynthia. "He inspires. The fact that you know Phil is going to cut your song is inspiring in the first place. You know that whatever you give him is going to be done right."

Barry said: "We flew out to California to work with Phil. He said he had this group, these two guys who sing, and that they'd had some hit records out of Orange County. He played us the records, and we really liked the way they sounded. So I came up with a melody, and an opening line: 'You never close your eyes anymore when I kiss your lips.' Cynthia took it from there, and wrote most of the lyrics. We felt pressure. We wanted to write a great song, and we loved the Righteous Brothers."

According to legend, it took some sixty takes to get the vocal parts down,

but Bobby insisted that it didn't take very long at all. The complete session, though, took nearly ten hours, and after the song was mixed down, Phil held a party at his house to celebrate. At the party, Phil played his masterwork over and over, for another five hours.

The Righteous Brothers first sang the song publicly on "Shindig" in October 1964. The TV exposure helped, and by February 1965 it was the number-one single in America.

"You've Lost That Lovin' Feelin'" was a complex, varied, dramatic record. Early critics said that it was slow and sounded as if it were playing at the wrong speed. Others claimed it was too long, and for that reason, Phillies deliberately mistimed its length on the label.

"If there hadn't been a Phil Spector, 'You've Lost That Lovin' Feelin' would never have happened," said Cynthia. "Any other producer would have said it was too weird, too strange, and too segmented. But Phil always understood."

(I Can't Get No) Satisfaction

THE ROLLING STONES

Mick Jagger and Keith Richards were childhood friends in England but slowly drifted apart. They met again on the campus of Sidcup Art School, where Keith was a student and Mick a vendor selling ice-cream cones. It wasn't until their paths crossed a third time—on a train in 1962—that the conversation turned to music, and they discovered a shared love of American R&B. From that talk arose the most controversial band of the mid-sixties—the Rolling Stones.

Rounding out the original line-up were Dick Taylor (guitar, bass), Brian Jones (guitar, vocals), Ian Stewart (piano), and Tony Chapman (drums). These six adopted their group name from a Muddy Waters song, "The Rolling Stones Blues."

The boys' first break came in June 1962, when they were heard on a BBC radio broadcast. Soon after, Dick Taylor and Tony Chapman left and were replaced, respectively, by Bill Wyman and Charlie Watts. In April 1963, Andrew Loog Oldham signed on as manager and began cultivating their "rebellious" public image. As Ian didn't look "punky" enough, he was dropped from the "official" line-up, yet continued to play live and on record with the rest of the group.

The first Stones single, "Come On," was released in June 1963; it was followed by "I Wanna Be Your Man" (a Lennon and McCartney song) and "Not Fade Away" (written by Buddy Holly; it made the American top fifty). After that came hit LPs (*The Rolling Stones, 12 × 5, Now*) and singles ("Tell Me," "It's All Over Now," "Time Is on My Side") on both sides of the Atlantic. In 1965, there was another hit, "Heart of Stone," and then a heavily soul-influenced album, *Out of Our Heads.* From it came "Play with Fire," "Get Off of My Cloud," and "(I Can't Get No) Satisfaction"—the Stones' very first number-one record.

"Satisfaction" was conceived in a dream by twenty-year-old guitarist Keith Richards. He awoke one night in a hotel with the basic riff and refrain pounding in his head. It felt pretty good, so he wrote it down, and the next day, he played it for Mick Jagger. Afterward, he almost apologized for his "silly kind of riff," but Jagger liked it and said it sounded like a folk song. Mick completed the words, and on May 13, the band committed it to tape in Los Angeles.

Keith was not happy with the recording. He thought it was "a bit basic" and "sounded too much like a dub." It needed horns or something "that could really knock that riff out." He also didn't care much for his fuzz guitar work and simply wanted to re-record the track. He certainly didn't want what they had released—especially as a single—as he was convinced that it wouldn't do very well.

Mick, on the other hand, felt it was a fine recording. "I don't think he listened to it properly," said Jagger. "That's the only time we have had a disagreement." Did Mick think, though, that it would go on to be a number-one record? "No, not at all."

According to Keith, "Satisfaction" was loosely based on Martha and the Vandellas' "Dancing in the Streets." However, other than the first five notes, it's hard to understand the connection. Musically, lyrically, and thematically, they're poles apart.

One critic called "Satisfaction" the greatest of the Stones' "gothic hymns." Another reported that it was full of "screaming, frustrated sex." One thing for sure was that it was the perfect Stones paradox—lyrics denying what the music delivered. Released in mid-June, it sold a million copies in two weeks and was number one for four weeks in July. Worldwide, it sold more than five million.

In a 1965 interview, Keith Richards was asked why the Stones had become so popular, so quickly. "I think it's a cross between the music, the image, and the time that we came along," he said. "I think we came along just at the right time, you know? It was luck."

I Can't Help Myself
THE FOUR TOPS

The four men who became the Four Tops first met as teen-agers in 1954. As veterans of neighborhood groups, they were asked to sing together at a high school party. Their vocal offering met with such praise and encouragement that they decided to stick together for a while and see what might happen. None of them could have guessed the heights they were to scale over the next quarter-century.

Abdul "Duke" Fakir, Levi Stubbs, Jr., Lawrence Payton, and Renaldo "Obie" Benson first decided to call them-selves the Four Aims. They played small clubs around their hometown of Detroit and in 1956 were signed by the Chess Record Company. The group changed their name to the Four Tops in time for their first release, "Kiss Me Baby," but the song was not a national success. Over the next few years, they were to cut sides for the Red Top, Riverside, Singular, and Columbia labels, all without making even the slightest dent on the record charts.

Then in 1963, the Four Tops went to see the founder and president of Motown, Berry Gordy, Jr. They had known him from back in his boxing

days, and he was well aware of the Four Tops' talent. They got a contract without an audition and were assigned to Motown's top songwriting and production team—Brian Holland, Lamont Dozier, and Eddie Holland. As major designers of the "Motown Sound," H-D-H had helped turn the Supremes, Mary Wells, and other singers into major pop stars. Berry Gordy believed they could do the same with the Four Tops.

In the fall of 1964, H-D-H wrote and produced the first Four Tops classic, "Baby I Need Your Loving." It was recorded in the wee small hours of an autumn morning, when everyone involved felt loose enough to offer a really heartfelt performance. All the Four Tops sessions—under H-D-H direction—were relaxed in the same kind of low-pressure way. Writers and singers would sit around and chat, try out a line or two, and slowly work out a feeling for the tune. Sometimes they'd send out for cold beer and sandwiches and then wait an hour for the food and drink to settle. Then they'd take another shot at the song. It was certainly a time-consuming and expensive way to make hit records. But it worked—and for years, million-

seller after million-seller rolled out of the Motown studios.

In the spring of 1965, the Four Tops recorded another H-D-H song, "I Can't Help Myself." Eddie Holland conducted the session, and, as usual, Levi Stubbs handled the lead vocals. After two or three takes, Levi asked if he could listen to what they had so far. At that point, Brian Holland walked in and was amazed to hear the tape as it was played back. "There's no point in going on," he said. "I don't think there's any way that we can improve on that."

Levi was stunned, as he didn't think he had done a very good job at all. "Let's give it another try," he pleaded, "just one more time."

"Tomorrow, Levi," they told him. "We'll try it again tomorrow."

There was, though, no "tomor-row," as Motown released one of those first few takes as the finished record. It broke onto the charts in May of '65 and within a month was the top-selling single.

The Four Tops went on to prove, over and over again, that they were one of the best R&B groups of the sixties. Among the nearly forty tunes they placed on the charts were "It's the Same Old Song" (1965), "Reach Out, I'll Be There" (number one in 1966), "Standing in the Shadows of Love" (1966), "Bernadette" (1967), "Walk Away Renee" (1968), and "It's All in the Game" (a Grammy nomi-nee in 1970). In 1972, they switched from Motown to Dunhill Records, and the hits continued with "Keeper of the Castle" (1972), "Ain't No Woman Like the One I've Got" (1973), and "Are You Man Enough" (1973).

The Four Tops specialized in songs of soulful hysteria—tunes that captured the anguish of a desperate lover. It's hard to pick a "best" or "most typical" hit from their long list of million-sellers. However, "I Can't Help Myself" sums up the Four Tops as well as any single record can.

Wooly Bully

SAM THE SHAM AND THE PHARAOHS

Domingo Samudio was born near Dallas, Texas, to a Spanish-speaking couple of Mexican descent. He made his singing debut while still in the second grade, representing his school in a live radio broadcast. Later, he took up guitar and formed a high school group with several of his friends, one of whom was Trini Lopez. After graduation, he joined the navy and lived in Panama for six years, until his discharge in 1962.

Back in the States, Domingo didn't know what kind of life's work to choose. He considered sports, heavy construction, and even crime, but finally decided to become a student. He enrolled at the University of Texas in Arlington and took courses in music history. "I was studying classical in the daytime and playing rock 'n' roll in clubs at night," he recalled. "That lasted two years. Then I dropped out and became a carny."

The carnival life paled after a short time, and Domingo returned to rock 'n' roll. Hocking everything he had, he bought an organ and three days later accepted a job with Andy and the Night Riders in Louisiana. "We became a popular roadhouse band," said Domingo, "playing mostly gun-and-knife clubs."

One night, David Martin, bass player in the group, told Domingo, "You know, there are people making thousands of dollars a night doing what we do, and they're not half as good as we are."

"Well," replied Domingo, "how do we make that kind of money?"

"There's only one way," David said. "It takes a gold record."

"O.K.," said Domingo, "let's go get one."

The two men shook, and their partnership was born.

One month later, two members of the Night Riders quit, including lead singer Andy Anderson. Two others replaced them, and Domingo took over control of the band. It was time for a new name.

"By that time, everyone was calling me Sam, short for Samudio," said the new leader. "And what I was doing, fronting the band and cutting up, was called 'shamming.' We got the rest of the name from the movie *The Ten Commandments.* Old Ramses, the King of Egypt, looked pretty cool, so we decided to become the Pharaohs."

In the summer of 1964, Sam the Sham and the Pharaohs finally got their chance to record. "We said we had something they might dig, a beat that was pretty popular around Dallas. The words we were using came from 'The Hully Gully,' and when we went into the studio, they said we couldn't use those words. I said, 'O.K., let's kick it off, and I'll make something up.' Now, the name of my cat was Wooly Bully, so I started from there. The countdown part of the song was also not planned. I was just goofing around and counted off in Tex-Mex. It just blew everybody away, and actually, I wanted it taken off the record. I was a little insecure, I guess. Anyway, we did three takes on it, all of them different, and all of them good. I think they took the first take and released it. From what I understand, it became the first American record to sell a million copies during the onslaught of all the British groups."

The lyrics of "Wooly Bully" were hard to understand, and some radio stations banned it, fearing that the words might be suggestive. They weren't, of course, and the record went on to sell more than three million copies. It was nominated for a Grammy Award and was named Record of the Year by *Billboard* in 1965.

Sam the Sham and the Pharaohs eventually toured the world and had several more hits, including "Little Red Riding Hood" in 1966. They broke up in 1967, unable to shake their image as comic entertainers. " 'Wooly Bully' was not a novelty song," said Sam. "It was a dance record, but not everybody realized that. They saw us as comedians, and that's a problem, especially when you come up with something serious."

1966

THE FIRST PSYCHEDELIC SHOPS opened in 1966, a year noted for the breakthrough of the tape cartridge. Iron Butterfly, the Capitols, Cream, and Buffalo Springfield all got together, while the Browns and the original Animals broke up. Gary Lewis got drafted, Jackson Browne left the Nitty Gritty Dirt Band, and John Lennon made an offhand remark about the Beatles being "bigger than Jesus." Names got changed in 1966: Vince Furnier became Alice Cooper; Gerry Dorsey, Englebert Humperdinck; and the Hi Fis turned themselves into the Fifth Dimension. Notable newcomers on the pop charts included B. J. Thomas ("I'm So Lonesome I Could Cry"), the Grass Roots ("Where Were You When I Needed You"), Neil Diamond ("Solitary Man"), and Senator Everett McKinley Dirksen ("Gallant Men"). TV shows by the Monkees and Roger Miller went on the air; "The Adventures of Ozzie & Harriet" went off. Jan Berry and Bob Dylan were hurt in separate vehicle crashes; Grace Slick joined the Jefferson Airplane. It was 1966—the year of graffiti on the wall of the men's room at Cambridge University Library: "To do is to be."—John Stuart Mill. And directly underneath: "To be is to do."—Jean-Paul Sartre. And followed by a third handwriting: "Do be do be do."—Frank Sinatra.

"Hullaballoo" was NBC's response to the great popularity of "Shindig," a rock 'n' roll variety series on ABC. Every week, a special guest introduced the line-up of pop stars, who would then sing their latest hits. For a time, a regular feature was a filmed segment on British rock, hosted by the Beatles' manager, Brian Epstein. One of the acts which appeared during the 1966 season was Motown's first successful girl group, the **Marvelettes,** who were then in the top ten with "Don't Mess with Bill."

Elvis appeared in three films in 1966—*Frankie and Johnny, Spinout,* and *Easy Come Easy Go.* Roy Orbison made his first motion picture appearance in a Civil War comedy *The Fastest Guitar Alive.* Lulu turned up in *To Sir with Love,* which also featured the Mindbenders. And country music was celebrated in *The Road to Nashville,* starring Johnny Cash, Marty Robbins, Bill Anderson, Faron Young, and Waylon Jennings.

Nineteen sixty-six was a year of many things, not least of which was the most successful "ghost" band in history—**Herb Alpert** and the Tijuana Brass. "The sound of the Tijuana Brass was the sound of my trumpet," said Herb. "I played all the trumpet parts on the records. There really was no group until 1965, after the *Whipped Cream* album. I got a group together then just to go on the road. The Brass was a lot of double trumpets, you know, and tricks and things, echo." It was also spectacularly successful in 1966: seven hit songs on the charts, five gold albums in the top twenty, and by year's end sales of thirteen and a half million in the United States alone. No other recording artist in history had accomplished that feat.

A one-time member of the Falcons, the "wicked" **Wilson Pickett** gained his greatest fame as a solo performer, belting out a hard, heavy brand of urban soul. Following his first major hits, "In the Midnight Hour" and "634-5789" (both cut in Memphis), Wilson changed his place of recording to Muscle Shoals in 1966. Out of those sessions came several classics of spontaneous rhythm and blues, including "Mustang Sally," "Funky Broadway," "I'm a Midnight Mover," and his first top-ten single, "Land of 1000 Dances." Pickett's string of driving, funky records remained staples of radio air play well into the early seventies.

The effervescent sound of the **Mamas and the Papas** was worked out in the Virgin Islands, where the group spent two summers lying on the sand and harmonizing. They returned to the mainland in September 1965, formally organized in October, recorded in November, and had a hit in January: "California Dreamin'." After that came "I Saw Her Again," "Words of Love," "Dedicated to the One I Love," "Creeque Alley," and their number one Grammy winner, "Monday, Monday." Leader "Papa" John Phillips and wife "Mama" Michelle seemed to live the ideal romance: the perfect California boy who wed the perfect California girl. But things fell apart in 1968; the couple split up, and the group disintegrated. John wound up a heroin addict; Michelle an unsuccessful actress. Another "Papa," Denny Doherty, became a Canadian talk show host. The fourth group member, "Mama" Cass Elliot, had a brief solo career ("Dream a Little Dream of Me," etc.) before dying of natural causes in 1974.

THE TOP 40

1. Ballad of the Green Berets, *S/Sgt. Barry Sadler*
2. Poor Side of Town, *Johnny Rivers*
3. You Can't Hurry Love, *Supremes*
4. Cherish, *Association*
5. Strangers in the Night, *Frank Sinatra*
6. Soul and Inspiration, *Righteous Brothers*
7. 96 Tears, *Question Mark and the Mysterians*
8. We Can Work It Out, *Beatles*
9. Last Train to Clarksville, *Monkees*
10. Good Lovin', *Young Rascals*
11. Sunny, *Bobby Hebb*
12. Hanky Panky, *Tommy James and the Shondells*
13. Monday Monday, *Mamas and the Papas*
14. Lightning Strikes, *Lou Christie*
15. See You in September, *Happenings*
16. Kicks, *Paul Revere and the Raiders*
17. These Boots Are Made for Walkin', *Nancy Sinatra*
18. Little Red Riding Hood, *Sam the Sham and the Pharaohs*
19. Groovy Kind of Love, *Mindbenders*
20. Sounds of Silence, *Simon and Garfunkel*
21. Reach Out, *Four Tops*
22. When a Man Loves a Woman, *Percy Sledge*
23. You Don't Have to Say You Love Me, *Dusty Springfield*
24. I Got You, *James Brown*
25. California Dreamin', *Mamas and the Papas*
26. Summer in the City, *Lovin' Spoonful*
27. Sunshine Superman, *Donovan*
28. What Becomes of the Broken Hearted, *Jimmy Ruffin*
29. Born Free, *Roger Williams*
30. Paint It Black, *Rolling Stones*
31. Uptight, *Stevie Wonder*
32. My Love, *Beatles*
33. Winchester Cathedral, *New Vaudeville Band*
34. Red Rubber Ball, *Cyrkle*
35. Cool Jerk, *Capitols*
36. No Matter What Shape, *T-Bones*
37. Wild Thing, *Troggs*
38. Ain't Too Proud to Beg, *Temptations*
39. Paperback Writer, *Beatles*
40. Daydream Believer, *Monkees*

In their earliest days, the *Hollies* made their mark by tightening and rocking up songs originally made famous by others. By 1966, though, the British quintet was writing their own material, such as their first major U.S. hit, "Bus Stop." "Stop Stop Stop," "On a Carousel," and "Carrie Anne" came after that; then, in 1969, Graham Nash left the group to form Crosby, Stills and Nash. "He Ain't Heavy He's My Brother" (featuring the piano talents of Elton John) was a Hollies million-seller in 1970; later gold included "Long Cool Woman in a Black Dress" (1972) and "The Air that I Breathe" (1974). Despite a distinctive three-part harmony style, the Hollies never developed much of an image in America—at least not one as clear-cut as the Beatles', Stones', or Kinks'.

THE TOP 10 LPs

1. The Sound of Music, *Original Soundtrack*
2. Whipped Cream and Other Delights, *Herb Alpert and the Tijuana Brass*
3. Going Places, *Herb Alpert and the Tijuana Brass*
4. Dr. Zhivago, *Original Soundtrack*
5. What Now My Love, *Herb Alpert and the Tijuana Brass*
6. South of the Border, *Herb Alpert and the Tijuana Brass*
7. If You Can Believe Your Eyes and Ears, *Mamas and the Papas*
8. Rubber Soul, *Beatles*
9. Best of . . ., *The Animals*
10. Best of . . ., *Herman's Hermits*

10

Good Lovin'
THE YOUNG RASCALS

Felix Cavaliere spent two years as a pre-med student before deciding that "my heart was in a different place." A long-time Ray Charles fan, he realized that music was the most important thing in his life.

He became the only white member of the Stereos, a soul group in his hometown of Pelham, New York. They had a top-thirty hit on Cub Records in October 1961: "I Really Love You." After that, he played with the Escorts, a band that included Mike Esposito (later of the Blues Magoos) and Neil Diamond. Finally he wound up as one of Joey Dee's Starlighters, performing at the Peppermint Lounge in New York City.

Also in the Starlighters were Eddie Brigati and Gene Cornish, who were fed up with playing twist music. In 1964, the trio split from Dee and added drummer Dino Danelli, whom Felix had met in Las Vegas. They holed up at Felix's house over the winter, working up a repertoire of twenty-five songs. It was there that Felix came up with their "sound concept": basing everything on his organ, as a blanket backdrop. Drums and guitar provided rhythm, with the organ and guitar completing the "orchestra." "I had to rethink my whole style of playing," said Gene. The boys also agreed on their name (adapted from the *Little Rascals* reruns on TV) and an early gimmick—dressing in Edwardian costumes. By January 1965 they were ready, and accepted a booking at the Choo Choo Club in Garfield, New Jersey (Eddie's hometown). They held one final rehearsal—for twenty-five hours straight.

The Choo Choo Club gig began early in February 1965. Dino was fifteen years old then, and the first time Felix had ever touched a big, professional Hammond B-3 organ was onstage. But he mastered it right away.

Their second booking was more prestigious: at the Hamptons on Long Island Sound. A real barge—cleverly called "The Barge"—had been refurbished into a chic floating discotheque for socialites. The Young Rascals thrilled the crowd with their raunchy renditions of R&B classics little known to the jet set. Their engagement was extended to two and a half months, and by the end of summer, the Young Rascals were the hottest new band in the New York area.

Concert promoter Sid Bernstein came to see them, and amid many bids from a flurry of record companies, signed the group to Atlantic. Their first single, "I Ain't Gonna Eat Out My Heart Anymore," was a regional hit, mainly on the east coast, in January 1966.

And then came "Good Lovin'."

The boys had a habit of visiting Harlem, browsing through record shops, looking for tunes not found in the pop top ten. They were after basic rhythmic R&B—the kind of stuff they could rework and knock people out with onstage. On one trip, they discovered "Good Lovin'," a crudely made record that had bombed in the black market for the Olympics (and had died at number eighty-one on the pop charts in May 1965). The Young Rascals decided to cut their own version under the direction of Arif Mardin and Tom Dowd (who would later join Jerry Wexler in producing the hits of Aretha Franklin).

"Good Lovin'" broke coast-to-coast in mid-March 1966, peaking at number one in April. It got heavy play in discotheques—both white and black—and remained a best-seller for fourteen weeks. It was featured on the Young Rascals' first self-titled album, which made the national LP top fifteen.

Later in 1966, the group went to England, where they impressed R&B loving bands such as the Animals, Stones, and Beatles. Back home again, they played Madison Square Garden with James Brown, and reportedly did a soulful version of "Good Lovin'" in their Little Lord Fauntleroy suits.

Last Train to Clarksville

The Monkees

The Monkees were put together by two TV executives, Bob Rafelson and Bert Schneider, who worked under the name of Raybert Productions. Both had admired the inspired lunacy of Beatles movies, such as *Help!* and *A Hard Day's Night,* and hoped to adapt the zany structure of those films for television. Originally, they planned to build a series around an existing band—an American counterpart to the Beatles—and chose the Lovin' Spoonful. Midway through negotiations, though, Bob and Bert realized that they'd have more control, and would be better off financially, if they assembled their own quartet. So, on September 8, 1965, an ad appeared in the *Hollywood Reporter*: "Wanted: Four insane boys, aged 17 to 21, to form a group for a TV show. The program will reflect the adventures of an unknown, young, long-haired, modern-dressed band, and their dreams on the way to fame and fortune." As fate would have it, those fictional dreams really were to come true.

Four hundred thirty-seven people auditioned for the parts, including Danny Hutton, who later found success in Three Dog Night. Those chosen were George Michael Dolenz, David Thomas Jones, Robert Michael Nesmith, and Peter Halsten Thorkenson. Dolenz, an actor, had once starred under the name of Mickey Braddock in a 1956–58 TV series, "Circus Boy." Jones, an Englishman, had performed on Broadway, most notably as the Artful Dodger in *Oliver.* Mike Nesmith had prior musical experience in Texas folk groups; Peter Tork had played banjo and sung in Greenwich Village as a member of the Phoenix Singers. Tork was the last to be hired; he heard about the project from his best friend, Stephen Stills. Stills, who also auditioned, would have gotten a role if he had only had better teeth.

The four Monkees spent the summer of '66 getting to know each other, and learning improvisational acting techniques. At the same time, their "sound" was being worked out at Screen Gems/Columbia Music. After several writers submitted ideas, the team of Tommy Boyce and Bobby Hart was selected to compose three songs for the pilot episode. They came up with the Monkees' theme, "I Wanna Be Free," and "Last Train to Clarksville."

Bobby Hart wrote most of the latter song. He'd been driving down Sunset Boulevard, and as he pulled into his driveway, a Beatles record he hadn't heard before came on the radio. He just caught the fade of it, and thought they were singing "take the last train to" something; he couldn't figure out what. Later he found out that the record was "Paperback Writer." "Well," thought Bobby, "if that's not the title of a Beatles' song, maybe we could make something of it."

Boyce and Hart then took their guitars and headed for an inspiring place—the beach at Malibu. Lying in the sun, they worked out a concept for their tune: a composite of two separate and unrelated ideas. The theme was farewell; a fellow at a train station, about to leave home. He wishes that the girl he loves would come to bid him goodbye, as he may never return again. "Clarksville" was tossed in by Bobby, as it was an Arizona town he used to like to visit.

The next day, Boyce and Hart sang their song for the Monkees and they all loved it. Later that week, Tommy and Bobby entered the studio and cut the basic tracks for the single. The Monkees then came in, overdubbed their vocal parts, and the record was complete.

"Last Train to Clarksville" was issued on August 16, 1966, the first release on the newly-formed Colgems label. Four weeks later, on September 12, the TV show premiered and the 45 took off. It reached number one in October, and at the end of that month was certified as a million-seller (eventual sales topped three million). The first Monkees album went gold in five weeks, and was number one for fifteen. It sold over 3,200,000 copies in less than three months—faster than the Beatles did at their launch in 1964. It wound up as the top-selling LP of the year.

And the Monkees were just getting started.

We Can Work It Out

THE BEATLES

The Beatles began 1966 on a triumphant note, with one of the best-selling singles of their career. Both sides became major hits, one song reaching number five and the other climbing all the way to the top of the charts.

The A side, "We Can Work It Out," was written mostly by Paul McCartney. John Lennon came up with the chorus; "The middle bit," as he called it, "the 'life is very short' stuff." Paul sang lead, with John providing backing vocals and harmonica. The other side of the record, "Day Tripper," was mostly John's creation ("I just liked the phrase," he said).

Both numbers were recorded early in November 1965 and were released during the first week in December. The single sold a million copies in England by December 20 and was the Beatles' tenth consecutive hit in that country to make number one overnight. In America, "We Can Work It Out" spent three weeks at the top of the charts, all in the month of January.

The Beatles sang both songs on American television, in their first and only appearance on NBC's "Hullaballoo." They were shown riding a fake train, lip-syncing along to their record. "Hullaballoo" was notorious for making its guests do this, and at one point, Lennon could be seen sneering at the camera and missing a finger note—all on purpose, of course. The Beatles only appeared on the show at the request of their manager, Brian Epstein, who hosted a regular "British Scene" segment of the series.

Over the next several months, the Beatles had four more hits—"Nowhere Man" in March, "Paperback Writer" in July, and "Yellow Submarine," backed with "Eleanor Rigby," in September. Then, in early fall, a British magazine quoted John Lennon as saying, "Christianity will go. It will vanish and shrink. I needn't argue about that; I'm right and I will be proved right. We're more popular than Jesus now; I don't know which will go first, rock 'n' roll or Christianity.

Jesus was right, but His disciples were thick and ordinary."

Those words set off angry reaction in all corners of the music world. Many radio stations banned Beatles records, with one deejay calling for a "Beatles bonfire" (he then broke the latest Beatles record on the air). Fiery editorials were written, and in some cities, anti-Beatles rallies were held. Finally, Lennon apologized for his statement, but added a condition. "Sorry or not, it's true," he said. "I suppose if I had said television was more popular than Jesus I would have gotten away with it. I wasn't saying we were greater or better. I'm just sorry I opened my mouth."

The Jesus controversy died down—we could work it out, and did. But, unfortunately, it timed exactly with the start of the Beatles' very last American tour. On August 29, 1966, the boys played Candlestick Park in San Francisco. Neither they nor we knew that they would never again grace a concert stage anywhere in the world.

96 Tears

QUESTION MARK AND THE MYSTERIANS

*S*aginaw, Michigan, 1962. An out-of-work bass player sits at home, watching a three-year-old Japanese sci-fi movie on television. It's about highly intellectual aliens; invaders, who try to take over Earth after their planet has been destroyed. The title of the film is *The Mysterians.*

And thus a band was born in the mind of Larry Borjas.

He contacted a cousin, guitarist Bobby Balderrama, and a drummer, Robert Martinez. Together as the Mysterians, they began to play teen clubs around the central Michigan area. Eventually, they picked up a fourth member, organist Franklin Rodriguez.

One night, while appearing at the Mount Holly Ski Lodge, the band was approached by an enigmatic stranger, who said he wanted to become their manager. They agreed. Later, they found out the man could sing, and made him their lead vocalist.

Not even the group was said to know his real name, or anything about his past. He never removed his sunglasses, and was known only by the mystic pseudonym, "Question Mark." He gave each member a secret initial—Y, X; other letters. The fellows were indeed grateful, but finally decided to keep their own names.

When the Vietnam War began to escalate, both Larry and Robert were drafted. They were replaced, respectively, by Frank Lugo and Eddie Serrato. Soon after, Question Mark revealed that he had written a poem, entitled "Too Many Teardrops." He invited the group to set his words to music, and they did so. However, Eddie felt a title change was in order. He suggested "69 Tears."

"We can't use that," said another member. "If you call it '69 Tears' they aren't gonna play it on the radio."

Somebody else chimed in, "Well, let's just turn the numbers around and call it '96 Tears.' " All the Mysterians thought that was a good idea.

"96 Tears" became a great crowd pleaser at the Mount Holly dance hall, and before long word had reached Lilly Gonzalez, the owner of Pa-Go-Go Records. She agreed to financially back the group in recording their song. The session took place in a makeshift two-track "studio"—actually, Lilly's living room. Afterward, there was disagreement as to which side of the record to promote. Several Mysterians opted for the flip, "Midnight Hour," because it was "more funky."

Question Mark, though, pushed "96 Tears," and when the tune began to take off locally, he got copies to Bob Dell, the program director of WTAC in Flint. Dell helped the group get better bookings, and before long "96 Tears" was the number-one request item at the station. Air play spread to Detroit, and when CKLW added the single, Cameo Records stepped in and bought the master for national release.

"96 Tears" broke coast-to-coast early in September 1966, and by October, it was the top-selling 45 in America. In November, twelve weeks after Cameo had picked it up, Question Mark and the Mysterians were presented with their gold record award, signifying over a million dollars in sales. In all, their tune spent nearly four months on the U.S. hit parade.

Question Mark and the Mysterians made several TV appearances, chiefly on shows like "Where the Action Is" and "American Bandstand." They also had a follow-up hit, "I Need Somebody," in December 1966. After that, though, Cameo Records went down the drain, taking most of their roster with them. In the summer of 1967, Question Mark and the Mysterians also agreed to say goodbye.

"We were something different," said Bobby Balderrama, "an all-Mexican band from Saginaw, Michigan." And Question Mark? "Oh, he was Robert's brother, and Eddie Serrato's brother-in-law: Rudy Martinez."

6

(You're My) Soul and Inspiration
THE RIGHTEOUS BROTHERS

The Righteous Brothers could do no wrong in 1965. Hollywood was on their heels, and live appearances were massive sellouts. Every week they were featured on "Shindig," one of TV's best-loved music shows. And the hits just kept on coming: "You've Lost That Lovin' Feelin'," "Just Once in My Life," "Unchained Melody," "Ebb Tide"—four consecutive top-ten singles. All were released on Phillies Records and were produced by Phil Spector.

"There was a definite 'Spector Sound,'" said Bobby Hatfield, the higher-voiced Righteous Brother, "and that's why we had to leave him. Phil called his thing 'controlled music,' and after a while, we called it 'stifling.' The vocal things Billy and I were doing were getting lost in the mix. Background effects and arrangement were coming through much stronger than we were. And I think any singer wants to be heard."

And so, shortly after the release of "Ebb Tide," the Righteous Brothers left Phillies, and signed a new contract with Verve Records. "The pressure was really on us now," recalled Bobby. "We had to prove that we could make it without Phil."

The Righteous Brothers had spent a long time building their musical reputation. Although not really brothers, they had a spine-tingling way of singing as kindred spirits. They didn't do duets, in the Everly Brothers' sense, but instead adapted a supportive, call-and-response approach. It was gospel rooted, and although they were white, the sound came out black. For this reason, they became known as singers of "blue-eyed soul"—one of the first acts to be so labeled.

"My definition of soul," said Bobby, "is that it's an inner feeling. It's a way of selling a song—projecting it and making it believable to the listener."

"(You're My) Soul and Inspiration" was their first single released by Verve Records. It was produced by the taller

Righteous Brother, Bill Medley, in a bombastic style that frankly imitated Phil Spector's. The composers were Barry Mann and Cynthia Weil, the same husband-and-wife team that came up with "You've Lost That Lovin' Feelin'." And like "Feelin'," "Soul and Inspiration" became a number-one record, all over the world.

The career of the Righteous Brothers went into a slow fade in 1966, despite later hits, such as "He" and "Go Ahead and Cry." After six weeks of deliberation, Bill Medley left the act in January 1968, walking out on more than three million dollars' worth of work. His first solo single, a complete flop, was prophetically titled "I Can't Make It Alone." Meanwhile, Bobby found a new partner, Jimmy Walker, formerly of the Knickerbockers, and tried to keep going as "the New Righteous Brothers." That venture was also doomed to failure.

By the early seventies, the separated Righteous Brothers had been reduced to playing some of the poorest lounges in Las Vegas. It was then that they decided to reunite and see if there was still room for them in the music business. They signed with Haven Records, a new label headed by the songwriting and production team of Dennis Lambert and Brian Potter. In the summer of 1974, the Righteous Brothers returned to the top of the charts with "Rock 'n' Roll Heaven," a million-seller composed by Alan O'Day.

The reunion didn't last long; there were two more hits, "Give It to the People" and "Dream On," and then Bobby and Bill split up once again. This time, though, the feelings were different—Bobby and Bill parted as friends. They were older and wiser and more confident—ready, at last, to "make it alone."

Strangers in the Night

FRANK SINATRA

F rancis Albert Sinatra was born an only child in a tough, ethnic neighborhood of Hoboken, New Jersey. It was there, at Demarest High School, that he first sang in public, in emulation of his idol, Bing Crosby. Frank first came to national attention on September 8, 1935, when he won first prize on Major Bowes's "Amateur Hour" on NBC radio. Then he sang on local stations until "rediscovered" by Harry James four years later. With the James orchestra, he cut "All or Nothing at All," a record that sold only eight thousand copies when first released.

From there, Frank joined the Tommy Dorsey orchestra as a featured vocalist. By 1941, he was America's most popular singer, according to surveys conducted by *Billboard* and *Downbeat* magazines. He left Dorsey in September 1942, and five months later became the host and star of "Your Hit Parade" over CBS radio. On June 1, 1943, he signed with Columbia Records and within a week had five titles out: "You'll Never Know," "Close to You," "Sunday, Monday and Always," "People Will Say We're in Love," and a reissue of "All or Nothing at All." All exploded into the top ten, and by the end of the year, Frank Sinatra was the highest-paid and most frantically worshiped star in history.

The hits rolled on with "I Couldn't Sleep a Wink Last Night" (1944), "Dream" (1945), "Five Minutes More" (1946; his first number-one record), "Mam'selle" (1947), "Nature Boy" (1948), "The Hucklebuck" (1949), "Good Night Irene" (1950), "Castle Rock" (1951), and over a dozen more on the Columbia label. Sinatra's film career, launched with *Las Vegas Nights* (1941), hit a peak in 1953, when he won an Academy Award for his role in *From Here to Eternity*. After that, he signed a new agreement with Capitol Records and he turned out a remarkable series of eighteen top-ten albums, several of which remained strong sellers year after year.

In 1965, Sinatra's producer, Jimmy Bowen, began looking for songs for Frank to record. "A publisher named Hal Fine came by, showed me some things, and then said, 'Let me play you some great new Bert Kaempfert melodies. The lyrics aren't written yet, but they're for the score of a James Garner movie called *A Man Could Get Killed*'. So he played this 'Strangers in the Night' melody, and I said—and this is the only time I've ever done this—'if you get me the right lyrics on that, Frank Sinatra will record it. It's just him, that melody.' "

Fine went back to New York and in a few months he sent the completed song. Bowen got in touch with Sinatra, but in the meantime, "Fine went ahead and got a Bobby Darin cut on it, a Jack Jones cut on it—I found out on a Friday that the Jack Jones record was coming out in three days!" Bowen said.

"I called Ernie Freeman, the arranger, and we picked the key it was going to be in, and at five o'clock Monday I had a full orchestra assembled. We ran the music down, getting everything the way we wanted it. Frank walked in at eight, and by nine, the song was cut." After working all through the night, they were able to get on the air, nationwide, by Tuesday evening.

"Strangers in the Night" turned out to be a multimillion-seller and Frank Sinatra's first number-one single in nearly twenty years. It won two Grammy Awards, as Best Male Vocal Performance and Song of the Year.

"Other than Frank's voice, I think it was the melody that made that song a hit," Bowen recalled. "Remember, the melody got to me before there was any lyric. And then the words—they were as perfect for Sinatra as were the lyrics of 'My Way.' I think those three elements combined just worked great. It's funny, though—I think he liked the record, but he never would sing the damn song at first. I saw Sinatra work a dozen times, and he never sang it. The only record I ever had with him that he did in person was 'That's Life.' I never saw him do 'Strangers in the Night.' "

Cherish

THE ASSOCIATION

The Association story began in the spring of 1965 at Doug Weston's Troubadour Club in Hollywood. A thirteen-man aggregate, the Men, made their debut there with a new kind of music called folk rock. They played several local dates and then, after one stormy rehearsal, angrily broke up. Five walked out with singer-songwriter Terry Kirkman, who led them back to his place for some drinks and consolation. As the wine flowed, someone suggested forming a new group, the Aristocrats. Terry's wife went to the dictionary to look up that word and found a better name for them on the very same page—the Association.

In May, they began six months of intensive rehearsals. Their hits would eventually bag them as a harmony pop group, similar in some ways to the Beach Boys, Vogues, or Four Preps. The Association, though, preferred the term *show rock,* and perhaps, ultimately, that description suited them best. Their repertoire was wide and varied, including not only folk but jazz, neoclassics, and even comedy routines. (One member, Jim Page, left at this point and was replaced by Jim Yester.)

In November 1965, the six-man band debuted at the Ice House in Pasadena. Early the next year, they signed with Four Star Television, which was just starting its own pop label, Valiant. One of their audition songs had been "Along Comes Mary," which wound up as the first Association hit. It was helped, and hindered, by drug lyric mania, which ran rampant in the summer of 1966. It seems incredible now, but certain social guardians insisted that "Mary" was a counter-culture code word for marijuana. Radio stations were bombarded with calls—usually from nonlisteners—demanding that "dangerous records" like "Along Comes Mary" be bounced from the airwaves. A few stations gave in to this, but most laughed it off,

turning "notoriety" into free publicity for the young sextet. The stage was set for their next single—the one that really established the Association, and put Valiant Records on firm financial footing.

Cherish, as it turns out, was not a word Terry Kirkman used very often in everyday life. However, one night he started thinking about it, rolling it over in his mind. He'd been trying to write a hit song for quite some time, and although this appeared to be a magic word, he just couldn't seem to force any ideas out of it. Three weeks later, after a long rehearsal, he was all keyed up and needed a way to wind down. He looked at his pad of song ideas, and there was the single word *cherish.* He picked up his pen, and thirty-six minutes later, the song was complete.

Terry enthusiastically auditioned his tune for a number of close friends. One of them, without his knowledge, picked up a lead sheet and sent it to the New Christy Minstrels. They performed the song live and got standing ovations with it every night. Terry was elated, but refused to let

them record what he knew would become a massive pop hit.

The Association was impressed with "Cherish" but felt the tune still needed a lot of work. He had conceived it as a slow, sad song of unrequited love—too slow, too sad, and too long, they said, for top-forty air play. The group rearranged the song, speeding it up considerably. After the session, they even speeded up the tape, half a tone. As a final step, the record label was deliberately mistimed.

"Cherish" was released in August 1966 and within two months was a million-selling single. By late September, it was number one in most cities. It remained at the top of America's pop charts for nearly a month. Oddly enough, the record did not do well overseas, perhaps because of poor distribution. The song did become an international hit in 1971, though, when recut by David Cassidy.

Ahead lay 1967, perhaps the most exciting period ever for the Association. Five of their songs were to make the charts that year, including "Windy" and "Never My Love."

You Can't Hurry Love

THE SUPREMES

The Motown Sound reached its summit in the sixties, and at the very peak of that summit was a black female trio called the Supremes. They'd risen from Detroit's dismal Brewster Housing Projects, and, by the end of the decade, had established themselves as the most important and successful girl group in the history of rock 'n' roll. With varying personnel, they stayed together for fourteen years and were stars for ten. Thirty-three of their songs reached the national top ten, and a dozen went all the way to number one.

Their forte was wide-eyed breathy soul; cool, clear, sophisticated, with a sharp, bitchy passion. Their appeal, visually and musically, depended on the growing idea that black women, in public roles, could be both beautiful and exciting. To that end, Motown Records established their Special Projects Department—a kind of charm school—to hone and perfect the sound, movement, look, and mystique of their stars. The resulting precision flattered audiences, impressed by the obvious heavy prep each act had gone through.

The prime attraction of the Supremes was lead singer Diana Ross, who had ambition and Berry Gordy's favor. Diana's voice purred, sighing and pausing in ways that were often more expressive than her words.

The Supremes' sweet soul sound was worked out by three house composer-producers, Brian Holland, Lamont Dozier, and Eddie Holland. H-D-H and the girls would get together in a little room over the session area and spend hours going over material. Eddie Holland would sing a line, Diana would hum along with him, and then sing the song herself the third time around. The combination worked well; they had parties together, even went to the race track together. And during that period, the hits were automatic. Between "Where Did Our Love Go"

and the end of 1967, all but two of the sixteen Supremes singles released made the top ten. Ten were number one.

"Where Did Our Love Go" was followed by "Baby Love" and "Come See About Me" in 1964. In 1965, there were "Stop! In the Name of Love," "Back in My Arms Again," "Nothing but Heartaches" and "I Hear a Symphony." "My World Is Empty Without You" and "Love Is Like an Itching in My Heart" came in 1966. And then came "You Can't Hurry Love."

All their records during this time kicked off with a different instrument—this one started out with bass; a socking rhythm designed to sound good on AM radio—"to have the quality," said Diana, "of making a nice, different kind of intro." Lamont worked with Mary and Flo to develop the counterpoint backgrounds; Diana, of course, sang lead.

"You Can't Hurry Love" was released in early August 1966, and peaked at number one in September. It spent three months on the chart, and was the Supremes' ninth million-seller.

There were many more hits: "You Keep Me Hanging On," "Love Is Here and Now You're Gone," and "The Happening." Then, in Las Vegas, original Supreme Florence Ballard was

mysteriously "retired" from the group. Amid much controversy, the three immediately became "Diana Ross and the Supremes," a semantic change obviously designed to hype their lead singer. Later, Florence filed a million-dollar lawsuit, claiming she had been "forced out," and promised a fortune that never came through. In 1971, her case was thrown out of court, and in 1976, while living on welfare, she died, the victim of "heart trouble."

Cindy Birdsong, a former member of Patti Labelle's Bluebelles, was hired to replace Florence, and the hits kept on coming. The emphasis in the girls' career at that point was on TV (they starred in a couple of show-bizzy specials), glamour, glitter, and a lot more of Diana Ross. In 1970, after the platinum single "Someday We'll Be Together," Ross was launched from the act to start a solo career.

Singer Jean Terrell replaced Diana, bringing a much-needed shot of Southern soul to the group. With Terrell, Wilson and Birdsong racked up four more gold records in the next eighteen months. In 1972, though, Cindy Birdsong retired, and the group's magical ride on the charts ended. The girls limped along for another five years until Mary Wilson, the last original Supreme, was dumped by the company.

Poor Side of Town

JOHNNY RIVERS

John Ramistella, the seventh son of a seventh son, grew up in Baton Rouge, Louisiana. "I didn't have any formal music education," he said. "Dad used to play the guitar and mandolin, and I just picked it up." As a teenager, he earned money by playing with his own group at local dances. Working at night, he would come to high school the next day and invariably fall asleep in class.

During summer vacation, Johnny visited New York and Nashville, hoping to break into the record business. On one trip he met deejay Alan Freed, who suggested a name change from Ramistella to Rivers.

In 1963, Johnny was asked to fill in for a few nights at Gazzarri's, an L.A. nightclub. He had no fancy act—just himself, sitting on a stool, singing and playing his guitar, with only a drummer as accompanist. Within three nights there were lines around the block.

Johnny accepted an offer to headline and record at L.A.'s leading discotheque, and from there his career exploded. His first album, *Johnny Rivers at the Whiskey Au Go Go*, became a national best-seller during its first two weeks of release.

Johnny's specialty was rock 'n' roll remakes—taking untouchable classic oldies and revitalizing them in his personal style. In the mid-sixties, every Rivers record was a hit, including "Memphis," "Maybellene" and "Mountain of Love" in 1964; "Midnight Special" and "Seventh Son" in 1965; and "Secret Agent Man" and "Muddy Water" in 1966. Then, in the fall of that year, Johnny tried something different—a slower song that he had written himself.

"It was kind of a gamble," he recalled, "a real departure for me. People were expecting another oldie, and I surprised them with a ballad—you know, lush strings and everything. That was the first time I expressed myself using my own words and music. It was a turning point. It took about two or three months, but I finally got it together. I think the real change in my music came with 'Poor Side of Town.'"

That single broke in mid-September 1966, and peaked on the charts two months later. It turned out to be Johnny's biggest hit, first number one, and first in a string of other mid-tempo tunes: "Baby I Need Your Lovin'," "The Tracks of My Tears," and "Summer Rain" (all 1967). Later hits included "Rockin' Pneumonia Boogie Woogie Flu" (1972), "Help Me, Rhonda" (1975), and "(Slow Dancin') Swayin' to the Music" (1977). By that time, Johnny had formed his own label (Soul City), earned two Grammy Awards, and sold more than twenty-five million records.

Ballad of the Green Berets

S/SGT. BARRY SADLER

The son of professional gamblers, Barry Sadler spent much of his youth in the back seat of a car. His parents moved around so much, following the games, that one year Barry attended nine different schools.

After graduating from high school, Barry took up the drums but found little work as a musician. He enlisted in the air force and spent four years in the service, finally getting out in 1962. A friend then taught him guitar, and for a brief time Barry made his living singing country and western music in bars. When his money ran out, Barry returned to the military, this time signing up for the army's airborne school. He specialized in medicine and after a year's rigorous training qualified as an army combat medic. He was given a green beret, symbol of the Special Forces unit established by President Kennedy in 1961.

Barry always carried a guitar strapped somewhere on his gear. On his way to Vietnam, he began to write songs, mostly about his military experiences. Once in the combat zone, he tried to entertain his fellow soldiers, but they'd often throw him out of the barracks, saying his voice was too bad. Barry would then go and sing to himself, seated on a box near the latrines.

One day, while on patrol, Barry stepped on a booby trap—a poisoned spear that punctured his leg. Between fainting spells, he treated the wound himself, and miraculously survived. However, his combat career was over, so he returned to music. At a friend's suggestion, he tried writing an anthem for the Special Forces.

"Ballad of the Green Berets" contained twelve verses when it reached Chet Gierlach, president of the Music Music Music publishing house. Gierlach showed the song to his friend Robin Moore, author of a best-selling book titled *The Green Berets.* Robin liked the tune and, with Barry's permission, selected two of the verses, wrote one of his own, and added a dramatic finale.

At first, Sadler recorded the song for the army, which released it as a "limited edition" to military personnel only. Moore thought it had more potential and got RCA to record a more professional version with full orchestral backup. The result was a runaway smash.

Released on January 11, 1966, "Ballad of the Green Berets" turned out to be the fastest-selling record in RCA history. It sold over a million copies in just a few days. Barry was stunned by his success, especially in light of the growing antiwar movement and previous hits such as Barry McGuire's "Eve of Destruction."

Barry went on tour, making over eight hundred appearances on behalf of the Special Forces. Over seventy-five artists recorded versions of the ballad, including nine in West Germany (East Germany banned the song, calling the Green Berets "fascist perverts").

Barry donated ten percent of his royalties to an educational fund set up to help the children of deceased Vietnam veterans. He admitted, though, that success came so fast that he really didn't earn very much money. More than a million dollars, he said, was skimmed off by "untrustworthy people" in Hollywood.

Barry's second single was "The 'A'

Team," a mild hit, later in 1966. He cut more records after that, but by then the spotlight had moved on. Eventually, he reenlisted in the army, but things just weren't the same. "They didn't have time for a sergeant who had made a lot of money."

In later years, Barry worked as a painter, a security guard, and even a life insurance salesman. He did a little TV acting and played a psychotic killer in the film *Dayton's Devils.* Ironically, in 1979, he was charged with second-degree murder in the shooting death of songwriter Lee Emerson Bellamy.

Not everyone liked "The Green Berets." Paul McCartney called it "a terrible record," and Mick Jagger claimed that it showed "what a warmongering race the Americans are." The public, though, didn't seem to agree, and made the ballad their most popular record of 1966.

 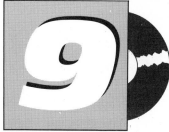  

1967

Jefferson Airplane took off in 1967, calling attention to the psychedelic rock scene in San Francisco with "Somebody to Love" and "White Rabbit"—two singles recorded in Los Angeles. Over that fabled "summer of love," S.F.'s Haight-Ashbury district became a magnet for hippies, flower children, and drug promoters from all over the world. It was a happening, well chronicled by the Animals in "San Franciscan Nights," and by Scott McKenzie in "San Francisco (Wear Some Flowers in Your Hair)." Oddly enough, very little *music* emerged from the city during this period, despite widespread media coverage. Most hometown bands remained strictly local in appeal, or developed only cult status (i.e., the Grateful Dead). A few groups developed national followings, but only after several years—and the psychedelic scene—had passed (Santana, Steve Miller, Boz Scaggs, etc.). Ironically, the most popular psychedelic rock was recorded *outside* the city by non-San Francisco groups (the Beatles, the Temptations, the Electric Prunes, Strawberry Alarm Clock, and others). As for the Airplane, their greatest success came in the late seventies, when, renamed Jefferson Starship, they cut "Miracles," "Play on Love," and "Count on Me"—middle-of-the-road material.

U.S. RECORD SALES topped the $1 billion mark for the first time in 1967, the year manufacturers raised the prices of mono releases to match those of stereo—a major step toward the creation of an all-stereo industry. At 94 Baker Street in London, the Beatles opened their Apple Boutique; in Las Vegas, Elvis Presley was married to his long-time sweetheart, Priscilla. Al Green played his first professional gig at the Apollo Theater in New York, and in Los Angeles, Jimmy Rodgers was beaten and left for dead in a savage freeway attack (from which he recovered). Composer Elton John met lyricist Bernie Taupin; newly-assembled groups included Fleetwood Mac, Steppenwolf, and Blood, Sweat and Tears. The Shangri-Las broke up; so did Buffalo Springfield, the Walker Brothers, Chad and Jeremy, the Crystals, Peter and Gordon, and Them (launching Van Morrison as a solo artist with "Brown-Eyed Girl"). The last Everly Brothers hit, "Bowling Green," came ten years to the month after their first success, "Bye Bye Love." Also saying goodbye were the Platters, whose final charted side was "Sweet Sweet Lovin'." New names on the pop scene included the Fifth Dimension and the Bee Gees, and the Who made their top-ten debut with "I Can See for Miles." It was 1967: the year the Stones gave in to censorship, turning "Let's Spend the Night Together" into "Let's Spend Some Time Together" in order to get the song televised on the "Ed Sullivan Show."

On February 5, a couple of folksinging satirists, **Tom and Dick Smothers,** made history by launching their second and most successful series. "The Smothers Brothers' Comedy Hour" was a broadcast landmark in many respects: as a showcase for artists rarely seen on television (such as the Who, the Beatles, Joan Baez, and Pete Seeger), as a launch pad for new talent (including Kenny Rogers, Glen Campbell, Mason Williams, and Steve Martin), and as a forum for decidedly one-sided political commentary. It was the brothers' use of their entertainment show as a personal soapbox that got them into trouble; eventually, affiliates were demanding to pre-screen episodes for questionable material. The Smothers' series was considered the hippest, most inventive, and most controversial program on television—when it was canceled by CBS on June 8, 1969.

Joan Baez co-starred with Bob Dylan in *Don't Look Back,* a cinema verité souvenir of their British tour with Donovan and a founding member of the Animals, Alan Price. The Animals themselves appeared in *It's a Bikini World,* along with the Castaways, Toys, and Gentrys. The talents of the Nitty Gritty Dirt Band could be found in *For Singles Only,* the Yardbirds in *Blow-Up,* Duane Eddy in *Kona Coast,* Marty Robbins in *Hell on Wheels,* and Fabian and Annette in *Thunder Alley.* Bobby Vee, Jackie DeShannon, and Eddie Hodges were seen in *C'mon Let's Live a Little*; Elvis' flicks were *Clambake, Double Trouble,* and *Easy Come Easy Go.*

According to one critic, it was "a super psychedelic LP that tops all toppers." Another reviewer called the album "the world's first forty-one-minute single" in tribute to its cohesion as a united work. *Sgt. Pepper's Lonely Hearts Club Band*—considered by many to be the Beatles'

finest work—took the Fab Four some seven hundred hours to complete, as opposed to just twelve hours for their first LP only three years before. It was the subject of lawsuits, 1001 rumors, and was described by the press as everything from "noise" to "a major musical achievement." Despite the popularity of such songs as "With a Little Help from My Friends" and "A Day in the Life," no 45s were pulled from the LP until 1978—and then only in response to the Bee Gees/Peter Frampton movie of the same name.

A preacher's daughter, **Aretha Franklin** found her style singing in church, where she also discovered that she had been blessed with a four-octave vocal range. At eighteen, she turned from gospel music to the blues, and on February 10, 1967, saw the release of her first Atlantic single, "I Never Loved a Man (the Way I Love You)." It was the start of a rock 'n' soul phenomenon: more than twenty million-selling discs, nineteen Grammy nominations, and ten Grammy Awards. Aretha set a record by winning Best Female R&B

Performance eight years in a row, between 1967 and 1974. Hundreds of singers from Bette Midler to Chaka Khan have been inspired by the one they dubbed "Lady Soul."

THE TOP 40

1. The Letter, *Box Tops*
2. To Sir with Love, *Lulu*
3. Ode to Billie Joe, *Bobbie Gentry*
4. Light My Fire, *Doors*
5. Windy, *Association*
6. I'm a Believer, *Monkees*
7. Can't Take My Eyes off You, *Frankie Valli*
8. Happy Together, *Turtles*
9. Groovin', *Young Rascals*
10. Something Stupid, *Frank and Nancy Sinatra*
11. Respect, *Aretha Franklin*
12. I Think We're Alone Now, *Tommy James and the Shondells*
13. Come Back When You Grow Up, *Bobby Vee*
14. Little Bit O' Soul, *Music Explosion*
15. Soul Man, *Sam and Dave*
16. Sweet Soul Music, *Arthur Conley*
17. Kind of a Drag, *Buckinghams*
18. I Was Made to Love Her, *Stevie Wonder*
19. Ruby Tuesday, *Rolling Stones*
20. Come On Down to My Boat, *Every Mother's Son*
21. Incense and Peppermints, *Strawberry Alarm Clock*
22. Apples, Peaches, Pumpkin Pie, *Jay and the Techniques*
23. The Happening, *Supremes*
24. Georgy Girl, *Seekers*
25. Never My Love, *Association*
26. Somebody to Love, *Jefferson Airplane*
27. I Got Rhythm, *Happenings*
28. Expressway to Your Heart, *Soul Survivors*
29. It Must Be Him, *Vikki Carr*
30. Reflections, *Diana Ross and the Supremes*
31. She'd Rather Be with Me, *Turtles*
32. Love Is Here and Now You're Gone, *Supremes*
33. For What It's Worth, *Buffalo Springfield*
34. Then You Can Tell Me Goodbye, *Casinos*
35. Gimme a Little Sign, *Brenton Wood*
36. All You Need Is Love, *Beatles*
37. A Little Bit Me, a Little Bit You, *Monkees*
38. Release Me, *Englebert Humperdinck*
39. The Rain, the Park and Other Things, *Cowsills*
40. Your Precious Love, *Marvin Gaye and Tammi Terrell*

THE TOP 10 LPs

1. Dr. Zhivago, *Original Soundtrack*
2. More of the Monkees, *Monkees*
3. The Sound of Music, *Original Soundtrack*
4. A Man and a Woman, *Original Soundtrack*
5. The Monkees, *Monkees*
6. S.R.O., *Herb Alpert and the Tijuana Brass*
7. Sgt. Pepper's Lonely Hearts Club Band, *Beatles*
8. Greatest Hits, *Temptations*
9. Surrealistic Pillow, *Jefferson Airplane*
10. Whipped Cream and Other Delights, *Herb Alpert and the Tijuana Brass*

Jann Wenner was an unemployed college dropout in 1967 when he got the idea for a new kind of youth publication—one that did more than supply singalong lyrics and pin-ups of teenybop rock idols. He conceived **Rolling Stone** as a well-written, carefully edited chronicle of the counterculture, or, as he put it, "the new America." "We're not just about music," Jann wrote in the first issue, "but also about the things and attitudes music embraces." *Rolling Stone* went on to document the pop scene all around the world, quickly becoming the most important consumer-oriented music magazine ever published. In 1973, its importance was celebrated in a hit by Dr. Hook and the Medicine Show: "The Cover of *Rolling Stone*."

Something Stupid

FRANK AND NANCY SINATRA

Frank Sinatra began his incredible career in the early 1940s while singing with the big band of Tommy Dorsey. Later, as a soloist, one of his many hits was a song, co-written by Phil Silvers, called "Nancy (with the Laughing Face)," which reached the national top ten in 1945. It had been inspired by Sinatra's five-year-old daughter. More than twenty years were to go by before the names of Frank and Nancy appeared on a record label again, but when they did, it would be on one of the most successful singles of the sixties.

While Nancy was growing up in the fifties, her dad established himself as one of the premier album artists of all time. He also, of course, had his share of hit singles, including "Young at Heart" and "Three Coins in the Fountain" (1954), "Learnin' the Blues" and "Love and Marriage" (1955), "Hey! Jealous Lover" (1956), "All the Way," (1957), "Witchcraft" (1958),, and "High Hopes" (1959).

Sinatra formed his own label, Reprise, in 1961, but didn't score a hit again until he began working with producer Jimmy Bowen. "Softly As I Leave You" became a top-thirty hit in 1964. It was followed by "Somewhere in Your Heart," and, in late 1965, "It Was a Very Good Year." Then, in 1966, along came "Summer Wind," "That's Life," and "Strangers in the Night."

Nancy also had a big year in 1966. She had been recording for some time on her father's label. After many flops in a soft vocal style, she put some sass in her voice and wound up with a number-one single of her own: "These Boots Are Made for Walkin'." Aggressive rock by women was a cause célèbre in 1966, and the way was opened for two other top-ten tunes from Nancy: "How Does That Grab You Darlin'?" and "Sugar Town."

Then, early in 1967, a song turned up that was to become Nancy's second, and Frank's third, number-one hit.

"Lee Hazelwood found the tune," said Jimmy Bowen. "He gave it to Nancy, and she showed it to her dad. Frank thought it was just perfect for the two of them—a sure hit—and they wanted to cut it right away. Since I was producing Frank at the time, and Lee was working with Nancy, Lee and I became co-producers on this particular track.

"The session itself was hilarious. It was on the first eight-track equipment any of us had used—a brand-new board at Western Recorders in Hollywood. Eddie Bracken was our engineer, the greatest there was, especially back in the days of three-track and four-track. He arranged the studio so that Frank and Nancy would be looking in the control room at us, side by side, the entire time. He also set up a producer's desk with two talk-back mikes, and a couple of name plates, you know, making kind of a light thing of it. That was because everyone was worried there'd be a lot of tension between Hazelwood and me. But we got the session done. I think it took about four takes. It was one of those that went real smooth.

"There was a lot of concern that the lyrics were not right for those two to be singing to each other—you know, a father and daughter. I remember one of the executives at the record company came up to me and said, 'Jimmy, that's incest. Tell Frank he can't do that.' I said, 'You tell Frank he can't do that.' He did, and Frank told him not to worry about the record company—we'd worry about the songs."

"Something Stupid," of course, became a multimillion-seller; yet it did not lead to further duets by the two. Nancy had several smaller hits in 1967 and 1968, some of which she sang with Lee Hazelwood. Frank went on to record "The World We Knew" (1967), "Cycles" (1968), and "My Way" (1969). He retired briefly in the early seventies but then came back for a series of well-received specials and concert tours. At the end of the decade, he released what many critics called the finest album package of his career—an ambitious three-record set called *Trilogy*.

Groovin'
THE YOUNG RASCALS

The mid-sixties was a golden age for blue-eyed soul—heart-felt R&B performances by such white acts as Tom Jones, the Box Tops, Mitch Ryder, and the Vanilla Fudge. In 1966, the Young Rascals added their name to that list with an explosive million-seller—the number-one hit, "Good Lovin'."

After that, most of their material was written by one or both of their lead singers. Eddie Brigati and Felix Cavaliere (who also played keyboards). Felix generally wrote the music and Eddie the lyrics. Rounding out the lineup were Gene Cornish (guitar) and Dino Danelli (drums).

Following "Good Lovin'" was "You Better Run," and in March 1967, "I've Been Lonely Too Long." By that time, the Young Rascals were headliners, constantly on the road, making innumerable TV and concert appearances. While on tour, they were known to relieve boredom by dropping water bombs out of hotel windows, or splashing around in the fancy fountains in front of them.

Occasionally, they got a day off to spend with girlfriends, and, more often than not, that day happened to be a Sunday. The idea of spending Sunday afternoon "groovin'" with a lady inspired Eddie and Felix to write "Groovin'" in the spring of 1967.

The song marked a change of direction for the band, which had previously built its sound around the lead of Felix's organ. "On our new single there isn't any organ," said Gene at the time. "There is no guitar and there are no regular drums. There's a bass, a harpsichord, a piano, a conga drum, tambourine, vibes, a harmonica, a vocal, and birds." "Groovin'," a reflective, sinuous record, was perhaps their most infectious creation. Its essential lightness was effectively balanced by the somber tone of Eddie's voice. On the track, he tried his best to sound like his idol, Ray Charles.

"Groovin'" broke in late April 1967, and spent four weeks at number one in May. In all, it clung to the charts for three months, becoming the Young Rascals' second million-seller. In September of that year, the song was covered by Booker T and the MGs, who made the top thirty with their instrumental version.

The Young Rascals had three more hits in 1967: "A Girl Like You," "How Can I Be Sure" (remade in 1972 by David Cassidy), and "It's Wonderful." Then, in 1968, they dropped the "Young" from their name, as the various members had all left their teenage years.

As the Rascals, they hit with "A Beautiful Morning" and "People Got to Be Free" in 1968. The latter tune came from their LP *Freedom Suite,* which sowed the seeds of the group's demise. As the band evolved, they moved away from basic R&B, drifted into a kind of cocktail jazz, and eventually wound up trying to go psychedelic. Although "People Got to Be Free" was a number-one record, their fans objected to the Rascals' flower power stance—Nehru jackets, love beads, and all. In 1969, there was a string of lesser hits: "A Ray of Hope," "Heaven," "See," and "Carry Me Back." That last song—ironically, a plea to return to their R&B roots—came too late to save the Rascals.

In 1971, Eddie and Gene quit; the other two tried to regroup on Columbia with new members. After two ill-fated LPs, they too gave up in 1972. Cornish and Danelli resurfaced in a band called Bulldog, and later, Fotomaker. Brigati, in 1976, tried to put out a new version of "Groovin'," but it was unsuccessful. Felix, though, had a mild solo hit: "Only a Lonely Heart Sees," in 1980.

Happy Together
THE TURTLES

The Turtles began in 1963 as a L.A. surf band called the Night-riders. They played high school dances, appeared on local TV, and abruptly fell apart. Two members, Howard Kaylan (vocals) and Al Nichol (guitar) then formed the Crossfires, adding Mark Volman (sax), Jim Tucker (rhythm guitar), Chuck Portz (bass) and Don Murray (drums). This sextet performed in small venues along the Southern California coast, often earning less than $200 a night. Eventually, it got to be an economic strain, especially since the money had to be split six ways. In 1965, while appearing at the Rebelaire Club in Redondo Beach, the group agreed to pack it in and say goodbye to the music scene.

Before they had a chance to quit, though, the band was approached by two men who offered them a contract with White Whale Records. The club owner, KRLA deejay Reb Foster, volunteered to manage the group. The Crossfires hastily reconsidered their plan, and quickly accepted both proposals.

Foster, however, insisted on one thing—the band had to come up with a better group name. He suggested "the Tyrtles," spelled with a "y" in emulation of the Byrds. They thought that was a bit much, but were willing to go along with just "the Turtles."

Next, they talked about their musical concept. At that time, they admired many performers, among them, the Zombies, a group that specialized in soft vocals over relatively hard instrumental tracks. They decided to modify that idea by starting softly, building to a rousing chorus, and then getting soft again. A song that fit that formula was Bob Dylan's "It Ain't Me Babe."

The Turtles' version was an instant hit—top ten in L.A. ten days after release. In September 1965, it entered the national top ten. Their next singles, "Let Me Be" (1965) and "You Baby" (1966) were also in the same bag. And then came "Happy Together."

That song was brought to the Turtles while they were on the road, appearing in a New York nightclub called The Phone Booth. The writers, Gary Bonner and Alan Gordon, were former members of the Magicians, a Gotham groups that had just broken up. They presented the tune as an awful-sounding dub, one that had already been turned down by a number of other artists. But for the Turtles, it had that soft beginning and rousing chorus that they loved. They tried it out on tour for about six weeks, perfecting the song, and the reaction was unbelievable. After they got home, they went right to the studio and cut it in January 1967.

"Happy Together" broke early the next month and spent three weeks at number one, starting in April. "It was 'our song' for millions of lovestruck couples, although the song's protagonist is actually wistfully imagining all that bliss," said the group. "Every time it comes on the radio, people still have an urge to start throwing their arms around each other."

On the record, John Barbata plays drums; he took over for Don Murray. Chip Douglas is on bass; he replaced Chuck Portz.

The Turtles went on to place ten more songs on the charts during the sixties; they included "She'd Rather Be with Me," "You Know What I Mean," and "She's My Girl" (all 1967); "Elenore" (1968); and "You Showed Me" (1969). Along the way, Jim Pons, formerly of the Leaves, came in on bass (Chip Douglas left to produce the Monkees), while ex-Spanky and Our Gang member John Seiter became drummer (John Barbata departed, eventually to join Jefferson Starship).

The Turtles broke up in 1970 amid a messy tangle of lawsuits. Without their star performers, White Whale folded, and years later, Volman and Kaylan were able to buy back their old masters. In 1975, they were reissued on the Sire label as a double LP, *Happy Together Again*.

Can't Take My Eyes Off You

FRANKIE VALLI

*F*rank Steven Castelluccio was born in Newark, New Jersey, where, at fifteen, he got a job singing and faking upright bass in a country and western band. After that, he joined a hometown lounge act called the Variety Trio. They turned into the Variatones, and then the Four Lovers. One night, his group auditioned to appear at a local bowling alley, but were turned down flat. Instead of just walking away, they copped the name of the place and became the Four Seasons.

The original quartet included Frank—by then known as Frankie Valli—Nick Massi, Tommy DeVito, and Bob Gaudio. It was Gaudio, either alone or with their producer, Bob Crewe, who wrote the bulk of the Seasons' material. Between 1962 and 1967 they placed thirty songs on the pop charts, nearly half of which made the top ten. All of the Four Seasons records were designed to showcase the remarkable falsetto of Frankie, whose range encompassed three and a half octaves.

In the mid-sixties, Frankie decided to try something Buddy Holly had done—establish a solo career without actually leaving his home group. His first attempt was in 1966 with "(You're Gonna) Hurt Yourself," a very mild seller. He then placed a call to the New York penthouse apartment of Crewe. Gaudio was there, and the three of them got into a multi-phone conversation. "Hey," said Valli, "I want you to write me a hit song. I want the greatest song you've ever written." It took a day—and Frankie was "blown away."

"Can't Take My Eyes Off You" was released in mid-May 1967, and peaked on the charts two months later. It sold in excess of two million copies, yet was a bittersweet victory for Valli.

You see, he couldn't hear it.

Doctors discovered that he had otosclerosis—a rare ear disease for which there is no real cure. One day,

Frankie just began to notice sounds around him dropping out. "I was destroyed," he said. "I mean, if I couldn't hear, I couldn't sing, so what was the point of living? I was ready to throw myself out a window."

Fortunately, delicate operations restored much of the loss, and many fans never learned anything of his crisis. Frankie went on singly, and with the Seasons, to further success in the seventies.

I'm a Believer

THE MONKEES

On record and on TV, the Monkees' star burned brightly in 1967. Their television series was a hit in the U.S., the U.K., and thirty-seven other countries around the world. More than eight million Monkees albums had been sold by the end of 1966, and Monkee merchandise had grossed over $20 million. They were offered and took songs by some of America's finest composers—Boyce and Hart, Lieber and Stoller, Linzer and Randell, Goffen and King, Mann and Weil, the Tokens, Nilsson, Neil Sedaka, John Stewart, Jeff Barry, Paul Williams, and many more.

Because the Monkees' show was a Screen Gems production, the boys were given free access to anything published by Screen Gems/Columbia Music. One of the bright young writers recently signed to that company was Neil Diamond. Neil had already begun to make a name for himself as a singer-composer; his "Cherry Cherry" had gone top ten in 1966.

Neil wrote the second Monkees hit, a record that confirmed their status as one of the best-loved rock groups of all time. "I'm a Believer" had advance orders of 1,051,280 copies *before anybody heard it*—before its release on November 26, 1966. It was the first time that RCA (which distributed Colgems) had had advance orders of over one million copies on any 45 (except a few by Elvis Presley). It was awarded an immediate gold disc, even before any copies had been shipped.

Prerelease expectations were more than justified once the record hit the air. It sold more than three million copies in two months, and was number one for seven weeks in the United States. "I'm a Believer" also topped the charts in England, Australia, Finland, New Zealand, Norway, Ireland and South Africa. Global sales were estimated at ten million copies.

The flip side of "I'm a Believer" was also a hit: "(I'm Not Your) Steppin' Stone." Both songs were included on the album *More of the Monkees*, issued on February 1, 1967. It had advance orders for 1,500,000 copies— the biggest ever for a vocal album. It was number one for eighteen weeks, selling over five million copies.

But the four Monkees were not happy: It seems that criticism had been leveled at them because they did not play all the instruments on their own albums. The Monkees sang the songs, but their uncredited back-up band was a studio group called the Candy Store Prophets. On TV, the Monkees only *pretended* to perform; they were actually faking along to prerecorded tracks.

Don Kirshner, who supervised the early Monkee sessions, felt there was "too much to risk" in allowing the quartet to play their own instruments. The Monkees battled with him and won, seizing control of their own records in 1967. They then spent six weeks cutting *Headquarters,* their third LP, and first effort as a real rock 'n' roll band. Despite prophecies of doom, it too became a giant seller.

The Monkees' hit streak continued through the sixties, often with both sides of their singles making the charts. In 1967, there was "A Little Bit Me, A Little Bit You," backed with "The Girl I Knew Somewhere"; "Pleasant Valley Sunday," backed with "Words"; and "Daydream Believer." In 1968 we heard "Valleri," backed with "Tapioca Tundra"; and "D. W. Washburn."

The Monkees toured worldwide in 1967 and 1968, and on one visit to London, Mickey Dolenz introduced the others to a little-known guitarist: Jimi Hendrix. Hendrix then joined the tour, and accompanied the group back to the States. He failed to make it as an opening act, though, and in many cities, was booed off the stage.

The Monkees' television show was cancelled on August 19, 1968. They then made a critically-acclaimed motion picture, *Head,* which co-starred Jack Nicholson, Annette, and Frank Zappa. Monkee money also went to finance the film *Easy Rider,* and to buy instruments for Three Dog Night.

Peter Tork left the group in 1968; Mike Nesmith in 1969. Davy Jones opened a boutique, and Mickey Dolenz made a movie with Linda Lovelace.

And as for Don Kirshner, he moved on to work with another group that presumably gave him less heartache—the Archies.

Windy
THE ASSOCIATION

The Association broke big in 1966, with two hot LPs (*And Then Along Comes the Association* and *Renaissance*) and a pair of back-to-back top-ten singles ("Along Comes Mary" and "Cherish"). The coming year was to bring even more good fortune, as no less than five of their songs were to make the national pop charts.

First, though, there were a couple of important career changes for the Association. Founding member Gary Jules Alexander left for a while to "unwind" in India (he was to rejoin the group two years later). His replacement was Hilario D. "Larry" Ramos, Jr., former lead singer of the New Christy Minstrels. The Association also moved to Warner Brothers, after that company bought out Valiant Records in order to acquire their hot young act. Everyone involved was poised and ready in 1967, with everything riding on that first Warner Brothers single.

No one really knew, however, just what the A side of that debut record would be. At Warners, tension began to mount as the weeks before the first company-sponsored tour began to slip away. At the last minute, on the morning before the group was to leave town, a song selection was finally made—"Windy."

At the time, the Association was renting what they called a "folk house"—a huge old mansion on Ardmore in Los Angeles that was nearing demolition. Six, seven, or eight people would split the rent on such places and then turn them into social and musical hangouts. The Association shared a structure that had been owned at one point by actress Faye Emerson, and opened its doors to any performers who happened to drift by. Among their drop-in guests were Donovan, Spanky McFarland (of Spanky and Our Gang), the Byrds, and a little-known folk singer by the name

of Ruthann Friedman. Ruthann had written a song about her "old man," Windy, and his free-wheeling lifestyle in San Francisco's Haight-Ashbury district. She played her song one night for the Association, and they were completely entranced. They knew that by simply changing the gender of "Windy," they had found a second number-one smash.

And so, on the day before their tour began, arrangements for the new song were sketched out over lunch. At 1 P.M., the Association entered the studio. They picked Russ Giguere and new member Larry Ramos, Jr., to share lead vocals, and a marathon session began. By 6:30 the next morning, the two men's voices were totally blown. For that reason, the vocals at the end of the record—a sheer crescendo of sound—were performed by everyone still awake in the studio at the time, including wives, girlfriends, engineers, the producer, and Ruthann.

"Windy" hit the top of America's pop charts early in July and remained there for nearly the entire month. Later

in the year, it was nominated for a Grammy Award, for Best Contemporary Group Performance, Vocal or Instrumental (it lost, however, to the Fifth Dimension's "Up, Up and Away").

In the fall, the Association had another million-selling single, "Never My Love" (revived in 1971 by the Fifth Dimension and again in 1974 by Blue Swede). In 1968, the group scored their fifth and final top-ten single, "Everything That Touches You."

After that, the Association went into a fairly rapid decline. They switched labels in 1972 to Columbia, but their only LP for the new company was a failure. Shortly afterward, founding member Brian Cole died, and there was a flurry of personnel changes. Three comeback attempts since then have all fizzled, on Mums (1973), RCA (1975), and Elektra (1981).

The Association was one of the finest pop harmony groups ever. They spent only three years in the musical spotlight, but that's all it took to assure them a permanent place in the history of pop music.

Light My Fire
THE DOORS

The story of the Doors began in July 1965, on a beach in Venice, California. Two friends from UCLA, Jim Morrison and Ray Manzarek, were walking along, talking about this and that, when Jim began to recite a poem he'd written called "Moonlight Drive." Ray was so impressed that he suggested forming a band to set those words to music.

In short order, he found Robbie Krieger and John Densmore, and the Doors were complete. The group played small clubs up and down Sunset Strip in Hollywood until they were signed by Elektra late in 1966.

"Our first album, *The Doors,* was released in January 1967," recalled Ray, "and nothing happened for six months. Then, 'Light My Fire' was pulled as a single.

"That song was pretty much the work of Robbie, our guitar player. He came up with most of the basic idea, and then we sat around and put the communal brain to work. John, our

drummer, gave it that Latinesque rhythm, and I worked out the keyboard parts. Most of our songs came together that way. Somebody would start something, and we'd all add our little touches."

While riding down Sunset one day, Jim asked the Doors' producer, Paul Rothchild, what he thought of the words to "Light My Fire." Paul, not knowing who had come up with what, assumed that Jim was the sole lyricist. "They're great," he said, "except for that bit about 'no time to wallow in the mire.'" As it turned out, that line was Morrison's only contribution to the song.

"Light My Fire" broke onto the charts early in June 1967, and reached number one in August. It was Elektra's first top-ten record after eighteen years of trying. The album it came off also reached number one, and remained a best-seller for one hundred four weeks.

"Light My Fire" opened the Doors

to worldwide success and eventual status as a legendary rock 'n' roll band. It was also a key to their demise. Jim Morrison came to hate the song—not just because he didn't write it, but because fans demanded it everywhere they played. After their third album, Jim lost enthusiasm for being lead singer of the group. He grew increasingly difficult to work with, both in the studio and on the road. The hits, though, continued: "People Are Strange" and "Love Me Two Times" (1967), "The Unknown Soldier" and "Hello, I Love You" (1968), "Touch Me" (1969), and finally, "Love Her Madly" and "Riders on the Storm" (1971).

Shortly after completing the last song, Jim went to Paris, where his heart stopped beating on July 3, 1971. His mysterious death, and the mystical, hypnotic music of the Doors has kept interest in the group high, many years after its demise.

Ode to Billie Joe

BOBBIE GENTRY

"Life in the South is very different from life in other parts of the country," said Bobbie Gentry. "The church was important. It was in the church that I learned my music."

Bobbie Gentry was born Roberta Lee Street on her grandfather's farm in Chickasaw County, Mississippi. Although she left the Delta region at thirteen to join her mother in California, she never forgot her Dixie roots.

Bobbie attended the Los Angeles Conservatory of Music, studying guitar, piano, vibes, banjo and bass. She appeared with several local vocal groups, and by seventeen was completely self-supporting through musical jobs. Eventually she worked her way to Las Vegas, where by 1966 she had organized her own singing and dancing revue.

In February 1967, Bobbie decided to concentrate on songwriting. She made a demonstration record of "Mississippi Delta," and placed it with publisher Larry Shayne. He took it to Kelly Gordon, an A&R director and producer at Capitol Records. All Bobbie wanted was to have the material presented, but Kelly liked her voice and the song. He signed her to Capitol, and asked for more numbers to fill out an album.

Bobbie leafed through her notebook of songwriting ideas, and came across the sentence, "Billie Joe McAllister jumped off the Tallahatchee Bridge." She worked through the night to finish the tune. The result was a ballad based on her memories of life around Greenwood, Mississippi. In the song, a family, at the dinner table, talks casually about Billie Joe McAllister, a young boy who committed suicide that day. Before his death, he and a girl had been seen throwing an object into the Tallahatchee river. Just what they might have tossed sparked a lot of controversy in the summer of 1967.

"To some people, it was an intriguing tale—a mystery," recalled Bobbie. "To me, the fact that the two of them threw something off the bridge was purely symbolic. People have found a lot more significance in that part than I had intended.

"Actually, I used the story of Billie Joe as a vehicle to point out man's indifference to man—people's lack of ability to relate to someone else's tragedy. I'm sure a lot of people missed that. There was a second message in there, too, about the generation gap. The girl in the story lost someone that she loved very much, and we find her mama asking, 'How come you're not eating?' She couldn't understand. Later, when the mother loses her own husband, she doesn't seem to be aware of any similarity. And her daughter, instead of consoling her, only wants to spend time up on the bridge. They've isolated themselves in their own personal tragedies, and never gotten involved with anyone else's."

On July 10, Bobbie cut the song in a half-hour in Capitol's Studio C, with her guitar as her only accompaniment (later, Jimmy Haskell added strings: a couple of cellos and six violins). Her original version ran more than seven minutes, and at the label's insistence, was shortened. Even so, at 4:13, it was deemed too long and too slow to get any air play. Capitol then decided to make it a B side, and slapped it on the back of "Mississippi Delta."

Deejays quickly flipped the record over and began to play "Ode to Billie Joe." In two weeks it was in the top thirty; in three weeks it had sold 750,000. It spent four weeks at number one in September—fourteen weeks in total on the charts. Global sales were estimated at more than five million copies.

"Ode to Billie Joe" led to three

Grammy Awards for Bobbie Gentry. She was named Most Promising Female Vocalist by the Academy of Country Music, Most Promising Singer of 1967 by *16* magazine, and was given an Appreciation Scroll by the Country Music Association. *Mademoiselle* magazine gave her their Merit Award, and the Board of Supervisors of Chickasaw County gave her a plaque on "Bobbie Gentry Day, 1967."

Bobbie never had another big hit record. Her one smash opened all the doors she wanted. In 1976, "Ode to Billie Joe" became a movie, starring Robbie Benson and Glynnis O'Connor. Bobbie wasn't seen onscreen, but once again her voice was heard— singing the haunting song that made her a star.

To Sir with Love

LULU

As the song says, most girls do progress "from crayons to perfume." However, few do it as memorably as Marie McDonald McLaughlin Lawrie did in 1967.

Born in Scotland, Marie got turned on to music by her family's record collection, which included the hits of Tommy Steele and Teresa Brewer. She sang along with them at home, and by age nine, she was imitating them in public, backed by a local accordion group.

She didn't take her singing seri-ously, though, and was about to enroll in hairdressing school when she met, and joined, a six-piece band called the Gleneagles. As their spunky lead singer, she quickly became the focal point of the group. Their manager took to referring to her as "a lulu of a kid," and eventually that stuck as a more distinctive stage name. The band, in turn, retitled themselves "Lulu and the Luvers."

Their first hit, "Shout," came along in 1964, and a year later, there was a second U.K. top-ten single, "Leave a Little Love." The group appeared on local TV and radio and toured Europe, including one time as an opening act for the Beatles. Lulu made her first film at about this time, the rarely seen *Gonks Go Beat* (1965). In 1966, she visited Poland, becoming the first British woman in history to perform behind the Iron Curtain.

By 1967, Lulu had left the Luvers and was recording on her own for Columbia. Early in the year, she scored two hits: "The Boat That I Row" (a Neil Diamond song) and "Let's Pretend." She went on tour with the Beach Boys, and that's where her international breakthrough began.

One night, after a show, director James Clavell came to see her and said, "You've got the part." She said, "What part?" He then explained the plot of the movie he was putting together: *To Sir with Love.*

In the film, Sidney Poitier plays a novice teacher assigned to a tough East End school in London. Slowly, he gains the respect of his rough-house gang of students—one of whom, a little Cockney kid, was Lulu. "I didn't read for it or anything," she recalled, "and I was afraid. All the other kids had been to acting school, and then working with Sidney Poitier! But it came naturally. When I first saw the movie, I thought, 'You cheeky thing, Lulu.' I crawled under the chair. All I could do was watch myself. The second time I saw it I enjoyed the whole movie."

Lulu sang the title tune (words by Don Black and music by Mark London) under the credits of the film. It's a remarkable song, condensing the entire plot in less than three minutes. It begins with tension, biting nails, embarrassment, awe, telling tales and schoolgirl days of astonishment, and emerges—with a sense of apprecia-tion—to hair curlers, young woman-hood, and a deep measure of maturity.

The song was released as a single on June 23, 1967, but didn't enter the U.S. charts until eleven weeks later. Once it did, it took off right away, spending over a month at number one, beginning in October. In November, it was certified a million-seller, with eventual sales topping two million. Strangely, it was a complete flop in England—and marked the first time that a U.K. disc reached number one in the States without even graz-ing the British charts.

This odd pattern continued with later Lulu hits; they made it in either the U.S. or the U.K., but rarely in both. Titles included "Best of Both Worlds" (U.S., 1967); "Me, the Peaceful Heart," "Boys," and "I'm a Tiger" (U.K., 1968); "Boom-Bang-a-Bang" (U.K., 1969); and "Oh Me Oh My I'm a Fool for You Baby" (U.S., 1970).

In 1969, Lulu got her own British television series, and in 1970, she turned up on American TV as a regu-lar on "The Ray Stevens Show." Also, on February 18, 1969, she had married Maurice Gibb of the Bee Gees. At the ceremony, police had to struggle to hold back a throng of uninvited guests—estimated at over 1,000. That marriage broke up in early 1973.

They called her "the British Brenda Lee" and "the little girl with the big, big voice." Today she's a nightclub performer, and a woman—having crossed that "crayons to perfume" threshold many, many years ago.

The Letter

BOX TOPS

Few groups looked whiter and sounded blacker than the Box Tops, a well-honed funk band that blended R&B grit with country rock. Thanks to the penetrating, rough-edged voice of lead singer Alex Chilton, they were among the leading exponents of mid-sixties blue-eyed soul, along with the Rascals, Vanilla Fudge, and the Righteous Brothers.

The original members of the Box Tops grew up in Memphis, where they played in various bands during their high school years. They met in college, forming the group in 1965. Besides Alex, the initial line-up included Gary Talley on lead guitar, Billy Cunningham on bass, John Evans on keyboards, and Danny Smythe on drums.

The fellows gigged around Memphis for about two years, slowly building a reputation at sock hops, school dances, and in clubs. Their manager, a local deejay, eventually put them in touch with Dan Penn, an independent record producer. Dan listened to the group, liked what he heard, and agreed to a session at American Recording Studios. It was

there, in the summer of 1967, that they cut "The Letter."

The tune had been written by Wayne Carson Thompson, one of a number of staff composers on the payroll at ARS. The Box Tops didn't choose the song; it was selected for them. However, Alex liked it, and felt he could do it justice.

The session for "The Letter" was the first time that any of the group had been inside a recording studio. To cut the track took about an hour and a half—not very long. Alex sang live on it, and there were no over-dubs. Afterward, the master was sold to Mala Records.

"The Letter" broke nationally in mid-August 1967, and moved up the charts very quickly. By September, it was the number-one song in the country, which it remained for four weeks. In all, the tune stayed nearly four months on America's hit parade. Globally, it sold more than four million copies.

"We made the record with adults as well as teenagers in mind," said Alex, at the time. "We hope to spread the Memphis sound abroad, and make

it as popular as the Tamla-Motown sound or the Stax sound." To that end, the group made several tours of Europe and Canada, often appearing in concert with the Beach Boys or Young Rascals.

The Box Tops followed "The Letter" with "Neon Rainbow," and then, in 1968, "Cry Like a Baby," "Choo Choo Train," and "I Met Her in Church." In 1969, there were "Sweet Cream Ladies Forward March" and "Soul Deep." Strangely, despite their live success, none of the Box Tops were allowed to play instruments on their later records. Alex Chilton still sang, but after "The Letter" their management insisted on using session musicians instead. Understandably, this demor-alized the group, and after four albums only Alex was left of the original line-up. His contract ran out in 1969, and when it did, he did.

As for "The Letter," it's come back two times since the Box Tops' version. It was a top-twenty hit for the Arbors in 1969, and a top-ten song for Joe Cocker in 1970.

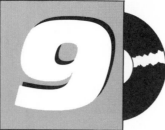

1968

THE YARDBIRDS BECAME Led Zeppelin in 1968, the year of three key musical marriages: Johnny Cash to June Carter, Phil Spector to Ronnie Bennett, and George Jones to Tammy Wynette. Doris Day got her own TV series, and another new program, "Laugh-In," introduced the world to Tiny Tim, and his hit, "Tiptoe Through the Tulips with Me." José Feliciano sang "The Star Spangled Banner" at the fifth game of the World Series; the Righteous Brothers split up, and so did the Seekers and the Mamas and the Papas. Frankie Lymon died from drug abuse in a New York tenement; Little Willie John died of pneumonia in prison. Spectrum became the Carpenters, the Golliwogs became Creedence Clearwater Revival, and Greg Webster and the Ohio Untouchables became the Ohio Players. Other new groups included Jethro Tull, the Doobie Brothers, Three Dog Night, Sweet, and Deep Purple. The Amboy Dukes' "Journey to the Center of the Mind" introduced gonzo rocker Ted Nugent; Linda Ronstadt was "featured" on the Stone Poneys' "Different Drum," and Kenny Rogers' "Just Dropped In" with the First Edition. Fats Domino's chart farewell was "Lady Madonna," and "Cab Driver" became a major hit for the Mills Brothers—a pop group formed in the thirties. It was 1968: the year good-time rock 'n' roll was labeled "bubblegum" and million-sellers included "Yummy Yummy Yummy," "Chewy Chewy," "Simon Says," and "Green Tambourine."

After seven months of experimentation and refinement, **Hair,** the "American tribal love-rock musical," opened on Broadway on April 29. It was an immediate sensation, and one of the most controversial productions ever to play New York (mainly due to its language, irreverence, and famous nude scene). Critics alternately hailed and condemned the show as "a theatrical landmark," "a pornographic riot," "a breath of fresh air," and "an anti-American cry for anarchy." Actually, *Hair* was a tuneful, topical celebration of the hippie lifestyle—its philosophy, morality, and attitude toward all things "establishment." Five numbers from the score became million-sellers for different artists: Oliver ("Good Morning Starshine"), Three Dog Night ("Easy to Be Hard"), the Fifth Dimension (a medley of "Aquarius" and "Let the Sunshine In"), and the Cowsills ("Hair"). Also, several notable performers emerged from the cast, including Diane Keaton, Ronnie Dyson, and Ellen Crawford. Strangely, a decade went by before the play became a motion picture and by that time, for most people, *Hair* had become a quaint period piece.

Former Beach Boy **Glen Campbell** did well enough as a regular on the old "Smothers Brothers' Comedy Hour" to warrant his own summer series in 1968, "The Summer Brothers' Smothers Show." During its run, America fell in love with the young man from Delight, Arkansas, and his simple, homespun pop-country style. Millions were turned on to a kind of music they had previously rejected as hick, nasal, and twangy. As the result of surprisingly strong ratings, the singer-guitarist returned to television in January 1969 with the "Glen Campbell Goodtime Hour," which remained on the network for three and a half years.

The blue-eyed soul of **Janis Joplin** electrified *Monterey Pop,* filmed at the 1967 International Pop Festival in Monterey, California (among the more than twenty other stars: Canned Heat, the Who, Otis Redding, the Mamas and the Papas, and Jimi Hendrix). The Rolling Stones appeared in *Voices* and *Sympathy for the Devil,* the Monkees in *Head,* Cream in *Cream Last Concert,* and Herman's Hermits in *Mrs. Brown You've Got a Lovely Daughter.* The Seeds and Strawberry Alarm Clock turned up in *Psych-Out;* Doris Day and the Grass Roots in *With Six You Get Eggroll.* Elvis' three movies were *Speedway, Stay Away Joe,* and *Live a Little, Love a Little.*

Hard-rocking **Steppenwolf** was formed in 1968 by an escapee from Communist East Germany, Joachim Krauledat. Under his anglicized name, John Kay, he led the band in developing a sound that came to be known as "motorcycle music"; raw, roaring "heavy metal thunder," typified by their first two gold singles, "Born to Be Wild" and "Magic Carpet Ride." "Rock Me" and "Move Over" were hits in 1969; in 1970, "Monster" and "Hey Lawdy Mama." After selling over $42 million worth of records, the group broke up in 1971, only to form again three years later for one final hit, "Straight Shootin' Woman."

Eric Clapton, Jack Bruce, and Ginger Baker came together in 1966 as the blues-rock trio **Cream**—so named on the arrogant assumption that they were the "cream" of British musicians. Their second album, *Disraeli Gears,* included "Sunshine of Your Love," three minutes of rumbling rhythm that made the U.S. top five in August 1968.

The same month, Clapton told the press that the group had "lost direction," and, coupled with the pressures of constant touring, would be separating. A series of fifteen "farewell" concerts were held over the next few weeks, as "White Room" and "Crossroads" also became hits.

THE TOP 40

1. Hey Jude, *Beatles*
2. Love Is Blue, *Paul Mauriat*
3. The Dock of the Bay, *Otis Redding*
4. Honey, *Bobby Goldsboro*
5. Mrs. Robinson, *Simon and Garfunkel*
6. This Guy's in Love with You, *Herb Alpert*
7. Young Girl, *Gary Puckett and the Union Gap*
8. Tighten Up, *Archie Bell and the Drells*
9. Harper Valley P.T.A., *Jeannie C. Riley*
10. Little Green Apples, *O. C. Smith*
11. Hello, I Love You, *Doors*
12. Sunshine of Your Love, *Cream*
13. Cry Like a Baby, *Box Tops*
14. Mony Mony, *Tommy James & The Shondells*
15. Judy in Disguise, *John Fred and the Playboy Band*
16. The Good, the Bad and the Ugly, *Hugo Montenegro*
17. People Got to Be Free, *Rascals*
18. I Wish It Would Rain, *Temptations*
19. Stoned Soul Picnic, *Fifth Dimension*
20. The Ballad of Bonnie and Clyde, *Georgie Fame*
21. Midnight Confessions, *Grass Roots*
22. Green Tambourine, *Lemon Pipers*
23. Yummy Yummy Yummy, *Ohio Express*
24. A Beautiful Morning, *Rascals*
25. Those Were the Days, *Mary Hopkin*
26. Lady Willpower, *Gary Puckett and and the Union Gap*
27. Grazin' in the Grass, *Hugh Masekela*
28. I've Gotta Get a Message to You, *Bee Gees*
29. Love Child, *Diana Ross and the Supremes*
30. Simon Says, *1910 Fruitgum Co.*
31. Turn Around Look at Me, *Vogues*
32. Dance to the Music, *Sly and the Family Stone*
33. The Horse, *Cliff Nobles and Co.*
34. La La Means I Love You, *Delfonics*
35. Bend Me Shape Me, *American Breed*
36. Jumpin' Jack Flash, *Rolling Stones*
37. Born to Be Wild, *Steppenwolf*
38. Spooky, *Gary Puckett and the Union Gap*
39. Lady Madonna, *Beatles*
40. Angel of the Morning, *Merrilee Rush and the Turnabouts*

THE TOP 10 LPs

1. Disraeli Gears, *Cream*
2. Are You Experienced?, *Jimi Hendrix*
3. The Graduate, *Original Soundtrack*
4. Magical Mystery Tour, *Beatles*
5. Parsley, Sage, Rosemary and Thyme, *Simon and Garfunkel*
6. Bookends, *Simon and Garfunkel*
7. Aretha: Lady Soul, *Aretha Franklin*
8. Blooming Hits, *Paul Mauriat*
9. Look Around, *Sergio Mendes and Brasil '66*
10. The Beat of the Brass, *Herb Alpert and the Tijuana Brass*

Elvis Presley had not appeared on television in more than eight years when it was announced that he would be making a "comeback special" for airing on NBC December 3. After his first number, "Hound Dog," Elvis grinned at the cheering crowd and said, "It's been a long time, baby." He continued through "Don't Be Cruel," "Jailhouse Rock," "Love Me Tender," and other songs, ending with a tune written especially for the program, "If I Can Dream." Lifted directly from the TV soundtrack, it became Presley's first million-selling single in nearly four years. Elvis collapsed as he left the stage and had to be carried to his dressing room, where he asked to be left alone. Through the door, one could hear the sound of the King of Rock 'n' Roll—in tears.

Little Green Apples

O. C. SMITH

A singer for as long as he could remember, Ocie Lee Smith was born in Mansfield, Ohio, and raised in Los Angeles. With the encouragement of his mother, a music teacher, he joined the high school choir and at the same time developed a great interest in the jazz and blues of Charlie Parker, B. B. King, Dizzy Gillespie, and Ray Charles.

After a short stay at Los Angeles City College, Ocie joined the air force in 1951. Originally an MP, he found himself attracted to the Special Services unit and wound up spending most of his time as a singer in camp shows. In 1953 he began to tour military bases, backed by the orchestra of Horace Heidt.

Ocie was discharged in 1955 and headed for New York, where he found work in nightclubs and resorts along the Catskill circuit. One show, at the Club Baby Grand, led to a job as featured vocalist with the Sy Oliver band. A short time later, he appeared on TV as a guest on Arthur Godfrey's "Talent Scouts." As a result, he won a contract with Cadence Records, although nothing of consequence came of it.

In 1961, Count Basie was looking for someone to replace Joe Williams. "The Count heard one of my dubs," recalled Ocie. "I met him in a hotel room one night, and he played piano while I auditioned. The next day, without rehearsal, I went on."

Ocie stayed with Count Basie for a number of years and then decided it was time to strike out on his own. His manager, Lee Magid, persuaded Columbia to give Ocie another shot at recording in 1966. It was at this time that Ocie decided to respell his first name, "to make it easier for billing purposes."

The first Columbia album, *The Dynamic O. C. Smith,* was less than dynamic at the cash register. O.C.'s A&R man, Jerry Fuller, felt that a change of material might do the trick. O.C. had already established himself as a "honey baritone"—a warm, highly believable singer with a finely honed yet gritty tone quality. All he needed was the right songs to sell. Jerry believed that "sophisticated country" was the answer.

"I recall one night at my home when Glen Campbell picked up a guitar and sang a song he'd learned earlier that night while playing on a Merle Haggard session," said Jerry. "That song was 'The Son of Hickory Holler's Tramp.' The next day, I presented it to O.C., and he agreed that we should record it for a single release."

"Hickory Holler" was delicate material—a young man's tribute to his mother, a courageous backwoods prostitute. Many radio stations found the subject "indelicate"; others banned it completely. It reached the bottom of the national top forty but vanished almost overnight.

O.C.'s second album was called *Hickery Holler Revisited.* On that LP was the tune that was to make O. C. Smith a star. Jerry Fuller explained: "We picked up on this Bobby Russell tune, 'Little Green Apples,' that was doing well on the country charts, via Roger Miller. We gave it a slight change of tempo and feel. We didn't want to get too 'uptown.' Then O.C. came up with that real smooth vocal performance."

"Little Green Apples" was a cute ballad of love's devotion. It said, in effect, "thank you for loving me, and putting up with me, for eternity." O.C.'s version earned two Grammy nominations, Top Male Vocalist and Best New Artist of the Year. Composer Russell walked away with two Grammy Awards for Best Country Song and Song of the Year. "Little Green Apples" has since been recorded by more than four hundred different artists.

As for O. C. Smith, he never really had another big record. In 1969, he cut "Daddy's Little Man," another delicate love song, this time directed at a child of divorce. It was a mild seller, peaking at number thirty-four.

Today, O. C. Smith is back where he started, playing the supper clubs and reprising his hits. There's a lot more jazz in his act now, and he's also introduced a synthesizer. But somewhere, in the middle, the end, or as an encore, there's always "Little Green Apples." O. C. Smith hasn't forgotten why the people come.

Harper Valley P.T.A.

JEANNIE C. RILEY

An aspiring country singer, Jeannie Carolyn Riley found work as a demo singer for the Wilburn Brothers and for Little Darlin' Records in 1966. She also toured with Johnny Paycheck, but by the spring of 1968 was forced to take a job as a secretary with Passkey Music.

Meanwhile, a fast-rising songwriter named Tom T. Hall was trying to place a tune he had based on an actual incident. Tom had grown up in Carter City, Kentucky, about four miles from the home of an attractive young widow. She was a flashy dresser with many friends, who would often sit with her on her porch, drinking beer and listening to music. This was considered sinful by the local P.T.A., which sent her a note telling her so. Tom updated the story with references to miniskirts and "Peyton Place," a popular TV soap opera of the time.

A demo was made using the voice of Alice Joy, who hoped that her recording might lead to a label contract. "Tom then brought the song to me," said producer Shelby S. Singleton, Jr. "I wasn't interested in Alice as a singer, because I thought her voice was too soft for the song. I wanted someone with a little sass.

"A disc jockey friend of mine, Paul Perry of WENO, was managing Jeannie at the time and played me a demo of her voice. I thought she had the right sound for the record, but I didn't know if she had the personality to carry it through. He brought her in and we talked about it, and I played her the song, and she didn't like it.

"For that reason I wasn't sure if she was going to show up on the night we had the studio booked. So we had a split session: two songs by another artist and two songs by her. But she did show up, and we got through one take O.K. Then somebody suggested that we change one line in the song: 'That's the day my mama *put down* the Harper Valley P.T.A.' 'Laugh-In' was popular at that time, and on that particular TV show, they used the phrase 'Sock it to me' a lot. So we just changed the line to 'the day my mama *socked it to* the Harper Valley P.T.A.'

"We cut it on a Friday night, and Saturday night I was shipping records. It wasn't two days after that that we started getting calls from distributors and disc jockeys and just every place. Once they put the record on the air, it was an instant request item.

"It went over a million in six days. I remember we had about twelve or fourteen pressing plants running at the same time. I personally took orders one day for 900,000 copies. That was the biggest day we ever had on the song. At last count it's sold over ten million copies."

"Harper Valley P.T.A." put Jeannie C. Riley on every important network TV variety show; she received four gold records—one for the single, one for the album, and two from overseas. She was the second artist ever to be presented with a Gold Tape Cartridge Award.

Jeannie was also honored with a Grammy (Best Female Country Vocal Performance), a Country Music Association Award, a Music Operators of America plaque, and citations from all the music trade magazines.

Seldom has a single record done so much for one artist. But the image it gave her—miniskirts and a certain worldly sophistication—was not, Jeannie said emphatically, her real self at all. "I want to change that image," she said in 1972. "I want to build a more wholesome image and convince people that I'm not like the heroine of 'Harper Valley P.T.A.' " She became a born-again Christian and turned her back on the record that had made her a star.

In 1978, "Harper Valley P.T.A." was made into a film starring Barbara Eden. Two years later, it was shown on television, attracting the largest audience of any program broadcast that week. NBC immediately ordered a series, which began on January 16, 1981.

"Barbara Eden is now associated with 'Harper Valley P.T.A.,'" said Jeannie. "Maybe she'll walk off with the image and set me free."

Tighten Up

ARCHIE BELL AND THE DRELLS

Archie Bell and the Drells began their career by winning talent shows in and around their hometown of Houston, Texas. It was Archie who invented the word *drell,* to rhyme with his name. Whenever anyone asked, he said that *drell* was short for "dressed well" and that his Drells were all sharp-looking young men.

The group played the southern circuit for about five years and then appeared on a talent show hosted by Skipper Lee Frazier, a Houston deejay and part owner of radio station KCOH. The boys won first prize, and afterward, the Skipper asked them if they'd like to cut some records. They jumped at the chance and by 1966 had scored several local hits on the tiny East-West label. They decided to try for a major record contract, but then Archie was drafted and wound up in the 101st Airborne Division.

Archie completed basic training and then was sent home for one weekend in September 1967. Knowing he was headed for Vietnam, he spent most of his time lying on the couch, feeling depressed. Then an old pal, Billy Buttier, came by, determined to cheer up poor Archie, and on the spot made up a funny little dance, right there in the living room.

Archie stared at his friend and said, "What's that you're doing?"

Billy laughed and replied, "Oh, just a little thing I call the Tighten Up."

Archie lunged for his pen and quickly wrote down a song to go along with the new dance idea.

The next day, the group cut a record entitled "Dog Eat Dog." With nothing else for a B side, Archie suggested "Tighten Up." The others agreed, and a simple arrangement was worked out. Then, at the last moment, Archie came up with an odd intro to the song. It grew, he explained, out of JFK's assassination in Dallas.

"I had been on the road at that time, and I heard this deejay cry that 'nothing good ever came out of Texas.' Well, I happen to be proud of my state, and my band, and I think that what happened in Dallas could have happened anyplace. So we wanted people to know that we were from Texas and that we were good."

A few hours after recording, Archie Bell was on his way to Vietnam, where he undertook a number of dangerous missions. Meanwhile, back in Texas, "Tighten Up" had become a local hit. Atlantic decided to buy the record, but on the strength of "Dog Eat Dog."

After four months, they agreed to flip the single. Within weeks, "Tighten Up" was selling more than 100,000 copies a day.

Archie Bell knew nothing of this; the week his record reached number one, he was in a military hospital in Worms, Germany. His leg had been shattered under fire, and doctors spent months trying to save it. Finally, Skipper Lee got through and gave Archie the news.

Archie sang at three more recording sessions over the next year, all held in New York City. He'd fly in from Germany, cut a few numbers, and then fly back, all on a weekend pass. "I Can't Stop Dancing" was a top-ten record in the summer of 1968, and "There's Gonna Be a Showdown" was a good-sized hit early in 1969.

Archie was discharged from the army on April 19, 1969. His leg made a complete recovery; sadly, though, his career did not. Imposter groups, posing as "Archie Bell and the Drells," had damaged his reputation. And to make matters worse, Atlantic had shifted their attention to newer bands, leaving Archie Bell far behind.

Archie Bell and the Drells spent most of the seventies on the road. They also cut a few more records, first for the Glades label and later for Philadelphia International.

"If I had known how rough show biz was going to be," said Archie, "I think I would have rather been a garbage man. Still, I'm happy for 'Tighten Up.' It sold nearly four million copies and won me twenty-three awards. Maybe someday, if I keep trying, that lightning will strike again."

Young Girl

GARY PUCKETT AND THE UNION GAP

Gary Puckett spent his early years in the northern Minnesota town of Hibbing, as did another singer-songwriter, Bob Dylan. He later lived in Washington state, and then Twin Falls, Idaho, where he graduated from high school. All during this time, he experimented with rock 'n' roll, playing and singing with friends at hops and area talent shows.

Eventually, Gary enrolled as a psych major at San Diego City College. He studied for about a year and then quit, preferring to hang out with local musicians. At one point, he put together an R&B group called the Outcasts, but they didn't last.

Next, he formed Gary and the Remarkables, a band which, while good, had nothing that was truly remarkable. Gary realized that he needed a gimmick—something that would attract attention and make his group really distinctive. After mulling it over, he decided on a military motif, costuming each member in a blue and gold Civil War uniform. As lead singer, lead guitarist and "General," he'd command "Sergeant" Dwight Bement (bass), "Corporal" Kerry Chater (rhythm guitar), "Private" Gary Withem (keyboards), and "Private" Paul Wheatbread (drums). Adapting the name of historic Union Gap, Washington, his new ensemble became "the Union Gap, featuring Gary Puckett."

That was January 1967, and the band quickly began to draw some attention in the San Diego area. "We were very serious and business-like," said Gary. "We made up a brochure with pictures, clippings, lyrics of our songs, and a demonstration record— actually my voice with another group, because we couldn't afford to make a Union Gap demo." Gary took this kit around to various record companies in L.A., and was turned down by all of them. Finally, before leaving town, he visited Columbia and was directed to singer-songwriter-producer Jerry Fuller. Jerry chuckled at the photos, listened to the demo, and agreed to come out and see the Gap on the second night of their regular weekend gig.

That booking happened to be in the lounge of a San Diego bowling alley, where the boys had to compete with the sound of rolling balls and crashing pins. Gary took it easy Friday, coasting through three rather routine sets. Then, to his shock, Jerry stepped forward, with a great big grin on his face. "Let's make some records," said Jerry.

The Union Gap signed contracts on June 21, 1967, and on August 17, cut their first single, "Woman Woman." Released one month later, it broke in Cleveland that November, rising to number four on the national charts.

"Naturally, since it was such a big hit, we were sent a lot of songs to use as a follow-up," said Jerry. "And I looked everywhere, even to the writer and publisher of 'Woman Woman.' But I just didn't hear the kind of song I wanted.

"Finally, I dug out a thing I'd given up on six months before that. I rewrote the song, and played it for the group. They didn't care too much for it, but I talked them into recording it.

"As far as what inspired 'Young Girl,' that's another story. I was on the road a lot as an artist, fronting various groups for many years. I guess every entertainer goes through a time when fourteen-year-olds look like twenty-five-year-olds. That's somewhat of an inspiration—not from my own experience, but just knowing that it happens."

"Young Girl" took off in early March 1968, and by the next month was one of America's best-selling singles. "Even today," said Gary, "people come up to me and say, 'We fell in love while listening to that song.'" All of the Union Gap records had a warm, romantic feel, and the hit streak continued with "Lady Willpower" (1968), "Over You" (1968), "Don't Give in to Him" (1969) and "This Girl Is a Woman Now" (1969).

"When you listen to those records today," said Jerry, "they sound fairly simple. We didn't try to get contrived, maybe because we just didn't know how. We always tried to make the music say what the lyrics did. We let the songs dictate our arrangements."

That philosophy must have worked, because in 1968, the Union Gap managed to outsell rock's number one group, the Beatles.

This Guy's in Love with You

HERB ALPERT

erb Alpert started playing the trumpet as a child. "In the mid-fifties," recalled Herb, "I wanted to be a jazz musician. I thought I was, until I started listening to some of my favorites, like Miles Davis and Clifford Brown. I found I wasn't really doing anything new. I was more or less trying to emulate what they had already done. It seemed like a very unsatisfying road for me to take."

Herb then turned to pop music and spent the late fifties and early sixties learning the business. He worked as a session musician and arranged Jan and Dean's first hit, "Baby Talk" (1959). In 1960, he co-wrote "Wonderful World" with Sam Cooke, and produced Dante and the Evergreens' "Alley-Oop."

In 1962, a friend, Sol Lake, came up with a melody called "Twinkle Star." In his garage studio, Herb tried recording it, over and over again, but somehow the song refused to jell. Finally, he decided to take a day off, and drove down to Mexico. There, for the first time, he was exposed to the multiple-brass sound of the mariachi. Herb applied what he heard to the tape of "Twinkle Star," and this time

the tune almost worked. But there was still something missing.

He talked about his trouble with another pal, Jerry Moss, who suggested adding the sound of a Mexican bullfight. The two recorded two hours of crowd noise at a Tijuana arena, and the effects transformed "Twinkle Star" into "The Lonely Bull." Jerry came up with a name—the Tijuana Brass—as well as half the money needed to press up first copies of the single. With that, A&M Records was under way—with a million-seller.

"The actual sound of the Brass," said Herb, "is sort of a combination between jazz and a slight touch of the flair of Mexico. But it was all my trumpet—one trumpet—overdubbed many many times. The lead lines of the tunes were not written down; they were played how they were felt at that particular time."

"A Taste of Honey" was the second top-ten single credited to "Herb Alpert and the Tijuana Brass." In 1965, it earned three Grammy Awards, including Best Instrumental Arrangement, Best Instrumental Performance (Non-Jazz), and Record of the Year. In 1966, those first two prizes again went

to Herb Alpert, for the single "What Now My Love."

The Tijuana Brass was primarily an album act, but Herb did place more than a dozen songs on the charts in the late sixties. By the end of 1967, he had released nine albums, all of which were strong, consistent sellers. Over a million advance orders awaited the tenth, *The Beat of the Brass,* due in the spring of 1968. To celebrate, Herb agreed to make, and star in, a CBS-TV special.

Herb asked two of the hottest songwriters of the day, Burt Bacharach and Hal David, to write a song expressly for the show. He told them that he wanted something warm and romantic, as he'd be singing it to his wife, Sharon. The tune they came up with was "This Guy's in Love with You."

On April 23—the day after the telecast—A&M, record shops, and radio and TV stations were flooded with requests for copies of the song. Herb put it out as a single right away. It jumped onto the charts and wound up as number one.

"This Guy's in Love with You" marked the high point—and the end—of Herb's hit streak. "Toward the end of '69 I found that my musical career had become a big burden," he said later. "I was boring myself musically, repeating myself." Herb stopped performing and spent the next four years winding down, and "making friends again" with his trumpet. In late 1973, he organized a new Tijuana Brass and began accepting occasional engagements.

Herb Alpert's main activity in the seventies was helping to run A&M Records, which grew into the largest independent label in America. But before the decade was over, Herb Alpert rose to the top one more time, with an undulating instrumental that earned him his sixth Grammy Award. What else could it be titled but "Rise"?

Mrs. Robinson

SIMON AND GARFUNKEL

Paul Simon and Art Garfunkel were born twenty-three days apart in Queens, New York City. Although only three blocks separated their homes, they didn't meet until the sixth grade, when both were cast in P.S. 164's version of *Alice in Wonderland.* Art played the Cheshire Cat, and Paul a rabbit.

They were drawn to each other because they were reluctant to join the crowd. "Paul always had a weird sense of humor," said Art. "One particularly nasty joke he cracked got us both sent to detention. Every day after that, during music period, we had to go to a little room in the tower to serve detention. Paul brought his guitar and we would sing every day."

With their friendship and musical ideals firmly intact, Paul and Art decided to go out and conquer the world. They recorded their first song in a twenty-five cent recording booth at the Coney Island amusement center in Brooklyn. When they were sixteen, calling themselves Tom and Jerry, they cut "Hey Schoolgirl" for Big Records. It climbed to number fifty-four in 1957, and got them a spot on "American Bandstand." After one tour, though, they were washed up.

Art eventually enrolled at Columbia University, and Paul at Queens College, where he began songwriting in earnest. In 1963, he composed "The Sounds of Silence," which the boys recorded on their first album two years later. The tune was ignored at first, but then a New York FM disc jockey discovered it and began giving the track heavy air play. Strong phone response convinced Columbia Records to issue it as a single, with added rock 'n' roll accompaniment. To the shock of Paul, Art, and everyone at the label, "The Sounds of Silence" became a number-one smash in January 1966.

Simon and Garfunkel were established, and the hits kept coming till the end of the decade and beyond.

Later in 1966, there were "Homeward Bound," "I Am a Rock," "The Dangling Conversation" and "A Hazy Shade of Winter"; in 1967, "At the Zoo" and "Fakin' It." They began 1968 with one of their prettiest songs: "Scarborough Fair/Canticle."

Simon and Garfunkel's best material had a gentle intimacy that was noticed by filmmaker Mike Nichols in 1968. For the motion picture, *The Graduate,* Nichols took existing Simon and Garfunkel tunes and re-edited parts of his film to fit them. He commissioned one original song—"Mrs. Robinson."

Paul and Art were working on their LP *Bookends* then. It was a typical S&G studio project: expensive, not because of musicians, but because of all the hours they burned up experimenting. Artie often made thirty-five or more takes on a song, and the two of them thought nothing of working all night. Their close-worked harmony was doubled, on tape, to four voices, by each singing his part twice. This effect was used on "Mrs. Robinson," turning the duo into a very effective "group."

The plot of *The Graduate* deals with a young man, played by Dustin Hoffman, who beds both a young lady (Katharine Ross) and her seductive mother (Anne Bancroft). The song is a series of questions, probing the character portrayed by Bancroft. Simon and Garfunkel spent a long time fine-tuning their recording, punching in a lot of retaken words, phrases, and even breaths. After many such edits, the track was released as a single in mid-April 1968.

"Mrs. Robinson" took off right away, rising to the top of the charts in June. It spent three weeks at number one, and thirteen weeks on the hit parade. It also won two Grammy Awards: as the Best Contemporary Performance by a Vocal Duo, and as Record of the Year.

"I write about personal things," said

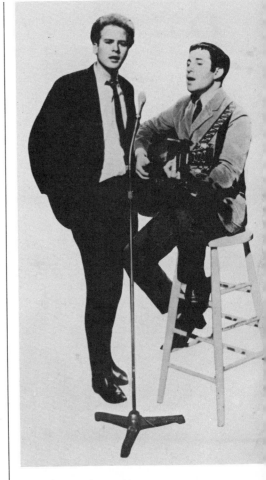

Paul, who composed nearly all of their material. "I can look into people and see scars in them. I write about what I know and observe—love relationships, craziness, happiness—it's all part of life." In the 1960s, he and Art chronicled life for millions—the frustrations and insecurities of a generation coming of age.

Their later hits included "The Boxer" in 1969, and in 1970, "Bridge over Troubled Water," "Cecelia," and "El Condor Pasa." They went their separate ways that year, but have since reteamed occasionally. In 1975, they made the top ten with "My Little Town," and in 1978 joined forces with James Taylor to record "(What a) Wonderful World."

Honey
BOBBY GOLDSBORO

Bobby's interest in music began to develop at the age of twelve when he dropped in at the home of a childhood friend. "This guy had received a ukulele as a gift, and was not musically inclined," he recalled. "So I began fooling around with it whenever I came by." Bobby quickly became rather skilled, and, as a Christmas gift, his parents bought him his own guitar. Before long, Bobby was spending nearly all his waking hours practicing, playing along with the radio, and working up his own songs.

In 1959, while still a high school student, Bobby formed his first rock band, the Webbs. Each member was required to wear a sport coat and tie, decorated with a design of spider webs. This group managed to stay together through his first two years at Auburn University, playing local clubs and dances.

"One day we heard that Roy Orbison was coming through town, and we were booked to back him up for four concerts. They must have gone pretty well, because afterward Roy asked us to go on the road as his regular band." The group accepted, and in deference to Roy's current hit, "Candy Man," the Webbs became the Candymen.

Bobby played guitar for Orbison for two years, studying his style and even writing a few tunes with him. Goldsboro's songwriting talents brought him to the attention of United Artists Records, with which he signed in 1963.

Bobby's first release for the label, "See the Funny Little Clown," was issued in January 1964. Despite Beatlemania and the British invasion, it became a top-ten single and paved the way for "Whenever He Holds You," "Little Things," "Voodoo Woman," "It's Too Late," and "Blue Autumn," all top-forty hits.

"Honey," ironically, was one of the few Goldsboro singles he did not write. The composer was Bobby

Russell, who also gave us "Sure Gonna Miss Her," "The Joker Went Wild," and "Little Green Apples." According to Russell, "The day I wrote 'Honey,' I was in an exceptional writing mood. I was going out for the night but at the last minute got inspired and decided to stay home and write. When we'd moved into this house, I hadn't noticed one particular tree outside. But lately it was getting my attention. I finally noticed how much it had grown in the last four years. As corny as it sounds, that's how 'Honey' started."

"Honey" was first recorded by Bob Shane, one of the original Kingston Trio. His single managed to sell about a hundred thousand copies in two weeks. Goldsboro was impressed and decided to see what he could do with the song. After the recording session, he felt very excited and seemed to know that he had just cut a pop classic. Even the singers, musicians, and studio engineers sensed something special.

"Honey" went on to sell more than five million copies and win the Country Music Association award for Song

of the Year. It was nominated for five Grammy Awards, including Record of the Year. More than three hundred versions of the song have been recorded since 1968.

Bobby Goldsboro has had his critics; some described "Honey" as "a mini soap opera." His 1968 reply: "The traditional June-moon love song doesn't make sense to today's youth. We grew up with the bomb, constant war, and the draft staring us in the face. We sing and think about death because we feel we can't plan for the future."

Since "Honey" came out, Bobby has had several other hits, including "Autumn of My Life," "The Straight Life," "Watching Scotty Grow," and "Summer (The First Time)." From 1972 to 1975, he hosted his own syndicated television show, seen in over a hundred forty markets worldwide. He also bought a five hundred-acre cattle ranch near Nashville, where he raises horses in his spare time. He still sings and writes, and dreams of someday topping his 1968 success with "Honey."

The Dock of the Bay
OTIS REDDING

Otis Redding, the son of a Baptist minister, was born in Dawson, Georgia, and raised in nearby Macon. A high school dropout, he tried to earn a living digging wells for $1.25 an hour and working as a hospital orderly. He was fired from the latter job for singing in the hallways.

As a teenager, Otis was impressed by the adulation heaped upon another hometown boy, Little Richard. He decided to become a performer himself and quickly mastered piano, guitar, drums, bass, and organ. Before long, he was working as road manager—and occasional singer—with Johnny Jenkins and the Pinetoppers.

In 1962, Otis drove the band to Memphis for a session at the Stax-Volt Studios. All through the date, Otis sat in the corner and every once in a while would say, "Man, I sure would like to cut a song." In the last twenty minutes, the group gave him a chance. He sang "These Arms of Mine"—his first top-twenty R&B hit.

Over the next five years, Otis put more than a dozen other tunes on the pop and R&B charts. Among the biggest were "I've Been Loving You Too Long" and "Respect" (1965); "Satisfaction" and "Fa Fa Fa Fa Fa" (1966); and "Shake" and "Try a Little Tenderness" (1967). Otis was equally expressive with fast and slow songs, and his distinctive, moving style earned him a nickname: "The Crown Prince of Soul." He was a tough singer, yet he could handle tender, sentimental ballads with ease. Many of his best records had themes of desperation and lost love. Another of his hits gave him a second nickname: "Mr. Pitiful."

In 1967, Otis became the only soul singer to show up at the Monterey Pop Festival. He was little known to the mostly white, flower-power audience, and came on late, well after midnight. The crowd was tired, and some people were dropping off to sleep when Otis hit the stage just before 1 A.M. Within seconds, they were on their feet, worked into a frenzy by his dynamic, exciting sound. Captured in the film and album *Monterey Pop,* it was said to be the greatest performance of Redding's life.

Apparently influenced by his new-found hippie friends, Otis came up with a song that matched their easy-going outlook. He wrote it while sitting in a houseboat anchored just off Sausalito, a few miles from San Francisco. It was a soft pop ballad that began with lapping waves and seagull cries, and rocked to a gentle beat. "(Sittin' on) The Dock of the Bay" had its own refined tension and expressed the wistful longings of a man alone.

The record was cut on December 7, 1967. Three days later, Otis ended a concert in Madison, Wisconsin, and boarded his brand-new twin-engine Beechcraft to fly to Cleveland. He was very proud of his plane because it showed that after all that time, he had finally begun to make it. *Melody Maker* had voted him Top Male Vocalist of the Year, an honor they'd given Elvis Presley the previous eight years. Thanks to Monterey, the pop market had discovered him, and everyone said that 1968 was going to be "his year."

The plane took off in heavy fog, and four miles out, dropped like a rock into Lake Monona. It sank within seconds; and Otis was gone.

For his funeral, 4,500 people filled the Macon City Auditorium. Joe Tex, Joe Simon, Johnnie Taylor, Don Covay, Percy Sledge, Solomon Burke, and Sam Moore (of Sam and Dave) were the pallbearers. He was buried on the ranch he loved so well in Round Oak, thirty miles out of town.

"Dock of the Bay" was released in January 1968 and three months later was the number-one song in the country. It went on to sell more than four million copies and earn two Grammy Awards (Best R&B Song and Best Male R&B Vocal Performance).

"It's his epitaph," said Jerry Wexler of Atlantic. "It proved that a singer could do his own thing and still be commercially successful. Otis is tremendously responsible for the fact that the young white audience now digs soul the way the black does."

Love Is Blue
(L'Amour Est Bleu)

PAUL MAURIAT
AND HIS ORCHESTRA

French-born Paul Mauriat descended from a long line of musicians, and first aspired to become a classical pianist. He studied music from the age of four, and after the family moved to Paris, he completed his studies at the Paris Conservatoire.

As a teenager, Paul became interested in jazz and pop music. At seventeen, he formed his own orchestra and began touring cabarets and concert halls all over Europe. Eventually, he returned to Paris and found work at various recording studios. He quickly built up a reputation as a top arranger and conductor, joining a select group which included Caravelli, Raymond Lafevre and Franck Pourcell. Those four regularly issued LPs of instrumental mood music—orchestrated arrangements of other people's hits (Pourcel's cover version of "Only You" made the U.S. top ten

in 1959). In 1963, Paul and Franck wrote an original song of their own entitled "Chariot." Translated into English, it became "I Will Follow Him," a million-seller in America for Little Peggy March.

The song "Love Is Blue" was written early in 1967 by Pierre Cour (words) and Andre Popp (music), and was chosen to represent Luxembourg in the Eurovision Song Contest that year. It came in fourth, as performed by Polydor artist Vicky (real name Vicky Leandros). She recorded it in several languages for nineteen different countries, but none of her versions became hits.

It was then that Paul Mauriat decided to give the song a try. He applied his own distinctive sound: soaring strings, muted horns, and a rocking rhythm. On his record, Paul arranged, conducted, and played harpsichord.

The single was released late in 1967, and broke in the U.S. right after New Year's, 1968. It reached number one in February and was certified gold in March. It spent more than a month as America's favorite 45 and eighteen weeks in total on the best-seller lists. Over four million copies were sold during that time. The album it came off, *Blooming Hits,* also became a chart topper.

Paul Mauriat's success with "Love Is Blue" inspired many other renditions, both instrumental and vocal (the English lyrics were written by Bryan Blackburn). Over three hundred artists, ranging from Al Martino to Claudine Longet, cut their own interpretations. In 1969, the Dells hit by working the song into a medley, "I Can Sing a Rainbow/Love Is Blue." Collective versions have sold more than ten million copies worldwide.

Hey Jude
THE BEATLES

One of the most remarkable things about the Beatles was their amazing ability to get better and better. Their standards never dropped, and each new record seemed to top what had come before. "Imagination," "first," "best," "success," "international significance"—those were the easy words, recycled in hundreds of reviews, articles, and personal profiles.

Nineteen sixty-seven had been a typical year of innovation, with two landmark albums. First there was *Sgt. Pepper's Lonely Hearts Club Band,* which *Rolling Stone* called "the superpsychedelic LP that tops all toppers." Then there was *Magical Mystery Tour,* the soundtrack from the Beatles' first self-produced TV special. The Beatles also appeared on "Our World," a global television spectacular viewed by an estimated hundred fifty million people. On the show, the boys were seen live in their studio in London, recording "All You Need Is Love."

In 1968, the Beatles formed Apple Corps, Ltd., both to manage their own affairs and to launch deserving new artists (among those given a boost were James Taylor, Billy Preston, Mary Hopkin, and Badfinger). In March, they released their thirty-second American hit single, "Lady Madonna," a pounding piano rocker dedicated to Fats Domino. On July 17, the film *Yellow Submarine* came out. It was the Beatles' first full-length animated motion picture and had been written, in part, by Eric Segal, later the author of *Love Story.*

And then they recorded their greatest hit.

"Hey Jude" came together in the summer of 1968, shortly after John and Cynthia Lennon split up. Paul McCartney had always been close to their son, Julian, and heard that he was very troubled over his parents' divorce. Paul decided to drive over and see the boy, and on the way, he began to make up a soft song of gentle consolation. Later, Paul refined "Hey Jules" into "Hey Jude"—giving it, in Paul's words, "a more country-western flavor."

"Hey Jude" was recorded on the night of July 31–August 1 with Paul on piano, singing as he played. As backup, George Martin assembled a forty-piece orchestra, and instructed the musicians to join in vocally at the end. This they did with great reluctance; one, in fact, asked for a special fee afterward.

The finished recording was a record-shattering production in many respects: At seven minutes and eleven seconds, it was the longest hit song ever played on American radio. It had the longest fade-out in history (about three minutes), and spent more time at number one than any other Beatles release (nine weeks).

The other side, "Revolution," was also a landmark. Written and sung by John, it was one of the Beatles' few obviously topical selections. At that time, rioters were battling police in Chicago at the Democratic National Convention, and political strife and paranoia were rampant on college campuses and in cities around the world. "Revolution," at first, seemed to be an anarchistic anthem, screamed and played with an intensity unequaled in any other Beatles recording. However, on closer inspection, it was actually an *antiprotest* song ("you can count me *out*"). This so delighted the conservative Young Americans for Freedom that they had posters printed up featuring the Beatles and all the words to the song. A slowed-down, more intelligible version of "Revolution" appears on the Beatles' *White Album,* their only LP release of 1968.

"Hey Jude," backed with "Revolution," spent nearly five months on the charts and sold over eight million copies.

1969

BY 1969, AMERICAN record sales were triple what they had been in 1956. John Lennon became the first recipient of *Rolling Stone*'s Man of the Year Award, and later was sued for plagiarism over his song "Come Together" (the first two lines were the same as Chuck Berry's "You Can't Catch Me"). Lennon wed Yoko Ono, and Linda Eastman married Paul McCartney (shortly before false rumors began of his "secret" passing). Death reports were real, though, in the cases of Shorty Long, Leonard Chess, Roy Hamilton, Tommy Edwards, and Judy Garland. Tom Jones, Johnny Cash, Andy Williams, and Debbie Reynolds all got their own television shows; the Smothers Brothers lost theirs. The original Manfred Mann broke up; so did Peter, Paul and Mary and the Zombies.

Instead, we got new faces: Argent, Bread, Mountain, Genesis, Brownsville Station, the Allman Brothers, and Grand Funk Railroad. The Turtles and the Temptations played the White House; the Doors played Florida (and were busted for obscenity). The Stones lost Brian Jones, added Mick Taylor, and formed their own record label. The Dells made the top ten with a remake of "Oh What a Night," a song they had first recorded in 1956. And in England, an LP called "Empty Sky" introduced the British public to a budding young talent, Elton John. It was a transitional time, a year of many contrasts. The single "Sugar, Sugar" and album *Blind Faith* each topped their respective charts simultaneously.

The crowning conclusion to the Age of Aquarius came the weekend of August 15–17 in a farmer's field in upstate New York. The **Woodstock** Music and Art Fair attracted nearly half a million free spirits, who laughed, played, and got rained on in what became the greatest rock 'n' roll party of all time. Entertainment was provided by Joan Baez; the Who; Crosby, Stills, Nash and Young; Richie Havens; Sha Na Na; Arlo Guthrie; Melanie; Ten Years After; John Sebastian; Santana; Jimi Hendrix; Jefferson Airplane; Sly and the Family Stone; Joe Cocker; Country Joe and the Fish; and others. Moviemaker Michael Wadleigh captured it all on film; his motion picture won a 1970 Oscar as the year's Best Documentary. The music of Woodstock was also released on five LP records.

On September 22, ABC premiered "The Music Scene," an ambitious and inventive series featuring performances by nearly every major pop artist available. **Joe Cocker** was one guest star. Comedian David Steinberg was the host, aided and abetted by others including Lily Tomlin (who later found more fame on "Laugh-In"). In retrospect, "The Music Scene" was clearly ahead of its time; that, and its irregular length (forty-five minutes) contributed to its early demise on January 12, 1970.

Guitar legend **Jimi Hendrix** starred in *Experience,* a motion picture record of songs from his first two albums. Arlo Guthrie brought to the screen *Alice's Restaurant,* while Donovan was heard on the soundtrack of *If It's Tuesday This Must Be Belgium.* Otherwise, it was a good year for country flicks: *From Nashville with Music* (with Marty Robbins, Merle Haggard, and Buck Owens), *Norwood* (with Glen Campbell), *Paint Your Wagon* (with the Nitty Gritty Dirt Band), and *Johnny Cash: The Man, His World, His Music* (with J.C., Carl Perkins, and Bob Dylan). Elvis' movies were *Charro, Change of Heart,* and *The Trouble with Girls.*

The most powerful and influential heavy metal band of the seventies was **Led Zeppelin,** the group that sprang from the ruins of the Yardbirds. Leader Jimmy Page was a one-time session man who had played guitar on records behind Petula Clark, Paul Anka, and Englebert Humperdinck. Together with John Bonham and John Paul Jones, Page invented a distinctly different hard rock sound—the perfect instrumental backup for lead singer Robert Plant. Zep's first major hit, "Whole Lotta Love," broke in November 1969; after that came "The Immigrant Song" (1970), "Stairway to Heaven" (never a single, but huge in 1971), "Black Dog" (1972), and "D'yer Mak'er" (1973). A year after their final hit, "Fool in the Rain" (1979), Led Zeppelin disbanded following the death of drummer Bonham.

The Who were identified as mod rockers until 1969 when they released "Tommy," the world's first rock 'n' roll opera. Pete Townsend wrote the work after reading a lot of Herman Hesse and becoming fascinated with the idea of a spiritual journey. "It's meant to be multi-leveled," Pete explained. "Tommy is a fantasy messiah—a phony one. He's deaf, dumb and blind because we're deaf, dumb and blind to spiritual potential that's within us." Added lead singer Roger Daltrey, "Everyone, at some stage in his life, feels like a Tommy: helpless, useless. I think that's what people identify with." The Who hits, "Pinball Wizard," "I'm Free," and "See Me, Feel Me," came out of "Tommy"; six years later, it became a motion picture starring Elton John, Eric Clapton, and the Who.

THE TOP 40

1. Sugar, Sugar, *Archies*
2. Aquarius/Let the Sunshine In, *Fifth Dimension*
3. Honky Tonk Women, *Rolling Stones*
4. Everyday People, *Sly and the Family Stone*
5. I Can't Get Next to You, *Temptations*
6. Dizzy, *Tommy Roe*
7. Crimson and Clover, *Tommy James and the Shondells*
8. Build Me Up Buttercup, *Foundations*
9. Hair, *Cowsills*
10. One, *Three Dog Night*
11. Crystal Blue Persuasion, *Tommy James and the Shondells*
12. I'll Never Fall in Love Again, *Tom Jones*
13. In the Year 2525, *Zager and Evans*
14. Get Back, *Beatles with Billy Preston*
15. Jean, *Oliver*
16. I Heard It Through the Grapevine, *Marvin Gaye*
17. Easy to Be Hard, *Three Dog Night*
18. Sweet Caroline, *Neil Diamond*
19. Hot Fun in the Summertime, *Sly and the Family Stone*
20. What Does It Take to Win Your Love, *Junior Walker and the All-Stars*
21. Green River, *Creedence Clearwater Revival*
22. Love Theme from "Romeo and Juliet," *Henry Mancini*
23. Wichita Lineman, *Glen Campbell*
24. Time of the Season, *Zombies*
25. Too Busy Thinking About My Baby, *Marvin Gaye*
26. Get Together, *Youngbloods*
27. It's Your Thing, *Isley Brothers*
28. Grazin' in the Grass, *Friends of Distinction*
29. Suspicious Minds, *Elvis Presley*
30. Touch Me, *Doors*
31. Proud Mary, *Creedence Clearwater Revival*
32. Hooked on a Feeling, *B. J. Thomas*
33. These Eyes, *Guess Who*
34. Bad Moon Rising, *Creedence Clearwater Revival*
35. Stormy, *Classics IV*
36. Spinning Wheel, *Blood, Sweat and Tears*
37. This Magic Moment, *Jay and the Americans*
38. In the Ghetto, *Elvis Presley*
39. Baby It's You, *Smith*
40. Wedding Bell Blues, *Fifth Dimension*

Despite or perhaps because of their total lack of psychedelic gimmickry, **Creedence Clearwater Revival** became the most successful band to emerge from the San Francisco area during the sixties. They made their mark with basic music: earthy, driving swampland vocals, set against Sun-style rockabilly backup. Their Southern feel was so authentic that even today many are convinced that Creedence must have been born on the bayou (even though it was some time after they hit that the group even ventured outside northern California). CCR really took off in January 1969 with the release of "Proud Mary," the first of eight gold singles and eight gold albums John Fogerty and the boys racked up over the next three years.

THE TOP 10 LPs

1. Hair, *Original Broadway Cast*
2. In-a-Gadda-da-Vida, *Iron Butterfly*
3. Blood, Sweat and Tears, *Blood, Sweat and Tears*
4. Led Zeppelin, *Led Zeppelin*
5. The Beatles (White Album), *Beatles*
6. Bayou Country, *Creedence Clearwater Revival*
7. Donovan's Greatest Hits, *Donovan*
8. Funny Girl, *Original Soundtrack*
9. Romeo and Juliet, *Original Soundtrack*
10. Greatest Hits, *Association*

One
THREE DOG NIGHT

Three Dog Night was conceived in Los Angeles by an Irish singer and record producer who had tried and failed to make it as a teen idol. He was twenty-six-year-old Danny Hutton, who had cut and released several flop singles on HBR Records in the mid-sixties.

In 1968, Danny went on the road with Sonny and Cher and an obscure group known as the Enemies. They were the house band at the Whiskey à Go Go in Hollywood, and although they never had any hits, they had managed to turn up in two pretty popular movies (*The Riot on Sunset Strip* and *Harper*). Danny was impressed by their version of "Hey Joe" and offered to produce a single of it by them at the end of the tour. The single was cut and released by MGM Records but went nowhere. Shortly thereafter, the Enemies broke up.

Danny kept in touch, though, with one former Enemy, Cory Wells, and later in the year called him up. They discussed forming a group with an unusual twist—three separate but equal lead singers. As a third member, Danny brought in Chuck Negron, whom he'd met a few months before at a party for Donovan.

After being turned down by several labels, the three signed with ABC Dunhill and recorded their first LP in two days. They still did not have a name, though, and after rejecting such suggestions as Tricycle and Six Foot Three, Danny's girlfriend, June Fairchild, came up with a solution. She'd been reading in *Mankind* magazine about the nocturnal habits of Australian aborigines. Apparently, when it got cold out there in the bush, the aborigines would keep warm by sleeping with their dogs. If it was a particularly chilly evening, they'd call it a "three dog night." The trio liked the offbeat nature of that name and decided to keep it.

Three Dog Night's first hit single was "Try a Little Tenderness," which reached the top thirty in the spring of 1969. A few weeks later, they released "One," which became their first top-five record.

"Both of those songs came from the first album," recalled Cory Wells. "They were produced by Gabriel Mekler, who also produced the hits of Steppenwolf. We tested all the material on that LP by playing in local clubs and high schools for about six months. The idea was to go in and record those songs just as we'd played them. After all that time we had them down cold; that's why we could cut that album so fast. We recorded live in the studio, with the singers in the same room as the musicians, and no overdubs.

"Chuck sang lead on 'One.' We'd been going through songs, and he brought that one in. He'd found it on an album; he said, 'I like this guy Nilsson,' and I said, 'I never heard of him.' Chuck said, 'Well, most people haven't, but listen to this,' so I listened, and I liked it. Danny said it was good; we had to change the arrangement a little bit. 'One is the loneliest number'— you know a lot of people didn't know what that meant. Some thought we were singing about marijuana being a number. We'd have people come up and say, 'Hey, I know what that song's about.' And we'd say, 'What?' And they'd say, 'The Trinity, right? The Father, Son, and the Holy Ghost, three into one, right?' And we'd say, 'No. . . .' "

Three Dog Night helped open the door for many obscure songwriters, including Nilsson, who sprang to fame immediately after "One." In fact, Nilsson's first hit as a performer, "Everybody's Talkin'," entered the pop charts in the very same week that "One" fell off.

For Three Dog Night, "One" began a string of eighteen consecutive top-ten singles in a row, stretched out over the next five years. "Easy to Be Hard" was next, and then came "Eli's Coming" and "Celebrate." Their fifth top-ten record went all the way to number one—"Mama Told Me Not to Come," in 1970.

Hair
THE COWSILLS

*I*n 1963, Chief Petty Officer Bud Cowsill retired from the navy after twenty years of service. Pension checks began arriving, but they didn't stretch far with his brood of seven children. A neighbor suggested that he capitalize on his houseful of talent. All the boys sang and played instruments in informal jams. Why not organize a family band?

The kids were intrigued, so a schedule was set up, using strict navy discipline. After schoolwork, there were two hours of rehearsal every day. Slowly, a repertoire of five hundred songs was built up—pop, country, folk, and rock 'n' roll. The long years of practice were costly, and before long, Bud was in debt to the tune of $100,000. The Cowsill home in Newport, Rhode Island, went neglected—the drive unattended to ward off creditors. When their oil was cut off one winter, the family kept warm by chopping and burning their furniture.

The Cowsills were just about ready to lose their house when they met writer-producer Artie Kornfield. Artie brought them to MGM, got them a contract, and helped them put together a hit single. It was called "The Rain, the Park and Other Things," and was a million-seller in the fall of 1967. In 1968, the boys added their sister and Mom to the act, and had two more big records, "We Can Fly" and "Indian Lake."

Then, in 1969, the group decided to record one of the big numbers from *Hair*, "the American Tribal Love-Rock Musical," then the hottest ticket on Broadway. They chose the title song, and immediately ran into flak from their record company. MGM objected to certain lyric lines, including a refer-

ence to the hair length of Jesus Christ. Bill and Bob Cowsill rearranged the song, dropping the offending words. The tune was then cut and released in early March 1969.

Reaction was immediate. The single jumped on radio playlists, and climbed steadily all through the month of April. In May, it peaked on the charts, having

gone gold a few weeks before. At the same time, Bill left the group to pursue a composing career.

The Cowsills never had another major hit, but lived on, in a sense, for several more years. Their story, style and sound served as the blueprint for a fictionalized TV imitation—"The Partridge Family" (1970–74).

Build Me Up Buttercup

THE FOUNDATIONS

Just about every act has to start at the bottom, and the Foundations were no exception. However, for this "underground band," that turned out to be literally the case.

Seven guys, aged nineteen to thirty-eight, formed the group in London in January 1967. Three of them were native sons, and the rest came from various parts of the Commonwealth. Tim "Sticks" Harris, from St. John's Wood, had been a drummer since leaving school. Alan Warner, lead guitarist, was a former printer who'd played in numerous bands around Britain. Bass man Peter Macbeth was an ex-teacher who'd spent some time in book publishing.

The other members came from all over the globe. Eric Allendale, on trombone, was born in the West Indies. He'd led his own group and performed with the Terry Lightfoot, Alex Walsh, and Hammersmith brass bands. Organist Tony Gomez, from Columbo, Ceylon, had worked in London's County Hall as a clerical officer. Lead singer Clem Curtis was a former metalworker and pro boxer who'd come to the U.K. in 1956 from Trinidad. Finally, there were Pat Burke (flute) and Mike Elliot (tenor sax), two Jamaicans who had moved to England in the early fifties.

The Foundations started out in a basement coffee bar called the Butterfly in Westbourne Grove, London. They'd sing a few numbers and then move about the crowd, serving up coffee. When the money ran low, they ate and slept in the basement. It was this subterranean lifestyle that eventually led to their group name.

Over the Butterfly was an office building, which included the quarters of record dealer Barry Class. He couldn't help hearing them, and after a while, he went downstairs to see what all the ruckus was about. He came away very impressed and contacted Tony Macaulay, a recording manager at Pye Records.

Tony agreed to record the group, and he and his partner, John McLeod, wrote their first hit, "Baby, Now That I've Found You." Released August 25, 1967, it spent three weeks at number one in England. It was a major hit in the United States as well, with worldwide sales topping three and a half million.

The single after that, "Back on My Feet Again," was less popular; a top-twenty entry in England, it generally flopped in America. At that point, lead singer Clem Curtis decided to quit and was replaced by Colin "Joey" Young, from Barbados, West Indies (Michael Elliot also left but was not replaced). The group was shaken by these changes but resolved not to break up. With new determination, they reentered the studio and emerged with their all-time classic.

Tony Macaulay and Mike D'Abo of Manfred Mann were the composers of "Build Me Up Buttercup." A bright, rhythmic, infectious song, it accomplished what the Foundations had set out to do: become the British counterpart to Motown. Their approximation of the Detroit sound was so exact that many deejays were amazed to learn that the record had been made outside the United States. They were also surprised to discover that the Foundations were a racially mixed group—one of the very few in all of pop music history.

Released in the U.K. on November 8, 1968, the song sold 250,000 copies in two months, eventually climbing to second place on the British charts. It came out in America a few weeks later, rising to number three. In March 1969, it was certified a million-seller in the U.S.; worldwide sales, one month later, topped four and a half million.

The Foundations continued to cut records for some time but never again recaptured the magic of "Buttercup" (one follow-up, "In the Bad, Bad Old Days," did make the U.K. top ten). Their last American chart entry, "My Little Chickadee," flickered briefly at number ninety-nine.

In the early seventies, the Foundations went their separate ways, several dropping out of the music business altogether. However, their place in rock history was assured, thanks to "Baby, Now That I've Found You" and, especially, "Build Me Up Buttercup."

Crimson and Clover

TOMMY JAMES AND THE SHONDELLS

Tommy James began playing the guitar in 1956 at the age of nine. Like millions of Americans, he was inspired by Elvis Presley, whom he'd seen on the "Ed Sullivan Show." Three years later, he was fronting his own band, which he named the Shondells. As Tommy remembered it, "The lead singer always walked off with the chicks. That was my reason for playing, back then."

In 1961, Tommy was asked by a local deejay to record a few songs for Snap, a tiny Michigan label. One of them, "Hanky Panky," started to take off but then died, a victim of poor distribution. Tommy quickly forgot about the record, and after a time, he and the Shondells broke up.

Five years went by, and then another deejay found a copy of the 45 in a stack of oldies. Not knowing that it hadn't been a real hit, he played it on the air in Pittsburgh, by mistake. To his amazement, delighted listeners demanded to know where they could get a copy of "the hot new single."

Sensing a hit, a local bootlegger taped the song off the air and began pressing illegal copies of it. Within ten days, more than eighty thousand copies had been sold. The Pittsburgh deejay finally tracked down Tommy James and informed him that his record was number one. Tommy almost hung up on the guy, but a week later, he was in New York, selling the original master of "Hanky Panky" to Roulette Records. One month later, it was number one nationwide.

Though the success of "Hanky Panky" may have at first seemed to be a fluke, subsequent hits, like "I Think We're Alone Now," "Mirage," "Gettin' Together," and "Mony Mony," were proof that Tommy was no one-shot wonder. The music industry recognized this as well, and *Billboard* voted Tommy Top Male Artist of 1967.

In 1968, Tommy decided to change his musical direction. " 'Mony Mony' was kind of the end of an era for me,"

he explained. "I thought we'd taken the hard rock sound about as far as it could go. I had learned a lot, and felt I knew my way around a studio. It was time now to not just write the hits, but produce them as well."

His first project was "Crimson and Clover." "I wrote that one with my drummer, Peter Lucia. When I went into the studio, I had some idea of what I wanted, but no idea that the song would come out the way it did. It was almost magic how it came together. I played all the instruments on that record, except the drums, and sang all the vocal parts. We knew it was a hit. We started that song and finished it in five and a half hours, God's truth. And you know, it sold five and a half million copies—that's one million records an hour.

" 'Crimson and Clover' combined two things I really like: simplicity and sound effects. I love to make sounds wiggle and twirl around. I think that it's important to keep records simple, but not empty. You have to start with the basics: a good hook, and then carefully add the right effects. Some

people called 'Crimson and Clover' a 'soft acid' record. I didn't care. The important thing was that I had created a new sound."

Tommy James continued to experiment with later hits, such as "Sweet Cherry Wine," "Ball of Fire," and "Crystal Blue Persuasion." In 1969 alone, he produced five gold singles and one platinum and one gold LP. In 1970, he wrote and produced "Tighter, Tighter," a major hit record for Alive and Kicking. He also split from the Shondells that year and launched a separate career. In 1971, there was a solo hit: the top-five single "Draggin' the Line."

Tommy James spent most of the seventies struggling with himself—clearing his head of pressures that built up during the sixties and groping for a new musical direction. He finally found it at the end of the decade, and in 1980, he returned to the charts in triumph, with "Three Times in Love." In 1982, "Crimson and Clover" became a hit all over again, when re-recorded by Joan Jett and the Blackhearts.

Dizzy
TOMMY ROE

Thomas David Roe had many friends as a kid; among them were Mac Davis, Joe South, Ray Stevens, and Billy Joe Royal. Another pal, Jerry Reed, helped out on guitar when Tommy recorded his first hit, "Sheila," in 1962. The next year Tommy toured England with Chris Montez. Among their supporting acts was a fast-rising group known as the Beatles. On the way home, Tommy wrote the song "Everybody," which became his second million-seller.

Tommy spent most of the mid-sixties on the road, playing clubs and concerts in nearly every American city. In 1966, he returned to the top ten with two gold singles in a row— "Sweet Pea" and "Hooray for Hazel." "I think I really knew how to write those three-minute singles," said Tommy. "Everything I did seemed to work." In 1968, he joined a Dick Clark Caravan of Stars package show. "We spent weeks and weeks crisscrossing the country in a cramped little bus. There was nothing else to do, so some of us started composing tunes.

"We were in the Midwest, and on board was Freddie Weller, a friend of mine from my home town of Atlanta, Georgia. He had just joined Paul Revere and the Raiders as a guitar player. I showed him the chorus of 'Dizzy'—I had that part done—but I was hung up on the rest of the song. We collaborated, and pretty much got it worked out. After the tour, we spent another couple of months polishing it.

"The chord progression in 'Dizzy' is unique. A lot of people think it's a simple song, but once you start playing it, it's very surprising. Some top musicians have said, 'Where does it go?' It kind of hangs them up. I think it was a well-constructed tune."

"Dizzy" was released in December 1968, but didn't take off for nearly two months. When it did, it rose quickly, peaking for four weeks in March 1969.

"It was the biggest thing I ever had," said Tommy. "It sold more than six million copies, worldwide." In November, he followed it with another top-ten single, "Jam Up Jelly Tight." By then, the end of the decade, he had sold over twenty million records.

5

I Can't Get Next to You

THE TEMPTATIONS

*I*n 1965, Smokey Robinson composed the Temptations' first number-one hit, "My Girl." After that came several more sweet Robinson ballads: "It's Growing," "Since I Lost My Baby," and "My Baby." "I'd always liked them and liked their sound," said Smokey, "because they reminded me of a church group. They had that churchy kind of feeling; the soulful sound, from the high tenor to the low bass." In 1966, though, the group adopted a more aggressive stance, and began working with writer-producer Norman Whitfield. "He just started to bang out hit after hit with them," recalled Smokey, who bowed out at that point. "That was my main reason—because I felt they were in good hands."

The first Whitfield-Tempts collaboration was a real shock for fans in the summer of 1966—"Ain't Too Proud to Beg." Nothing in the group's past had prepared listeners for the tough new sound of that single. It sold well, though, opening the door for even more adventuresome records. Later in 1966, "Beauty Is Only Skin Deep" and "(I Know) I'm Losing You" both made the national top ten. "All I Need" and "You're My Everything" did likewise in 1967. Later releases included "It's You That I Need," and in 1968, "I Wish It Would Rain," "I Could Never Love Another" and "Please Return Your Love to Me."

Then in July 1968, lead singer David Ruffin was asked to leave the group amid charges that he had become "an insufferable egotist." Ruffin responded by calling the Temptations' records "patent leather products," hardly in the "soul bag" he wanted to get into. The title of his first solo effort was, appropriately, "My Whole World Ended (the Moment You Left Me)." It would be his only solo hit for more than six years, until "Walk Away from Love" in 1975.

The Tempts struggled to downplay the loss of David, who really had become their star performer. He was replaced by Dennis Edwards, who had formerly sung lead with the Contours. At that point, the rest of the line-up consisted of Otis Williams, Paul Williams (no relation), Eddie Kendricks, and David English (who had used the name "Melvin Franklin" previously to avoid confusion with Ruffin).

It was then that producer Whitfield ushered the group into the era of psychedelic soul and social commentary. In the winter of 1968, "Cloud Nine" marked a turning point—a complete about-face—from the ballads upon which the Tempts had built its reputation. For the rest of the decade, its sound would be raw-edged, furious and driving: an inescapable whirlwind of funk and rhythm that resembled Sly Stone more than anything else. Public reaction to the Tempts' new look and pace was encouraging. "Cloud Nine" became a gold record and won a Grammy Award as the Best R&B Performance by a Duo or Group.

More progressive soul tunes followed: "Runaway Child, Running Wild" and "Don't Let the Joneses Get You Down," both in 1969.

And then came their biggest ever in that style—"I Can't Get Next to You."

The song was written by Norman Whitfield and Barrett Strong (Barrett having been the singer of Motown's first hit record, "Money," in 1960). In arranging "I Can't Get Next to You," Whitfield chose to adopt the Family Stone technique of trading off vocals: having several group members take brief turns at the lead mike. In this instance, the idea worked with spectacular results.

"I Can't Get Next to You" broke in mid-August 1969, and peaked at number one in October. It remained on the charts for seventeen weeks—longer than any other Temptations single, before or since.

It was their last record of the sixties and a precursor of many more hits to come.

Everyday People
SLY AND THE FAMILY STONE

Chalk in hand, a schoolboy faced the blackboard. He was supposed to write out his name, but it was such a big word, and so easy to misspell. Slowly, he started: S-L-Y, and then the other kids began to laugh. Little Sylvester grinned and dropped the chalk, not realizing that he had just given himself a very fitting nickname—one that he'd make world-famous as leader of Sly and the Family Stone.

Sly began singing at the age of four in a San Francisco gospel group. While still in high school, he formed the Viscanes and with them had a local pop hit. Sly studied musical theory and composition for three years at Vallejo Junior College and by age eighteen had mastered more than a dozen instruments. He also took some broadcasting courses, and by 1963, he was one of the most listened-to deejays in the Bay Area. His boss, Tom Donahue, owned Autumn Records and invited Sly to try his hand at record production. Several hits came out of that, including "The Swim" by Bobby Freeman (1964), "Laugh, Laugh" and "Just a Little" by the Beau Brummels (1965), and "Sit Down I Think I Love You" by the Mojo Men (1967).

In December 1967, Sly met with his brother Freddie, a lead guitarist; his sister, Rosie, who played electric piano; trumpeter Cynthia "Ecco" Robinson; bassist Larry Graham; sax man Jerry Martini; and drummer Gregg "Hand Feet" Errico. With these six people, he formed Sly and the Family Stone—and introduced "psychedelic soul."

Up until that time, most R&B records were simple and straightforward. A single "sound idea" would suffice for an entire song (and sometimes a whole career). Sly and the Family Stone changed all that by specializing in surprise—rapid-fire tradeoffs between key instruments and the four lead singers. A switch could come at any time; in mid-song, mid-line, and even mid-word. The contrast between traditional R&B and the Family's splintered sound images was unbelievable. It was bold, outrageous, incredible—a flashing light show on record.

The new era in soul began with "Dance to the Music," a top-ten single the following spring. That summer, the group was featured in "new talent competition" on an NBC variety series, "Showcase '68." The TV experience was a big boost to the band, giving them instant nationwide visual exposure. And they were a sight to be seen, decked out in the most extraordinary clothes. They were beaded, fringed, and feathered to a fare-thee-well. Cynthia wore a blond Shirley Temple wig, while others sported multicolored afros. Overnight, they caused a fashion revolution among blacks.

In November 1968, Sly and the Family Stone released what was perhaps their quintessential single, "Everyday People." It was a song of sweet complexity—a brotherhood tune—which became an anthem for the public that Sly tried most of all to reach. "What I write is people's music," he said. "I want everybody, even the dummies, to understand what I'm saying. That way they won't be dummies anymore. You gotta write your tunes, and arrange 'em, in a way that the message gets through. That's what I did on 'Everyday People.'"

"Everyday People" became a gold record in February 1969 and concurrently was the number-one single in America. Two months later, it turned up on an album, *Stand,* which was also socially oriented.

The Family continued to rock and shock for another five years, cutting hits like "Hot Fun in the Summertime" (1969); "Thank You," backed with "Everybody Is a Star" (both number one in 1970); "Family Affair" (another number one in 1971); and "If You Want Me to Stay" (1973).

Sly Stone operated by his own rules, and in doing so, destroyed a remarkable career. He was consistently late for his own concerts, if he showed up at all. Sly was caught in several well-publicized drug raids, and by 1975 his golden group was no more.

Sly and the Family Stone broke up just as a "new" kind of pop record was starting to take off. It was called "disco," a style many historians trace back to 1968 and "Dance to the Music."

Honky Tonk Women

THE ROLLING STONES

Early in the Stones' career, they were called "the bad boys of rock 'n' roll." They cursed and sneered, hurled cream pies at reporters, and were branded "dirty, unwashed enemies of the public decency."

"I think everyone associates long hair with dirtiness," said guitarist Keith Richards. "I don't know why. Something to do with a Victorian thing. I don't really care what they write about us, as long as they write about us."

Producer-manager Andrew Loog Oldham encouraged the Stones' rebel image and carried their crudeness right into the studio. Unlike the four adorable moptops, the Stones had a raw and raunchy sound, combining compelling guitar with a tough, aggressive stance. Their first recordings, made in the early sixties, were basically punk remakes of R&B material. Then, as Richards and Mick Jagger sharpened their own songwriting skills, more and more original tunes began to turn up. In 1965, two of their creations, "Satisfaction" and "Get Off My Cloud," became number-one hits.

The next year, the Stones' "brute force" began to soften and was replaced by tenderness, impatience, and a streak of sardonic humor. The hits, of course, rolled on: "As Tears Go By," "19th Nervous Breakdown," "Paint It Black," "Mother's Little Helper," and "Have You Seen Your Mother, Baby, Standing in the Shadows?" "Ruby Tuesday" and "Dandelion" came along in 1967, "Jumping Jack Flash" in 1968. And there were the albums: *December's Children; High Tide & Green Grass, Aftermath, Got Live If You Want It, Between the Buttons, Flowers, Their Satanic Majesties' Request,* and *Beggar's Banquet.*

Hypocrisy and decay were favorite subjects of the Rolling Stones, who also wrote with equal gusto about sex. Group compositions appeared under the pseudonym Nanker Phelge; otherwise, Mick wrote the words and Keith the music. They were influenced by "a lot of people," according to Keith: Chuck Berry, Jimmy Reed, the Miracles, Marvin Gaye, and others. Keith himself was also a great fan of country and western, especially Hank Williams. It was a Williams hit, in fact, that inspired "Honky Tonk Women."

While vacationing on a ranch in South America, Keith got "into a cowboy thing," as he put it. The muse struck to turn Hank's "Honky Tonk Blues" into a rollicking rock 'n' roll song. Actually, he and Mick pulled two tunes out of the idea: "Honky Tonk Women" and an even more down-home number, "Country Honk." But it was "Honky Tonk Women" that became the single, and the classic.

"It's a tantalizing taste of everything they do well," bubbled one critic. "The strongest three minutes of rock 'n' roll released in 1969." It was their last single for London, last hit of the sixties, and first to feature twenty-year-old Mick Taylor, the new guitarist they'd just acquired from John Mayall's Bluesbreakers.

Taylor replaced founding member Brian Jones, who, earlier in the year, had announced that he was leaving the group. A few days later, Brian was found dead, floating in his backyard pool. On July 3, the day after his funeral, the Stones played a free memorial concert in Hyde Park.

"Honky Tonk Women" was released on July 4, 1969, and by August was the top-selling single in America. It spent four weeks at number one, nearly four months, in total, on the chart.

In the seventies, the Stones formed their own label and went on to even greater success. Their hits included "Brown Sugar" (1971); "Tumbling Dice" (1972); "Angie" (1973); "Doo Doo Doo Doo Doo," "It's Only Rock 'n' Roll," and "Ain't Too Proud to Beg" (1974); "Fool to Cry" (1976); "Miss You" and "Beast of Burden" (1978). In 1980, "Emotional Rescue" became their fortieth chart entry.

Easily one of rock's most durable bands, the Rolling Stones were also one of the most influential—lyrically, musically, stylistically, visually, and philosophically. Many place them second only to the Beatles in historical importance. They were arguably the best hard-rock band of all time.

Aquarius/Let the Sunshine In

THE FIFTH DIMENSION

At a beauty pageant in Los Angeles in 1963, Florence LaRue, the new Miss Bronze California, was being crowned by the previous year's winner, Marilyn McCoo. Suddenly, a photographer, Lamont McLemore, broke through the crowd and snapped the girls' picture. Little did they know, but within a few short years, those three people would become part of one of the hottest groups in pop history.

After the show, Lamont struck up a conversation with Marilyn, and the two discovered a mutual interest in R&B music. They got together with Harry Elston and Floyd Butler and formed the Hi-Fis. Ray Charles helped them cut a single, "Lonesome Mood." It was a flop, though, and Harry and Floyd quit—only to turn up years later in the Friends of Distinction.

Lamont then looked up Florence, whom he'd kept in touch with for modeling assignments. He also called his cousin Billy Davis and an old friend from St. Louis, Ron Townson. This group became the Versatiles, and they were directed to a new label being formed by Johnny Rivers. Johnny liked their sound but didn't care much for the group's name. At his insistence, Ron came up with an alternative—the Fifth Dimension.

In 1967, the group debuted with two impressive hits: "Go Where You Wanna Go" and "Up-Up and Away." The latter song, written by Jimmy Webb, became a million-seller and led to an unprecedented five Grammy Awards—Best Performance by a Vocal Group, Best Contemporary Group Performance, Best Contemporary Single, Song of the Year, and Record of the Year.

Two more big hits, "Stoned Soul Picnic" and "Sweet Blindness," followed in 1968. Then, in the summer of that year, the group took in a New York play—Hair, the "American Tribal Love-Rock Musical." The show began with "Aquarius." Afterward, the five agreed that they had to record that tune. They called their producer, Bones

Howe, and were amazed when he tried to talk them out of it. Other singers had tried and failed with "Aquarius," he argued. What made them feel that they could do any better?

Bones talked about the problem with a friend of his, who suggested "lightening" the song by combining it with "Let the Sunshine In" (heard in a later scene of Hair). That sounded like a good idea to Bones, so he called the group back and said that he and arranger Bob Alcivar were going to try to put the two songs together.

A background rhythm was recorded in Los Angeles in October 1968. Two months later, the group overdubbed their vocal parts in a small studio in Las Vegas. They were very close to the railroad tracks, and while they were singing the final chorus, a train rumbled by. By that time, the song was so raucous that it blended right in. You can still hear the locomotive, though, just barely, on the finished master.

"Aquarius/Let the Sunshine In" was released in February 1969. By April it was the number-one song in the country and had been certified gold by the RIAA. It sold another million copies in two weeks and by the end of the year was over the three-million mark. It also earned two Grammy Awards, as Best Contemporary Vocal Performance by a Group and Record of the Year.

The Fifth Dimension went on to score several other big hits during 1969–1972. In November 1975, Marilyn and Billy left the group to begin a separate career as a duo. They scored a couple of hits of their own, won a Grammy Award, and starred in a six-week summer TV series for CBS in 1977.

The Fifth Dimension was one of the classiest and most imitated pop groups of the late sixties and early seventies. They were also among the best liked, placing thirty songs on the pop charts between 1967 and 1976.

Sugar, Sugar
THE ARCHIES

The Archies grew out of a comic strip about a group of teenagers: "Archie," first drawn by John L. Goldwater in 1942. Twenty-six years later, the fun-loving cartoon characters became rock 'n' roll wonders when their singing voice was born. In real life, that voice belonged to Ron Dante.

"Before I started professionally," Ron recalled, "I did demos for Burt Bacharach, Carole King, and Neil Sedaka and worked as a backup musician.

"In 1964, I got to sing on a real hit. The Shangri-Las were big with 'Leader of the Pack,' and Paul Vance and Lee Pockriss thought it would be fun to write a parody of that song. It came out as 'Leader of the Laundromat,' by the Detergents. It was a top-twenty record nationwide, until the Shangri-Las sued.

"Don Kirshner signed me to his publishing company, and that led to the Archies. They were to star as an animated cartoon on TV Saturday mornings. I was hired to do all the voices. Jeff Barry wrote enough songs to last two or three seasons—about sixty in all.

"The TV show debuted with 'Bang-Shang-a-Lang' September 14, 1968. That song became the first Archies hit. When it made the charts, I decided to keep a low profile. Not even Don Kirshner could get me on the phone. I just hid.

"And 'Sugar, Sugar'—most of my friends hated me for doing that record. They came around and said, 'What are you doing, singing with this group? This could be the worst thing that ever happened to your career.' But I liked it. I thought it was a cute little song. Toni Wine was the girl's voice on that, and Ray Stevens was one of the handclappers.

"In 1969, it was very unhip to like records like 'Sugar, Sugar.' We were in the middle of a war, people were getting killed, and all kinds of terrible things were going on. I was still worried about getting drafted. And then this group with a light sound and memorable melody comes through without any relevance, except that it's fun music.

"After finishing those Archie songs, I accepted another job with the Cuff Links. I sang all the vocal parts on their only hit record, 'Tracy,' which came out right after 'Sugar, Sugar.' It was funny because at the same time 'Sugar, Sugar' was number one, the Cuff Links' record was number five. No one caught on that it was the same person.

" 'Sugar, Sugar' sold about ten million copies worldwide. After that, the Archies had another top-ten record, 'Jingle Jangle.' It sold about two million. Those records were called 'bubblegum,' and that label stuck to me—no pun intended—for at least five years.

"The problem with the Archies was that there wasn't any group. People couldn't identify with them. They liked the sound, but there wasn't anybody who went out and performed and won fans. I was offered big bucks at the time to go out on the road and sing live with either the Archies or the Cuff Links, and I turned them both down. You know, you work a long time to get somewhere in this business and earn some respectability. You work tours and seedy nightclubs, and then when you finally get some recognition, it's under the auspices of a cartoon group! I didn't really want to be a star from that.

"For the next four or five years, it seemed like I'd made a big mistake, because my own recording career

didn't take off. Instead, I sang more than fifty commercials. At one session, there were three of us 'unknowns': Valarie Simpson, Melissa Manchester, and Barry Manilow. Barry and I hit it off right away, and today I'm his musical director. We co-produce all of his records, and he and I sing all the backgrounds.

"Unfortunately, I think the Archies will always be remembered whenever someone wants to put down 'fun music' as light and superficial. They'll say the Archies as a group and 'Sugar, Sugar' as a record did not have enough depth and emotion. But there had to be more than fourteen-year-old girls buying that record or it wouldn't have been the biggest hit single of 1969."

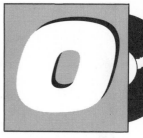

1970

RECORD SALES IN THE UNITED STATES nearly doubled in the ten years between 1960 and 1970. As the new decade began, RCA and Motorola introduced the first compatible four-channel eight-track cartridge system—Quad 8. In New York, Barry Manilow met Bette Midler at the Continental Baths, while in L.A., Elton John made his American debut at the Troubadour. Janis Joplin began working with the Full Tilt Boogie Band, Phil Spector was hurt in an auto crash, and music was heard on the Isle of Wight and at the Atlanta Rock Festival. Englebert Humperdinck, Bobby Sherman, Ray Stevens, and the Everly Brothers all won and lost their own television series. TW4 became Styx, and new bands included Aerosmith, the Electric Light Orchestra, and the Atlanta Rhythm Section. The Union Gap lost Gary Puckett, Tommy James left the Shondells, Curtis Mayfield said goodbye to the Impressions, and Spencer Dryden took wing from Jefferson Airplane. Jimi Hendrix died, and so did Billy Stewart, Slim Harpo, James "Shep" Sheppard, Tammi Terrell, George Goldner, Earl Grant, and Alan Wilson (of Canned Heat). "Rubber Duckie" became a hit for Ernie of "Sesame Street," "Fire and Rain" introduced James Taylor, and we first heard from Gordon Lightfoot with "If You Could Read My Mind." After many years, B.B. King entered the top fifteen for the first time with "The Thrill Is Gone"; and a Dutch group, the Shocking Blue, reached number one with "Venus," an English-language song that they had to learn phonetically. It was 1970—Elvis Presley had sold over a hundred sixty million disc units around the world, with gross returns to RCA of $280 million.

Every album was gold, every single a hit. In little more than five years, the **Beatles** put more than sixty songs on the charts, over half of which were top ten. Twenty of their tunes reached number one, an unprecedented achievement in the recording industry. They sold more than eighty-five million albums, one hundred twenty million singles, enough to wrap around the world four times. They were criticized, heralded, banned, and condemned—but most of all, loved. They were the Beatles, and in 1970, they reached the end of their long and winding road.

On September 25, ABC premiered **"The Partridge Family,"** a half-hour sitcom about five kids and their mother who decided to form a rock 'n' roll band (the premise, of course, was stolen directly from the real-life story of the Cowsills). As in another Screen Gems production, "The Monkees," an integral part of each episode was the performance of new songs, released concurrently on Bell Records. The first Partridge Family single, "I Think I Love You," sold over four million copies, and there were ten more hits before the series was canceled in 1974.

The Isley Brothers appeared and sang the title song in *It's Your Thing,* a concert picture that also included the Five Stairsteps, Ike and Tina Turner, and the Edwin Hawkins Singers. Mick Jagger starred in *Performance* and joined the other Stones for *Gimme Shelter. Sweet Toronto* captured, onstage, Bo Diddley, Chuck Berry, Little Richard, and Jerry Lee Lewis; while *Supershow* featured Eric Clapton, Glen Campbell, and Led Zeppelin. Olivia Newton-John was seen in *Toomorrow,* Alice Cooper in *Diary of a Mad Housewife,* and Mr. Presley in *Elvis: That's the Way It Is.*

On January 14, **Diana Ross** resigned as lead singer of the Supremes, following a farewell performance at the Frontier Hotel in Las Vegas. The last number she performed with her old cronies was "Someday We'll Be Together," their twelfth and final number-one song. Diana was then replaced by Jeanne Terrell, the sister of former heavyweight boxer Ernie Terrell. The Supremes went on to score several more major hits, including "Up the Ladder to the Roof," "Stoned Love," and "River Deep Mountain High" before breaking up in 1977. Diana, of course, blossomed into one of the premier female soloists of the seventies.

One of the most durable *groups* of the seventies was **Chicago,** the most successful jazz-rock ensemble of all time. Formed in the late sixties, they gigged around their namesake city and Los Angeles before being signed by Columbia Records. Their first release, "Chicago Transit Authority," came out in 1969, but it wasn't until 1970 that they really emerged with the LP *Chicago,* which was voted Album of the Year by *Cashbox* magazine. It included three of their most popular songs: "Make Me Smile," "25 or 6 to 4," and "Color My World." The group continued to score major hits every year through the decade, selling more than thirty million records in the process.

THE TOP 40

1. Bridge over Troubled Water, *Simon and Garfunkel*
2. American Woman, *Guess Who*
3. Get Ready, *Rare Earth*
4. Band of Gold, *Freda Payne*
5. Raindrops Keep Fallin' on My Head, *B. J. Thomas*
6. ABC, *Jackson Five*
7. Let It Be, *Beatles*
8. Close to You, *Carpenters*
9. Mama Told Me Not to Come, *Three Dog Night*
10. War, *Edwin Starr*
11. Spirit in the Sky, *Norman Greenbaum*
12. Make It with You, *Bread*
13. Venus, *Shocking Blue*
14. Ball of Confusion, *Temptations*
15. Spill the Wine, *Eric Burdon and War*
16. Which Way You Goin' Billy?, *Poppy Family*
17. Everything Is Beautiful, *Ray Stevens*
18. Lay Down, *Melanie with the Edwin Hawkins Singers*
19. Candida, *Dawn*
20. Thank You, *Sly and the Family Stone*
21. Ain't No Mountain High Enough, *Diana Ross*
22. I'll Be There, *Jackson Five*
23. Instant Karma, *John Lennon*
24. Signed, Sealed, and Delivered, *Stevie Wonder*
25. Hitchin' a Ride, *Vanity Faire*
26. Hey There Lonely Girl, *Eddie Holman*
27. I Want You Back, *Jackson Five*
28. Ride Captain Ride, *Blues Image*
29. Ooh Child, *Five Stairsteps*
30. Something's Burning, *Kenny Rogers and the First Edition*
31. All Right Now, *Free*
32. Love on a Two-Way Street, *Moments*
33. Reflections of My Life, *Marmalade*
34. Julie, Do Ya Love Me, *Bobby Sherman*
35. Up Around the Bend, *Creedence Clearwater Revival*
36. Green-Eyed Lady, *Sugarloaf*
37. Turn Back the Hands of Time, *Tyrone Davis*
38. Love Grows Where My Rosemary Goes, *Edison Lighthouse*
39. The Rapper, *Jaggerz*
40. In the Summertime, *Mungo Jerry*

And 1970 also bore witness to the rise of **Bread,** a soft-rock partnership between veteran session men David Gates, Jim Griffin, and Robb Royer (fourth member Mike Botts was added later; then Robb was replaced by Larry Knechtal). This collective specialized in thoughtful, romantic records, flawlessly written, arranged and produced. "Make It with You" and "It Don't Matter to Me" both made the top ten in 1970; later singles included "If," "Baby I'm A-Want You," "Everything I Own," and "Lost Without Your Love." After Bread crumbled in 1977, lead singer and chief composer Gates had some solo success, most notably with the theme from *The Goodbye Girl.*

THE TOP 10 LPs

1. Bridge over Troubled Water, *Simon and Garfunkel*
2. Chicago, *Chicago*
3. Abbey Road, *Beatles*
4. Led Zeppelin II, *Led Zeppelin*
5. Santana, *Santana*
6. Get Ready, *Rare Earth*
7. Déjà Vu, *Crosby, Stills, Nash, and Young*
8. Joe Cocker, *Joe Cocker*
9. Easy Rider, *Original Soundtrack*
10. Butch Cassidy and the Sundance Kid, *Original Soundtrack*

War

EDWIN STARR

Edwin Starr was born Charles Hatcher in Nashville, Tennessee, and grew up in Cleveland, Ohio. In 1957, while attending high school, he formed his own group, the Future Tones, which played on local bills alongside Lloyd Price, Chuck Jackson, and Billie Holiday.

In 1962, Edwin hit the road as a featured singer with the band of Bill Doggett. Over the next few years, Edwin learned the ropes of the recording industry and wrote the song that was to become his first hit single.

In 1965, he left the Doggett band and signed as a solo artist with Ric Tic Records. His debut disc became a good seller and led to his early nickname: "Agent Double-O-Soul." The next year, he found a vocal quartet, the Shades of Blue, and wrote and produced their biggest hit, "Oh How Happy."

After a while, Ric Tic was bought out by Motown Records. Edwin became a part of the Motown family and was assigned to the Gordy label. In 1969, he entered the national top ten for the first time with "Twenty-five Miles," a soul stomper he wrote back in his Cleveland days. Edwin was rising fast, and he knew that the coming decade would bring him his greatest popularity ever.

In 1970, Edwin began work with one of Motown's finest writers and producers, Norman Whitfield, who had been responsible for the continuing success of the Temptations. It was Norman and composer Barrett Strong who came up with perhaps the label's most controversial hit single ever.

" 'War' was originally recorded by the Temptations," recalled Edwin. "It was buried on one of their albums. But then a lot of mail came in, mostly from students, asking why they didn't release it on a 45. Well, that was a touchy time, and that song had some very funny implications. It was a message record, an opinion record, and stepped beyond being sheer entertainment. It could become a smash record, and that was fine, but if it went the other way, it could kill the career of whoever the artist was."

Apparently, the Temptations were afraid of the song, and so it was given to Edwin Starr.

"Nobody really understood what we were talking about on that song," he continued. "It wasn't about Vietnam. It never once mentioned the war in Vietnam. It just so happened that, at the time, the war was going on, and the words just lent themselves to the occasion. Actually, we were talking about a war of people—the war people wage against each other on a day-to-day basis. All the words are applicable to neighbors who fight with each other, you know, 'War, what is it good for?' That's what the song was about, at least for me."

"War" became a political anthem in 1970 and soared to number one during the long, hot summer. It sold more than three million copies and earned a Grammy Award nomination for Best Male Rhythm and Blues Vocal Performance.

"Afterward, I recorded another song called 'Stop the War Now.' I didn't like that song. I thought it was much too similar. I tried to say, 'Hey, let's go another way completely,' but I didn't have much say in the matter. I have always contended that that was part of the reason I fell off the charts. You see, Motown did the formula many times. They'd do 'I Can't Help Myself,' and then come right back with 'The Same Old Song,' with the same sound but different lyrics."

Edwin finally left Motown in the mid-seventies, frustrated at being unable to come up with another hit. In later years, he recorded for Granite and 20th Century Records. Sales were small, but at least there was a kind of satisfaction.

"I'm back now in the soul vein," he said proudly. "Back in the bag I was in with 'Twenty-five Miles' and 'Agent Double-O-Soul.' I write for myself and produce by myself. As far as I'm concerned, the 'war' is over, and I thank God for that."

Mama Told Me (Not to Come)

THREE DOG NIGHT

Three Dog Night touted itself on being "pure entertainment" in an era of musical messages. They were there to look good and make hit records, and that's exactly what they did, amassing fourteen gold or platinum awards between 1969 and 1976. They outlasted nearly all of their contemporaries, and most of their critics.

"We were blasted back then," said co-founder Danny Hutton, "by people who thought 'commercial' was a dirty word. Yeah, we weren't 'purists.' Purists believe there's some virtue in being unknown and living in poverty. We weren't into poverty. We wanted to play music that would have a broad appeal—please the greatest number of people. If being commercial meant satisfying your audience, then yes, we were commercial. And proud of it."

Three Dog Night began their streak in 1969 with "Try a Little Tenderness," "One," "Easy to Be Hard," and "Eli's Coming." In 1970, the hits continued with "Celebrate," "Mama Told Me (Not to Come)," "Out in the Country" and "One Man Band." Cory Wells, another founder (along with Chuck Negron), talked about the biggest of those songs.

" 'Mama Told Me (Not to Come)' was a tune that I had been doing before Three Dog Night, when I still had my old group in Arizona," he said. "I used to buy all these bizarre records—still do—and one of them was a Randy Newman album. On it was 'Mama Told Me,' and I became a tremendous fan, long before Randy Newman became 'in.' I used to play the album for other people, and they'd go, 'Oh my God, who is that? That's terrible! That's horrible!' But see, you had to listen to what the man was *writing.* He's not a performer, he's a composer.

"When I brought the song to the other guys, they didn't like it. They hated it. Matter of fact, it took me three albums for them to accept it. I kept saying, 'Please listen to this song. It's a hit song. Man, will you please listen to it?' And they said, 'Cory, it just doesn't have it. Why don't you try some other song instead?'

"I pushed so hard for 'Mama Told Me.' In my guts, I wasn't relieved, I hadn't climaxed, I hadn't gotten the song done, you know? Those were the days when we were having a lot of problems trying to give everybody equal say about our material. But a song can get so worn down, with everyone going, 'No, I'd rather have it this way,' and so forth. After a while you just want to say 'Screw it. I don't even want to do the song anymore.' 'Mama Told Me' was a little easier than that. I had more control over it in direction, and the other guys were a little more open to listen. And, of course, they contributed their ideas and things and it turned out to be what it was.

"The president of Dunhill at that point was Jay Lasker, last of the old-time record tycoons. He had a big cigar, and was the typical 'come here, boy, I'm gonna make you a star' kind of guy. He came into the studio and said, 'Let's hear this stuff.' 'Mama Told Me' was in its raw form, not mixed or anything, just the basic track and vocals. After we played it for him, he became so excited he said, 'I'd like to buy you boys something. What do you want? What do you want?' At the time, we weren't making a whole lot of money, so he shouted, 'TV sets! You want TV sets?' The guys said, 'Yeah, sure,' and then he came up to me and said, 'Hey Cory! Want a TV set?' I said, 'No, man, I've gotta be honest with you. The place I'm living

in, I'm sleeping on the floor. I'd really appreciate a bed.' So he bought me a bed, believe it or not."

"Mama Told Me (Not to Come)" was released in May 1970, and reached the top of the charts in July. "We were in rehearsal in New York, and our road manager came running down the aisle, waving this telegram. It was from Dunhill, telling us that we had just scored number one!" Days later, "Mama Told Me" was certified a million-seller. After it passed the three-million mark, Randy Newman phoned the group to offer his congratulations. "He said, 'Cory, thanks for putting my kid through college,' " recalled Wells. "And then he hung up."

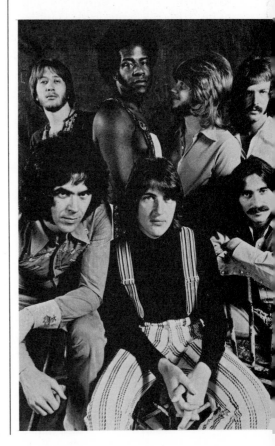

Close to You
THE CARPENTERS

Karen and Richard Carpenter grew up in New Haven, Connecticut, where, at an early age, Richard developed an interest in pop records. He studied music for a while at Yale and even played in some local jazz bands.

In the early sixties, the family moved to Downey, California, then hometown for a number of seminal surfing groups like the Chantays. At the age of sixteen, Karen took up the drums. In 1965, the two siblings launched the Carpenter Trio, along with friend Wes Jacobs. The following year, they won a Battle of the Bands at the Hollywood Bowl. RCA stepped up with a recording contract, but nothing ever came of it.

In 1967, the group expanded into Spectrum, but after a short time was back to a duo. Karen and Richard retreated to the garage studio of a friend, Joe Osbourne, where they began cutting demonstration tapes.

"We went to all the record labels trying to get a recording contract—twice," said Karen. Capitol wanted them to sound like Bobbie Gentry. And Warners wanted them to sound like Harper's Bizarre. "We'll sign you if you do 'Anything Goes' type of stuff," they said. Richard replied, "Hey, we have our own sound." Talk-folk records like Dylan's "Like a Rolling Stone" were big at that time, and "Columbia told us they could use us if we could redo our songs so they could be talked," Richard said. "I said, 'We don't want them to be talked.' And they said, 'Well, we're not interested.' And that was that.

"Finally, through a friend of a friend, we got a tape to Herb Alpert at the A&M label."

The Carpenters signed with A&M on April 22, 1969. Alpert gave them free reign, total control of their music. And he brought them "Close to You." It was a song Burt Bacharach had intended for Alpert himself. "But Herbie couldn't bring himself to sing about 'moondust in your hair,'" Richard said. "He said, 'I'm going to give you this lead sheet, and I want you to do your own arrangement.' So I made a shuffle, put the doo-wahs at the end, and the whole thing. We cut it, and I remember sitting on the steps of the recording studio. Herbie said, 'Well, what do you think?' And I said, 'I think it's either going to be a number-one record or one of the biggest stiffs of all time.'"

"Close to You" had been written in 1964, first turning up on the debut album of Dionne Warwick. Far from being a stiff, it became a number-one record for the Carpenters in the summer of 1970. With their royalties, they bought an apartment building and named it—what else?—"Close to You."

The Carpenters blossomed into one of the most successful pop groups in the history of the recording industry, scoring more than a dozen major hits in the seventies. They earned three Grammy Awards and a reputation for crafting some of the best sound recordings ever made.

Let It Be

THE BEATLES

The project that came to be known as *Let It Be* began at a Beatle rehearsal in the fall of 1968. The boys were looking for new ways to package their material, perhaps as a live show, television date, or some kind of special event. Finally, Paul McCartney suggested making a documentary movie—a diary of the next Beatle album in progress. Camera crews could follow the boys through every phase of production, and, in the end, there'd be an intimate record of just how musical magic was made.

John, George, and Ringo agreed to this idea, and in January 1969, filming began at Apple headquarters on Saville Row. Among the tunes performed was the title theme, which Paul had written as a quiet tribute to his mother. One of the Beatles' old pals from Hamburg, Billy Preston, happened to be around at the time and was invited to sit in as organist. John was on bass guitar, while Paul played the piano and sang. This particular number—just for fun—was recorded on the roof of the building, where giant speakers echoed the sound for miles across London. Complaining neighbors summoned policemen, and in fact, you can see bobbies in the picture, trying to break up the session and restore the peace.

Over the weeks that *Let It Be* was in production, the Beatles were constantly tripping over cameras, lights, and moviemaking people. Paul McCartney kept his composure, but he turned out to be the only one who did. Tempers grew thin, and as days rolled into months, there were wrangles—even punch-ups—in the studio.

John, by that time, appeared to be perpetually stoned and, to the others' great annoyance, was inseparable from Yoko Ono. He also argued continually with producer George Martin over content, musical style, and even the recording technique. John insisted that *Let It Be* should be an "honest" album, without overdubs,

mixing, or even editing. "I want them to hear us, warts and all," he said. Thirty hours of music were put on tape before everyone agreed that that approach was simply not going to work. At that point, George Martin left and was replaced by Phil Spector. Phil offered to "salvage" the tapes, and the boys—sick of the whole thing—gave him their blessing. He immediately went to work, adding strings, horns, celestial choirs—in short, the whole Phil Spector "Wall of Sound." The result was the most heavily produced of all Beatles LPs—the complete reversal of what John Lennon had argued for.

The release of *Let It Be* was held up until the album, single, and movie could all be ready at the same time. In the interim, three more 45s were issued: "Get Back," "The Ballad of John and Yoko," and a two-sided hit, "Come Together," backed with "Something." There were also two other albums: *Hey Jude,* a patchwork compilation; and *Abbey Road,* the Beatles' last collaborative effort.

On March 16, 1970, the single

version of "Let It Be" was finally released, a year and two months after being recorded. A week later, it was on the charts, and by early the next month, it was the number-one song in America. The timing was perfect, because on April 11, Paul McCartney shocked the world by announcing that he was ready to "let it be." He was leaving the Beatles—or, in his words, the Beatles left him: "No one wants to be the one to say the party's over." Within a few days, John, Paul, and Ringo confirmed that the group had broken up. "We just got sick of being side men for Paul," said John. "We had fun doin' it, but it's ended, mate."

On May 13, the movie *Let It Be* opened in New York. Not one Beatle attended the premiere. The album came out soon afterward and, of course, shot to the top of the LP charts. It spawned a final hit single, "The Long and Winding Road." That too, was number one.

It was June of 1970, and the magical mystical musical mystery tour was over.

ABC
JACKSON FIVE

The Jackson Five was the brainchild of Joseph Jackson, a steel mill crane operator from Gary, Indiana. Frustrated as a musician, he formed his own blues band in 1951, the Falcons, and held group rehearsals at home. His three young sons, Jackie, Tito, and Jermaine, watched these sessions with fascination and, after the adults had gone, picked up the same instruments and tried to imitate what they had seen. By 1959, it was evident that the Falcons' career was not going anyplace, and Joseph decided to transfer his dreams for a show biz career to his children.

Joseph began the process by carefully studying the techniques of successful black recording acts. He discovered that it was usually the tallest or shortest member of a group that emerged as the flashy front man. The others would croon at his side or behind him, providing both an audio and visual backdrop. Careful choreography, impeccable harmony, and a distinctive lead singer seemed to be the elements that set the superstars ahead. Joseph committed himself to making sure that his boys had all of those things, and more.

The family diet suffered first; grocery money was rechanneled into bigger and better guitars, amplifiers, and other equipment. The boys happily fell into a routine of practicing for four hours a day, seven days a week. After more than a year of polish and rehearsal, they began to turn up at talent shows, winning nearly everything they entered. Midwestern tours came next, including dates with the Chi-Lites, the Emotions, Gladys Knight and the Pips, and their early idols, the Temptations. New brothers Michael and Marlon joined the group in the early sixties, and by the end of the decade, the Jackson Five were primed, precise, and ready for the big time.

In the summer of 1969, the boys appeared at a charity concert hosted by the mayor of their hometown, Richard Gordon Hatcher. According to legend, Diana Ross was in the audience and was "genuinely astounded" at their performance. She persuaded Berry Gordy to audition the group, and in August 1969, they were signed to Motown. Their first single, "I Want You Back," was released in October and within six weeks had sold more than two million copies. Shortly after Christmas, it entered the top ten, and by mid-January, the Jackson Five had the number-one record in the country.

On February 24, Motown issued a second Jackson Five single, "ABC." Like the first, it was written and produced by a faceless team, known only as "the Corporation." Later, they were identified as some of the cream of Motown's writing and production staff: Freddie Perren, Fonzo Mizell, Deke Richards, and Berry Gordy himself. Those four men designed "ABC" as a high-energy showcase for their youngest and tiniest protégé, eleven-year-old Michael Jackson. In his whirling, free-wheeling live performances, Michael was already being described as "a miniature James Brown," "an unabashed child prodigy."

"ABC" quickly outstripped "I Want You Back," selling more than two million copies in less than three weeks. It was followed in May by "The Love You Save," backed with "I Found That Girl." In September, Motown issued "I'll Be There." All five Jackson Five titles reached number one in 1970—an unprecedented achievement.

The Jackson Five were easily among the most innovative and imitated pop groups of the early seventies. They pioneered the sound of bubblegum soul and, in doing so, outsold every other recording act in Motown history.

Raindrops Keep Fallin' on My Head

B. J. THOMAS

Billy Joe Thomas started singing at the age of fourteen with a church choir in Houston. While in high school, he joined the Triumphs, a country-rock band that played dates all over the Southwest. On one Fourth of July weekend, they were heard performing in a state park by Charles Booth, the owner of a tiny label, Pacemaker. He put the group under contract and cut fifteen sides with them. Later, he sold that contract and the tapes to Scepter Records, which had national distribution. In the spring of 1966, one tune, a version of Hank Williams' "I'm So Lonesome I Could Cry," became a coast-to-coast top-ten million-seller on Scepter. It looked like a great start for the Triumphs, as well as their engaging lead singer, B. J. Thomas.

However, the band refused to go on the road. They had school and other local interests, and did not want to leave the area. So, B.J. took off on his own, touring primarily with the Dick Clark Caravan of Stars. After two more 1966 hits, "Mama" and "Billy and Sue," B.J. was given a *Cashbox* award as the Most Promising Vocalist of the Year.

There were no big hits in 1967, but in 1968 B.J. bounced back with "The Eyes of a New York Woman," and his second million-seller, "Hooked on a Feeling." A fellow Scepter artist, Dionne Warwick, was impressed enough to take a copy of the latter single to composer Burt Bacharach, who was then working on a score for the film *Butch Cassidy and the Sundance Kid.* She convinced him to pitch some songs to B.J., and with great reluctance, Burt finally asked Thomas to sing the main theme—"Raindrops Keep Fallin' on My Head." He failed to mention that the song had already been turned down by two major artists, Bob Dylan and Ray Stevens.

B.J. had laryngitis at the time, but that didn't stop him from accepting Bacharach's offer. He went to a doctor,

got loaded down with throat medications, and hopped a plane to Los Angeles. Once in the studio, it took five takes to get "Raindrops" down right for the soundtrack. "I don't think I could have made it through one more time," said B.J. Fortunately, the movie producers liked the gruffness in his throat.

A few weeks later, the pop version of the song was recorded in a different studio. That take was released by Scepter in October 1969. It broke nationally early in November, and within a month was certified gold. "Raindrops" peaked in January 1970, spending four weeks at the top of the charts. In all, it remained a best-seller for twenty-two weeks. It won the Oscar as Song of the Year, and a Grammy as the Best Original Score Written for a Motion Picture or TV Special.

B.J. had several other 1970 hits: "Everybody's Out of Town," "I Just Can't Help Believing," and "Most of All." "No Love At All" and "Mighty

Clouds of Joy" came along in 1971, and in 1972, "Rock and Roll Lullaby."

By the age of 29, B.J. had become a superstar, having sold more than sixteen million records. But he was also a drug addict, and had been since the age of fifteen. He estimated that he had spent between two and three million dollars on drugs during that time, with the worst years coming in the mid-seventies. Despite many attempts on four labels, only one tune became a hit for him then: "(Hey Why Don't You Play) Another Somebody Done Somebody Wrong Song," in 1975.

On January 28, 1976, B.J. became a born-again Christian, and quit drugs cold turkey. He began recording gospel songs, and soon amassed four Grammys for his efforts. In concert, he still performed the gold records, but added a little testimony to his act. Audiences didn't seem to mind, and in the summer of 1977 he racked up another pop hit, "Don't Worry Baby."

Band of Gold

FREDA PAYNE

Freda Payne began her career at the age of five, studying piano at the Detroit Institute of Musical Arts. She soon performed at teas, banquets, and other social functions, and at thirteen added singing to her repertoire. "I was turned on early by applause," she said.

Freda entered a hometown amateur contest, and won a radio. "For that one glowing moment, I felt I was somebody," she recalled. "Right then I decided to become a professional vocalist." She then appeared on "Ed MacKenzie's Dance Hour," a local TV talent show. "I won three times," she laughed. From there she went to Ted Mack's "Original Amateur Hour," and made her national television debut. On that program, she came in second place, behind an Italian opera singer.

Berry Gordy took an interest in Freda, and supervised her first recording sessions. At that point, he hadn't yet formed Motown Records, and planned to place her tapes with an existing major label. He drove Freda and her mom to New York to sign contracts, but at the last moment, Mrs. Payne changed her mind. "My daughter is not going to become a rock 'n' roll singer," she announced, and that was that.

Freda graduated from high school, and spent a year cutting jingles for radio commercials. Finally, she landed a spot in the chorus of Pearl Bailey's revue. After that, she met Duke Ellington, who offered her an exclusive ten-year contract singing with his band. She worked with him for six months in Las Vegas, but then walked out—it was too much of a tie-down.

Freda moved to New York, and got a job as a telephone operator. Her singing ceased, and she considered becoming a dancer instead. Quincy Jones talked her out of that, and invited her to sing with his band at the Apollo. She toured Europe with him, performing in Norway, Sweden, Germany, Spain, and England.

Back in the States, Freda became the understudy for Leslie Uggams in the Broadway musical, *Hallelujah Baby*. "I geared and polished myself into being a sophisticated and well-rounded entertainer," she remembered, "and the very first night I went onstage, I received a standing ovation."

In 1969, Freda ran into an old friend, Brian Holland, of the writing and production team of Holland-Dozier-Holland. He asked her to join their newly-formed label, Invictus Records. "Up until that point, I had had good luck, good gigs, the right ability—everything but the proper backing and right promotion. They were prepared, and so was I."

Holland-Dozier-Holland convinced Freda to move from straight jazz into a more popular vein. "The first song they handed me was 'Band of Gold,'" she recalled, "and my initial reaction to it was 'What?' Lines like 'we stayed in separate rooms' made me think that this song was for a seventeen-year-old. She's copping out, doesn't understand her own womanhood and is really frigid, you know. So I said, 'Hey, I'm not frigid. Why should I sing about somebody who is?' They explained to me that the idea was to get the feeling over, and sell the song.

"Well, I worked on about twenty tunes over six months and 'Band of Gold' was the first one we sat down with and started rehearsing. I didn't know it was going to be a big hit, but it sure wound up that way."

"Band of Gold" was released in April 1970, and by July was one of the top-selling singles. It clung to the charts for twenty weeks, and quickly earned Freda her first gold record. A few months later, "Deeper and Deeper" became a second top-thirty hit.

In 1971, Freda recorded "Bring the Boys Home," a topical tune about the Vietnam war. The U.S. Command banned the song from the American Forces Network, claiming it would "give aid and comfort to the enemy." Stateside, it gained heavy air play and became a third million-seller.

Freda didn't have any more major hits after that, although she did appear in a 1973 movie, *Book of Numbers*. She also accepted a few television acting roles. Primarily, she's a supperclub singer today.

"Whatever I was before, I'm even better now," she said in 1979. "I never stop reaching for the stars."

Get Ready
RARE EARTH

Their sound was a combination of hard rock and funky blues, and for that reason, millions assumed that the five men in the band were black. They weren't. In reality, Rare Earth was a blue-eyed soul group—the first white act to cut hits under the Motown banner.

John Persh, Gil Bridges and Pete Riveria grew up in Detroit on a steady diet of rhythm and blues. The three attended elementary and high school together and started rehearsing as a trio in their mid-teens. In 1961, as the Sunliners, they began playing parties, dances, and "whatever paid" around the Motor City area. They continued to build a local following all through the sixties, and in 1969 decided to reorganize. They added guitarist Rob Richards and keyboard player Kenny James and renamed themselves Rare Earth.

The quintet then ran into Dennis Coffey, an arranger and session man who helped the group produce a medley of old Motown hits. The recording was released on Verve Records and impressed the people at Motown. It paved the way to a Motown contract—with one unusual wrinkle. For the first time in its history, Motown was setting up a subsidiary label to be named after its leading act. In that way, Rare Earth Records was formed.

Their first album release was, as before, built around Motown gold. The band decided to reinterpret "Get Ready," which had been a top-thirty hit for the Temptations in 1966. On

July 4 at 1 A.M., Rare Earth began recording, and when they were through, they had stretched the song out to twenty-one and a half minutes. It took up the entire second side of that first LP, issued in the fall of 1969.

The album was given heavy Motown promotion and broke nationally early in December. By far, the most popular cut for air play was the long version of "Get Ready." Reversing the usual procedure, the hit LP spawned a hit 45—a cut-down version of the song—which took off in mid-March. By June, it was one of the best-selling pop singles in the country, and was getting R&B play as well. "At first," said Gil, "everybody on the soul stations thought we were black. When they found out we

weren't, we were knocked off by some deejays. They would be playing the song one week, and then—gone!" The record wound up, though, in the R&B top twenty.

Rare Earth followed this success with another remake of a Temptations song, "I Know I'm Losing You." In 1971, they had three more hits: "Born to Wander," "I Just Want to Celebrate," and "Hey Big Brother." After that, though, dissension, dropouts and lawsuits decimated the band. Some former members ended up doing session work for Motown.

In its prime, Rare Earth was one of the most popular live groups of the early seventies. It was, in fact, the topselling white act to blacks—until displaced in 1975 by AWB.

American Woman

THE GUESS WHO

For more than a decade, despite major personnel changes, the Guess Who remained one of the world's most popular rock bands.

They began in 1963 as Al and the Silvertones in Winnipeg, Canada. In their early days, they were heavily influenced by British musicians. They cut a few local singles, and eventually became known as Chad Allan and the Expressions, which they remained until 1965, when Chad Allan left the line-up.

It was about then that an American label, Scepter, laid plans to release some of their records in the United States. As a promotional gimmick, a contest was held in which people sent in suggestions for a new group name. Meanwhile, their version of a Johnny Kidd song, "Shakin' All Over," was issued as a 45, with the artist listed simply as "Guess Who?" Before a winner could be chosen in the competition, "Shakin' All Over" became a U.S. hit, establishing the band down under as the Guess Who. The fellows figured that name was as attention-getting as any, and decided to keep it. They then began extensive American tours, starting in the summer of 1965. In the fall of 1966, the quartet got its own television show, "Let's Go," which ran for two years on the Canadian network. By that point, the group consisted of lead singer Burton Cummings, lead guitarist Randy Bachman, bass player Jim Kale, and Gerry Peterson on drums.

In 1968, after recording a premium disc for Coca-Cola, the Guess Who met Jack Richardson, who signed them to his Nimbus 9 label. He became their producer, and got them U.S. distribution through RCA Records. In 1969, along came the LP *Wheat-field Soul,* and from it, a tune called "These Eyes." It became a million-seller—their first of four such singles in a row.

The second Guess Who album, *Canned Wheat,* contained three more Guess Who classics. "Laughing," another song in the same bag as "These Eyes," was coupled on a 45 with "Undun," and both sides became hits. Also off the same LP: "No Time," which went top five in February 1970.

And then came "American Woman."

"It started as a jam," said co-writer Kale. "We were playing in Ontario after being on the road in the States, trying to solidify our hold in the American marketplace with 'These Eyes.' We were playing a two-set situation, and for one reason or another we were late getting back onstage for the second set. In order to dispel the ominous air that was hanging over the place—as we raced on the stage, one by one we picked up on just this simple rhythm. Cummings came up, ad-libbed some lyrics, and it worked. We recorded it just like that. It was an accident—completely spontaneous.

"'American Woman' was also controversial. The popular misconception was that it was a chauvinistic tune, which was anything but the case. The fact was, we came from a very strait-laced, conservative, laid-back country, and all of a sudden, there we were in Chicago, Detroit, New York— all these horrendously large places with their big city problems. After that one particularly grinding tour, it was just a real treat to go home and see the girls we had grown up with. Also, the war was going on, and that was terribly unpopular. We didn't have a draft system in Canada, and we were grateful for that. A lot of people called it anti-American, but it wasn't really. We weren't anti-anything. John Lennon once said that the meanings of all songs come after they are recorded. Someone else has to interpret them."

"American Woman" broke in the U.S. late in March 1970. It spent three weeks at number one in May, fifteen weeks on the charts.

In June 1970, Randy Bachman quit the group and later formed his own outfit, Bachman-Turner Overdrive. He was replaced by Greg Leskiw and Kurt Winter; Kurt being the author of "Hand Me Down World," the next Guess Who hit. Over the next few years, a number of people floated in and out of the band, and the hits continued. Among the more successful singles were "Share the Land" (1970); "Albert Flasher" and "Rain Dance" (1971); "Star Baby," "Clap for the Wolfman" and "Dancin' Fool" (1974). After another year, Burton Cummings dissolved the group in order to launch his solo career. He had his own hit in 1976—a top-ten tune called "Stand Tall."

Bridge over Troubled Water

SIMON AND GARFUNKEL

*I*n 1969, Paul Simon, his wife Peggy, Art Garfunkel and some other people rented a house for the summer on Bluejay Way in the Hollywood hills. The same house, a few years earlier, had inspired George Harrison to write the Beatle song, "Bluejay Way." This time around though, it served as a backdrop for the creation of Simon and Garfunkel's greatest hit: the biggest pop record of 1970.

Art was in Mexico for much of the summer, making his acting debut in a Mike Nichols film, *Catch 22* (1969). When he returned, Paul presented him with a tune written in his absence— "Bridge over Troubled Water." Surprisingly, Art said he didn't want to sing the song, and suggested that Paul do it instead. Paul wouldn't hear of that, and later regretted "giving the song away." In concert, Art wound up singing the song solo, with Paul sitting, brooding, off to one side. It was that kind of resentment—ironically, over a song of unity—that lead to their breakup a short time later.

By that point, Simon and Garfunkel had been stars for more than four years, and were tiring of the grind. From September to October, they taped an acclaimed TV special, "Songs of America," which CBS telecast on

November 30. In October, they embarked on yet another concert tour, which kept them on the road and out of the studio until mid-December. When they finally did begin recording, they were, in Paul's words, "totally exhausted." But somehow they came through with the best album they ever made.

The title track, "Bridge over Troubled Water," started out as a simple two-verse melody, written by Paul in the key of G. As Art's key was E-flat, the chords had to be transposed, and were by Jimmy Haskell (who later picked up a Grammy as "co-arranger"). Another musician, soon to be a founding member of Bread, was hired to play piano: Larry Knechtal. "I want a gospel kind of feel," Paul said, and over a four-day period, Larry honed the tune in exactly that manner. Eventually, his part of the song became so elongated that, in the studio, Paul decided to tack on a third verse. Later, Paul would point out how you could "clearly hear" the addition, because "it didn't sound at all like the first two verses."

The piano part done, Joe Osbourne then played two bass lines, which were mixed in. Next, vibes were added to make the second verse "ring a little bit." After that came the drums,

recorded in an echo chamber with tape reverb to give an afterbeat effect.

Paul hired an outsider to write the string arrangement, and mailed a copy of the rough mix on a demo tape. Apparently the vocal work on that tape was a little garbled, because the sheet music came back entitled "Like a Pitcher of Water." Garfunkel's name was also misspelled. Paul rejected that arrangement and demanded that it be completely rewritten.

All of the above was completed in Los Angeles. Simon and Garfunkel stopped for Christmas and then went to New York, where Artie spent several days on vocals. In all, "Bridge" took about two weeks to record, not counting the final mix-down.

The *Bridge over Troubled Water* album was supposed to have twelve tunes on it. However, Paul and Artie fought over the final cut. Simon wanted to include another of his songs, while Garfunkel insisted on a Bach chorale. Finally, Paul threw up his hands and ordered the LP released "as is," with only eleven tracks. Simon and Garfunkel then split, each taking a long and separate vacation.

The single version of "Bridge" broke in early February 1970, and spent six weeks at the top of the charts. It was gold by March, platinum by April, and by the end of the year had sold over five million copies. The LP was number one simultaneously, and by 1975 had sold more than ten million copies. It's still one of the best-selling albums in music history.

Collectively, as an LP and 45, "Bridge over Troubled Water" won an unprecedented six Grammy Awards: Single of the Year, Album of the Year, Song of the Year, Best Arrangement, Best Engineering, and Best Contemporary Song. By the end of 1970, Simon had earned over $7 million from the tune. He waited a couple of years, and then launched his own successful solo career.

1971

On July 31, **George Harrison** played host at a rock 'n' roll benefit held in New York's Madison Square Garden—The Concert for Bangla Desh. The production, filmed for theatrical release, was also issued as a three-record box set, complete with souvenir booklet (the LP package later won a Grammy Award). Among the stars who stopped by to perform that night were Billy Preston, Badfinger, Leon Russell, Ringo Starr, Bob Dylan, and Eric Clapton. The concert sold twenty thousand tickets in two hours, and raised more than $4.5 million for that impoverished Asian country. Harrison added to that total by starting the Material World Charitable Foundation, and, as the first contributor, pledged all the publishing royalties from his next album, *Living in the Material World.* That LP sold a million copies in two days.

CBS/SONY PREVIEWED the SQ disc—a compatible four-channel disc system—in 1971, the year that most major labels dumped the four-track tape configuration. Bill Graham closed his rock palaces, the Fillmores East and West; in Houston, Texas, Mickey Gilley opened the largest nightclub in the world (total capacity: 5,500 people). Chicago became the first rock group to play Carnegie Hall; Frank Sinatra retired (briefly); and wedding bells rang for Stevie Wonder, Donovan, and Mick Jagger. The Jackson Five, Carpenters, and Sonny and Cher all got their own network television programs; Lawrence Welk lost his, but returned the next week in syndication, stronger than ever (also taking the independent TV route: Kenny Rogers and the First Edition). Martha and the Vandellas split up; so did Free and the Sir Douglas Quintet. Several groups lost members: War (Eric Burdon), Blood Sweat and Tears (David Clayton-Thomas), the Temptations (Eddie Kendricks and Paul Williams), Procol Harum (Robin Trower), the Hollies (Allan Clarke), and Creedence Clearwater Revival (Tom Fogerty). Nilsson wrote, scored, and sang all the tunes in *The Point,* an animated "ABC Tuesday Movie of the Week." "If Not for You" introduced Olivia Newton-John to America, "I'm Eighteen" was our first peek into the bizarre world of Alice Cooper, and Judy Collins had a hit with a celestial hymn—"Amazing Grace." "Charity Ball" became the first top-forty single by an all-girl rock band—Fanny. It was 1971: the year that Barry McGuire found Christ and renounced his biggest hit, "The Eve of Destruction."

Former deejay Don Cornelius created, produced, and hosted **"Soul Train,"** an hour series he introduced nationally via syndication in 1971. Originally a local show in Chicago, the program began as a black version of "American Bandstand," but later found its own identity. Over the years, hundreds of stars stopped by to lip-sync their hits; most were black, but a few were white (such as David Bowie). In 1974, a theme from "Soul Train," "T.S.O.P.," became a major hit single for MFSB.

The music and the movie: Eric Segal's *Love Story* captured the hearts of countless couples across the nation. (Composer Francis Lai had a hit with the title theme, as did Andy Williams and Henry Mancini.) The Three Degrees were heard in *The French Connection,* James Taylor in *Two Lane Blacktop,* and Frank Zappa in *200 Motels.* It was a good year for concert pictures: *Celebration at Big Sur* (with Joni Mitchell, John Sebastian, and Crosby, Stills, Nash and Young), *Soul to Soul* (with Santana, Wilson Pickett, and Ike and Tina Turner), *Stamping Ground* (with Jefferson Airplane, Pink Floyd, and the Byrds), *Medicine Ball Caravan* (with B. B. King, Alice Cooper, and Delaney and Bonnie), and *Mad Dogs and Englishmen* (with Joe Cocker, Leon Russell, and Rita Coolidge).

In 1965, an unsuccessful pop lyricist named Tim Rice met Andrew Lloyd Webber, who had a burning desire to write musicals. After several misfires, they came up with *Jesus Christ Superstar,* an eighty-nine-minute rock opera that critics both hailed and blasted (it did take great liberties with biblical history). Two hit songs came from the score: the title theme, sung by Murray Head and the Trinidad Singers; and "I Don't Know How to Love Him," recorded by Yvonne Elliman and covered by Helen Reddy (it was the first chart single for each). Initially, *Superstar* was released as an album, and only staged after it had proven a success. In October 1978, the 2,620th performance was given in London, making it the longest-running musical in the history of England. Over one and a half million people saw the show before it closed in August 1980. *Superstar* is in the *Guinness Book of World Records* as the largest-selling album ever recorded in Britain.

We lost many good people in the fall of 1971—star performers in every category of music. The first was **Jim Morrison,** enigmatic lead singer of the Doors. In January, he left for Paris on an extended holiday; on July 3, his heart suddenly stopped beating, for reasons doctors have yet to explain. Three days later, jazz great Louis Armstrong passed away. Country satirist Henry Haynes (the Homer of Homer and Jethro) died on August 7; on August 13, King Curtis was stabbed to death in front of an apartment house he owned in New York City. A drug overdose claimed Janis Joplin on October 4; bleeding ulcers took the life of Gene Vincent nine days later. Then, on October 29, Duane Allman of the Allman Brothers was killed in a grinding motorcycle crash.

But even as we mourned our losses, the new sounds of the seventies were taking shape, growing and developing each day. In January, "Your Song" became the first top-ten hit for **Elton John,** while in February, Gordon Lightfoot emerged with "If You Could Read My Mind." In April, "Another Day" kicked off the solo career of Paul McCartney, who went on to form Wings in August. That same month, "Take Me Home, Country Roads" introduced John Denver, we first heard of Olivia Newton-John via "If Not for You," and a California band got together as the Eagles. Other groups that formed in 1971 include Supertramp, Foghat, Kansas, and Queen.

THE TOP 40

1. Joy to the World, *Three Dog Night*
2. It's too Late, *Carole King*
3. How Do You Mend a Broken Heart?, *Bee Gees*
4. Indian Reservation, *Raiders*
5. One Bad Apple, *Osmonds*
6. Go Away Little Girl, *Donny Osmond*
7. Just My Imagination, *Temptations*
8. Take Me Home, Country Roads, *John Denver with Fat City*
9. Maggie May, *Rod Stewart*
10. Knock Three Times, *Dawn*
11. Want Ads, *Honey Cone*
12. Treat Her Like a Lady, *Cornelius Brothers and Sister Rose*
13. She's a Lady, *Tom Jones*
14. Smiling Faces, *Undisputed Truth*
15. Me and Bobby McGee, *Janis Joplin*
16. The Night They Drove Old Dixie Down, *Joan Baez*
17. Signs, *Five Man Electrical Band*
18. What's Going On, *Marvin Gaye*
19. You've Got a Friend, *James Taylor*
20. Tired of Being Alone, *Al Green*
21. Ain't No Sunshine, *Bill Withers*
22. Rose Garden, *Lynn Anderson*
23. Never Can Say Goodbye, *Jackson Five*
24. Uncle Albert/Admiral Halsey, *Paul McCartney*
25. Draggin' the Line, *Tommy James*
26. Put Your Hand in the Hand, *Ocean*
27. Bridge Over Troubled Water, *Aretha Franklin*
28. Doesn't Somebody Want to Be Wanted, *Partridge Family*
29. Temptation Eyes, *Grass Roots*
30. Don't Pull Your Love, *Hamilton, Joe Frank and Reynolds*
31. Mr. Big Stuff, *Jean Knight*
32. Do You Know What I Mean?, *Lee Michaels*
33. It Don't Come Easy, *Ringo Starr*
34. Superstar, *Carpenters*
35. Mercy Mercy Me, *Marvin Gaye*
36. I've Found Someone of My Own, *Free Movement*
37. Superstar, *Murray Head*
38. Amos Moses, *Jerry Reed*
39. For All We Know, *Carpenters*
40. Rainy Days and Mondays, *Carpenters*

The Top 10 LPs

1. Jesus Christ Superstar, *Various Artists*
2. Tapestry, *Carole King*
3. Pearl, *Janis Joplin*
4. Tea for the Tillerman, *Cat Stevens*
5. Abraxas, *Santana*
6. Close to You, *Carpenters*
7. Paranoid, *Black Sabbath*
8. Golden Bisquits, *Three Dog Night*
9. The Partridge Family Album, *Partridge Family*
10. Sticky Fingers, *Rolling Stones*

Knock Three Times

DAWN

The son of a Greek furrier, Michael Anthony Orlando Cassivitis grew up in perhaps the worst slum in New York City—a run-down, crime-ridden neighborhood known as Hell's Kitchen. Determined to escape his unhappy environment, Tony turned to music, singing at first for pennies on the subway and later with his own vocal group, the Five Gents.

In 1960, Aldon Music owner Don Kirshner hired young Tony as a demo singer for a then-unknown composer named Carole King. "I worked with her for seven months," Tony recalled. "On my first demo session, I cut 'Will You Love Me Tomorrow?,' 'Take Good Care of My Baby,' and 'Halfway to Paradise.'" The latter song, released as a single, became Tony's first hit in 1961. His next record, "Bless You," did even better, and Tony was, overnight, a teen pop star. He did live dates, appeared on "American Bandstand," and then vanished. The hits had ended as quickly as they had begun.

In the fall of 1963, Tony joined April-Blackwood Music, and by 1970 he had risen to the rank of general professional manager. It was then that Dave Appell and Hank Medress walked into his office with a demo they'd produced called "Candida." Tony tried to place the song with Bell Records, but it was rejected, with a note that the lead vocal was too weak. Dave and Hank asked Tony to re-record the song himself, in the style he had used while working for Carole King. "Fellows, I don't do demos anymore," Tony objected, but finally he agreed. April-Blackwood approved as well, as long as Tony did not take label credit. Instead, Hank used the name Dawn, which was the name of their production manager's daughter. After the recording, Dave

and Hank dubbed in the voices of two background singers, Telma Hopkins and Joyce Vincent Wilson, long time friends who had sung together anonymously on hundreds of sessions since 1964 (it was Telma, for instance, who told Isaac Hayes to "shut your mouth" on "Shaft").

Eight weeks later, "Candida" was a smash. (Tony couldn't remember the name of the song; his secretary had to look it up for him.) Calls began to come in from people hoping to book "that hot new 'Candida' group." But there was no Dawn—in fact, Tony and the girls had not even met. To fill the void, over a dozen fake Dawns began to pop up everywhere. Bell whipped out $100,000, begging Tony to sign with them. Reluctantly, he agreed. Later, the $100,000 was spent suing the imposter groups and establishing the real identity of Dawn.

" 'Knock Three Times' was the follow-up to 'Candida' and came from the same album," said Tony. "It was a simple story about two people in love in a tenement building somewhere in New York City. One interesting thing about the record comes at the very end, at the bomp-bomp-bomp. We really used the ceiling in the recording studio to get that sound, and the last time you hear the drum, you can also hear the studio ceiling falling down. On some radio stations it distorts, but it's really just the whole ceiling, falling on our heads."

"Knock Three Times" was released in November 1970 and within a month had sold its first million. The record reached number one in January 1971 and went on to sell more than seven million copies worldwide. As with "Candida," Tony and the girls recorded their parts separately—he in New York and they in Los Angeles. The three

still did not meet until after they had sold nine million records.

The success of Dawn was "overwhelming," Tony told the press. "You say, 'Well, that ain't never going to happen to me—no way! 'Course, if I ever had the chance I might . . . but what am I even thinking about it for?' And then, boom! Fantasy becomes reality! I think some fantasies should stay fantasies, because they're really much nicer that way. But in this case—thank the good Lord—everything turned out to be everything I imagined it to be."

Maggie May

ROD STEWART

Roderick David Stewart was born in the Highgate section of North London, where his parents ran a small general store. In school, he was captain of the soccer team and also found time to play guitar and banjo.

In the early sixties, Rod pretty much led the "beatnik" life, leading protesters in song during "ban the bomb" marches. In doing so, he was heavily exposed to folk music. That sound, combined with his other, eclectic tastes—Sam Cooke, Al Jolson, and Eddie Cochran—formed the earliest semblance of a Rod Stewart "style."

Rod held a number of odd day jobs: building fences, framing pictures, digging graves, and working as a box boy. At night, he visited London rock clubs, where the Who, the Stones, the Yardbirds, and other new groups were getting their acts together. In 1963, Mick Jagger showed him how to play the harmonica, which led to a part-time gig with the Five Dimensions.

In 1964, Long John Baldry gave Stewart his first chance as a vocalist. "I had heard Rod before," he recalled, "playing harmonica, but never singing. I discovered him at the Twickham railway station, waiting for a train. Roddy was sitting on the platform, singing the blues. He rather impressed me, so I asked him how he'd fancy a gig. So Rod joined my band as a vocalist."

During his tenure with Long John Baldry's Hoochie Coochie Men, Stewart was given the nickname "Rod the Mod" because of his style of dress and grooming. "I used to worry more about how I looked than the music," he admitted. He was very shy and developed the habit of ignoring the audience while he was singing. Observers thought this was very cool, and it only added to his following.

After the Hoochie Coochie Men broke up, Rod worked with the Soul Agents, Steampacket, Shotgun Express, and finally the Jeff Beck Group. It was with the last band that Rod finally began to attract some attention in America.

In 1968, the Jeff Beck Group cut the LP *Truth,* for which Stewart and Ron Wood wrote several songs. It was a good seller, as was *Beck-Ola* (1969), which marked a shift from blues to "heavy metal." When Beck broke up his band, Stewart and Wood joined the Faces, where they remained for seven years.

At the same time, Rod signed a solo recording contract with Mercury Records. *The Rod Stewart Album* (1969) and *Gasoline Alley* (1970) sold fairly well, but it was the *Every Picture Tells a Story* LP, released in June 1971, that rocketed him to superstardom.

Rod has always felt that "performing is where it's at" and for that reason has always played down his songwriting. For him, composing is "a hard slog," something better suited for those "brimming with ideas and thought." He just writes "words that rhyme," dipping into his memory and experiences. Out of that memory, and perhaps his experience, came

"Maggie May"—the tale of a schoolboy's liaison with a hooker—written with Martin Quittenton.

"Maggie May" broke in America in July of 1971 and slowly rose to number one, where it stayed for five weeks. The flip side, "Reason to Believe," was a moving song written by Tim Hardin. In most markets, it was played almost as much, making the single a double chart-topper. At one point, in September 1971, both the album and single were number one simultaneously, in the United States and England. In 1979, Rod pledged all his royalties from the song to UNICEF, as part of the Year of the Child campaign.

Also pulled from *Every Picture Tells a Story* was "(I Know) I'm Losing You," a soul number that made the top thirty in December.

Stewart and the Faces spent the next five years touring all over the world, selling out halls to wildly appreciative crowds. As a regular part of the act, he'd kick soccer balls out to the fans, whom he referred to as "the Tartan hordes."

Take Me Home, Country Roads

JOHN DENVER

Henry John Deutschendorf, Jr., was born in Roswell, New Mexico, but grew up all over the country. His father, an air force pilot, was constantly on the move, shifting from one military base to another. The elder Deutschendorf managed to set three world records in aviation, inspiring his son to have similar ambitions. However, such was not to be; the air force rejected Henry Jr. as too nearsighted.

The young man then turned to music, and was given a 1910 Gibson guitar by his grandmother. He spent hours in his room, picking and singing, and imitating Elvis Presley. Later, at Texas Tech, he abandoned plans to become an architect, and moved instead toward a show biz career.

Henry changed his name to John Denver (after his favorite city) and started playing folk clubs around the Southwest. One night, while appearing in Phoenix, he was "discovered" by a member of the Brothers Four. John was told to head for L.A., where auditions were being held to fill a spot in the Chad Mitchell Trio. On July 4, 1965, he got the job over two hundred fifty other applicants. Denver stayed with the group for more than three years, until they broke up in November 1968.

He tried making it on his own, and signed with RCA Victor. His first solo album, *Rhymes and Reasons,* featured his own composition, "Leaving on a Jet Plane." Peter Paul and Mary covered it, and had a number-one hit with the song in 1969. Two LPs followed—*Take Me to Tomorrow* and *Whose Garden Was This?*—before John Denver found the tune that was to make him a star.

It happened in Washington, D.C., during an engagement at a folk club called the Cellar Door. John was sharing the bill with Bill Denoff and Taffy Nivert, who worked under the name of Fat City. After opening night, the three piled into Bill's car and headed back to his place for an impromptu jam. On the way, though, there was a crash, and John's thumb was broken. He had to be taken to the hospital, where a splint was applied to his hand. By the time they got back to the house, John was, in his words, "wired, you know."

Bill and Taffy then told him about a song they'd been working on for about a month. The inspiration had come while they'd been driving to a family reunion of Taffy's relatives in Maryland. To pass the time en route, Bill had made up a ballad about the little winding roads they were taking. Later, he changed the story to fit that of an artist friend, who used to write to Bill about the splendors of the West Virginia countryside. The second verse of the tune was a bit risque—making reference to naked ladies and such—so Bill and Taffy figured their song would never ever get played on the radio.

They sang it for John, and, as he recalled, "I flipped." The three of them then stayed up until 6 A.M., changing words and moving lines around. When they finished, John announced that the song had to go on his next album—and it did.

"Take Me Home, Country Roads" appeared on the LP *Poems, Prayers and Promises,* and was released as a 45 in the spring of 1971. It broke nationally in mid-April, but moved up the charts very slowly. After several weeks, RCA called John and told him that they were giving up on the single. "No!" he screamed. "Keep working on it!" They did, and on August 18 it was certified as a million-seller.

"Take Me Home, Country Roads" spent nearly six months on the hit parade, establishing John Denver as a force to be reckoned with in the pop, country, and easy listening fields. Fat City later evolved into the Starland Vocal Band, winner of two 1976 Grammy Awards, including Best New Artist of the Year.

And Bill and Taffy? "Someday," they said, "we'll have to vist West Virginia."

Just My Imagination (Running Away with Me)

THE TEMPTATIONS

*I*n the late sixties, writer-producers Norman Whitfield and Barrett Strong began to create an entirely new musical environment for the Temptations, beginning with "Ain't Too Proud to Beg" in 1966. Instead of melodious tunes like "My Girl" or "Since I Lost My Baby," the group fell into a new bag of psychedelic soul, hard rock, and social commentary. Taking a cue from Sly and the Family Stone, they rapidly evolved their look and sound, putting a heavy emphasis on musical messages. Although they still sang love songs with their sister group, the Supremes ("I'm Gonna Make Me Love Me," "I'll Try Something New"), they were strictly in a guest-starring role. In 1970, the Tempts really laid it on thick with "Psychedelic Shack" and "Ball of Confusion," two of their most topical records.

It was quite a shock then, in 1971, for the quintet to make another complete and abrupt about-face. This time they went backward—beyond their own earliest hits—all the way to their streetcorner days in the fifties, as a Detroit doo-wop group.

Whitfield and Strong wrote "Just My Imagination" as a billowy showcase for the lilting voice of Eddie Kendricks, one of three lead singers in the Tempts. The track appeared on the album *Sky's the Limit,* which reflected the changing political mood of America. There were still psychedelic tunes and social comments on the LP, but it was clear that sixties revolutionary fervor was beginning to wear thin. "Just My Imagination" became the most famous song on the album, and a platinum single to boot.

The track was released as a 45 in February 1971, and took off right away. It peaked at number one in April,

spending fifteen weeks on the charts. During that period, it sold in excess of two million copies.

By that time Eddie Kendricks was no longer a Temptation. He quit the group to embark on a solo career—one that really didn't get off the ground for more than two years. Finally, in 1973, "Keep On Truckin'" became his first big hit; "Boogie Down" and "Son of Sagittarius" followed in 1974. In 1975 he hit again with "Shoeshine Boy," and in 1976, "He's a Friend."

Paul Williams also left the Temptations in March of 1971, but continued to draw a salary as an advisor. Williams was separated from his wife, said to have owed $80,000 in back taxes, and was being treated for alcoholism. Friends said Paul was putting away two fifths of cognac a day. On August 17, 1973, at the age of thirty-four, he committed suicide in Detroit. He was buried two blocks from the Motown offices where he and the other Tempts had cut their first record nearly ten years before.

As for the Temptations, they kept going with new members. Three hundred auditioned to fill Eddie's shoes (Damon Harris got the nod), while Richard Street replaced Paul Williams. Late in 1971, they made the top twenty with an offbeat single, "Superstar (Remember How You Got Where You Are)".

The Temptations' last number-one record came in 1972: "Papa Was a Rolling Stone." They won two Grammy Awards for it: Best R&B Performance by a Group and Best R&B Instrumental Performance. Whitfield and Strong also picked up individual awards for writing the tune. The Tempts followed it in 1973 with "Masterpiece," another top-ten 45. Six

other singles made the top forty over the next two years.

A tribute was made to the group by their own congressman, John Conyers, Jr., who spoke of their contribution to music in the 91st U.S. Congress' Congressional Record. "Their involvement is total and sincere," it reads in part, "and whether they are communicating with young people on the basketball court, the baseball field, by personal appearances or through their music, the effect has been inspirational to many, and appreciated by all."

Go Away Little Girl
DONNY OSMOND

The seven performing Osmonds actually made up five different recording "units": the Osmonds as a group; Donny and Marie as a team; and then Donny, Marie, and Jimmy separately. By far, the most successful was Donny, with eleven hits as a soloist.

Donald Clark Osmond broke into show biz at age four at a nightclub in Lake Tahoe, Nevada. His older brothers Jay, Alan, Wayne, and Merrill were appearing there as the opening act for Phyllis Diller. Donny, billed as "a special added attraction," made his entrance in a top hat and tux, descending a long staircase, singing, "I'm a Ding Dong Daddy from Dumas."

That was in 1962, while the Osmond Brothers were still a barbershop quartet. The same year, he made his TV debut on the "Andy Williams Show" and also appeared in a musical special, "The Seven Little Foys." In 1966, Donny became an official member of his brothers' group, and soon after they shortened their name to simply "The Osmonds."

Throughout the sixties, the boys recorded for MGM, Uni, and Barnaby. All of their singles were total failures—until "One Bad Apple." The secret of their success turned out to be Donny, who was not only cute but obviously was a fine lead singer as well.

With "Sweet and Innocent," Donny soared into the top ten on his own in the summer of 1971. At the same time, he was also singing lead on the current Osmonds' hit, "Double Lovin'." Over the next few years, Donny alone and Donny with the Osmonds took turns on the charts; the next release, a solo effort, turned out to be Donny's biggest hit single ever.

That, of course, was "Go Away Little Girl," a song created by Gerry Goffin and Carole King in 1962 (the same year Donny made his debut as a show biz toddler). It was written for Steve Lawrence, who had a number-one hit with it in 1963. At first, the Osmonds weren't sure if this was an appropriate tune for thirteen-year-old Donny. It dealt with dating, and the Osmond parents forbade dating until the age of sixteen. (As Mormons, the family shunned premarital sex, drugs, alcohol, and even caffeine.) Eventually, though, the decision was made to take the "risk" and record the tune, under Rick Hall's direction, in Muscle Shoals. Almost immediately after its release in August 1971, the record began to bound up the charts, and by the next month it was the best-selling single in the country. On Halloween, it was certified gold, and soon after, platinum.

"Go Away Little Girl" was one of the few songs to reach number one by two different artists at two different times. It also demonstrated how timeless tunes can be resurrected every few years and resold to an entirely new audience. Donny, in fact, spent the rest of his solo career remaking oldies: "Hey Girl" in 1971; "Puppy Love," "Too Young," "Why," and "Lonely Boy" in 1972; and "The Twelfth of Never" and "Are You Lonesome Tonight?" in 1973. In 1974, Donny teamed with his sister, Marie, and they remade three more successful oldies: "I'm Leavin' It Up to You" in 1974, "Morning Side of the Mountain" in 1975, and "Deep Purple" in 1976.

Besides records, Donny also starred in three ABC-TV series during the seventies: "The Osmonds" (an animated cartoon); "Donny and Marie" (a variety program); and "The Osmond Family Show" (an attempt to rekindle the success of "Donny and Marie" later in 1979). In December 1979, NBC tried to revive "Donny and Marie" with only "Marie"; that show ran only four weeks. Donny and Marie also made a film together in 1978 called *Goin' Cocoanuts,* but it went nowhere.

Donny hopes to spread out into more areas of show business. He and his family should have no problems with working space. From their earnings in the seventies, the Osmonds built a $4-million studio complex near Salt Lake City. It'll be the launch pad, they say, for future homemade Osmond productions.

One Bad Apple
THE OSMONDS

The Osmonds began singing as a family pastime when their father, George Osmond, taught Alan, Jay, Wayne, and Merrill how to sing "The Old Oaken Bucket" in a simple barbershop style. By 1960 the brothers had begun performing locally, at small parties, church events, and civic club dinners. Then, in the spring of 1962, they made their first appearance outside the state at a barbershop convention in Pasadena, California. Since Anaheim was nearby, the boys took in Disneyland, where they stopped to watch another barbershop quartet. The latter group, seeing the brothers' identical suits, asked them if they'd like to sing. The Osmonds did, and drew such strong applause that they were signed to sing regularly at the park.

A few weeks later, the father of Andy Williams visited Disneyland and saw the four boys. Impressed by their clean-cut look, young talent, and MOR appeal, he offered them a five-year contract to co-star on Andy's new TV series. The Osmonds hesitated; they had never heard of Andy and were, in fact, dreaming of a spot on the "Lawrence Welk Show." When Welk failed to come through, however, they went with Williams in November 1962. With a big smile, Andy introduced his "discovery" as the "the Ogden Brothers, from Osmond, Utah."

During the 1963–1964 season, the boys picked up a second TV job playing the Kissel brothers on an ABC western, "The Travels of Jamie McPheeters." They cut the theme song as a single in 1963, but it bombed, as did every other record they cut during the decade.

In 1966, little brother Donny joined the group, and three years later, along came the Jackson Five with their explosive, high-energy, "black bubblegum" sound. It was fast, euphoric, and, best of all, a fun kind of music, and the Osmonds were obviously impressed. After four J5

records hit number one in a row, the Osmonds decided it was time to modify their style. They headed for Muscle Shoals, Alabama, where they booked time at the Fame Recording Studios, noted for their unique "Muscle Shoals Sound." There, under the direction of producer Rick Hall, they put together "One Bad Apple," written by George Jackson. Musically, it was a complete departure for the Osmonds, with a touch of Muscle Shoals soul and a more rocking, R&B feel.

"One Bad Apple," featuring the lead voice of thirteen-year-old Donny Osmond, broke onto the charts during the first week of January 1971. It took off so fast that the boys had to leave the "Andy Williams Show" the very same month to begin an exhausting round of live appearances. By February 2, it was certified gold, and before long, platinum, selling in excess of three million copies. It spent five weeks at number one—almost four months on the charts in total. In 1971, the Osmonds were hailed as the Top New Group of the Year by all three music magazines—*Billboard*, *Cashbox*, and *Record World*.

"Osmondmania" continued for the rest of the decade. In mid-1972, MGM announced that the five Osmond brothers had achieved eleven gold albums and singles in a one-year period, thus surpassing marks previously held by the Beatles (nine) and Elvis Presley (eight). By 1976, they had twenty-six gold records and had sold seventy million albums and singles worldwide. Their combined annual income was estimated at more than $10 million.

The Osmonds had nearly two dozen hits, despite opposition from many deejays who considered it "unhip" to program their records.

The Osmonds' response was "You're Mine," a single mailed to radio stations in 1979 without any artist credit. Disc jockeys raved about the record and played it heavily, until they learned who the "mystery group" was. At that point, the record died.

"It's a little unfair," said Wayne, "but once a person gets a hit with one or two of the same type of record, you know they're bagged for life." For that reason, and out of a need to establish their own identities, the Osmonds disbanded as a working unit in the summer of 1980. In 1982, however, they re-formed—as a country act.

Indian Reservation
(The Lament of the Cherokee Reservation Indian)

THE RAIDERS

Mark Lindsay, a runaway who never finished high school, was once a delivery boy in Boise, Idaho. Among his stops was a drive-in restaurant owned by a former barber, Paul Revere. Mark learned that Paul had a local group called the Downbeats, and that they had an opening for a musician. Mark raced home, taught himself enough saxophone to fake it, and began a remarkable musical career.

The Downbeats evolved into Paul Revere and the Raiders. In 1961, Gardena Records released a raucous instrumental, "Like Long Hair," which became their first national top-forty hit. After that, their regional fame mushroomed, and by 1963, they were one of the hottest bands in the Pacific Northwest. Deejay Roger Hart paid for a demo tape session and the boys recorded a favorite, "Louie Louie." Although a rival group, the Kingsmen, beat them to the charts with the song, the Raiders did wind up with a new label contract, making them the first hard rock band signed by Columbia Records.

In 1965, Dick Clark signed the boys to appear regularly on "Where the Action Is," a daily musical-variety series. It premiered over ABC-TV on June 27, and six months later the Raiders were off and running with their first major vocal hit, "Just Like Me." It was followed by "Kicks," a powerful anti-drug song; and then, from the LP *Spirit of '67*, "Hungry," "The Great Airplane Strike" and "Good Thing."

"Ups and Downs" was their first hit in 1967, and after that came a down—the cancellation of "Where the Action Is." The hits continued, though, with "Him or Me (What's It Gonna Be)" and "I Had a Dream," both from the album "Revolution." Then, on January 6, 1968, the Raiders returned to TV as the stars of "Happening '68." Over the summer, that show expanded to six days a week, and

became known as "It's Happening." From the LP *Something Happened* came two good sellers: "Too Much Talk" and "Don't Take It So Hard."

In the spring of 1969, the Raiders made the top twenty for the ninth time with "Mr. Sun, Mr. Moon." By then, they were clearly one of America's favorite rock bands, yet their records were rarely played on "progressive" FM stations. To counter this, the boys sent out test pressings of their next LP under the name of Pink Puzz. FM programmers played it heavily and endorsed the "new band" until they found out it was really Paul Revere and the Raiders. From that album came another major single, "Let Me."

Later in '69, "Happening" went off the air and Mark Lindsay, the group's focal point, lead singer and chief songwriter, began a concurrent solo career with the top-ten tune "Arizona." That million-seller was followed in 1970 by "Silver Bird."

The Raiders' biggest problem— endless personnel changes—had taken its toll. Only Lindsay, Revere, and former lead guitarist (now drummer) Michael "Smitty" Smith remained from the original line-up. Freddy Weller had taken over lead guitar, and Keith Allison had come in on bass.

The band decided to cut down their concert schedule. That pace had

allowed only two or three days to knock out an album, two or three takes to cut a single. With the added time, they hoped to accomplish something that they had come close to but hadn't yet achieved—a number one record.

They came across a lament written by country songwriter John D. Loudermilk. It concerned the plight of the Cherokees who, in 1791, were moved from their home in Georgia to Oklahoma. Mark, whose ancestry was part Indian, thought that this would be a good tune to try. It had already been a hit once—in 1968—for Don Fardon.

The track was almost released as a Mark Lindsay record, but at the last minute, the group decided to put their collective name on it. Paul Revere then took a seven thousand mile motorcycle ride, visiting three stations a day, to help promote it. The song broke nationally in mid-April 1971, beginning a twenty-two week run on the charts. By July, it was the most popular tune in America.

"Indian Reservation" wound up being not only the Raiders' biggest hit, but the best-selling single Columbia Records had issued. Indians in Salt Lake City even used it as a publicity song in their struggle for civil rights.

In the fall of 1971, the Raiders had one final hit, "Birds of a Feather," after which they finally went their separate ways.

How Do You Mend a Broken Heart?

THE BEE GEES

It was the success and flash of Elvis Presley that inspired the Gibb brothers to make their first public appearance as contestants in a hometown talent show. At that time—June 1956—their leader and main writer, Barry, was nine years old; his twin brothers, Robin and Maurice (pronounced "Morris") were seven.

Coached by their father, Hugh, a bandleader, the boys began singing at speedway stadiums around Brisbane, Australia. Race driver Bill Good, impressed by their vocal harmony, introduced them to local deejay Bill Gates. Gates, in turn, started playing tapes of the group on his "Midday Platter Chatter" radio show, which helped build a local following. "Because of our names, we became known by the three initials B.G.'s," said Maurice. "Later we changed that to 'Bee Gees,' after the words 'Brothers Gibb.'"

By 1960, the boys had their own regional TV show, and in 1962, they signed with the Festival label. Four years and a dozen singles later, the Gibb family departed for England. Their last Festival recording, "Spicks and Specks," became a number-one hit Down Under after they arrived in England.

Before leaving Australia, the Bee Gees had sent audition tapes to the Beatles' manager, Brian Epstein, at NEMS Enterprises. They were heard by managing director Robert Stigwood, who was impressed. He put the brothers under contract, along with two backup musicians, guitarist Vince Melouney and drummer Colin Petersen.

On Valentine's Day, 1967, this quintet recorded a stark, Gothic ballad entitled "New York Mining Disaster 1941." Released amid a massive publicity campaign, the record was a million-selling sensation. It sounded so much like the Beatles that many were convinced that "Bee Gees" was simply a pseudonym for "Beatles Group." When critics attacked the Gibbs as Beatles imitators, the brothers lashed back that the Beatles' sound was actually a ripped-off Bee Gees sound! This bizarre controversy came to an ironic end in 1978, when the Bee Gees starred in a film of Beatles music—*Sgt. Pepper's Lonely Heart's Club Band.*

The Bee Gees had three other hits in 1967: "To Love Somebody" (which they wrote for Otis Redding), "Holiday," and "(The Lights Went Out in) Massachusetts." In 1968, they entered the American top ten for the first time with "I've Gotta Get a Message to You" and "I Started a Joke."

The sixties were crazy days, and the Bee Gees, caught up in the lunacy of their own rise to stardom, broke up in early 1969. Robin left, upset over "musical direction." Colin was fired and tried to sue, claiming that the others could not go on as "the Bee Gees" without him (he lost). Then Vince quit, formed his own group, and promptly sank from sight. Barry and Maurice tried to forge on as a two-man Bee Gees, but with little success. Finally, in November 1970, the three brothers agreed to reunite.

The second phase of their career was the ballad period (1970–75). It began with "Lonely Days," a comeback record noted for its jagged rhythm. Released late in 1970, it bounced up the chart to number three, becoming the boys' biggest pop single. They were ecstatic, and wondered if they could top it.

They did—in the summer of 1971. "How Can You Mend a Broken Heart?" was an anguished, yet soothing ballad, composed expressly for Andy Williams. When Williams turned it down, the Bee Gees decided to record it themselves. "The writing of it was neither a struggle nor a hardship," said Robin. "The whole thing took about an hour to complete. The song reached the number one spot, to our great satisfaction."

"How Can You Mend a Broken Heart?" took off in late June, and spent four weeks at the top of the charts, cresting in August. It solidified the return of the Bee Gees. In 1972, there were two more lush ballad hits: "My World," and "Run to Me." The best was yet to come.

It's Too Late
CAROLE KING

*I*n 1957, Carole Klein was a Brooklyn high school student with more than a passing interest in a local combo called the Tokens. Although warned by her parents that they were a bad influence, she steadily dated their lead singer—a pudgy young pianist named Neil Sedaka. In emulation, she formed her own group, the Cosines, and even adopted a professional name—Carole King.

Sedaka finally left the Tokens and went out on his own as a soloist. Meanwhile, Carole enrolled at Queens College, where she met fellow student Gerry Goffin, who enjoyed matching his lyrics to her melodies. Before long, they quit school, got married, and signed with Neil's publisher, Aldon Music, as staff songwriters.

Gerry and Carole were assigned a small, one-bench, one-piano cubicle, similar to those shared by the other cogs in Aldon's hitmaking factory—Sedaka and Greenfield, Barry and Greenwich, Lieber and Stoller, and Mann and Weil. Over the next eight years, the fusion of Goffin's words and King's music would result in three dozen top-forty hits, running the gamut from passionate surrender to vengeful fury. The simple, direct, highly personal romanticism of their songs was tempered, but not undermined, by their own New York street sense. Gerry and Carole's talents were in full flower from the very start, as their first effort, "Will You Love Me Tomorrow," became a number-one smash for the Shirelles in 1960.

Goffin and King broke up—professionally and personally—in 1968, with Carole moving to L.A. to rebuild her career. She lacked confidence in herself and was terrified of "forgetting the words" in live appearances. James Taylor offered encouragement and took her along with him on the road. She played backup piano.

In December 1970, James introduced Carole to his audience at Toronto's Massey Hall. Accompanying herself on the piano, she got through ten songs and earned a rousing ovation. A solo album was made, *Writer,* and for the first time, Carole began thinking of herself seriously as a lyricist, as well as a composer. She credited James Taylor as a major influence: "James has a strong but gentle quality about his lyrics, and it was like that opened up that side of me, and I felt another way to go. It resulted in *Tapestry.*"

The LP *Tapestry,* released early in 1971, included "I Feel the Earth Move," an upbeat example of Carole's resilient piano technique. It was chosen as the A side for a single. As a flip, the company picked "It's Too Late," a medium-tempo lament of resignation. Many observers feel that "It's Too Late" was inspired by a short-lived romance with James Taylor, who later was to court and marry Carly Simon. Carole has never said; but then again, she's hardly ever said anything to the press.

"I Feel the Earth Move" got air play right away; but then, after a few weeks, deejays discovered the brooding power of the record's B side. Before long, both tunes were getting heavy exposure, with a decided listener preference for "It's Too Late." By June the single was topping the charts, and on July 21, it was certified gold by the RIAA.

"It's Too Late" went on to win a Grammy Award as Record of the Year. The LP it came from, *Tapestry,* won two: Album of the Year and Best Female Pop Vocal Performance. The Grammy-winning Song of the Year, "You've Got a Friend," was also featured on *Tapestry* (although the hit version, with Carole on piano, was cut by James Taylor).

Tapestry was a record-breaking record in every sense of the word. It stayed on the LP charts for over six years, selling more than thirteen million copies. Until 1976, it was the largest-selling album ever.

One other single was pulled from *Tapestry*—"So Far Away," backed with "Smackwater Jack." Predictably, both sides became major hits. After that, Carole cut seven more albums for Ode, all of which eventually went gold. From them came the singles "Sweet Seasons" and "Been to Canaan" (1972); "Believe in Humanity" and "Corazon" (1973), "Jazzman" (1974), "Nightingale" (1975) and "Only Love Is Real" (1976). In 1977, "Hard Rock Cafe" became a top-thirty hit on her own label, Avatar.

Joy to the World
THREE DOG NIGHT

I think our versatility had a good part to do with our longevity," said Cory Wells. "Not only did Three Dog Night have three lead singers, but also three distinctive styles. Chuck Negron was our ballady Johnny Mathis type, I was hard R&B, and Danny Hutton was a sort of middle-of-the-road kind of singer. Put together, we made our own kind of California sound."

After an impressive debut in 1969, Three Dog Night emerged as one of the most successful rock groups of the early seventies. They scored eighteen top-twenty hits in a row—twenty-one hits in total—before their farewell concert at L.A.'s Greek Theater in July 1976.

"We never tried to push our product on the public," Cory said. "Our whole idea was to record every song, taking the approach that it was the single. We'd record 'em, put 'em in an album, and then release the album. The public knew what they wanted, what they liked; why should we try to outguess them? Whatever tracks got the best response we'd then issue as 45s."

In 1971, four of their tunes became singles, and all of them made the national top ten: "Joy to the World," "Liar," "An Old Fashioned Love Song," and "Never Been to Spain." Cory recalled the biggest of that group, the best-selling single the band—or ABC Records—ever produced.

"'Joy to the World'—now that was a four- to five-million-seller," he said. "Hoyt Axton brought it into the studio one night; we were all there. He walked in wearing Captain America golf shoes, I remember that. They were red, white and blue; everything was red, white and blue in those days, with stars and things. And he took his shoes off, handed them to me and said, 'Hey, Cory. You're Captain America. You should wear these now.' Hoyt's about 6'3", 240 in weight, and I thought, 'How am I going to wear these big shoes?' Then he said, 'Plus, there's a song I want you to hear.'

"He had mentioned before that he was writing a ninety-minute animated children's TV show called "The Happy Song." It was the story of a bunch of children in a fantasy land and their adventures and misadventures. He wrote it so it could be played at any time of the year—Christmas, Halloween, New Year's—any holiday.

"Well, Hoyt never got it together, really, never finished it. So he decided to peddle the songs around to various artist friends. One of those tunes was 'Joy to the World.'

"Hoyt played it for us right there on his guitar, which was not the usual way we auditioned material. It's hard to get the idea of a tune that way because you get into the performance instead of the song. But we knew Hoyt personally; he'd traveled with us many times as an opening act. He's a very close friend of the group.

"As he stood there, playing the song for us, I remember not liking it that well. There are certain songs where you can say 'that's a smash' but you wouldn't want to sing 'em. I knew it was gonna be a hit, but 'Joy' was too

light for my taste. I tend to lean toward heavier sorts of music. The other guys, though, thought it was great, and I remember recording the song and Chuck singing it.

"We were out working maybe three hundred fifty days a year then, moving faster than the music was behind us. We were just zooming along, and everything was a collage of Holiday Inns, airports, and backs of limos. I couldn't even tell you where I was when it reached number one, it sold so many copies so fast."

Hoyt Axton added a footnote. "Actually, I didn't expect 'Joy to the World' to be a hit at all," he said. "After Three Dog Night cut it, they played the tape for me and I thought it was terrible. Then that son-of-a-gun was on top of the charts for six weeks across the board. I looked in *Billboard* magazine, and saw that in Singapore and Malaysia, the song was number one. That made me feel great, because I could imagine all those little kids with holes in their shirts and no shoes rockin' around singing 'Jeremiah was a bullfrog.' I mean, that cracked me up."

Led Zeppelin scored three major hits in 1972: "Black Dog," "Rock and Roll," and their almost eight-minute classic, "Stairway to Heaven" (which bore no relation to Neil Sedaka's 1960 song of the same name). The latter piece, although never released commercially on a 45, became their most popular number ever, and one of the most requested tunes of all time on radio stations from coast to coast. The song was available only as a track on their untitled *Runes* album (an LP so named because it bore only four cryptic symbols as identification). To the great confusion of music merchants and buyers, neither title, artist, label, nor any other information appeared on the record jacket.

At the end of the decade, Little Roger and the Goosebumps cut a perfect parody of the Led Zeppelin sound: an exact reproduction of "Stairway to Heaven," substituting the words of the "Gilligan's Island" TV theme. Led Zeppelin was not amused and sued—and won.

Salvadore Bono and Cherilyn La Piere met on a blind date in Hollywood, and spent the first year of their marriage trying to cut a hit record. When they finally broke through in the fall of 1965, they had five of them—all on the charts simultaneously—including their number-one theme song, "I Got You Babe." **Sonny and Cher** not only helped popularize folk rock, but also set fashion and social trends, proving it was O.K. to be young, mod, and married. Their career went into a tailspin in 1968, but the Bonos hung on, and in 1971 made a dramatic comeback with the hit "All I Ever Need Is You." They were given a CBS-TV summer show, and did well enough to land a regular variety

THANKS TO REVISED copyright laws, sound recordings were given greater federal protection in 1972, the year RCA, Japan Victor, and Panasonic introduced their own four-channel disc systems. New demand for quadrophonic music boosted U.S. record sales past the $1.3 billion mark for the first time—an increase of nearly eleven percent over 1971. So far, total sales in the seventies exceeded $3.3 billion, a figure greater than that for the entire decade of the fifties. New stars made their debuts via landmark singles: "Take it Easy" (the Eagles), "You Don't Mess Around with Jim" (Jim Croce), "Doctor My Eyes" (Jackson Browne), "Taxi" (Harry Chapin), "Go All the Way" (the Raspberries), "Tightrope" (Leon Russell), and "Do You Wanna Dance?" (Bette Midler). Other 45s of distinction included "Layla" by Derek and the Dominoes (actually Eric Clapton and friends in disguise), "Back Stabbers" by the O'Jays (their first biggie after struggling four-

teen years), "My Ding-a-Ling" by Chuck Berry (his best seller ever and only number one), "I Am Woman" (Helen Reddy's feminist anthem), "Popcorn" by Hot Butter (the first big synthesizer hit), and "Burning Love" (Elvis Presley's last top-ten single). The Byrds broke up; so did Steppenwolf, Iron Butterfly, the Youngbloods, Delaney and Bonnie, and Creedence Clearwater Revival. The Four Tops moved to ABC, Joe Tex retired, James Taylor and Carly Simon got married, and Smokey Robinson left the Miracles. We lost the Chipmunks' creator, David Seville; also Billy Williams, Brian Cole (of the Association), Clyde McPhatter (of the Drifters), and Phil King (of Blue Oyster Cult). John and Yoko separated, but reunited two months later for a benefit concert for the Willowbrook Home for Retarded Children. It was 1972—the year Apollo 100 brought Bach into the top ten with "Joy" (an adaptation of his classical work "Jesu, Joy of Man's Desiring").

series, "The Sonny and Cher Comedy Hour," two days after Christmas. It swiftly became a 1972 sensation, and before long was television's top-rated variety program. Unfortunately, their marriage and the series fell apart in 1974. After that, Sonny and Cher had only spotty success, either alone or in reunions.

Carlos Santana and the group that bore his name performed in *Fillmore*, a movie record of the last show staged in Bill Graham's legendary San Francisco rock music hall (also on hand: Boz Scaggs, the Grateful Dead, Elvin Bishop, and other local regulars). Donovan contributed to *The Pied Piper*, Curtis Mayfield to *Superfly*, and Joe Cocker to *Groupies* (which also featured Gary Wright in Spooky Tooth). Diana Ross launched her acting career in *Lady Sings the Blues*, while Mr. Presley was seen in *Elvis on Tour*.

In October 1971, **Rick Nelson** and the Stone Canyon Band appeared in concert at New York's Madison Square Garden. After running through a number of early hits, they launched into relatively recent material, including a version of "Honky Tonk Women." Segments of the crowd, there more to relive their past than to enjoy classic rock 'n' roll, began to boo. Rick was unnerved, but then moved to write a sequel to his ten-year-old ballad, "Teenage Idol." The new song, "Garden Party," recounted his New York experience, and reminded fans that old tunes could be more than mere stepping stones to nostalgia. "If memories are all I sing," he said, "I'd rather drive a truck." After a slow, steady start, "Garden Party" emerged as one of the top records of 1972, and Nelson's biggest hit in nearly nine years. By the next March, Rick and the band were back in New York, this time playing Carnegie Hall.

If ever a group had a sound that was cosmic, it was the **Moody Blues,** creators of some of the most ethereal albums of all time. Their blend of impassioned vocals and elaborate orchestrations came to be known as "symphonic rock," a new kind of melodramatic music. They were always considered far ahead of their time, and were one of the first rock groups to openly collaborate with classical musicians. In 1967, when the Moodies recorded "Nights in White Satin," they proved to be exactly five years ahead of their time, as that song did not reach number one until the fall of 1972.

THE TOP 40

1. American Pie, *Don McLean*
2. Alone Again (Naturally), *Gilbert O'Sullivan*
3. Without You, *Nilsson*
4. Brand New Key, *Melanie*
5. I Gotcha, *Joe Tex*
6. Daddy Don't You Walk So Fast, *Wayne Newton*
7. Let's Stay Together, *Al Green*
8. The First Time Ever I Saw Your Face, *Roberta Flack*
9. Brandy, *Looking Glass*
10. Lean on Me, *Bill Withers*
11. If Loving You Is Wrong, *Luther Ingram*
12. Baby Don't Get Hooked on Me, *Mac Davis*
13. Heart of Gold, *Neil Young*
14. Candy Man, *Sammy Davis, Jr.*
15. Nice to Be with You, *Gallery*
16. The Lion Sleeps Tonight, *Robert John*
17. Slippin' into Darkness, *War*
18. I'll Take You There, *Staple Singers*
19. Long Cool Woman, *Hollies*
20. Horse with No Name, *America*
21. Outa Space, *Billy Preston*
22. Oh Girl, *Chi-Lites*
23. Song Sung Blue, *Neil Diamond*
24. Family Affair, *Sly and the Family Stone*
25. Rockin' Robin, *Michael Jackson*
26. My Ding-a-Ling, *Chuck Berry*
27. Back Stabbers, *O'Jays*
28. Everybody Plays the Fool, *Main Ingredient*
29. Last Night (I Didn't Get to Sleep at All), *Fifth Dimension*
30. Betcha by Golly Wow, *Stylistics*
31. Precious and Few, *Climax*
32. Ben, *Michael Jackson*
33. Cherish, *David Cassidy*
34. How Do You Do?, *Mouth and MacNeal*
35. I'm Still in Love with You, *Al Green*
36. Down by the Lazy River, *Osmonds*
37. Scorpio, *Dennis Coffey*
38. Popcorn, *Hot Butter*
39. Go All the Way, *Raspberries*
40. Too Late to Turn Back Now, *Cornelius Brothers and Sister Rose*

THE TOP 10 LPs

1. Tapestry, *Carole King*
2. Harvest, *Neil Young*
3. American Pie, *Don McLean*
4. Teaser and the Firecat, *Cat Stevens*
5. Music, *Carole King*
6. Hot Rocks 1964–1971, *Rolling Stones*
7. America, *America*
8. Let's Stay Together, *Al Green*
9. The Concert for Bangla Desh, *Various Artists*
10. First Take, *Roberta Flack*

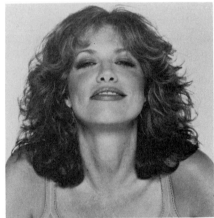

Carly Simon was born rich, the daughter of an obscure New York book publisher. She began her hit career in 1971 with a ballad she wrote, "That's the Way I've Always Heard It Should Be." A top-ten smash, it was followed by "Anticipation," a tune later reworked into an ad jingle for ketchup. In 1972, she won a Grammy Award as the Best New Artist of the Year, and also recorded the LP *No Secrets,* a turning point in her musical direction. As she said, "I was tired of self-pity." What came from that feeling was "You're So Vain," an accusative song that caused much speculation about the identity of its central character (actually, it was a composite of men in her life, but most notably actor Warren Beatty). In November, Carly ended all romantic trauma by marrying a longtime friend, James Taylor. Both went on to score several more hits, both separately and together, before splitting in 1981.

10

Lean on Me
BILL WITHERS

For most of his youth, Bill Withers was what you might call the strong, silent type. Because he stuttered so badly, he was embarrassed to say anything to anybody. But at thirty-three, he became a soft-spoken yet nonstop talker—and a singer-songwriter with his first of several gold records.

Bill, who was born in Slab Fork, West Virginia, spent nine years in the navy—"to get away from people," he said. Afterward he found work delivering milk and then as a mechanic for the Ford Motor Company. Next he got a job as a computer operator for IBM. Eight months later, Bill left for California and was hired by Lockheed Aircraft to make bathrooms and air stairs and kitchens for 747s. In his free time, he hung around clubs, listening to the singers. "They seemed to be pretty contented people," he recalled, "and I guess I thought I could sing as well as them."

He began writing his songs because "I figured if I was going to be a singer, I'd have to have some tunes." Instead of making the usual rounds of the record companies and begging for a chance to be heard, he decided to make his own record. "I just saved my money and read the backs of album covers to find out who could play. Then I got a license from the musician's union and hired a few."

A piano player who helped out on the demo introduced Bill to Chico Hamilton's son, Forrest. In turn, Forrest took Bill to Clarence Avant, president of Sussex Records. In the spring of 1970, Bill was given a producer, Quincy Jones, and the recording process began.

His first single release was "Ain't No Sunshine," in 1971. "If you listen to it, you'll realize that the first half of the record is nothing but a guitar riff and my foot stomping on a board." It became a gold record, and won a Grammy Award as Best R&B Song of the Year. Bill was also nominated in

two other categories, including Best New Artist of 1971.

The next year was even more successful. His second album, *Still Bill,* featured two more tunes that would go on to become R&B classics. The first was "Lean on Me."

"I was still working in the factory when I wrote that tune," Bill recalled. "None of us were really making much money, and we came to depend on each other for favors. You know, most songs are about romantic love, perhaps the most inconsistent kind there is. Well, there's another kind of love where people are vulnerable enough to say, 'Hey, if there's anything I can do for you, let me know.' At the same time, they're smart enough to say, 'And if there's any way you can help me out, I'd sure appreciate it.' Well, at the factory, there was always somebody there to help you—if you were fixin' your car and there was something too heavy for you to handle by yourself, or you needed five bucks. We all needed some little thing from each other. The song grew out of that environment."

"Lean on Me" entered the pop charts in April of 1972 and three

months later was number one. It was followed by "Use Me," another million-seller, which made number two.

"I loved working at Sussex Records, because we kind of grew up together," said Bill. "When I came about, nobody had heard much of Sussex Records, or me either. So we just had a lot of fun. Nothing can ever replace that first situation, you know. It's kind of like your first girlfriend."

Sussex Records folded in the mid-seventies, though, and Bill moved on to the Columbia label. His old masters were bought by Columbia at auction. In 1978, Bill had another mild hit, "Lonely Day." He returned to the top ten in 1981 with "Just the Two of Us," a single cut in collaboration with Grover Washington, Jr.

"A person's either musical or not," Bill said. "I was fortunate in that I was able to be reasonably successful without being too cultivated. The longer I make records, the more sophisticated I become. But all I'll ever be able to do is say the things that are available to me in my mind. I write and sing about whatever I'm able to understand."

Brandy
LOOKING GLASS

The group Looking Glass was formed in 1969, at Rutgers University in New Brunswick, New Jersey. The four members—Elliot Lurie (lead guitar), Lawrence Gonsky (piano), Pieter Sweval (bass), and Jeff Grob (drums)—all shared a common love of rock 'n' roll and, in particular, the sound and style of the Young Rascals.

The band played the usual round of bars, dances, and frat parties until their graduation rolled around. It was then that they decided to pool their funds and make a firm commitment toward their communal future. Taking a cue from what the Rascals had done, they began looking for a group home—an isolated structure in which to live, develop their act, and refine material. They finally found one near the Pennsylvania border, in Glen Gardner, New Jersey. It was an aging farmhouse surrounded by eighty-two acres of open country. The boys plunked down their rent and made a pact to spend one year at the farmhouse, rehearsing, writing songs, and in general, "polishing the Looking Glass."

By 1971, the group felt confident enough to begin circulating a demo tape to record companies. After several rejections, it came to the attention of Clive Davis, then head of Columbia Records. He came out and watched the band perform at a bar in New York City. Among the songs in their set was "Brandy," a tune written and sung by Elliot. Clive liked what he heard and saw, and signed the group to Columbia's subsidiary, Epic Records.

The song had been inspired by a girl in Elliot's life who had a name similar to "Brandy." He started the song as a guitar instrumental and then had Larry play the melody over and over on the piano. Slowly, through free association, Elliot put together a story for his song and filled in the lyrics. He later admitted that although the girl

was real, most of the ballad was fictional.

Looking Glass cut the song at least three times, first as a part of their demo and then at an unsuccessful session in Memphis. The third version was recorded in New York, in a marathon production that ran many hours. After being disappointed before, the group redid the song three or four times, until guitars, drums, and voices blended perfectly. Then the track was added to their first album, which was issued by Epic early in 1972.

"Brandy" was not the label's first choice as a single. However, the song was picked off the album by a deejay in Washington, D.C., who played the song heavily and built up a strong local demand. When finally issued as a 45, "Brandy" sold slowly, but eventually gained momentum and finally peaked at number one in August 1972. The same month, it was certified as a million-seller by the RIAA.

More than a year went by before

Looking Glass scored a follow-up hit, but it finally came in September 1973. However, "Jimmy Loves Marrianne" was only a mild seller. Soon after, Elliot Lurie, who'd written and sung lead on both Looking Glass hits, announced he was leaving the group to begin a solo career. The others replaced him and then changed the group's name to one word—Lookinglass. However, the whole band fell apart soon afterward.

Looking Glass suffered from a problem common to many groups— a wide rift between their live sound and their sound on vinyl. People came to Looking Glass concerts expecting the same kind of New York pop sound they'd heard on "Brandy." They'd hear that sound, but it was mixed in with hard-rock remnants of the boys' bar-band background. Everyone knew "Brandy," but not the group Looking Glass—four men who never quite established their own musical identity.

The First Time Ever I Saw Your Face

ROBERTA FLACK

"I was born in Asheville, North Carolina, but grew up in Virginia," said Roberta Flack. "I began playing the organ at the age of four and started piano lessons when I was nine. Later on, it was a great honor for me to accompany the junior high chorus. Eventually I won a full scholarship to Howard University, where I earned my degree as a music major. I then taught music, math, and English in Farmville, North Carolina, and after that, I joined the Washington, D.C., school system.

"During summer vacations, and even through the winter, I worked part time at a fancy restaurant called the Tivoli. My job there was to accompany opera singers. It was my first public exposure as a performer, and I never even thought about singing."

In the spring of 1967, though, Roberta decided to try making it as a vocalist. She soon was attracting such crowds at one nightclub that an extra room was added solely to showcase her talents. In the summer of 1968,

she appeared at the Bohemian Gardens as part of a benefit for the Ghetto Children's Library. Jazz pianist Les McCann was in the audience, and he was so impressed that he arranged an audition for her with Atlantic Records. The result, in 1969, was a well-received debut album, *First Take*.

"One of my friends in Washington was a folk entertainer named Donal Leace," Roberta continued, "and one day he turned me on to a record by the team of Joe and Eddie. It was 'The First Time Ever I Saw Your Face.' A British folk singer, Ewan McColl, wrote it in 1963 for his wife, Peggy Seeger, who was also a folk singer and the sister of Pete Seeger. I thought it was just beautiful and had to add it to my first album.

"A lot of people ask me what I was thinking about while I was recording that song. Actually I was thinking about a little black cat that someone had given me, named Sancho Panza. I had just gotten back from being on the road for the first time, and I

discovered that he had been killed. I only had one pet, and when I went into the studio, two days later, he was still on my mind.

"After the album was released, a disc jockey in New Orleans started a one-man campaign to get the song pulled off the album as a single. Nobody at Atlantic, though, paid any attention to him. Then, three years later, Clint Eastwood called and said that he loved the song and wanted to use it in a movie. They were making this film based around the Monterey Jazz Festival, and they were using jazz and jazz musicians."

The picture was *Play Misty for Me* (1971), which turned out to be one of Eastwood's most popular movies ever. "First Time" was used in a steamy love scene between Eastwood and Donna Mills. Moviegoers inundated record shops for copies of what they'd heard. "When it was finally picked as a single," said Roberta, "obviously because of the Clint Eastwood thing, I was happy that the young man in New Orleans got credit as the one who broke the record."

Atlantic, incidentally, did not release "First Time" exactly as it had appeared on the album. They believed, and rightly so, that it was an unusual track and, at nearly five and a half minutes, a little long for AM radio play. So they lopped off sixty-six seconds, making the time a more comfortable 4:15.

Roberta Flack went on to be named Top Female Vocalist of the Year both by *Cashbox* and at the Second Annual Soul and Blues Award Night in L.A. *Record World* called her the Top Jazz, Top Album, and Top Pop Artist of 1972. She won *Billboard's* Trendsetter Award, for "moving jazz into the pop market with her soft, delicate style." At the Grammys, "The First Time Ever I Saw Your Face" was hailed as Record of the Year, while its composer, Ewan McColl, was cited for writing the Song of the Year. Not bad for a three-year-old recording of a ten-year-old song.

Let's Stay Together
AL GREEN

Al Green grew up in Grand Rapids, Michigan, amid influences that were both musical and religious. Until he was sixteen, he sang with a family gospel group, the Green Brothers, which toured the Midwest extensively. His parents, though, did not allow pop music in their house, so Al had to go to the local record shop to listen to his early idols, Jackie Wilson, Sam Cooke, Otis Redding, and James Brown.

In the early sixties, Al and a couple of friends formed the Creations, which played the "chitlin circuit" in the Midwest. Then, in 1967, group member Palmer Jones persuaded Al to record a song he had written, titled "Back Up Train." The single was released on Hot Line Records, a small independent label, and Al was an overnight success—but without a follow-up, it didn't last long.

While playing a small club in Midland, Texas, Al met Willie Mitchell, a pianist who had backed dozens of performers on record. Since 1964, he'd fronted his own instrumental combo, churning out a string of mild-selling funk singles for Hi Records in

Memphis. In Al, Willie felt he'd found the perfect vocal counterpart to his own taut, seductive rhythm. He guaranteed that he could make Al a star in a couple of years. Exactly two years later, in the fall of 1971, the first hit came along—"Tired of Being Alone." It sold more than a million copies.

The follow-up single was "Let's Stay Together," a carefully plotted blues record, despite its live, almost stream-of-consciousness feel. Al's vocal style was deliberately underplayed, generating a sensual, almost hypnotic emotional tension. The rhythm behind him was controlled and edged with tension—the ideal backdrop for sudden yet perfectly timed bursts of falsetto. It was soul with a twist—painfully sweet, not at all gruff like the music of many of his predecessors.

"Let's Stay Together" broke onto the national charts early in December 1971 and slowly rose to the number-one spot, which it occupied in mid-February 1972. It sold more than three million copies and was the number-one single of the year in the 1972 *Cashbox* polls, as well as top soul

song of the year according to *Billboard.* Al quickly followed it with three more top-five hits in a row: "Look What You Done for Me," "I'm Still in Love with You," and "You Ought to Be with Me." In all, Al sold ten million "units" in 1972, and he closed out the year by being named the Top Male Singer of 1972, at the Second Annual Soul and Blues Night, held in L.A.

Al Green continued to place records in the top twenty for three more years. "Call Me" and "Here I Am" in 1973, "Livin' for You" and "Sha La La" in 1974, and "L-O-V-E" in 1975. Some complained that they were too repetitious, joking that Al had recorded just one marathon selection and was slowly releasing it in three-minute bits. Al Green hardly varied his formula, but it seldom got boring. His distinctive vocal screech and unusually soft sound brought a strange yet exciting kind of sexy showmanship to R&B.

Besides musical waves, Al Green made headlines on October 18, 1974, when a girlfriend, Mary E. Woodson, poured a pot of boiling grits over Al as he was getting out of his bathtub, because he had refused her proposal of marriage. A few minutes later, she committed suicide. Al recovered physically from his second-degree burns, but the tragedy left deep emotional scars.

"The Prince of Love" was one of a number of nicknames that Al picked up during his career; others included "the mean Al Green," "Green Power," "the lean Al Green," and "the Soul Doctor." But in 1976 he acquired the title he cherishes the most—"the Reverend Al Green." He entered the ministry, and opened his own nonde-nominational church in Memphis, the Full Gospel Tabernacle. It had been thirteen years since he'd left home, bitter over his father's refusal to let him buy rock 'n' roll records. But now he had returned, once more to be surrounded by the gospel trappings he'd walked away from years before.

6

Daddy Don't You Walk So Fast

WAYNE NEWTON

Wayne Newton was born in Norfolk, Virginia, and began singing there at the age of six. Along with his brother, Jerry, he formed a duo that appeared at county fairs, church functions and school events. Most of their repertoire was country and western; Wayne strummed along on his Hawaiian guitar. They were known as the Rhythm Rascals.

In 1952, Wayne developed bronchial asthma, and for his health, the family moved to Phoenix, Arizona. Soon after, the boys landed a daily TV show over KOOL. They kept it until 1959, when Las Vegas beckoned. The Fremont Hotel offered them a five-year contract: six nights a week, six shows a night, as a lounge act. They accepted, even though Wayne was barely sixteen at the time. As he was too young to enter the casinos, Wayne had to spend most of his time in his hotel room, talking to his pet skunk.

In the summer of 1962, Wayne was invited to appear on the fall premiere of the "Jackie Gleason Show." It was his first national TV exposure, and one of the people watching was Bobby Darin. Darin signed Newton to his production company, TM Music, and got him a contract with Capitol Records. The next year, Darin gave Wayne a song he himself had planned to record. That tune, "Danke Schoen," became the first Wayne Newton hit, in the summer of 1963. Two years later, there was a second hit, "Red Roses for a Blue Lady."

Wayne spent most of the sixties developing a nightclub act specifically aimed at Las Vegas audiences. It seemed to work. By the end of the decade, he was one of the highest-paid performers in the city. Wayne's weekly take was estimated at $52,500, which works out to $6 million a year. Clearly, he was doing something right—live, in person, onstage. The problem was out of town, where, across America, Wayne was still being

perceived as an ultra-square, squeaky-voiced wimp. His record sales were a joke, and no label wanted to take him.

Then, in 1972, Wes Farrell decided to take a chance. He signed Wayne as the first artist on his new Chelsea label. As a debut single, they came up with "Daddy Don't You Walk So Fast."

The song had already been a hit a few months before in England, for pop singer Daniel Boone (Daniel was later to have a U.S. hit, "Beautiful Sunday," in the fall of 1972). Wayne liked it for its unstated theme of divorce—something his Las Vegas fans could surely identify with. He also felt it "tugged at the heartstrings."

"I seem to lean toward emotional songs," he said, "and there's a reason for it." He offered a cinematic analogy. "If you go to see a comedy, you laugh a lot, and come out saying, 'I really liked that.' But you'll never go back. It's kind of like hearing the same

joke twice. But if you go to a movie and cry when you leave, you might go back and see it nine or ten times. Don't ask me why, but it's a human trait, and that's the way I am. If something truly touches me that deeply, I'll want to see it, or sing it, or hear it again."

"Daddy Don't You Walk So Fast" was released in April 1972, and peaked on the charts in July. The same month, Wayne received his gold disc for sales topping one million copies.

Since that time, Wayne has concentrated mainly on raising horses, exercising his three-octave vocal range, and building a business empire. In 1980, he and a partner bought the Aladdin Hotel in Las Vegas for $85 million, assuring Newton of a perpetual place to play.

When asked for his mood at that time, Wayne just smiled at the reporters. "It's a wonderful feeling," he said.

I Gotcha

JOE TEX

Joe Tex was a southern soul singer who spent ten years looking for his place—recording everything from rock 'n' roll to crying blues. Finally, with a blend of gospel and country music, he gained fame as a down-home storyteller—the "master rapper" of the sixties.

His motivation for entering show biz, he explained, was to make enough money to buy homes for the two women he admired most—his mother and his grandmother. He started singing as a child and sang in the school chorus and, on weekends, with pop and gospel groups. In 1954, at the age of eighteen, he entered a hometown talent contest and won first prize—a two-week trip to New York City. He turned up at the Apollo Theater on amateur night and again walked off with top honors. He was given an extended four-week booking, which led to offers from rival nightspots.

In 1956, while singing at the Celebrity Club on Long Island, Joe was discovered by a scout from King Records. His audition song, "Davy You Upset My Home," became his first single release. It flopped, as did five other 45s he cut for the company.

He moved to the Ace label in 1957, and over the next four years, issued another half dozen discs. Somehow, though, tunes like "Little Baby Face Thing," "Yum Yum Yum," and "Charlie Brown Got Expelled" failed to catch on with the public.

Then, in 1961, Joe signed with Dial, a new firm headed by Buddy Killen, based in Nashville. Buddy was sure he could help Joe find a successful formula, even though it might take a while to develop.

Joe had been a long-time admirer of country music, especially tunes that were essentially morality narratives. With Buddy's help, he discovered that such material, delivered in a black "preacher" style, was both effective and ear-catching. Joe began to write a series of folksy little sermons: some on the state of the world, but mostly on man's responsibility to women. For inspiration, he drew on true-life experiences—his own, or those of people he met. To have hits, he reasoned, people must identify.

Late in 1964, Joe pulled a piece of paper out of his pocket with four lines scribbled on it. From that, he and Killen created "Hold What You've Got," which became a gold record in January 1965. It was the first of two dozen such songs Tex would place on the charts over the rest of the decade. They included "I Want To," and in 1966, "A Sweet Woman Like You" and "S.Y.S.L.J.F.M. (The Letter Song)." In 1967, there was "Show Me," followed by "Skinny Legs and All" (a million-seller in 1968) and "Men Are Gettin' Scarce."

Before recording these tunes, Joe used to make himself hoarse. He felt that he sounded better that way, and also more authentic, as he really did start to rasp while on long concert tours. The concept worked well for four years, but began to run out of steam in 1969.

Then, in 1972, Joe made an impressive comeback with the biggest 45 of his career. There had always been a sly, cunning, almost smug sound to his releases, but nothing like the raving self-confidence of "I Gotcha." Issued late that January, it made a slow climb to number two. The single was certified gold on March 22 and hung in for twenty-one weeks on the hit parade.

Soon after, Joe stunned the music world by announcing his retirement. He was to become a Muslim minister and assume the name of Joseph X (later, Yusuf Hazziez).

Joseph X left Dial Records and went

on a speaking tour on behalf of his new religion. It didn't last long. Once home, he got his band together and tried recording again for Mercury. Four singles were made, but none of them sold.

Joe Tex did return, however, and as Joe Tex. In 1977, he had one final hit with "Ain't Gonna Bump No More (With No Big Fat Woman)." It reached number twelve on the Epic label.

Today he's a television scriptwriter.

Brand New Key
MELANIE

Melanie Safka was born in Astoria, New York, where she learned to play the ukulele at the age of four. There was always music around the house—her uncle sang folk songs; her mother, jazz and blues.

At sixteen, Melanie was already singing in nightclubs and coffeehouses. She also studied drama for a while, at New York's Academy of Fine Arts.

One day, she went to a building on Broadway, looking for an acting audition. The doorman misdirected her instead to the offices of Buddah Records. The company owners saw she was carrying a guitar, so they auditioned her, and signed her to their label. In the process, they introduced her to her future producer and husband, Peter Schekeryk.

Not much happened until the fall of 1969, when Melanie sang at the famous Woodstock festival. As it began to rain, hundreds of candles suddenly appeared, glowing in the darkness. From that experience came her first hit, "Lay Down (Candles in the Rain)," which she recorded with the Edwin Hawkins Singers. Later in 1970, she made the top forty again, with "Peace Will Come (According to Plan)."

In 1971, Melanie and Peter formed their own label, Neighborhood Records. The first release was a single—"Brand New Key."

"I like all kinds of music," she said, "but what I like best is to blend different styles so well in one song that both the song and I transcend categories. I hate being pegged as anything—country, pop, whatever. The trick is to become a timeless musical being, with timeless musical songs.

"'Brand New Key' I wrote in about fifteen minutes one night. I thought it was cute; a kind of old thirties tune. I guess a key and a lock have always been Freudian symbols, and pretty obvious ones at that. There was no deep serious expression behind the song, but people read things into it. They made up incredible stories as to what the lyrics said and what the song meant. In some places, it was even banned from the radio.

"My idea about songs is that once you write them, you have very little say in their life afterward. It's a lot like having a baby. You conceive a song, deliver it, and then give it as good a start as you can. After that, it's on its own. People will take it any way they want to take it."

"Brand New Key" broke on American radio in October 1971 and reached the top of the charts in December. For nearly four months, confused record buyers flooded the stores asking for "The Roller Skate Song," "I've Got a Brand New Pair of Roller Skates," and even "The Bicycle Song." Fortunately, all finally were steered to the right record.

"I used to love singing 'Brand New Key,'" said Melanie, "at first. It had great shock value, dropped in the middle of one of my concerts. I'd be singing along about Suffering and the Trials of Man, and then suddenly, 'I've got a brand-new pair of roller skates. . . .' It had a great effect. After it became a hit, though, the fun kind of wore off, at least for me. Some things, I think, are better left a surprise."

Without You

NILSSON

Harry Edward Nilsson was born in Bushwick, a tough neighborhood in Brooklyn, New York. In the early fifties, his family moved to California, where Harry began to get into rock music. After high school, he started work as a computer supervisor at the First National Bank of Van Nuys. In his free time, he wrote songs, came up with commercial jingles, and sang demos for music publishers. Once his voice was heard, off camera, singing on an episode of "I Spy."

He got his first real break from producer Phil Spector, who had the Ronettes record two Nilsson songs. After that, other artists began to use his material, including the Turtles, the Yardbirds, Blood, Sweat and Tears, Rick Nelson, Lulu, Herb Alpert, Glen Campbell, the New Christy Minstrels, Jack Jones, and Harry Belafonte. One day, after hearing the Monkees sing his "Cuddly Toy" on the radio, Nilsson decided to make music his full-time occupation.

In 1967, he signed with RCA and put out the LP *Pandemonium Shadow Show.* It used twenty voices, all his, and featured "You Can't Do That," an eleven-song montage of Beatle tunes. John Lennon heard it and immediately called Nilsson his "favorite American singer."

His second album was *Aerial Ballet,* titled after his grandparents' turn-of-the-century circus act. On it was "Everybody's Talkin'," which became his first hit in the fall of 1969. The song, written by Fred Neil, was used on the soundtrack of *Midnight Cowboy.* Nilsson had also written a tune for the movie, but it was rejected by the film's producers. Instead, Nilsson released it as a follow-up single, and "I Guess the Lord Must Be in New York City" became his second hit.

In 1971, Nilsson wrote the story and songs for an animated TV special, "The Point." It was the story of Oblio, a little boy banished to the Pointless

Forest because his round head made him different. From that soundtrack came Nilsson's third hit, "Me and My Arrow," which was later rewritten into a TV commercial for Plymouth Arrow automobiles.

And then came the big time—Nilsson's first number-one record. He ventured to England for a whole new tone and feel to his music, and met up with producer Richard Perry. The two began to map out an LP, which came to be known as *Nilsson Schmilsson.* Almost immediately, Richard came up with the first song—a tune he'd found on the first Badfinger album. Group members Pete Ham and Tom Evans had written "Without You," and Richard was certain it would be an excellent tune for Nilsson to record. Harry wasn't quite so sure, and it wasn't until the middle of their sessions that he agreed to give it a try.

"It was a different record for its time," Richard recalled. "It was a big ballad with a heavy backbeat, and although many artists have cut songs like it since, no one was doing it then. It has a very romantic feel, and you know who was playing piano on that? It was Gary Wright, and that was years before he hit it big with 'Dream Weaver.' "

"Without You" was released as a single in December 1971 and spent four weeks at the top of the charts that February. In March, Nilsson received an RIAA Gold Disc Award, for sales surpassing one million copies. Soon after that, he also picked up a Grammy, for Best Male Pop Vocal Performance. "Without You" itself was nominated for Record of the Year and *Nilsson Schmilsson* for Album of the Year.

That LP also produced Nilsson's next couple of hits, "Jump into the Fire," and "Cocoanut," both in 1972. Later in the year, Nilsson had another hit, "Spaceman," on which he was joined for the first time by Ringo Starr.

In 1974, Ringo and Nilsson made a movie together, *Son of Dracula,* which featured "Without You," "Jump into the Fire," and a new hit single, "Daybreak."

One oddity about Nilsson can be traced to his amazing studio wizardry. He has a three-octave vocal range and for that reason sings nearly all the parts on all his records. The final effect would be almost impossible to duplicate live, so Nilsson has never tried. When asked when he'll give a concert performance, Nilsson just shrugs and says, "I don't know."

Alone Again (Naturally)

GILBERT O'SULLIVAN

*T*he Beatles touched many lives in the early sixties, including that of Raymond Edward O'Sullivan, an Irish-born art student living in England. After being inspired by their music, he junked his major and talked his mother into buying him a piano. He began to practice at home, but played so loud (he still breaks notes) that his mother made him move the piano out into the garden shed. Before long, he was writing and arranging his own songs, and he found work in a number of local bands.

After college, Ray headed for the bright lights of London, but ended up in the mail room of a large department store. He wouldn't give up, though, and at night made tapes, which he sent out to anyone who would listen. On a rainy Sunday in 1969, one found its way to Gordon Mills, the manager of Tom Jones and Englebert Humperdinck. Gordon liked what he heard and set Ray up in a small bungalow, just down the road from his own house. In order to make his new protégé feel right at home, he also trucked in all of Ray's personal possessions, which included, among other things, four pianos and a giant collection of ancient bus tokens.

At that time, Ray was a rather eccentric dresser. He was nearly twenty-three years old, yet he looked like a ten-year-old schoolboy. He wore shorts cut off at the knee, shirts with upturned collars, and a funny little cap that was far too small for him. Gordon changed all that, putting Ray into a letterman's sweater, complete with a capital *G* (this idea came from an old Jerry Lewis movie), and getting him to grow sideburns. Gordon also wanted Ray to change his name. Reluctantly, he decided to adapt the names of the popular nineteenth-century operettists Gilbert and Sullivan.

In 1970, Gilbert O'Sullivan released his first single, "Nothing Rhymed," which became a number-one record in England. A couple more hits followed, and then came the song that established his name on both sides of the Atlantic—"Alone Again (Naturally)."

"Everyone wants to know if it's an autobiographical song," said Gilbert, "based on my father's early death [when Ray was only eleven]. Well, the fact of the matter is, I didn't know my father very well, and he wasn't a good father anyway. He didn't treat my mother very well."

"Alone Again (Naturally)" was first released in the States in the summer of 1972 and first caught fire in Philadelphia. Before long, it had sold more than three million copies and earned three Grammy Award nominations (Best Male Pop Vocal Performance, Song of the Year, and Record of the Year). In his native Ireland, Gilbert was voted Top International Singer of 1972, and in England, he was named Songwriter of the Year by the Songwriters' Guild of Great Britain. UPI also offered an award, but it's doubtful that Gilbert

accepted. They called him "the worst potential influence on the direction of pop music since Tiny Tim." They gave his record their "Schlock Rock Trophy" of the year.

Gilbert went on to score one other platinum single in 1972, "Clair," his ode to the young daughter of his manager, Gordon Mills. The next year there were three more good sellers: "Out of the Question," "Get Down," and "Ooh Baby." After that, though, success seemed to elude him. "It was like being on a conveyor belt," said O'Sullivan, "and suddenly stopping halfway there." He tried several other numbers, but nothing else would click. By the end of the decade, he had stopped recording completely.

"Show business," said O'Sullivan, "is the phoniest, most ridiculous business in the world." Nevertheless, in the early eighties, Gilbert began a slow comeback, by signing with Epic Records. "Writing music is all I live for, and everything else comes a poor second."

American Pie

DON McLEAN

According to his parents, Don McLean knew more than one hundred songs by the time he was two years old. Born and raised in New Rochelle, New York, he suffered from asthma, which limited his sports play. Instead, he turned to music, and became a fan of Little Richard and Buddy Holly.

"Buddy was the person who made me learn the guitar," recalled Don. "To me, he had a certain energy, and I loved the way he played. I knew I was going to make a living at music for the simple reason that I didn't want to have to wear a suit or take a day job."

For a brief time, Don did hold down daytime employment as a paper boy, at age twelve. Later, he would mention that fact in the opening lyrics of "American Pie."

While in high school, Don developed an interest in native American music, especially instrumentals that he could play on the guitar or banjo. He performed at parties, and after graduation, started to work the folk club circuit. Don was quickly accepted by such veterans as Josh White, Fred Hellerman, and Pete Seeger, and in 1967, began writing songs.

In 1970, Don put several tunes on tape and went shopping for a label deal. He was turned down by thirty-seven companies before signing with Media Arts. They released his first LP, *Tapestry,* and a single from it, "Castles in the Air." Both were flops.

Media Arts was bought out by United Artists, and Don was added to the UA roster. Shortly thereafter, he began work on "American Pie." It was a slice of what he'd been thinking about for ten years, and was conceived as a rousing encore to his live show.

"That song didn't just happen," said Don. "It grew out of my experiences. 'American Pie' was part of my process of self-awakening; a mystical trip into my past."

Don explained how he came to be a spokesman for the suburban middle class. "I try to create music that represents me—where I came from and who I am. I'll sing about my experiences, growing up white and middle class in New Rochelle."

Don called his song a complicated parable, open to different interpretations. "People ask me if I left the lyrics open to ambiguity. Of course I did. I wanted to make a whole series of complex statements. The lyrics had to do with the state of society at the time."

In the late sixties and early seventies, Don was obsessed with what he called "the death of America"—the loss of many things he believed in while growing up. "In that sense, 'American Pie' was a very despairing song. In another, though, it was very hopeful. Pete Seeger told me he saw it as a song in which people were saying something. They'd been fooled, they'd been hurt, and it wasn't going to happen again. That's a good way to look at it—a hopeful way."

"American Pie" was released in November 1971, and moved up the charts faster than any other UA record in history. It reached number one in January 1972, and stayed on the hit parade for nearly four months. It sold more than three million copies as a single, five million as an album.

Don followed his hit with a ballad, "Vincent." On the flip side was "Castles in the Air." Both sides became radio staples in 1972, as did another song, "Driedel." In 1973, Don appeared at L.A.'s Troubadour Club before a packed house, including singer Lori Lieberman. Her experience of watching Don perform "American Pie" inspired the biggest hit of that year, "Killing Me Softly with His Song." Don then faded from public view, only to stage a comeback in 1981 with "Cryin'."

1973

SALES OF QUADROPHONIC music doubled in 1973, the first year overall record sales topped the $1.4 billion mark. Pablo Cruise, Abba, and Bad Company took shape; the Everly Brothers and Bread broke up, and Frank Sinatra came out of retirement. Elton John organized his Rocket Record label, Stevie Wonder was hurt in an auto crash, and Fabian posed nude for *Playgirl* magazine. The Watkins Glen Rock Festival was heard by six hundred thousand fans. In California, a man named Roger English set a new twisting record: 102 hours, 28 minutes, and 37 seconds. Another fellow, Jerry Cammarata, set a record for solo singing: seventy-five hours in a bathtub in the back of a truck. Rita Coolidge married Kris Kristofferson, Elvis Presley got divorced, and so did Lulu, who split from Maurice Gibb of the Bee Gees. "Boogie Woogie Bugle Boy" was revived by Bette Midler; she reached number one

on Mr. Blackwell's annual list of the ten worst dressed women (number ten was David Bowie). "Don Kirshner's Rock Concert" premiered on NBC; Bobby Goldsboro got his own TV series, and so did Helen Reddy and Bobby Darin (who died on December 20). Besides Mr. Darin, we also lost gospel singer Clara Ward, big band baritone Vaughn Monroe, Paul Williams (of the Temptations), Gram Parsons (of the Byrds), Hugo Winterhalter, Alan Sherman, and Jim Croce. "Money" became the first pop hit for Pink Floyd, while in San Francisco, KSFX broke Dobie Gray's "Drift Away" by playing it continuously for eight and a half hours. It was 1973—the year that Dr. Hook and the Medicine Show landed on the cover of *Rolling Stone*, after recording their second million-seller, "The Cover of *Rolling Stone*."

It was a milestone in entertainment—the fruition of a year-long dream of Colonel Tom Parker—and regarded as Elvis's most memorable performance. **The Aloha Satellite Show** was a benefit concert, telecast from Honolulu and beamed by Globcom satellite to a worldwide audience estimated at over one and half *billion.* Twenty-eight European countries watched via a Eurovision simulcast; in America, NBC carried the show in a ninety-minute version on April 4. Elvis was seen live in prime time in Australia, Korea, New Zealand, South Vietnam, and the Philippines; in Japan, he broke all Japanese television records, capturing an incredible ninety-eight percent share of the audience. It was the most expensive entertainment special ever staged, costing $2.5 million, $1 million of which went to Elvis himself. Days after the concert, RCA issued a two-record quadrophonic LP version simultaneously around the globe. Elvis was then thirty-eight years old.

On February 2, NBC premiered "The Midnight Special," network television's first regularly scheduled foray into late late night programming (it ran Fridays from 1 to 2:30 A.M.). The first emcee of this ninety-minute rock music show was Helen Reddy; various guest hosts followed until she returned on a "permanent" basis in 1975 (she left again after a couple of seasons). Over the years, hundreds of performers, such as **Sam and Dave** were showcased. Wolfman Jack was the announcer; the title theme was specially recorded by Johnny Rivers as a variation on his 1965 hit.

Teen culture circa 1962 was celebrated in ***American Graffiti,*** a movie with literally nonstop oldies on the soundtrack (**Wolfman Jack** played the deejay). Rock 'n roll history was also the backdrop for *That'll Be the Day* (with David Essex, Ringo Starr, and Keith Moon) and *Let the Good Times Roll* (with Chuck Berry, Little Richard, and Jerry Lee Lewis). Ritchie Havens was seen in *Catch My Soul,* Jimi Hendrix in *Hendrix,* T. Rex in *Born to Boogie,* and Melanie in *Glastonbury Faire. Wattstax* captured, in concert, Isaac Hayes, the Emotions, Johnny Taylor, and the Staple Singers. And Kris Kristofferson starred in *Pat Garret and Billy the Kid,* the picture that marked the acting debut of Bob Dylan.

The Allman Brothers Band—"six enlightened rogues," according to leader Duane Allman—was formed in Jacksonville, Florida in 1969. Despite the loss of Duane and bassist Berry Oakley in separate motorcycle accidents, the group continued to build a strong following, peaking in 1973. It took only three weeks that year for their album *Brothers and Sisters* to reach number one and spawn a chart-topping single, "Ramblin' Man." The remaining Allman brother, Gregg, also put out a solo LP in 1973, *Laid Back,* which included the hit "Midnight Rider." But success came too strong and too fast; after five gold albums, the band broke up amid chaos in 1976.

Formed in 1952, **Gladys Knight and the Pips** became hitmakers in 1961 with the release of "Every Beat of My Heart"—on three different labels simultaneously. In 1967, they joined Motown, and almost immediately recorded that label's best-selling single, "I Heard It Through the Grapevine." Despite frequent hits in the late sixties and early seventies, GK&TP never managed to rise above second-class status at Motown, and switched labels to Buddah in 1973. The experts called it "professional suicide," but it was a godsend for Gladys and the group. They wound up with several albums and five big 45s issued by one company or the other. In 1974, the momentum continued, as Gladys Knight and the Pips became the most successful recording act of the year.

THE TOP 40

1. Tie A Yellow Ribbon Round the Ole Oak Tree, *Dawn*
2. Bad, Bad Leroy Brown, *Jim Croce*
3. Crocodile Rock, *Elton John*
4. My Love, *Paul McCartney and Wings*
5. Let's Get It On, *Marvin Gaye*
6. Touch Me in the Morning, *Diana Ross*
7. Delta Dawn, *Helen Reddy*
8. Playground in My Mind, *Clint Holmes*
9. Killing Me Softly with His Song, *Roberta Flack*
10. Me and Mrs. Jones, *Billy Paul*
11. Will It Go Round in Circles, *Billy Preston*
12. Brother Louie, *Stories*
13. The Night the Lights Went Out in Georgia, *Vicki Lawrence*
14. Drift Away, *Dobie Gray*
15. Half Breed, *Cher*
16. You're So Vain, *Carly Simon*
17. Shambala, *Three Dog Night*
18. Love Train, *O'Jays*
19. That Lady, *Isley Brothers*
20. Why Me, *Kris Kristofferson*
21. Loves Me Like a Rock, *Paul Simon*
22. Pillow Talk, *Sylvia*
23. Say, Has Anybody Seen My Sweet Gypsy Rose, *Dawn*
24. Superstition, *Stevie Wonder*
25. Clair, *Gilbert O'Sullivan*
26. Rocky Mountain High, *John Denver*
27. Last Song, *Edward Bear*
28. Midnight Train to Georgia, *Gladys Knight and the Pips*
29. Frankenstein, *Edgar Winter Group*
30. Stuck in the Middle with You, *Stealers Wheel*
31. Little Willy, *Sweet*
32. You Are the Sunshine of My Life, *Stevie Wonder*
33. Danny's Song, *Anne Murray*
34. We're an American Band, *Grand Funk Railroad*
35. Right Place Wrong Time, *Dr. John*
36. Wildflower, *Skylark*
37. The Morning After, *Maureen McGovern*
38. Rockin' Pneumonia and the Boogie Woogie Flu, *Johnny Rivers*
39. Oh, Babe, What Would You Say, *Hurricane Smith*
40. Natural High, *Bloodstone*

Steely Dan was one of the few studio-based groups that avoided derision by reviewers and fans. They remained critical favorites throughout their existence, despite a dearth of live performances. Steely Dan had a powerful, intricate sound—a unique blending of pop, rock, and jazz textures. College friends Walter Becker and Donald Fagen were the founding members; they had spent time together on the road in the backing band of Jay and the Americans and formed Steely Dan in 1972. Their first album, *Can't Buy a Thrill,* featured two 1973 singles: "Do It Again" and "Reeling in the Years." Later LPs included the hits "Rikki Don't Lose That Number" (1974), "Peg" (1977), "Deacon Blues" (1978) and "Hey Nineteen" (1980). In 1981, Becker and Fagen abandoned the Steely Dan concept in favor of solo projects.

THE TOP 10 LPs

1. The World Is a Ghetto, *War*
2. Talking Book, *Stevie Wonder*
3. Dark Side of the Moon, *Pink Floyd*
4. No Secrets, *Carly Simon*
5. They Only Come Out at Night, *Edgar Winter Group*
6. Lady Sings the Blues, *Original Soundtrack*
7. Rocky Mountain High, *John Denver*
8. The Captain and Me, *Doobie Brothers*
9. Seventh Sojourn, *Moody Blues*
10. Diamond Girl, *Seals and Crofts*

Me and Mrs. Jones

BILLY PAUL

Born and raised in Philadelphia, Paul Williams began his singing career at the age of eleven, thanks to a neighborhood friend by the name of Bill Cosby. It was Cosby who helped the young man land a singing spot on WPEN, which led to a string of local radio appearances. Listening at home to his family's collection of 78s, Paul began to develop a vocal style that would eventually incorporate traces of jazz, R&B, and pop.

"That's how I really got indoctrinated into music," he recalled. "My mother was always buying and collecting records. She would buy everything from *Jazz at the Philharmonic* to Nat King Cole."

As the young man grew, so did his interest in music. Seeking to increase his technical skills, he attended Temple University, West Philadelphia Music School, and Granoff Music School. Before too long, he was appearing in local clubs—and discovered that he had to change his name, to avoid confusion with another Paul Williams, who was then singing lead with the Temptations.

As Billy Paul, he soon became an underground phenomenon in Philadelphia. Switching from rock to pop to soul ballads, he began getting national recognition and turned up in concert with Dinah Washington, Nina Simone, Miles Davis, the Impressions, Sammy Davis, Jr., and Roberta Flack.

Billy formed a trio and cut his first record, "Why Am I," for Jubilee Records, before being drafted into the armed services. After his release came a quick stop with the Flamingoes and a brief stand-in for one of the Blue Notes with Harold Melvin. (More than one reviewer described Billy's "saxophonic baritone" as resembling that of the Blue Notes' Teddy Pendergrass.)

His first album, *Feelin' Good at the Cadillac Club,* was a commercial flop but did mark the beginning of his

relationship with the writing and production team of Kenny Gamble and Leon Huff. They put the LP together and released it on their own Gamble label. They also assembled his second album, *Ebony Woman,* which bombed on their Neptune label. In the early seventies, Kenny and Leon formed another record company, Philadelphia International, and one of the first artists they signed was their old friend Billy Paul. His first LP for the new firm was entitled *Going East,* and it, too, went right down the drain. By that time the year was 1972.

Billy's fourth album was designed to show him off as "an all-round entertainer." In fact, it was called *360 Degrees of Billy Paul.* Among the tracks was a tune that Gamble and Huff had helped write—a soul ballad about the touchy theme of adultery.

"I knew that, 'Me and Mrs. Jones' would be a hit even before it was released," said Billy. "It's a song that everybody can relate to."

Not everyone agreed with that philosophy—in fact, a number of

stations refused to play the record because it discussed an "immoral" theme without condemning it. Regardless, "Me and Mrs. Jones" became one of the largest-selling singles of the year, with sales topping four and a half million copies.

Billy Paul went on to win a Grammy Award for "Me and Mrs. Jones," for the Best Male Rhythm and Blues Performance. Later, it was voted Song of the Year at the Second Annual Soul and Blues Night in Los Angeles.

"Me and Mrs. Jones" peaked on the charts in December 1972, yet remained a strong seller for another two months. Then, in April, the next Billy Paul single was released, and *it* nearly killed his career. Radio program directors recoiled, fearing community reaction to the mere title alone. For that reason, "Am I Black Enough for You?" received almost no air play and faded in five weeks. It took until the spring of 1974 for Billy to score another top-forty hit, and even then, only barely. Its ironic title: "Thanks for Saving My Life."

Killing Me Softly with His Song

ROBERTA FLACK

*I*n 1971, Roberta Flack proved that she could be a hitmaker with "You've Got a Friend," her duet with Donny Hathaway. (It grazed the top thirty.) In 1972, she proved that she could be a star, by cutting the Grammy-winning Record of the Year—"The First Time Ever I Saw Your Face." A riveting love song, it became a number-one hit.

Later in the year, she had another million-seller, "Where Is the Love," again sung with Donny Hathaway. "My first two albums were gold, and they were selling worldwide," recalled Roberta. "They'd been on the charts fifty-some weeks by that time.

"I got on a flight from L.A. to New York, and on the plane was in-flight entertainment—eight different chan-nels of music you could listen to on a personal headset. I ran down the list of song titles on this one channel and got to 'Killing Me Softly with His Song.' I thought, 'Hmm, that's differ-ent,' and instantly plugged in. I said, 'I'm gonna wait for that,' and sat back and waited for it to come on. And when I heard it, I freaked. I absolutely freaked. When I got to New York, I went to the hotel and called Quincy Jones. I said, 'Tell me how to find the guys that wrote this song—Charles Fox and Norman Gimbel.'

"I got it from Charles Fox that they wrote the song, in its final form, based on the feelings of Lori Lieberman. At first, the tune was called 'Killing Me Softly with His Blues.' Similar, but not really the same song. Then Lori went and had the experience of seeing Don McLean perform at the Troubadour."

The song that moved Lori so much was "American Pie." Fox and Gimbel completed their tune and then had Lori record it for Capitol Records. Although it did get "air play" in the sky, Lori's version did not sell at all on the ground.

Roberta previewed "Killing Me Softly" live, without rehearsal, at a concert held in L.A.'s Greek Theater. Afterward, Quincy Jones, the other act on the bill, leaned over and said, "Don't you ever sing that song again until you get it recorded. Don't you know that that the crowd is full of singers looking for material?"

Roberta then went into the studio with producer Joel Dorn and arran-ger Eumir Deodato (himself to become famous within weeks, with the hit instrumental "2001"). They released "Killing Me Softly" in late January 1973, and within a month, it had been certified gold by the RIAA. The song took just four weeks to reach number one, and it remained a good seller for more than a dozen more.

Over fourteen months were spent crafting an album around, and named after, "Killing Me Softly with His Song." When it finally came out, it included a small follow-up hit, "Jesse." After that, Roberta "retired" for a while and studied record production, studio technique, and classical music. When she returned, it was with the LP *Feel Like Makin' Love.* The title track from that album became a number-one million-seller in the fall of 1974.

Roberta's next three years were spent, again, out of the spotlight. She came back in 1978 with her fifth gold single, "The Closer I Get to You" (another duet with Donny Hathaway). A few months later, there was one more small hit, "If Ever I See You Again."

"Hits are important," said Roberta, "because they mean that you are successful at what you're trying to do. A hit is a sign that people have accepted what you're trying to share with them. And the fact that you get paid for them at all is fantastic." Her hopes, though, for more hits with Donny Hathaway were dashed on January 13, 1979, when he was killed in a fall from his hotel window.

Roberta, however, vowed to march on. "Ten years from now, I expect to be alive," she said. "I expect to be healthy. I expect to be a mother. I expect to be everything that I want to be. It'll take all those things and more for me to be truly happy. I require a lot out of life."

Playground in My Mind

CLINT HOLMES

I was born in England," said Clint Holmes, "but grew up in Farnham, New York. My mother was a British opera singer. In fact, everybody in my family sang. When people ask me when I decided to become a singer, my answer is that it was never a conscious decision. It was always something I did. As far as how I got into it professionally, I was in the army chorus in the mid-sixties as part of my military career. When I got out, I started playing little clubs and kind of sang around until I got a following and became a local name in Washington, D.C. An agent from New York saw me, and I began working on a bigger scale, and things got better and better.

"One night I was singing in the Bahamas, on Paradise Island, Nassau. Paul Vance, who had produced Johnny Mathis, walked by the club and heard me do my little comic impression of Mathis. He laughed, came in, and saw the rest of the show. Afterward, he came up to me and said that he and his partner, Lee Pockriss, had a couple of songs and they were looking for a singer. Paul thought that I would be terrific. So, when I got back home two or three weeks later, I went to see them and listen to what they had.

"The one that they were real high on was 'Playground in My Mind.' Paul had four kids, and his inspiration came from watching them play. I thought it was a cute song. I didn't have, of course, the entire production concept that they had in mind.

"The other song was 'There's No Future in My Future,' which honestly I liked a whole lot better. I told them so, and then we agreed to cut the two sides and see which one turned out better.

"The biggest memory I have of recording 'Playground' was when we tried to match vocals with Paul's son, Phillip, who was the little boy's voice on the record. He was eight or nine years old at the time, and not a professional singer by any means. I put my vocal down and then we tried to have him sing along with me. Eventually, we had to reverse it and have me sing along with him. I remember having to sing softer and softer to try to get some kind of vocal blend. I was so afraid of overpowering him.

" 'Playground' was recorded in May 1972 and released by Epic in June. It got played in a few places, but for all intents and purposes, the record flopped, and we went on to other things.

"Then in November a programer in Wichita, Kansas, put it on as a Christmas record. He thought it had a Christmasy sound. The record had never made any kind of impact, but now it was getting really heavy phone response. It spread all over the Midwest. A few weeks later, I got a call from Epic in New York. Don Ellis, the head of A&R, said, 'We've got to get you out to L.A. to finish an album. Your record's gonna hit the Hot 100 this week, and it looks like it could make the top forty.' I didn't even know what record he was talking about. I was amazed.

"By springtime I was in New Orleans and 'Playground' was a solid hit. Everywhere I went, I heard that song being played on the radio. Don Ellis had said he thought it had a *chance* at the top twenty. He was *certain* it wouldn't go to top five—and then it wound up as number one. By June, it was a million-seller.

"You know, in some sense 'Playground' hurt me. It branded me as a novelty singer because I didn't follow it up with something more substantial. We recorded another song in a similar vein, which I did not want to do. It was called 'Shiddle-ee-Dee,' and the very title tells you what the song was like—a bomb.

"Now I'm trying to create a new image, which is why I don't do the song in my act anymore. 'Playground' was an excellently made record, but it could have been almost anybody singing it. It didn't have to be me; therefore, it was not a career-making record. It didn't bear the stamp of Clint Holmes. I think that's why, even today, a lot of people remember the song but not the fellow who sang it."

Delta Dawn

HELEN REDDY

Her backers called her "the female Frank Sinatra"; her critics "the hip Julie Andrews." Alice Cooper named her "the Queen of Housewife Rock"—a definition of which she highly approved.

Helen Reddy was born in Melbourne, Australia, the daughter of show business parents. In 1966, she won a television talent contest, and was sent to America in search of fame and fortune. Within a few months, she'd met and married an assistant mailroom boy, Jeff Wald, who became her manager. Twenty-seven labels rejected Helen before she was finally signed by Capitol Records in 1970.

Her first charted song, "I Don't Know How to Love Him," was one Helen never liked, and agreed to record as a B side for one of her singles. However, Jeff, armed with a credit card and a phone, worked eighteen hours a day, phoning radio stations, pleading for air play. His efforts turned "I Don't Know How to Love Him" into a top-twenty hit in the spring of 1971.

In 1972, Helen wrote a feminist anthem, "I Am Woman," which became a number-one record and earned her a Grammy. Her next single, "Peaceful," was also a hit. And then came the high water mark of her career: an enigmatic number, "Delta Dawn."

"It's a song about women's liberation," explained co-composer Alex Harvey. "That was a big deal at the time, and I guess it still is.

"I like images a lot, and mystery, and I think the mystery of 'Delta Dawn' is what pulled it together. The song basically came out of a feeling that I had for my mother, but I'm not really sure.

"I cut the song in Nashville for my first Capitol album. One of the background singers on that session was Tracy Nelson, who had her own band, Mother Earth. She got booked at the Bottom Line in New York City, and added 'Delta Dawn' to her act. A fan of hers, Bette Midler, heard the tune and was hypnotized by it. She came every night and learned the song exactly the way Tracy did it. Bette then began to perform the song at the Continental Baths in New York. It got an immediate reaction. She sang the song three different times on the Johnny Carson show.

"Billy Sherrill, who worked for Columbia-Epic, had a thirteen-year-old girl named Tanya Tucker under contract. He was going to produce her, but hadn't yet chosen any material. Once he heard Bette do 'Delta Dawn' on TV, he knew the song could be a smash. So, right after the release of Bette's first album, *The Divine Miss M,* he put out a country version by Tanya.

"Well, that single began to take off. Then, Tom Catalano, who was producing Barbra Streisand, decided that Barbra could cut 'Delta Dawn' for the pop market and have a big hit. In her absence, he cut an instrumental backing track, brought her down to the studio, and then played it for her. She didn't like the tune, and refused to put her voice on it. So, Wally Schuster—a song plugger for United Artists Music—called up Jeff Wald and asked if Helen might be interested. They made a deal, Helen put her voice on the track, and the rest was history. Helen's single took off immediately in the summer of 1973.

"I think 'Delta Dawn' became a hit primarily because of all the exposure that it was given on the "Tonight Show." The song was rightfully Bette Midler's hit. It was her image, and would have been a great image builder for her, especially in light of the mystique that she carries around with her today. The Reddy record came out two days before Bette was to release her version as a 45. Bette's record then had to be flipped, making 'Boogie Woogie Bugle Boy' the A side, and her 'Delta Dawn' was forgotten."

Helen Reddy went on in the seventies to solidify her position as one of the most successful female hitmakers of the decade. Later in 1973 she scored with "Leave Me Alone (Ruby Red Dress)"; and in 1974, "Keep On Singing," "You and Me Against the World" and "Angie Baby." In 1975 there were "Emotion," "Bluebird," "Ain't No Way to Treat a Lady" and "Somewhere in the Night." Her last big singles were "I Can't Hear You No More"/"Music Is My Life" (1976) and "You're My World" (1977).

Touch Me in the Morning

DIANA ROSS

Diana Ross was one of six kids who slept in the same room, three to a bed, with a kerosene jar lighted to keep the insects away. Her dad worked two jobs in order to keep the family going. Diana escaped her ghetto surroundings by immersing herself in music: singing in the church choir, and by starring in little shows on the back porches of her friends' homes.

She often walked to school singing gospel or R&B songs, along with two neighbors, Mary Wilson and Florence Ballard. When Diana was fifteen, they became the Primettes, a sister group to the all-male Primes. Both acts sang frequently around the Detroit area, performing nights and on weekends. To earn extra money, the Primettes also took straight jobs—Diana in Hudson's Department Store, working as a cafeteria busgirl.

Once signed by Motown Records, the Primettes were renamed the Supremes, and went on to become that label's consummate commercial coup. Over a ten-year span, they racked up thirty-three top-forty hits— nineteen in the top ten; twelve of which reached number one. They performed in a gospel call-and-response pattern, set to a vibrant dance beat; and were sweetness, energy, and vulnerability all in one attractive package. Compared to other girl groups, such as the meek Shirelles or tough Ronettes, Mary, Flo and Diana came on as mature young women—respectable, but accessible to those who really cared. In person or on record, they epitomized the essence of Motown magic: slick, sophisticated soul, engineered with machine-like precision.

The Supremes' golden decade lasted from 1963 to 1972, but their musical world began to crumble long before that. On January 15, 1970, at the Frontier Hotel in Las Vegas, Diana bid farewell to the group and began her own solo career. When she did,

she took with her the attention of label president Berry Gordy, Jr., and thus all of Motown. The Supremes began to falter, even though they continued to turn out a number of exceptional records. Perhaps it was a little embarrassing that the group continued to have success without Diana, whose own career was floundering at that point. But whatever the reason, the Motown Record Corporation seemed to lose interest in the Supremes sometime in the early seventies.

Diana's debut solo single was "Reach Out and Touch," a song she had selected over heavy objections from Berry Gordy, Jr. In June of 1970, it peaked at number twenty. Next, she covered "Ain't No Mountain High Enough," first recorded by Marvin Gaye and Tammi Terrell in 1967. It turned out to be a number-one record for Diana in September 1970. After that, there were four 45s in 1971: "Remember Me," "Reach Out I'll Be There," "Surrender," and "I'm Still Waiting," each one placing progressively lower on the charts.

In 1972, there were no hits at all, as Diana turned her attention toward motion pictures. She made *Lady Sings the Blues,* co-starring Billy Dee Williams, Richard Pryor, and James Callahan. It was a highly fictionalized biography of jazz singer Billie Holiday, and earned Diana an Academy Award nomination. One song from the soundtrack, "Good Morning Heartache," barely made the top forty in March 1973.

By that time, Diana had gone nearly three years without a really big hit. She needed one to reassert her position as a major recording artist, and to dwarf the continuing popularity of her old group. At Berry Gordy's direction, an aching ballad was written especially for her by Michael Masser and producer Ron Miller. It was "Touch Me in the Morning," released in May 1973.

The single took off in April, slowly

building through the summer until it peaked at number one in August. In all, it spent twenty-one weeks on the chart, longer than anything Diana had ever recorded, either by herself or with the Supremes.

It was a plaintive, longing, emotionally rich record—proof that Diana Ross still had it, after more than a decade as a superstar.

Let's Get It On

MARVIN GAYE

Marvin Gaye, Jr., began singing in his father's church in Washington, D.C., taking his first solos at the age of three. His dad encouraged him to vocalize and play organ, and at Cardoza High, Marvin joined the school band.

At seventeen, he enlisted in the air force. After his discharge, Marvin began his musical career in earnest, hoping to become a jazz singer in the mold of his idol, Nat King Cole. He joined a local group, the Rainbows, and later the Marquees, who were chosen by the leader of the Moonglows, Harvey Fuqua, to become the new Moonglows in 1958. Marvin played drums, piano, and sang with them for the next four years.

In 1962, the Moonglows were booked at a nightclub in Detroit. Marvin took the opportunity to entertain at a private party, and was observed by the president of Motown, Berry Gordy, Jr. Gordy persuaded Gaye to go solo, and offered him a contract as a session drummer. Marvin accepted, and was soon playing percussion behind the Miracles, Mary Wells, and others.

His fourth vocal single, "Stubborn Kind of Fellow," was a regional hit in November 1962. After that came "Hitchhike" (top thirty), "Pride and Joy" (top ten) and "Can I Get a Witness," all in 1963. In 1964, there were "You're a Wonderful One," "Try It Baby," "Baby Don't You Do It" and "How Sweet It Is (to Be Loved by You)." He also hit with some duets: "What's the Matter with You Baby" and "Once Upon a Time," both with Mary Wells.

His streak continued into 1965 with "I'll Be Doggone," "Pretty Little Baby" and "Ain't That Peculiar." In 1966 there was "One More Heartache" and in '67 "Your Unchanging Love." The same year, he sang with Kim Weston and Tammi Terrell, who died of a brain tumor in 1970.

Marvin was devastated by Tammi's death and went into a self-imposed exile from live concerts. In the interim, more of their duets became major sellers: "If I Could Build My Whole World Around You," "Ain't Nothing Like the Real Thing," "You're All I Need to Get By," "Keep On Lovin' Me Honey" (all 1968) and "Good Lovin' Ain't Easy to Come By" (1969). Concurrently, Gaye hit the charts by himself with "You," "Chained," and his first number one, "I Heard It Through the Grapevine" (all 1968). In 1969 there were "Too Busy Thinking About My Baby" and "That's the Way Love Is"; in 1970, right after Tammi's passing, he sang "The End of Our Road."

In 1971, Marvin signed a new Motown contract. He immediately cut an LP entitled *What's Going On,* a clear break from his previous three-minute dance-rock 45s. Motown executives were skeptical of its commercial potential, but it turned out to be the best-selling album of Marvin's career to that point. Three gold singles came from it: the title track, "Mercy Mercy Me" and "Inner City Blues."

Gaye's next assignment was a soundtrack: *Trouble Man.* He had by then appeared in two motion pictures: *The Ballad of Andy Crocker* in 1969 and *Chrome and Hot Leather* in 1971. The title tune from *Trouble Man* became a top-ten hit in January 1973.

And then came "Let's Get It On."

Reviewers were blown away by the work. "Perhaps the best overtly sensual music anyone in rock has ever made," wrote one critic. "The sexiest record Motown has ever produced." "Irresistible." "Pure eroticism," said others. "Another magnum opus." "One of the most joyous celebrations of sex ever recorded."

"Let's Get It On" was another complete departure for Marvin and one of the largest-selling singles in Motown history. It sold two million copies in six weeks and stayed on the charts for more than four months, selling in excess of three million copies.

Gaye also hit in 1973 with "Come Get to This" and "You're a Special Part of Me," the latter a duet with Diana Ross. In 1974, Gaye and Ross returned with "My Mistake." Marvin tried to repeat his erotic success that year with "You Sure Love to Ball," but it bombed.

Marvin Gaye dubbed himself "Mr. Perfectionist," and for a while would perform for no less than $100,000 a night. "The only thing between me and Beethoven is time," he said in the mid-seventies.

In the spring of 1981, Marvin left for London, where he planned to live. L.A. was "a psychological hellhole," he noted, complaining that he wanted "more love and more respect as an artist" than he was getting on this side of the Atlantic. He also planned to spend some time at a home he owned in Senegal, West Africa, and start a record label there.

My Love
PAUL McCARTNEY AND WINGS

*I*magine what it must be like to have a romantic love ballad, written just for you, become one of the hottest-selling singles of the year. Well, to Linda Eastman McCartney, it happened not once, but three times—with two different songs—in three different decades.

The first time came when Linda's father, a New York attorney, introduced her to one of his clients, songwriter Jack Lawrence. She was a toddler, but inspiration enough for "Linda," a charming ballad recorded by big band crooner Buddy Clark. It was a million-seller in 1947, and sixteen years later, the song came back in rock 'n' roll form, as sung by Jan and Dean.

It was the sixties; Linda married a Princeton man and followed him to the University of Arizona. There he became immersed in graduate research, and Linda, lonely, took up photography to pass the time. Eventually, she got a divorce, returned to Manhattan, and found work as a receptionist for *Town & Country* magazine at $65 a week.

As part of her job, Linda opened mail, and one day she came across a photographer's pass to a Rolling Stones concert. She grabbed her camera, saw the show, attended the press party, and—incredibly—was the only "newsperson" admitted into the Stones' quarters. She walked away with a scoop, exclusive photographs, and a nickname given to her by the other reporters: "The Park Avenue Groupie." By 1967 she was "big enough" to arrange a meeting with Paul McCartney. She slipped him her phone number, he called, and a romance dreamed about by millions was on. After a whirlwind courtship, they were married on March 12, 1969.

The Beatles broke up a few months later; Paul was the first to leave and first to release a solo LP. That record, *McCartney,* included an early testament to his beloved bride, "The Lovely Linda."

"I remember John Lennon saying, 'I didn't think that was your taste in women,' " recalled Paul. "But it doesn't matter what your taste was for when your *wife* comes along, if it's someone you love. I never really had a home for a long time, and I started to realize that I wanted that kind of warmth. When you're eighteen you can sneer at such things, but once you turn thirty, you reconsider. Mind you, I could have said to John, 'Well, look at you. You must be joking.' But we all grow up, get older and wiser."

Paul's first solo single came out in the spring of 1971: "Another Day," backed with "Oh Woman Oh Why." Both sides made the top five. After that, he made a momentous decision: "about the craziest thing I could do," he admitted. He brought his wife—who had no previous musical experience—into the act.

"At first, Linda was terrified out of her mind," said Paul, "and picked on something silly. She *was* absolute rubbish you know, but has improved as a keyboards player. But then again you don't always form technical groups." Linda was given equal billing on Paul's next project, the LP *"Ram,"* and the number-one single that came from it, "Uncle Albert/ Admiral Halsey."

Next, the McCartneys formed Wings, by adding former Moody Blues member Denny Laine on guitar and session man Denny Seiwell on drums. Later, ex-Grease Band guitarist Henry McCullough joined up, although he left, along with Seiwell, after the group made their first tour of England.

Wings debuted in 1972 with "Give Ireland Back to the Irish," a political single immediately banned by the BBC. McCartney responded—tongue-in-cheek—by making their next 45 a nursery rhyme, "Mary Had a Little Lamb."

And then came "My Love."

Paul considered this tune to be one of his two best of the decade. It was a lush, syrupy valentine to his wife: "A smootchy ballad," as McCartney would say. His first single of the year, it was also the first release (and first number one) credited to Paul McCartney and Wings, the name they used in 1973 and 1974. Issued in mid-April 1973, it was certified a million-seller in less than three months.

"My Love" was the only 45 issued from *Red Rose Speedway,* Paul's fourth LP after leaving the Beatles. Both the album and single reached number one simultaneously in early June. Ironically, the record displaced by *Red Rose Speedway* was a Beatles compilation, "1967–1970." *Red Rose Speedway* was also notable for the Braille message embossed on the back of the jacket. Intended for Stevie Wonder, it read: "We love you, baby."

Crocodile Rock

ELTON JOHN

R eginald Kenneth Dwight began teaching himself to play the piano at the age of four. He got good grades at London's Royal Academy of Music, but wasn't entirely satisfied with the sound of the "classic masters." Then one day, his mom bought him copies of "Heartbreak Hotel" and Bill Haley's "ABC Boogie." "I couldn't believe how great they were," he grinned. "And from then on, rock 'n' roll took over." He soon left the academy, much preferring to stay home imitating Little Richard or Jerry Lee Lewis.

At thirteen, he put together his first band, the Corvettes, and two years later, helped form a backup band, Bluesology. It was then that he decided to change his name, because Reg Dwight "sounded too much like a laboratory assistant, or cement mixer, or something." He lifted "Elton" from Elton Dean, the sax man in Bluesology, and "John" from R&B singer Long John Baldry.

In 1967, Elton John answered an ad placed by Liberty Records. He was given an audition, but failed, due to "weak words in my songs." Liberty suggested that he get in touch with a lyricist, and teamed him with Bernie Taupin. For six months, the two collaborated entirely by mail—Elton writing music to fit Bernie's poetry. To supplement his income, Elton took a number of odd jobs: playing piano for the Hollies (on "He Ain't Heavy He's My Brother") and singing back-up for Tom Jones (on "Delilah" and "Daughter of Darkness").

Eventually, Elton and Bernie met face-to-face, and got a job together as staff songwriters for Dick James Music. Finally, one of the staff salesmen had the guts to tell them their work really stunk, and the only way they'd ever get anywhere was to write in their own natural style. The boys wholeheartedly agreed, and from then on, it was uphill.

In America, Elton's career was ignited on August 25, 1970, the night of a remarkable showcase performance at the Troubadour in Los Angeles. Many members of the pop press were there, and they quickly spread the word about "England's brilliant new superstar" (Bernie elected to remain in the background). That first U.S. album, *Elton John,* featured the hit "Your Song," which went top ten in January 1971.

The floodgates were open, and five more LPs were rapidly released:

Tumbleweed Connection, 11-17-70 (a radio soundtrack), *Friends* (a movie soundtrack), *Madman Across the Water,* and *Honky Chateau.* As his popularity snowballed, Elton took a few weeks out to record still another album—*Don't Shoot Me, I'm Only the Piano Player.* He cut it in Paris at the "Honky Chateau"—his name for the Chateau d'Herouville.

In the fall of 1972, EJ embarked on his most elaborate American tour. On it, he introduced a tune that some referred to as "the British answer to 'American Pie.' " It was Elton's distillation of his record collecting interest, and clearly, the most potent cut on his brand-new LP.

"Crocodile Rock" was a celebration, of sorts, of rock's earlier days, and in many respects echoed the sounds and styles of Elton's lifelong idols. From a construction standpoint, it was akin to early sixties records, such as those of Neil Sedaka. Elton gave it a carnival feel by playing the farfisa organ, strongly reminiscent of Del Shannon's "Runaway."

The story line concerns happy, carefree teenage years, as fictitious (at least in Elton's case) as the dance the song "recalls." "I had such a miserable time as a child and a teenager," said Elton, who spent much of his youth as a fat, lonely kid. "That's why I'm making up for it now. I regard myself as a teenager today, even though I'm in my mid-twenties."

"Crocodile Rock" was issued about two months ahead of the LP it came off, and broke in the U.S. in early December 1972. By March of '73, it was a million-seller, and the number-one single in America. Elton's record company had an extra reason to celebrate, as it was also their first release under a new name—MCA Records. With one swoop, both the label and the song were established in the marketplace.

Bad, Bad Leroy Brown

JIM CROCE

I never really thought of my neighborhood in South Philly as being a neighborhood," said Jim Croce. "It was more a state of mind. For people who aren't familiar with those kinds of places, it's a whole different thing. Like 42nd Street in New York City is a state of mind. I think that if 42nd Street were in China, they'd probably call it the Street of the Living Gargoyles. You see some very unusual people there, lurking in doorways. The people who live in phone booths are strange, too."

Jim Croce grew up in Philadelphia, watching his favorites perform on "American Bandstand."

"Certain groups really knocked me out—Fats Domino, the Coasters, and the Impressions. The things the Coasters used to do, their visual act, was something I could always get into. It was something you could see around the neighborhood, too. It was real.

"That music was really goodtime music. There wasn't any heavy message in the delivery and the subject matter was just 'stomp your feet, get up and have a good time, dance, laugh, and forget yourself.' It wasn't the morbid 'ain't it terrible' school of songwriting. The stuff just feels good when you listen to it; you feel like moving around. I think people want to hear goodtime music."

The music of Jim Croce expressed many emotions, and much of it was goodtime. It was also real—about ourselves, and characters we see on the street, everyday.

"Well, they're real people, and I think that anybody who's either traveled from one place to another or been in the service or worked, whether it's in a factory or an office building, will have seen the kind of people I sing about. 'Rapid Roy,' for example, with a pack of cigarettes wrapped up in his T-shirt sleeve."

The Croce hit streak began in 1972, with "You Don't Mess Around with Jim" and "Operator." Then, in 1973, he introduced his most famous character, "Bad, Bad Leroy Brown."

"I met him at Fort Dix, New Jersey. We were in lineman (telephone) school together. He stayed there about a week, and one evening he turned around and said he was really fed up and tired. He went AWOL, and then came back at the end of the month to get his pay check. They put handcuffs on him and took him away. Just to listen to him talk and see how 'bad' he was, I knew someday I was gonna write a song about him."

To emphasize the character even more, Jim described him in the lyrics as "meaner than a junkyard dog."

"Yeah, I spent about a year and a half driving those $29 cars, so I drove around a lot looking for a universal joint for a '57 Chevy panel truck or a transmission for a '51 Dodge. I got to know many junkyards well, and they all have those dogs in them. They all have either an axle tied around their necks or an old lawnmower to keep 'em at least slowed down a bit, so you have a decent chance of getting away from them."

"Bad, Bad Leroy Brown" was released in April 1973, and peaked at number one in July. It was still on the charts on September 20, the day Jim died in a plane crash in Natchitoches, Louisiana. He was thirty years old.

Tie a Yellow Ribbon Round the Ole Oak Tree

DAWN

By 1973, Tony Orlando and Dawn had come quite a way since their first hit, "Candida," three years before. They had become the second biggest seller of singles in America, without ever having made a major concert tour or appeared on a television show. England's *New Musical Express* voted them the Number One Vocal Group in Europe, and they were also named Most Popular Group in England, Italy, France, Germany, Australia, South America, and Japan. They had sold nine million records before their first live gig—at Carnegie Hall—and since that time had sold six million more.

Early in 1973, Tony and Dawn cut the single that was to become their all-time classic—"Tie a Yellow Ribbon Round the Ole Oak Tree."

The song was based on an actual incident that occurred aboard a southern bus bound for Miami. One of the passengers explained to the driver that he was just out of prison, having served three years for passing bad checks. In a letter to his wife, he had written that she didn't have to wait for him; but, if she was still interested, she could let him know by tying a yellow ribbon around the only oak tree in the city square. As the bus rolled down U.S. 17, nearing the man's hometown of White Oak, Georgia, the driver was asked to slow down so that all could see whether the ribbon was in place. To the man's tearful relief, it was. The driver pulled over and phoned the story in to the wire services, which spread it all over the country. Songwriters Irwin Levine and L. Russell Brown read it in the newspaper, then put together their million-selling ballad.

"Tie a Yellow Ribbon" was released by Bell in February 1973, and by April it was the number-one record in the country. In all, it spent more than five months on the charts and sold more than seven million copies. The song was so popular that over one hundred cover versions were cut by other artists, all around the world.

Tony Orlando and Dawn had another big hit in 1973: "Say, Has Anybody Seen My Sweet Gypsy Rose." After that, CBS called and offered the trio their own four-week summer show, which aired in July 1974. In the fall, "Steppin' Out" became a top-ten record for the group and in December, they returned to TV in a comedy-variety series that lasted for two full seasons. In 1975, there were three more big singles: "Look in My Eyes Pretty Woman," "He Don't Love You" (another number one), and "Mornin' Beautiful," the latter two songs on the Elektra label.

When asked to explain the group's secret of success, Tony said, "In our case, we like each other. That's number one. Number two, we have no intentions of breaking up. A lot of groups with a name like Tony Orlando and Dawn, Dion and the Belmonts, Diana Ross and the Supremes, it's inevitable to think that someday the leader will go off alone. In this case, I don't ever want to break up this group."

"The Tony Orlando and Dawn Rainbow Hour" was canceled on December 28, 1976; the group lasted just seven months more. On July 22, 1977, at the South Shore Music Circus in Cohasset, Massachusetts, Tony shocked the crowd—and his partners—by announcing his retirement from show business. He suffered a nervous breakdown on stage and spent the next six months in a New York psychiatric hospital. After his release, Tony began to pick up the pieces of his career—without Dawn.

As for "Tie a Yellow Ribbon," the song made a dramatic comeback of its own, eight years after being recorded. The yellow ribbon as a symbol of loyalty was a natural to express the nation's feelings for the fifty-two American hostages held in Iran, and when they returned after 444 days of captivity on January 20, 1981, the song was played throughout the land as a joyous homecoming theme.

At one time, **disco** was a kind of secret music, hidden behind the locked doors of certain private clubs in New York, L.A., and Europe. In the mid-seventies, disco became popularized, sanitized, merchandised, and internationally franchised. According to one estimate, there were about twenty thousand places in the U.S. that called themselves discos, and they ranged from the exclusive Studio 54 in New York City to tiny corner bars with a record player and a lot of imagination. Disco became an entire industry built around a peppy, dance-oriented kind of music that stressed a number of key features. Usually, it was brightly orchestrated with a high-stepping beat. The beat was all-important. The lyrics and melodies tended to be repetitive, even to the point of being mechanical, so as not to interfere with the dancers getting lost in their movements. It was escapist music, totally self-oriented, and Americans spent an estimated $8 billion dollars a year under those flashing lights. That figure, incidentally, was only for club admissions, food, and the beverages sold in discos. Clothing, sound and light equipment, and of course record sales, were on top of that.

DESPITE RISING COSTS, record sales were nearly five times what they'd been when Elvis arrived, and had nearly tripled since the Fab Four first broke in America. George Harrison was busy organizing his Dark Horse Records; John Lennon was tossed out of the Troubadour Club with Harry Nilsson for heckling the Smothers Brothers. Cass Elliot of the Mamas and Papas died in Nilsson's London apartment. (The same flat would later be the scene of Who drummer Keith Moon's death.) Other notable passings: Duke Ellington, Bobby Bloom, and Ivory Joe Hunter. Robbie McIntosh of the Average White Band died of poisoning at a party, nearly the entire group Chase perished in a plane crash, and we lost western star Tex Ritter. Tex's reading of "The Americans" was one of *three* versions of that radio editorial to chart during the year. Other singles included revivals of the Beach Boys' "Surfin' U.S.A." and Bill Haley's "Rock Around the Clock," a pop version of "The Lord's Prayer" by Sister Janet Mead, and a name-dropping music history review, "Life Is a Rock (But the Radio Rolled Me)," by Reunion. Danny Seraphine of Chicago opened a nightclub called "B. Ginnings"; the Grand Ole Opry settled into new quarters, and Connie Francis was raped in a motel room. Mac Davis, the Hudson Brothers, Bobbie Gentry, and Tony Orlando and Dawn each got a TV series; Dean Martin and the Partridge Family lost theirs. The Righteous Brothers got back together (for "Rock 'n' Roll Heaven"), the New Seekers split up, and Sonny and Cher were divorced. It was 1974—the year Jefferson Airplane became Jefferson Starship, and Dolly Parton began her dramatic rise to stardom.

On January 15, ABC premiered a half-hour sitcom set in the fifties: "Happy Days," featuring Ron Howard, star of the 1973 film, *American Graffiti.* The show didn't really take off, though, until the emphasis was shifted to **Henry Winkler,** who played Arthur "Fonzie" Fonzarelli, a leather-jacketed wise guy who seemed to know a lot about cars, girls, and being "cool." Bill Haley's "Rock Around the Clock" was the original series theme; its weekly exposure actually put the song back in the national top forty for the first time in nearly twenty years. Later, an original "Happy Days" tune was substituted; it became a top-five hit for Pratt and McClain in 1976. At decade's end, Suzi Quatro joined the cast as Leather Tuscadero, a macho female rock 'n' roller. Soon after, she had her first United States success with "Stumblin' In," a duet with Chris Norman.

The Sting sparked a national revival of ragtime music, with one of the movie's themes, "The Entertainer," becoming a left-field pop hit for pianist Marvin Hamlisch (later he'd help write "The Way We Were"). Gary Glitter starred in *Remember Me This Way,* Nilsson and Ringo Starr in *Son of Dracula;* Ringo also turned up in *Stardust,* along with David Essex, Adam Faith, and Dave Edmunds. Major concert movies included *Ladies and Gentlemen, The Rolling Stones, Pink Floyd Live at Pompeii,* and *Save the Children* (with Jerry Butler, Marvin Gaye, the Jackson Five, Roberta Flack, the Temptations, the O'Jays, and Gladys Knight and the Pips).

On March 2, country singer **Charlie Rich** won a Grammy Award for "Behind Closed Doors," the single that rescued him from near-obscurity at the age of forty-two. Suddenly an industry pet, "the Silver Fox" put six songs on the pop charts in 1974, including "The Most Beautiful Girl," "There Won't Be Anymore," and "I Love My Friend." Other stars staging comebacks in 1974: Paul Anka, Al Wilson, the Three Degrees, Andy Kim, Bobby Vinton, the Tymes, Dionne Warwick, and the Righteous Brothers.

Born in Brooklyn, **Barry Manilow** worked in Columbia Records' mailroom while studying at the New York College of Music and Juilliard. He broke into the business singing commercials for soft drinks, fast foods, and other products. Barry was filling in as a pianist at the Continental Baths in 1972 when he met Bette Midler and became her musical director. He toured with Midler, performing his own songs as her opening act. In 1974, Manilow went off on his own and soon came across a Scott English 45 called "Brandy." To avoid confusion with the Looking Glass hit of the same name, he changed the title to "Mandy," and released his own version late in 1974. Within a few weeks it was number one and a million-seller. Over the next four years, he put fourteen more singles in the top twenty, most of them ballads of emotional regret.

THE TOP 40

1. The Way We Were, *Barbra Streisand*
2. Come and Get Your Love, *Redbone*
3. Seasons in the Sun, *Terry Jacks*
4. Show and Tell, *Al Wilson*
5. Love's Theme, *Love Unlimited Orchestra*
6. Locomotion, *Grand Funk*
7. Benny and the Jets, *Elton John*
8. You Make Me Feel Brand New, *Stylistics*
9. Sunshine on My Shoulders, *John Denver*
10. T.S.O.P., *MFSB*
11. Rock On, *David Essex*
12. The Most Beautiful Girl, *Charlie Rich*
13. Spiders and Snakes, *Jim Stafford*
14. Rock Me Gently, *Andy Kim*
15. The Streak, *Ray Stevens*
16. Dancing Machine, *Jackson Five*
17. Band on the Run, *Paul McCartney and Wings*
18. You're Sixteen, *Ringo Starr*
19. Let Me Be There, *Olivia Newton-John*
20. The Joker, *Steve Miller Band*
21. You're Having My Baby, *Paul Anka*
22. Annie's Song, *John Denver*
23. One Hell of a Woman, *Mac Davis*
24. Billy Don't Be a Hero, *Bo Donaldson and the Heywoods*
25. Until You Come Back to Me, *Aretha Franklin*
26. You Haven't Done Nothin', *Stevie Wonder*
27. Nothing from Nothing, *Billy Preston*
28. Jungle Boogie, *Jethro Tull*
29. Midnight at the Oasis, *Maria Muldaur*
30. Hooked on a Feeling, *Blue Swede*
31. Dark Lady, *Cher*
32. Top of the World, *Carpenters*
33. Time in a Bottle, *Jim Croce*
34. Sundown, *Gordon Lightfoot*
35. Side Show, *Blue Magic*
36. The Night Chicago Died, *Paper Lace*
37. Goodbye Yellow Brick Road, *Elton John*
38. You're the Best Thing That Ever Happened to Me, *Gladys Knight and the Pips*
39. If You Love Me Let Me Know, *Olivia Newton-John*
40. Hello It's Me, *Todd Rundgren*

THE TOP 10 LPs

1. Greatest Hits, *John Denver*
2. Goodbye Yellow Brick Road, *Elton John*
3. Band on the Run, *Paul McCartney and Wings*
4. Behind Closed Doors, *Charlie Rich*
5. You Don't Mess Around with Jim, *Jim Croce*
6. Innervisions, *Stevie Wonder*
7. The Sting, *Original Soundtrack*
8. Bachman-Turner Overdrive II, *Bachman-Turner Overdrive*
9. American Graffiti, *Original Soundtrack*
10. The Singles 1969–1973, *Carpenters*

Ray Stevens was the guy who started his career in 1961 with a hit called "Jeremiah Peabody's Polyunsaturated Quick-Dissolving Fast-Acting Pleasant-Tasting Green and Purple Pills." From there, he developed into a first-rate singer, writer, arranger, producer, musician, and studio wizard. In 1962, "Ahab the Arab" became his first gold record; after that came message music ("Mr. Businessman"), rock revivals ("Along Came Jones"), novelty humor ("Harry the Hairy Ape"), satire ("Gitarzan"), country ("Misty") and straight pop ("Everything Is Beautiful")—the latter two both Grammy Award winners. In 1974, Ray decided to capitalize on the newest campus fad—sprinting around *au naturale*. "The Streak" showed off Mr. Stevens' vocal impersonations and a gaggle of nudity puns. The single rose quickly, selling nearly four million copies in less than five weeks.

T.S.O.P.
MFSB

"Most people think that our show *adopted* 'T.S.O.P.' as a theme song," said the tall, cool TV emcee. "But that's not the way it was. Actually, 'T.S.O.P.' was 'The Theme from Soul Train' at first. Only later was the name changed."

Don Cornelius, the creator, producer, and host of "Soul Train," did not start out to make his mark in music. He spent time as a Marine and an insurance agent before getting into broadcasting. After taking a $400 disc jockey course, he was offered an announcing job at radio station WVON in Chicago.

"A practice that jocks were into then was finding a little-known or forgotten record with a special quality and using it as a theme song," Don recalled. "Whenever I did a show, I would open and close with my personal theme, which was 'Hot Potatoes' by King Curtis. It wasn't in anybody's catalog anymore—so it was mine alone."

In 1970, Don got the idea to put together a black-oriented TV dance show, something along the lines of "American Bandstand." Numerous potential sponsors turned him down, but then Sears indicated a willingness to take a chance. With their backing, "Soul Train" premiered over WCIU-TV on August 17, 1970.

"A little over a year later we began making a syndicated version—a little more sophisticated—in Los Angeles. I was still hanging in there with 'Hot Potatoes,' and made some inquiries as to how I could acquire ownership of the song. I found out that it was too complicated; King Curtis had passed on, and his people were not exactly the kind one could negotiate with. So I decided what we needed was an *original* theme.

"People in music were just starting to hear about the show when I happened to run into Kenny Gamble in New York. We really hit it off, and I mentioned that I wanted to do a special song for the show. He was all excited, so we made a date, met in Philadelphia, and sort of co-produced a rhythm track. It was done more or less to my specifications.

"It was Kenny who came up with the basic melody. We started the session with seven or eight notes and the rest evolved from the contributions of musicians, as musicians will do once they tune in on a particular groove. We laid a foundation that we all felt had some magic in it, and then Kenny, Leon, and Bobby Martin did the bulk of the arranging.

"Several months went by before the song was released as a single. I was trying to hang on to it as an exclusive, which was a mistake. Finally, Kenny called me and said, 'This doesn't make a lot of sense. When you have a record like this, Don, you have to put it out.' So I said, 'O.K. Put it out.' However, I wasn't satisfied that everything in our agreement was coming true. So I told him not to use "Soul Train," our service mark, on the record. Kenny then changed the title of the song to 'T.S.O.P.,' meaning 'The Sound of Philadelphia.' "

MFSB stood for "Mother Father Sister Brother"—not a family band, but rather a group of thirty-four resident studio musicians at Philadelphia's Sigma Sound Studios. Their ages ranged from twenty-six to seventy-three, and they had played on dozens of hit records over the years. Twenty-eight contributed to "T.S.O.P.," including Kenny Gamble (keyboards), Norman Harris (guitar), Roland Harris (guitar), Ron Kersey (guitar), Bobby Eli (bass), Ronnie Baker (bass), Zack Zacherly (sax), Lenny Pakula (organ), Vince Montana (vibes), Larry Washington (percussion), Earl Young (drums), and Don Renaldo (contractor for strings, reeds, and horns).

"T.S.O.P." was introduced as the "Soul Train" theme in November 1973. The single version broke nationally in March 1974, reaching number one in April. It spent eighteen weeks on the charts, and won a Grammy as the "Best R&B Instrumental Performance of the Year."

Sunshine on My Shoulders

JOHN DENVER

John Denver's hit career began in 1971 with "Take Me Home, Country Roads," from his LP *Poems, Prayers and Promises.* For many, that song served as an introduction to one of the most pastoral of all American singer-songwriters. John Denver's music was described as a cross between contemporary folk, country, and pop: a joyous celebration of nature and the simple pleasures of rural living. In 1972, "Rocky Mountain High" continued that philosophy, inspiring Baskin-Robbins to invent a "natural" ice cream flavor of the same name. John also brought his folksy demeanor to television, serving as the first host of "The Midnight Special" when it premiered on NBC in August.

Clearly, by 1973, Denver was a man to be reckoned with when it came to colorful characters on the U.S. pop scene. It was natural that he would be asked to expand into motion pictures, even if it was only to help score a made-for-TV movie.

The feature was called *Sunshine,* and was a character study based on a real-life journal excerpted in the L.A. *Times.* It told the story of a terminal cancer case: a nonestablishment couple and the doctor who tried to save the young woman. Joseph Sargeant directed, Cliff DeYoung starred, and Cristina Raines played his wife. Also in the cast were Brenda Vaccaro, Meg Foster, Billy Mumy, and Corey Fischer. CBS drew high ratings when they aired the film on November 9, 1973.

MCA issued a *Sunshine* soundtrack LP, with performances by a number of cast members (in the picture, DeYoung, Mumy, and Fischer portrayed a singing trio). One of the tunes tackled was a Denver composition, "My Sweet Lady." Released as a 45 in the spring of 1974, it became a left-field top-twenty hit.

The flip side of that single featured DeYoung alone, crooning "Sunshine on My Shoulders." Dick Kniss, Mike Taylor, and John Denver had written that song in 1971, and it had been included on John's *Poems, Prayers and Promises* LP. Denver had even used it as the B side of one of his own singles in 1972. DeYoung's version was a high point of *Sunshine,* but it failed to gain much air play.

At that time, RCA was just about to issue an LP called *John Denver's Greatest Hits.* Embarrassed by some of the early material, John insisted on re-recording several of the tracks. He was so pleased with the new version of "Sunshine on My Shoulders" that he asked that it be released as his next single. It was, in January 1974.

"Sunshine on My Shoulders" reached number one in March, becoming John Denver's first chart-topping 45. Its success can be attributed to both his moving rendition and the TV exposure his composition got. The tune was certainly an inspiring one, and not only in the context of the movie. In May 1974, New York policeman Ben Huggard swam one hundred sixty-five miles from the Florida Keys to the Bahamas listening to it and other John Denver music. And when seventeen-year-old Lyn Cox swam Cook's Strait in New Zealand— a cold, angry stretch of water—the tune that ran endlessly through her mind, she said, was "Sunshine on My Shoulders."

You Make Me Feel Brand New

THE STYLISTICS

In the spring of 1968, two Philadelphia vocal groups competed for first prize in a high school talent show. The winners were the Monarchs, featuring Airrion Love, James Smith, and Russell Thompkins, Jr. The Percussions, with Herb Murrell and James Dunn, came in a close second. Soon after, college and the draft took several members from both groups. The remaining five decided to merge and become the Stylistics.

"We were close from the beginning," recalled Russell. "We realized early that there was a chance that success could hurt us, so we sat down and talked it over. We pointed out what *could* happen and agreed to remain conscious of potential problems."

The group developed its early style by emulating the Temptations, the Impressions, and especially the Platters. They came to be known as a kind of up-to-date Mills Brothers, purveyors of sweet, delicate R&B harmonies.

In 1969, their road manager, Marty Bryant, and the boys' guitarist, Robert Douglas, wrote a song called "You're a Big Girl Now." The fellows added it to their act, and one night it was heard by Bill Perry, the owner of Sebring Records. At the cost of $400, he had the tune recorded and released on his own label, and it became a local hit in Philadelphia, New York, Washington, and Baltimore. Avco Records bought the master in late 1970 and issued it coast-to-coast in 1971. The single barely dented the national charts, but at least the Stylistics were on their way.

Avco vice presidents Hugo Peretti and Luigi Creatore placed the group in the hands of producer Thom Bell, who had been working with the Delfonics. The first thing Bell did was lower Russell Thompkins' voice. Thom was impressed by Russell's memory—an ability to sing songs back exactly as he had been taught them. As a result, ten tunes could be mastered in four hours—an album cut in three.

The Stylistics' first session with Bell produced "Stop, Look, Listen (to Your Heart)," a top-forty single in the summer of 1971. Their second date yielded "You Are Everything" and "Betcha By Golly, Wow," both of which made it into the top ten. After that, there was no stopping the group: in 1972, there were "People Make the World Go Round" and "I'm Stone in Love with You"; in 1973, "Break Up to Make Up," "Rockin' Roll Baby," and "You'll Never Get to Heaven (If You Break My Heart)." All of their hits (except the latter) were composed by Thom Bell, with lyrics by Linda Creed, a white, French, Jewish girl who sang backup vocals.

"We owe everything to Thom and Linda," said Herb Murrell. "To say that he's a genius is only half the story. You know, those two can sit down anytime and write about everyday feelings that everyone can identify with."

As the months went by, Thom began spending time honing the Stylistics' sound. He distilled what they had down to pure emotion. "Every track he put down on us," said Love, "he worked on like it was a potential single." This caused friction between Bell and the group, with things coming to a head at the close of 1973.

"You Make Me Feel Brand New" was, in Thom's words, his "parting shot." It was unique among Stylistics' records in that it featured two lead vocals, Airrion Love and Russell Thompkins, Jr. Released as a single in March 1974, it quickly scaled the pop, soul, and easy listening charts. On May 22, it was certified gold—the sixth and last million-seller for the Stylistics.

Hugo and Luigi then took over production and writing, Van McCoy arranging and conducting for the group. Their well-titled next effort was "Let's Put It All Together," a top-twenty entry in the fall of 1974. But the Stylistics weren't really able to put it together after that. They're still together and still hoping that their blend of doo-wop and strings will make a comeback.

Benny and the Jets
ELTON JOHN

Benny and the Jets." A great name for something, right? Lyricist Bernie Taupin—the man who wrote the words for Elton John—talked about how he turned such phrases into solid gold rock 'n' roll.

"I'm a title freak," explained Bernie. "My usual method of writing is by titles. If I come up with a really good title, then I'll build a song around it. I'll be walking down the street, or in the bath, scrubbing my back. I'll think of a line and say, 'Now that's good. I'll have to build a song around it.' Or, I'll just think of a subject."

In 1974, there was one subject that Bernie and Elton could hardly keep from thinking about, and that was the worldwide record industry. As the hottest single performer of the seventies, Elton got to witness and experience far more of the multifaceted music scene than nearly any other participant. He was, at once, a pop fan, record collector, record producer, performer, singer, songwriter, spokesman, musician, actor, and owner-director of his own label (Rocket Records). He was also, to millions, the logical successor to Elvis Presley and the Beatles—a kind of bizarre but beloved musical messiah.

Heady stuff.

"Pop music is fun," laughed Elton, "and there's only one way to keep your sanity in it. Don't take yourself seriously. I don't. I love pop music. It's my whole life. I love it because it *is* fun. People say, 'Why do you wear flamboyant clothes, and why do you do this and that?' It's fun! I mean, I really have a ball dressing up, wearing the crazy clothes. But there's one thing I do take seriously, and that's the quality of the music. The music has to be there."

With their every waking hour steeped in pop music culture, it's logical that eventually Elton and Bernie would come up with a song that commented on all the craziness. They

did—a tune that Elton described as "one big hook. The strangest cut on the album *Goodbye Yellow Brick Road*—I think I sound like Frankie Valli on the song."

"Benny and the Jets" was written as a satire, lyrically poking fun at the trendy nature of the mid-seventies music scene. Oddly enough, though, it was nearly not pulled as a single. MCA fully intended to release another LP track, "Candle in the Wind." However, WJLB, Detroit's number one black station, began playing "Benny" experimentally as an album cut. Within a matter of days, 80 percent of all phone requests were for "Benny and the Jets." Rival CKLW then added the song, and MCA was forced to issue it as a 45.

That was in February 1974. By April, "Benny and the Jets" was a gold

record, and America's number-one hit, both pop and R&B. Elton helped that along by visiting both kinds of deejays, and making a rare TV appearance on the dance show, "Soul Train." "Benny and the Jets" clung to the charts for more than four months, selling over two million copies.

The album it was off didn't do too poorly, either. *Goodbye Yellow Brick Road* remained in the LP top ten for three-quarters of the year. "It is like the ultimate album for me," said Elton. "It takes in everything I've ever written, or sounded like. Now I've got to start all over again."

To help get things rolling, Elton renegotiated his contract with MCA. He walked away with an $8 million deal—the largest figure ever given to a record artist to that time.

The Locomotion
GRAND FUNK

Simply put, Grand Funk was one of the best loved and least liked groups in pop history. Critics hated them; even other stars, like Rod Stewart, put them down. But Grand Funk became an unqualified success in the early seventies by finding and filling a public need for basic, sledge-hammer rock 'n' roll.

The group specialized in drum and guitar solos played at levels that seemed designed to blister paint. "We were loud," admitted their leader, Mark Farner, "but there was a reason. We wanted to create an atmosphere in which nothing existed but the music."

Mark had been swept into music in high school. He honed his style in two Flint, Michigan, bands: the Bossmen and Terry Knight and the Pack. In the late sixties he formed his own group with Don Brewer (from the Pack) and Mel Schacher (from Question Mark and the Mysterians). Adapting the name of Michigan's Grand Trunk Railroad, Grand Funk Railroad was born.

The boys made a splashy debut in July 1969, when, unpaid, and unbilled, they opened the Texas International Pop Festival. Their audition tape, already turned down by several labels, was then picked up by Capitol. A debut LP, *On Time,* faced further rejection—this time by radio—yet, through word of mouth, managed to sell nearly a million copies by Christmas.

And so it went for Grand Funk Railroad—air play and acclaim eluding them, even as concert halls around the world were crammed (the Beatles took three weeks to sell out Shea Stadium; Grand Funk did it in three days). Capitol estimated that they were selling one Grand Funk LP every four seconds, yet there were few radio hits. As consolation, the group was given its own custom label; the first release, *E Pluribus Funk,* was issued in a round, silver dollar jacket.

In 1972, things began to look up. Organist Craig Frost was added, and the word "Railroad" was dropped from their name. "Footstompin' Music" and "Rock 'n' Roll Soul" both made the national top thirty. Then, in 1973, the group scored its first number-one hit single. "We're an American Band!" became the title of a chart-topping 45 and an LP, both pressed in gold vinyl.

In January 1974, after nine consecutive million-selling albums, the group announced plans for an LP to be called *Shinin' On.* Todd Rundgren would again produce. The LP featured a remake of "The Locomotion," originally popularized by Little Eva in 1962. As an added gimmick, the package design would be an industry first: a jacket in 3-D with a 3-D poster inside. Star-shaped 3-D glasses were also thrown in as a punch-out bonus.

The track was released as a single in late February 1974, and broke nationally early in March. On April 24 it was certified gold, and in May "The Locomotion" was at the top of the charts. It was one of the few times in pop history in which a particular tune had been taken to number one by two different artists. Oddly enough, the only previous instance involved another Goffin-King song, "Go Away Little Girl."

Grand Funk then embarked on a sold-out, forty city American tour, and in keeping with the *Shinin' On* concept, "mysteriously" lit up in the dark during their live performances. To close the shows, they went into an encore of "The Locomotion," heightening the effect by showing a filmed train collision behind them. After the tour, manager Andy Cavaliere received a Jaguar XKE from the band, and road manager Louis Pulver got a pie in the face.

The song "Shinin' On" became a hit in August 1974; in 1975, "Some Kind of Wonderful" and "Bad Time" both made the top five. The group moved to MCA in 1976, cut one LP, and broke up. By that time, Grand Funk had sold over thirty million dollars worth of albums.

Mark Farner was interviewed at that point. "As old as I am," he said (he was twenty-five), "I've accomplished what people eighty years old have been trying to accomplish, financially, that is, and that made me realize a lot. Being in the business we're in makes you grow up faster. I don't have a high school education, but I feel like I got a college degree.

"Please tell all our brothers and sisters how grateful we are to them for voting us Best Rock Group in the United States. The critics might not be happy, man, but we sure are. That's the real power of people."

Love's Theme

THE LOVE UNLIMITED ORCHESTRA

Barry White was born in Galveston, Texas, but grew up in Los Angeles, where he began singing in the church choir at the age of eight. By the time he was ten, he was playing the church organ, and helping to serve as choir director. Over the next few years, his musical interest led to the mastery of several instruments.

At sixteen, Barry joined a local group called the Upfronts, and gained experience as a singer and pianist in small R&B clubs. He also started to write and produce records, working with such artists as Bob and Earl ("The Harlem Shuffle"), Jackie Lee ("The Duck"), and Felice Taylor ("It May Be Winter Outside").

In 1968, Barry met three young black girls, Diane Taylor and Linda and Glodean James, who aspired to professional acceptance as a singing trio. Barry devoted the next few years to grooming this group, which he called Love Unlimited. In 1972, their first single, "Walkin' in the Rain with the One I Love," turned out to be a million-seller. On their record, Barry was heard very briefly as a voice on the telephone.

The next year, Barry launched his own singing career, with "I'm Gonna Love You Just a Little More Baby." It was a startlingly different sound, lushly orchestrated, with bedroom lyrics that were half-spoken and half-sung. Barry called his pillow-talk style "sensual soul," and a few months later, we were to call it disco." Oddly enough, Barry always viewed that genre of music with disdain, even though he was clearly one of its founding fathers.

Barry had a second hit in the same style in the fall of 1973: "Never Never Gonna Give You Up." He then returned to his protégés, writing and producing their album, *Under the Influence of Love Unlimited.* To help pad out the LP, he threw together a filler instrumental, "Love's Theme," which he cut with his forty-piece orchestra.

The track worked so well that he decided to release it as a single, credited to the "Love Unlimited Orchestra."

"I conduct the Love Unlimited Orchestra," said Barry. "I also arrange and play many of the instruments. That's the backing I've used on every one of the fifty-seven gold records I've won, worldwide. That's a lot of records. I didn't go on trips. I didn't get high. I went into the studio and made music. That's the only reason I have so many gold records. I didn't go in there loaded, talking about 'Let's dream up this.' I knew what I wanted when I went in there. I went in, got it, and I left."

"Love's Theme" took off early in December 1973, reaching number one in February 1974. It hung around for five months, becoming one of the top-selling singles of the year. Afterward, Barry had four more major vocal hits: "Can't Get Enough of Your Love Babe" (1974), "You're the First, the Last, My Everything" (1974), "What Am I Gonna Do with You" (1975), and "It's Ecstasy When You Lay Down Next to Me" (1977).

"The hardest kind of superstar to be is a black one," said Barry. "I can't make black music. I have to make worldwide music—music that appeals to everybody, not just black, white, Puerto Rican, Italian, Jewish, African, Australian—for the world.

"The supreme gift that I have is rhythm, and everybody has that, whether they know how to dance, sing, compose, or not."

Show and Tell

AL WILSON

Al Wilson was born and raised in Meridian, Mississippi, where he acted in school plays. Later he won talent shows as a singer and took first prize in an art contest. By the age of twelve, he had earned money as a country and western singer, formed his own spiritual quartet, and was singing in the church choir.

"Our preacher never had any formal music training," said Al. "But when he laid down a beat and established the root bass, it was a thrill. No singer could miss."

As a teenager, Al moved to San Bernadino, California, where he continued to work to help support his family. Between odd jobs as a letter carrier, clerk, janitor, and laborer, he took up the drums and practiced pounding out seductive rhythms in his spare time.

After two years in the navy, where he sang with an enlisted men's combo, Al came to Los Angeles. Alone and unknown, he made the rounds of cabarets and nightclubs, singing wherever he could. One day he decided that he had to either live on his earnings as an entertainer or get out of the business.

In 1959, he joined the Jewels, by then a fast-fading R&B group. He stayed with them briefly, then moved on to the Rollers. When they broke up, he formed the Souls, his own instrumental quartet. After a while, Al began to wonder if he would ever click in the music world. He developed a stand-up comedy routine—just in case.

In 1966, Al met Marc Gordon who agreed to become his personal manager. Marc introduced the young singer to Johnny Rivers, who auditioned Al, a cappella, for the Soul City label. Al was accepted, but it took another two years for his contract to pay off. In 1968, he recorded "The Snake," which sold nearly half a million copies. Al was on his way, but sadly, he was unable to score another hit for Soul City.

Eventually, Marc Gordon formed his own label, Rocky Road Records, and Al was one of the first artists signed to that company. Al was assigned a producer, Jerry Fuller, and the two began to sift through songs, looking for appropriate material. Finally, Jerry sat down at the piano and began playing some of his own compositions. When he got to "Show and Tell," Al expressed interest. Jerry explained that he had written the song especially for Johnny Mathis and that Mathis had had an "easy listening" hit with it in 1972. Al was thrilled with the song, and was convinced that he could turn it into a monster pop record as well. Jerry agreed to give it a try.

Their finished master was released in late fall 1973 and entered the pop charts in October. On December 17, it was awarded an RIAA gold disc. In January, it reached number one. Eventually it sold more than three million copies.

For a follow-up, Al recorded another of Jerry's tunes, "Touch and Go." However, it sounded very similar to "Show and Tell" and was not a very good seller. Later in 1974, Al again ran into trouble when both he and O. C. Smith recorded versions of "The La La Peace Song." The two singles split air play and sales, with neither one really making much of an impact.

In 1976, Al tried recording again, this time for Playboy Records. He cut "I've Got a Feeling," but it, too, was only a moderate seller. He cited poor

promotion as the reason and tried to get off the label. When they refused to let him go, Al decided to sit out his contract. As things turned out, Al lasted longer than Playboy Records, which folded two years later.

"I think it's very important to be on the charts, because it keeps your name alive," said Al. "But I'd rather disappear than make records for companies that don't do *their* job. I'm a professional, and I think people should always do their best, no matter what their job is. It's like singing. If you do a thing well, it doesn't matter if it's a ballad, soul, blues, or rock. You can reach people of many different tastes, and please them all."

Seasons in the Sun

TERRY JACKS

Canadian-born Terry Jacks grew up admiring American rock 'n' roll, especially the Everly Brothers, Elvis Presley, and Buddy Holly. "Buddy was the greatest," Terry recalled. "I used to have a job delivering papers in the morning, and all the money I earned was spent buying Buddy Holly 45s."

Terry began his own career as rhythm guitarist and lead singer for a Vancouver group, the Chessmen. They recorded extensively in Nashville and Los Angeles, but never managed to have a hit. "It was frustrating," said Terry, "and I had to find out why. So, whenever I could, I'd hitchhike down to L.A. and study the record trade."

One night, while playing with the Chessmen on Canadian TV's "Music Hop," Terry met a young singer named Susan Pesklevits, who was then making her national debut. The two decided to team up, personally and professionally, as a husband-and-wife duo: the Poppy Family. Susan was lead vocalist, while Terry composed, arranged, and produced all their material. One tune, written quickly to fill up a B side, became a huge Canadian hit early in 1970. American listeners whose radios picked up the song from over the Canadian border demanded its U.S. release. The London label obliged, and before long, "Which Way You Goin' Billy?" reached number two in the States. In Canada, the tune was voted "Song of the Year" by *RPM*, the Canadian music industry trade paper.

The Poppy Family had one other top-thirty single, "That's Where I Went Wrong," issued later in 1970. After that, everything seemed to go wrong. "We stayed together as long as possible," Terry explained, "but it got to be too much for us. I liked making records, and sometimes singing live, but hated to go on the road. Susan enjoyed traveling." By mid-1973, both their marriage and their act had broken up.

Terry continued to write and produce for Susan, but was then open to outside projects. The Beach Boys called and asked him to supervise one of their sessions. In the studio, he had them cut one of his favorite tunes, "Seasons in the Sun." When the group refused to release the finished track, Terry began to consider singing the song himself.

"Seasons in the Sun" had been written in French in 1961 under the title of "Le Moribond" (The Dying Man), by Belgian poet-composer Jacques Brel. In 1964, it was translated into English by Rod McKuen and recorded by Bob Shane of the Kingston Trio. Although that version didn't sell well, Terry heard it, and the tune remained in the back of his mind. The Beach Boys' rejection—coupled with the death of a close personal friend of Terry's, which made the song's theme more meaningful to him—finally sent Terry back into the studio, accompanied by guitarist Link Wray.

Terry received permission, but not credit, for changing part of "Seasons in the Sun." He rewrote the last verse and rearranged the words and chords in the chorus in order to "lighten up" the song. He released it on his own label, Goldfish Records, and was amazed when it became the largest-selling single in Canadian history—more than 285,000 copies sold in a matter of weeks. Bell's A&R vice president, Dave Carrico, heard the record, flew to Vancouver, and snapped up the American rights. On February 14, 1974, it earned its first RIAA Gold Award, for sales of over a million copies. Eventually, it sold more than three million copies in the United States alone. Worldwide, the figure is over six million.

"Seasons in the Sun" is the story of a dying man, bidding farewell to loved ones who have shared his life. Shortly before Terry's recording came out, Jacques Brel retired, at the peak of his popularity. Fans around the world were stunned, but the composer would give no reason. Finally, the truth was revealed. After a quiet, six-year battle against cancer, Brel succumbed to the disease and died, on October 9, 1978.

Come and Get Your Love

REDBONE

Their sound was rough and funky—melodic chants set to a jerky Cajun beat. It was a mix of black and tribal influences, and many called their style "swamp music." They named themselves Redbone, and they were one of the very few rock groups to be fully staffed by genuine American Indians.

The key men behind Redbone were Pat and Lolly Vegas, brothers who grew up together near Fresno, California. Their grandparents, who were from Texarkana, turned the boys on to the southern sounds, as well as their own Yaqui Indian heritage. As children, the two developed a great liking for what they heard, and R&B in general.

In the early sixties, Pat and Lolly moved to L.A. to try their luck as musicians and songwriters. They wound up doing session work with Dr. John, Leon Russell, Glen Campbell, Johnny Rivers, and many others. They also recorded under their own names for Reprise, Apogee, Mercury, and Audio International.

Their biggest break came in 1964 when they became regulars on the ABC-TV series, "Shindig." Three years later, a Vegas Brothers song, "Niki

Hoeky," became a hit single for P. J. Proby. Suddenly, their material became popular with other performers, such as Bobbie Gentry, Aretha Franklin, and the Righteous Brothers.

Pat and Lolly then formed their own group, called the Crazy Cajun Cakewalk Band. Soon after, they added Tony Bellamy, a flamenco guitarist. Rounding out the line-up was Peter De Poe, a drummer whose Cheyenne Indian name was Last Walking Bear. In 1968, these four decided to call themselves Redbone, after a derogatory Indian slang term meaning "half-breed." They chose to bear that name with pride—and a touch of humor.

From the start, the band tried to capitalize on their unusual heritage. They wore buckskins and moccasins onstage, and promoted themselves as "the Injun band." It was a gimmick, but it seemed to work, and slowly their reputation grew on the west coast nightclub circuit. In 1970, they signed with Epic Records.

Their first chart single was "Maggie," "a song," said Lolly, "about the way some girls prostitute themselves in life." It became a regional hit in some parts of the country in September 1971. Then, in February

1972, along came "The Witch Queen of New Orleans." It reached number twenty-one in the States, and in England climbed to number two. The stage was set for the most successful record Redbone would ever release.

"Come and Get Your Love" was the most commercial—and least Indian—of all the Redbone recordings. Their strained vocals were perfectly suited to the song, which was cast in a Marvin Gaye mold. The single took off in January 1974, and on April 22 was certified a million-seller.

The group tried following that hit with a tune called "Suzie Girl," which got limited play at year's end but did not chart. Later releases reflected their Indian background even more strongly, but still the sales were not there. In 1978, a final comeback attempt fizzled on RCA Records.

By that time, only Pat and Lolly remained on the original quartet. They announced plans to slowly delete the Redbone name, and simply call themselves Pat and Lolly Vegas.

"Nobody ever took us seriously," said Lolly, in retrospect. "We were ignored."

The Way We Were
BARBRA STREISAND

According to experts, Barbra Streisand was born with a technically perfect voice: dynamic range, flawless control, and impeccable pitch. From there, she developed a dramatic, emotional way of selling a song; a delivery that seemed gutsy in comparison with many other middle-of-the road performers. It's no wonder that, once exposed to the public, she became an "overnight sensation" in 1964, riding her first hit single, "People."

That song opened the door to a vast, hungry audience—the large group of more conservative folks who needed an answer to Beatlemania and the jangling sounds of rock 'n' roll. Barbra was the right person with the right style at the right time, and she became their heroine.

In 1965, the LPs *My Name Is Barbra* and *My Name Is Barbra, Two* became top sellers, and earned Streisand a Grammy Award for Best Female Vocal Performance. In April, her first TV special was aired, and it led to two Emmy Awards. Later, she held "A Happening in Central Park"—a free, one-woman concert that drew over 135,000 enthusiastic fans. In 1966, "Color Me Barbra" became both a TV spectacular and a million-selling album (another LP, *Je M'Appelle Barbra,* also went gold). The next year, she starred in a musical made for television, "The Belle of Fourteenth Street."

Streisand's film career took off in 1968 with *Funny Girl,* for which she won an Oscar (in the picture, she performed "People"). Her next film project was *Hello, Dolly!* She made two movies in 1970, *The Owl and the Pussycat* and *On a Clear Day You Can See Forever.*

Despite the quality of Streisand's films, many appeared dated, as if they'd been made for an earlier time. The market for "Broadway and Hollywood"-type material went into a sharp decline during the sixties, as enter-tainment in general underwent a rapid metamorphosis. Barbra, immersed in show tunes and "period" motion pictures, insisted on recording the works of her friends—sadly, few of whom were in vogue. She lost touch with her own generation, and by mid-1970, her record sales had fallen to less than one-third their former strength.

Columbia chief Clive Davis then hired producer Richard Perry, who managed to coax Barbra back onto the contemporary music scene. With great reluctance, she cut an LP of current tunes, including a version of Laura Nyro's "Stoney End." In 1970, that song became Barbra's biggest hit since "People," and led to more experiments with Billy Preston and the all-girl group, Fanny.

Barbra was still uneasy with rock material, and longed for the security of standards and melodramatic show tunes. Finally, in 1973, she was cast opposite Robert Redford in *The Way We Were.* Much to her relief, the title theme turned out to be a shivery ballad of love gone awry—exactly the kind of song she'd been waiting for.

Marvin Hamlisch came up with the melody; he was asked to write in the minor mode, but instead wrote in the major. "If I'd written in a minor mode, it might have told you too much in advance," he said, "that Streisand and Redford were never going to get together. So, I wrote a melody that was sad, but also had a great deal of hope in it." The tune was completed by a husband-and-wife songwriting team, Marilyn and Alan Bergman.

Streisand's single broke in late November 1973, and reached number one in mid-February 1974. It was her first number-one hit, and first 45 to stay on the charts for more than five months. It earned an Academy Award as the Best Film Song of 1973, *Billboard's* award as the Top Pop Single of 1974, and a Grammy as Song of the Year.

As for the film, it re-established the "Streisand character"—a brassy young girl who chases her "golden boy." Frazzled, earnest, and slightly ridiculous, she's also touching; a woman who doesn't quite understand her own feelings of loneliness. The screenplay was written by Arthur Laurents, who adapted it from his novel, which was set during Hollywood's "Blacklist Era."

THANKS TO SPIRALING INFLATION, the price of singles rose from a dollar to $1.29, with LPs and tapes also up about the same amount. Despite that, record and tape retail chains proliferated in 1975, the year that most labels dumped their budget lines in favor of steady catalog sellers—at $4.99. Business was so good that the industry now dwarfed all U.S. film, television, and sports interests combined. Record sales had nearly doubled since 1970 and were more than six times what they'd been in 1956. So far in the seventies, more records had been sold than in the entire decade of the sixties. Stevie Wonder knew how to strike when the poker was hot; on August 5, he signed the most lucrative recording contract in history up to that time—guaranteeing him, over the next seven years, a minimum of $13 million. The Raspberries and Guess Who split up; Mick Taylor left the Stones, and Jermaine Jackson quit the Jackson Five. Sal Mineo died; so did Cannonball Adderly, and Pete Ham of Badfinger. It was 1975: a year of TV triumph for Cher, Bobby Vinton, Donny and Marie, and Gladys Knight and the Pips. It was also the year that an unknown, John Travolta, was cast on the TV series "Welcome Back, Kotter."

The **Who** starred in the motion picture version of their rock opera *Tommy,* along with Elton John, Tina Turner, and Eric Clapton. Robert Altman's *Nashville* included Keith Carradine's Oscar-winning hit "I'm Easy," while *Shampoo* featured a Beach Boys' oldie, "Wouldn't It Be Nice." Barbra Streisand sang in *Funny Lady;* the Staple Singers in *Let's Do It Again. Jaws* inspired two hits: the title theme (for composer John Williams) and a crazed novelty ("Mr. Jaws") for satirist Dickie Goodman.

After spending a semester at Arizona State University, **Linda Ronstadt** formed the Stone Poneys with two friends and cut one hit record, "Different Drum," in 1967. The group then broke up, leaving Linda to drift around the L.A. country-rock scene until 1974, when ex-singer Peter Asher became her manager. Under Peter's direction, Linda recorded *Heart Like a Wheel,* the landmark LP that made her one of the brightest new stars of 1975. The album featured her first number-one single, "You're No Good," as well as another million-seller, "When Will I Be Loved." A few months later, there was "Heat Wave" and "Love Is a Rose," and after that there was no stopping the young lady from Tucson. For the rest of the decade, Linda specialized in rock 'n' roll remakes, making old hits her own in much the same way as Johnny Rivers had a decade earlier. "That'll Be the Day," "Blue Bayou," "It's So Easy," "Back in the U.S.A.," "Ooh Baby Baby" and "Hurt So Bad" all made the top twenty over the next five years.

At 11:30 P.M. on October 11, millions watched the premiere of NBC's **"Saturday Night Live,"** a freewheeling ninety-minute comedy-variety series starring the Not Ready for Prime Time Players—originally, Dan Aykroyd, John Belushi, Chevy Chase, Jane Curtin, Laraine Newman, and Gilda Radner. Each week, a musical guest was featured in a couple of spots, exposure that quickly became the most important single showcase for performers in broadcasting. Some of the offbeat sketches led to books, albums, television specials and motion pictures. The most successful outside projects were those of Dan Aykroyd and John Belushi as the Blues Brothers, on LP and film. Their first album, *Briefcase Full of Blues,* was one of the fastest-selling records in history, and featured the hit single "Soul Man."

A piano prodigy, **Neil Sedaka** switched from classical to pop music in order to win friends and gain favor in high school (one classmate, who became his girlfriend, was Carole King). Neil began to compose songs with a neighbor, Howard Greenfield, and their first major effort, "Stupid Cupid," became a million-seller for Connie Francis. Between 1959 and 1963, Sedaka had a hand in writing seventy-five top-ten hits, six of which he sang himself. After that, he was blown off the charts by the Beatles and others. Neil remained out of the spotlight until late 1974, when he was signed to Rocket Records by label owner Elton John. "Laughter in the Rain," which reached number one in January 1975, re-established Sedaka in the comeback of the year.

The ubiquitous **Van McCoy** began his career in the early sixties, swiftly establishing himself as a prolific writer, producer, arranger, and record company executive. Starting with the Shirelles, he went on to work with Gladys Knight and the Pips, Aretha Franklin, and more. In 1975, while writing and arranging for the Stylistics, Van got a chance to cut his own album, *Disco Baby.* It included a song about a

Latin step that McCoy had only been told about. However, his conception of what "The Hustle" was like became what the *New York Times* called "the biggest dance record of the seventies." It won a Grammy as the Best Pop Instrumental of the Year. Van continued his grueling schedule until July 1979, when he died of heart disease at age thirty-eight.

THE TOP 40

1. Love Will Keep Us Together, *Captain and Tennille*
2. Rhinestone Cowboy, *Glen Campbell*
3. Fame, *David Bowie*
4. Shining Star, *Earth, Wind, and Fire*
5. My Eyes Adored You, *Frankie Valli*
6. Thank God I'm a Country Boy, *John Denver*
7. Philadelphia Freedom, *Elton John*
8. One of These Nights, *Eagles*
9. Pick Up the Pieces, *Average White Band*
10. At Seventeen, *Janis Ian*
11. Kung Fu Fighting, *Carl Douglas*
12. Boogie On Reggae Woman, *Stevie Wonder*
13. Laughter in the Rain, *Neil Sedaka*
14. Black Water, *Doobie Brothers*
15. Lady Marmalade, *Labelle*
16. Why Can't We Be Friends, *War*
17. The Hustle, *Van McCoy*
18. Best of My Love, *Eagles*
19. Wasted Days and Wasted Nights, *Freddy Fender*
20. Before the Next Teardrop Falls, *Freddy Fender*

21. Some Kind of Wonderful, *Grand Funk*
22. Island Girl, *Elton John*
23. Lovin' You, *Minnie Riperton*
24. Jive Talkin', *Bee Gees*
25. Mandy, *Barry Manilow*
26. Please Mr. Postman, *Carpenters*
27. Have You Never Been Mellow, *Olivia Newton-John*
28. Jackie Blue, *Ozark Mountain Daredevils*
29. Ballroom Blitz, *Sweet*
30. Another Somebody Done Somebody Wrong Song, *B. J. Thomas*
31. He Don't Love You, *Tony Orlando and Dawn*
32. Feelings, *Morris Albert*
33. I'm Not in Love, *10cc*
34. Games People Play (They Just Can't Help It), *Spinners*
35. Love Won't Let Me Wait, *Major Harris*
36. Angie Baby, *Helen Reddy*
37. I'm Sorry, *John Denver*
38. Fight the Power, *Isley Brothers*
39. Lady, *Styx*
40. Fire, *Ohio Players*

THE TOP 10 LPs

1. Greatest Hits, *Elton John*
2. That's the Way of the World, *Earth, Wind and Fire*
3. Captain Fantastic and the Brown Dirt Cowboy, *Elton John*
4. Heart Like a Wheel, *Linda Ronstadt*
5. Back Home Again, *John Denver*
6. Average White Band, *Average White Band*
7. Have You Never Been Mellow, *Olivia Newton-John*
8. Physical Graffiti, *Led Zeppelin*
9. Phoebe Snow, *Phoebe Snow*
10. Tommy, *Original Soundtrack*

New Jersey-born **Bruce Springsteen** began his recording career in 1973, but didn't gain much more than local fame until two years later when *Rolling Stone* magazine discovered him and began hyping him as "the future of rock 'n' roll" (by an odd coincidence, Bruce's original producer had just been replaced by *Rolling Stone* writer Jon Landau). Columbia Records fanned the flames with an all-out publicity campaign that resulted—incredibly—in *Time* and *Newsweek* cover stories on the "new Dylan." Hysteria mounted until the release of *Born to Run* as an album and as a single—and then everything backfired. The LP, according to critics, failed to capture Springsteen's live excitement, while the 45 fizzled out without even making the top twenty. Contract disputes kept Bruce out of the studios and away from the public for the next three years. In 1978, he began a comeback with the album *Darkness at the Edge of Town.* It wasn't until 1980, though, and the LP *The River* that Springsteen finally scored with a major hit song: the top-five single, "Hungry Heart."

10

At Seventeen

JANIS IAN

The childhood of Janis Ian Fink was hardly stable. By the time she was fifteen, she had already lived in thirteen places around the New York area. High school teachers disliked her, calling her "a disruptive influence."

One day, while waiting for a guidance counselor, she felt suddenly moved to write a song that symbolized her youthful frustration. She called it "Society's Child."

"It was a good song for the time," she said. "A good song for a fourteen- or fifteen-year-old to write. I don't think the song holds up today as well as it did. I don't sing it anymore."

"Society's Child" stirred up a storm of controversy in 1967. Its themes of interracial love and adult hypocrisy caused it to be banned by many radio stations. In Louisiana, one deejay was actually murdered for playing it on the air.

The record made Janis an overnight sensation, and, in her own words, "a precocious, snotty kid. I was so serious. My God, I thought I was heavy . . ."

Her parents' marriage collapsed, and Janis ran off to Philadelphia with a photographer friend. Over the next few years, she turned out a half-dozen albums of stark, unhappy music, which she later called "lousy." At nineteen, confused and numb, she completed a Philharmonic Hall concert, strode off stage, and "dropped out."

After two years of psychoanalysis, and numerous ventures into the mystical world of drugs, Janis hit rock bottom. Nearly broke, she seriously considered becoming a secretary, but then decided to give the music business just one more try.

After several embarrassing auditions for various labels, she was signed by Columbia in 1972. Her first album for them, *Stars,* included the lonely blues ballad, "Jesse." Roberta Flack turned it into a top-thirty hit in 1973.

The next Ian LP, *Between the Lines,* featured her long-sought follow-up to "Society's Child." Like that early tune, it was an introspective recollection of her own romantic and sexual frustration—"At Seventeen."

"I wrote that song at my mother's house," recalled Janis. "I was sitting and reading the *New York Times* when I came across an article about debutantes and proms. In it was the line 'I learned the truth at seventeen,' or something like that. My guitar was handy, so I started playing around with this little bossa nova riff, the one that opens the song. I finished up the first verse and chorus, and then a couple of days later, the last verse and that chorus. The middle part came two weeks after that.

"I think 'At Seventeen' is a good song. It does what a good song should do, which is strike a nerve, communicate to any age group, cross class and cultural boundaries. The prob-

lem with protest stuff like 'Society's Child' is that I was singing to people who felt the same way I did. I wasn't changing anybody, or making any difference to the people. I think 'At Seventeen' may make some difference to some kid in junior high. A lot of people seemed to relate to it, anyway."

"At Seventeen" broke onto the charts in mid-June 1975, and peaked in September. In total, it spent nearly five months on the best-seller lists. It also earned Janis a Grammy for Best Female Pop Vocal Performance.

"It seems like a good thing to be able to say, 'I wrote a song everyone can believe,' " said Janis. "I started out wanting to be a star. I guess everyone begins that way. I wanted to be Baez, or Odetta, so I sang. But I love songwriting best. That's what I'd like to be when I grow up. A songwriter."

Pick Up the Pieces
THE AVERAGE WHITE BAND

Although raised in Scotland, the six men who came to form the Average White Band grew up listening to and playing the music of black Americans: R&B, jazz, and the Motown hits of the sixties.

Bassist Alan Gorrie, along with Onnie McIntyre, led an R&B band called Forevermore, while attending college in Perth. It was there that they first heard the Dundee Horns, a rival group that featured Roger Ball and Malcolm "Molly" Duncan.

Alan had written some songs he wanted to experiment with, so he booked some time in a local studio. He got Onnie, Roger, Malcolm, and some other friends to play on the session. When it was over, they realized that they had created their own individual sound, a kind of jazz-oriented soul, modeled after American bands such as James Brown's and Booker T and the MGs.

In 1972, the four joined Robbie McIntosh and Hamish Stuart to form a sextet. It was Bonnie Bramlett, of Delaney and Bonnie, who suggested their name—the Average White Band. The group debuted later in the year at the Lincoln Festival in England. They did a lot of work all over Europe, playing American bases in Germany and many black clubs.

In January 1973, the band achieved a major breakthrough by appearing as the supporting act at Eric Clapton's comeback concert at the Rainbow Theatre in London. After that, they entered a cheap demo studio and produced their first album, *Show Your Hand,* which they sold to MCA. In November, they made their first American tour, using equipment borrowed from the Who, and doing their own road work. The tour and the album were both bombs, and the group was quickly dumped from the MCA roster.

Jerry Wexler, a co-founder of Atlantic Records, then signed the band and put them in the studio with arranger-producer Arif Mardin. He turned out to be just the man they needed to bring them their first real success.

By the fall of 1974, things were looking up. The group had a new album in the can, a road crew, and—at last—their own equipment. On September 22, they attended a party held in their honor in West Hollywood, California. Sometime during the night drummer Robbie McIntosh was sold a small amount of cocaine, which had been spiked with strychnine. Before he left, Alan Gorrie sampled it and soon after began displaying the symptoms of poisoning. Another party guest, Cher Bono, kept him awake and out of a coma, until the crisis passed. However, the next day, Robbie was found dead, alone, in his motel room. It was thought that the band might break up, but in January 1975, Steve Ferrone, a close friend of Robbie's, stepped in as their new drummer. The "White" band now had a black member.

Their second album, *Average White Band,* was full of disco music. The highlight was an instrumental, "Pick Up the Pieces," written by Roger and Hamish. It featured a tenor sax solo by Malcolm and the dual guitars of Onnie and Hamish. At first, the song was shunned by black stations because the band was chiefly white. But black youngsters—and deejays—loved it, and helped the band top the LP and singles charts simultaneously in February 1975. "Pick Up the Pieces" was certified a million-seller by the RIAA on March 6 and was later nominated for a Grammy Award as Best R&B Instrumental of the Year (it lost, to MFSB's "T.S.O.P."). In the summer of 1975 there was a second top-ten hit, "Cut the Cake."

The music trade magazines were overflowing in awards to AWB, as they eventually came to be known, and awards from other publications, such as *Playboy,* were also numerous. Their "overnight" success left them reeling and wealthy—so much so that they left Glasgow to become tax exiles in America.

"In the United States," said Ferrone, "there is music all the time. This is the place to be."

One of These Nights

THE EAGLES

Glenn Frey was an out-of-work musician in 1971 when he was hired to play guitar in Linda Ronstadt's road band. She also needed a drummer, so Glenn recruited Don Henley from the bar in L.A.'s Troubadour Club. The two men became friends and decided it would be fun to start their own group. Weeks later, Ronstadt's bass player quit, and was replaced by Randy Meisner, formerly of Poco. During the weeks of rehearsals that followed, Randy agreed to join the new band. At that point, Bernie Leadon, who had played with Ronstadt in the past, began to sit in with the other three. In August of 1971, they officially became a quartet. At first, as a joke, they called themselves Teen King and the Emergencies. Then Bernie began reading about the Hopi Indians and the spiritual significance that eagles had in their culture. Don liked the idea of calling the group the Eagles, and so did Glenn, who thought it made them sound like a street gang from Detroit.

Their first LP, *The Eagles,* produced three hits in a row in 1972: "Take It Easy," "Witchy Woman," and "Peaceful Easy Feeling." Critics characterized their style as "the laid-back sound of L.A.," even though the entire album was recorded in London. Their second LP, *Desperado,* and most of their third, *On the Border,* were also cut overseas.

During the sessions for *On the Border,* the band went through what Glenn called their "midlife crisis." They changed producers, added guitarist Don Felder, and returned to L.A., where the album was completed. In late 1974, it yielded their first number-one single, "Best of My Love."

From the beginning, the Eagles' music explored the emotional side effects of pursuing one's goals. "I think you write about what moves you," said Glenn. "I mean, I'm all in favor of singing a love song that has no message at all, you know, concerning politics or ecology, if it's a well-writ-ten song where the words really mean something for somebody who listens to it. I just think there's a need for lyrics that you can get your teeth into."

In 1975, the Eagles released their fourth album, *One of These Nights.* Among other songs, Glenn conceived the title track. "It's about putting things off. We've all said, 'one of these nights I'm gonna do something—get that girl, make that money, find that house.' We all have our ultimate dreams—a vision we hope will come true someday. When that 'someday' will come is up to each of us."

"One of These Nights" is perhaps the quintessential Eagles song. "All our records have the same theme, and that is *the search,*" said co-writer Don. "It doesn't matter if it's romance, money, or security; it's the act of looking for it. Your whole life is one long journey, and getting there is more important than the journey's end."

In July 1975, "One of These Nights" became the Eagles' second number-one single. The album included two other hits, "Lyin' Eyes" (a Grammy winner) and "Take It to the Limit." At year's end, Bernie Leadon left the band and was replaced by Joe Walsh.

The Eagles went on to further assert themselves as a premier rock group of the decade. Their 1977 LP, *Hotel California,* sold over nine million copies and led to two more Grammys. "New Kid in Town" (later number one) won Best Vocal Arrangement, while the title song (another chart-topper) was named Record of the Year. The album also contained "Life in the Fast Lane."

In 1978 came a Yuletide 45, "Please Come Home for Christmas." Then, in 1979, the Eagles released their seventh LP, *The Long Run.* It featured three hit singles: "Heartache Tonight" (their fifth number one), the title track, and "I Can't Tell You Why."

At the decade's close (according to their label), the Eagles had sold more records during the 1970s than any other American recording act. It was shortly after that point that they decided to break up—for, as Glenn explained, "I don't want to be thirty-nine years old with a beer belly singing 'Take It Easy' because I need the money. I think there's a time and place for everything."

Philadelphia Freedom

ELTON JOHN

Elton John had always been a big sports fan, and for that reason, it was a great thrill for him, at a party, to meet one of his athletic idols: tennis pro Billie Jean King. They became good friends, and afterward, he always tried to attend her matches, whenever he could. Sometimes, Elton got in on the action, in celebrity benefit games.

One day, Billie surprised Elton with a special track suit, customized just for him. Elton was so touched that he promised to dedicate one of his "next big hits" to her. She laughed and thanked him, assuming he'd quickly forget such an off-the-cuff vow.

A short time later, Billie was in Denver, embroiled in a crucial playoff game. Suddenly, Elton entered her locker room, bearing a hand-held tape recorder. With a nervous grin, he punched up a track he had just completed, and awaited her reaction. For many long minutes, the tune played on. And then she smiled. Billie Jean King loved the song.

Single copies of "Philadelphia Freedom" carry Elton's dedication to "B.J.K.," as well as to "the soulful sounds of Philadelphia"—a clear nod to the Gamble-Huff-Bell school of R&B. The record was Elton's answer to dance music mania, and was, in fact, one of the largest-selling disco singles of all time. It was also one of the longest—and on purpose, too. In the months before, a national programer had lashed out at Elton for releasing 45s that clocked in at over four minutes. They were lousing up his formats, and therefore, the man announced a boycott of any future Elton John records that violated his time restrictions. Elton's response was "Philadelphia Freedom"—a hit so big that the man was forced to program it.

Elton liked to make his singles as collectible as possible, and did this by filling his B sides with otherwise

Elton John and Bernie Taupin

unavailable material. The flip of "Philadelphia Freedom" is perhaps the most famous of these, "I Saw Her Standing There." It's the only recorded live duet between Elton and John Lennon, and was John's way of thanking his friend for singing along on "Whatever Gets You Through the Night."

"Philadelphia Freedom" broke in America in early March 1975, and by April, was a gold record, the top-selling single in the country. It quickly became Elton's most popular 45 yet, a fact that didn't surprise his lyricist, Bernie Taupin. Bernie, though, downplayed his role in the song's success.

"I'm quite honest about it," he said. "I'm sure fifty percent of the people who liked it never even listened to the words. People don't buy a record because the words are good, or the words sound nice. They buy it for the old thing melody, or 'It's got a good beat, man. Yeah, I can dance to that one.' The words, at least in the beginning, are secondary.

"Later on they may play a part, because you have to have something to sing along to. But on 'Philadelphia Freedom,' or any of the uptempo things, the words just aren't that important. If they're palatable, and you can sing them, that's all that matters."

Thank God I'm a Country Boy

JOHN DENVER

By 1975, John Denver had been singing and writing about the beauties of nature and of romanticism for a long time. The man and his music had become symbols—simple, wholesome, sometimes corny—but, in many ways, said much as a voice for Middle America. His records seemed to have a therapeutic effect, and millions, all across the country, listened and bought. In 1975, John Denver was the largest-selling recording artist in the United States.

He achieved that feat with old standbys, really; love, peace, and homespun happiness served as subject matter for most of his tunes. In troubled times, cheerful, nostalgic songs hold wide appeal for almost everyone—everyone, that is, except the rock press. Critics especially loathed his optimism (as they hate anyone who appears to be more happy than they are). Perhaps it was John's unremitting sincerity that made it all work, and made him the Norman Rockwell of popular music. Denver sang from the perspective of a "country boy," reflecting on the joys of rural living, and since he had lived that experience, he was certainly a qualified spokesman for it.

John first recorded "Thank God I'm a Country Boy" for his LP *Back Home Again,* issued in 1974. That record, which spent four weeks at the top of the album chart, was certified gold one month after release (and ultimately sold more than three million copies). It included his second number-one tune, "Annie's Song" (written for his wife), as well as the hits "Back Home Again" and "Sweet Surrender." "Thank God I'm a Country Boy" was, at that point, just another track, in its original studio version.

But then, in the summer of 1974, John appeared at the Universal Amphitheater in Los Angeles. His engagement there set a house record by selling out seven nights' performances in twenty-four hours. All the

shows were taped for television and an eventual live LP.

That album—a double set—was released in February 1975 as *An Evening with John Denver.* It shipped gold, peaked at number two, and spent fifty weeks on the best-seller lists. Among the many tunes featured were "Take Me Home, Country Roads," "Rocky Mountain High," "Annie's Song," "Sweet Surrender," and "Thank God I'm a Country Boy."

Somehow the vibes on one magic night—John's interaction with the fans—helped make the latter song a high point of the entire concert run. The tune, written only months before, was composed by John Sommers, a guitarist in Denver's backup group. It was pulled for release as a single in February 1975, and broke onto the charts a month later. In June, it reached number one, and was certi-

fied as a million-selling 45. In all, it spent twenty-two weeks on the pop charts.

John went on to score three more hits in 1975: "I'm Sorry," "Calypso," and "Fly Away." He also did well on the LP charts with *Windsong* and *Rocky Mountain Christmas* (both of which went gold on advance orders alone). His "Rocky Mountain Christmas" TV special was watched by sixty-five million people—the largest audience to that time for an ABC music program. And the TV special "An Evening with John Denver" won an Emmy as the Best Musical Variety Special of the 1974–75 Season.

John closed out the decade by revealing his sales figures to an astonished pop press. By January 1979, he had sold over one hundred million records.

My Eyes Adored You

FRANKIE VALLI

Frankie Valli was twenty-eight before he scored his first success with "Sherry" in 1962. As lead singer of the Four Seasons, he'd helped that group sell more than eighty million records in the sixties.

In 1971, Frankie signed with Motown, with the understanding that he'd be getting the personal attention of label president Berry Gordy, Jr. That support, according to Valli, never came, due to Gordy's involvement with Diana Ross and her film, *Lady Sings the Blues.*

While with Motown, Frankie recorded a sentimental ballad, written by a former Season, Bob Gaudio, and the group's long-time producer, Bob Crewe. It was inspired by Valli's relationship with his second wife, twenty-four-year-old Mary Ann. The first time she heard it, she knew "My Eyes Adored You" was a hit.

Motown sat on the track for a year and a half without issuing it. Finally, when Frankie's contract ran out in 1973, he bought back the master for $4,000.

Right about that time, Larry Uttal was organizing his new label, Private Stock. He needed a first release, and called Bob Crewe. At a dinner party, Crewe played the song, explaining that it would make a good B side for something else. Uttal disagreed; that tune was an A side all the way.

"My Eyes Adored You" was shipped to radio stations in October 1974. It started to get a little play in November, breaking out in various parts of the country. It wasn't until after Christmas, though, that the record broke wide open. By March 1975, it was the number-one song in the country.

In celebration, Mary Ann had a special gold record medallion made, which reads "My Eyes Adored You." Frankie wears it around his neck to this day.

Shining Star
EARTH, WIND AND FIRE

Earth, Wind and Fire was formed late in 1970 by a Chicago session musician who had worked for Motown, Chess, and several Windy City stars. Maurice White conceived his group one night on paper, while sitting alone at his kitchen table. He'd been reading a book entitled *The Laws of Success* and felt inspired to put together a band "with a dynamic name and new musical message." He outlined the kind of group he wanted to form and even drew pictures of the way he wanted them to look (later, the members did resemble those early sketches). He then thought about a name, "Fire," but rejected it as not comprehensive enough to describe his dream band. Turning to an astrological chart, he discovered that air and earth were elements of his birth sign, Sagittarius. By substituting the word *wind* for *air*, he devised "the perfect name" for his group.

Earth, Wind and Fire began as a straight jazz band, cutting a couple of flop LPs for Warner Brothers. After being dumped by the label in 1971, Maurice fired most of his players and regrouped. A third album, issued by Columbia, did even worse in 1972—selling fewer than fifty thousand copies. Desperate, Maurice took his band on the road, touring mostly black middle-class college towns. He experimented with the group sound and made careful note of audience reaction to his ideas. Slowly, their style began to evolve, with less emphasis on jazz and more on basic R&B. Maurice simplified Earth, Wind and Fire, borrowing concepts from War, Santana, the Ohio Players, and Sly and the Family Stone. Costumes, sets, and stunts were added to their live show, turning them into one of the most theatrical of all black groups. Record sales began to climb, until finally Earth, Wind and Fire was outselling every other act on the Columbia roster, except Chicago.

Their sixth LP, *That's the Way of the World,* released in February 1975, was the soundtrack from a movie of the same name, about a record company executive who tries to promote a new group. The band in the film was played by members of Earth, Wind and Fire.

"In our efforts to communicate," wrote Maurice in the liner notes, "we've set a new goal in the presentation of this album. This is a musical score, put together with you in mind. Each song is an event relative to an experience we've lived while trying to achieve perfection in our everyday lives. We laugh, we cry, we worship, we enjoy. You might recall an old saying: 'You reap what you sow.' That's the way of the world."

"Shining Star" was the first song on side one of the album. It related the group's belief that everyone has the potential to become a star in his or her own way. Amid lusty instrumental backing, it spoke a new kind of philosophical gospel. The single was released in March 1975 and immediately took off as a heavily played disco record. By May, it was number one on the pop charts, and on June 19, it received gold certification from the RIAA. Months later, when the Grammies were passed out, "Shining Star" earned the award for Best R&B Performance by a Vocal Group.

"Shining Star" kicked off a long string of pop hits for Earth, Wind and Fire, including "Sing a Song," "Getaway," "Serpentine Fire," and "Got to Get You into My Life" (the Beatles song sung by them in the 1978 movie *Sgt. Pepper's Lonely Hearts Club Band*). Another hit was the title track from the LP *That's the Way of the World.*

"Shining Star," like nearly all Earth, Wind and Fire material, was built around simple R&B percussion. The same could be said about many disco records in the seventies, yet "Shining Star" was different—it was lyrically strong as well.

Earth, Wind and Fire enjoyed a good, clean image in the seventies; most of the members were vegetarians, and none smoked, drank, or took drugs. They gathered regularly to meditate and achieve "oneness of mind" before performing. Maurice White summed up their attitude in this way: "We live in a negative society. Most people can't see beauty and love. I see our music as medicine."

Fame

DAVID BOWIE

David Bowie (born David Robert Haywood-Jones) began his odd musical odyssey in the early sixties. He worked with a mime troupe, and through them developed an interest in theatrics and abstract characterizations. He also formed and played in several rock bands, and wondered if somehow he might be able to link the two.

In 1966, he changed his last name from Jones to Bowie to avoid confusion with the Monkees' Davy Jones. He also began recording but didn't get anywhere until 1969, the year man landed on the moon. That event inspired "Space Oddity," his first major U.K. hit. Almost immediately, David staged his first in a career of publicity stunts—his "retirement" to an arts lab in Beckingham.

In 1970, he returned in a new guise—a transvestite—posing for photos in ankle-length skirts. This gimmick caught the attention of RCA Records. They signed Bowie to a lucrative, long-term contract. Their hope was to turn flash into figures: through heavy promotion, make David Bowie out to be "the Elvis of the seventies."

On January 22, 1972, the campaign took off with a "shocking announcement"—David's famous admission to the press that he was gay. Taking a cue from *A Clockwork Orange,* he cropped his hair, dyed it orange, and started appearing in modified space suits. This visual image tied in with the new LP, *Ziggy Stardust and the Spiders from Mars.* Amid a huge publicity push, it became a successful album, and David Bowie was on his way.

Within a few months, David was the best-selling recording act in England. Then, on July 3, 1973, he announced his second "retirement"—this time, he assured fans, he meant business. Bowie kept his word, and vanished entirely from the music industry—for a few weeks.

In 1974, David made a "comeback" tour of America, cutting a live LP in the process. RCA released new figures, trumpeting cumulative Bowie sales, by then, of "one million albums, and one million singles." The BBC chimed in with numbers of their own: in a survey of favorite record stars in Britain, Bowie had finished third in the Best Male category, and first in Best Female. He had become the "King of Glitter Rock"—and perhaps the "Queen" as well.

In 1975, Bowie turned his back on all that, and entered an R&B bag. "He'd been working to put together a soulful sound for years," said co-producer Tony Visconti. "Every British musician has a hidden desire to be black." David entered the Sigma Sound Studios in Philadelphia, and, backed by the city's top session men, recorded the LP *Young Americans.*

"It wasn't a statement album," said Bowie. "It was a Polaroid album. I took a snapshot of music in America as I saw it at the time. I don't play *Young Americans* much. I think it's one of the most unlistenable albums I ever made."

The title track made the U.S. top thirty—the first time a Bowie song had done that since "Space Oddity." Then, in late June, a second tune was pulled off the album—"Fame."

"Now that's a happy song," David continued. "Everything about it, the melodic feel, is happy. The whole disco thing, I think I anticipated the whole plastic soul thing with that LP."

Bowie wrote "Fame" in the studio, along with his guitarist, Carlos Alomar, and a new-found friend, John Lennon. John, whom David called "the last great original," can be heard joining in with Bowie toward the end of the song.

"Fame" reached number one in September 1975, and was certified as a million-seller on October 17. Six months later, his last major hit, "The Golden Years," entered the top ten. Since that time, Bowie has concentrated on acting.

"I'm a corporation of characters," he said, "naturally, ahead of my time. I'm not part of rock 'n' roll. I used rock 'n' roll. I've rocked my roll and it's finished."

Rhinestone Cowboy
GLEN CAMPBELL

I'm not a country singer per se," said Glen Campbell. "I'm a country boy who sings." Perhaps that's one reason for Glen's remarkable rise from rural poverty to big city acclaim.

Campbell left school at fourteen, "because they didn't teach me what I wanted to know, which was pickin' and grinnin'." He worked his way to Los Angeles, where he became one of the highest-paid session musicians in the business. In the late sixties, his singing career took off, aided immeasurably by weekly TV exposure on the "Glen Campbell Goodtime Hour." By 1975, he had a dozen gold records, and had recorded nearly thirty LPs.

And the best was yet to come.

"I heard 'Rhinestone Cowboy' on the radio," he said. "It was a track off Larry Weiss' album, and I immediately got a cassette of it. I actually learned the song while we were on a tour of Australia in November of '74. When I got back to the States, I went into Al Coury's office at Capitol and he said, 'I've got a great song,' and he played 'Rhinestone Cowboy' for me. Well, I was familiar with the song by that time. The airlines had been on strike in Australia, which meant that we had plenty of driving time to spend listening to the cassette. And let me tell you, the freeway over there is something else—from Sydney to Brisbane—some 650-odd miles. So, by the end of that drive, I *knew* 'Rhinestone Cowboy.' I could've whistled it backwards. But I related to the lyrics immediately. In the first verse he says, 'There's been a load of compromising on the road to my horizon.' Then later he says, 'There'll *be* a load of compromising on the road to my horizon." And the truth in that struck me; I think that's what sold me on the song, much more than even the hook itself, the 'rhinestone cowboy' stuff."

Glen's version of "Rhinestone Cowboy" first appeared on his 1974 LP, *Houston (I'm Coming to See You).*

In May of 1975, it was released as a single, and took off right away, selling eighteen to twenty thousand copies a day. It went gold on September 5, and, at the same time, hit the top of the charts.

"I'd had number-one albums before, but never a number-one pop single," said Glen. "But I really had a feeling about 'Rhinestone Cowboy.' It went way beyond anything that I had ever visualized for it. I thought it would be a hit record, but I honestly had no idea that it would be as big as it was."

Love Will Keep Us Together

CAPTAIN AND TENNILLE

Toni Tennille was born in Montgomery, Alabama, where she sang with her sisters and had nine years of classical piano training. In 1964, the family moved to Los Angeles, where the California sunshine delighted Toni. She got her first job as a file clerk, and hummed her way to and from the office.

Her first professional experience was with the South Coast Repertory Theater. She and a friend, Ron Thronson, wrote a rock-ecology musical for the theater called *Mother Earth.* The show ran in San Francisco to good reviews, and had a short run in Los Angeles. During the San Francisco run, the show needed a new keyboard player: enter Daryl Dragon, who was in town between Beach Boy tours.

Daryl, the son of conductor Carmen Dragon, had studied classical piano for ten years. During the run of *Mother Earth* Daryl became impressed with Toni's writing and singing and persuaded her to join the Beach Boys as pianist on their next tour. She was the first and only "Beach Girl." Daryl wound up being nicknamed "Captain Keyboard" by Mike Love, because he always wore a naval captain's cap on stage, so when he and Toni teamed up, they naturally became the Captain and Tennille.

Toni and Daryl were unable to land a recording contract, so with $500 of their own money, they cut a single and released it on their own Butterscotch Castle label. "The Way I Want to Touch You" became a regional hit, and before long, the duo was signed to A&M Records.

Toni and Daryl first heard "Love Will Keep Us Together" when Kip Cohen, vice president of A&M, called them into his office and played the song from a Neil Sedaka album. It was love at first hearing, and Kip suggested they release it as a single. They agreed.

"I call it circus music," said Daryl. "I don't know if anyone else does. Remember that sort of happy feeling in Billy Swan's 'I Can Help'? It came through on his record, and that was my goal; I said, 'I wish we could make one just like his' when we recorded 'Love Will Keep Us Together.' It's just relaxation time, three minutes of letting your mind wander. That's the only way I can explain it. To me, there's no message, although a lot of people, even little kids, say they like the lyrics."

"Love Will Keep Us Together" broke on American radio in mid-April 1975, and climbed steadily through the month of May. It reached number one in June, and spent nearly six months on the charts. Over two and a half million copies of the single were sold in both English and Spanish. It won the 1975 Grammy as Record of the Year, gained instant recognition and enormous popular acclaim for the duo, and became their signature tune. The album of the same title went on to sell over a million copies, established them as pop stars, and opened the avenues that led to their ABC-TV series.

1976

REEL-TO-REEL TAPE SALES were abandoned by most labels in 1976, the year that Johnnie Taylor (and "Disco Lady") won the first award ever given for a platinum single. Al Green opened a church in Memphis, while elsewhere in that city, Isaac Hayes declared bankruptcy (he was $6 million in the hole). Kiss made publishing history by donating their own blood to be mixed with the ink for *Kiss Comics* (sales were anemic). Brian Wilson rejoined the Beach Boys, adding that he was giving up sex to better channel his music-making energies. (Mrs. Wilson was reportedly not pleased by that announcement.) The Who, live in London, put out one hundred twenty decibels at thirty yards—the loudest pop concert ever held. At the second televised "Rock Music Awards," Sara Miles announced the winner of Best Song as "Fifty Ways to *Lose* Your Lover," by Paul *Williams.* Later in the show, Diana Ross was named as "the female entertainer of the *century."* Commander Cody and his Lost Planet Airmen broke up; so did Deep Purple, and Loggins and Messina. Marilyn McCoo and Billy Davis quit the Fifth Dimension; Rod Stewart left the Faces. We lost Flo Ballard of the Supremes, Buster Brown, and Howlin' Wolf; also Keith Relf of the Yardbirds and Paul Kossoff of Free. And an unknown group called Boston sold over a million copies of their first album in two and a half months. It was 1976: the year that Gary Glitter retired and George Harrison was found guilty of plagiarism—lifting the melody of the Chiffons's "He's So Fine" for his own "My Sweet Lord."

British-born **Peter Frampton** established himself as a singer-songwriter-guitarist in two late-sixties bands, the Herd and Humble Pie. By 1975, though, he was $300,000 in debt and working solo for $500 a night. In desperation, he took the best songs he'd written over the past few years and re-recorded them in concert, hoping to capture some of that in-person excitement on vinyl. The resulting album was a two-record set, *Frampton Comes Alive,* which sold over thirteen million copies. Not only was it the biggest double album to that time, but it was also number one for an incredible seventeen weeks. Three hit singles came out of that package: "Show Me the Way," "Baby I Love Your Way," and "Do You Feel Like We Do." The next year, Frampton struck again with "I'm in You" and a remake of Stevie Wonder's "Signed, Sealed, Delivered." In 1978, Peter co-starred with the Bee Gees in the film *Sgt. Pepper's Lonely Hearts Club Band,* and in 1979 had his last hit of the decade, "I Can't Stand It No More."

Kiss—the most successful gimmick band of all time—made their television debut as guests on a Paul Lynde Halloween special for ABC. Formed in 1972, the hard rock group decided to call attention to themselves through the use of outlandish effects: explosive devices, snow machines, police lights, rocket-firing guitars, levitating drums, bizarre make-up, outrageous costumes, and a bass player who both ate fire and spit blood. By the mid-70s, Gallup pollsters were reporting that Kiss was the most popular act in teenage America. Ironically, three of the four band members did not even perform on their biggest hit single, a lilting 1976 ballad, "Beth." Only drummer Peter Criss (who wrote the song) showed up for the session, at which he was accompanied by a twenty-six piece orchestra and a thirty-voice boys choir.

Nineteen seventy-three concert footage was mixed with fantasy sequences to create *The Song Remains the Same,* a **Led Zeppelin** documentary. Bobbie Gentry's *Ode to Billie Joe* became a motion picture, and David Bowie went scifi in *The Man Who Fell to Earth.* The Pointer Sisters appeared in *Car Wash,* but it was Rose Royce who cleaned up with the title tune. *Mahogany* starred Diana Ross, whose own story with the Supremes served as a general inspiration for *Sparkle,* the movie that introduced Irene Cara (later to find fame in *Fame).*

And with the spring came summer—**Donna Summer**—who began her streak to the top in response to a dare. Could she, a mere studio background singer, cut a record to top the eroticism of the then-hot single "Je T'aime"? "I came up with a title," she said, "and some of the music, but hadn't really finished writing the song before the session. We cut a basic rhythm track. I sat down, listened to the music a few times, jotted down a couple of lines—I really wanted to feel a certain way. No one was allowed in the studio. The lights were all turned out, except for the small red light on the control panel. It was unlike anything I had ever recorded. At first I resisted singing the song the way I felt it. Finally, I just let myself go. 'Love to Love You Baby'—I think it was the hardest song I have ever attempted recording."

Born in India and raised in England, **Cliff Richard** spent nearly twenty years as a major star in virtually every country except the United States. Although second only to Elvis in number of British hit singles, he had flickered in America just twice, with "Living Doll" in 1959, and "It's All in the Game" in 1963. Thirteen years later, signed to Elton John's Rocket label, he finally made the U.S. top ten with "Devil Woman," a raucous, yet inviting performance that he called his "best work ever." "To make it in this country, the fatherland of rock 'n' roll, is a dream come true," he said. More stateside hits followed, including "We Don't Talk Anymore" (1979), "Dreaming" (1980), and "A Little in Love" (1981).

THE TOP 40

1. Disco Lady, *Johnnie Taylor*
2. Don't Go Breaking My Heart, *Elton John and Kiki Dee*
3. Play That Funky Music, *Wild Cherry*
4. Tonight's the Night, *Rod Stewart*
5. Kiss and Say Goodbye, *Manhattans*
6. Silly Love Songs, *Paul McCartney and Wings*
7. A Fifth of Beethoven, *Walter Murphy*
8. Love Machine, *Miracles*
9. 50 Ways to Leave Your Lover, *Paul Simon*
10. December, 1963 (Oh, What a Night), *Four Seasons*
11. Love Hangover, *Diana Ross*
12. Shake Your Booty, *K.C. and the Sunshine Band*
13. I'd Really Love to See You Tonight, *England Dan and John Ford Coley*
14. Sara Smile, *Hall and Oates*
15. Boogie Fever, *Sylvers*
16. Afternoon Delight, *Starland Vocal Band*
17. Misty Blue, *Dorothy Moore*
18. Disco Duck, *Rick Dees and His Cast of Idiots*
19. More, More, More, *Andrea True Connection*
20. Love Is Alive, *Gary Wright*
21. You'll Never Find Another Love Like Mine, *Lou Rawls*
22. I Write the Songs, *Barry Manilow*
23. You Don't Have to Be a Star, *Marilyn McCoo and Billy Davis*
24. Dream Weaver, *Gary Wright*
25. If You Leave Me Now, *Chicago*
26. Fly Robin Fly, *Silver Convention*
27. Rock 'n' Me, *Steve Miller Band*
28. Get Closer, *Seals and Crofts*
29. Bohemian Rhapsody, *Queen*
30. Welcome Back, *John Sebastian*
31. Theme from "S.W.A.T.," *Rhythm Heritage*
32. Get Up and Boogie, *Silver Convention*
33. Hot Line, *Sylvers*
34. Wreck of the Edmund Fitzgerald, *Gordon Lightfoot*
35. You Sexy Thing, *Hot Chocolate*
36. Let 'Em In, *Paul McCartney and Wings*
37. Love Hurts, *Nazareth*
38. You Should Be Dancing, *Bee Gees*
39. Rubberband Man, *Spinners*
40. Take It to the Limit, *Eagles*

THE TOP 10 LPs

1. Frampton Comes Alive, *Peter Frampton*
2. Fleetwood Mac, *Fleetwood Mac*
3. Greatest Hits, *Eagles*
4. Wings at the Speed of Sound, *Wings*
5. History: America's Greatest Hits, *America*
6. The Dream Weaver, *Gary Wright*
7. A Night at the Opera, *Queen*
8. Gratitude, *Earth, Wind and Fire*
9. Breezin', *George Benson*
10. Silk Degrees, *Boz Scaggs*

The Band, Bob Dylan's one-time backup group, held the rock 'n' roll concert of the year Thanksgiving night at the Winterland Ice Palace in San Francisco. Five thousand fans paid $25 apiece for tickets to the event, which included not only live music but catered turkey dinners for everyone. The Band—formed in Toronto in 1959—dubbed the show "The Last Waltz"; their final onstage appearance before withdrawing from live dates. Original leader Ronnie Hawkins was just one of many guest stars who showed up; also on the bill were Eric Clapton, Neil Diamond, Dr. John, Muddy Waters, Joni Mitchell, Van Morrison, Neil Young, and Bob Dylan. A year and a half later, "The Last Waltz" came out as a three-record set and as a documentary movie, directed by Martin Scorsese.

December, 1963 (Oh, What a Night)
THE FOUR SEASONS

Making a remarkable comeback in 1975 was Frankie Valli and the Four Seasons. Mainstays of the sixties, the Seasons, led by Valli, had done a slow fade at the end of the decade. By 1970, original members Nick Massi and Tommy DiVito had quit, and Bob Gaudio had retired from the road. Gaudio and Valli remained business partners, though, owning all rights to the group name, and all of their old masters as well.

Frankie kicked off the resurgence with "My Eyes Adored You" in the spring of 1975. That number one was followed by a second top-ten hit, "Swearin' to God." Then, in August, a disco single, "Who Loves You," introduced us to the new Four Seasons: John Paiva (guitar), Don Ciccone (bass), Lee Shapiro (keyboards), and Gerry Polci (drums). Over them, Valli sang lead, backed by two ex-Seasons, Gaudio and Joe Long.

The record reached number three nationally, and inspired an album of the same name. From that LP came "December, 1963 (Oh, What a Night)."

That song was written by Bob Gaudio, along with a lady friend, Judy Parker. At first it was about the repeal of Prohibition, and was called "December 5th, 1933." Judy wasn't pleased with that concept, though, and said that the words were a little "too cute." New lyrics were written, and the melody reworked. The result was a tune that everyone seemed to like—except for one man. "Me," said John Paiva. "I'm the guy who predicted 'December '63' would be a bomb."

Fans, already shocked by the group's turn to disco, were in for another surprise. Frankie Valli gave up most of his lead vocal to Gerry and Don. "That was intentional," explained Gaudio. "We wanted to mix up the voices so the group could broaden its identity. It was a specially-designed piece of material."

In the words of one reviewer, "December, 1963" was "catchy, semi-erotic car radio fare." It broke right around Christmas of '75, and slowly climbed to number one by mid-March. The song spent six months on the charts, and sold more than three million copies. Ironically, that made it the Four Seasons' best-selling single ever.

"It's been almost like a double life for me," said Valli, in a 1977 interview. "What we're hoping for is to get the group to a point where it can exist completely on its own, without me at all. That way, I'll be able to put more emphasis on my solo career."

50 Ways to Leave Your Lover

PAUL SIMON

*I*n the 1960s, no one spoke from the heart and from the head quite like Simon and Garfunkel. They truly were spokesmen for a generation, and when they broke up many wondered if the two men could be as successful separately as they had been together.

Art went off hoping for an extensive career as a motion picture actor, but in eleven years made only three films: *Catch 22* (1969), *Carnal Knowledge* (1971), and *Bad Timing* (1980). Of his eight chart singles during that period, two were "reunion" efforts with Paul, and only one solo song, "All I Know" (1973), managed to crawl into the national top ten. For a while, Art even gave up show business altogether, and became a math teacher.

His former partner, however, had better luck, even though Simon's mother conceded that Garfunkel had the better voice. What Paul had on his side was songwriting ability, and while he had seen Simon and Garfunkel as a three-way partnership (with engineer and co-producer Roy Halee), musically they were just not a creative team. Paul wrote, played, vocalized and worked out in the studio, while Artie only sang. During the sessions for "Bridge over Troubled Water," Artie was not even there much of the time, and does not appear at all on some of the LP tracks.

Dissolving Simon and Garfunkel relieved Paul of a lot of pressure, leaving him free to experiment with other kinds of music. He developed a taste for reggae, gospel, and unusual rhythms.

His first solo hit came along in the spring of 1972, and was inspired by the name of a chicken and egg dish Paul had in a Chinese restaurant. "Mother and Child Reunion" quickly became a gold record, and was followed later that year by "Me and Julio Down by the Schoolyard." In 1973, his album *Rhymin' Simon* included "Kodachrome" and "Loves Me Like a Rock"—both million-sellers—along with "American Tune."

In 1975, Paul recorded two duets: the first, "Gone at Last," with Phoebe Snow. He then took Garfunkel to Muscle Shoals, to show him where and with whom he'd cut *Rhymin' Simon.* The two friends then put together "My Little Town," a top-ten tune and their first collaboration in more than five years.

But Paul's big project in 1975 was an autobiographical LP, one that dealt with adjustment, a favorite theme in Simon songwriting. As he had in the sixties, Paul continued to document the trials and tribulations of his generation: the baby boom kids now facing the crises of adulthood. They and he could still grin, sigh, and admit that they were "Still Crazy after All These Years."

Paul Simon's marriage had broken up by the mid-seventies. Rather than make it a negative experience, Paul decided to tackle the issue in a humorous vein, and in doing so, managed to come up with "50 Ways to Leave Your Lover." He gave his song a basic rhythm, and added one coloring instrument—martial drums—in order to avoid clutter. He recorded the song in a small studio in New York City, in the heart of Broadway's theater district.

"50 Ways to Leave Your Lover" broke nationally in late December 1975, and spent three weeks at number one in February 1976. It was certified gold on March 11, and remained a best-seller for nearly five months.

The title track from *Still Crazy* became a top-forty hit later in 1976, while the LP itself won a Grammy as Album of the Year. In 1977, Paul returned with "Slip Slidin' Away"; and in 1978, "(What a) Wonderful World" (sung with Garfunkel and James Taylor). Simon changed labels to Warner Brothers in time for the new decade, and hit with "Late in the Evening" and "One Trick Pony" in 1980. The latter tune was the title song from Paul's first starring motion picture. In it, the thirty-nine-year-old singer-songwriter played an aging rock star, trying to revive a sagging career. "It touches on the problem of prolonged adolescence," said Paul. "The movie had a lot to do with what happened to the sixties generation—my generation—in rock."

Love Machine
THE MIRACLES

The Miracles' saga began in 1955, in a Detroit junior high. Ronnie White and Pete Moore, who'd known each other since kindergarten, formed a vocal group with Bobby Rogers and thirteen-year-old William "Smokey" Robinson. Smokey brought along his girlfriend, Claudette, who in 1959, became his wife.

For four years, the Matadors (as they were called) polished their singing style, appearing locally whenever they could. In search of a break, they eventually auditioned for Jackie Wilson's manager. He was not impressed with what he heard, but there was a man in the audience who was—an up-and-coming songwriter-producer, Berry Gordy.

Gordy was impressed by the fact that the group did not attempt to emulate other artists, but presented original material in their unique way. He took the five under his wing, and gave Smokey a few pointers on composition. In 1958, they began recording under a new name—the Miracles.

Not much happened until late 1960, when "Shop Around" put the Miracles and Gordy's new label on the musical map. It was the first million-seller for both, and over the next dozen years, there were many more hits, among them "You've Really Got a Hold on Me" and "Mickey's Monkey" (1963), "Ooh Baby Baby" and "The Tracks of My Tears" (1965), "I Second That Emotion" (1967), "Baby, Baby Don't Cry" (1969), and their first number one single, "The Tears of a Clown" (1970). Smokey wrote or co-wrote nearly all of the forty-three songs charted by the Miracles between 1959 and 1973.

Soulful lyrics, intricate harmony, and Smokey's soft, caressing tenor helped make the Miracles one of the best-loved of all sixties groups. They were a cornerstone in the Motown empire, and played a major part in erasing the color barrier in popular music. By 1973, they were a rock 'n' roll legend—and that's when Smokey decided to bail out.

"We'd been doing it for seventeen years," he said, "and with the traveling and the hotels and the food—I had really had it."

So, in the summer of 1973, there was a farewell tour, ending with the introduction of Smokey's replacement. He was William "Bubbey" Griffin, who'd grown up in Baltimore idolizing the Miracles. Griffin was chosen because, in his own words, "I looked and sang like Smokey."

"We were not in demand at all," recalled Pete Moore. "Promoters and bookers thought the Miracles without Smokey weren't very potent. We played some nice engagements, but also some places that weren't so nice. The thing is, we wanted to work, so we did 'em. We were just waiting for the hit that would change it all."

That hit was a long time coming—more than three years, in fact. "Do It Baby" marked the Miracles' comeback in October 1974.

"As writers, we really hadn't done anything since Bill joined the group," explained Pete. "We concentrated on getting him acclimated. Our next album, though, was completely written by Bill and me."

That LP was *City of Angels,* an ambitious concept work. Its loose theme was "life in Los Angeles."

"We wanted to make sure all the songs on the album could stand alone," he said. "We didn't want to tie them too closely, so that if one was pulled as a 45, it wouldn't need the others to make sense. We did, though, make sure that the music told a story when all the songs were played in sequence.

"One of the characters in the story was a guy named Michael, who becomes an L.A. superstar. When he does, he describes himself by singing the song 'Love Machine.'"

In early October 1975, Motown split "Love Machine" in half, and released it as two sides of a single. Part I took off almost immediately, steadily climbing to the top of the charts in February 1976. In all, it spent more than six months on the best-seller list, and ironically—without Smokey—became the Miracles' biggest hit.

A Fifth of Beethoven

WALTER MURPHY

Walter Murphy began his musical training at the age of four, with Rosa Rio, an organist on radio soap operas. She gave lessons in a Manhattan music store, and because Walter could not read at the time, she used colors to teach him the notes. He became so proficient that he appeared in Hammond organ commercials and also in concert with Rio.

By the time Walter graduated from high school, he had mastered classical and jazz piano. He enrolled in the Manhattan School of Music as a composition major, and even before graduating, he was writing arrangements for Doc Severensen and the "Tonight Show" orchestra. A final year of college kept Walter from relocating in California with the show in 1972.

Instead, he entered the mad world of Madison Avenue, writing ad jingles. Among his clients were Revlon, Woolworth's, Lady Arrow, Viasa Airlines, and Korvette's. He also wrote for the children's TV show "The Big Blue Marble" and several made-for-TV films (*The Savage Bees, The Night They Took Miss Beautiful,* and others).

Walter's interests included rock recordings, especially those adapted from classical themes. The Toys, for example, hit in 1965 with "A Lover's Concerto"; Apollo 100 sold a million copies of "Joy" in 1972.

"I had this crazy idea to take symphonic music and combine it with contemporary rhythm," he said. "Nobody had done it in a while, and nobody had done it in this particular way. It was an experiment—taking an instrumental that was about as far from pop music as you could get, and making a hit single out of it.

"I made up a demo tape of several songs and took it around to all the record companies in New York. Nobody liked any of them, except 'A Fifth of Beethoven.'

"I wrote the song, arranged it, played most of the parts; it was basi-

cally my own doing. Then, after it was made, Private Stock told me that we would have a better chance of getting air play if it was credited to a group. I wasn't really in favor of this but went along, and we came up with the name Big Apple Band. The record had been out two days when we learned there already was a Big Apple Band. We changed to the Walter Murphy Band, and then just plain Walter Murphy.

"The first time I heard the song on the air, I was driving in my car and almost hit a tree. It was really exciting. I knew it was being played in some parts of the country, but not

New York. It wound up selling about two million singles, and about 750,000 albums. But the best was yet to come.

"Early in 1977, the people at RSO called up Private Stock and said they were making a movie with John Travolta called *Saturday Night.* Nobody knew what it was about, but they wanted to use 'A Fifth of Beethoven' on the soundtrack. We said it was fine, to go ahead. Little did we know that it would turn out to be *Saturday Night Fever*—the largest-selling album in music history. I'd say that was a lucky turn of events."

Silly Love Songs
WINGS

Paul McCartney spent the seventies making hits—more than two dozen, in fact, beginning with "Another Day" in 1971. As the leader of Wings, he cut all kinds of records, from mellow ballads to surging rockers, and nearly all made the national top ten. In a sample year, 1973, there was a raver ("Hi, Hi, Hi"), a sentimental crooner ("My Love"), and a dramatic James Bond movie theme ("Live and Let Die"). After cutting the latter with a forty-piece orchestra, Wings reverted to primal scream for their next number, a raucous song inspired by Paul's nickname for his battered Land-Rover.

That tune, "Helen Wheels," came from *Band on the Run,* Wings' most popular LP of the decade. It was recorded in an eight-track studio, built over a swamp, in Lagos, Nigeria. The album included "Jet" (named after the McCartneys' little black dog) and the title track, both of which became top pop singles in the States. Their final record of 1974 was cut in Nashville: "Sally G," backed with "Junior's Farm" ("Junior" was lead guitarist Jimmy McCullough). Both sides of that 45 also got a lot of air play.

In 1975, Wings switched labels to Capitol, and recorded *Venus and Mars* in L.A. and New Orleans. That LP amassed orders of one-and-a-half million copies before release. Afterward, it yielded three major hits: "Listen to What the Man Said," "Letting Go," and "Venus and Mars Rock Show."

By 1976, Paul McCartney had certainly established himself as the consummate hitmaker—composer, arranger, publisher, producer, bandleader, singer and musician. No one doubted his ability to *make* hits, but some criticized the sentimental way he sometimes did it. Even during his Beatle days, McCartney had been called a romantic, a softie, and he was never embarrassed by it. "I'm a fan of old-fashioned writing," he admit-

ted. "I do like rhyme, when it comes off. I hate silly rhymes, but when they work, they're the greatest little things in songwriting."

John Lennon used to say that Paul's material was "a lot of rubbish," and that he "couldn't rock if he tried." "He sounds like Englebert Humperdinck," said Lennon, who further attacked his old partner in "How Do You Sleep?," a cut off the *Imagine* album.

"I listened to him for a few years," said Paul, "and used to think, 'I can't write another of those soppy love songs. We've got to get hard and rocky now.' In the end, though, I realized that I just had to be myself. It's bolder, you know, to say, 'What's the difference? *I* like it.'"

And with that, McCartney composed "Silly Love Songs"—a tune that overcame its own silliness by its obvious sincerity. Its mass acceptance proved McCartney's point, much to his satisfaction.

"The fact is, deep down, people are very sentimental," he said. "If they watch a sentimental movie at home, they cry, but in public they won't. We don't like to show our emotions; we

tend to sneer at that. And in the same way, people may not admit to liking love songs, but that's what they seem to crave."

Wings' single came out in mid-April 1976, just before the final leg of a tour that took them to the U.S., the U.K., Australia, and five cities in Europe (in Berlin, Paul and Linda painted the lyrics of "Silly Love Songs" on a bedsheet and paraded it along the Berlin Wall). In every town, the specter of Paul's former group was there—in America, where a ten-year-old Beatle track, "Got to Get You Into My Life," had been revived; and in England, where almost a quarter of Britain's top-one hundred single records were old Lennon-McCartney songs. In concert, post-Beatles material was emphasized, and the result was a rousing string of celebrative events. "Paul confronted his legacy," wrote one reviewer, "and was not engulfed by it."

And of course, to make things sweeter, both Wings' new album (*At the Speed of Sound*) and single ("Silly Love Songs") reached number one while they were on the road.

Kiss and Say Goodbye

THE MANHATTANS

"We went to high school together," said Winfred "Blue" Lovett. "Edward 'Sonny' Bivins, Kenneth 'Wally' Kelly, Richard 'Ricky' Taylor, and Gerald 'Smut' Alston. We loved sports—baseball, preferably—and singing. When we weren't playing ball in the daylight, we'd entertain ourselves just singing. I guess singing was our main thing.

"The Apollo Theater in New York had an amateur night, and we being from New Jersey, it was no problem for us to go there and audition. On this particular night, we came in third, and a gentleman by the name of Joe Evans was there. He signed us to his label, which was called Carnival Records.

"At that time, we were the Dulcets. It didn't sound that exciting; *dulcets* means 'melodic tones'—but how could you explain that to the public? We needed a catchy name that would last. So, with the cocktail theme in mind—not the borough of Manhattan—we picked the name Manhattans.

"We spent four years with Carnival, four years with Starday-King Deluxe, and then signed with CBS [Columbia Records] in 1973. The years before we hit were not easy. We were limited in the places we could play, and our sales were mediocre. To keep our families going, we all had to get part-time jobs.

"There were lots of songs I sat down and composed. I did big arrangements on 'em—worked on 'em for a week—and nothing happened. A lot of times I heard songs in my sleep, but I was too tired to get up and struggle in to where the piano was.

"But this particular night, I just couldn't lie there. I heard the melody. Everything was there. I got up about three o'clock in the morning and jotted down the things I wanted to say. I just put the words together on my tape recorder and little piano.

"I've always thought that when you

write slow songs, they have to have meaning. In this case, it's the love triangle situation we've all been through. I figured anyone who's been in love could relate to it. And it seemed to touch home for a lot of folks.

"To me, 'Kiss and Say Goodbye' was a country tune. I didn't really mean it for the Manhattans. I wrote it for Glen Campbell, Charley Pride, one of those people. I didn't think the Manhattans were ready for it, being labeled rhythm and blues artists.

"I did the background parts; Bobby Martin did the arrangement. He and I sat together and I showed him how I wanted the rhythm to go. Then I talked to our lead singer, Gerald. He's a real soulful, gospel guy, and I told him I wanted it straight, with no rhythm. I heard this as a strictly country-type thing, sung by a black person.

"The record lay in the can for fourteen months before it was released. I was a hundred percent disappointed that they shot it out when they did, because disco was peaking at the time. Dorothy Moore had a song out then ['Misty Blue'], and our record and Dorothy's creeped very slowly up the charts. I watched it week by week just

to see how it competed. Diana Ross and the Brothers Johnson also had stuff out then, and they zoomed past us like we were standing still. But we still made it up the chart, and reached number one.

"We were on tour when we heard it had gone gold, and we celebrated for a week. After eleven years, we had gotten our first gold! It didn't really hit us that it was as big as it was until it had gone platinum.

"We'd always thought kids had a lot to do with a song selling that well, but it isn't true. This wasn't a teen-age-type record at all. And there were so many records before that we thought were going to be hits, and they weren't. It's funny, because before it made it, no one in the group had anything good to say about 'Kiss and Say Goodbye.' I was critical, a perfectionist in the studio, and there are still parts of it that make my skin crawl. For example, in one place, the background vocals go off pitch. Somehow, though, that didn't seem to bother anyone else. We wound up selling more than four million copies of 'Kiss and Say Goodbye.'"

Tonight's the Night
ROD STEWART

F ollowing his 1971 solo success with "Maggie May," Rod Stewart toured the world with the Faces, a band notorious for their love of beer, soccer, Cockney humor, and wild parties. As the Small Faces, they'd had one U.S. pop hit—a psychedelic, flower-power classic, "Itchycoo Park" (1968). After Rod joined in 1969, they dropped the "Small" and had one other American hit, "Stay with Me,"

off their 1972 LP, *A Nod's as Good as a Wink to a Blind Horse.*

Rod cut seven albums with the group, all of which were overshadowed by what he was able to do by himself. His fourth solo LP, *Never a Dull Moment,* produced two top-forty hits in 1972: "You Wear It Well" and "Angel" (the latter released as a single without Rod's consent). *Sing It Again, Rod,* a 1973 "best of" collection, was a good seller, as was *Smiler* (1974), his last album of new material for Mercury.

In May of 1975, Stewart signed with Warner Brothers, and not long afterward, he took up residence in Los Angeles. His debut solo effort for the label, *Atlantic Crossing,* was released in the summer of '75. Veteran producer Tom Dowd supervised the recording sessions at Muscle Shoals and Los Angeles; joining Stewart were the Muscle Shoals and Memphis Rhythm Sections, as well as other top studio musicians. The album went gold in America without the help of a hit single (although in other countries, "Sailing" did become a million-selling 45). Then, in December, Rod made official what everyone had expected for months: He was leaving the Faces and from then on would be working "alone."

A Night on the Town was Rod's first LP without a single member of his old band on it. This fact was underlined on the jacket by the cryptic words "All selections written or selected by R.S." Again, Tom Dowd handled production, with sessions held in California at Cherokee Studios and in Alabama at Muscle Shoals.

The album was well promoted: A special, called "A Night on the Town,"

was put together and shown on the British independent TV channel. The BBC ran its own film, "Rod the Mod Comes of Age." Stewart was very happy about this, and quite proud of his LP. The press, though, gave it a lukewarm reception, and, oddly enough, most early reviews ignored what was to become its most famous cut.

Rod wrote four of the nine tunes on the album, including the one that kicks off the "slow side." "Tonight's the Night" is a song of seduction, filled with barely restrained, gleeful anticipation. "It's as erotic as 'Je T'aime,'" wrote one critic. "The string background and tenor sax solo are as romantic as dinner by candlelight." The track ends with breathy female moans, a sexy voice purring in French. That unbilled cameo was provided by Rod's girlfriend at the time, Swedish actress Britt Ekland.

"Tonight's the Night" was released as a single in the fall of 1976, and immediately ran into controversy. Many programers objected to phrases in the song, which described a girl losing her virginity. Some tried to tape the tune and hack out offensive lines like "Angel, spread your wings and let me come inside." Others just banned the record completely. Even in Europe, it received spotty air play.

However, enough stations did play it to create a demand, and after a few weeks, most radio people were forced—by listener request—to air the song. In October, it entered the national pop charts, and by November it was the number-one single in the country. It stayed there for seven weeks—longer than any other record in 1976.

Play That Funky Music

WILD CHERRY

"What I wanted to do was cross R&B and pop music," said Rob Parissi, lead singer of Wild Cherry. "That's why I put a band together in 1970. Shortly after that, I wound up in the hospital for a few days, and the other guys came to see me. They brought me a bunch of stuff—they were clowning around—and one of the things was a box of cough drops. As they were getting ready to leave, one said, 'Hey, we don't have a name for our band.' So I held up the box of cough drops, as a joke, and said, 'You can call it this,' and pointed to the words 'Wild Cherry.' They liked it, and I hated it. I said, 'Are you serious?' It took me a long time to get used to that name.

"Anyway, we signed with Brown Bag Records—Terry Knight's label—but nothing really came of it. We went through some changes and broke up in 1975. I sold all my equipment and went to manage some Bonanza steakhouses. I listened to the radio as we closed up each night and heard things like 'Fame' by David Bowie and 'You're No Good' by Linda Ronstadt. I started saying that the trend was changing—that we were getting back to the roots of rock 'n' roll.

"So I got out of the steakhouses, got another bunch of fellows together, and formed a second attempt at Wild Cherry. We started playing all the rock clubs, but then they started to disappear, and we wound up having to work in discos, including a place in Pittsburgh called the 2001. We played too much rock, I guess, because people came up to us and said, 'Play that funky music.'

"In the dressing room, I told the guys that we had to find a rock 'n' roll way to play this disco stuff. Our drummer said, 'Well, I guess it's like they say—"You gotta play that funky music, white boy."' I said, 'That's a great idea.' I grabbed a bar pad, the kind used to take down drink orders, and began to write.

"A couple of months later, the Commodores came out with a song called 'I Feel Sanctified,' which I thought would be a good A side for us. So we went into the studio and cut that, along with 'Funky Music' as a B side. While I was laying down my vocal part on 'Funky Music,' our engineer called up some friends across town and said, 'I think you ought to come in here—I think we've got a hit.' So this guy came over and listened to it, and said, 'Yeah, when you get through with that, let me have it.'

"Well, I didn't take his opinion alone, so I took the song to New York and played it for a few labels, but nobody was really that much into dealing for it. I was pretty disgusted, and after a few weeks, I was ready to throw the thing away. Then that first guy called me back and said he'd played it for Epic Records.

"I knew enough about the record business to know that we had to capture the biggest cities. But to me, to get a breakout in Pittsburgh, our hometown, was something that we needed badly. When I first heard the song on the air in Pittsburgh, it was a real exciting thing. It just became everything I'd hoped it would be. And all the things that followed! *Billboard* called us the Best Pop Group of the Year; we got the American Music Award for the Top R&B Single of the Year; and there were two Grammy nominations, for Best New Vocal Group and Best R&B Performance by a Group or Duo. We got gold records from Canada and a lot of other foreign countries.

"After that, we started to overproduce our records, and that's probably why we never had another major hit. A lot of that was my fault, striving to sound different. We cut our last album in February 1979 and then just kind of fell apart.

"I think rock music is getting back now to pure forms. I grew up on Bo Diddley, Duane Eddy, the Animals, the Easybeats, the Yardbirds, the Ventures, Sly and the Family Stone—all pure forms of their own kind. I'm a firm believer in cutting things in their purest form, with each guy playing something interesting, and complementary to the song. That's what happened with 'Play That Funky Music.' Every guy had a designated part, and it all came together, and sounded good."

Don't Go Breaking My Heart

ELTON JOHN AND KIKI DEE

"It sounds terribly robotized, but it's the way we've always worked," said Bernie Taupin. "I totally write the whole lyric first, and then just take it to him and say, 'Here,' you know. And he sits down at the piano and works around it. It's not the old two-people-at-the-piano, hammering out songs, going 'Moon and June, silver spoon,' and sitting there, working together. It's not that sort of established way of writing at all. It's very very methodical. It's 'Here, this is my bit, you do your bit.' And it works out. We could never sit at the piano and write together. It would be impossible. We'd drive each other mad.

"Well, we were in Barbados for Christmas, and he came to me and said, 'I really want to write something uptempo, like a disco soul thing.' So I went upstairs and started banging away on the typewriter. In five minutes I'd done something, came downstairs, and just gave it to him. In the next five minutes, he finished it, and it was great. It was just one of those things that sparked off immediately. As soon as he played it, I said, "Well, that's gonna be the next single. That's a hit.' "

What Elton and Bernie had come up with was "Don't Go Breaking My Heart," and both agreed it was a special number. Elton then suggested recording it as a duet, with his favorite female singer, Kiki Dee.

Kiki, whom Elton said "has one of the greatest voices of all time," was the first artist signed to his Rocket Records label. Born Pauline Matthews in Bradford, England, she had been given her strange stage name in the mid-sixties. "It was a time when everything was kinky or kooky," she explained. "I was told that they had to call me something unusual if they were going to make me a star. I said, 'Call me anything you like. I just want to sign a recording contract.' "

Many years and many labels later, Kiki finally had a hit in 1974, "I've Got the Music in Me," on Rocket. However, nearly two years had passed since then, and Elton felt his protégé needed a second boost.

He called her and explained his idea for the song. She was more than willing, and met him in the studio. Elton actually taught her the tune during the recording process. This added to its spontaneity, and, in Kiki's words, made it "a whole lot of fun."

"Don't Go Breaking My Heart" took off early in July 1976, and by August, was America's favorite top-forty single. It hung around for nearly five months, becoming the biggest hit yet for either Kiki or Elton John.

By that point, Elton had sold over forty-two million albums and eighteen million singles throughout the world. Ten of his albums had gone over the million mark in the U.S. alone, and before the decade was out, his sales were to top one hundred million. The magnitude of this success was not lost on Elton or his lyricist, Bernie Taupin.

"The thing that I always say about our records, our music, our songs," said Bernie, "is that I'm happy that they sell as many copies as they do. This is not purely because I'm making a lot of money. I just love the thought of knowing that millions of people are listening to what we've written. That's a great feeling—I mean, a *really* great feeling. That's what really makes me happy."

Disco Lady

JOHNNIE TAYLOR

Johnnie Taylor's first public appearance was at age eight, in church, on an Easter Sunday program. Through his early teens, he performed with various church choirs and groups around Memphis and Kansas City, while absorbing the singing styles of the current top gospel and blues talents.

He moved to Chicago at age fourteen and shortly thereafter became lead singer of the Highway QCs, one of the area's top gospel groups. But even before that, he had been part of Kansas City's Melody Masters. That group had the honor of opening several local dates for the Soul Stirrers as far back as 1951, which marked Johnnie's first meeting with his idol, Sam Cooke. Cooke was then lead singer of the Soul Stirrers, the group that set the pace for intense, inspirational gospel quartet singing.

A friendship developed, which led Johnnie to replace Cooke in the Soul Stirrers when the latter made his crossover into pop music. One of Johnnie's recordings with the Soul Stirrers was "Stand by Me, Father," a song later adapted into the pop hit "Stand by Me" by Ben E. King. Eventually, Johnnie also got the urge to switch over—a decision that was hard to make.

"Really, I had little choice," he recalled. "They had cut gospel music off the radio. We could not be heard, we could not make a living, so it was kind of a forced issue. I spent two years in California, trying to get myself together. Finally I decided I couldn't sit on the fence any longer. If you can't make a living at your craft, you've got to do something else. So conse-quently I had to go with what was being heard on the radio."

When Cooke formed SAR Records in 1960, Johnnie became the first artist signed to the label. Nothing came of it, though, and when Cooke died in 1965, SAR folded up. Johnny returned to Memphis and, on impulse, dropped in at the office of Stax Records.

"I knew Al Bell, the executive vice president of Stax, when he used to be a disc jockey," Johnnie said. "We talked about old times, and I mentioned that I had gotten into rhythm and blues and pop music. Two weeks later, I signed a contract."

It took Johnnie an album and eight or nine singles before he struck gold in 1968, with "Who's Makin' Love?" After that smash, there was a string of small hits: "Take Care of Your Homework" and "Testify" in 1969; "Steal Away" and "I Am Somebody" in 1970; and "Jody's Got Your Girl and Gone" in 1971. In 1973, Johnnie recorded two big sellers, "I Believe in You" and "Cheaper to Keep Her." But as he entered the mid-seventies, he faced his most difficult challenge yet. With the bankruptcy of Stax, he had to redirect his career, which had been moving in a classy pop direction, toward the more youth-oriented disco dance style.

Eargasm, his debut album for Columbia in 1976, put it all together, spearheaded by the single "Disco Lady."

"I've been singing for a lot of years and I've paid a lot of dues, so when that record hit, I was ready," said Johnnie. "You build up quite a following after so long, and I think when you get a 'Disco Lady,' it just kind of pushes you over the top. It created more work for me, but my style of living didn't change."

"Disco Lady" was Johnnie's first single for Columbia Records, and the first single of any kind to be certified platinum. With its throbbing, pulsating rhythms, "Disco Lady" perfectly captured the commercial moment, at the same time commanding media attention for its evasive lyrics.

In retrospect, it was a little jarring for long-time fans, used to his romantic, astringent records, to see Johnny embroiled in a controversy over one of his songs. But it's true—many radio stations banned "Disco Lady" because of its "suggestive" lyrics.

"Disco Lady" triumphed, though, and went on to become the best-selling record in Columbia's history.

1977

U.S. RECORD SALES were up nearly twenty-eight percent in 1977, topping the $3 billion mark for the first time. Direct-to-disc recording was revived, as quad and the eight-track tape configuration were fading away. The Beach Boys signed a contract guaranteeing them a minimum of $1 million per album. Not to be outdone, the Stones closed a six-year deal calling for royalties of $21 million. *Rolling Stone* magazine celebrated its tenth anniversary with a lavish CBS-TV special; celebrities from Steve Martin to Bette Midler showed up for what critics termed "an unqualified disaster." Diana Ross got divorced, Chic got together, and the Starland Vocal Band got their own summer TV series. We lost Mr. New Year's Eve, Guy Lombardo; also Tommy Bolin of Deep Purple, William Powell of the O'Jays, and Dr. Peter Goldmark (the perfecter of the LP). Gene Chandler went to prison for selling narcotics; Johnny Rivers sued United Artists Records for millions in unpaid royalties. On October 20, a plane carrying the Lynyrd Skynyrd band went down in the deep South; several members were killed. Country superstar Dolly Parton crossed over into the pop market with "Here You Come Again"; Bob Seger made a dramatic comeback with "Night Moves"; and "I Go Crazy" by Paul Davis set a pop chart endurance record—*forty* consecutive weeks on America's best-seller lists. It was 1977—the year that Tom Johnston left the Doobie Brothers, and Stevie Wonder turned down an invitation to play at Jimmy Carter's inauguration.

Sha Na Na, a group that specialized in satirizing 50s rock 'n' roll, brought their comic posing to television in 1977 in a weekly syndicated half-hour. The ten members got together at Columbia University in 1968, adopting their name from the background chant of the Silhouettes' 1958 hit "Get a Job" (the real lyric of which, incidentally, is "sha *da da*"). Sha Na Na's line-up included Lenny Baker, Denny Greene, Johnny Contaroo, Dirty Dan McBride, Jocko Marcellino, Chico Ryan, Screamin' Scott Simon, Dan York, Tony Santini, and John "Bowser" Bowman (the unofficial leader of the gang).

Fleetwood Mac was formed in 1967 by bass guitarist John McVie and drummer Mick Fleetwood, both refugees from John Mayall's Bluesbreakers. In 1970, John's then-wife Christine came in on keyboards, along with guitarist Bob Welch. When Welch left in 1974, guitarist Lindsey Buckingham and vocalist Stevie Nicks were added, creating the group's best-known and most successful line-up. This quintet recorded the LP *Fleetwood Mac*, which featured the band's first major U.S. hits: "Over My Head," 'Rhiannon," and "Say You Love Me." In February 1977, they released *Rumours,* an album that got immediate air play and spent six months at the top of the LP charts. It earned a Grammy Award as Album of the Year and sold in excess of thirteen million copies (a record at that time). *Rumours* included four hits: "Go Your Own Way," "Dreams," "Don't Stop," and "You Make Lovin' Fun." Fleetwood Mac returned to the top ten with "Tusk" in 1979; in 1980 there was "Sara" and "Think about Me."

Star Wars, of course, was the year's big cinema blockbuster; the title theme was a hit for both composer John Williams and disco arranger Meco Monardo. Carly Simon crooned "Nobody Does It Better" in *The Spy Who Loved Me* (a 007 flick), while Bill Conti contributed "Gonna Fly Now" to the soundtrack of *Rocky.* Thelma Houston, the O'Jays, the Commodores, and Donna Summer were all heard in *Looking for Mr. Goodbar;* Debby Boone was not in *You Light Up My Life.* Also on hand: Kris Kristofferson and Barbra Streisand in their remake of *A Star Is Born.*

On February 19, **Stevie Wonder** swept the Grammy Awards by winning four key honors: Best Male Pop Singer, Best Male Rhythm and Blues Singer, Best Producer and Best Album (for *Songs in the Key of Life*). That two-record LP package was hailed by the critics as a musical milestone and one of the best record sets ever released. Among the twenty-one selections were two tunes that became number-one hits for Stevie in 1977: "I Wish" and "Sir Duke" (the latter a tribute to Duke Ellington and other personal idols). Later in the year, forty songs from Stevie's past were assembled in *Looking Back,* a three-record retrospective.

It's been said that there are four things America has contributed to this world—baseball, Coca-Cola, Mickey Mouse, and **Elvis Presley.** According to estimates, Elvis generated, in his lifetime, a total in excess of $43 billion. This staggering sum includes more than twenty-three years of record and tape sales, motion picture grosses, and live concert receipts. His 1962 soundtrack LP *Blue Hawaii* sold more than five million copies, while his biggest two-sided smash single, "Hound Dog" / "Don't Be Cruel," topped the eleven-million mark. In all, he earned fifty-five gold singles and 24 gold albums, and sold more than six hundred million records around the world. Despite claims of sagging popularity, nearly one-sixth of that total was sold between 1975 and the day he died—August 16, 1977. He had more top-ten singles, more consecutive top-ten records, more charted record sides, and more number-one records than any other performer in the history of recorded music. His voice has been heard in every corner of the globe, by more people, than that of any other individual of any era. He was without question the most important single force in the development of popular music. He was, and always will be, the King of Rock 'n' Roll.

Bing Crosby may not have been exactly a rock star, but he was the most durable recording artist in the history of the medium. His incredible career took him through every area of show business—radio, TV, films, theater, records—all conquered with his customary easy grace. Starting in the 1920s, when pop singers tended to overinterpret in a semioperatic style, Bing introduced warmth and intimacy to records and made himself the first legitimate pop idol. Between 1931 and 1957, he cut about eight hundred fifty records, with at least twenty achieving gold record status. Among them was his greatest achievement, "White Christmas." Recorded in 1942, it is still the largest-selling single in the history of the industry. Bing was the first record star to make pop singing "human," and managed to remain his unpretentious, witty, and charmingly hip self for more than seventy years. Bob Hope, Crosby's lifelong friend, summed it all up pretty well. "We've lost the most recognizable voice in the world," he said. "Bing called it 'groaning.' We called it 'magic.'"

THE TOP 40

1. You Light Up My Life, *Debby Boone*
2. I Just Want To Be Your Everything, *Andy Gibb*
3. A Star Is Born (Evergreen), *Barbra Streisand*
4. Undercover Angel, *Alan O'Day*
5. I Like Dreamin', *Kenny Nolan*
6. Dancing Queen, *Abba*
7. Torn Between Two Lovers, *Mary MacGregor*
8. Higher and Higher, *Rita Coolidge*
9. Best of My Love, *Emotions*
10. Southern Nights, *Glen Campbell*
11. Angel in Your Arms, *Hot*
12. Don't Leave Me This Way, *Thelma Houston*
13. I'm Your Boogie Man, *K. C. and the Sunshine Band*
14. Margaritaville, *Jimmy Buffett*
15. When I Need You, *Leo Sayer*
16. Telephone Line, *Electric Light Orchestra*
17. Rich Girl, *Hall and Oates*
18. Slow Dancin', *Johnny Rivers*
19. Star Wars, *Meco*
20. Rocky (Gonna Fly Now), *Bill Conti*
21. Things We Do for Love, *10cc*
22. Weekend in New England, *Barry Manilow*
23. Hotel California, *Eagles*
24. You Make Me Feel Like Dancing, *Leo Sayer*
25. Nobody Does It Better, *Carly Simon*
26. Whatcha Gonna Do, *Pablo Cruise*
27. I've Got Love on My Mind, *Natalie Cole*
28. On and On, *Stephen Bishop*
29. Do You Wanna Make Love, *Peter McCann*
30. Sir Duke, *Stevie Wonder*
31. Got to Give It Up, *Marvin Gaye*
32. Dreams, *Fleetwood Mac*
33. Carry On Wayward Son, *Kansas*
34. Easy, *Commodores*
35. Lonely Boy, *Andrew Gold*
36. Feels Like the First Time, *Foreigner*
37. You and Me, *Alice Cooper*
38. Car Wash, *Rose Royce*
39. Keep It Comin' Love, *K. C. and the Sunshine Band*
40. Don't Give Up on Us, *David Soul*

THE TOP 10 LPs

1. Rumours, *Fleetwood Mac*
2. Songs in the Key of Life, *Stevie Wonder*
3. Hotel California, *Eagles*
4. Boston, *Boston*
5. A Star Is Born, *Original Soundtrack*
6. Frampton Comes Alive, *Peter Frampton*
7. Fly Like an Eagle, *Steve Miller Band*
8. Night Moves, *Bob Seger and the Silver Bullet Band*
9. A New World Record, *Electric Light Orchestra*
10. Leftoverture, *Kansas*

Southern Nights

GLEN CAMPBELL

Glen Campbell was eminently qualified to sing of "Southern Nights," as he lived them for all of his growing-up years.

Raised on a farm near Delight, Arkansas, he first learned to pick tunes on the family guitar. Then, when he was four years old, his parents gave him one of his own, a five-dollar model, bought from the Sears catalog. Since he couldn't read music, Glen learned whatever he could from wherever he could: first from his family and friends, and later from listening to the radio. He also practiced his singing in the local Church of Christ.

"I spent the early part of my life looking at the north end of a southbound mule," he said. "It didn't take long to figure out that a guitar was a lot lighter than a plow handle."

Campbell left Arkansas as a teenager in the early fifties, but stayed in the south, living in New Mexico and Houston, Texas. His first music jobs were with his uncle, Dick Bills, touring the southwest and playing in what Glen called "dancin' and fightin' clubs." Soon he formed his own band.

In the sixties, Glen became a leader in country-pop music. His impressive hit string included "By the Time I Get to Phoenix," "Gentle on My Mind," "Wichita Lineman," "Galveston," and "Try a Little Kindness." He made films, starred in his own top-rated TV musical series, and won four Grammy Awards. By the end of the decade, he was the highest-paid concert performer on the country music scene.

In the seventies, Glen concentrated on live appearances. He still made the charts every year, with songs like "It's Only Make Believe," "Rhinestone Cowboy," and "Country Boy (You Got Your Feet in L.A.)."

Then, in 1977, Glen recorded "Southern Nights." He chose it because it reminded him of his rural roots—his early days on the farm in Arkansas. "My dad told me when I

was a kid, 'You're having the best time of your life, and you don't even know it.' Sure enough, he was right. Now I really feel the need to go back home, float down the Missouri River, and fish for bass and crappies. It's real peaceful, and remote from things like telephones. My head is still there."

"Southern Nights" was released in January 1977, and peaked at number one in April. It was Glen's twenty-eighth single to make the charts, in a pop career that spanned sixteen years.

"There's an old saying," he recalled. "It's easy to come, and easy to go. The hard thing is to remain."

Best of My Love
THE EMOTIONS

The Emotions, known originally as the Heavenly Sunbeams, began performing as children, singing gospel music in their hometown of Chicago. Their father and manager, Joe Hutchinson, taught them how to sing, how to read music, and how to harmonize.

Wanda, Shelia, and Jeanette made their first TV appearance in 1958, and a few years later, they hosted their own radio show of religious music. Eventually, the program evolved into a Sunday morning TV series, and the fame of the singing Hutchinsons spread.

As the Sunbeams' reputation continued to grow, they began to record, releasing product on several labels before signing with Volt Records in 1968. It was at that time that the group became known as the Emotions.

"We made the transition from gospel to pop at that time," recalled Wanda. "It was then that several friends told our father about how our singing affected them. They said it kind of brought chills, you know, an emotional response. So he thought the best thing to call us would be the Emotions."

Producers Isaac Hayes and David Porter were instrumental in the development of a new pop sound for the Emotions. The result was "So I Can Love You," which reached the bottom of America's top forty in July 1969. Several follow-up records became R&B hits, and in 1973, the girls made their movie debut in the concert documentary, *Wattstax*.

In 1975, their label folded, and the group found themselves without a recording contract. Maurice White, the leader and founder of Earth, Wind and Fire, then signed them to his company, Kalimba Productions. In February 1976, they recorded *Flowers*, their first album under his direction. Released the following summer, it quietly went gold while the girls were in the midst

of a sixty-city tour. March of 1977 saw the Emotions and White back in the studio, recording their follow-up album. They decided to call it *Rejoice*.

"We arrived in Los Angeles with a bunch of songs we'd written, ready to show Maurice," said Wanda. "He had a few of his own, including 'Best of My Love,' which he had not yet completed. He had the rhythm down and had sung the song on a demo tape, even though the words weren't all finished. But that hook line was there—'Oh, oh, you've got the best of my love.' I learned the song off that demo and practiced singing it in the same register that he had.

"Well, the day we went to rehearse the song in the studio, he said, 'No, Wanda, I meant for you to sing it an octave higher.' So I said, 'Maurice,' I'ver never sung that high in that range.' And he said, 'Well, you don't know if you don't try it.' So we did it, but I was still pretty doubtful.

"Well, we were in Baton Rouge on June 29, and we heard the song for the first time on the radio. I still hadn't gotten used to hearing me sounding way up there. But what happened was that when my range got higher, the intensity of my vibrato sharpened a

little. It got a cut on it, and people like it. And I've got to say, I've come to like it myself, now."

"Best of My Love" broke onto the pop charts in June 1977 and spent twenty-three weeks on the best-seller lists. Five of those weeks were spent in the number-one position. Later, the record was to earn the Emotions their first Grammy Award, for Best R&B Vocal Performance by a Duo, Group, or Chorus.

"Best of My Love" turned out to be a tough act to follow. However, another hit finally came in 1979—"Boogie Wonderland," performed in conjunction with Earth, Wind and Fire.

"The definition of gospel music, as we understand it, is 'good news,'" said Wanda, "and we don't feel we've ever moved away from music that brings good news. We appreciate our roots. They're our foundation. They keep us remembering, and always grateful and humble to the Father for having blessed us so. Although our songs are not all directly ones that can be sung in church, they do lift up the spirit. So, in a way, we're still singing the same kind of music we always have."

Higher and Higher
RITA COOLIDGE

Born in Nashville and raised in East Tennessee, Rita Coolidge was the daughter of a minister at a small church outside of Lafayette. He positioned her at the center of his choir, and young Rita quickly learned to sing and perform.

Her first group was the Coolidge Sisters, which included siblings Priscilla and Linda. The trio won local state fairs and talent contests before eventually going their separate ways. Rita went to Florida State University to pursue a degree in art.

While still a student, Rita returned to music, mainly to help pay for art supplies. First she sang locally, then ventured into Memphis to work at a jingles company. Through that association, she recorded her first single, "Turn Around and Love You," for Pepper Records.

Memphis, meanwhile, was being rediscovered by a whole new crop of southern rockers like Leon Russell and Delaney and Bonnie. When the latter duo visited town, they were impressed by Rita's voice and took her back with them to Los Angeles to sing on one of their albums.

"When I got to L.A.," recounted Rita, "I just couldn't believe it. Everyone knew who I was." Sure enough, "Turn Around and Love You" had been a top-ten hit, but only in L.A.

In 1969 Rita accepted a job singing on Joe Cocker's "Mad Dogs and Englishmen" tour. "It was a circus," she recalled. "It was an incredible time. We were always moving, always traveling. There was no time for anything." Rita, though, was a survivor, and in tribute, another tour member, Leon Russell, wrote a song about her—"Delta Lady."

On November 9, 1970, in the Los Angeles airport, on the runway and waiting to board a flight for Memphis, Rita met singer-songwriter-actor Kris Kristofferson. Both were getting on the same flight. Kristofferson was headed to Nashville for a magazine cover-story interview. Rita was getting off at the first stop, Memphis. Kristofferson got off in Memphis, too, and not long afterward, they were wed.

In 1971, Rita signed with A&M Records and began to cut a string of mild-selling albums. On them, she covered everything from gospel to pop, from R&B to rock. "I came out of that searching period learning you touch people's hearts quietly, and it could have had as much impact as making them dance in the streets. I realized I didn't need to rock and roll to move an audience. I found my strength lay in ballads."

In May of 1977, Rita Coolidge was five months pregnant. "I was really taking care of myself, watching my diet, sleeping right, and was in excellent health. My baby was alive and kicking. I heard the heartbeat and then, for some reason, no one knows why, it just stopped."

Having something to do right afterward made the loss of her baby easier for Rita to bear. She threw herself into her next album, *Anytime ... Anywhere.* "It became a very important project for me," she said. "I gave it all my energy, and wanted to make it an 'up' album. With a lot of help from Jerry Moss [of A&M Records], it was."

Rita was persuaded to spice up the LP with remakes of some of her favorite oldies from the sixties. Among them was "Higher and Higher," which had been a million-seller for Jackie Wilson just a decade before. Rita slowed it down and understated the song, singing it in a sleepy, almost detached kind of way. The low-pressure approach worked, and Rita wound up with one of the biggest hits of the year.

"Higher and Higher" was her first platinum single—and a smash in nearly every city around the world. Oddly, though, it was not a hit in Singapore, where it was banned as a "drug record."

Rita placed more songs on the pop charts in later years, including "We're All Alone," "The Way You Do the Things You Do," and "You." Sadly, her marriage to the man who's love had taken her higher and higher did not last. However, by that time, Rita had ceased being merely "Mrs. Kris Kristofferson." She had become a star in her own right, with a permanent niche in the history of American pop.

Torn Between Two Lovers

MARY MacGREGOR

Mary was born in St. Paul, Minnesota, where she studied classical piano from the age of six. Within eight years, she was singing professionally with a local big band. After attending the University of Minnesota, where she continued singing with Minneapolis and St. Paul groups, Mary began touring the rest of the country with various folk, R&B, and rock bands.

It was during one of these national tours that she caught the attention of Peter Yarrow of Peter, Paul and Mary. Impressed with her double-octave range, Yarrow invited her to join him on a national tour as a backup vocalist. His next step was putting her voice on vinyl: Mary was heard singing backup on Yarrow's *Love Songs* album. Her blossoming vocal talent led to her first solo endeavor, produced by Yarrow, the fateful "Torn Between Two Lovers."

"I never liked the song too much, and I still don't," said Mary. "There are just some songs I like, and some I don't, and this is one of them. Peter and I had a very long relationship. We're both very emotional people, and whenever we got together it was a very volatile experience. Sometimes it was positive, sometimes negative, and on this particular song we had a lot of fights. Was it really good? Was it going to make it? We had a lot of discussions about this song.

"For me to sing anything, I have to get emotionally involved. That's what really makes it for me. I didn't like 'Torn' mostly because it was boring to sing. It's a real 'sleeper' kind of ballad. Peter thought it was a real statement, and he wanted it to happen. He wanted a woman to sing it, and he wanted that woman to be me.

"I recorded the song in Muscle Shoals, Alabama, while standing in a bathroom. It was a room that was actually part of the studio, just sort of built-in there. They had a boom stand with a microphone on the end of it. The boom was in the studio, and the mike kind of stuck in through the door, hanging over the mirror. It was a tiny little room, but I finally worked things around so I didn't have to stare at myself singing. It's a great place. You get a lot of natural echo in bathrooms."

Mary was trembling when she recorded her big song, and not from the studio air conditioning. At the time, she'd been happily married for five years, and just the thought of being unfaithful to her husband, Don, was traumatic. But then came stardom, and the hopes, pressures, fears, and disappointments that come with it. On May 25, 1978, Mary filed for divorce, citing "irreconcilable differences." Her next release—a flop—was called "Memories."

"A lot of people are torn between two lovers," said Mary, "or have been, or will be. The single itself must have touched a lot of them, because it sold more than two million copies, worldwide."

"Torn Between Two Lovers" began its rise in November 1976, finally peaking at number one in February 1977. It put Mary in the spotlight—for the moment—but ruined her career singing advertising jingles.

"I'm in a dilemma because I'm too well known to return to being an anonymous singer for a bank, but I'm not well known enough to get bookings. I never thought about being a success until 'Torn.' I was trying to make a career out of doing commercials. Now I can't.

"Success is so fickle," she warned. "You're only as good as your next hit."

Dancing Queen
ABBA

*T*he Abba story began with Bjorn Ulvaeus, who was born in Göteborg, on the Baltic coast of Sweden. He and some friends, fans of the music of the Kingston Trio and the Brothers Four, formed their own folk group, the West Bay Singers. Later, they were to change their name to the Hootenanny Singers.

Meanwhile, there was a pop group knocking around Scandinavia known as the Hep Stars. They were the most popular band in Sweden, with more than a dozen hits, many of which had been written by one member, Benny Andersson.

In the summer of 1966, Bjorn and Benny met at a party and discovered that they had pretty much the same ideas on music. Over the next few years, they got together whenever they could, writing songs and placing them with other acts. After a while, they started performing their own material in nightclubs and cabarets. At one booking, the management insisted that they "brighten up the stage" with some female accompaniment. Bjorn called on his girlfriend, a singer named Agnetha Faltskog, and Benny found Annafrid Lyngstad. Together, they made their debut on November 1, 1970, as the Festfolk Quartet (*festfolk* could be translated either as "party people" or "fiancés").

On July 7, 1971, Bjorn and Agnetha were married, and on the same day, Bjorn was offered a job as staff producer at the Polar Recording Company. Bjorn insisted that Benny come along, too. The label explained that they had only enough money to hire one person, but Bjorn said that was all right; he'd just split his salary with Benny.

The pair wrote and produced a number of records in the early seventies, including several of which were credited to "Bjorn and Benny." The girls sang background vocals at first, but as time went on, they began to take over more and more of the leads.

Eventually the labels credited all four singers' names. Their manager got tired of repeating all those names in interviews, so one day, as a joke, he strung the initials of their first names together to form the name Abba.

Abba first gained worldwide attention in 1974, when they performed "Waterloo" in the 19th Annual Eurovision Song Festival, an event televised to an estimated half-billion viewers in thirty-two countries. Abba won the festival, and their record became their first U.S. hit, selling more than five million copies around the globe. It was followed, in America, by "Honey Honey" (1974), "S.O.S." (1975), "I Do I Do I Do I Do I Do" (1976), and "Fernando" (1976). In the summer of 1976, these songs were collected in the album *Abba's Greatest Hits,* which sold over seven million copies.

In early November 1976, "Dancing Queen," after weeks as the number-one record in England, throughout Europe, Australia, and the Far East, broke out as an "import" item on several U.S. radio stations. The unde-

niable new hit picked up steam as the stations began to play it right from Abba's brand-new album, *Arrival,* still unreleased in the U.S. at that point.

On November 18, Atlantic seized the initiative and rush-released "Dancing Queen" in North America, simultaneously issuing the tune as the latest entry in its limited-edition twelve-inch DiscoDisc series. By March, it was the number-one song in America, with sales ultimately topping six million. The LP, certified gold one month later, sold in excess of nine million copies. In all, during 1977, Abba earned well over $10 million.

Abba went on to score other hits in the seventies, and they also made a film, *Abba: The Movie,* in 1978.

By the end of the decade, the group owned their own studio, film production works, a movie theater, and an art gallery, and were investing heavily in hotels and restaurants. Their "aural candy," as one critic put it, had made them the largest single corporation in Sweden. Volvo was number two.

I Like Dreamin'

KENNY NOLAN

"Music has always been my love," said Kenny Nolan. "My mother bought me an accordion when I was thirteen. The same year, I won a scholarship to USC for composition. I went for about five or six months, and then got bored. At fifteen, I changed to piano, and at seventeen, I won another scholarship to Chiounard. I went there for about six months, and got bored again. I just had to do it on my own. I couldn't learn the conventional way."

Kenny began honing his style in a succession of high school bands. In the late sixties, he embarked on a songwriting career, sending material to everyone from the Osmonds to the Grass Roots. In 1975, three of his tunes became million-sellers: "My Eyes Adored You," recorded by Frankie Valli; "Lady Marmalade," performed by Labelle; and "Get Dancin'," cut by Disco Tex and his Sex-O-Lettes.

Kenny sang on that last record, adding the falsetto that helped make it a major hit. After that, he became the voice of two studio groups, Firefly and the Eleventh Hour. In 1976, he "broke them up," and decided to become himself.

"It was a totally different feeling, because when I sang as Kenny Nolan, it was me. All I did was sing in my normal voice. I was so used to doing that high disco screaming that finally, when I sang 'I Like Dreamin',' it was a total departure.

"I do like dreaming. I dream songs, and actually get melodies and lyrics in my sleep. I then rush to my living room. While radio stations and the rest of the world are off in sleep, I turn on my cassette, and proceed to capture a dream."

Kenny wrote "I Like Dreamin' " on assignment for a major pop star. It was turned down, frustrating Kenny enough to make him want to sing the song himself. After being released, it sat around for six months, and looked like a total dud. Then a few stations in Louisiana started to play it, and slowly its popularity spread.

"I Like Dreamin' " broke onto the national charts in early November, 1976. For three months, it crept higher and higher, finally peaking in February 1977. In all, it spent more than six months on America's hit parade. A follow-up, "Love's Grown Deep," also made the national top twenty. As a result, Kenny was named the Number One New Pop Singles Artist of 1977, by *Billboard* magazine.

" 'I Like Dreamin' is a lot like all my songs," said Kenny, "love-related. Situations between a man and a woman—something that anybody can relate to and understand."

Undercover Angel

ALAN O'DAY

Alan O'Day's father was a news-paper photographer and a music lover. "He used to give me back rubs," recalled Alan, "with syncopated hand-pat drum figures." His mother was a newspaper writer, schoolteacher, and music lover as well.

Alan's first musical memory is of creating tunes on a xylophone at the age of six. By the fifth grade, his favorite artist was Spike Jones, and he was serenading his class on the ukulele. At Coachella Valley Union High, he started his first rock 'n' roll band, with heavy influences from Jerry Lee Lewis, Little Richard, Elvis, and Fats Domino.

It was at this point that Alan began to write his own songs. "When I was in high school, to be a songwriter was tantamount to being a bum, at least as far as the prospects were concerned. I had never even given it much thought. I just did it for fun. I wrote songs when I was in high school as a way of getting acceptance from my peer group."

Alan spent most of the sixties on the road with a four-piece band. He scored some films, and appeared on the "Ed Sullivan Show," but still felt his career was going nowhere.

"When I was twenty-eight years old, I was completely miserable," he said. "I couldn't see what my future would be. I'd been playing in bars and clubs with various groups for years, waiting for that break that would catapult me to stardom. I had a few near misses, but they always fell short."

Then, in 1971, Alan signed with Warner Brothers Music, and wrote "The Drum," which became a hit single for Bobby Sherman. In 1974, three more of his songs did well: "Train of Thought," recorded by Cher; "Rock 'n' Roll Heaven," cut by the Righteous Brothers; and "Angie Baby," sung by Helen Reddy. "Well-known artists, good production, distribution, air play; it was the first time that these things just clicked in, one right after

another. I said to myself, 'My God, that's what it feels like when everything goes right.' "

In 1977, Warner Brothers Music decided to form a special label for their composers who also performed. "Songs which otherwise would have been channeled to major recording artists," said president Ed Silvers, "we will now be able to exploit on Pacific Records, via the original song-writers." The first artist signed was

Alan O'Day, and the first release—"Undercover Angel."

Alan described that tune as a "nocturnal novelette." It was put out, without fanfare, in February 1977. Four months later, it was the number one song in the country, and certified gold to boot. "It's wonderful when you find out what feels right," said Alan, "and then it also feels right to other people. That's a songwriter's dream."

A Star Is Born (Evergreen)

BARBRA STREISAND

Kris Kristofferson and Barbra Streisand

A Star Is Born started out in 1937 as an early Technicolor feature film. It told the story of two stars whose marriage goes on the rocks because one is on the way up and the other is on the way down. Fredric March played the loser, an aging, self-destructive type; Janet Gaynor was his wife, a young movie hopeful. The picture itself won an Oscar for Best Original Story, which was something of a lark; its premise, in fact, had been lifted from *What Price Hollywood?*, a feature made in 1932 by George Cukor.

Ironically, it was Cukor who directed *A Star Is Born* when it was remade in 1954, with James Mason. The plot was rewritten a little bit to allow musical numbers by Mason's co-star, Judy Garland. A high point was Judy's classic rendition of "The Man Who Got Away"; her "love theme" from *A Star Is Born.*

The next twenty years were peaceful on the retread front; everyone assumed that *A Star Is Born* was "dated" property, and two versions were more than enough. But then, somebody got the bright idea of changing the setting—adapting the old concept to the world of rock music. In 1974, rumors began: Streisand was up for the female lead in *Rainbow Bridge,* a third remake of *A Star Is Born.* Cher and others had been in the running; Kris Kristofferson was pretty much set for the male lead. Then, in April 1975, a source close to Elvis Presley said that he would "definitely co-star in the movie, newly titled *Rainbow Road.*" That bit of inspired casting never came off, of course, and is one of the great rock 'n' roll "ifs." We can only speculate as to the kind of sparks Streisand and Presley might have struck if they'd been able to work together onscreen.

Kris Kristofferson wound up with the part, and, quite credibly, made it very much his own. A gifted singer-songwriter, he'd gained great fame in the early seventies with such tunes as "Why Me" and "Loving Her Was Easier" (he'd also written "Help Me Make It Through the Night"). Thanks to his popularity (and Barbra's), the film found a huge fan market—even though the critics, by and large, were less than impressed.

Their main gripe was with the movie music, which they said was middle of the road, passed off as rock 'n' roll. Indeed, most of the score was by soft pop composers: Kenny Loggins, Paul Williams, and the team of Marilyn and Alan Bergman. Kris himself was not really a rock singer, and neither was Barbra, who took screen credit for the picture's "musical concept."

"In many respects, this is a filmed Streisand concert," wrote one reviewer. "It's simply set against a soggy soap opera. As in *Funny Girl* and *The Way We Were,* there's a brassy woman, intent on a guy less strong than she is. She can't control her ambitions, and in the end, her main squeeze is lost. How many times is Barbra going to play the same role?"

Streisand served as the picture's executive producer; her boyfriend, Jon Peters, was producer. The two edited their film at home, allowing no one to see it before the world premiere. It was finally released on December 18, 1976. Within eighteen months, it had earned back a spectacular profit—more than $65 million.

Barbra also came up with the title theme, which she wrote with Paul Williams. Despite its greeting card sentimentality, it became enormously popular, and is still a standard song chosen by many couples to be sung at weddings. Streisand's version broke in mid-December 1976, and reached number one in March 1977. In all, it spent nearly six months on the charts. Later, it earned three Grammy Awards: Best Female Vocal Performance, Best Arrangement Accompanying a Vocalist, and Song of the Year. The soundtrack album was a pretty big hit too, despite carrying the highest list price of any pop LP to that time—$8.98. After seven months in the top twenty, it had sold over three and a half million copies.

I Just Want to Be Your Everything

ANDY GIBB

*T*he Bee Gees' little brother, Andy, wasn't quite sure what kind of career he should carve for himself as he entered his teens. He'd grown up in the shadows of fame his entire life, and didn't know if show business was the right approach to take. He decided to give it a try, and spent several years honing his voice, writing, and performing talents. As a Gibb brother, he was very much aware of the fact that he had to come on like a seasoned veteran from the moment of his pro debut.

In 1977, the Bee Gees' manager, Robert Stigwood, decided that eighteen-year-old Andy was ready. He was summoned, along with Barry, to Stigwood's island retreat in Bermuda. He was given a contract, and instructed to come up with a hit song—a super song—worthy of a Bee Gee brother.

"Well, it was Barry who came up with the tune," said Andy. "We needed a single, and locked ourselves in a bedroom at my manager's big estate there. I think we wound up writing four songs in two days.

"The first day we came up with a nice ballad that was never used. Then, that afternoon, on his own, Barry came up with 'I Just Want to Be Your Everything.'"

To Barry, the word "just" was vital to the song; it was the sentiment he wanted to express. He spent a long time looking for a way to put emphasis on that word, and finally made "I" a long note, instead of putting it in the same line as the rest of the title. Stigwood liked the song, but planned to make "Love Is (Thicker Than Water)" Andy's actual debut single. Three days before the scheduled release date, he changed his mind.

"I Just Want to Be Your Everything" broke in late July 1977, and sped to the top of the charts. It stayed there for four weeks, and remained on the best-seller list for an incredible seven months.

"I think Barry pinpointed the

reason," explained Andy. "He said it all works with the time of year. If you release a song in the summer that's right for summer, and it's a happy song, then it's bound to become a hit. 'I Just Want to Be Your Everything' was that perfect song. Everybody sang along to it. In fact, it was a big hit within the industry before it was even released. Acetates went around to people at different companies, and they rang us up, saying, 'This is amazing. Everybody at our label is singing that song here.' It was a big hit because it was an up, happy, summer song.

"I remember when it entered the top thirty. It was exciting—God, it was

incredible! It was making big jumps, but then it began to slow down. It got to number twenty and made an astonishing jump to thirteen. I thought, ooh, and it picked up again, and everyone thought, gee, this could be big. It went thirteen to seven; I thought, oh no, I don't believe it, this could be a number one record, my first! The first time, as much as you want that number one—it's what you've been dreaming about all your life—when it happens, you can't really face the fact that you could have a number-one record on your hands. At times I thought it wasn't going up there, but it did."

You Light Up My Life

DEBBY BOONE

Debby Boone was, among other things, one of the very first *third-generation* pop stars. In 1950, her grandfather, Red Foley, topped the charts with "Chattanooga Shoeshine Boy." A few years later, her father, Pat Boone, had the number-one single of 1957, "Love Letters in the Sand." It was twenty years after that that Debby's turn came, and with her first solo release she scored one of the biggest hits of the rock 'n' roll era.

Debby was born in Hackensack, New Jersey, and moved with her family to the Los Angeles area when she was four. Thanks to her father's success, she was able to lead a sheltered life, and was content to do so. "I never felt a need to know everything that was going on," she said. "Really, what's the point of knowing about the smutty things in life?"

As a result of her attitude, Debby developed an image of unusual wholesomeness—saying yes to spiritual matters, but no to smoking, drinking, drugs, and premarital sex. What rebellious years she had came in the late sixties and early seventies, after seeing the film *Easy Rider* (1969). She announced plans to buy a

motorcycle and head for San Francisco, but never got around to making the trip. Instead, she hung out in places where she wasn't supposed to go, and admittedly "smoked cigarettes."

It was about then that her dad decided to incorporate his wife and four daughters into a family-oriented concert act. They played state fairs, hotels and amusement parks around the world. Eventually, the team began to break up, as each girl entered college, got married, or pursued other interests. As for Debby, she elected to stay home with her parents, claiming that she couldn't handle the "high pressure atmosphere" of university life. Instead, she enrolled at Bible school, and worked briefly with emotionally disturbed children.

By 1977 though, Debby's lifestyle was getting her down—visiting friends, working out at her gym, and accompanying Dad and Mom on trips was boring, and "making her crazy." It was then that producer Mike Curb approached her with "You Light Up My Life."

"I'm pleased that my first release was a ballad," said Debby. "I like some rock music, but I'm not really a rock 'n' roller. Middle America, the bulk of

the nation, isn't into one extreme or the other, and enjoys this sort of thing. I think the song is a change, different from what we've been hearing. It's refreshing."

Debby freely acknowledged that she had a spiritual, rather than a romantic idea in mind when she recorded "You Light Up My Life."

"When I first heard the song, I knew it was probably written about a male-female relationship, but I hadn't seen the movie. For me, it lent itself to these spiritual feelings I was having. People always ask me if I was singing it to some special person, and I have to say no. You see, as far as I'm concerned, it's my love song to God. My life is centered around Him, and that's not something predominant in the music business."

"You Light Up My Life" was the title theme from a movie about making it in the record industry. The project was conceived and produced by Joe Brooks, an award-winning commercial jingle writer. He had been making half-a-million dollars a year in advertising, but in 1975 simply quit to try something new. He wrote a screenplay and hired Kacey Cisyk to sing five songs for the soundtrack, including the title theme. Later, Kacey claimed she was never paid for that recording session, and her name did not appear in the movie credits. When the soundtrack album came out, her name was misspelled and she was listed as a "background singer."

Recorded in late May, the single came out in late August and was used in a TV spot plugging the film. Within seven weeks the song had rocketed all the way to the top.

"You Light Up My Life" was number one longer than any other song in 1977, and longer than any recording by a female artist in a quarter century. It sold nearly five million copies, outdistancing even her father Pat's biggest hit. It also garnered an Oscar and two Grammy Awards.

1978

THE MUSIC INDUSTRY boomed in 1978, with U.S. record sales nearly eleven times what they'd been in 1956. Total receipts were up eighteen percent, topping the $4 billion mark for the first and only time. In April, the RSO label placed six singles in the *Billboard* top ten, while their soundtrack album *Saturday Night Fever*, became the best-selling LP ever. Another of their soundtracks, from the film *Sgt. Pepper*, became the first double album to ship triple platinum, with orders for more than three and a half million copies. Kenny Rogers and "Lucille" swept the Academy of Country Music awards, picking up four trophies; CMA winners included Crystal Gayle and "Don't It Make My Brown Eyes Blue." Marvin Gaye dedicated what appeared to be a deliberately bad album, *Here My Dear,* to his ex-wife (who was given all the LP royalties by the court). Later, Marvin filed for bankruptcy, claiming to be $2 million in debt.

Evelyn "Champagne" King, who was discovered while working as a janitor in the Philadelphia International studios, recorded one of the year's biggest disco numbers, "Shame" (another top dance hit, "Got to Be Real," was cut by former "Gong Show" winner Cheryl Lynn). In October, Toto's "Hold the Line" became a 45 RPM picture disc record; in December, Bobby Caldwell scored with a heart-shaped single, "What You Won't Do for Love." We lost Johnny Bond, Louis Prima, and big band leader Ray Noble; also Terry Kath of Chicago, Victor Ames of the Ames Brothers, Keith Moon of the Who, and Bill Kenny (the last of the original Ink Spots). Nineteen seventy-eight was the year of a Beatles spoof—the Rutles—as well as attractions like Cal Jam II and a Presley festival in Las Vegas. The latter events drew record-setting crowds; the Rutles generated enough excitement to last a lunch hour.

"The new generation takes few risks; it graduates, looks for a job, endures. And, once a week, on Saturday night, it explodes." So wrote Nik Cohn in a cover story for *New York* magazine in June 1976. It told of young people in Brooklyn's Bay Ridge district, who, every weekend, escaped their humdrum existence by dancing their cares away at a local disco. Cohn zeroed in on the club's best dancer, who was admired by all the guys and pursued by all the girls. Slowly, the young dancer came to realize that his time at the top would be as fleeting as it was then absolute. Cohn's article, "Tribal Rites of the New Saturday Night," was turned into a film in 1978 starring John Travolta and Karen Gorney. Titled **Saturday Night Fever,** the picture earned over $108 million by the end of the year (and was the first R-rated movie to top $100 million in rentals). By April, the soundtrack LP had sold over ten million copies, making the two-disc set the largest-grossing album to that time. It in itself was a first-rate disco sampler, featuring old and new tracks by the Bee Gees, Kool and the Gang, K.C. and the Sunshine Band, the Trammps, MFSB, Walter Murphy, Tavares, Yvonne Elliman and others.

What a year for music movies! The Bee Gees, having contributed heavily to *Saturday Night Fever* and *Grease.* came on screen themselves (with Peter Frampton) in the motion picture version of *Sgt. Pepper's Lonely Hearts Club Band.* Cheech and Chong went *Up in Smoke,* Diana Ross and Michael Jackson met *The Wiz,* and Stephen Bishop met his match (John Belushi) in *Animal House* (Bishop and Linda Ronstadt also turned up in *FM*). Kris Kristofferson helped turn C.W. McCall's hit "Convoy" into a movie; Donna Summer sang "Last Dance" in *Thank God It's Friday.* There were also two major biopics: *The Buddy Holly Story* and *American Hot Wax* (about deejay Alan Freed, and featuring Chuck Berry and Jerry Lee Lewis).

The only live entertainment show of the 1978–79 season was **"Dick Clark's Live Wednesday,"** a brave attempt to revive Ed Sullivan-style variety on television. Although Dick presented many kinds of acts, he naturally put the emphasis on pop music performers. On one program, Connie Francis appeared and sang publicly for the first time in more than four years (since her 1974 motel room rape). After its premiere on September 20, low ratings dogged the series; after three months, ABC dropped the show.

It was a textbook case of media manipulation. **The Sex Pistols,** a cacophonous band of British punkers, bamboozled the American press into making them one of the most talked-about new groups in years. Led by Johnny Rotten (so named because he never brushed his teeth), the Pistols specialized not in music, but in brutal rudeness, spitting, cursing, and vomiting on their audiences. Their U.S. tour was a media circus and a total disaster, ending in an angry break-up in San Francisco. Later, bass player Sid Vicious allegedly knifed his girlfriend to death, and then took his own life through a drug overdose. The whole fiasco was over in a few months, with almost no record sales. "If you really want to know, I think we failed," said Rotten, "miserably." He then announced plans to form a new band—to be called the Carnivorous Buttocks Flies.

Legendary programer Bill Drake narrated the most ambitious and expensive radio show ever produced: **"The History of Rock 'n' Roll,"** a 52-hour musical documentary. Hundreds of original hits, and quotations from the stars who made them, told the story, both chronologically and in chapters covering specific artists, styles, and periods. The finale was a forty-minute montage of clips from every number-one record since 1956, in sequence. Engineer Mark Ford assembled the show from a script written by an obscure pop musicologist. Over four hundred radio stations around the world aired the epic, which earned a *Billboard* Award as The Top Special Program of the Year.

THE TOP 40

1. Night Fever, *Bee Gees*
2. Shadow Dancing, *Andy Gibb*
3. Stayin' Alive, *Bee Gees*
4. Kiss You All Over, *Exile*
5. Three Times a Lady, *Commodores*
6. Boogie Oogie Oogie, *A Taste of Honey*
7. Baby Come Back, *Player*
8. Emotion, *Samantha Sang*
9. You're the One That I Want, *Olivia Newton-John and John Travolta*
10. Grease, *Frankie Valli*
11. Miss You, *Rolling Stones*
12. Hot Child in the City, *Nick Gilder*
13. MacArthur Park, *Donna Summer*
14. How Deep Is Your Love, *Bee Gees*
15. Love Is Thicker Than Water, *Andy Gibb*
16. Lay Down Sally, *Eric Clapton*
17. Just the Way You Are, *Billy Joel*
18. Baker Street, *Gerry Rafferty*
19. If I Can't Have You, *Yvonne Elliman*
20. I Can't Smile Without You, *Barry Manilow*
21. It's a Heartache, *Bonnie Tyler*
22. With a Little Luck, *Paul McCartney and Wings*
23. We Are the Champions/We Will Rock You, *Queen*
24. Sometimes When We Touch, *Dan Hill*
25. I Go Crazy, *Paul Davis*
26. Short People, *Randy Newman*
27. Too Much, Too Little, Too Late, *Johnny Mathis and Denice Williams*
28. Feels So Good, *Chuck Mangione*
29. You're in My Heart, *Rod Stewart*
30. You Needed Me, *Anne Murray*
31. Dance, Dance, Dance, *Chic*
32. Hot Blooded, *Foreigner*
33. Hopelessly Devoted to You, *Olivia Newton-John*
34. Love Is Like Oxygen, *Sweet*
35. Jack and Jill, *Raydio*
36. The Closer I Get to You, *Roberta Flack and Donny Hathaway*
37. Dance with Me, *Peter Brown*
38. Reminiscing, *Little River Band*
39. Two Out of Three Ain't Bad, *Meatloaf*
40. Last Dance, *Donna Summer*

THE TOP 10 LPs

1. Saturday Night Fever, *Original Soundtrack*
2. Grease, *Original Soundtrack*
3. The Stranger, *Billy Joel*
4. Rumours, *Fleetwood Mac*
5. Point of Know Return, *Kansas*
6. Aja, *Steely Dan*
7. The Grand Illusion, *Styx*
8. Slowhand, *Eric Clapton*
9. Simple Dreams, *Linda Ronstadt*
10. Running on Empty, *Jackson Browne*

Styx's history began in Chicago in 1963 when twin brothers Chuck and John Panozzo learned to play bass and drums, respectively, and were joined by neighbor Dennis DeYoung on accordion. By 1970, the trio had added two guitarists and adopted their group name. "Lady," a three-year-old album cut, became their first top-ten hit in 1975, and after that Styx could not be stopped. Their seventh LP, *The Grand Illusion,* stayed on the charts almost two years, sold over three million copies, and featured their 1978 gold 45, "Come Sail Away." Later that year, the album *Pieces of Eight* and a triumphant tour solidified their popularity, and in 1979, Styx struck again with their first number one single, "Babe."

Grease
FRANKIE VALLI

American high school life in the fifties was the inspiration for *Grease,* one of the most popular and longest-running of all Broadway musicals. In 1978, the film version spawned four top-five hits: the title theme, "You're the One That I Want," "Hopelessly Devoted to You," and "Summer Nights." Surprisingly, only one of them—the latter song—actually came from the original score.

One reason for this was the movie's musical director, Bill Oakes, who'd spent his own high school years in England. He's seen the live show, and simply "wasn't knocked out" by what he heard. When the motion picture rights were negotiated, a clause was worked in, allowing him to "punch things up" with extra material. Twenty-three songs wound up on the final soundtrack—ten of them from outside sources. Ironically, the title tune was among them.

The film *Grease,* like *Saturday Night Fever,* was co-produced by Robert Stigwood, the RS of RSO Records (the O stands for "Organization"). He agreed that a song called "Grease" was needed, and asked Barry Gibb of the Bee Gees to write one. It was not an easy assignment. What can you make out of a word like "grease"? Finally, Barry decided that "grease" was *"the* word." It didn't make any sense, but perhaps with a good rhythm, nobody would notice.

At that time, the Bee Gees were the most heavily-played recording group on the radio. To avoid further overexposure, it was agreed that the song had to be given to some other performer.

"I had met Barry during the filming of *Sgt. Pepper,*" said Frankie Valli. "I played a cameo role at the very end. We started talking; in fact, every time we ran into each other we talked about doing something together. One day, Barry told me that he was involved in a project, and it was something that he was sure was right for me. I had

no idea what it was, because he said he couldn't talk about it. A month later, he sent me the song, and I flipped. I thought it would be a hit the day I heard it—which doesn't mean anything, of course. The public has to like it."

The single "Grease" came out in late May 1978, and made a slow, steady ascent to number one. It hit that peak in August, spending more

than five months on the charts. Lead guitar on the record, incidentally, was played by Peter Frampton.

And, oh, yes—it came sixteen years after we first heard of Frankie Valli, then lead singer of the Four Seasons. "Grease" turned out to be the largest-selling record of his career, topping everything he had ever done alone, or with his former group.

You're the One That I Want

OLIVIA NEWTON-JOHN AND JOHN TRAVOLTA

John Travolta was inspired to get into acting by his mother, a drama teacher in Englewood, New Jersey. He turned pro at sixteen, and at eighteen went to New York, where he landed a small role in the stage production of *Grease.* His next step was a trip to Hollywood and his television debut in an episode of the CBS drama "Medical Center." After that, the job offers dried up, so John went back to Broadway and appeared in *Over There,* a musical with the Andrews Sisters. Then, in the fall of 1975, he was cast as Vinnie Barbarino, a swaggering, street-wise high school punk in the ABC comedy series "Welcome Back, Kotter."

Within a few months, John was pulling some eight thousand pieces of viewer mail a week, far more than the star of the show, Gabe Kaplan. His face was beginning to turn up on posters, T-shirts, and fan magazines, and there was even a top-ten hit, "Let Her In," in the summer of 1976. In less than a year, Travolta had become the hottest property at ABC-TV.

Meanwhile, producer Allan Carr had bought up the rights to *Grease,* mainly as a vehicle for his friend Ann-Margret and her friend, Elvis Presley. Sadly, that casting never came through, so the lead was offered instead to Henry Winkler, then on "Happy Days" and at the peak of his fame. Amazingly, Winkler turned it down, saying the part was too much like his TV character, "The Fonz."

Carr didn't know where to turn, and while mulling it over, flipped on his TV. By accident, he tuned in "Welcome Back, Kotter," which he decided to watch out of loyalty to Kaplan (who'd opened for Ann-Margret in Las Vegas many times). To his surprise, "out came this charismatic kid, this wonder, John Travolta." He called his partner, Robert Stigwood, and shouted, "Get to a TV!" Both men agreed that they had found the perfect lead—their Danny Zuko—for *Grease.*

Snags postponed the start of the *Grease* project, so Carr and Stigwood cast John in another project, *Saturday Night Fever.* It, of course, exploded into a film and record phenomenon, making John's participation in *Grease* an even more valuable asset.

His co-star, though, was not cast until the company was already into prefilming rehearsals. "I had met Olivia at a small dinner party given by Helen Reddy and Jeff Wald about four months earlier," recalled Carr. "I'd never seen her in person before, and I couldn't resist telling her that she really should be doing movies. I mean, she's just adorable and yet she has a very special sophistication about her, too. I knew if we could just capture that on film, we would have our Sandy."

Olivia agreed to do the picture, partly because it was a musical, and partly because it gave her a chance to play two different kinds of women. Because of her involvement, her musical director, John Farrar, was asked to write a couple of new tunes for her. The first turned out to be a wistful ballad, "Hopelessly Devoted to You." And then came the film finale—

a rousing scene, set at a carnival, in which Olivia learns to "outgrease" Travolta. For that, Farrar came up with "You're the One That I Want."

"I had a ball doing that part of the picture," said Olivia. "It was so much fun to shoot. All through production, the crew treated me like I was Sandy—this seventeen-year-old naïve lady." Then, in the last reel, she's transformed into a black-leather-clad biker, complete with skintight satin pants, red stiletto heels, and vampy makeup. The change made for a stunning climax—both for the film and for a phase of Olivia's career. "I was usually pretty virginal," she said, "and I was hoping I wouldn't lose all my fans. But this side of me is much more fun than the sweet virginal side. Doing *Grease* and cutting 'You're the One That I Want' was an opening-up for me. It made me want to try different things.

"I was thrilled with the film. Maybe another one like it will never come along. But I'll always know that I was in one of the biggest films of all time."

And to help her remember, Olivia can always look at her bankbook. Her work in *Grease* reportedly earned her over $10 million.

Emotion
SAMANTHA SANG

amantha Sang was born in Melbourne, Australia, where her father ran a singing school. She became hooked on music by the age of eight, and sang on the radio as "Cheryl Gray." Her father, a vocalist, was known as "Reg Gray" professionally, because he thought his real last name, Sang, sounded "too stagy."

When she was fifteen, Samantha began to tour with her parents, who were kind of the Steve Lawrence and Eydie Gorme of Australia. She earned a reputation as "the little girl with the big voice," because of her robust, dramatic singing style. Samantha started a recording career, and in 1969, had a European hit with "Love of a Woman." The same year, she met Barry Gibb, who suggested that she try a softer vocal approach. To demonstrate, he wrote and produced her on a single, "Don't Let It Happen Again." Unfortunately, that record bombed.

Samantha continued performing in Europe and Australia, cutting four LPs, and playing clubs and outdoor concerts. At one show, a wasp flew into her open mouth and down her throat. She kept on singing, though, and the wasp was blown out.

Samantha's real dream was to crack the American market, but somehow, her plans always seemed to fall through. Then, in 1977, she heard that Barry was back in Paris.

"We were in the middle of the *Saturday Night Fever* soundtrack," he recalled. "She flew in with her manager, not to my knowledge, confronted me, and said, 'Would you write me a song?' I said, 'Great, I'd love to, but that's as far as it can go.' Six months later, she rang up and said nobody would produce the song, because it was so Bee Gees influenced. We should produce it, and nobody else. So I said, 'Let's see if we can fit it in.' She came to Miami for a week, we cut it, and that was it."

The Bee Gees wrote "Emotion" in about an hour's time. Samantha was actually given her choice of that song or "Our Love (Don't Throw It All Away)." When she chose "Emotion," "Our Love" was given to Andy Gibb, who had a top-ten hit with her reject in 1978.

"Emotion" was produced as a duet, with Barry and Samantha each singing eight harmonies. Their voices blended so well that critics called her "the female Bee Gee." At first, she was flattered, but later grew to resent that term. "We didn't set out to do it that way," she said. "Barry just thought that soft and very sensuous sound would work best on that record. It did, but it's only one of many styles I use."

"Emotion" wound up sounding just like another Bee Gees record, and for that reason, many labels eagerly bid for it, including those who had rejected Samantha in the past. She wanted to sign with RSO, but owner Robert Stigwood, her former manager, doubted Sang's ability to sell records without a Bee Gee connection. The master was finally placed with Private Stock, a company famed for its skill with singles.

It broke in America in mid-November 1977, and peaked on the charts in March 1978. In all, it spent more than six months on the best-seller list.

And Robert Stigwood was right. Samantha Sang never did have another major hit record in the United States.

Baby Come Back
PLAYER

Peter Beckett grew up in Liverpool, England, where he spent four years playing in a band called Palladin. He quit to come to America and join another group, Friends, which recorded for MGM. After a short time, they evolved into Skyband, which released one album on the RCA label. Skyband lasted long enough to play one concert in L.A. and tour abroad before breaking up.

In 1976, he slipped on his jeans and attended a classy Hollywood party. To his surprise, everyone there was wearing white except for one other guest, who had also come in Levi's. Peter figured the other guy had to be a musician, so they sat down together and began to talk. As it turned out, he was John Charles Crowley, a singing, songwriter guitarist from Galveston Bay, Texas. The two hit it off, and made a date to listen to each other's material.

A few days later, Peter and J.C. held a jam session, and afterward decided to form a band. They added Ron Moss, a bass player from L.A., and veteran of two bands: Punk Rock and Count Zeppelin and his Fabled Airship. Ron brought along a high school friend, John Friesden, who, at one time, had toured the world as the assistant producer and drummer with the Ice Follies. Keyboard man Wayne Cook came abroad just a little too late; he missed being included in the photo used on their first LP cover.

The boys were spotted by the production team of Dennis Lambert and Brian Potter, and signed to their company, Haven. Lambert and Potter then negotiated a deal with RSO. A debut album was planned, which one critic was to call "a ten-song exercise in straightforward romantic pop." One of those tunes was "Baby Come Back."

"We wrote that pretty quickly," recalled Peter. "It took about three hours one night, and then we spent about an hour the next night polish-ing it up. J.C. and I had just broken up with our girlfriends, and we were still feeling the sting. When we sat down to write, our moods just blended, and it came out as 'Baby Come Back.'

"I remember rehearsing the song in J.C.'s garage studio. It was the middle of summer, hotter than hell, and there we sat with our acoustic guitars, working it up amid the spiders and cockroaches. We knew it sounded like a hit, though. There was so much personal feeling in the song that we knew it had to be something special."

"Baby Come Back" broke on the radio in October 1977 and reached number one early in January. It spent three weeks at the top—more than seven months on the charts. During that time, over two million copies were sold.

This infuriated some critics, who felt that the boys' style was a "blatant carbon" of several other groups. However, reviewers couldn't seem to agree as to the source of their familiar sound. Various writers claimed that "Baby Come Back" was an imitation of Hall and Oates' "She's Gone," while others insisted the band copied Foreigner, the Bee Gees, Steely Dan, the Eagles, Journey, and even Andy Gibb.

"Just call it rock 'n' soul," said Ron Moss. "We pull from the best of both worlds."

Player didn't perform live until November 1977, when they appeared as the opening act for Gino Vanelli. Later, they toured with Heart, Boz Scaggs, Kenny Loggins, and Eric Clapton. Their second single, "This Time I'm in It for Love," was a top-ten hit in the spring of 1978.

And their name? The reason they chose it was simple. They wanted people to be able to hold up their album, point to it, and say, "That's a great record, Player."

Boogie Oogie Oogie

A TASTE OF HONEY

The nucleus for A Taste of Honey was formed in 1971, through the friendship of Perry Kibble and Janice Johnson. At the time, Perry was working as a bassist with a soul trio, the Exits, while Janice was singing in a group called Soundstage #1. When those two acts fell apart, Perry and Janice decided to join forces.

The two added a couple of friends and landed a job at a nearby beer joint, L.C.'s Hideaway, for $50 a night. They went through several drummers before finding Donald Johnson (no relation to Janice), who was hired and appeared with the group during their three-month run at the club.

By the summer of 1972, they had adopted their unusual name, taken from the 1965 hit by Herb Alpert and the Tijuana Brass. They had also added another singer and conga player, and had become a six-piece band. They signed their first management contract and were immediately shipped overseas on a six-week USO tour. Over the next four years, they alternated between stateside dates and tours of other countries. Among dozens of stops were spots in Spain, Morocco, Taiwan, Japan, Thailand, and the Philippines. Along the way, various performers joined and left the act, but the three key members—Perry, Janice, and Donald—always remained.

In early 1976, the group's lead singer, Gregory Walker, suddenly quit and joined a rival band, Santana. The others decided they'd had enough of floating personnel and elected to form a permanent four-piece line-up. By that time, Janice was not only singing but also playing lead guitar. To complement her, they hired a second female lead guitarist, Hazel Payne. After five years of experiments, A Taste of Honey had finally come together and was ready for the big time.

A friend, Dr. Otto Stallworth, saw them perform at a backyard wedding in Los Angeles and arranged for the group to meet Larry and Fonce Mizell, producers of hits for the Jackson Five, L.T.D., and other acts. Larry and Fonce liked what they heard and were particularly fascinated by the novelty of two female lead guitarists. They arranged for the band to meet Larkin Arnold, then a vice president of Capitol Records. Arnold auditioned the group in early 1978, but then hesitated. Three months later, they were asked to do a repeat audition. Finally, Capitol signed them, and work began on their debut release, "Boogie Oogie Oogie."

"It's funny how that song came about," said Janice, who co-wrote the tune. "We played a lot of military bases around the world, and one night we were playing this certain Air Force club. We were knocking ourselves out but getting no reaction from the crowd. In fact, they seemed to have contempt for two women who thought they could front a band, get out and strut their stuff and all. Well, it didn't take me long to come up with a good lyric. When we got home, I picked up my bass, and with our keyboard man, Perry Kibble, we worked out a melody. Next time you hear 'Boogie Oogie Oogie,' listen to the words!

"We picked the song to be our first single right away. But it didn't break in L.A., our hometown. It took off in New York and shot through the Midwest, and didn't get to L.A. until many weeks later. This is a crazy market. It broke out of the discos first, and then radio picked it up."

"Boogie Oogie Oogie" became a number one across-the-board hit and the first platinum single in Capitol Records' history. The group's debut album, *A Taste of Honey,* sold nearly two million copies, and they became the first black group to win the Grammy for Best New Artist of the Year. They were also the only group ever to have both their debut single and debut album certified platinum and to win the coveted Best New Artist award all in the same year.

"Boogie Oogie Oogie" has been called everything from disco at its worst to one of the best R&B singles of the decade. It was, at least, a fascinating souvenir of the time—a record that encapsulated all the carefree abandon that made disco so popular.

Three Times a Lady
THE COMMODORES

The story of the Commodores began in 1967, on the campus of Alabama's Tuskegee Institute. While walking along, sax in hand, Lionel Richie was stopped by guitarist Thomas McClary. Thomas wanted to meet girls, and figured a good way was to form an act for the freshman talent show. Was Lionel interested in joining him? What a question.

Together they found William King, a trumpeter in the school band, and rehearsed assiduously. Calling themselves the Mystics, they brought down the house at the talent show. After that, they began to play dances, and talked about someday being "bigger than the Beatles." When another campus group, the Jays, broke up, keyboard man Milan Williams came in. In honor of their new member, the others decided to rename the band. William threw a dictionary up in the air, stuck his finger in at random, and pulled out a plum of a name—the Commodores. For years afterward, they were to joke about how close they came to being called "the Commodes."

The Commodores played locally for $15 to $20 a night, and all the fish sandwiches they could eat. In 1969, they added drummer Walter Orange and bassist Ronald LaPread. By 1970, they were touring extensively.

Motown signed the Commodores in 1971, and let them open shows for the Jackson Five. "We kind of became big brothers to the J5," recalled Lionel. "We stayed with them for almost three years." Finally, in 1974, the Commodores began to record.

The group's early hits, such as "Machine Gun" (1974) and "Slippery When Wet" (1975) were ragged, funky R&B, appealing mainly to blacks. Then, in 1976, their first ballad, "Sweet Love," became a top-five pop hit. After that, their records were unpredictable—slow, fast, hard, soft—even country and gospel. "People know us but they don't know us," said Ronald.

"We're six different writers, six different producers, six different arrangers, and we come from six different ways." It showed, too, in such diverse hits as "Just to Be Close to You" (1976), "Easy" (1977), and "Brick House" (1977).

Then, at a 1978 sound check, Lionel got the idea for the Commodores' first number-one single. "My father told me that in thirty-five years of marriage, he'd never told my mother how much she meant to him. I decided that I wasn't going to wait thirty-five years to tell my wife, Brenda."

The ballad he came up with, "Three Times a Lady," was released in early June 1978. Seven weeks later, it was the number-one song in the country.

In all, it spent more than five months on the charts.

In 1979, there were two more big hits: "Sail On" and "Still." In 1980, "Old Fashioned Love" became a top-twenty single. By then, the Commodores had sold more than twenty-five million albums, and the end was nowhere in sight.

"There's something different about us," said Ronald. "Maybe it's just a feeling, but six little country boys have evolved into a pretty fantastic musical force. The people we once looked up to are now looking up to us. We like to think that once you have been exposed to the Commodores, you will never settle for anything less than the best."

Kiss You All Over

EXILE

We came from a town in Kentucky with a population under 10,000," said guitarist Jimmy Stokely. "Back in '63, we had hair to our shoulders and beards, and played rock 'n' roll. The townspeople tended to regard us as outcasts—or 'exiles.' When we'd walk down the street, people would point at us, and laugh at us. Sometimes, they'd throw things at us."

In the early sixties, Exile was a local band in the strictest sense—they'd never played more than thirty miles from home. Their music was in a soul/R&B vein, with leader Stokely in a James Brown/Wilson Pickett bag. Over the next decade, though, the group toured endlessly, cutting hundreds of flop singles for dozens of obscure labels. It seemed like they'd never get a break and then . . .

"We mailed a demo to a deejay friend in Florida, who sent it on to a guy in L.A.," recalled Jimmy. "It was taken in a stack of about fifteen tapes by different bands to Mike Chapman's house one evening. Mike was looking for an American group to produce, and out of the stack, he picked us.

"He sent us this song he had written on a demo he had made himself. We fell in love with it, you know. We recorded it along with the rest of our first LP for Warner-Curb. It was our consensus, as well as his and others, that it should be the single.

"We made it quite a bit funkier than he had it, you know. His demo was just two guitars, bass, one vocal, and a drum machine. You can't get very funky with that. He gave us his tape, and said, 'Do with it what you feel best. Put your own pieces into it; I'll come back and take a listen.' He did, and said, 'I like it.'"

"Kiss You All Over" broke onto the charts in July 1978, but didn't reach the top until October. It remained America's favorite record for four weeks, and stayed on the best-seller list for nearly six months.

"We were in the offices of Warner-Curb when we heard it had gone all the way," said Jimmy. "We all almost fainted. It was very—well, after fifteen years, there were a few tears rolling, you know. We were shocked, just really blown away. We thought 'Kiss You All Over' would probably make the charts, but we had no idea that it would go to number one. We're just very lucky, very thankful."

Stayin' Alive
THE BEE GEES

The Bee Gees' saga can be neatly divided into four parts: their Days of Development (1956–66), the Ethereal Era (1967–69), the Ballad Boom (1970–74), and the Disco Deluge (1975–79). The latter period, of course, was when they hit their peak—creatively, and commercially.

Their immense popularity, though, was a distant dream in 1974. The group had been making two million a year in the late sixties, but then, after a string of hits, they fell apart. A comeback in the early seventies yielded such million-sellers as "Lonely Days" and "How Can You Mend a Broken Heart," but that success was short-lived.

Then, in 1975, the rhythm of their car tires on a Florida bridge inspired "Jive Talkin'," their first number-one hit in four years. They thought of it as just an R&B tune, but when the record took off in dance halls, the Bee Gees were suddenly cast as "disco kings." Barry, Robin, and Maurice were not entirely sure as to what that meant, but were determined to find out. By the end of the decade, they had not only mastered the music, but defined, shaped, and epitomized its potential.

Each hit after "Jive Talkin' " seemed more impressive than the last, as the brothers explored and shattered the limits of disco. In 1975, there were "Nights on Broadway" and "Fanny (Be Tender with My Love)"; in 1976, "You Should Be Dancing" and "Love So Right." They started 1977 with their sixth major dance record, "Boogie Child."

And then they got a phone call.

It seems that their manager, Robert Stigwood, had been talking to an English writer, Nik Cohen, who was based in New York. Nik told Robert that he'd send him some ideas for movies. Stigwood saw Cohen's *New York* magazine cover story about discomania, and rang him up.

"Who needs ideas?" said Stig-wood. "Let's do your magazine piece."

"He rang us up," said Robin, "and said, 'Would you like to do the soundtrack for a film? We said, 'What film?' He said, 'A film I'm making. I haven't even got a title for it yet. Maybe you could think of that, too.' 'How many songs?' 'Oh, about six or seven.' I said, 'Well, that's about one a day. When will you send us the script?' He said, 'Well, I don't have a script. You'll just have to get on with the soundtrack.' 'Well,' I said, 'You haven't got a script, and we haven't got any songs, so we're equal, we're even.' I put down the phone, and we went to work."

The brothers actually wrote "Stayin' Alive" on a staircase at the chateau.

"Years ago, there were many porno films made here," said Robin. "The staircase where we wrote 'Stayin' Alive,' 'How Deep Is Your Love,' and all those songs was the same staircase used in about six classic porno movies."

Barry recalled other details of "Stayin' Alive," which he called "a desperate plea for help."

"Robert wanted a scene that was eight minutes long, where Travolta was dancing with this girl," he said. "It would have a nice dance tempo, then a romantic interlude, and all hell breaking loose at the end. I said, 'Robert, that's crazy. We want to put this song out as a single, and we don't think the rhythm should break. It should go from beginning to end with the same rhythm, and get stronger all the way. To go into a lilting ballad just doesn't make sense.' The film got changed."

"Stayin' Alive" wound up opening *Saturday Night Fever,* as John Travolta struts along a city sidewalk. A teasing thirty seconds of that scene was shown in fifteen hundred theaters a week before the movie actually opened. A record was not yet available, but people began calling RSO anyway, asking for "Stayin' Alive."

The single broke in mid-December 1977, spending four weeks at number one in February 1978. It was on the charts for more than six months, and won a Grammy for Best Arrangement for Voices.

"'Stayin' Alive' is about survival in the big city—any big city—but basically New York," said Robin. "When we saw the film we were surprised that it fit so well. It just amazed us, since we'd never even seen the script."

Shadow Dancing

ANDY GIBB

Andrew Roy Gibb was born two years after his older brothers, Robin, Barry and Maurice, formed the Bee Gees. For that reason, he's been "dancing in the shadows" all of his life.

Andy was never accepted by the other kids his age; they knew he was "the Bee Gees' brother," and resented seeing him picked up after classes every day in a Rolls Royce. He was picked on, hated it, and eventually quit public school at the age of thirteen.

Barry gave him a guitar, and with it, Andy made his performing debut at a nearby tourist bar. He worked cheap—for tips, in fact—and appeared on a fairly regular basis. Occasionally, his brothers showed up, and supplied harmonic accompaniment.

In 1973, Andy got his first real job in the music biz. He formed a band with some local rock 'n' rollers, and for over a year, kept himself employed by playing two clubs on the Isle of Man. Then, in 1975, he moved to Australia, on the advice of his family.

"They said to go there, and spend some years like we did," Andy recalled. "With all due respect to Australia, in a way it's a great training ground, because you can become the biggest star there and still not be heard of anyplace else. It's a crying shame, too, because there are so many great artists and groups there. I planned to stay about five years, but then I got a contract, a record deal, and put out a single that I wrote called 'Words and Music.' It was a moderate success; didn't get to the top ten, but did get me television exposure."

Robert Stigwood, the president of RSO Records, then called Barry and asked him if he thought Andy would be interested in signing with RSO.

"Andy's very willing to come over and talk," replied Barry.

"Well," said Stigwood, "can you and Andy meet me in Bermuda?"

"Certainly." So the two brothers packed their bags, flew to Bermuda, and consummated a deal. Within a few hours, Barry had also written Andy's first U.S. hit: "I Just Want to Be Your Everything."

In the summer of 1977, that record exploded, topping the charts for a month, and remaining a best-seller for more than thirty weeks. The follow-up, "(Love Is) Thicker Than Water," did nearly as well, thanks in part, to an unbilled guitar solo by Joe Walsh (who just happened to be working in the studio next door). Both of those tracks appeared on Andy's first LP, *Flowing Rivers,* which was certified platinum by the RIAA.

In 1978, Andy recorded his second album, *Shadow Dancing,* which was certified platinum within weeks of its release. The title cut—his third number-one in a row—was a fast-rising chart record even before the LP was released. As a 45, "Shadow Dancing" broke in mid-April 1978, and by July was the best-selling single in the country. It remained that way for seven weeks, and in total, spent nearly six months on the pop charts.

Also in July, Barry, Robin and Maurice surprised Andy by walking out and joining him onstage during a show at the Jai-Alai Fronton Studios in Miami. It was the first time all four brothers had performed live together in concert, and the Bee Gees' only concert appearance of 1978. The song they did? What else, but "Shadow Dancing."

Andy went on to rack up several more hits over the next few years, including "An Everlasting Love" and "Our Love (Don't Throw It All Away)" in 1978. In 1980, there were "Desire," "I Can't Help It" (a duet with Olivia Newton-John), and "Time Is Time." By then, Andy was twenty-two years old.

"I feel I've done very little," he said, of his accomplishments. "I know I've been very lucky, and wouldn't have gotten as far as I have so quickly if it hadn't been for my family. I'm making music for now, and it's what's selling now. It won't stay that way. It's going to change, and I'm going to change with the times. I know the public's going to change with me."

Night Fever
THE BEE GEES

*I*t was mid-December 1977, and RSO label chief Al Coury felt relaxed. His latest LP, the soundtrack of *Saturday Night Fever,* had just been released—a million copies to the stores, 750,000 more stockpiled in the warehouse. That was enough for a good three or four weeks, *easily.* With great confidence, he left on a one-week Christmas vacation.

Four days later, everything was gone—sold—every album, eight-track, and cassette. "That's when we felt the real impact of the film," he said.

No one had seen such record sales since the advent of the Beatles, fourteen years before. In less than six months, *Saturday Night Fever* shattered all previous highs to become the largest-selling album in history. It set another record by climbing to the top of the LP charts for an amazing ten weeks. Industry "experts" were dumbfounded: this package broke three cardinal rules of merchandising. Soundtracks, various artist compilations, and anything containing oldies were traditionally thought of as poor sellers. Yet this monster was all three, rolled into one.

K. C. and the Sunshine Band, Tavares, Kool and the Gang, Ralph McDonald, MFSB, and David Shire all contributed tracks to *Saturday Night Fever.* In addition, there were hits by the Trammps ("Disco Inferno"), Yvonne Elliman ("If I Can't Have You"), Walter Murphy ("A Fifth of Beethoven"), and the Bee Gees ("Jive Talkin'," "You Should Be Dancing," "How Deep Is Your Love," "Stayin' Alive" and "Night Fever"). The latter song worked so well that the movie title actually changed to fit it.

"Robert Stigwood, the producer, wanted to call the film *Saturday Night,*" said Robin Gibb. "And we had already written the song 'Night Fever.' We told him we didn't like the title *Saturday Night,* and he said he didn't want to call the movie just *Night Fever.* So he thought it over for a while, called

us back, and said, 'O.K., let's compromise. Let's call it *Saturday Night Fever.*' We said, 'All right, that's great. So we'll keep it at that.' "

The song "Night Fever" was actually the first one written by the Bee Gees for the picture. Released as a single early in February 1978, it peaked in April, spending eight weeks at the top of the chart. In all, it spent nearly five months on the best-seller list. The record was also a hit in England—their first number-one song there in nearly ten years.

Nineteen seventy-eight was truly the time of the Bee Gees. Because they had made Criteria Studios in north Miami their second home, the Governor of Florida made Barry, Robin and Maurice honorary citizens of the state. Governor Jim Williams said the Bee Gees' presence "enhanced the quality of the musical and entertainment community in the state, and is reflective of the outstanding technical facilities and personnel available in Flor-

ida." The Miami Beach Tourist Development Authority then jumped in, and asked the boys to compose an official Miami Beach theme song. They respectfully declined, and to this day, the beach town's official theme song remains "The Miami Beach Rhumba."

The *Saturday Night Fever* project led to *five* Grammy Awards for the Bee Gees: Album of the Year (as artists), Album of the Year (as producers), Best Pop Vocal Performance by a Duo, Group or Chorus, Best Arrangement for Voices (for "Stayin' Alive"), and Producers of the Year. In addition, "How Deep Is Your Love," one of the "oldies" on the set, was a previous Grammy winner, as Best Pop Vocal Performance by a Duo, Group or Chorus.

Incredibly, despite the immense impact of the film and its music, not a single song from *Saturday Night Fever* earned an Academy Award nomination.

1979

Harry Casey's first job in the music industry was stacking product in the TK Records warehouse in Miami. After a while, he and a friend, Richard Finch, began hanging out after hours in the company's recording studio. Eventually, they mastered the equipment and developed a disco style which they came to call "the Sunshine Sound." In 1975, it exploded nationwide via two back-to-back number-one singles: "Get Down Tonight" and "That's the Way (I Like It)." A year later, they topped the charts again with "(Shake Shake Shake) Shake Your Booty." In 1977, they reached number one for a fourth time with "I'm Your Boogie Man," and also sold a million copies of "Keep It Comin' Love." **K.C. and the Sunshine Band** was one of the few disco acts to remain popular throughout the craze; K.C.'s personality, professionalism, and good-natured music were clearly the reasons why. In 1979, the group recorded a ballad, "Please Don't Go"; it became their fifth and final number-one hit.

More patchwork. On February 9, ABC presented *The Heroes of Rock 'n' Roll*, perhaps the best musical documentary ever broadcast on television. Twenty-five years of pop history were evoked through the masterful use of old TV and film clips, including prime footage of 50s legend **Gene Vincent** (of "Be-Bop-a-Lula" fame). Producers Andrew Solt and Malcolm Leo were to team again on a similar project: the compilation-documentary *This Is Elvis*.

AFTER A STEADY decline in the seventies, sales of 45 RPM records surged 36 percent in 1979 to 353.6 million. This was attributed, in part, to the incredible popularity of disco—a kind of music most people seemed to prefer listening to on singles as opposed to LPs. The high price of albums also discouraged shoppers, who, for the same money, could pick up a handful of 45s. The Bee Gees were given a star on the Hollywood Walk of Fame, the fifth singing group to be so honored (they joined the Spinners, the Mills Brothers, Crosby, Stills and Nash, and the Sons of the Pioneers). Chuck Berry left prison after serving a hundred days for income tax evasion (he made good use of his time, completing a 328-page autobiography). In Cincinnati, eleven fans died in a massive human crunch outside the doors of Riverfront Coliseum before a Who concert. New artists making chart debuts included Pat Benatar, Blondie, Dire Straits, G.Q., Rickie Lee Jones, the Knack, Nick Lowe, M, and the Police. On television, PBS—always on the lookout for money—aired a six-hour fundraiser, "Live from the Grand Ole Opry." "Puff the Magic Dragon" became an animated CBS-TV special, and ABC devoted three hours to a dramatic biography starring Kurt Russell as *Elvis*. It was 1979: the year the Capricorn and Infinity labels folded, and Kris Kristofferson and Rita Coolidge split up after six years of wedded bliss.

The history of the **Who** was documented in *The Kids Are All Right*, a compilation of their TV and concert appearances (the group was also behind a second '79 motion picture, *Quadrophenia*). Rock culture was also portrayed in three movies set in the sixties: *The Wanderers* (soundtrack music by the Four Seasons and Dion), *More American Grafitti* (with an avalanche of oldies) and—of all things—a cinema version of *Hair* (only a decade too late). The Doors were heard in *Apocalypse Now,* Abba in *Abba: The Movie,* and Eddie Rabbitt in *Every Which Way but Loose.* The title theme from *The Main Event* became a major hit for that picture's star, Barbra Streisand.

Jackson Browne and Tom Petty were just two of the stars who performed in Madison Square Garden during five nights of charity concerts (September 19–23). The cause was a non-nuclear future, sponsored by MUSE (Musicians United for Safe Energy). The coalition said that they were making "a statement against the dangers of nuclear technology and the emerging 'plutonium economy.' " Also in the show (and subsequent album and film) were the likes of Nicholette Larson, Poco, Raydio, Carly Simon, James Taylor, Bruce Springsteen, the Doobie Brothers, and Crosby, Stills, and Nash.

And speaking of the **Doobie Brothers,** in the early seventies they were just a northern California bar band, making ends meet with food stamps, often playing gigs for drinks "and whatever we would find under the tables at closing time." Then, in 1972, "Listen to the Music" introduced their style to a coast-to-coast crowd. Such hits as "Long Train Runnin'," "China Grove," "Black Water," "Take Me in Your Arms" and "Takin' It to the Streets" turned them into one of the hottest bands of the seventies. After a couple of slow years, the Doobies bounced back in 1979 with their best-selling album ever, *Minute by Minute.* It featured the much-imitated sound of keyboard player Mike McDonald, as well as their biggest hit of the decade, "What a Fool Believes."

THE TOP 40

1. My Sharona, *Knack*
2. Le Freak, *Chic*
3. Do Ya Think I'm Sexy? *Rod Stewart*
4. Bad Girls, *Donna Summer*
5. YMCA, *Village People*
6. Reunited, *Peaches and Herb*
7. Ring My Bell, *Anita Ward*
8. I Will Survive, *Gloria Gaynor*
9. Too Much Heaven, *Bee Gees*
10. Hot Stuff, *Donna Summer*
11. Sad Eyes, *Robert John*
12. What a Fool Believes, *Doobie Brothers*
13. Heart of Glass, *Blondie*
14. Fire, *Pointer Sisters*
15. Good Times, *Chic*
16. Tragedy, *Bee Gees*
17. A Little More Love, *Olivia Newton-John*
18. Knock on Wood, *Amii Stewart*
19. Babe, *Styx*
20. Shake Your Body, *Jacksons*
21. When You're in Love with a Beautiful Woman, *Dr. Hook*
22. Pop Muzik, *M*
23. Makin' It, *David Naughton*
24. Don't Stop Till You Get Enough, *Michael Jackson*
25. Rise, *Herb Alpert*
26. My Life, *Billy Joel*
27. I Want You to Want Me, *Cheap Trick*
28. I'll Never Love Like This Again, *Dionne Warwick*
29. You Don't Bring Me Flowers, *Barbra Streisand and Neil Diamond*
30. We Are Family, *Sister Sledge*
31. No More Tears (Enough Is Enough), *Barbra Streisand and Donna Summer*
32. Sail On, *Commodores*
33. Logical Song, *Supertramp*
34. Stumblin' In, *Suzi Quatro and Chris Norman*
35. Chuck E's in Love, *Rickie Lee Jones*
36. Lead Me On, *Maxine Nightengale*
37. Main Event, *Barbra Streisand*
38. Don't Cry Out Loud, *Melissa Manchester*
39. Music Box Dancer, *Frank Mills*
40. Just When I Needed You Most, *Randy Van Warmer*

Keyboards also played a key role in the success of **Supertramp.** Almost a decade after their founding in London as a heavy metal band, the group hit the big time by moving to the U.S. and issuing their sixth album, *Breakfast in America.* It included three major hits: "Take the Long Way Home," "Goodbye Stranger," and their first million-selling single, "The Logical Song" (quickly parodied by the Barron Knights as "The Topical Song"). In July, the members of Supertramp displayed their logic by walking into Butnum's Music and buying, at one time, five Wurlitzer pianos—all the same model. The reason? The piano heard on their gold 45 happened to be a Wurlitzer, purchased at that same store just one year before.

THE TOP 10 LPs

1. 52nd Street, *Billy Joel*
2. Minute by Minute, *Doobie Brothers*
3. Breakfast in America, *Supertramp*
4. Spirits Having Flown, *Bee Gees*
5. Bad Girls, *Donna Summer*
6. Blondes Have More Fun, *Rod Stewart*
7. At Budokan, *Cheap Trick*
8. Get the Knack, *Knack*
9. 2 Hot, *Peaches and Herb*
10. In Through the Out Door, *Led Zeppelin*

10

Hot Stuff
DONNA SUMMER

I was born in Boston," said Donna, "and began singing at the age of ten. I practiced every day. Mahalia Jackson was my idol. She was the only singer I had ever heard who had the type of volume and control I wanted. At first, I couldn't even get into the church choir, but I worked at my music, almost fanatically. Finally, I was accepted. I'll never forget that day. My whole family started crying. I don't know if they were proud, shocked, or overwhelmed. All I knew was that if I hadn't made up my mind before, I did at that instant. I knew I was going to be a singer.

"I left Boston for New York, where I met someone connected with the production of *Hair.* Then things started happening to me overnight. Within a week, I was in Europe, with one of the title roles in the German company! I could hardly speak any of the language then, but by the time I got home again, I was speaking it like a native.

"While doing *Hair,* I got a lot of other stage offers, because, at that time, there weren't many blacks in Europe doing that type of theater. I also did some background singing on quite a few German films. I spent about one year with *Hair* in Germany, and then joined the Vienna company. I also worked with the Vienna Folk Opera. We did *Porgy and Bess* and *Show-boat* as light operas. It was an incredible experience. Then I returned to Germany, and legit theater, where I did *Godspell* and *The Me Nobody Knows.*

"One day, while recording some demos, I met Pete Bellotte and Giorgio Moroder. Pete was in the studio doing a demo for Three Dog Night. We got along well together and tried a few recordings, but nothing seemed to happen with them."

Then, in 1976, "Love to Love You Baby" hit the American music scene like a hurricane. The lyrics of the song, and the sensual way they were sung,

stirred up a whirlwind of controversy. Donna was praised—and blasted—as the new "Queen of Sex Rock." Many dismissed her as a flash-in-the-pan novelty success.

"I knew the industry refused to consider me a legitimate singer," she said, "but it just made me work harder. A lot of people run from obstacles, but I'm just the opposite. I love challenges. I said, 'Let's show 'em.' "

And that's exactly what she did, cutting seven remarkable LPs in less than three years. *Love to Love You Baby, A Trilogy of Love, Four Seasons of Love, I Remember Yesterday, Once Upon a Time,* and the soundtrack of *Thank God It's Friday* all became million-selling albums. In 1978, an in-concert set, *Live and More,* went double platinum.

Donna Summer emerged as the most versatile and adventurous of all disco performers. But, as she told the press, she didn't want to "die with disco." She wanted "validity," like that of stars such as Aretha Franklin and Barbra Streisand.

To that end, she sat down and sketched out "Hot Stuff," an ener-

getic blend of disco, R&B, and hard rock 'n' roll (her inspiration: separation from Bruce Sudano, a guitarist with Brooklyn Dreams, and her future husband). Donna took the song to label chief Neil Bogart, who became alarmed when she explained she wanted to "expand" her sound. He suggested she give the tune to Cher instead. With that, Donna exploded, vowing to "go back to singing in church" before she'd continue being "stuck doing something that had been choking me to death for three years." Finally, Neil agreed to let half her next album, *Bad Girls,* be "rock-oriented."

"Hot Stuff" turned out to be the opening track—a raunchy pulse highlighted by the blazing guitar of Jeff "Skunk" Baxter (an original member of Steely Dan and later of the Doobie Brothers). It quickly became the hottest song in the nation's discos and by May was a number-one pop hit as well. Today it ranks as one of the best—and most successful—examples of rock-disco fusion, along with the Stones' "Miss You" and Rod Stewart's "Do Ya Think I'm Sexy?"

Too Much Heaven

THE BEE GEES

In 1978, the Bee Gees—brothers Robin, Maurice and Barry Gibb—held a news conference at the United Nations to announce their donation of an unidentified song to the U.N.'s Children's Fund. About three hundred fans jammed the room to hear Robin say, "We hope this is only the beginning." U.N. Secretary-General Kurt Waldheim replied, "This is an outstanding and generous initiative." At that point, UNICEF Executive Director Henry Labouisse chimed in with his own personal thanks, during which he cheerfully referred to the group as the "Beatles."

Later, President Carter met with the Bee Gees at the White House to thank them for their fundraising efforts. After Carter congratulated them, the brothers presented him with one of their black satin tour jackets. Carter grinned, and admitted that he was "not much of a disco fan." However, he was familiar with the Bee Gees' music, because Amy played their records "all the time."

The Bee Gees' contribution was the first in a new project called Music for UNICEF. It was launched officially in January 1979, when the International Year of the Child began. Other artists who pledged song royalties included John Denver, Earth, Wind and Fire, Andy Gibb, Donna Summer, Rod Stewart, Olivia Newton-John, Abba, Kris Kristofferson and Rita Coolidge. Many of these stars appeared on a worldwide television special, aired in about seventy countries, which also benefited the fund.

The Bee Gees' donation was "Too Much Heaven," which also turned out to be the first number-one record of the year. It was a slow, lush ballad, and the first track off their new album, *Spirits Having Flown.* "We wanted to move in an R&B direction," said Barry, "still maintaining our lyric power, and our melody power as well. A lot of good rhythm is essential today. We want to keep our lyrics strong, and our melodies strong as well."

The phrase "Too Much Heaven" pretty much described the state the Bee Gees were in in 1979. Their previous album, *Saturday Night Fever,* had sold over twenty-five million copies—more than double any other LP in history. Their annual earnings were over $50 million, topping the paychecks of Barbra Streisand, Robert Redford, and Johnny Carson put together. From their start in the family basement in 1956, the Bee Gees had risen to become the highest-paid stars in the world.

"A pop idol of today receives the same amount of attention as a pop idol of twenty years ago," said Barry. "But I think people expect more of an artist than they did before. It's surprising how many artists got through with very little to offer."

He explained the Bee Gees' longevity this way. "It's very simple, really. We've been able to adapt our music around various scenes. We saw the Beach Boys come; we were making records then. We saw Jan and Dean and 'Surf City' and the hootenanny craze and all that. The Beatles—we saw them come. We were making records before the Beatles. We've seen so many phases and exciting times. We just change with them, and make our music for now."

I Will Survive

GLORIA GAYNOR

Gloria Gaynor's early heroes were the Everly Brothers, Buddy Holly, and Frankie Lymon. "When Frankie was thirteen, I was eight, and I could sing exactly like him," she said. "If you heard me from behind a door you'd swear it was him. I figured if he could sing, so could I." She studied male singers, chiefly for technique. "I tried to stay away from females," she explained, "because I didn't want to be compared with anybody else."

Gloria's taste widened as she entered her teens, stretching to include Nat King Cole (for diction), Sarah Vaughan (for phrasing), and Marvin Gaye (for style). Unable to afford singing lessons, she studied recordings, learning how to put emotion into a song. "I loved Nancy Wilson, Frank Sinatra, and Ella Fitzgerald," she recalled. "It always amazed me how they could sing so many words in a single line and you could still understand every one."

When she was eighteen and a sales auditor, she got her first professional singing job, replacing a singer in a band in Canada. "I'd never been out of Newark, but I quit my job and told everybody I was going to be a big star. We were there two weeks. Then I worked for a week in New Jersey and that was it. My career was at a standstill for almost six years."

In 1971, Gloria joined a house band in Newark, the Soul Satisfiers, and then formed her own group, City Life. They played the East Coast circuit, working nightclubs, supper clubs, and hotels, playing six shows a night, six nights a week. In eighteen months, she had just two weeks off.

Finally, in 1972, Gloria was given the chance to make her recording debut. "I was looking for the easiest way to make it in the record business," she explained. "I was tired of struggling. My manager, my producers, and I felt disco was new and open.

We all thought that I could get in on the ground floor and grow with it." Her first record, "Honey Bee," was a mild R&B hit and failed to make the pop charts.

Gloria then switched labels, from Columbia to MGM, and fell in with a new production team: Monardo, Bongiovi, and Ellis. With their aid, she cut "Never Can Say Goodbye," a tune composed by comedian Clifton Davis of ABC's comedy series "That's My Mama." The song had been successful before, both times in 1971, as a mid-tempo ballad for the Jackson Five and Isaac Hayes. But now, thanks to an effervescent, rip-roaring arrangement, Gloria transformed the tune into something akin to a Broadway show-stopper, spiraling strings and all. "I felt the time was right for a woman's version of the song," she said, and obviously was right. It was a disco smash, a big pop hit, and led, in March of 1975, to her actual coronation, at a New York performance, as Queen of the Discos.

Gloria's reign as a musical monarch was short-lived, however. Subsequent singles all bombed, as did four follow-up albums. By the spring of 1976, her crown had been snatched away by newcomer Donna Summer.

Gloria kept on singing, though, performing mostly in Europe. During one show, she suffered a fall that put her out of commission for months. From March through October of 1978 she was bedridden as a result of spinal surgery. To cap off her troubles, Gloria's mother, to whom she had been very close, died at about the same time.

"I knew I had to get back in there and survive," she recalled. After leaving the hospital, she hooked up with the writing and production team of Freddie Perren and Dino Fekaris. For her, they came up with "I Will Survive," a woman's inspiring declaration of strength after being emotionally abused by a lover. Gloria did not consider herself a feminist, however; she explained that she was too busy "trying to hook a man" to be into "women's lib."

Polydor promoted "I Will Survive" as "more than a hit—it's a way of life." Gloria was even induced to record the song in Spanish, as "Yo Viviré." Another version, with new lyrics, was used as the theme of the 1979 Easter Seals Telethon. The recording sessions were video-taped, with a special message from Gloria, and then broadcast repeatedly throughout the program. Polydor even donated a gold record of the song to the first person pledging $5,000 to the Telethon.

Interviewed late in 1979, Gloria reaffirmed her complete devotion to the disco movement. "I give the people what they want and what they need. They come up and thank me for this song. They say that it changed their lives." And perhaps it did. It certainly changed the life of Gloria Gaynor.

Ring My Bell

ANITA WARD

Anita Ward was born in Memphis, the eldest of five children. She was always interested in music, and while still a student, sang with the Rust College A Cappella Choir on an LP with Metropolitan Opera star Leontyne Price. Later, she put out another album with her own gospel quartet.

After graduation, Anita got a job as a substitute teacher in the Memphis elementary schools. It was all right, but she longed for a show biz career. Finally, through her manager, she met singer-songwriter Frederick Knight. He knew what it was like to have a hit record; "I've Been Lonely for So Long" had made the top thirty for him in the summer of 1972.

Frederick agreed to help Anita by producing a three-song session with her. Shortly after recording began, though, he became "so impressed by her ability, that we went on and completed an entire LP. Out of that," said Frederick, "came 'Ring My Bell.'"

Actually, that song was not intended to be on the album. Basic tracks were completed, but after they were played back, everyone agreed that the LP needed one more up-tempo tune. Frederick went home, and the next day returned with "Ring My Bell." Anita had a few doubts about the song, but wound up cutting it anyway.

The original "Ring My Bell" was written for eleven-year-old Stacy Lattisaw, whom Frederick had hoped to sign to his production company. "It was then a teenybopper type of song, about kids talking on the telephone. It was conceived strictly for Stacy, because I believe a kid that young needs a special piece of material. 'Ring My Bell' was something real special, and unique." However, Stacy signed with Henry Allen and Cotillion Records.

"I had to rewrite 'Ring My Bell' when Anita did it," explained Frederick. "The title was so catchy I kept that, but changed the lyrics. They kind of suggest that we play around, but I let the people make up their own meanings.

"I played keyboards and all the percussion parts on the record, including the syn-drum, which stands for 'synthesized drums.' It was one of the first tunes to feature the effect of syn-drums. I also arranged the background vocals with two girls, Valerie Williams and Cheryl Bundy. As a singer myself, that part was pretty easy, since my roots are in barbershop harmony.

"That entire record came together very quickly. In fact, I remember how long the whole production took us— two days."

It didn't take much longer than that for "Ring My Bell" to start ringing the chimes of radio stations all across the country. After breaking in mid-May, it bounded to the top of the charts in June 1979, and remained a strong seller all summer and into the fall. In total, the song kept ringing for an impressive five months.

"Ring My Bell" was an insidiously infectious record, and a far cry from the gospel Anita had been singing just eighteen months before. It was also an immense disco hit, which surprised Anita, who have never even been to a disco before her first promotion tour.

"Anita is a very clean-cut person," said Frederick. "We're trying to build a respectable image for her. The lyrics of 'Ring My Bell' haven't hurt her. They speak of an everyday situation— something you'd never be ashamed of in front of the kids."

Reunited
PEACHES AND HERB

Herb Fame began singing at the age of seven, in a Washington, D.C., church choir. After high school, he got a job in a hometown record shop, frequented by music industry personnel. One day, he spotted writer-producer Van McCoy in the store, and decided that this was his big chance to break into show business. He cornered Van, and offered a vocal audition right on the spot. Van then left the store—and returned one week later, contract in hand.

Herb was signed to Date Records, but after his first single flopped, things looked a little shaky. Then Date executive Dave Kapralik hit upon the plan of teaming Herb with Francine Day, who was one-third of a struggling girl group called the Sweet Things.

The new duo was dubbed Peaches and Herb, and billed by their record company as "The Sweethearts of Soul." Many got the impression that the two were childhood lovers, or at least were going steady. However, their musical romance was just as phony as their stage name.

"We're good friends," said Herb, in 1967. "A lot of our fan mail asks if we're married, and so many people want to know if we've 'set the date.' I guess to our fans we're sweethearts. That's our image, so I guess we've got to uphold it."

And uphold it they did, through five top-forty hits in a row in 1967: "Let's Fall in Love," "Close Your Eyes," "For Your Love," "Love Is Strange," and "Two Little Kids." However, later Peaches and Herb records did not do as well.

By 1971, Francine had had enough of show biz. She broke up the act, and enrolled in a self-improvement course, mainly to lose weight. "I want to settle down and get married," she said, "and become a songwriter." Herb returned to Washington, D.C., and found work as a policeman.

Then there was nothing, for five years.

Finally, Herb decided he had to find out if it was possible for him to make a comeback. He contacted Van again, who suggested reviving the team with a new "Peaches." They held extensive auditions, and then picked Linda Greene, a young model who lived only a couple of blocks from Herb. The two rehearsed, and in January 1977, broke in their act in small clubs. At the same time, Van lined up a record deal, and in September 1977, the new duet made its official debut on MCA Records.

And no one bought. They bombed.

Herb and Linda were crushed, but unwilling to give up. They next contacted Freddie Perren, a former pianist who was then starting his own record company. Freddie agreed to make Peaches and Herb's next effort the first release on his new Polydor/MVP label.

That turned out to be "Shake Your Groove Thing," issued in mid-December 1978. Within three months, it was a million-seller, and the most famous track on Peaches and Herb's LP, *2 Hot.* "But it was a disco number," said Herb, "and we didn't want to get typecast as a disco group. So we decided to make our next release something totally different. We went for an R&B ballad, and that was 'Reunited.' "

"That was the ultimate song on the album for me," said Linda. "It was overwhelming just to listen to the words of that song. It was not written about myself and Herb as a couple's relationship. Dino Fekaris and Freddie wrote it for the people who could truly relate to it.

"I remember, on one promotion tour I got to visit a little elementary school. These kids were in first, second and third grades, and when I asked them what their favorite song was, they all shouted 'Reunited.' A lot of kids said, 'That song was played when my Mommy and Daddy got back together,' and it just made me feel so good."

"Reunited" spent four weeks at number one, peaking in May of 1979. In all, it sold more than three million copies, and remained a best-seller for nearly six months. In 1980, the duo had another top-twenty hit, "I Pledge My Love."

Incidentally, Linda was often asked how long it took her to assemble her multi-beaded hairdo. The answer: up to twelve hours. The effect lasted for about two months, and then had to be all torn down and rebuilt.

YMCA
THE VILLAGE PEOPLE

French composer-producer Jacques Morali came to the United States as the winner of a 20th Century-Fox slogan contest. While in New York, he attended a costume ball at Les Mouches, a gay disco in Greenwich Village. As he gazed around the room, Morali was impressed by all the "macho male stereotypes" portrayed by the party guests. The idea came to him: Why not put together a group of singers and dancers, each one playing a different gay fantasy figure?

Felipe Rose, a professional dancer, came that night as an American Indian. He was cast as the first "image." Next came singer Alexander Briley, as the uniformed GI/sailor. Victor Willis, who had been in such Broadway musicals as *The Wiz* and *The River Niger*, rounded out the trio as lead singer and lyricist. His role was as the naval commander and part-time policeman. As all had been recruited from Greenwich Village, Morali decided to call them the Village People.

Their first LP, *The Village People*, was released in 1977 and aimed directly at the gay market. Soon after it hit, auditions were held for three more members. TV actor Randy Jones was hired as a cowboy. Glenn Hughes, a former Brooklyn Battery Tunnel toll collector, came in as a leather-clad biker (a role he played in real life as well, he claimed). And last but not least was David "Scar" Hodo, the muscular construction worker in mirrored shades. A great lover of bizarre stunts, his passion for roller skating while eating fire had landed him on "What's My Line?"

The title cut from their second album, *Macho Man,* was a small hit in the summer of 1978 (the LP itself went platinum). Then in the fall, they released their third album, *Cruisin'.* From that came their biggest single, "YMCA."

"We were always very positive about our energy and what we did," said Randy. "We never sang about broken hearts, lost love, or shattered dreams. We always dealt with positive things, and a very positive place is the YMCA. I think people had forgotten about Y's and their positive qualities. They've provided food, shelter, and spiritual encouragement for a lot of people for more than a century. They provide excellent physical programs for young and old, and it's a very positive institution. That's why we decided to sing about it."

At first, Y officials were alarmed by the song. They didn't know who the Village People were or what they represented (although they certainly heard stories). They also weren't sure if the tune was a tribute, a ripoff, or a slap in the face.

"We understood their point of view," Randy explained, "and we talked about it before we cut the song. YMCA is a trademark, and a trademark must be protected. If they allowed one person or one group to violate their rights, that would make YMCA public domain, and there'd be YMCA toothpaste, YMCA T-shirts, YMCA towels, everything. David and I tried to communicate this to our producers, but couldn't get through. Then, when 'YMCA' became a big hit, there was a legal decision that those letters are the property of the Young Men's Christian Association. By that time, though, the Y was thinking of our song

as a free commercial, so everything was cool."

According to *Rolling Stone,* "YMCA" sold more than twelve million copies, worldwide. It spent a full half-year on the charts, peaking in February 1979.

The Village People had one other major hit, "In the Navy," in the spring of that year. Then, in the fall, lead singer Willis, dissatisfied with their direction, quit the group "by mutual agreement." This happened days before shooting was to begin on their first motion picture, *Can't Stop the Music.* Ray Simpson was brought in to replace Willis, but somehow things just weren't the same. Released in June of 1980, the film—which featured "YMCA"—was a box-office disaster.

In 1981, the Village People reorganized and renounced their disco roots. Full-page ads in the music trades displayed their new look and future sound—as Bowiesque punk rockers.

Bad Girls
DONNA SUMMER

*T*ime magazine described Donna Summer's first hit, "Love to Love You Baby," as a "marathon of twenty-two orgasms. The lyrics are stunningly simple," they wrote, "mostly five words, repeated twenty-eight times. Her message is best conveyed in grunts and groans and languishing moans." Yet she was a woman who, after performances, wouldn't go anywhere until every last speck of glitter was removed from her eyelids. "I don't want to look like a hooker," she said.

Born LaDonna Andrea Gaines, Donna Summer was easily the most important artist to emerge from the seventies disco craze. She was called The Queen of Disco, a title she came to resent. "I do not consider myself a disco artist," she said. "I am a singer who has done disco songs. Despite the way it may have seemed to the public, I have always been rock-oriented. For me, *Bad Girls* is far more rock than disco."

Bad Girls, Donna's most ambitious LP, was also her best seller and final new release of the decade. It was a "concept" album, as was the earlier *Once Upon a Time.* On this double set, though, the design was clearly different. Instead of being a Cinderella story, the theme was "romantic reflection." It was much more loosely constructed and, as such, left lots of room for experimentation.

In its sweep of fifteen songs—eight of which Donna had a hand in writing—she and her producers, Giorgio Moroder and Pete Bellotte, embraced new stylistic ground. The funky, get-on-up beat of disco still reigned supreme, but in many of the tunes there was a lusty rock 'n' roll bite. "Hot Stuff" certainly had it, and there was also the title track—the most popular cut pulled from the album as a single. Donna's steamy vocal—a hooker's chant—taunted, teased, and cajoled over a swirling synthesizer track. In July 1979, "Bad Girls" bounded to the top of the charts. Both the album and the single were number one simultaneously, week after week after week.

And then Donna Summer became a born-again Christian.

"I went from poverty to riches, but when I got there, I found it wasn't so great," she said. "I had neglected the spirit—my spiritual needs. I hadn't been to church in almost ten years.

"I started crying like a baby. All the stuff that had been keeping me so tense got released. I've gone down the wrong paths, had the life of sin and decadence, but I'm different now. It was the most wonderful experience of my life."

And there were more surprises. In January 1980, after selling more than twenty million records, Donna sued her label, charging "undue influence, misrepresentation, and fraud." Two weeks later, Casablanca president Neil Bogart resigned, freeing her to sign with some other company. She chose Geffen, and a few months after that, released her first new album of the eighties, *The Wanderer.*

"I have miles to go before I sleep," said Donna, who became the most successful female hitmaker of the seventies. "I've really only started to say what I want to say. I've paid a lot of dues. The years have not been easy. There's so much I want to do. I'm going to try to branch out even more. I don't want to stay with any one thing. I like to think of myself as a beautiful plant that changes—grows leaves, loses them, and every day looks different. I want to have an image follow me, not have me follow the image.

"I'm a normal human being who can sing a lot of kinds of songs. I can be classy and versatile. Besides, when you start out whispering, the only way is up."

Do Ya Think I'm Sexy?

ROD STEWART

All through the seventies, Rod Stewart stuck to a simple musical philosophy: Give the people exactly what they want. And what they wanted from him was spectacle, showmanship, and his own brand of earthy sensuality.

Rod developed into one of the most moving singers of the decade. His voice was little more than a hoarse rasp, yet was capable of both hard rock and deep emotion. He was streetwise tough with a soft heart—and millions thought he was very sexy indeed.

In 1976, his "Tonight's the Night" became the largest-selling single in Warner Brothers history. It came from

the album *A Night on the Town,* the first album released on his own label, Riva (distributed by Warner Brothers). Off that same LP came two other top-thirty hits in 1977, "The First Cut Is the Deepest" and "The Killing of Georgie." With a new backup band, Stewart then cut *Footloose and Fancy Free.* It featured "You're in My Heart"—"a very confused song," according to Rod, "about women, Scotland, and two soccer teams." Also on that album was another pair of top-thirty hits, released as singles in 1978: "Hot Legs" and "I Was Only Joking." The latter tune was written to explain his unfaithful lifestyle to Britt Ekland, his former girlfriend.

In 1978, Rod bolstered the band by adding Nicky Hopkins on piano and Carmen Appice on drums. Together, they recorded his most spirited album of the seventies—*Blondes Have More Fun.* "It's Stewart in a playful mood," wrote one critic. "The music is rowdy and irreverent." Another called it "smutty self-indulgence." Regardless, it sold nearly four million copies in six months. Additionally, the LP was released in a limited edition of 100,000 picture discs, featuring disc imprints of front- and back-cover album graphics, as well as a cardboard pull-out of Stewart's face, also taken from album artwork.

The standout track, of course, was "Do Ya Think I'm Sexy?" "I wrote the verse, chords and the melody for the bridge," recalled Carmen Appice. "Rod wrote the bridge. It's the kind of stuff he likes—sort of singalong music. And when we do the song live, the audience reaction, worldwide, has been amazing. Whenever we start playing

it, they start singing it. And when you get fifteen or twenty thousand people going 'Do ya think I'm sexy, da-da-dada-da-da,' it's incredible. Even in Japan, where they don't even speak English, they were singing along anyway."

In concert, Rod's rendition of "Do Ya Think I'm Sexy?" was met by a tidal wave of screaming fans—mostly female—shouting, "YES!" It underlined his image as "rock's premier playboy of the seventies."

"Do Ya Think I'm Sexy?" was selling 250,000 copies a week in February 1979, the month it made number one. It was the fastest-selling single in Warner history and their first platinum single of the year. A special twelve-inch version was said to be the first forty-eight-track disco mix ever made (only 300,000 copies were pressed as collector's items). The song topped charts in eleven countries, including France, Germany, Holland, Sweden, Norway, Italy, Belgium, England, Australia, and Canada. In Brazil, singer Jorge Ben cried "ripoff," claiming the tune was too similar to his work, "Taj Mahal" (he later withdrew the complaint).

The record also sparked a parody, "Do You Think I'm Disco?," recorded by Chicago deejay Steve Dahl. An antidisco anthem, it sold over 300,000 copies for Ovation Records, without breaking the national top forty.

Rod didn't make much money off "Do Ya Think I'm Sexy?" since he donated all his publishing royalties to UNICEF. But he did get an answer to his question on April 6, 1979, when former model Alena Collins Hamilton became his bride.

Le Freak
CHIC

I'm from North Carolina," said Bernard Edwards, "and Nile was born in New York. We met in the Bronx in 1970, just out of high school. I was working in the post office during the day, and my girlfriend's mother introduced us. We got jobs in nightclubs and doing weekend things. We made $15 apiece."

Nile Rodgers interrupted. "They paid you fifteen?" (General laughter all around.)

"We just stuck together," Bernie went on. "It was like two guys that just had something in common. We never talked about it. I didn't know he wrote songs; he didn't know that I wrote."

In 1972, the two began playing in the Big Apple Band, backing New York City ("I'm Doing Fine Now"). When that group broke up, they toured with Carol ("Doctor's Orders") Douglas for six months. At the close of 1976, they decided to form their own band.

"We had two amplifiers and two guitars, and we just started to play. We met Tony Thompson, our drummer, and none of us had any money. But we stuck it out."

In February 1977, they began laying down rough rhythm and vocal tracks for a demo. Since Walter Murphy had adopted the Big Apple Band's name, a new moniker—Chic—was coined in June. They were turned down by every major label in New York, until finally, in September, Atlantic agreed to give Chic a chance. From their tape, a single, "Dance Dance Dance," was released. In less than a month, it had sold well over a million copies.

"That first hit had different voices on it," explained Bernie. "After the record was made, we found the two girls who are in Chic today. Alfa Anderson, our lead singer, was teaching school in New York. Luci Martin was a dancer and singer in clubs in

Canada, and she had toured in *Hair* and *Jesus Christ Superstar*."

"At that time, Studio 54 was real big in New York," recalled Nile. "A lot of people tried to get into the club, but couldn't. It was real popular with models and people who are not inhibited, more or less. They came out late at night after working all day and were just having fun. Anyway, they had this dance they called the Freak, and it was very, very unorthodox."

In order to Freak, two dancers bend at the knees, spread their legs, and bump their pelvises together, in time to the music.

"The public began to pick up on it, and they made a more 'commercial' Freak. That's what we saw in the discos and started to write about. We thought it could be like the Twist. Everyone said, 'You're crazy. There'll never be another dance craze in the U.S.' But we wrote the song anyway to go along with the dance.

"At first, reaction was bad because of the word *freak*. A lot of stations just didn't want that word on the radio. But suddenly they just started playing it, and within two or three weeks it had sold over a million copies."

"Le Freak" went gold in Belgium, Italy, South Africa, England, France, Brazil, and most of the rest of the world. In Canada, it became the best-selling song in the nation's history. In America, it was number one for five weeks, and eventually it sold more than five million copies. It was Atlantic Records' all-time biggest hit.

"We try to please the public," said Nile. "We're not interested in the critics that much. They don't buy records."

His partner agreed. "We're trying to establish an entertaining kind of music. We don't have any heavy message; no moral issues, no heavy problems. When you get off work, come and see us, have fun, and split—that's all. We're just trying to have a good time."

My Sharona

THE KNACK

The Knack—lead singer/guitarist Doug Fieger, lead guitarist Berton Averre, drummer Bruce Gary, and bassist Prescott Niles—formed in May 1978, in Hollywood, California. All had previously played in unsuccessful bands or as studio musicians.

Their aim was to bring back "teenage rock 'n' roll"—"high school songs with a teenage viewpoint." They put together a demo tape and sent it around to every major label in town. After being completely rejected, the group decided to "show everybody" and blitz the local rock club scene. They caused such a sensation that thirteen labels reportedly came by to make offers. After much consideration, the group signed with Capitol, which guaranteed $500,000 for two LPs.

Mike Chapman, who heard about the Knack from an L.A. writer, was chosen by the band to produce their debut album. The reason given was that "his pop sensibilities and vision paralleled the Knack's." Of course, Chapman's number-one singles by Blondie, Nick Gilder, and Exile over

the last year didn't hurt his chances either. Almost all the tracks were cut live in one take; there were overdubs (mostly lead guitar) on only a few tracks. The entire LP was recorded, mixed, and in the can in eleven days flat. Total cost: $18,000.

It was perhaps the cheapest platinum album ever made. Released on June 11, it went gold in thirteen days—the fastest climb by any new group in years. It went platinum on August 3 and eventually sold more than four million copies.

Doug Fieger, who described his most distinguishing feature as "smirk on face," listed his favorite pastime as "writing nasty songs about girls that I know." One was a young groupie named Sharona.

"Berton had this basic guitar and drum riff lying around for a long time," he said, "even before the Knack got together. He played it for me, and I really liked it. I said we would do it someday, but I didn't know how we could use it at the time. Then, at the same time the Knack started, I met a little girl named Sharona, whom I fell in love with. When I would think about

Sharona, Berton's riff came to mind. So Berton and I got together and worked out a structure and a melody and the words. The result was 'My Sharona.' "

With its slamming drums, driving guitar work, and simple, infectious beat, "My Sharona" caused a sensation in 1979. Released June 18, the single went gold in eight weeks, reaching number one in early August.

The Knack had their detractors: Some were offended by their Beatle-like album cover, the title of which was a play on the Fab Four's debut, *Meet the Beatles.* One critic called the Knack "an arrogant hype," while another termed leader Fieger "obnoxious." Still another reviewer said, "The ugly sexism of these corrupt creeps is an affront to women. The Knack delivers time-warped heartless junk with a contemptuous sneer." San Francisco artist Hugh Brown invented the "Knuke the Knack Kit": a button, a bumper sticker ("Honk If You've Slept with Sharona"), and a *Jaws*-style T-shirt (a swimmer is shown being attacked by a shark wearing a Knack T-shirt; the slogan reads, "Just When You Thought It Was Safe to Listen to the Radio"). Amused, the Knack bought four of the shirts and wore them to rehearsal the next day. However, when kit sales picked up, they stopped smiling, took them off, and threatened to sue.

The band's success—labeled "The Big Knack Attack"—brought dozens of talent scouts into L.A., hoping for a similar miracle. There were none. The group had a lesser hit, "Good Girls Don't," and then cut their second LP. Producer Chapman gleefully bragged that it cost even *less* to make than the first album. "It cost more to mix than make," he said. "Everything was cut in one take. I'd say we spent less than $10,000 on it." The biggest single pulled from it, "Baby Talks Dirty," was a flop; critics called it "My Sharona Part II." The Knack broke up in 1982.

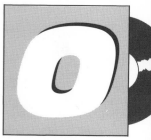

1980

On December 8, two months after his fortieth birthday, **John Lennon** left a New York recording studio with his wife, Yoko, and headed home. They were in good spirits; their album, *Double Fantasy,* was selling briskly, and John's new single, "(Just Like) Starting Over," was on its way to number one. The Lennons' limo stopped in front of their apartment building, the Dakota, and the couple stepped out onto the sidewalk. Moments later, several shots rang out. "They were loud, ear-shattering," said a witness. "I am shot! I am shot!" John cried out, staggering into the courtyard. Bystanders seized Mark David Chapman, who reportedly stood nearby with a pistol. "I just shot John Lennon," he's said to have remarked as Yoko watched in horror. John was taken to the emergency room of Roosevelt Hospital, where doctors worked on him as the Muzak played "All My Loving." At 11:15 P.M., he died, ending one of the most remarkable careers in music history.

THE HIGH-FLYING STATUS of New York's Studio 54 disco came to an end in 1980 when owners Steve Rubell and Ian Schrager were fined and sent to prison for income tax evasion. Dance music itself was declared dead by *Variety* and many other trades, despite its continued popularity on the record charts. Donna Summer left the Casablanca label amid $10 million in lawsuits; soon after, the Bee Gees filed against their manager, Robert Stigwood, and the Polygram Group for more than $200 million. At Tokyo's International Airport, Paul McCartney was arrested for possession of nearly half a pound of marijuana (his tour was canceled, and he was sent home). We lost Mantovani, André Kostelanetz, and AC/DC leader Ben Scott; also John "Bonzo" Bonham, the pyrotechnic drummer man for Led Zeppelin. RCA issued an eight-record set, *Elvis Aron Presley,* retailing at $69.95; and, not to be outdone, George Harrison offered a 400-page autobiography, *I Me Mine,* at $354 a copy. CBS Records swept the Academy of Country Music Awards, and no wonder: they instructed all employees to vote as a bloc and then cast ten times as many votes as the next largest label. It was 1980: the year MCA debuted the Discovision video disc, and Geffen Records was formed (their first three acts: John Lennon, Donna Summer and Elton John).

John Travolta, having already made fifties punk and seventies disco fashionable, sparked a country craze with his performance as the *Urban Cowboy.* The disco sound, meanwhile, went down the tubes in *Can't Stop the Music,* a Village People movie that not only could stop the music, but did. "Saturday Night Live" stars Dan Aykroyd and John Belushi brought their *Blues Brothers* characters to the screen, along with James Brown, Ray Charles and Aretha Franklin. Olivia Newton-John visited *Xanadu,* Irene Cara found *Fame,* Bette Midler became *The Rose,* and Paul Simon rode *One Trick Pony.* Alice Cooper, Meatloaf and Deborah Harry turned up in *Roadie* (Harry also sang "Call Me" in *American Gigolo*). On the country side, Willie Nelson made *Honeysuckle Rose,* Mac Davis was in *Cheaper to Keep Her* and the life story of Loretta Lynn was retold in *Coal Miner's Daughter.*

After a shaky start in 1978, **"WKRP in Cincinatti"** emerged as the first successful television series set in a rock 'n' roll radio station. Gary Sandy played Andy Travis, the program director who attempted to cope with a staff full of broadcast crazies. The use of actual hits on the soundtrack added a touch of realism, as did the casting of former jock Howard Hessman as deejay Dr. Johnny Fever.

Kenny Rogers scored his first number-one pop hit in 1980 with "Lady," a song written and produced by Lionel Ritchie of the Commodores. Kenny was in the New Christy Minstrels until 1967, when he and Terry Williams left that group to form the First Edition. They had about a half-dozen hits between 1968 and 1970 ("Just Dropped In," "Ruby Don't Take Your Love to Town") and a TV series before fading in the early seventies. Kenny then went solo, switched from folk-rock to country, and began a string of million-selling ballads with "Lucille" in 1977. By the end of the decade, he was clearly the number one artist in the pop-country field.

After "Ramblin' Gamblin' Man" in 1968, **Bob Seger** was considered a one-hit wonder everywhere except around Detroit, where his brand of all-out basic rock remained a hometown favorite. Then, in 1976, Bob discovered an untapped market: the multitude of music fans who had outgrown their teens but not their love of rock 'n' roll. Bob became a spokesman for the dreams, cries, and reminiscences of a grown-up generation through such hits as "Night Moves," "Still the Same," and "Old Time Rock 'n' Roll." In 1980, his twelfth LP became his first number one—more songs for a growing older crowd.

THE TOP 40

1. Call Me, *Blondie*
2. Another Brick in the Wall, Part II, *Pink Floyd*
3. Rock with You, *Michael Jackson*
4. Magic, *Olivia Newton-John*
5. It's Still Rock and Roll to Me, *Billy Joel*
6. Funkytown, *Lipps, Inc.*
7. The Rose, *Bette Midler*
8. Upside Down, *Diana Ross*
9. Do That to Me One More Time, *Captain and Tennille*
10. Coming Up (Live at Glasgow) *Paul McCartney and Wings*
11. Crazy Little Thing Called Love, *Queen*
12. Lost in Love, *Air Supply*
13. Ride Like the Wind, *Christopher Cross*
14. Little Jeannie, *Elton John*
15. Working My Way Back to You / Forgive Me Girl, *Spinners*
16. Cruisin', *Smokey Robinson*
17. Another One Bites the Dust, *Queen*
18. Lady, *Kenny Rogers*
19. Cars, *Gary Numan*
20. Woman in Love, *Barbra Streisand*
21. Escape, *Rupert Holmes*
22. Biggest Part of Me, *Ambrosia*
23. Take Your Time, *S.O.S. Band*
24. Longer, *Dan Fogelberg*
25. Steal Away, *Robbie Dupree*
26. Coward of the County, *Kenny Rogers*
27. Sailing, *Christopher Cross*
28. Yes, I'm Ready, *Teri De Sario with K.C.*
29. The Wanderer, *Donna Summer*
30. Sexy Eyes, *Dr. Hook*
31. Don't Fall in Love with a Dreamer, *Kenny Rogers and Kim Carnes*
32. Please Don't Go, *K. C. and the Sunshine Band*
33. Cupid / I've Loved You for a Long Time, *Spinners*
34. With You I'm Born Again, *Billy Preston and Syreeta*
35. Shining Star, *Manhattans*
36. Still, *Commodores*
37. Emotional Rescue, *Rolling Stones*
38. All Out of Love, *Air Supply*
39. I'm Coming Out, *Diana Ross*
40. This Is It, *Kenny Loggins*

THE TOP 10 LPs

1. The Wall, *Pink Floyd*
2. Off the Wall, *Michael Jackson*
3. Glass Houses, *Billy Joel*
4. The Long Run, *Eagles*
5. Against the Wind, *Bob Seger and the Silver Bullet Band*
6. Damn the Torpedoes, *Tom Petty and the Heartbreakers*
7. Christopher Cross, *Christopher Cross*
8. On the Radio (Greatest Hits Vols. I & II), *Donna Summer*
9. Phoenix, *Dan Fogelberg*
10. The Game, *Queen*

Mild-mannered **Christopher Cross** called his music "pop 'n' roll," and many were stunned when he came out of nowhere to capture Grammy Awards in four categories: Song of the Year, Record of the Year, Album of the Year and Best New Artist. Actually, Cross's unprecedented feat was not surprising. Through a combination of personal taste, good timing and luck he had stumbled onto a style that seemed to find favor with everyone. "Ride Like the Wind," "Sailing" and "Say You'll Be Mine" were soft, romantic, charming, and very easy on the ears. While there was no Chris Cross mania, no one really tuned out his sound either, which was all radio programers wanted to know. They gave him all the air support he needed to pull off the greatest sweep by a new act in the twenty-three-year history of the awards.

10

Coming Up
(Live at Glasgow)
PAUL McCARTNEY AND WINGS

*I*n October 1979, Paul McCartney was given a special medallion by the staff of the *Guinness Book of World Records.* He earned it by appearing in their pages so often: as the most successful composer of all time, with forty-three songs written between 1962 and 1978 that had each sold more than a million copies; for having a record number of gold discs; and for being the world's most successful recording artist, with estimated global sales of a hundred million singes and a hundred million albums. Paul was thirty-seven years old.

Already the world's wealthiest rock star, McCartney next signed an astonishing record deal—a guarantee of $20 million for his next three LPs. He also won the most generous royalty ever offered an artist: a minimum of $1.40 per album.

It was a great year for Paul, as well as his former writing partner, John Lennon. Together, they earned an estimated $40 million from the films *Sgt. Pepper* and *I Wanna Hold Your Hand,* and the musical *Beatlemania.* Paul himself earned $30 million in 1977, $40 million in 1978, and over $50 million in 1979. Part of that income came from songs he had "collected": publishing properties such as "Autumn Leaves," "Sentimental Journey," tunes from *Annie, A Chorus Line, Grease,* the Buddy Holly catalog, even college fight songs.

"The money doesn't matter anymore," he admitted. Paul then recalled riding in his Rolls, watching a "common man" walking his dog. "I wonder," he mused, "which one of us really got it right."

In the late seventies, the answer to that question sure seemed to be Paul McCartney and Wings. Their 1976 LP, *At the Speed of Sound,* featured two gold singles, "Silly Love Songs" and "Let 'Em In." A concurrent U.S. tour—McCartney's first in ten years—resulted in a double live album, *Wings Over America* (and from it, the hit "Maybe I'm Amazed"). In 1977, their "Mull of Kintyre" became the most popular 45 in U.K. history; over two million copies were sold. And in 1978 Wings' *London Town* LP yielded three more hits: "With a Little Luck," "I've Had Enough," and the title track—all recorded aboard the yacht "Fair Carol," in the U.S. Virgin Islands.

Wings changed labels to Columbia in 1979, and scored right away with "Goodnight Tonight," "Getting Closer," and "Arrow Through Me," all from the album *Back to the Egg.* Like nearly all their material, those songs were cut outside England, for tax reasons. "I have to *write* outside the country, too," complained McCartney. "Otherwise, the government steps in and takes all the money back to Britain. I'm in the ninety-eight percent tax bracket there. So I write on tour, whether I'm in Venice or downtown Burbank."

McCartney was on the road in January 1980, when he was arrested for smuggling seven ounces of marijuana. While incarcerated, Paul was grilled several times, fed clear soup and seaweed, and forced to sleep on a mattress on the floor of a tiny cell. He spent much of his "free" time in a communal bath with other prisoners, leading them in rousing rounds of "Yesterday."

Once safely home again, Paul embarked on a new recording project—"something that didn't sound anything like me," he explained. Bypassing the console, he plugged a single mike into a sixteen-track tape machine and began building overdubs—one voice, one instrument, one effect after another. The idea was to make a crazy cassette; something to play in his car but not release. In the end, though, friends said, "Say, that's your new album," and he said, "You're probably right." Thus was born *McCartney II,* his second totally solo LP.

One of the tunes invented was "Coming Up," which Paul had cut using a sped-up, gimmicky voice. Later, on the road with Wings, he thought about trying the song out onstage, just for reaction. They were in Glasgow, the last night of the tour. In his normal tone, Paul sang the song once, as recording engineers captured the performance.

Columbia was impressed with that live take, and wanted to put it on *McCartney II* instead of the original version, but Paul refused: "I mean, if you do that, it isn't a solo album anymore." Finally, they agreed to include it as a separate single, packaged with the LP.

Radio programmers were then mailed "Coming Up" as a 45, with the studio version on Side A, and the live take on Side B. Overwhelmingly, they jumped on the B side, making "Coming Up (Live at Glasgow)" one of the first gold records of the new decade.

Do That to Me One More Time

CAPTAIN AND TENNILLE

In 1975, "Love Will Keep Us Together" swept the world to become one of the best-selling love anthems of all time. It was the biggest song of the year, and the Captain (Daryl Dragon) and Tennille (Toni Tennille) emerged as a popular and promising musical force.

Besides the title track, their debut album also included "The Way I Want to Touch You," which became a coast-to-coast hit in the fall of 1975. Their second LP, *Song of Joy*, provided them with three gold singles: "Lonely Night (Angel Face)," "Shop Around," and "Muskrat Love," all in 1976.

That same year, the Captain and Tennille became TV personalities. Fred Silverman, president of ABC Entertainment, saw them performing in concert. Silverman became an instant fan and asked them to do an ABC summer special. The show received a tremendous rating, and "The Captain & Tennille Show" was added to ABC's fall schedule. At first, the program reached a wide audience. However, stilted production and unfunny scripts took their toll, and by March of 1977, the series was off the air. There was some consolation: a few weeks later, "Can't Stop Dancin'," off their third album, *Come In from the Rain*, became a major hit.

The Captain and Tennille left TV frustrated and discouraged. The show had reduced them to caricatures: a wooden Captain, and goody-goody Tennille. Their wholesomeness, a plus in the beginning, was ruining their career. Something had to be done. And something was.

On their next album, Toni and Daryl added a mildly suggestive cut—"You Never Done It Like That." Released as a single in the fall of 1978, it rocketed them back into the top ten. "That's the direction we're planning to go in," said Toni, early in 1979. "More of a sensual, sexy sound." To complete their change of image, they left A&M, and signed with Casablanca.

"She's a blonde, streamlined temptress, more appealing than the plain, giddy Pollyanna of old," wrote one critic, reviewing the "new" Toni Tennille. "Her ammunition includes a dress with a hip-high slit that elicits waves of wolf whistles." Also in her arsenal was a new song—the most daringly lusty record Toni and Daryl had ever produced. "Do That to Me One More Time" was a far cry from the apple-pie style of their first hit, five years before.

"Do That to Me One More Time" broke in mid-October 1979, and reached number one the following February. In all, it spent more than six months on the charts—and was the biggest hit ever for the Captain and Tennille.

Upside Down

DIANA ROSS

The year was 1970. The former lead singer of the Supremes was making her solo debut at Hollywood's Coconut Grove. "Welcome," she said, "to the 'Can Diana Ross Make It on Her Own' Show." She laughed nervously, as the line had been spoken only partially in jest. She had just come from the most popular girl group in rock history—a pretty tough act for anyone to follow. How successful could she be? Millions were wondering, including Diana, the staff at Motown Records, and her mentor, label owner Berry Gordy, Jr.

Berry had been captivated by the magnetic, sexy presence of Diana. He envisioned her as a black Barbra Streisand—a superstar singer, dancer, actress—and lover. For years, they had denied any romance, but Gordy finally admitted, "It would have been hard to work with her and not fall in love." Over the dozen years of Supremes success, Berry avoided all talk of marriage while Diana pined for a family of her own. Finally, she cut her "Gordyan Knot" (emotionally, but not professionally) and married a white man, Bob Silberstein. She had met him in an L.A. men's shop, while picking out a gift for Berry. Silberstein was unemployed at the time. They were wed in 1971.

Diana's solo career began with "Reach Out and Touch," followed by "Ain't No Mountain High Enough" and "Remember Me." Then, in 1973, she cut her biggest hit single to that point—"Touch Me in the Morning." After that, she experimented by recording with Marvin Gaye. In November 1973, "You're a Special Part of Me" was their first duet; five months later they returned with "My Mistake." Also in 1974, Diana made the top twenty with "Last Time I Saw Him."

In 1975, Ross made her second motion picture, *Mahogany,* with co-stars Billy Dee Williams and Anthony Perkins. Berry Gordy directed the story of a fashion designer who becomes famous but only finds love in the arms of her less successful boyfriend (déjà vu?). Diana, who had studied costume illustration in high school, actually designed some of the clothes she wore in the picture. The film theme song, "Do You Know Where You're Going To?" became her third number-one single in January 1976.

Later that year, Diana topped the charts again with "Love Hangover" (beating out a cover version by the Fifth Dimension). After that came "One Love in a Lifetime" (1976) and "Gettin' Ready for Love" (1977).

In 1978, Diana appeared in a third movie, *The Wiz,* which was a black version of *The Wizard of Oz.* Sidney Lumet directed; the cast included Michael Jackson, Nipsey Russell, and Ted Ross (no relation). Diana, at the age of thirty-four, was cast—at her insistence—in the juvenile role of Dorothy. Nothing could save the resulting disaster, and no singles from the soundtrack managed to make the top forty.

Things looked up, though, in 1979. In October, "The Boss" became Diana's first top-twenty hit in more than two years. Soon after, a deal was struck that promised to take the Ross career to even greater heights. Bernard Edwards and Nile Rodgers, the masterminds behind Chic, agreed to help Diana put together her follow-up LP.

Bernard and Nile had gained great fame in the late seventies for their spare, lean production work. They had made major stars of Chic, Sister Sledge, and several other acts. The hope was that they could assist Diana in stripping away years of show biz gloss. The soul of Diana Ross was under there somewhere, if they could find it.

They did, although critics claim that the sound they used was too reminiscent of Chic records. The cutting edge that sparked Chic hits was in sharp contrast with Ross' style: a smooth, velvety approach. However, that dichotomy seemed to work on the LP *Diana.* It featured some of Ross' most confident singing in years, and was, on balance, a fun, playful album. It was also her biggest seller ever.

"Upside Down," a song written by Bernard and Nile, was the first track pulled from the LP as a single. It broke in mid-July 1980, and spent four weeks at number one in September. In all, it spent twenty-nine weeks on the charts.

Diana had more hits in 1980: "I'm Coming Out" and "It's My Turn." Then, in 1981, it was. She ended a nearly twenty-year association with Motown by signing with RCA.

The Rose
BETTE MIDLER

"The first time I saw the film I was nauseated. I'd had this mental picture of myself, and then on screen was this ratty, broken-down creature. I jumped in my car and looked for a bridge to drive off—only there aren't any in L.A.!"

That's how Bette Midler described her reaction to *The Rose,* the 1980 quasi-biography of Janis Joplin that brought Bette her first number-one record.

Born in Hawaii, Bette Midler moved to New York in 1965 and got a job in the Broadway chorus of *Fiddler on the Roof.* At the same time, she began to assemble her own bizarre night-club act, which she called "Trash with Class." It included everything from a Mae West impression to girl-group parodies, and it went over particularly well at the Continental Baths, a gay hangout (her piano player then was unknown Barry Manilow). Word spread about "the last of the truly tacky ladies" (her own description), and before long, she was being hailed in the press as the "Queen of Tasteful Vulgarity."

Bette burst onto the pop scene in late 1972 amid a shower of glitter, sass, and her own self-mocking humor. Her first album, *The Divine Miss M,* yielded four top-forty tunes, including "Do You Want to Dance" and "Boogie Woogie Bugle Boy." In 1973, she won her first Grammy Award as the Best New Artist of the Year.

Bette spent most of the seventies in one outrageous revue after another. Every once in a while there was a new LP: *Bette Midler, Songs for the New Depression, Broken Blossom, Live at Last,* and *Thighs and Whispers.* Then, at the end of the decade, Bette entered the final frontier—the world of motion pictures.

At first, Bette did not set out to make a film like *The Rose.* She wanted to do a traditional musical comedy, like *Singing in the Rain,* with laughter, dancing, and a happy ending. "That kind of movie is in my bones," said Bette. "But there's a problem. Film companies don't make 'em anymore."

Bette spent a well-publicized year trying to find such a property and finally gave up. It was then that she turned to the project that became *The Rose.* Originally, it was very much a Janis Joplin story, and in that form, Midler turned it down flat. Only after the script was rewritten and made much more general did she agree to play the part.

"I didn't want to imitate Janis because I have too much respect for her memory," explained Bette. "The first draft was even titled *Pearl,* which, of course, was her nickname. I changed that to 'May Rose,' along with a lot of other details about her character. I made her more of an R&B singer as well. There's a little Tina Turner and even Jim Morrison, in May Rose. She may have had the roughness of Janis Joplin, but really not a whole lot else."

Still, the parallels exist. *The Rose* plot chronicles the last eight days in the life of a self-destructive rock star: a woman riddled with drugs, drink, and hypertension. In triumph, she returns to her hometown for a spectacular concert, showing up all the people who had put her down for years. Janis's final public appearance, at her ten-year high school reunion, was similarly vindictive.

The song "The Rose" was actually written two years before the film was conceived. Bette decided to use it in the picture because, by sheer accident, it neatly sums up the lost inno-cence of her character. The tune was composed by an out-of-work actress, Amanda McBroom, who took up songwriting as a hobby. When she completed "The Rose," she realized it didn't have a bridge or a hook and in fact broke most of the rules of conventional pop structure. "The emotion seems to be what made the record work," said Amanda. "It's real and poignant because Bette just sounds so whipped."

The single took off in mid-March 1980, reaching number one in July. In all, it spent nearly six months on the charts, earning both a Golden Globe (for Best Song) and a Grammy Award (as Best Female Pop Vocal Performance).

Funkytown
LIPPS, INC.

Lipps, Inc., was really only two people: Cynthia Johnson, who sang all the vocals, and Steven Greenberg, who wrote, produced, and played most of the instruments. Their creation, "Funkytown," was number one in more than twenty countries around the world and was the first platinum single of 1980.

Steven Greenberg began his career at the age of fifteen as a professional rock 'n' roll drummer. In 1971, he wrote and produced his first single and took it to L.A., hoping it could open a few doors for him. However, the record industry wasn't interested, and Steven had to return home without a contract.

Over the next six years, he strengthened his musical skills, first as half of a singing duo known as Atlas and Greenberg. He then launched the "Discomobile," a state-of-the-art traveling party service. Later, he became a partner in an entertainment production company, working with local and regional talent.

Eventually Steven grew tired of "telling people what to do, and them not doing it." Deciding to take matters in his own hands, he wrote and recorded "Rock It." He played all the instruments except bass, pressed five hundred copies, and promoted the record all over Minneapolis. Before long, it climbed to number one on KFMX.

Soon after, in June of 1979, Greenberg began auditioning singers for a new group, Lipps, Inc. Cynthia was then performing with her own band, Flyt Tyme, but was looking for something else. After her audition for Steven, both knew they had found what they wanted. They recorded a demo, which Steven took around to record companies in New York and Los Angeles. After many rejections, it was finally accepted by Casablanca, which commissioned an LP.

Assembling that LP was "a nerve-racking experience," Greenberg recalled. He had sold his concept on the basis of only one song, "Rock It," and was now expected to come up with six or seven more. He wrote three new tunes in a week, but after that, inspiration stopped. "I tried for a couple of weeks, but nothing came out," he explained, "so I just lengthened the four tracks I had."

Another problem was the rapid decline of disco popularity, which had begun even as he entered the studio. "I didn't know what to do," he said. "The whole scene was changing, and I didn't know where music was heading. I wanted to redo parts of the album—change this, change that. I was turning into a maniac."

Greenberg tried several experiments and then settled on a slowed-down, danceable style. It was a combination of electronic disco and hard-core R&B, offset by Cynthia's shrieking vocals.

The idea for "Funkytown" came about while Steven was still in Minneapolis, brooding over that first LP. His hometown seemed dull and boring, and he began daydreaming about being somewhere else. "Everyone feels that way sometimes, about where they live," he explained. "You've got to get up and get away to a more funky place." Minneapolis, he pointed out, had a small black population. "There's no market here for disco and R&B. In fact, not a single major radio station in town played my record."

"Funkytown," though, was played in nearly every other American city and soon soared to the top of the disco, R&B, and pop charts. In fact, it was rumored that it had become the favorite song of "champagne music" star Lawrence Welk. "I had hoped it would get on the pop charts, but even I was surprised by its performance," Greenberg said. "I would have been happy if it had just broken even and the company gave me a chance to make another record."

Despite the message of "Funkytown," Steven Greenberg still lives, writes, and records where he always has—right in the heart of Minneapolis. "I was born and raised here," he admitted, "and I guess I feel safe and secure. If you must know, I really don't want to leave."

It's Still Rock and Roll to Me

BILLY JOEL

Billy Joel got into music at the age of four, when his parents signed him up for piano lessons. His father was devoted to the classics and hoped that someday his son would become a concert pianist. Billy had other ideas and infuriated his father by playing the classics boogie-woogie style. Eventually the elder Joel left home, leaving the young piano man to chart his own path through the bewildering world of music.

Billy began listening to the radio and was electrified by artists such as James Brown. He got into fifties rock 'n' roll, Sam and Dave, Wilson Pickett, and the records of Phil Spector. In 1964, the Beatles came along, and Billy Joel was blown away. "I remember when I used to go out and buy Beatles records, and it's almost a cliche to say, but every song was great. I became a Beatles baby, and they had to be the biggest influence on my music. Paul McCartney was my biggest influence as a melody writer. I saw *A Hard Day's Night* and knew I had to go out and start my own rock 'n' roll band."

Billy formed the Echoes (not the "Baby Blue" group), and played up and down Long Island. Later, he joined the Hassles and sang briefly in a twosome known as Atilla. He did session work and at one time backed up the Shangri-Las. He also took a few nonmusical jobs, just for the money. He painted Piping Rock Country Club in Locust Valley, worked in a factory, wrote some criticism for *Changes* magazine, and even recorded a pretzel commercial with Chubby Checker.

In 1971, Billy cut his first solo album, *Cold Spring Harbor,* which went nowhere. He became frustrated and moved to L.A., where he took a string of low-paying jobs as a barroom pianist. Those small-time experiences inspired "Piano Man," which he wrote and recorded in 1974. It

wasn't a big seller, but did impress the media. *Music Retailer* named him Male Artist of the Year, while *Cashbox* voted him the Best New Vocalist. *Stereo Review* liked his single and called it their Record of the Year.

In 1977, the public discovered Billy Joel and bought many copies of his LP, *The Stranger.* In fact, it turned out to be the best-selling album in Columbia Records' history. Four hit singles were pulled from *The Stranger,* including "Just the Way You Are," a song that sounded very much like an Elton John record. It won two Grammy Awards, as both Song and Record of the Year.

The album *52nd Street* came out in 1978 and featured another gold single, "My Life." His record sales doubled and quadrupled, and by the end of 1979, he had sold more than nine million units for Columbia. That made him the most successful solo artist ever signed to that label.

As the eighties began, the music scene shifted again, bringing back simple, hard-edged rock 'n' roll. Echoes of Elvis, Eddie Cochran, the Beatles, the Kinks, the Dave Clark Five,

and other acts were everywhere. It was a recycled style, and it was given a recycled name: punk rock.

"Back when I was with the Echoes, we were called punks," said Billy. " It was the mid-sixties then, but we didn't call ourselves punks. We thought we were hoods. I was called a punk when I started because a real wise guy was a punk. I remember when they called Elvis Presley a punk, and I thought the Young Rascals were punks."

After a few late-seventies groups muddied the term *punk rock,* the music was given an even more ludicrous name: "new wave." The irony of it all was not lost on Billy Joel, who had seen the same fads and fashions come and go several times over. For his album *Glass Houses,* he composed a song that perfectly expressed his viewpoint. Although each season brings its own trimmings, and each wave of trendsetters makes their own rules, the bottom line of contemporary pop always remains the same: "Hot funk, cool punk, even if it's old junk, it's still rock and roll to me."

Magic
OLIVIA NEWTON-JOHN

Born in Cambridge, England, and raised in Australia, Olivia Newton-John was fifteen when she formed a folk group, the Sol Four, which played at dances and parties. Later, Olivia sang solo every weekend in a coffeehouse owned by her brother-in-law.

At sixteen, she had her own local television program and became known as "Lovely Livvy" of "The Happy Show." The next year, in talent competition, she won a trip to England, where she eventually hooked up with a song-and-dance group called Tomorrow. With them, she made her first, rarely seen film, *Double-O.*

Olivia's recording career took off in 1971 with a Bob Dylan song, "If Not for You." In 1971 and 1972, she was voted the Best British Girl Singer of the Year by readers of the pop music paper *Record Mirror.* In 1973, she earned her first Grammy for the single "Let Me Be There." After that, there were more Grammy Awards, American Music Awards, and multiple honors from *Record World, Billboard, Cashbox,* the Academy of Country Music, the Country Music Association, AGVA, ASCAP, and others.

And, of course, there were hits: "If You Love Me, Let Me Know" and "I Honestly Love You" (a number-one song) in 1974; "Have You Never Been Mellow" (another number one), "Please Mr. Please," and "Something Better to Do" in 1975. The next year, her songs made less impact, but she still made the charts with "Let It Shine," "He Ain't Heavy, He's My Brother," "Come On Over," and "Don't Stop Believin'." In 1977, "Sam" became a top-twenty hit. By that time, Olivia had sold over twenty-five million records.

Her next move was to make a film. Critics who had already assailed her as "the voice of a singing bunny rabbit" now accused her of wanting to become "the Doris Day of the seventies." But as it turned out, the film *Grease* enabled Olivia to break away from her "Miss Goody Two-Shoes" image.

Olivia also made a dramatic image change with her next album, *Totally Hot,* which consisted of up-tempo, aggressive rock 'n' roll. At the same time, she looked at scripts, turning them all down as "inappropriate." Finally, Olivia read a thirty-page treatment of *Xanadu.* She instinctively felt that it was right, and so, two years after *Grease,* she embarked on her second Hollywood motion picture.

Xanadu, as it turned out, was an update of *Down to Earth,* a 1947 musical fantasy that starred Rita Hayworth as Terpsichore, the daughter of Zeus and goddess of dance and music. In the original film, the goddess takes human form and helps Larry Parks stage a Broadway show. In *Xanadu,* Olivia (as Terpsichore) befriends an aging clarinet player, portrayed by Gene Kelly. To Kelly, Olivia is the reincarnation of a singer he once loved in the big-band days. With her help, and that of a young painter (Michael Beck), he opens the nightclub of his dreams—Xanadu—"where all your wishes come true."

From a musical standpoint, it was quite a film, blending the big-band sound of the 1940s with the rock band sound of the 1980s. But even more remarkable was the mix of Olivia Newton-John with the Electric Light Orchestra. Such a combination—an "easy listening" queen with one of the most thundering of all rock 'n' roll bands—was unthinkable only a few years before. But since then, both acts had made dramatic moves toward the mainstream of popular music. A collaboration of Olivia and ELO not only became feasible, but came off, with the hit title theme.

The song "Magic" was also an integral part of the film. Like nearly all of Olivia's material, it was written by her long-time producer, John Farrar (to whom she dedicated her *Greatest Hits* album). Critics praised "Magic" for its "subtle charm, owing as much to her beguiling vocal, as to the song's hypnotic rhythm."

Olivia's own magic had made her second only to Donna Summer as the most successful female soloist of the seventies.

Rock with You

MICHAEL JACKSON

The Jackson Five made an impressive debut in 1970—four number-one records in a row, including both sides of their third release ("The Love You Save" / "I Found That Girl"). In only nine months, the quintet sold over ten million singles—far more than the Beatles had sold in an equal period of time. Those early hits, which included "I Want You Back," "ABC," and "I'll Be There," shaped and defined the sound of bubblegum soul. For six years, the J5 reigned as pop *Wunderkinder,* thanks to such tunes as "Mama's Pearl," "Never Can Say Goodbye," and "Dancin' Machine."

In the fall of 1971, lead singer Michael Jackson entered his teens and began a concurrent solo career. His first release was a hit: "Got to Be There." He followed that ballad with an even bigger hit, "Rockin' Robin," his own version of a song that had been on the charts the day he was born. After that was "Ben," the most successful Michael Jackson single of the early seventies. The title theme from a low-budget horror movie, it ranks as the most popular love song ever written about a rat.

As the decade wore on, the Jackson Five grew increasingly restless under the corporate thumb of Motown. The brothers had written some of their own material, but the company steadfastly refused to let them record any of it. Finally, in the summer of 1975, four of the brothers broke away amid a flurry of lawsuits. The move cost the boys more than $600,000, as well as their group name, which Motown retained. Their biggest loss, though, was Jermaine, who had married into the Gordy family and elected to stay (he'd already launched a solo career anyway, with "Daddy's Home" in 1972). The others replaced him with Randy, the youngest Jackson brother, and forged ahead, beginning in March 1976.

Their new recording home was Epic Records, and their new collective name was the Jacksons. But even at Epic the boys weren't given the chance to write and record their own material at first. They recorded two albums under the direction of Kenny Gamble and Leon Huff, a veteran songwriting-production team best known for their lush "Philadelphia-styled" orchestral R&B. It was a fine sound, said the brothers, and resulted in

another hit single, "Enjoy Yourself," in 1977. But it was still not really *them.*

The turning point came in 1978, when the Jacksons, for the first time in their careers, assumed responsibility for their own recordings. *Destiny,* written and produced by the brothers, became the biggest-selling LP ever in the Jacksons' catalogue. A platinum LP, it contained the hit singles "Shake Your Body (Down to the Ground)" and "Blame It on the Boogie." Significantly, the LP established the Jacksons as major songwriters and producers of mainstream pop music.

Right on the heels of *Destiny,* Michael Jackson released *Off the Wall,* his first solo album in nearly five years. It was a very carefully crafted LP, masterminded by R&B veteran Quincy Jones. The result was the best-selling LP—solo or group—in the family's history.

"Rock with You," the second single taken from *Off the Wall,* became the first new number-one single of 1980 in all three music trades. In January, on the American Music Awards show, Michael shared honors with Donna Summer as the recipients of the most awards for 1979—three each. Michael won top honors in three soul categories: Favorite Male Vocalist, Album (*Off the Wall*), and Single ("Don't Stop till You Get Enough").

Off the Wall sold more than five million copies, yet marked only one more milestone in the remarkable career of Michael Jackson, with and without his family. According to a broadcast special on the brothers, aired in 1980 on ABC-TV, the Jacksons are the largest-selling rock group in history, after the Beatles, with ninety-three million records sold.

Another Brick in the Wall, Part II

PINK FLOYD

*I*n 1965, a common love of rock 'n' roll brought together six students at London's Regent Street Polytechnic Architectural School. Roger Waters (bass, vocals), Richard Wright (keyboards, vocals), Nick Mason (percussion), Clive Metcalf (bass), Keith Nobel (vocals) and Juliette Gale (vocals) formed a group called the Sigma Six; later, the Tea Set, and then the Architectural Abdabs. Metcalf, Noble and Gale quit after a few months (Juliette became Mrs. Richard Wright) and were replaced by Roger "Syd" Barrett, a guitarist from Beckenham Art College. Barrett suggested another name change to the Pink Floyd Sound, in honor of Georgia bluesmen Pink Anderson and Floyd Council. It was accepted, and streamlined to Pink Floyd.

The band's initial style was straight R&B, but at Syd's insistence, they moved toward psychedelic music in 1966. By 1967, their live concerts were mixed-media events, complete with light shows, twenty-minute "scream-ups," and an array of special effects. Two singles became U.K. hits that year: "Arnold Layne" and "See Emily Play." There was also a debut album, *Piper at the Gate of Dawn.*

In April 1968, Barrett—a drug casualty—was replaced by David Gilmour. Roger Waters then took control of the group, writing and directing nearly all of the material. After that, LPs came about once a year: *A Saucerful of Secrets* (1968), *More* and *Ummagumma* (1969), *Atom Heart Mother* (1970), *Meddle* (1971), and *Obscured by Clouds* (1972).

In 1973, Pink Floyd took about nine months to record *Dark Side of the Moon* (with the aid of engineer Alan Parsons). It was still on the charts some eight years later, having sold more than seven million pressings. The LP featured Pink Floyd's first U.S. pop hit, "Money," which included the word "bullshit." Harvest Records thoughtfully supplied each deejay with a specially-edited single, but left the regular store copies intact—much to the surprise of many American parents. In 1975, they cut *Wish You Were Here;* and in 1977, their tenth album, *Animals.*

And then came *The Wall.*

It was a project conceived in 1977, following a disastrous tour of North America. Rapport between the audience and the band was so bad that at one point Waters found himself onstage spitting at his own fans. Once home, he began to plot a way to "get back" at the crowds, and everyone else who had ever made his life miserable. He wrote all the lyrics and most of the music and then mailed demo tapes to the various band members, each of whom added their own little parts. The result was a double LP that took over a year to record—and was so unnerving to make that each man told producer Bob Ezrin, "I'll never do this again."

The Wall tells the story of a rock star, Mr. Floyd (a/k/a Waters) who battles with an absent father, smothering mother, vicious schoolteacher, insistent fans, and an unfaithful spouse. Every assault adds another brick to his wall of defenses until he's left a shell-shocked, neurotic mess. Seventy-five minutes into his nightmare, he's convicted of "numbness, savagery, and fecklessness" in a courtroom trial presided over by a worm. He is sentenced to be "exposed before his peers," as the magistrate shouts, "Tear down the wall."

Pink Floyd's stage version was a re-creation of the album, complete with an actual wall, 35 feet high and

210 feet wide. At the start of the show, stagehands began stacking huge cardboard blocks—340 of them—until, by intermission, the band itself was completely hidden from the audience. During the second half, strategic blocks were removed, giving the fans "peekholes" through which they could glimpse the group. Finally, on cue, the entire structure crashed down, amid an ear-splitting crescendo.

Other gimmicks included huge floats, representing major characters—a 30-foot inflatable Mom, a fanged Wicked Wife, and a 25-foot marionette of the Schoolmaster. When the latter creature came lurching into view, a piped-in chorus of schoolboys sang "Another Brick in the Wall, Part II"—the part of the work selected as the first single's release.

As a 45, "Another Brick in the Wall Part II" broke in mid-January 1980. It reached number one in March, spending four weeks at the top of the charts. The disc remained on the hit parade for nearly six months, during which both it and the LP it came from became platinum sellers.

Call Me

BLONDIE

"The first thing I wanted to be when I grew up was a roller derby queen," said Deborah Harry. "Then I went through all these stages of wanting to be a ballet or tap dancer; I even wanted to be in the circus." Most of all, though, Debbie wanted to be a singer, and to that end, she started practicing in church and school plays. As a teenager, she hung out in New York's Greenwich Village, where she met and joined a folk group called Wind in the Willows.

After that, Debbie held a number of nonmusical jobs, as a beautician, Playboy bunny, and barmaid at Max's Kansas City. While working at Max's, she and two other girls formed the Stilletos, a kind of sleazy glitter-rock trio. When that outfit broke up in early 1975, she and guitarist Chris Stein laid plans for their own rock 'n' roll band, Blondie, which they named after the comic strip.

The couple auditioned over fifty drummers before choosing Clem Burke, and then signed keyboard player Jimmy Destri. In the summer of 1977, Frank "The Freak" Infante replaced their original second guitarist, Gary Vallentine. The line-up was completed in October of that year with Nigel Harrison on bass.

The group played around the New York area for several months, gaining a reputation as one of the best punk bands in the city. Eventually, with the aid of producer Richard Gottehrer (a former member of the Strangeloves) Blondie got a chance to audition for Private Stock Records. Frankie Valli, a part-owner of the label, dropped in and caught their act at CBGB's, a Manhattan new-wave club. "I was so thrilled when Frankie came," recalled Debbie. "I almost asked him to come onstage to sing a duet." That wasn't necessary; Frankie liked what he heard and approved a recording contract. However, their self-titled debut LP turned out to be less than a major success.

The band then moved to Chrysalis, but a second album, *Plastic Letters,* didn't sell much better. The group brought in a new producer, Mike Chapman, to supervise their third LP, *Parallel Lines.* From that album came "Heart of Glass," a number-one single in the spring of 1979; and "One Way or Another," which got to twenty-four during the summer. In the fall of 1979 there was a third top-thirty hit, "Dreaming."

It was about then that filmmaker Paul Schrader was putting the finishing touches on his first motion picture, *American Gigolo.* Music for the project was being directed by Giorgio Moroder. Giogio called on Blondie to contribute one song to the soundtrack, and the result was "Call Me."

Actually, Debbie was Moroder's second choice. He wanted Stevie Nicks of Fleetwood Mac, but she was on tour at that point, and having troubles with her voice. Giorgio had no choice—he had to use Blondie.

As things worked out, "Call Me" was played during the opening credits of the film, and was, as one critic put it, "appropriately seductive." After three weeks in five hundred seventy theaters, the movie grossed over $11.5 million—more than twice the production cost. And the soundtrack album made the LP top ten.

"Call Me" was a number-one smash—the biggest single of the year. After breaking in mid-February, it spent six weeks at the top of the charts, beginning in May. It remained a bestseller for twenty-five weeks. Its success offset some of Debbie's disasters that year: a role in the motion picture *Roadie* (the film bombed), her endorsement of a line of Murjani jeans (the deal fell through), and her being named one of the ten Worst Dressed Women by fashion designer Mr. Blackwell. Blondie, though, went on to score two more hits in 1980: "Atomic" and "The Tide Is High." They came from the LPs *Eat to the Beat* and *Autoamerican,* respectively.

THE POPULARITY OF DISCO eroded further in 1981, as country sounds and mainstream rock continued to dominate the American record industry. Key musical figures—the ones who most stimulated U.S. cash registers—included Kenny Rogers, Pat Benatar, and REO Speedwagon. Joining them from the C&W field were such names as Alabama, the Oak Ridge Boys, and Johnny's daughter, Rosanne Cash. Stars who had first gained fame in groups launched successful solo careers: Lindsay Buckingham and Stevie Nicks from Fleetwood Mac, Marty Balin from Jefferson Airplane/Starship, Phil Collins from Genesis, and Steve Winwood from the Spencer Davis Group. But the biggest trend was the newfound,

continued or renewed popularity of women in often aggressive musical roles, frequently featured with or leading their own top forty groups. Abba, Blondie, Kim Carnes, the Carpenters, Sheena Easton, Terri Gibbs, the Go Gos, Emmylou Harris, Juice Newton, the Pointer Sisters, Quarterflash, A Taste Of Honey, Diana Ross (with and without Lionel Richie), Barbra Streisand (with and without Barry Gibb), and Olivia Newton-John all participated in the movement. The most remarkable fad was the medley craze, sparked by Stars on 45, and perpetuated by the Beach Boys and the Royal Philharmonic Orchestra (under the direction of Louis Clark). An old Elvis record, "Guitar Man," was remade and revived; For-

eigner brought back Junior Walker (in a sax solo on their hit "Urgent"). Comebacks of the year were staged by Gary U.S. Bonds, Lulu, Rick Springfield, Carl Carlton, Del Shannon, and Bill Withers. Donna Summer changed her style and tried to return as a born-again Christian; her record, "Who Do You Think You're Foolin'," was only a mild success. We lost Bob Hite of Canned Heat, folksinger Harry Chapin, and reggae star Bob Marley. Two rock 'n' roll pioneers slipped away: R&B great Roy Brown and the legendary Bill Haley. Lloyd's Of London paid off $82,000 when Rod Stewart sprained his big toe and had to cancel a concert in Washington. The same firm granted "paternity insurance" to Van Halen's David Lee Roth after he convinced them that debauchery was "instrumental" to his work. Daryl Hall and John Oates had their biggest year yet with "You Make My Dreams" and three key number-one hits: "Kiss On My List," "Private Eyes," and "I Can't Go For That (No Can Do)." And three of the Beatles reunited on a tribute to John Lennon, "All Those Years Ago" (background vocals by Paul McCartney, Ringo Starr on drums, and George Harrison taking the lead). It was 1981—the year Quincy Jones won five Grammy Awards, and Fantasy Records discovered that their "British" Creedence Clearwater Revival album, *The Royal Albert Hall Concert*, actually had been recorded in Oakland, California.

THE TOP FORTY

1. Physical, *Olivia Newton-John*
2. Bette Davis Eyes, *Kim Carnes*
3. Endless Love, *Diana Ross & Lionel Richie*
4. Jessie's Girl, *Rick Springfield*
5. Keep On Loving You, *REO Speedwagon*
6. Celebration, *Kool & the Gang*
7. Theme from *The Great American Hero* (Believe It Or Not), *Joey Scarbury*
8. 9 to 5, *Dolly Parton*
9. Queen Of Hearts, *Juice Newton*
10. Slow Hand, *Pointer Sisters*
11. Rapture, *Blondie*
12. Kiss on My List, *Daryl Hall & John Oates*
13. Being with You, *Smokey Robinson*
14. Morning Train, *Sheena Easton*
15. Medley: Venus—Sugar, Sugar—No Reply—I'll Be Back—Drive My Car—Do You Want to Know a Secret—We Can Work It Out—I Should Have Known Better—Nowhere Man—You're Going to Lose That Girl—Stars on 45, *Stars on 45*
16. The Tide Is High, *Blondie*
17. Woman, *John Lennon*
18. Lady, *Kenny Rogers*
19. I Love a Rainy Night, *Eddie Rabbit*
20. Starting Over, *John Lennon*
21. Angel of the Morning, *Juice Newton*
22. Elvira, *Oak Ridge Boys*
23. Private Eyes, *Daryl Hall & John Oates*
24. The One That You Love, *Air Supply*
25. Arthur's Theme (Best That You Can Do), *Christopher Cross*
26. Just the Two of Us, *Grover Washington, Jr. (Bill Withers, vocal)*
27. Waiting for a Girl Like You, *Foreigner*
28. A Woman Needs Love (Just Like You Do), *Ray Parker, Jr., & Raydio*
29. Let's Groove, *Earth Wind & Fire*
30. Take It on the Run, *REO Speedwagon*
31. I Love You, *Climax Blues Band*
32. Oh No, *Commodores*
33. Best Of Times, *Styx*
34. Sukiyaki, *A Taste Of Honey*
35. The Winner Takes It All, *Abba*
36. Love on the Rocks, *Neil Diamond*
37. Who's Crying Now, *Journey*
38. Every Woman in the World, *Air Supply*
39. Here I Am, *Air Supply*
40. For Your Eyes Only, *Sheena Easton*

TOP TEN ALBUMS

1. Hi Infidelity, *REO Speedwagon*
2. Greatest Hits, *Kenny Rogers*
3. Double Fantasy, *John Lennon & Yoko Ono*
4. Paradise Theatre, *Styx*
5. Crimes Of Passion, *Pat Benatar*
6. Christopher Cross, *Christopher Cross*
7. 4, *Foreigner*
8. Escape, *Journey*
9. The Jazz Singer, *Neil Diamond*
10. Back in Black, *AC/DC*